# The 1100 Most Frequently Used Russian Adjectives: Save Time by Learning the Most Frequently Used Words First

Ivan Ivanov

# Contents

# The 1100 Most Frequently Used Russian Adjectives: Save Time by Learning the Most Frequently Used Words First

Ivan Ivanov

# About the Author

Ivan Ivanov was born in Moscow, Russia in 1975. He grew up in a bilingual household, speaking both Russian and English fluently. Ivanov attended Moscow State University, where he studied linguistics and literature. After graduation, he worked as a language teacher and translator for several years before deciding to pursue a career as a writer.

Ivanov is best known for his language-learning books for Russian language learners. His books are popular among both beginners and advanced learners, as they provide a comprehensive and engaging approach to learning the language. Ivanov's writing style is clear and concise, making his books accessible to a wide range of readers. He continues to write and publish new language-learning books, and is considered one of the leading experts in the field of Russian language education.

# Other Works by This Author

## Series: Learn Russian Grammar With Flashcards

Explore Russian with a unique series focusing on learning through context-rich example sentences. Enhance your understanding with intuitive grammar insights, supplemented by practical flashcards. Ideal for all levels, this approach promises a natural and effective mastery of Russian.

- Learn Russian Grammar with Flashcards vol. 1: Understanding the Basic Structure
- Learn Russian Grammar with Flashcards vol. 2: A Deep Dive into Naming Words - Nouns
- Learn Russian Grammar with Flashcards vol. 3: Action, State, and Linking Words Unveiled - Verbs
- Learn Russian Grammar with Flashcards vol. 4: The Art of Description - Adjectives
- Learn Russian Grammar with Flashcards vol. 5: Amplifying Meaning - Adverbs
- Learn Russian Grammar with Flashcards vol. 6: Mastering the Stand-ins - Pronouns
- Learn Russian Grammar with Flashcards vol. 7: Navigating Space, Time, and More - Prepositions
- Learn Russian Grammar with Flashcards vol. 8: Connecting Thoughts - Conjunctions
- Learn Russian Grammar with Flashcards vol. 9: Expressing Emotion and Interruption - Interjections
- Learn Russian Grammar with Flashcards vol. 10: Indicating Quantity and Possession - Determiners

## Series: Most Frequently Used Words

Introducing a unique Russian language book series, prioritizing the most frequently used words. Covering nouns, verbs and adjectives, it's perfect for enhancing spoken and written skills. Words are sorted by frequency, each with English translations and example sentences for comprehensive learning. Ideal for all levels, it's a great tool to master Russian vocabulary effectively.

1. The Most Frequently Used Russian Nouns: Save Time by

Learning the Most Frequently Used Words First

2. The Most Frequently Used Russian Adjectives: Save Time by Learning the Most Frequently Used Words First
3. The Most Frequently Used Russian Verbs: Save Time by Learning the Most Frequently Used Words First

# Introduction

Welcome to the enchanting world of Russian adjectives, the colorful words that paint our conversations and writings with vivid detail and emotion. This book is your comprehensive guide to mastering the most frequently used Russian adjectives, an essential toolkit for anyone eager to deepen their understanding and use of the language. Adjectives play a crucial role in language, allowing us to describe nouns, giving life to our descriptions, and making our communications more precise and interesting. Whether you're starting your journey into Russian or looking to enrich your existing skills, this collection of adjectives will expand your ability to express yourself with greater clarity and richness.

Adjectives are the words we use to modify or describe nouns and pronouns, offering additional information about an object's size, shape, age, color, origin, or material, among other qualities. They help us create a vivid picture in the listener's or reader's mind, enhancing our expressions and communications. For example, words like "beautiful," "large," "ancient," and "silky" transform simple sentences into more detailed and engaging narratives. "A beautiful garden," "a large room," "an ancient city," and "silky hair" not only tell us more about the nouns they describe but also evoke feelings and images, making the language more impactful and memorable.

In addition to the rich array of adjectives, this book also introduces you to the most frequently used adverbs, further enriching your vocabulary and expressive capabilities. Adverbs modify verbs, adjectives, or other adverbs, providing additional information about how, when, where, and to what extent an action is performed. For example, "quickly," "very," "yesterday," and "extremely" are adverbs that can describe how fast someone runs, the intensity of a feeling, the timing of an action, and the degree of a quality. By mastering the use of adverbs, you'll be able to convey your thoughts and actions with greater precision and nuance, making your Russian even more dynamic and expressive.

This book is designed not only to enhance your vocabulary but also to provide you with the tools to use adjectives and adverbs effectively in real-life contexts. Through practical examples and and comprehensive explanations, you'll learn how to select the perfect words to convey your thoughts and emotions accurately. As you progress through the chapters, you'll discover new ways to describe the world around you, enriching your conversations, writings, and understanding of the Russian language. Let's embark on this colorful journey together, unlocking the power of adjectives and adverbs to make your Russian more vivid and expressive than ever before.

— Ivan Ivanov

# Contents at a Glance

# 1. Full List

Initially, the words will be presented according to their *frequency of use*: starting with the most frequently used words, then slowly going to the least frequently used words. After this, the words will be organized alphabetically.

In the sections containing example sentences, English translations are provided separately, allowing you to concentrate on deciphering the meaning in English before consulting the provided translations for verification.

**1. так** — *so* — 'Так' is used to emphasize a quality or degree of something, to express agreement or confirmation, or to introduce a consequence or result. It can also be used to compare two things.
● *1. Я надеюсь, что это так. 2. Это так? 3. Ты так думаешь? 4. Полагаю, что так. 5. Нет, я так не думаю.* ● *1. I hope so. 2. Is that so? 3. You think so? 4. I guess so. 5. No, I don't think so.*

**2. просто** — *just, simply, merely* — 'Просто' is used to indicate simplicity or lack of complexity in a situation. It can also be used to emphasize the straightforwardness or ease of an action or task.
● *1. Просто иди. 2. Просто расслабься. 3. Просто сделай это. 4. Просто так. 5. Просто шучу. 6. Я просто не могу. 7. Довольно просто. 8. Просто невероятно. 9. Десерт был просто великолепен. 10. И тогда однажды он просто перестанет. 11. Он был просто сторонним наблюдателем. 12. Шум был просто случайным. 13. Она просто притворялась. 14. Роль была просто второстепенной. 15. Задача была просто формальностью.* ● *1. Just go. 2. Just relax. 3. Just do it. 4. Just like that. 5. Just kidding. 6. I simply can't. 7. Quite simply. 8. Simply incredible. 9. The dessert was simply marvellous. 10. And then, one day he will simply stop. 11. He was merely a bystander. 12. The noise was merely incidental. 13. She was merely pretending. 14. The role was merely incidental. 15. The task was merely a formality.*

**3. верно** — *right* — 'Верно' is used to indicate correctness or accuracy in a statement or action. It can also be used to express agreement or certainty. It is a versatile word that can be used in

various contexts to convey the idea of being correct or right.
● *1.* О верно. *2.* Верно-верно. *3.* Это не верно. *4.* Верно, сэр. *5.* Совершенно верно. ● *1.* Oh, right. *2.* Right, right. *3.* It's not right. *4.* Right, sir. *5.* Quite right.

**4. выше** — *up, above* — 'выше' is used to indicate a higher position or level in relation to something else. It can be used to describe physical height, rank, or quality. It is often used in comparisons to show something is above or superior to another.
● *1.* Выше голову. *2.* Все вышеперечисленное. *3.* Ни один из вышеперечисленных. *4.* Я выше мелких споров. ● *1.* Chin up. *2.* All of the above. *3.* None of the above. *4.* I'm above petty arguments.

**5. действительно** — *really, actually, indeed* — This word is used to emphasize the truth or reality of something, to confirm a statement, or to express surprise or admiration. It can also be used to convey a sense of sincerity or genuineness.
● *1.* Я действительно так делаю. *2.* Я действительно. *3.* Я действительно не знаю. *4.* Вы действительно так думаете? *5.* Действительно хорошо. *6.* Вы действительно в это верите? *7.* Ты действительно пришел. *8.* Ты действительно здесь. *9.* Это действительно может сработать. *10.* Мы действительно это сделали. *11.* О да, действительно. *12.* Нет, действительно. *13.* О, действительно. *14.* Я действительно являюсь. *15.* Я действительно делаю. ● *1.* I really do. *2.* I really am. *3.* I really don't know. *4.* You really think so? *5.* Really good. *6.* You actually believe that? *7.* You actually came. *8.* You're actually here. *9.* This might actually work. *10.* We actually did it. *11.* Oh, yes, indeed. *12.* No, indeed. *13.* Oh, indeed. *14.* I am indeed. *15.* I do indeed.

**6. более** — *more* — Used to compare two or more things, indicating that one has a higher degree of a certain quality or quantity than the other(s). Can also be used to emphasize a comparison or to express a preference for one option over another.
● *1.* Вы можете быть более конкретным? *2.* Гораздо более. *3.* И более. *4.* Но не более того. *5.* Тем более причина. ● *1.* Can you be more specific? *2.* Much more. *3.* And more. *4.* But no more. *5.* All the more reason.

**7. очень** — *very, extremely, highly, awfully* — 'Очень' is used to intensify the meaning of an adjective or adverb, indicating a high degree of the quality being described. It is commonly used in everyday speech to emphasize emotions, opinions, or physical attributes.

● *1.* Очень хорошо. *2.* Очень хороший. *3.* Очень смешно-. *4.* Очень. *5.* Очень хорошо, сэр. *6.* Мне очень жаль. *7.* Очень хорошо. *8.* Это очень срочно. *9.* Это очень любезно с вашей стороны. *10.* Очень вряд ли. *11.* Я в этом очень сомневаюсь. *12.* Я очень рекомендую это. *13.* Его очень - рекомендуют. *14.* Очень заразна. *15.* Мне очень жаль. *16.* Очень жаль. *17.* О, мне очень жаль. *18.* Нам очень жаль.

● *1.* Very well. *2.* Very good. *3.* Very funny. *4.* Very much. *5.* Very good, sir. *6.* I'm extremely sorry. *7.* Extremely well. *8.* It's extremely urgent. *9.* That's extremely kind of you. *10.* Highly unlikely. *11.* I highly doubt it. *12.* I highly recommend it. *13.* He comes highly recommended. *14.* Highly contagious. *15.* I'm awfully sorry. *16.* Awfully sorry. *17.* Oh, I'm awfully sorry. *18.* We're awfully sorry.

**8. немного** — *little, slightly* — 'немного' is used to indicate a small amount or degree of something, often implying a sense of scarcity or insufficiency. It can be used to describe quantities, qualities, or actions that are limited or minimal.

● *1.* Немного. *2.* Немного больше. *3.* Только немного. *4.* Да, немного. *5.* Я немного нервничаю. *6.* Немного выше оценк-и! *7.* Я знал Эдвардса лишь немного. ● *1.* Just a little. *2.* A little more. *3.* Just a little bit. *4.* Yeah, a little. *5.* I'm a little nervous. *6.* Slightly higher grades! *7.* I knew Edwardes only slightly.

**9. жалкий** — *sorry, miserable, pathetic, wretched* — 'Жалкий' is used to describe something or someone as pitiful, pathetic, or wretched. It conveys a sense of sorrow or sympathy towards the subject being described.

● *1.* Мне жалко его. *2.* Он жалкий негодяй. *3.* Это жалко. *4.* Как жалко. *5.* Насколько это жалко? *6.* Это было жалко. *7.* Ты такой жалкий. *8.* Он был жалким оправданием для человека. ● *1.* I feel sorry for him. *2.* He's a miserable wretch. *3.* It's pathetic. *4.* How pathetic. *5.* How pathetic is that? *6.* That was pathetic. *7.* You're so pathetic. *8.* He was a wretched excuse for a man.

**10. верный** — *sure, correct, loyal, faithful* — 'Верный' is used to describe something or someone that is reliable, trustworthy, accurate, or faithful. It conveys a sense of certainty and loyalty in various contexts, such as relationships, beliefs, or actions.

● *1.* Мы этого не знаем наверняка. *2.* Вы этого не знаете наверняка. *3.* Одно можно сказать наверняка. *4.* Мы не - знаем наверняка. *5.* Я не знаю наверняка. *6.* Это верно. *7.* Да это верно. *8.* Совершенно верно. *9.* Это верно? *10.* Это верно, Майкл. *11.* Их колли был верным компаньоном. *12.* Он верный товарищ. *13.* Напарник пиджа был верным проводником. *14.* Колли был верным компаньоном. *15.* Она верный товарищ. *16.* Мой верный щит! *17.* Она была верным другом. *18.* И навсегда они остались верны делу. *19.* Собака была верна своему хозяину. ● *1.* We don't know that for sure. *2.* You don't know that for sure. *3.* One thing's for sure. *4.* We don't know for sure. *5.* I don't know for sure. *6.* That is correct. *7.* Yes, that is correct. *8.* Quite correct. *9.* Is this correct? *10.* That's correct, Michael. *11.* Their collie was a loyal companion. *12.* He is a loyal companion. *13.* The pidge's partner was a loyal guide. *14.* The colley was a loyal companion. *15.* She's a loyal comrade. *16.* My faithful shield! *17.* She was a faithful friend. *18.* Evermore, they remained faithful to the cause. *19.* The dog was faithful to its owner.

**11. первый** — *first* — 'Первый' is used to indicate the initial or primary position in a sequence or ranking. It can also be used to describe something as being the earliest or most important of its kind.

● *1.* Вы первый. *2.* Перво-наперво. *3.* Я пойду первым. *4.* Это впервые. *5.* Кто первый? ● *1.* You go first. *2.* First things first. *3.* I'll go first. *4.* That's a first. *5.* Who's first?

**12. великий** — *great, grand* — 'Великий' is used to describe something of significant size, importance, or excellence. It can be used to emphasize the grandeur or greatness of a person, event, or object.

● *1.* Это звучит великолепно. *2.* Ты был великолепен. *3.* Она великолепна. *4.* Он великолепен. *5.* Они великолепны. *6.* Разве любовь не велика? *7.* Дворец халифа великолепен. *8.* Его великая идея была всего лишь фантазией. *9.* Резиденция губернатора великолепна. *10.* Ты великий. ● *1.* That sounds great. *2.* You were great. *3.* She's great. *4.* He's great. *5.* They're great. *6.* Ain't love grand? *7.* The khalifa's palace is grand. *8.* His grand idea was a mere fantasy. *9.* The governor's residence is grand. *10.* You're grand.

**13. последний** — *last, final* — 'Последний' is used to refer to the final or most recent item in a series or sequence. It can also indicate the last in a line or queue, or the ultimate occurrence of an event.

• *1.* Последний шанс. *2.* Это ваш последний шанс. *3.* Когда вы видели его в последний раз? *4.* Одна последняя вещь. *5.* Последний. *6.* Космос, последний рубеж. *7.* Это ваше последнее предупреждение. *8.* Это мое последнее предложение. *9.* Последнее предупреждение. *10.* Мое последнее предложение. • *1.* Last chance. *2.* This is your last chance. *3.* When was the last time you saw him? *4.* One last thing. *5.* Last one. *6.* Space, the final frontier. *7.* This is your final warning. *8.* That's my final offer. *9.* Final warning. *10.* My final offer.

**14. лучше** — *better* — 'лучше' is used to compare two or more things, indicating that one is superior to the others. It can also be used to express improvement or preference in a situation or action.

• *1.* Так-то лучше. *2.* Намного лучше. *3.* Даже лучше. *4.* Чувствуете себя лучше? *5.* Как нельзя лучше. • *1.* That's better. *2.* Much better. *3.* Even better. *4.* Feeling better? *5.* Never better.

**15. новый** — *new, fresh* — 'Новый' is used to describe something that is recently made, acquired, or discovered. It can also be used to indicate a change or a beginning of something. It conveys the idea of freshness and novelty.

• *1.* Как новый. *2.* Это новый. *3.* Он новый. *4.* Это был новый век. *5.* Совершенно новый. *6.* Новый старт. *7.* Это новый старт. *8.* Свежий апельсиновый сок. • *1.* Good as new. *2.* That's a new one. *3.* He's new. *4.* It was a new age. *5.* Brand new. *6.* Fresh start. *7.* This is a fresh start. *8.* Fresh orange juice.

**16. старый** — *old* — This word is used to describe something or someone that has been in existence for a long time or has a significant amount of age. It can also be used to indicate that something is outdated or no longer in its prime.

• *1.* Как в старые времена. *2.* Я стар. *3.* Привет, старый друг.

*4.* Мы старые друзья. *5.* Старый друг. ● *1.* Just like old times. *2.* I'm old. *3.* Hello, old friend. *4.* We're old friends. *5.* An old friend.

**17. большой** — *big, great, high, large* — This word is used to describe something that is of significant size or importance. It can refer to physical dimensions, quantities, or qualities. It is versatile and can be used in various contexts to convey a sense of magnitude.

● *1.* Это не большое дело. *2.* Большое дело. *3.* Это не имеет большого значения. *4.* Оно большое. *5.* Большой. *6.* У меня большие успехи. *7.* Это большая честь. *8.* Большие огненные шары! *9.* С большим удовольствием. *10.* Большой белый буйвол. *11.* Мы больше не учимся в старшей школе. *12.* Идите по большой дороге. *13.* У меня были такие большие надежды. *14.* Я возлагал на тебя такие большие надежды. *15.* Он возлагал большие надежды на фильм. *16.* На сколько большой? *17.* Большой. *18.* Очень большой. *19.* Турнир по лакроссу собрал большое количество зрителей. *20.* Ярость собрала большую толпу. ● *1.* It's no big deal. *2.* Big deal. *3.* It's not a big deal. *4.* It's big. *5.* A big one. *6.* I'm doing great. *7.* It's a great honor. *8.* Great balls of fire! *9.* With great pleasure. *10.* Great white buffalo. *11.* We're not in high school anymore. *12.* Take the high road. *13.* I had such high hopes. *14.* I had such high hopes for you. *15.* He held high expectation for the movie. *16.* How large? *17.* A large one. *18.* Very large. *19.* The lacrosse tournament drew a large crowd. *20.* The rager attracted a large crowd.

**18. приятный** — *nice, pleasant* — 'Приятный' is used to describe something that brings a sense of enjoyment or satisfaction. It can be used to describe a person, object, experience, or feeling that is pleasing or agreeable.

● *1.* Приятно познакомиться. *2.* Приятно видеть вас снова. *3.* Легко и приятно. *4.* Было приятно познакомиться. *5.* Разве это не приятно? *6.* Какой приятный сюрприз. *7.* Очень приятно. *8.* Это приятный сюрприз. *9.* Мне не приятно. *10.* Спуститесь ниже, где лежат приятные фонтаны. ● *1.* It's nice to meet you. *2.* Nice to see you again. *3.* Nice and easy. *4.* It was nice to meet you. *5.* Isn't that nice? *6.* What a pleasant surprise. *7.* Very pleasant. *8.* This is a pleasant surprise. *9.* It's not pleasant. *10.* Stray lower, where the pleasant fountains lie.

**19. добрый** — *kind* — 'Добрый' is used to describe someone who is friendly, generous, and considerate towards others. It can also be used to describe actions or gestures that are done with good intentions and a caring attitude.

● *1.* Вы слишком добры. *2.* Вы очень добры. *3.* Вы были очень добры. *4.* Ты так добр. *5.* Ты добр. ● *1.* You're too kind. *2.* You are very kind. *3.* You've been very kind. *4.* You're so kind. *5.* You're kind.

**20. левый** — *left* — 'левый' is used to describe something that is located on the left side or is associated with the left side. It can also be used figuratively to mean something that is incorrect or fake.

● *1.* Левый. ● *1.* The left one.

**21. достаточно** — *enough, sufficient* — This word is used to indicate that there is an adequate amount of something, or that a certain condition has been met. It can also be used to express that something is satisfactory or sufficient.

● *1.* Достаточно. *2.* Недостаточно. *3.* Этого не достаточно. *4.* Достаточно близко. *5.* Разве этого недостаточно? *6.* Этого достаточно? *7.* Этого достаточно. *8.* Недостаточно для выборов. ● *1.* That's enough. *2.* Not enough. *3.* It's not enough. *4.* Close enough. *5.* Isn't that enough? *6.* Is that sufficient? *7.* That's sufficient. *8.* Not sufficient for election.

**22. неправильный** — *wrong* — 'неправильный' is used to describe something that is incorrect, inaccurate, or not done in the right way. It can refer to actions, decisions, answers, or anything that deviates from what is considered to be right or proper.

● *1.* Не поймите меня неправильно. *2.* Неправильный номер. *3.* Это вышло неправильно. *4.* Опять неправильно. *5.* Вы идете неправильным путем. ● *1.* Don't get me wrong. *2.* Wrong number. *3.* That came out wrong. *4.* Wrong again. *5.* You're going the wrong way.

**23. плохой** — *bad, poor* — 'плохой' is used to describe something that is of low quality, not good, or unfavorable. It can be used to express dissatisfaction or disapproval towards a person, object, situation, or outcome.

● *1.* Неплохо. *2.* Это очень плохо. *3.* Насколько плохо? *4.*

Это не так уж плохо. *5.* Это плохо. *6.* Он плохо запоминал детали. • *1.* Not bad. *2.* That's too bad. *3.* How bad is it? *4.* It's not that bad. *5.* This is bad. *6.* He had poor retention of details.

**24. собственный** — *own* — 'Собственный' is used to indicate possession or ownership of something. It can also be used to emphasize that something belongs exclusively to a particular person or entity.

• *1.* Это ваша собственная вина. *2.* Мой собственный. *3.* Это для вашей собственной защиты. *4.* Получите свой собственный. *5.* Его собственный. • *1.* It's your own fault. *2.* My own. *3.* It's for your own protection. *4.* Get your own. *5.* His own.

**25. следующий** — *next* — 'Следующий' is used to refer to something that comes after the current one in a sequence or order. It can be used to indicate the next item, person, event, or action in a series.

• *1.* Кто следующий? *2.* В следующий раз. *3.* Возможно, в следующий раз. *4.* Увидимся на следующей неделе. *5.* Ты следующий. • *1.* Who's next? *2.* Next time. *3.* Maybe next time. *4.* See you next week. *5.* You're next.

**26. многие** — *many* — 'Многие' is used to describe a large quantity or number of people or things. It can be used to indicate a general sense of abundance or a significant portion of a group.

• *1.* Очень много. *2.* Много раз. *3.* Не много. *4.* Их слишком много. *5.* Так много вопросов. • *1.* Too many. *2.* Many times. *3.* Not many. *4.* There's too many of them. *5.* So many questions.

**27. лучший** — *best* — 'лучший' is used to describe something that is superior in quality or performance compared to others. It can also be used to indicate a preference or ranking among choices or options.

• *1.* Ты мой лучший друг. *2.* Всего наилучшего. *3.* Это для лучших. *4.* Он лучший. *5.* Это лучшее, что ты можешь сделать? • *1.* You're my best friend. *2.* All the best. *3.* It's for the best. *4.* He's the best. *5.* Is that the best you can do?

**28. реальный** — *real* — 'Реальный' is used to describe something that is genuine, authentic, or true. It can also be used to emphasize that something is tangible or concrete, rather than imaginary or hypothetical.

● *1.* Это реально. *2.* Это нереально. *3.* Это не реально. *4.* Это реально? *5.* Все это нереально. ● *1.* It's real. *2.* It's not real. *3.* This isn't real. *4.* Is it real? *5.* None of this is real.

**29. живой** — *live, lively* — 'Живой' is used to describe something that is alive, lively, or full of energy. It can refer to living organisms, as well as to things that are vibrant or active.

● *1.* У нас есть живой. *2.* Революция будет живой. *3.* Традиционное фанданго имело живой ритм. *4.* Анимация мультфильма была красочной и живой. ● *1.* We got a live one. *2.* The revolution will be live. *3.* The traditional fandango had a lively rhythm. *4.* The toon animation was colorful and lively.

**30. готовый** — *ready* — 'готовый' is used to describe something that is prepared or completed and can also be used to indicate readiness or willingness. It can be used to describe objects, people, or situations.

● *1.* Вы готовы? *2.* Я готов. *3.* Приготовься. *4.* Мы готовы. *5.* Готов идти? ● *1.* You ready? *2.* I'm ready. *3.* Get ready. *4.* We're ready. *5.* Ready to go?

**31. счастливый** — *happy, lucky* — This word is used to describe a feeling of joy or contentment, as well as to express good fortune or luck. It can be used to describe a person's emotional state or a positive outcome.

● *1.* Вы счастливы? *2.* Я счастлив. *3.* Я так счастлив. *4.* Ты счастлив? *5.* Счастлив теперь? *6.* Ты счастливчик. *7.* Ты был счастливчиком. *8.* Это твой счастливый день. *9.* Я счастливчик. *10.* Счастливая девочка. ● *1.* Are you happy? *2.* I'm happy. *3.* I'm so happy. *4.* You happy? *5.* Happy now? *6.* You're lucky. *7.* You were lucky. *8.* It's your lucky day. *9.* I'm lucky. *10.* Lucky girl.

**32. такой** — *such* — 'Такой' is used to describe a specific quality or characteristic of a person, thing, or situation. It can also be used to emphasize the degree of something or to refer to a particular item or person.

● *1.* Такой как? *2.* Я такой идиот. *3.* Нет такой вещи. *4.* Нет такой удачи. *5.* Ты такой идиот. ● *1.* Such as? *2.* I'm such an idiot. *3.* No such thing. *4.* No such luck. *5.* You're such an idiot.

**33. хорошенький** — *pretty* — 'Хорошенький' is used to describe something as pretty or attractive in a slightly informal or endearing way. It is often used to compliment someone's appearance or to describe something as cute or charming.

● *1.* Она хорошенькая. *2.* Очень хорошенькая. *3.* Такая - хорошенькая девочка. *4.* Разве она не хорошенькая? *5.* Не беспокой свою хорошенькую головку. ● *1.* She's pretty. *2.* Very pretty. *3.* Such a pretty little girl. *4.* Ain't she pretty? *5.* Don't worry your pretty little head.

**34. целый** — *whole* — 'целый' is used to describe something that is complete or entire, without any parts missing. It can also be used to emphasize the entirety of something or to indicate that something is not divided or broken.

● *1.* Целый год? *2.* Целый месяц? *3.* Там целый мир. *4.* Целый новый мир. *5.* Целый шар воска. ● *1.* A whole year? *2.* A whole month? *3.* There's a whole world out there. *4.* A whole new world. *5.* The whole ball of wax.

**35. жесткий** — *hard, tough, stiff* — 'Жесткий' is used to describe something that is firm, rigid, or unyielding. It can refer to physical objects, rules, or people's behavior. It conveys a sense of toughness or strictness.

● *1.* Вы заключаете жесткую сделку. *2.* Жестко налево! *3.* Действительно, милорд, это последовало жестко. *4.* Ты жесткий. *5.* Жестко! *6.* Она жесткая. *7.* Он жесткий. *8.* Жесткий призыв. *9.* Ну, жестко. *10.* Жесткая комната. *11.* Ты слишком жесткий. *12.* Легкий, как перышко, жесткий, как доска. *13.* Немного жестковат. *14.* Ты такой жесткий. *15.* Просто немного жестковат. ● *1.* You drive a hard bargain. *2.* Hard left! *3.* Indeed, my lord, it followed hard upon. *4.* You're hard. *5.* Hard alee! *6.* She's tough. *7.* He's tough. *8.* Tough call. *9.* Well, tough. *10.* Tough room. *11.* You're too stiff. *12.* Light as a feather, stiff as a board. *13.* A little stiff. *14.* You're so stiff. *15.* Just a little stiff.

**36. открытый** — *open* — 'Открытый' is used to describe something that is not closed or sealed. It can also be used to describe someone who is open-minded or welcoming. It can be used as an adjective or adverb in various contexts.

● *1.* Открыто. *2.* Держать глаза открытыми. *3.* Дверь была открыта. *4.* Дверь открыта. *5.* Двери открыты. ● *1.* It's open. *2.* Keep your eyes open. *3.* The door was open. *4.* The door's open. *5.* Door's open.

**37. немногие** — *few* — 'немногие' is used to describe a small number or amount of something. It indicates that there are not many of the specified item or group. It is often used to emphasize scarcity or rarity.

● *1.* Немного. *2.* Немногословный человек. *3.* Один из немногих. *4.* Я выпил немного. *5.* Мы выпили немного. ● *1.* Just a few. *2.* A man of few words. *3.* One of the few. *4.* I had a few drinks. *5.* We had a few drinks.

**38. истинный** — *true* — 'Істинный' is used to describe something that is genuine, real, or authentic. It can also be used to emphasize the truthfulness or accuracy of a statement or claim. It is often used to convey a sense of sincerity or honesty.

● *1.* Истинно верующий. *2.* Маска скрывала его истинные эмоции. *3.* Его видимость доброты скрывала его истинные намерения. *4.* Маскарад раскрыл ее истинную личность. *5.* Она могла сделать вывод о его истинных чувствах. ● *1.* A true believer. *2.* The mask hid his true emotions. *3.* His veneer of kindness hid his true intentions. *4.* The masquerade revealed her true identity. *5.* She could infer his true feelings.

**39. прекрасный** — *beautiful, lovely* — 'Прекрасный' is used to describe something that is visually appealing or delightful. It can be used to compliment a person, object, or experience. It conveys a sense of beauty, charm, and admiration.

● *1.* Ты выглядишь прекрасно. *2.* Ты прекрасна. *3.* Она прекрасна. *4.* Это прекрасно. *5.* Разве они не прекрасны? *6.* Это прекрасно. *7.* Вы прекрасно выглядите. *8.* Она прекрасна. *9.* Они прекрасны. *10.* Это было прекрасно. ● *1.* You look beautiful. *2.* You're beautiful. *3.* She's beautiful. *4.* This is beautiful. *5.* Aren't they beautiful? *6.* It's lovely. *7.* You look lovely. *8.* She's lovely. *9.* They're lovely. *10.* That was lovely.

**40. вероятно** — *probably* — 'Veroiatno' is used to indicate a high likelihood or probability of something happening or being true. It is often used to express uncertainty or speculation about a situation or event.

● *1.* Вероятно, он прав. *2.* Вероятно, так. *3.* Вероятно, она права. *4.* Вероятно, так и есть. *5.* Вероятно, это был просто ветер. ● *1.* He's probably right. *2.* Probably so. *3.* She's probably right. *4.* Probably is. *5.* It was probably just the wind.

**41. поздно** — *late* — 'поздно' is used to indicate that something is happening or done after the expected or desired time. It can refer to being late for an appointment, arriving late to a meeting, or completing a task after the deadline.

● *1.* Извините, я опоздал. *2.* Слишком поздно. *3.* Ты опоздал. *4.* Уже поздно. *5.* Становится поздно. ● *1.* Sorry I'm late. *2.* It's too late. *3.* You're late. *4.* It's late. *5.* It's getting late.

**42. молодой** — *young* — 'Молодой' is used to describe someone or something that is youthful or in the early stages of development. It can refer to age, freshness, or newness. It is often used to describe people, animals, or objects.

● *1.* Ты молод. *2.* Ты слишком молод. *3.* Я был молод. *4.* Она молода. *5.* Так молод. ● *1.* You're young. *2.* You're too young. *3.* I was young. *4.* She's young. *5.* So young.

**43. второй** — *second* — 'второй' is used to indicate the second in a series or sequence. It can also be used to compare two items or people, with one being the first and the other being the second.

● *1.* Второй этаж. *2.* Второй. *3.* А второй? *4.* Второй шанс. *5.* Второстепенные мысли? ● *1.* Second floor. *2.* The second one. *3.* And the second? *4.* A second chance. *5.* Second thoughts?

**44. сумасшедший** — *crazy, mad* — This word is used to describe someone or something that is behaving in an irrational or unpredictable manner. It can also be used to emphasize extreme emotions or actions.

● *1.* Он сумасшедший. *2.* Я не сумасшедший. *3.* Ты сумасшедший? *4.* Она сумасшедшая. *5.* Я сумасшедший? *6.* Почему ты сумасшедший? *7.* Он, должно быть, сумасшедший. *8.* Ты совершенно сумасшедший. *9.* Ты выглядишь сумасшедшим. *10.* Это был сумасшедший шлюха. ● *1.* He's crazy. *2.* I'm not crazy. *3.* You crazy? *4.* She's crazy. *5.* Am I crazy? *6.* Why are you mad? *7.* He must be mad. *8.* You're completely mad. *9.* You look mad. *10.* A whoreson mad fellow's it was.

**45. ровно** — *exactly* — 'ровно' is used to indicate precision or accuracy in describing a specific time, quantity, or measurement. It emphasizes that something is exact or precise without any deviation or variation.

• *1.* Взлом кабеля продлится ровно 60 секунд. *2.* Посылка весила ровно один килограмм. *3.* У вас есть ровно одна минута. • *1.* The cable hack will last exactly 60 seconds. *2.* The package weighed exactly one kilo. *3.* You have exactly one minute.

**46. дальний** — *far, distant* — This word is used to describe something that is physically far away or distant in space or time. It can also be used to describe something that is remote or removed in a figurative sense.
• *1.* Дальний угол. *2.* На дальней стороне. *3.* Родственники приехали из ближнего и дальнего зарубежья. *4.* Он дальний родственник. • *1.* Far corner. *2.* On the far side. *3.* The kinfolk came from near and far. *4.* He is a distant relative.

**47. внутри** — *inside* — 'Inside' is used to describe the location of something within a confined space or container. It can also be used to indicate a sense of containment or enclosure.
• *1.* Входи внутрь. *2.* Давай зайдем внутрь. *3.* Он внутри. *4.* Вернитесь внутрь. *5.* Она внутри. • *1.* Come inside. *2.* Let's go inside. *3.* He's inside. *4.* Go back inside. *5.* She's inside.

**48. различный** — *different, various* — 'Различный' is used to describe things that are not the same or are diverse in some way. It can be used to indicate a variety of options or choices, or to highlight differences between objects or ideas.
• *1.* Различные места. *2.* Различные люди. *3.* В книге обсуждались различные типы неврозов. *4.* Они исследовали различные методологии в полевых работах. *5.* Они изучали различные точки зрения. *6.* Он страдает различными недугами. *7.* Спортивный клуб предлагает различные спортивные программы. *8.* Центр предлагает различные мероприятия. *9.* Будучи дилетантом, он занимался различными хобби. *10.* Теория применима в различных областях. • *1.* Different places. *2.* Different people. *3.* The book discussed different neurosis types. *4.* They explored different methodologies in fieldwork. *5.* They studied different viewpoint perspectives. *6.* He suffers from various ailments. *7.* The athletic club offers various sports programs. *8.* The centre offers various activities. *9.* He pursued various hobbies as a dilettante. *10.* The theory is applicable in various fields.

**49. дорогой** — *dear, expensive* — 'Дорогой' is used to describe something that is considered valuable or costly. It can refer to both material possessions and emotional connections. It can also be used to address someone in an affectionate or respectful manner.

● *1.* Да, дорогой. *2.* Спасибо, дорогой. *3.* Привет, дорогой. *4.* Нет, дорогой. *5.* Мой дорогой. *6.* Это дорого. *7.* Очень дорого. *8.* Слишком дорого. *9.* Это слишком дорого. *10.* Это дорого? ● *1.* Yes, dear. *2.* Thank you, dear. *3.* Hello, dear. *4.* No, dear. *5.* My dear. *6.* It's expensive. *7.* Very expensive. *8.* Too expensive. *9.* It's too expensive. *10.* Is it expensive?

**50. близко** — *close* — 'Влизко' is used to indicate proximity or closeness in physical distance, time, or relationship. It can also be used to convey a sense of intimacy or familiarity in a figurative sense.

● *1.* Это было близко. *2.* Достаточно близко. *3.* Так близко. *4.* Как близко? *5.* Очень близко. ● *1.* That was close. *2.* Close enough. *3.* So close. *4.* How close? *5.* Very close.

**51. наименее** — *least* — 'Наименее' is used to indicate the lowest degree or amount of something. It is often used to compare different options or qualities and to express that something is the least in a particular context.

● *1.* Это наименьшая из ваших проблем. *2.* Это наименьшая из наших проблем. ● *1.* That's the least of your problems. *2.* That's the least of our problems.

**52. вполне** — *quite* — 'Вполне' is used to indicate a high degree of certainty or completeness. It can also be used to express agreement or approval. It is often used to emphasize that something is satisfactory or adequate.

● *1.* Да, вполне. *2.* Я вполне согласен. *3.* Вполне возможно. *4.* Вполне нормально. *5.* Я вполне понимаю. ● *1.* Yes, quite. *2.* I quite agree. *3.* Quite possibly. *4.* Quite all right. *5.* I quite understand.

**53. важный** — *important, newsworthy* — This word is used to describe something that holds significance or is of great importance. It can be used to highlight the importance of a person, event, or piece of information.

● *1.* Это важно. *2.* Это не важно. *3.* Это очень важно. *4.* Это действительно важно. *5.* Это важно? • *1.* It's important. *2.* It's not important. *3.* It's very important. *4.* It's really important. *5.* Is it important?

**54. больше не** — *anymore* — This word is used to indicate that something is no longer happening or will not happen in the future. It is often used to express a change in circumstances or behavior.

• *1.* Я больше не могу это терпеть. *2.* Я больше не знаю. *3.* Нет, больше нет. *4.* Но не больше. *5.* Я больше не могу этого делать. • *1.* I can't take it anymore. *2.* I don't know anymore. *3.* No, not anymore. *4.* But not anymore. *5.* I can't do it anymore.

**55. позади** — *behind* — 'позади' is used to indicate a position or direction behind something or someone. It can also be used metaphorically to refer to something that is in the past or has already happened.

• *1.* Никто не остается позади. *2.* Я оставил его позади. *3.* Я остаюсь позади. *4.* Мы никого не оставляем позади. *5.* Мы оставили его позади. • *1.* No one gets left behind. *2.* I left him behind. *3.* I'm staying behind. *4.* We leave no one behind. *5.* We left him behind.

**56. почти** — *almost, nearly* — 'почти' is used to indicate that something is very close to being true or complete, but not quite there. It is often used to express a high degree of approximation or proximity to a certain state or condition.

• *1.* Мы почти там. *2.* Почти готово. *3.* Я почти забыл. *4.* Я почти закончил. *5.* Я почти на месте. *6.* Мы почти у цели. *7.* Я почти там. *8.* Почти сделано. *9.* Я почти забыл. *10.* Вы почти у цели. • *1.* We're almost there. *2.* Almost there. *3.* I almost forgot. *4.* I'm almost done. *5.* I'm almost there. *6.* We're nearly there. *7.* I'm nearly there. *8.* Nearly done. *9.* I nearly forgot. *10.* You're nearly there.

**57. в состоянии** — *able* — This word is used to indicate the ability or capability of a person or thing to perform a certain action or task. It implies that the subject has the necessary skills, resources, or conditions to successfully complete the specified action.

• *1.* Я должен быть в состоянии сделать это. • *1.* I should be able to do this.

**58. бесплатно** — *free* — This word is used to describe something that does not require payment or cost. It can be used to indicate that a service, product, or event is provided without charge.

● *1.* Это бесплатно. *2.* Бесплатно. *3.* Они бесплатны. *4.* Оружие бесплатно. *5.* Первый бесплатно. ● *1.* It's free. *2.* For free. *3.* They're free. *4.* Weapons free. *5.* First one's free.

**59. глупый** — *stupid, silly, foolish* — This word is used to describe someone or something that lacks intelligence or common sense. It can be used to criticize someone's actions or decisions, or to describe something that is nonsensical or foolish.

● *1.* Не будь глупым. *2.* Это глупо. *3.* Не делай ничего глупого. *4.* Это было глупо. *5.* Я такой глупый. *6.* Не глупи. *7.* Это глупо. *8.* О, не глупи. *9.* Не глупо. *10.* Нет, не глупи. *11.* Не будь глупым. *12.* Это глупо. *13.* Не делай ничего глупого. *14.* Глупая девчонка. *15.* Я был глуп. ● *1.* Don't be stupid. *2.* It's stupid. *3.* Don't do anything stupid. *4.* It was stupid. *5.* I'm so stupid. *6.* Don't be silly. *7.* That's silly. *8.* Oh, don't be silly. *9.* No, silly. *10.* No, don't be silly. *11.* Don't be foolish. *12.* That's foolish. *13.* Don't do anything foolish. *14.* Foolish girl. *15.* I was foolish.

**60. передний** — *front* — 'Передний' is used to describe something that is located at the front or front-facing. It can refer to physical objects, positions, or directions. It can also be used figuratively to describe something that is leading or forefront.

● *1.* Она сидела в передней части. ● *1.* She sat in the front section.

**61. прохладный** — *cool* — This word is used to describe something that is slightly cold or refreshing, such as a breeze, weather, or a drink. It can also be used to describe a person's demeanor or attitude as calm and collected.

● *1.* Прохладный напиток был освежением. *2.* Она искупалась в прохладной воде. *3.* Они почувствовали прохладный ветерок на крыльце. *4.* Утро было туманным и прохладным. *5.* Наступившая ночь принесла прохладный ветерок. ● *1.* A cool drink was a refreshment. *2.* She took a dip in the cool water. *3.* They felt a cool breeze on the porch. *4.* The morning was misty and cool. *5.* The nightfall brought a cool breeze.

**62. полный** — *full, complete, total, thorough* — 'Полный' is used to describe something that is full, complete, total, or thorough. It can be used to emphasize the extent or intensity of a situation or to indicate that something is done to the fullest extent.

● *1.* Радуйся, Мария, полная благодати. *2.* Полная остановка. *3.* Я беру на себя полную ответственность. *4.* Полный импульс. *5.* Полное раскрытие. *6.* Задание выполнено. *7.* Полная трата времени. *8.* Ты полный идиот? *9.* Я полностью контролирую ситуацию. *10.* Я не полный идиот. *11.* Полная чушь. *12.* Это полная чушь. *13.* Это полная потеря. *14.* Это было полной неожиданностью. *15.* Это не была полная потеря. *16.* Горничная тщательно выполняла свою работу. ● *1.* Hail Mary, full of grace. *2.* Full stop. *3.* I take full responsibility. *4.* Full impulse. *5.* Full disclosure. *6.* Mission complete. *7.* A complete waste of time. *8.* Are you a complete idiot? *9.* I'm in complete control. *10.* I'm not a complete idiot. *11.* Total bullshit. *12.* This is total bullshit. *13.* It's a total loss. *14.* It was a total surprise. *15.* It wasn't a total loss. *16.* The housemaid was thorough in her work.

**63. иногда** — *sometimes, occasionally* — This word is used to indicate that something happens at irregular intervals or not very often. It is used to describe actions or events that occur occasionally or from time to time.

● *1.* Да, иногда. *2.* Иногда бывает. *3.* Ну, иногда. *4.* Я иногда так делаю. *5.* Иногда они это делают. *6.* Да, иногда. *7.* Она пекла иногда. *8.* Иногда они ходили в поход. ● *1.* Yeah, sometimes. *2.* It happens sometimes. *3.* Well, sometimes. *4.* I do that sometimes. *5.* Sometimes they do. *6.* Yes, occasionally. *7.* She baked occasionally. *8.* Occasionally, they went camping.

**64. снаружи** — *outside* — This word is used to describe something that is located or happening outdoors or beyond the confines of a particular space. It can also be used to indicate a perspective or viewpoint that is external or from the outside.

● *1.* Подожди снаружи. *2.* Я буду снаружи. *3.* Я подожду снаружи. *4.* Они снаружи. *5.* Это снаружи. ● *1.* Wait outside. *2.* I'll be outside. *3.* I'll wait outside. *4.* They're outside. *5.* It's outside.

**65. световой** — *light* — The adjective/adverb 'световой' is used to describe something related to light, such as brightness, illumination, or radiance. It can also refer to objects or devices that emit or reflect light.

● *1.* В нескольких миллиардах световых лет от дома. ● *1.* Several billion light years from home.

**66. жаркий** — *hot* — 'Жаркий' is used to describe something that has a high temperature or produces a lot of heat. It can also be used to describe intense emotions or passionate feelings.

● *1.* Жарко. *2.* Мне жарко. *3.* Тут жарко. *4.* Слишком жарко. *5.* Так жарко. ● *1.* It's hot. *2.* I'm hot. *3.* It's hot in here. *4.* It's too hot. *5.* It's so hot.

**67. смешной** — *funny, ridiculous* — This word is used to describe something that is humorous or absurd. It can refer to a joke, situation, or person that is funny or ridiculous in nature.

● *1.* Очень смешно. *2.* Что смешного? *3.* Это не смешно. *4.* Это очень смешно. *5.* Не смешно. *6.* Это смешно. *7.* Ты ведешь себя смешно. *8.* Ты выглядишь смешно. *9.* О, это смешно. *10.* Ну, это смешно. ● *1.* Very funny. *2.* What's so funny? *3.* That's not funny. *4.* That's very funny. *5.* Not funny. *6.* That is ridiculous. *7.* You're being ridiculous. *8.* You look ridiculous. *9.* Oh, that's ridiculous. *10.* Well, that's ridiculous.

**68. ясный** — *clear* — The word 'ясный' is used to describe something that is clear, bright, or easily understood. It can refer to clear weather, clear instructions, or a clear mind.

● *1.* Колокольчик издал ясный звон. ● *1.* The bell gave a clear ting.

**69. черный** — *black* — 'черный' is used to describe something that is the color black. It can also be used to describe something as dark, gloomy, or sinister.

● *1.* Он черный. *2.* Кофейный, черный. *3.* Оно черное. *4.* Черное и белое. *5.* Черный или белый? ● *1.* He's black. *2.* Coffee, black. *3.* It's black. *4.* Black and white. *5.* Black or white?

**70. белый** — *white* — The word 'белый' is used to describe something that is the color white. It can also be used to describe something that is pure, clean, or innocent.

● *1.* Красный или белый? *2.* Это белый. *3.* Ты белый. *4.* Он белый. *5.* Черный или белый? ● *1.* Red or white? *2.* It's white. *3.* You're white. *4.* He's white. *5.* Black or white?

**71. малый** — *small* — 'Малый' is used to describe something that is small in size or quantity. It can also be used to indicate a young age or low importance. It can be used as both an adjective and an adverb in Russian language.

● *1.* Малый калибр. ● *1.* Small caliber.

**72. больной** — *sick, ill, sore* — The word 'больной' is used to describe someone or something that is experiencing physical discomfort or illness. It can also be used to describe a situation or feeling that is causing pain or discomfort.

● *1.* Вы больной. *2.* Она больна. *3.* Она больна? *4.* Вы не больны. *5.* Это больной. *6.* Она больна. *7.* Она больна? *8.* Ты выглядишь больным. *9.* Она очень больна. *10.* Моя мать больна. *11.* Больное горло? *12.* Тебе больно? *13.* Больная тема. *14.* Он наносил мазь на больные мышцы. *15.* Мне больно. ● *1.* You're sick. *2.* She's sick. *3.* Is she sick? *4.* You're not sick. *5.* It's sick. *6.* She's ill. *7.* Is she ill? *8.* You look ill. *9.* She's very ill. *10.* My mother is ill. *11.* Sore throat? *12.* Are you sore? *13.* Sore subject. *14.* He applied liniment to the sore muscles. *15.* I'm sore.

**73. безопасный** — *safe, secure* — This word is used to describe something that is free from harm, danger, or risk. It can refer to physical safety, security, or emotional well-being. It implies a sense of protection and assurance.

● *1.* Ты в безопасности. *2.* Теперь ты в безопасности. *3.* Это небезопасно. *4.* Быть безопасным. *5.* Это безопасно. *6.* Это безопасно. *7.* Мы в безопасности. *8.* Все безопасно. *9.* Сокровищница была в безопасности. *10.* Они находились в безопасном хранилище весь день. ● *1.* You're safe. *2.* You're safe now. *3.* It's not safe. *4.* Be safe. *5.* It's safe. *6.* It's secure. *7.* We're secure. *8.* Everything's secure. *9.* The treasury was secure. *10.* They were in the secure vault all day.

**74. специальный** — *special* — This word is used to describe something that is unique, particular, or designed for a specific purpose. It can also be used to emphasize the importance or significance of something.

● *1.* Специальная доставка. *2.* Специальный агент Гиббс. *3.* Специальное издание! *4.* Специальный агент Джек Мэлоун. *5.* Специальный агент Джонсон. ● *1.* Special delivery. *2.* Special Agent Gibbs. *3.* Special edition! *4.* Special Agent Jack

Malone. *5.* Special Agent Johnson.

**75. серьезный** — *serious, grave, severe* — This word is used to describe situations, people, or actions that are significant, important, or require careful consideration. It can also be used to convey a sense of severity or gravity in a given context.

● *1.* Ты серьезно? *2.* Я серьезно. *3.* Нет, я серьезно. *4.* Вы серьезно? *5.* Это серьезно. *6.* Вы находитесь в серьезной опасности. *7.* Вы совершаете серьезную ошибку. *8.* Проблема с родинками была серьезной. *9.* Его проблемы с желудком были серьезными. *10.* Высыпания прыщей были серьезными. *11.* Анафилаксия вызвала серьезную реакцию. *12.* Последствия лжесвидетельства могут быть серьезными. ● *1.* Are you serious? *2.* I'm serious. *3.* No, I'm serious. *4.* You serious? *5.* This is serious. *6.* You are in grave danger. *7.* You're making a grave mistake. *8.* The mole problem was severe. *9.* His gastric issues were severe. *10.* The acne breakout was severe. *11.* The anaphylaxis caused a severe reaction. *12.* The consequences of perjury can be severe.

**76. красный** — *red* — 'Красный' is used to describe objects, people, or situations that are red in color. It can also be used to describe something that is intense, bright, or vivid.

● *1.* Оно красное. *2.* Красный. *3.* Оно было красным. *4.* Твои глаза красные. *5.* Отмените красный сигнал тревоги. ● *1.* It's red. *2.* The red one. *3.* It was red. *4.* Your eyes are red. *5.* Cancel red alert.

**77. возможный** — *possible* — 'Возможный' is used to describe something that can happen or exist. It can also be used to express a potential or hypothetical situation. It is often used to discuss options or outcomes that are within the realm of possibility.

● *1.* Возможно. *2.* Это невозможно. *3.* Как это возможно? *4.* Это возможно? *5.* Невозможно. ● *1.* It's possible. *2.* That's not possible. *3.* How is that possible? *4.* Is that possible? *5.* Not possible.

**78. верхний** — *top, upper, overhead* — 'Верхний' is used to describe something that is located at the top or upper part of something else. It can also be used to indicate something that is overhead or above another object.

● *1.* Верхний этаж. *2.* Верхний ящик. *3.* Верхняя полка. *4.* Верхний левый. *5.* В правом верхнем углу. *6.* Она занимала верхний бер. *7.* На верхних этажах было тихо. *8.* Держите верхнюю губу твердой. *9.* Они жили в верхней квартире. *10.* Она получила травму верхней части тела. *11.* Свои вещи - он хранил в верхнем отсеке. ● *1.* Top floor. *2.* Top drawer. *3.* Top shelf. *4.* Top left. *5.* Top right. *6.* She occupied the upper ber. *7.* The upper floors were quiet. *8.* Keep a stiff upper lip. *9.* They lived in the upper apartment. *10.* She suffered an upper body injury. *11.* He stored his belongings in the overhead compartment.

**79. радостный** — *glad, joyful, joyous* — This word is used to describe a feeling of happiness or joy. It can be used to express a positive emotion or to describe something that brings joy or happiness.

● *1.* Быть радостным. *2.* Радостное веселье продолжалось. *3.* Уличное веселье было радостным. *4.* Он отпраздновал это радостным танцем. *5.* Радостная новость. *6.* Триумф б-ыл радостным. *7.* Юбилей был радостным событием. *8.* Эта новость вызвала радостные слезы. ● *1.* Be glad. *2.* The joyful frolic continued. *3.* The revel in the streets was joyful. *4.* He celebrated with a joyous dance. *5.* Joyous news. *6.* The triumph was joyous. *7.* The jubilee was a joyous occasion. *8.* The news brought joyous tears.

**80. холодный** — *cold, chilly* — This word is used to describe something that has a low temperature or lacks warmth. It can refer to weather, objects, or emotions. It conveys a sense of coolness or frigidity.

● *1.* Холодно. *2.* Мне холодно. *3.* Тебе холодно? *4.* Мне так холодно. *5.* Это холодно. *6.* Холодно. *7.* Здесь холодно. *8.* Мне немного холодно. *9.* Холодный ветер прорезал ее пальто. *10.* Холодная погода была неожиданностью. ● *1.* It's cold. *2.* I'm cold. *3.* Are you cold? *4.* I'm so cold. *5.* That's cold. *6.* It's chilly. *7.* It's chilly in here. *8.* I'm a little chilly. *9.* The chilly wind cut through her coat. *10.* The chilly weather was unexpected.

**81. быстрый** — *fast, quick, swift, rapid* — This word is used to describe something that moves or happens at a high speed. It can refer to physical movement, mental processes, or the passing of time. It conveys a sense of efficiency and urgency.

● *1.* Не так быстро. *2.* Это было быстро. *3.* Сделай это быстро. *4.* Все произошло так быстро. *5.* Это произошло так быстро. *6.* Это было быстро. *7.* Я буду быстрым. *8.* Приходи быстро! *9.* Быстрее. *10.* Давай, быстро. *11.* Быстрое течение унесло лодку. *12.* Их контратака была быстрой и эффективной. *13.* Возмездие за его действия было быстрым. *14.* Осуждение было быстрым. *15.* Гильотина принесла быстрый конец. *16.* Она приняла быстрое решение. *17.* В этой тематической - области наблюдался быстрый рост. *18.* Компания пережила быстрый поворот. *19.* Его сердцебиение было быстрым. *20.* Река имела быстрое течение. ● *1.* Not so fast. *2.* That was fast. *3.* Make it fast. *4.* It all happened so fast. *5.* It happened so fast. *6.* That was quick. *7.* I'll be quick. *8.* Come quick! *9.* Be quick. *10.* Come on, quick. *11.* The swift current carried the boat away. *12.* Their counterattack was swift and effective. *13.* The retribution for his actions was swift. *14.* The condemnation was swift. *15.* The guillotine brought a swift end. *16.* She made a rapid decision. *17.* The focal area experienced rapid growth. *18.* The company experienced a rapid turnaround. *19.* His heartbeat was rapid. *20.* The river had a rapid current.

**82. сладкий** — *sweet, sugary* — This word is used to describe something that has a sweet or sugary taste, such as candy, desserts, or drinks. It can also be used to describe something that is overly sentimental or overly affectionate.

● *1.* Сладкие сны. *2.* Ты такой сладкий. *3.* О сладкий. *4.* Разве он не сладкий? *5.* Сладкая поездка. *6.* Употребление сладких напитков вредно для здоровья. *7.* Я должен избегать сладких напитков. ● *1.* Sweet dreams. *2.* You're so sweet. *3.* Oh, sweet. *4.* Isn't he sweet? *5.* Sweet ride. *6.* The consumption of sugary drinks is unhealthy. *7.* I must avoid sugary drinks.

**83. удачливый** — *lucky, weirdly* — 'Удачливый' is used to describe someone who is fortunate or lucky in a strange or unusual way. It can also be used to describe a situation or event that is oddly fortunate or lucky.

● *1.* Удачливый ублюдок. *2.* Ты очень удачливая девушка. *3.* Я чувствую себя удачливым. *4.* Он очень удачливый человек. *5.* Ты очень удачливый человек. ● *1.* Lucky bastard. *2.* You're a very lucky girl. *3.* I feel lucky. *4.* He's a very lucky man.

*5.* You're a very lucky man.

**84. тихий** — *quiet, silent, pacific* — This word is used to describe something or someone that is calm, peaceful, or not making much noise. It can refer to a quiet place, a silent person, or a peaceful atmosphere.

• *1.* Почему ты такой тихий? *2.* Очень тихий. *3.* Ты ужасно тихий. *4.* Ты очень тихий. *5.* Ты такой тихий. *6.* Тихий, но смертоносный. *7.* Сильный и тихий. *8.* Ты очень тихий. •
*1.* Why are you so quiet? *2.* Very quiet. *3.* You're awfully quiet.
*4.* You're very quiet. *5.* You're so quiet. *6.* Silent but deadly. *7.*
Strong and silent. *8.* You're very silent.

**85. осторожный** — *careful, wary, cautious, discreet* — This word is used to describe someone who is cautious and attentive in their actions, making sure to avoid potential dangers or mistakes. It can also refer to being discreet and thoughtful in decision-making.

• *1.* Осторожно, осторожно. *2.* Теперь осторожно. *3.* И будьте осторожны. *4.* Мы должны быть осторожны. *5.* Осторожнее с этим. *6.* Будьте осторожны. *7.* Мы должны быть осторожны. *8.* Она осторожный инвестор. *9.* Давайте будем осторожны. *10.* Она подошла к делу осторожно. *11.* Но будьте осторожны. *12.* Будьте осторожны. *13.* Но будьте осторожны. *14.* Посредник был надежным и осторожным. *15.* Мы должны быть осторожными. *16.* Она была осторожна со своими секретами. • *1.* Careful, careful. *2.* Careful now. *3.* And be careful. *4.* We have to be careful. *5.* Careful with that. *6.* Be wary. *7.* We must be cautious. *8.* She is a cautious investor. *9.* Let's be cautious. *10.* She took a cautious approach. *11.* But be cautious. *12.* Be discreet. *13.* But be discreet. *14.* The intermediary was reliable and discreet. *15.* We have to be discreet. *16.* She was discreet with her secrets.

**86. секретный** — *secret* — This word is used to describe something that is kept hidden or not known by others. It can also be used to describe actions or behaviors that are done in private or without others knowing.

• *1.* У правительства есть секретная система. *2.* У меня есть секретное оружие. *3.* Я секретный агент. *4.* Встретимся в секретной пещере. *5.* Секретное оружие? • *1.* The government has a secret system. *2.* I have a secret weapon. *3.* I'm a secret agent. *4.* Meet us down in the secret cave. *5.* Secret weapon?

**87. прямой** — *straight, direct, straightforward* — The word 'прямой' is used to describe something that is straight, direct, or straightforward. It can be used to indicate a direct path, a straightforward approach, or a blunt manner of speaking.

● *1.* Позвольте мне объяснить это прямо. *2.* Прямо. *3.* Встать прямо. *4.* Ты не думаешь прямо. *5.* Смотреть прямо вперед. *6.* Прямое попадание. *7.* Это прямой приказ. *8.* Вы не подчинились прямому приказу. *9.* Вы очень прямолинейны. *10.* Это прямая цитата. *11.* Прямой ответ был оценен по достоинству. *12.* Ее прямой подход к решению проблем оказался эффективным. *13.* Он ценил ее прямую честность.

● *1.* Let me get this straight. *2.* Straight ahead. *3.* Stand up straight. *4.* You're not thinking straight. *5.* Look straight ahead. *6.* Direct hit. *7.* That's a direct order. *8.* You disobeyed a direct order. *9.* You're very direct. *10.* That's a direct quote. *11.* The straightforward answer was appreciated. *12.* Her straightforward approach to problem-solving was effective. *13.* He appreciated her straightforward honesty.

**88. безумный** — *mad, insane, certifiable* — The word 'безумный' is used to describe something or someone as mad, insane, or certifiable. It conveys a sense of extreme irrationality or craziness.

● *1.* Ты звучишь безумно. *2.* Ты ведешь себя безумно. *3.* Ты звучишь безумно. *4.* Совершенно безумный. *5.* Ты выглядишь безумным. *6.* Раздался безумный смех. ● *1.* You sound mad. *2.* You're acting insane. *3.* You sound insane. *4.* Completely insane. *5.* You look insane. *6.* The insane laughter echoed.

**89. замечательный** — *wonderful, remarkable, admirable* — 'Замечательный' is used to describe something or someone that is exceptional, outstanding, or deserving of admiration. It conveys a sense of wonder and appreciation for the qualities or characteristics being described.

● *1.* Это замечательно. *2.* Это было замечательно. *3.* Ты замечательный. *4.* Это было бы замечательно. *5.* Она замечательная. *6.* Это замечательно. *7.* Замечательно, не так ли? *8.* Замечательная женщина. *9.* Замечательный человек. *10.* Он замечательный. *11.* Это замечательно. *12.* Она проявила замечательный такт. • *1.* It's wonderful. *2.* It was wonderful. *3.* You're wonderful. *4.* That would be wonderful. *5.* She's wonderful. *6.* It's remarkable. *7.* Remarkable, isn't it? *8.* Remarkable woman. *9.* A remarkable man. *10.* He's remarkable. *11.* That's admirable. *12.* She showed admirable tact.

**90. чистый** — *clean, pure, neat, sheer* — 'Чистый' is used to describe something that is clean, pure, neat, or sheer. It can refer to physical cleanliness, purity of a substance, tidiness, or transparency.
• *1.* Он чистый. *2.* Чисто. *3.* Я чист. *4.* Они чистые. *5.* Она чистая. *6.* Чистый и простой. *7.* Это чисто. *8.* Чистое зло. *9.* Такой чистый. *10.* Чистый гений. *11.* В комнате было чисто и порядок. *12.* Двор был чистым и опрятным. *13.* Он сказал это из чистой злости. *14.* Чистая решимость привела к успеху. *15.* Поступок был чистой глупостью. • *1.* He's clean. *2.* It's clean. *3.* I'm clean. *4.* They're clean. *5.* She's clean. *6.* Pure and simple. *7.* It's pure. *8.* Pure evil. *9.* So pure. *10.* Pure genius. *11.* The room was neat and orderly. *12.* The yard was neat and tidy. *13.* He said it out of sheer spite. *14.* Sheer determination led to success. *15.* The act was sheer stupidity.

**91. странный** — *strange, odd, weird, bizarre* — This word is used to describe something that is unusual or out of the ordinary, often in a way that is unsettling or unexpected. It can refer to both physical objects and behaviors.
• *1.* Это странно. *2.* Странно. *3.* Как странно. *4.* Очень странно. *5.* Странно, не так ли? *6.* Странно. *7.* Как странно. *8.* Это странно. *9.* Ну, это странно. *10.* Разве это не странно? *11.* Это странно. *12.* Это было странно. *13.* Ты странный. *14.* Это так странно. *15.* Странно, да? *16.* Это странно. *17.* Это было странно. *18.* Это так странно. *19.* Действительно странно. *20.* Как странно. • *1.* That's strange. *2.* It's strange. *3.* How strange. *4.* Very strange. *5.* Strange, isn't it? *6.* That's odd. *7.* How odd. *8.* It's odd. *9.* Well, that's odd. *10.* Isn't that odd? *11.* That's weird. *12.* That was weird. *13.* You're weird. *14.* It's so weird. *15.* Weird, huh? *16.* It's bizarre. *17.* It was bizarre. *18.* This is so bizarre. *19.* Really bizarre. *20.* How bizarre.

**92. сильный** — *strong, intense, severe, potent* — This word is used to describe something that is powerful, intense, severe, or potent. It can be used to describe physical strength, emotions, flavors, or any other quality that is strong or intense.

● *1.* Будь сильным. *2.* Ты сильная. *3.* Оставайся сильным. *4.* Это сильно. *5.* Он сильный. *6.* Это было сильно. *7.* Это сильно. *8.* Ну, это было сильно. *9.* Его увлечение ею было сильным. *10.* Боль была мучительно сильной. *11.* У него была сильная аллергия. *12.* Растяжение связок было сильным. *13.* У нее были сильные спазмы во время менструации. *14.* Мальчик испытывал сильную боль из-за аппендицита. *15.* Сильное обморожение потребовало медицинской помощи. *16.* Экстракт кураре был сильнодействующим. *17.* Лекарство оказалось сильным стимулятором. ● *1.* Be strong. *2.* You're strong. *3.* Stay strong. *4.* It's strong. *5.* He's strong. *6.* That was intense. *7.* That's intense. *8.* Well, that was intense. *9.* His infatuation with her was intense. *10.* The pain was excruciatingly intense. *11.* He had a severe allergy. *12.* The ligament strain was severe. *13.* She experienced severe cramps during menstruation. *14.* The young boy experienced severe pain from appendicitis. *15.* The severe frostbite required medical attention. *16.* The curare extract was potent. *17.* The medicine was a potent stimulant.

**93. общая** — *general* — 'Общая' is used to describe something that is common, shared, or overall in nature. It can be used to refer to a general concept, idea, or characteristic that applies to a group or situation as a whole.

● *1.* Это общая идея. *2.* Это была общая идея. ● *1.* That's the general idea. *2.* That was the general idea.

**94. занятой** — *busy* — 'Занятой' is used to describe someone who is occupied with tasks or responsibilities. It can also be used to describe a place or object that is in use or unavailable.

● *1.* Я занят. *2.* Я был занят. *3.* Вы заняты? *4.* Он занят. *5.* Ты занят? ● *1.* I'm busy. *2.* I've been busy. *3.* Are you busy? *4.* He's busy. *5.* You busy?

**95. полностью** — *completely, entirely, fully, totally* — 'Полностью' is used to emphasize that something is done or exists in its entirety, without any exceptions or omissions. It indicates a state of completeness or fullness in relation to a particular action, object, or concept.

● *1.* Я полностью понимаю. *2.* Не полностью. *3.* Я полностью согласен. *4.* Полностью отличается. *5.* Я полностью

доверяю тебе. *6.* Это полностью зависит от вас. *7.* Я не б-
ыл с тобой полностью честен. *8.* Вина полностью моя. *9.*
Я полностью намерен это сделать. *10.* Я полностью согласен. *11.* Мы полностью забронированы. *12.* Полностью
работоспособен. *13.* Он полностью загружен. *14.* Да, полностью. *15.* Я полностью понимаю. *16.* Полностью понима-
ю. *17.* Полностью согласен. *18.* Я это полностью понимаю.
● *1.* I understand completely. *2.* Not completely. *3.* I agree
completely. *4.* Completely different. *5.* I trust you completely.
*6.* It's entirely up to you. *7.* I haven't been entirely honest with
you. *8.* The fault is entirely mine. *9.* I fully intend to. *10.* I fully
agree. *11.* We're fully booked. *12.* Fully operational. *13.* It's fully
loaded. *14.* Yeah, totally. *15.* I totally understand. *16.* Totally
understand. *17.* Totally agree. *18.* I totally get that.

**96. круглый** — *round* — 'Круглый' is used to describe objects
that have a circular shape or are spherical in form. It can also be
used to describe events or situations that are complete or whole.
● *1.* Земля круглая. *2.* Пуля была круглой. *3.* Ее кот был к-
руглым масляным шариком. ● *1.* The earth is round. *2.* The
pellet was round. *3.* Her cat was a round butterball.

**97. синий** — *blue* — The word 'синий' is used to describe objects, places, or feelings that are of a blue color. It can also be
used to describe something that is sad or melancholic in nature.
● *1.* Код синий! *2.* Это синий. *3.* Это синий? *4.* Он синий. *5.*
Черный и синий. ● *1.* Code blue! *2.* It's blue. *3.* Is it blue? *4.*
He's blue. *5.* Black and blue.

**98. страшный** — *terrible, scary, fearsome, grisly* — This word is
used to describe something that is causing fear or terror, something that is terrible or grisly in nature. It is often used to convey
a sense of horror or dread.
● *1.* У меня есть страшная тайна. *2.* Страшная война. *3.* Он
в страшной опасности. *4.* Вы находитесь в страшной опасности. *5.* Это страшно. *6.* Это было страшно. *7.* Страшно, не
так ли? *8.* Довольно страшно, да? *9.* Я знаю, это страшно.
*10.* Страшная буря бушевала. ● *1.* I have a terrible secret. *2.*
A terrible war. *3.* He's in terrible danger. *4.* You are in terrible
danger. *5.* It's scary. *6.* It was scary. *7.* Scary, isn't it? *8.* Pretty
scary, huh? *9.* I know it's scary. *10.* The fearsome storm raged
on.

**99. определенно** — *definitely* — 'Определенно' is used to express certainty or assurance about a statement or opinion. It emphasizes the speaker's confidence in the truth or accuracy of what they are saying.

- *1.* Определенно да. *2.* Нет, определенно нет. *3.* О, определенно. *4.* О да, определенно. *5.* Это определенно он. ● *1.* Yeah, definitely. *2.* No, definitely not. *3.* Oh, definitely. *4.* Oh, yeah, definitely. *5.* It's definitely him.

**100. навсегда** — *forever* — 'навсегда' is used to indicate that something will last indefinitely or for an extremely long time. It conveys a sense of permanence and can be used to describe relationships, commitments, or promises.

- *1.* Не навсегда. *2.* Всегда и навсегда. *3.* Сейчас и навсегда. *4.* Прощай навсегда. *5.* Это было навсегда. ● *1.* Not forever. *2.* Always and forever. *3.* Now and forever. *4.* Goodbye forever. *5.* It's been forever.

**101. откровенный** — *frank, outspoken* — The word 'откровенный' is used to describe someone who is honest and direct in their communication, not holding back their thoughts or feelings. It conveys a sense of openness and sincerity in expressing one's opinions or emotions.

- *1.* Могу я быть откровенным? *2.* Давайте будем откровенны. *3.* Позвольте мне быть откровенным. *4.* Она откровенный трансвестит. ● *1.* Can I be frank? *2.* Let's be frank. *3.* Let me be frank. *4.* She is an outspoken transvestite.

**102. серьезно** — *seriously, gravely* — 'Серьезно' is used to convey a sense of seriousness or gravity in a situation. It can indicate that something is important, significant, or requires careful consideration.

- *1.* Нет, серьезно. *2.* Я имею в виду, серьезно. *3.* Я серьезно в этом сомневаюсь. *4.* Да, серьезно. *5.* Чувак, серьезно? *6.* Доктор серьезно посмотрел на нее. *7.* Лицо солдата было серьезно повреждено. *8.* Он сообщил эту новость серьезно. *9.* Выражение ее лица было очень серьезным. *10.* Он серьезно высказался о ситуации. ● *1.* No, seriously. *2.* I mean, seriously. *3.* I seriously doubt that. *4.* Yeah, seriously. *5.* Dude, seriously? *6.* The doctor looked at her gravely. *7.* The soldier's face was gravely injured. *8.* He delivered the news gravely. *9.* Her expression was gravely serious. *10.* He spoke gravely about the situation.

**103. простой** — *simple, plain, mere, idle* — 'Простой' is used to describe something that is straightforward, uncomplicated, or basic. It can also refer to something that is plain or ordinary, as well as something that is idle or not busy.

● *1.* Это не так просто. *2.* Это просто. *3.* Это очень просто. *4.* Это так просто. *5.* Просто как тот. *6.* Легко и просто. *7.* Это просто грубо. *8.* Просто как день. *9.* Отель был ничем не примечательным и простым. *10.* Одеяние монаха было простым и незамысловатым. *11.* Простая формальность. *12.* Это было простое совпадение. *13.* Задача была просто детской игрой. *14.* Их вместе свела простая случайность. *15.* Машина простаивала. ● *1.* It's not that simple. *2.* It's simple. *3.* It's very simple. *4.* It's that simple. *5.* Simple as that. *6.* Plain and simple. *7.* That's just plain rude. *8.* Plain as day. *9.* The hotel was unremarkable and plain. *10.* The monk's robe was simple and plain. *11.* A mere formality. *12.* It was a mere coincidence. *13.* The task was mere child's play. *14.* It was mere happenstance that brought them together. *15.* The machine lay idle.

**104. средний** — *middle, average, intermediate, middling* — This word is used to describe something that is in the middle or average in terms of size, quality, or quantity. It can also refer to something that is intermediate or middling in comparison to other things.

● *1.* Средний. *2.* Какой был средний? *3.* Он среднего роста, веса, интеллекта. *4.* На тесте она получила средний балл. *5.* Он был среднего роста. *6.* Еда была в лучшем случае средней. *7.* Его музыкальные способности находились на среднем уровне. *8.* Средний уровень требует некоторого опыта. *9.* Поход имел средний уровень сложности. *10.* От среднего до среднего. *11.* Ее оценки были средними. *12.* Она была довольна своим средним успехом. ● *1.* The middle one. *2.* What was the middle one? *3.* He's of average height, weight, intellect. *4.* She received an average score on the test. *5.* He was of average height. *6.* The food was average at best. *7.* His musical skills were at an intermediate level. *8.* The intermediate level required some experience. *9.* The hike had an intermediate level of difficulty. *10.* Fair to middling. *11.* Her grades were middling. *12.* She was content with her middling success.

**105. короткий** — *short, brief* — This word is used to describe something that is not long in length or duration. It can refer to physical objects, time periods, or descriptions. It is the opposite of something that is long or lengthy.

● *1.* Жизнь коротка. *2.* Жизнь слишком коротка. *3.* Спасибо, что пришли в такой короткий срок. *4.* Коротко и мило. *5.* Слишком короткий. *6.* Объятие было неловким и коротким. *7.* Поездка включала короткую остановку в Чикаго. *8.* Она коротко улыбнулась. *9.* У них произошла короткая размолвка. *10.* Короткий перерыв помог ей сосредоточиться. ● *1.* Life is short. *2.* Life's too short. *3.* Thank you for coming on such short notice. *4.* Short and sweet. *5.* Too short. *6.* The hug was awkward and brief. *7.* The trip included a brief stopover in Chicago. *8.* She gave a brief smile. *9.* They had a brief tiff. *10.* A brief break helped her refocus.

**106. одинокий** — *single, lonely, lone* — This word is used to describe someone or something that is alone or isolated, lacking companionship or support. It can also convey a sense of solitude or being the only one of its kind.

● *1.* Он одинок. *2.* Ты одинок. *3.* И одинокий. *4.* Как ты до сих пор одинок? *5.* Ты одинок, да? *6.* Я одинок. *7.* Я был одинок. *8.* Я так одинок. *9.* Ты одинок? *10.* Одиноко. *11.* Одинокий волк. ● *1.* He's single. *2.* You're single. *3.* And single. *4.* How are you still single? *5.* You're single, right? *6.* I'm lonely. *7.* I was lonely. *8.* I'm so lonely. *9.* Are you lonely? *10.* It's lonely. *11.* A lone wolf.

**107. нормальный** — *normal* — 'нормальный' is used to describe something that is considered standard, average, or typical. It can also be used to indicate that something is functioning properly or is in a satisfactory condition.

● *1.* Это нормально. *2.* Это нормально? *3.* Это ненормально. *4.* Веди себя нормально. *5.* Вернуться к нормальной жизни. ● *1.* It's normal. *2.* Is that normal? *3.* It's not normal. *4.* Act normal. *5.* Back to normal.

**108. ключевой** — *key* — 'Key' is used to describe something that is essential, crucial, or pivotal to a situation or outcome. It can also refer to something that unlocks or opens up new possibilities or solutions.

● *1.* Моли была ключевым ингредиентом. *2.* Консистенция

является ключевым моментом в выпечке. *3.* Поставщик был ключевым партнером. *4.* Эффективное общение является ключевым моментом. *5.* Вольфрам был ключевым ресурсом. ● *1.* Moly was a key ingredient. *2.* Consistency is key in baking. *3.* The supplier was a key partner. *4.* Effective communication is key. *5.* Wolfram was a key resource.

**109. быстро** — *quickly, fast, quick* — The word 'быстро' is used to describe actions or movements that are done with speed or efficiency. It can be used to indicate the rapidity of a process or the swiftness of a person's actions.

● *1.* Сделайте это быстро. *2.* Быстро, быстро. *3.* Давай, быстро. *4.* Быстро идти. *5.* Быстрее пожалуйста. *6.* Не так быстро. *7.* Это было быстро. *8.* Сделай это быстро. *9.* Все произошло так быстро. *10.* Это произошло так быстро. *11.* Это было быстро. *12.* Я буду быстрым. *13.* Приходи быстро! *14.* Быстрее. *15.* Давай, быстро. ● *1.* Do it quickly. *2.* Quickly, quickly. *3.* Come on, quickly. *4.* Go quickly. *5.* Quickly, please. *6.* Not so fast. *7.* That was fast. *8.* Make it fast. *9.* It all happened so fast. *10.* It happened so fast. *11.* That was quick. *12.* I'll be quick. *13.* Come quick! *14.* Be quick. *15.* Come on, quick.

**110. личный** — *personal* — This word is used to describe something that is related to or belongs to a specific individual. It can also be used to emphasize the personal nature of something.

● *1.* Это личное. *2.* Ничего личного. *3.* Могу я задать тебе личный вопрос? *4.* Это не личное. *5.* Это не было личным. ● *1.* It's personal. *2.* Nothing personal. *3.* Can I ask you a personal question? *4.* It's not personal. *5.* It wasn't personal.

**111. глубоко** — *deep, deeply* — This word is used to describe something that is deep in a physical or metaphorical sense. It can also be used to describe the intensity or extent of a feeling or emotion.

● *1.* Сделайте глубокий вдох. *2.* Глубокий вдох. *3.* Дышите глубоко. *4.* Это глубоко. *5.* Как глубоко? *6.* Глубоко дышать. *7.* Просто дышите глубоко. *8.* Я глубоко тронут. *9.* Дышите глубоко. *10.* Фолликул был глубоко укоренен. ● *1.* Take a deep breath. *2.* Deep breath. *3.* Breathe deep. *4.* That's deep. *5.* How deep? *6.* Breathe deeply. *7.* Just breathe deeply. *8.* I'm deeply moved. *9.* Breath deeply. *10.* The follicle was deeply rooted.

**112. определенный** — *certain, specific, definite* — This word is used to describe something that is known or specified, rather than general or vague. It is used to indicate a particular item or idea, rather than something uncertain or unspecified.

• *1.* Фетва запрещала определенные виды деятельности. *2.* В обществе существуют определенные правила. *3.* Была предрасположенность к определенному поведению. *4.* Ничего определенного. *5.* В этом есть определенная мистика. *6.* Компания ориентировалась на определенную аудиторию. *7.* Стоматолог порекомендовал определенный тип жидкости для полоскания рта. *8.* Церковь принадлежит к определенной конфессии. *9.* У каждого компонента есть определенные потребности. *10.* Это не определенно. *11.* Был определенный план. *12.* Это определенно? *13.* Наиболее определенно. *14.* У него было определенное мнение. • *1.* The fatwa banned certain activities. *2.* Society has certain rules. *3.* There was a predisposition to certain behaviors. *4.* Nothing for certain. *5.* There's a certain mystique about it. *6.* The company targeted a specific demographic. *7.* The dentist recommended a specific type of mouthwash. *8.* The church is of a specific denomination. *9.* Each constituent has specific needs. *10.* It's not definite. *11.* There was a definite plan. *12.* Is it definite? *13.* Most definite. *14.* He had a definite opinion.

**113. умный** — *smart, clever, intelligent* — 'Умный' is used to describe someone who is intelligent, clever, or smart. It is often used to compliment someone's mental abilities or problem-solving skills. It can also be used to describe objects or actions that are clever or well-thought-out.

• *1.* Он умный. *2.* Умный ход. *3.* Умный человек. *4.* Какой ты умный. *5.* Ты умный парень. *6.* Умный мальчик. *7.* Ты умный. *8.* Ты очень умный. *9.* Ты такой умный. *10.* Я умный. *11.* Очень умный. *12.* Ты умный человек. *13.* И умный. *14.* Он очень умный. *15.* Умный робот может выполнять сложные задачи. • *1.* He's smart. *2.* Smart move. *3.* Smart man. *4.* You're so smart. *5.* You're a smart guy. *6.* Clever boy. *7.* You're clever. *8.* You're very clever. *9.* You're so clever. *10.* I'm clever. *11.* Very intelligent. *12.* You're an intelligent man. *13.* And intelligent. *14.* He's very intelligent. *15.* An intelligent robot can perform complex tasks.

**114. сердитый** — *angry* — The word 'сердитый' is used to describe someone or something that is feeling or showing anger. It can be used to express frustration, irritation, or displeasure in various situations.

● *1.* Не сердитесь. *2.* Вы сердитесь на меня? *3.* Пожалуйста, не сердитесь. *4.* Пожалуйста, не сердитесь на меня. *5.* Ты выглядишь сердитым. ● *1.* Don't be angry. *2.* Are you angry with me? *3.* Please don't be angry. *4.* Please don't be angry with me. *5.* You look angry.

**115. богатый** — *rich, wealthy, plentiful, opulent* — This word is used to describe someone or something that has a lot of money or possessions, or something that is abundant or luxurious. It can also refer to something that is full or rich in flavor.

● *1.* Мы богаты! *2.* Я богат. *3.* Это богато. *4.* Ты богат. *5.* Мы будем богатыми. *6.* Семья Кларенса богата. *7.* На вечеринке присутствовала богатая элита. *8.* Им посчастливилось быть богатыми. *9.* Очень богатый. *10.* Владелец плантации был богатым и влиятельным человеком. *11.* Поместье было богатым. *12.* Пышная демонстрация богатства была экстравагантной. ● *1.* We're rich! *2.* I'm rich. *3.* That's rich. *4.* You're rich. *5.* We're gonna be rich. *6.* Clarence's family is wealthy. *7.* The wealthy elite attended the party. *8.* They were fortunate enough to be wealthy. *9.* Very wealthy. *10.* The plantation owner was wealthy and powerful. *11.* The estate was opulent. *12.* The opulent display of wealth was extravagant.

**116. золотой** — *gold, golden* — 'Золотой' is used to describe something that is gold in color or made of gold. It can also be used figuratively to describe something as being of high value or quality, similar to the precious metal gold.

● *1.* На пиджаке были золотые пуговицы. *2.* Ох уж эти золотые тапочки! *3.* Молчание - золото. *4.* Мы золотые. *5.* Золотое солнце наполнило комнату. *6.* Золотой орел. ● *1.* The blazer had gold buttons. *2.* Oh, dem golden slippers! *3.* Silence is golden. *4.* We're golden. *5.* The golden sunshine filled the room. *6.* A golden eagle.

**117. гордый** — *proud, prideful* — The word 'гордый' is used to describe someone who feels a sense of satisfaction and self-respect in their achievements or qualities. It can also be used to describe something that evokes a feeling of pride or admiration.

• *1.* Я так горд тобой. *2.* Ты должен гордиться. *3.* Вы, должно быть, очень гордитесь. *4.* Заставить меня гордиться. *5.* Вы должны гордиться. *6.* Она стояла гордая и гордая. *7.* Он был слишком горд, чтобы признать поражение. *8.* Его гордый характер отталкивает. *9.* Она чувствовала гордость за свои достижения. *10.* Гордые отношения могут быть вредными.
• *1.* I am so proud of you. *2.* You should be proud. *3.* You must be very proud. *4.* Make me proud. *5.* You must be proud. *6.* She stood proud and prideful. *7.* He was too prideful to admit defeat. *8.* His prideful nature is off-putting. *9.* She felt prideful of her achievements. *10.* A prideful attitude can be harmful.

**118. общественный** — *public, societal* — This word is used to describe something that is related to or involves the general public or society as a whole. It can refer to public institutions, events, or attitudes that impact the community at large.
• *1.* Это общественное место. *2.* Он общественный деятель. *3.* Это общественная собственность. *4.* Общественность требовала ответов. *5.* Она избегала проблем с общественным транспортом. *6.* Он чувствовал принуждение общественных ожиданий. • *1.* This is a public place. *2.* He's a public figure. *3.* This is public property. *4.* The public demanded answers. *5.* She avoided the hassle of public transportation. *6.* He felt the coercion of societal expectations.

**119. печальный** — *sad, grievous, lamentable* — This word is used to describe something that evokes feelings of sadness, grief, or lament. It is often used to express a sense of sorrow or disappointment in a situation or person.
• *1.* Печально. *2.* Это печальная история. *3.* Насколько это печально? *4.* Разрушение здания было печальным. *5.* Печальный день. • *1.* That's sad. *2.* It's a sad story. *3.* How sad is that? *4.* The ruination of the building was sad. *5.* Sad day.

**120. английский** — *english* — This word is used to describe something or someone related to the country, language, or culture of England. It can also be used to refer to the English language itself.
• *1.* Я английский. *2.* Где ты выучил английский? *3.* Класс на английском языке. *4.* Я подозреваю, что вы английский шпион. *5.* В колледже она изучала английскую литературу.
• *1.* I'm English. *2.* Where did you learn English? *3.* The class

is in english. *4.* I suspect you may be an English spy. *5.* She studied English literature in college.

**121. голодный** — *hungry* — This word is used to describe the feeling of needing to eat food. It can also be used to describe a place or situation where there is a lack of food or resources.

● *1.* Вы голодны? *2.* Вы, должно быть, голодны. *3.* Она - голодна. *4.* Мы голодны. *5.* Ребята, вы голодны? ● *1.* Are you hungry? *2.* You must be hungry. *3.* She's hungry. *4.* We're hungry. *5.* You guys hungry?

**122. третий** — *third* — 'Третий' is used to indicate the position of something in a sequence, with two items coming before it. It can also be used to describe the order in which something occurs or is ranked.

● *1.* Третий этаж. *2.* А третий? *3.* Третий раз на этой неделе. *4.* Третий раз - это прелесть. *5.* Это уже третий раз. ● *1.* Third floor. *2.* And the third? *3.* Third time this week. *4.* Third time's the charm. *5.* This is the third time.

**123. часто** — *often, frequently, oft* — This word is used to describe how frequently something occurs or is done. It indicates a high frequency or repetition of an action or event. It is often used to convey a sense of regularity or routine.

● *1.* Вы сюда часто ходите? *2.* Как часто? *3.* Не часто. *4.* Вы часто сюда приезжаете? *5.* Приезжают сюда часто? *6.* Да, часто. *7.* В книге автор часто использовал слово «раскавычивать». *8.* Она часто бывала в парке. *9.* Она часто обедала в ресторане «Бист». *10.* Часто меняющиеся погодные условия. ● *1.* Do you come here often? *2.* How often? *3.* Not often. *4.* You come here often? *5.* Come here often? *6.* Yes, frequently. *7.* The author used 'unquote' frequently in the book. *8.* She frequently visited the park. *9.* She frequently dined at the bist. *10.* Frequently changing weather patterns.

**124. честный** — *honest* — The word 'честный' is used to describe someone or something that is truthful, sincere, and fair. It can also be used to describe actions or behavior that are morally upright and free from deceit or fraud.

● *1.* Будь честным. *2.* Будем честны. *3.* Я просто говорю честно. *4.* Могу ли я быть честным? *5.* Это была честная ошибка. ● *1.* Be honest. *2.* Let's be honest. *3.* I'm just being honest. *4.* Can I be honest? *5.* It was an honest mistake.

**125. кровавый** — *bloody* — The word 'кровавый' is used to describe something that is related to blood or has a bloody appearance. It can also be used figuratively to describe something violent or intense.

● *1.* Кровавый ад. *2.* Кровавая Мэри. *3.* Кровавый идиот! *4.* Какой кровавый беспорядок. *5.* Кровавый дурак. ● *1.* Bloody hell. *2.* Bloody Mary. *3.* Bloody idiot! *4.* What a bloody mess. *5.* Bloody fool.

**126. частный** — *private, proprietary* — The word 'частный' is used to describe something that is private or proprietary, typically referring to ownership or individual rights. It can also be used to indicate something that is not public or shared.

● *1.* Это частная собственность. *2.* Я частный детектив. *3.* Это частная вечеринка. *4.* Частная вечеринка. *5.* Это частный разговор. ● *1.* This is private property. *2.* I'm a private investigator. *3.* This is a private party. *4.* Private party. *5.* This is a private conversation.

**127. невозможно** — *impossible* — 'невозможно' is used to describe something that cannot be done or achieved. It conveys the idea of impossibility or something that is not feasible or realistic.

● *1.* Это невозможно. *2.* Но это невозможно. *3.* Нет, это невозможно. *4.* Ты невозможен. *5.* Это не невозможно. ● *1.* That's impossible. *2.* But that's impossible. *3.* No, that's impossible. *4.* You're impossible. *5.* It's not impossible.

**128. особенно** — *especially, particularly, notably, singularly* — 'особенно' is used to emphasize a specific quality or characteristic that stands out from the rest. It is often used to highlight something as being particularly important, significant, or unique in comparison to other things.

● *1.* Особенно ты. *2.* Не особенно. *3.* Особенно меня. *4.* Особенно сейчас. *5.* Особенно этот. *6.* Не особенно. *7.* Нет, не особенно. *8.* Ой, не особенно. *9.* Особенно сейчас. *10.* Собака была особенно разговорчива. ● *1.* Especially you. *2.* Not especially. *3.* Especially me. *4.* Especially now. *5.* Especially this one. *6.* Not particularly. *7.* No, not particularly. *8.* Oh, not particularly. *9.* Particularly now. *10.* The dog was feeling particularly talky.

**129. французский** — *french* — 'французский' is used to describe something or someone that is related to France or the French language. It can also be used as an adverb to describe actions or behaviors that are characteristic of French culture.

● *1.* Это французский. *2.* Простите за мой французский. *3.* Французский тост. *4.* Извините за мой французский. *5.* Французская рыбка! ● *1.* It's French. *2.* Pardon my French. *3.* French toast. *4.* Excuse my French. *5.* French fish!

**130. зеленый** — *green* — This word is used to describe objects, plants, or landscapes that have a color similar to that of grass or leaves. It can also be used to describe someone who is inexperienced or naive.

● *1.* Это зеленый. *2.* Все зеленое. *3.* Зеленая. *4.* Свет зеленый. *5.* Сойлент зеленый – это люди. ● *1.* It's green. *2.* All green. *3.* The green one. *4.* The light's green. *5.* Soylent green is people.

**131. милый** — *cute, lovable, likeable, cutesy* — 'Милый' is used to describe someone or something as cute, lovable, likeable, or cutesy. It is often used to express affection or admiration towards a person, animal, or object.

● *1.* Он милый. *2.* Он такой милый. *3.* Ты такой милый. *4.* Разве он не милый? *5.* Он милый? *6.* Ты милый. *7.* Милый персонаж, на самом деле. *8.* Я милый. *9.* Он такой милый, когда ему страшно. *10.* Вот почему он такой милый. ● *1.* He's cute. *2.* He's so cute. *3.* You're so cute. *4.* Isn't he cute? *5.* Is he cute? *6.* You're lovable. *7.* A lovable character, really. *8.* I'm lovable. *9.* He's so lovable when he's scared. *10.* That's why he's so lovable.

**132. святой** — *holy, saintly, sainted* — 'Святой' is used to describe someone or something as holy, saintly, or sainted. It is often used in religious contexts to refer to individuals who are considered to be exceptionally virtuous or sacred.

● *1.* Святое дерьмо. *2.* Святая корова! *3.* Святая моли. *4.* Святая скумбрия! *5.* Святой дым! *6.* У него была святая аура. *7.* Он святой персонаж. *8.* Святый поступок доброты. *9.* Святая женщина помогла всем. *10.* У нее святая натура. *11.* Святый лидер был символом надежды. *12.* Святитель был известен своей щедростью. *13*. Она молилась святым предкам. *14*. Ег-о святая мать всегда была доброй. *15*. Святитель почитался многими. • *1*. Holy crap. *2*. Holy cow! *3*. Holy moly. *4*. Holy mackerel! *5*. Holy smokes! *6*. He had a saintly aura. *7*. He is a saintly figure. *8*. A saintly act of kindness. *9*. The saintly woman helped everyone. *10*. She has a saintly nature. *11*. The sainted leader was a symbol of hope. *12*. The sainted man was known for his generosity. *13*. She prayed to the sainted ancestors. *14*. His sainted mother was always kind. *15*. The sainted figure was revered by many.

**133. злой** — *evil, wicked* — 'Злой' is used to describe someone or something as evil or wicked. It can be used to convey a sense of malice or ill-intent. It is often used to describe a person's behavior or a situation.

• *1*. Ты злой. *2*. Он злой. *3*. Я не злой. *4*. Ты злой! *5*. Ты не злой. *6*. Злой – это хорошо. *7*. Ты злой! *8*. Я не злой. • *1*. You're evil. *2*. He's evil. *3*. I'm not evil. *4*. You evil! *5*. You're not evil. *6*. Wicked is good. *7*. You're wicked! *8*. I'm not wicked.

**134. медленный** — *slow* — This word is used to describe something that is not fast or quick in movement, speed, or progress. It can be used to describe a person, object, or action that is deliberate or unhurried.

• *1*. Красиво и медленно. *2*. Слишком медленно. *3*. Двигайся медленнее. *4*. Медленно, но уверенно. *5*. Медленно вперед. • *1*. Nice and slow. *2*. Too slow. *3*. Go slow. *4*. Slow and steady. *5*. Slow ahead.

**135. огромный** — *huge, enormous, vast, massive* — This word is used to describe something that is very large in size or quantity. It emphasizes the immense scale or magnitude of an object or concept, conveying a sense of grandeur or overwhelming size.

• *1*. Это огромная. *2*. Это огромно. *3*. Это место огромно. *4*. Вы совершаете огромную ошибку. *5*. Это было огромно. *6*. Это огромно. *7*. Это место огромно. *8*. Они огромны. *9*. Халифат претендовал на огромные территории. *10*. Империя магната была огромной. *11*. Саванна была огромной и изобиловала дикой природой. *12*. Болото огромное. *13*. Каньон был огромным и глубоким. *14*. Это огромно. *15*. Это место огромное. *16*. На поляне они заметили огромного лося. *17*. Люди восхищались огромным дирижаблем. *18*. Поместье Бернсайдов огромно. • *1.* It's huge. *2.* This is huge. *3.* This place is huge. *4.* You're making a huge mistake. *5.* It was huge. *6.* It's enormous. *7.* This place is enormous. *8.* They're enormous. *9.* The caliphate claimed vast territories. *10.* The tycoon's empire was vast. *11.* The savannah was vast and teeming with wildlife. *12.* The swamp is vast. *13.* The canyon was vast and deep. *14.* It's massive. *15.* This place is massive. *16.* They spotted a massive elk in the clearing. *17.* People marveled at the massive zeppelin. *18.* The Burnside estate is massive.

**136. грязный** — *dirty, muddy, filthy, messy* — This word is used to describe something that is not clean or tidy, often referring to dirt, mud, or filth. It can also be used to describe messy or disorganized situations or environments.

• *1.* Это грязно. *2.* Ты грязный. *3.* Ты грязный ублюдок! *4.* Мне нравится, когда ты говоришь грязно. *5.* Я чувствую себя грязным. *6.* Даг был грязным от дождя. *7.* Это грязно. *8.* Ты грязный. *9.* Убери от меня свои грязные руки! *10.* Это место грязное. *11.* Я грязный. *12.* Это грязно. *13.* Это может стать грязным. *14.* Это немного грязно. *15.* Довольно грязно. *16.* Его волосы были неопрятными и грязными. • *1.* It's dirty. *2.* You're dirty. *3.* You dirty bastard! *4.* I love it when you talk dirty. *5.* I feel dirty. *6.* The dag was muddy from the rain. *7.* It's filthy. *8.* You're filthy. *9.* Get your filthy hands off me! *10.* This place is filthy. *11.* I'm filthy. *12.* It's messy. *13.* This could get messy. *14.* It's a little messy. *15.* Pretty messy. *16.* His hair was unkempt and messy.

**137. немедленно** — *immediately, forthwith* — 'Немедленно' is used to convey a sense of urgency or immediacy in a situation. It is often used to emphasize the need for prompt action or a quick response to a request or command.

• *1.* Вступает в силу немедленно. *2.* Немедленно эвакуируйтесь. *3.* Мы должны уйти немедленно. *4.* Да, немедленно. *5.* Вы должны немедленно уйти. *6.* Им было приказано немедленно явиться. *7.* Вопрос должен быть решен немедленно. *8.* Он приказал им немедленно уйти. • *1.* Effective immediately. *2.* Evacuate immediately. *3.* We must leave immediately. *4.* Yes, immediately. *5.* You must leave immediately. *6.* They were ordered to report forthwith. *7.* The matter must be resolved forthwith. *8.* He ordered them to leave forthwith.

**138.  обычно** — *usually, normally, generally, ordinarily* — 'Обычно' is used to describe actions or situations that occur on a regular basis or are typical. It indicates a common occurrence or standard behavior without any specific emphasis on time or frequency.

● *1.* Я обычно так делаю. *2.* Обычно они так и делают. *3.* Обычно они есть. *4.* Обычно я так и делаю. *5.* Обычно это так. *6.* Обычно да. *7.* Не обычно. *8.* Обычно я этого не делаю. *9.* Обычно все идет не так, как надо. *10.* Обычно он приносит обед. *11.* Обычно откладывать дела на потом -- плохая идея. *12.* Обычно он приходил на встречи заранее. *13.* По выходным они обычно спали. *14.* Обычно он ездил на поезде. *15.* По воскресеньям магазин обычно был закрыт. *16.* Обычно она бы отказалась, но сделала исключение. *17.* Задача была обычно простой. ● *1.* I usually do. *2.* They usually do. *3.* They usually are. *4.* I usually am. *5.* It usually is. *6.* Normally, yes. *7.* Not normally. *8.* I don't normally do that. *9.* Things don't normally go wrong. *10.* He normally brings lunch. *11.* It's generally a bad idea to procrastinate. *12.* He generally arrived early to meetings. *13.* They would ordinarily sleep in on weekends. *14.* He would ordinarily take the train. *15.* The shop was ordinarily closed on Sundays. *16.* She would ordinarily decline but made an exception. *17.* The task was ordinarily easy.

**139.  грандиозный** — *grand, grandiose* — 'Грандиозный' is used to describe something on a large scale, impressive, or magnificent. It conveys a sense of grandeur and importance, often used to emphasize the size or significance of something.

● *1.* Разве это не грандиозно? *2.* Дворянин устроил грандиозный бал. *3.* Церемония инаугурации была грандиозной. *4.* Парад представлял собой грандиозное шествие. *5.* Это грандиозная идея. *6.* Он говорил в грандиозных терминах. *7.* Грандиозное здание стояло высоко. *8.* Его грандиозные планы были амбициозными. *9.* Она описала грандиозное -событие. *10.* Они надеялись на грандиозное торжество. ● *1.* Isn't it grand? *2.* The nobleman held a grand ball. *3.* The inauguration ceremony was grand. *4.* The parade featured a grand procession. *5.* That's a grand idea. *6.* He spoke in grandiose terms. *7.* The grandiose building stood tall. *8.* His grandiose plans were ambitious. *9.* She described a grandiose event. *10.*

They hoped for a grandiose celebration.

**140. наихудший** — *worst* — 'Наихудший' is used to describe something that is the most unfavorable or least desirable out of a group. It emphasizes the extreme negative quality of the noun it is describing.

**141. нервный** — *nervous, neural, jumpy* — The word 'нервный' is used to describe someone or something that is feeling anxious, tense, or easily agitated. It can also refer to actions or behaviors that are driven by nerves or anxiety.

● *1.* Ты нервничаешь? *2.* Не нервничайте. *3.* Я нервничаю. *4.* Я не нервничаю. *5.* Я немного нервничаю. *6.* Травма повлияла на ее нервные функции. *7.* Нервные пути были повреждены. *8.* У нее начинается нервный шок. *9.* Ты нервный. ● *1.* Are you nervous? *2.* Don't be nervous. *3.* I'm nervous. *4.* I'm not nervous. *5.* I'm a little nervous. *6.* The injury affected her neural functions. *7.* The neural pathways were damaged. *8.* She's going into neural shock. *9.* You're jumpy.

**142. окончательный** — *final, definitive, irrevocable, conclusive* — This word is used to describe something that is ultimate, conclusive, or definitive, indicating that there is no possibility of change or reversal. It signifies a final decision, outcome, or result.

● *1.* Это окончательно. *2.* Мое решение окончательное. *3.* Это ваш окончательный ответ? *4.* Окончательное предложение. *5.* И это окончательно. *6.* Результаты были убедительными и окончательными. *7.* Решение было окончательным и окончательным. *8.* Результаты были убедительными и окончательными. *9.* Они не были окончательными. ● *1.* That's final. *2.* My decision is final. *3.* Is that your final answer? *4.* Final offer. *5.* And that's final. *6.* The results were conclusive and definitive. *7.* The decision was conclusive and final. *8.* The results were conclusive and definitive. *9.* They weren't conclusive.

**143. невинный** — *innocent* — 'невинный' is used to describe someone or something that is free from guilt or wrongdoing. It can also be used to describe a situation or action that is not harmful or malicious.

● *1.* Невинные люди. *2.* Такой невинный. *3.* Ты такой невинный. *4.* Это невинный вопрос. *5.* Это было невинно. ● *1.*

Innocent people. *2.* So innocent. *3.* You're so innocent. *4.* It's an innocent question. *5.* It was innocent.

**144. беременная** — *pregnant* — This word is used to describe a female who is expecting a baby. It can also be used to describe something that is full or filled with something else, similar to the concept of being pregnant.

● *1.* Я беременна. *2.* Она беременна. *3.* Вы беременны. *4.* Ты беременна? *5.* Я не беременна. ● *1.* I'm pregnant. *2.* She's pregnant. *3.* You're pregnant. *4.* Are you pregnant? *5.* I'm not pregnant.

**145. виновный** — *guilty, culpable* — 'виновный' is used to describe someone who is responsible for a wrongdoing or offense. It can also be used to describe a feeling of guilt or culpability in a situation.

● *1.* Мы признаем подсудимого виновным. *2.* Признать себя виновным. *3.* Мы считаем подсудимого невиновным. *4.* Виновная совесть. *5.* Они были виновны в растрате. ● *1.* We find the defendant guilty. *2.* Plead guilty. *3.* We find the defendant not guilty. *4.* Guilty conscience. *5.* They were guilty of embezzlement.

**146. классно** — *awesome* — 'Классно' is used to describe something as excellent, great, or fantastic. It is a positive expression used to show enthusiasm or approval for something.

● *1.* Он классный. *2.* Классно, чувак! ● *1.* He's awesome. *2.* Awesome, dude!

**147. пустой** — *empty, blank, null* — The word 'пустой' is used to describe something that lacks content, is devoid of substance, or is unoccupied. It can also refer to a blank space or a void.

● *1.* Оно пустое. *2.* Опустошите карманы. *3.* Там было пусто. *4.* Дом пуст. *5.* Я пуст. *6.* Это пусто. *7.* Они пусты. *8.* Форма была пустой. *9.* У пациента, подвергшегося лоботомии, было пустое выражение лица. *10.* Страница пуста. ● *1.* It's empty. *2.* Empty your pockets. *3.* It was empty. *4.* The house is empty. *5.* I'm empty. *6.* It's blank. *7.* They're blank. *8.* The form was blank. *9.* The lobotomy patient had a blank expression. *10.* The page is blank.

**148. свежий** — *fresh, crisp, breezy* — This word is used to describe something that is new, recently made, or has a cool and invigorating quality. It can refer to food, air, or anything that feels refreshing and revitalizing.

● *1.* Свежий воздух. *2.* Это свежо. *3.* Мне нужен свежий воздух. *4.* Свежее мясо. *5.* Подышите свежим воздухом. *6.* Листовая зелень была свежей и хрустящей. *7.* Салат был свежим и хрустящим. *8.* Воздух был свежим и прохладным. *9.* Сельдерей был свежим и хрустящим. *10.* Капуста была свежей и хрустящей. *11.* Он любил гулять на свежем воздухе. ●
*1.* Fresh air. *2.* It's fresh. *3.* I need some fresh air. *4.* Fresh meat. *5.* Get some fresh air. *6.* The leafy greens were fresh and crisp. *7.* The salad was fresh and crisp. *8.* The air was crisp and cool. *9.* The celery was fresh and crisp. *10.* The cabbage was fresh and crisp. *11.* He liked to take breezy walks.

**149. любимый** — *favorite, favourite* — 'Favorite' is used to describe something that is preferred or cherished above others. It can refer to a person, object, or activity that holds a special place in one's heart.

● *1.* Мой любимый. *2.* Ваш любимый. *3.* Это мой любимый. *4.* Это моя любимая часть. *5.* Какой ваш любимый цвет? *6.* Мой любимый. *7.* Твой любимый. *8.* Это мой любимый. *9.* Они мои любимые. *10.* Это моя любимая часть. ● *1.* My favorite. *2.* Your favorite. *3.* It's my favorite. *4.* This is my favorite part. *5.* What's your favorite color? *6.* My favourite. *7.* Your favourite. *8.* It's my favourite. *9.* They're my favourite. *10.* This is my favourite part.

**150. двойной** — *double, dual, binary* — The word 'двойной' is used to describe something that is double or dual in nature, or to indicate a binary relationship or structure. It can be used to emphasize the presence of two distinct elements or components.

● *1.* Двойной или ничего. *2.* Сделайте его двойником. *3.* Двойное время. *4.* Теперь я двойной агент ЦРУ. *5.* Сделайте мою двойную. *6.* У нее двойное гражданство. *7.* Нож двойного назначения удобен. *8.* Двойное управление обеспечивает гибкость. ● *1.* Double or nothing. *2.* Make it a double. *3.* Double time. *4.* Now I'm a double agent for the CIA. *5.* Make mine a double. *6.* She has dual citizenship. *7.* The dual purpose knife is convenient. *8.* The dual controls allow for flexibility.

**151. проклятый** — *goddamn, damnedest, accursed* — 'Проклятый' is used to express strong negative emotions or frustration towards a person, situation, or thing. It conveys a sense of anger, annoyance, or disappointment. It is often used in informal speech or writing.

• *1.* Проклятье! *2.* Будь ты проклят! *3.* Проклятый человек! *4.* Будь он проклят. *5.* Проклятая семья так и не обрела покоя. *6.* Проклятая земля принесла только лишения. *7.* Он проклял проклятое сокровище. *8.* Они стремились снять проклятое проклятие. • *1.* Goddamn it! *2.* Goddamn you! *3.* Goddamn, man! *4.* Goddamn him. *5.* The accursed family never found peace. *6.* The accursed land brought only hardship. *7.* He cursed the accursed treasure. *8.* They sought to lift the accursed curse.

**152. нелепый** — *ridiculous, preposterous, ungodly* — 'Нелепый' is used to describe something that is absurd, nonsensical, or completely unreasonable. It conveys a sense of disbelief or incredulity towards the situation or idea being described.

• *1.* Это нелепо. *2.* Эта ситуация становится все более и более нелепой. *3.* Весь план нелеп. *4.* Они выглядят нелепо. *5.* Это нелепый разговор. *6.* Это нелепо. *7.* Ну, это нелепо. *8.* О, это нелепо. • *1.* This is ridiculous. *2.* This situation is getting more and more ridiculous. *3.* The whole plan is ridiculous. *4.* They look ridiculous. *5.* This is a ridiculous conversation. *6.* That's preposterous. *7.* Well, that's preposterous. *8.* Oh, that's preposterous.

**153. медицинский** — *medical, medicinal* — The word 'медицинский' is used to describe things related to medicine or health. It can refer to medical treatments, equipment, facilities, or practices. It is often used to indicate something that is used for healing or treating illnesses.

• *1.* Пожалуйста, укажите характер неотложной медицинской помощи. *2.* Неотложная медицинская помощь. *3.* Ему нужна медицинская помощь. *4.* У нас неотложная медицинская помощь. *5.* Это неотложная медицинская помощь. • *1.* Please state the nature of the medical emergency. *2.* Medical emergency. *3.* He needs medical attention. *4.* We have a medical emergency. *5.* This is a medical emergency.

**154. спящий** — *asleep, dormant* — This word is used to describe something or someone that is currently in a state of sleep or dormancy. It can refer to physical sleep or a state of inactivity or lack of development.

● *1.* Крепко спящий. *2.* Спящий вулкан проснулся. ● *1.* Sound asleep. *2.* The dormant volcano awoke.

**155. дополнительный** — *extra, additional, auxiliary, supplementary* — This word is used to describe something that is added to what is already present, providing more of something or serving as a supplement. It emphasizes the idea of something being extra or additional.

● *1.* Без дополнительной оплаты. *2.* Дополнительно, дополнительно! *3.* Дополнительный кредит. *4.* Это дополнительно. *5.* Они наняли дополнительную охрану. *6.* Он попросил дополнительное время, чтобы закончить. *7.* Для торта требовался дополнительный сахар. *8.* Она заказала дополнительные материалы. *9.* Боковая панель предоставляет дополнительную информацию. *10.* Дополнительная информация была полезна. *11.* Он установил в машину дополнительный аккумулятор. *12.* Капитанский журнал, дополнительный. ● *1.* No extra charge. *2.* Extra, extra! *3.* Extra credit. *4.* That's extra. *5.* They hired extra security guards. *6.* He requested additional time to finish. *7.* The cake needed additional sugar. *8.* She ordered additional supplies. *9.* The sidebar provides additional information. *10.* The additional information was helpful. *11.* He installed an auxiliary battery in the car. *12.* Captain's log, supplementary.

**156. тяжелый** — *heavy, severe, grievous* — 'Тяжелый' is used to describe something that is physically heavy or emotionally burdensome. It can also be used to describe a difficult or severe situation.

● *1.* Это тяжело. *2.* Это слишком тяжело. *3.* Это тяжело? *4.* Слишком тяжелый. *5.* Твои веки тяжелые. *6.* Симптомы Эболы тяжелые. *7.* У нее был тяжелый грипп. *8.* Симптомы тифа тяжелые. *9.* Инфекция была тяжелой. *10.* Последствия были невообразимо тяжелыми. ● *1.* It's heavy. *2.* It's too heavy. *3.* Is it heavy? *4.* Too heavy. *5.* Your eyelids are heavy. *6.* The symptoms of ebola are severe. *7.* She had a severe influenza. *8.* The symptoms of typhus are severe. *9.* The infection was severe. *10.* The consequences were unimaginably severe.

**157. знаменитый** — *famous, renowned, illustrious* — 'Знаменитый' is used to describe someone or something that is well-known and highly regarded for their achievements or reputation. It is often used to highlight the fame or prestige of a person, place, or thing.

● *1.* Ты знаменит. *2.* Он знаменит. *3.* Она знаменита. *4.* Я не знаменит. *5.* Я знаменит. *6.* Они восхищались знаменитым шеф-поваром. *7.* Она посетила знаменитый музей. ● *1.* You're famous. *2.* He's famous. *3.* She's famous. *4.* I'm not famous. *5.* I'm famous. *6.* They admired the renowned chef. *7.* She visited the renowned museum.

**158. дикий** — *wild* — The word 'дикий' is used to describe something that is untamed, uncivilized, or uncontrollable. It can refer to wild animals, nature, behavior, or places that are not domesticated or civilized.

● *1.* Он дикий. *2.* На родео был дикий бык. *3.* Ты дикий человек. ● *1.* He's wild. *2.* The rodeo had a wild bull. *3.* You're a wild man.

**159. превосходный** — *excellent, superb, tiptop* — 'Превосходный' is used to describe something of exceptional quality or excellence. It conveys a sense of superiority and is often used to express admiration or praise for something that is considered outstanding or top-notch.

● *1.* Это превосходно. *2.* Это было превосходно. *3.* О, это превосходно. *4.* Самый превосходный. *5.* Последняя еда была превосходной. *6.* Еда была превосходной. *7.* Написание было превосходным. *8.* Спектакль был превосходным. *9.* Вид был превосходным. *10.* Качество фотографий было превосходным. ● *1.* That's excellent. *2.* It was excellent. *3.* Oh, that's excellent. *4.* Most excellent. *5.* The last meal was excellent. *6.* The meal was superb. *7.* The writing was superb. *8.* The performance was superb. *9.* The view was superb. *10.* The photographic quality was superb.

**160. ответственный** — *responsible, liable, answerable* — This word is used to describe someone who is trustworthy and can be relied upon to fulfill their duties or obligations. It can also refer to someone who is accountable for their actions and decisions.

● *1.* Я несу ответственность. *2.* Я чувствую ответственность. *3.* Я несу ответственность за тебя. *4.* Я ответственный. *5.*

Вы несете ответственность. *6.* Она понесла ответственность за свои действия. *7.* Компания понесла ответственность. *8.* Владелец был привлечен к ответственности. *9.* Он нес ответственность за причиненный ущерб. *10.* Они несли юридическую ответственность. ● *1.* I'm responsible. *2.* I feel responsible. *3.* I'm responsible for you. *4.* I am responsible. *5.* You're responsible. *6.* She was liable for her actions. *7.* The company was liable. *8.* The owner was held liable. *9.* He was liable for the damages. *10.* They were legally liable.

**161. общий** — *common* — 'Общий' is used to describe something that is shared or mutual among multiple people or things. It can also be used to indicate something that is general or universal in nature.
● *1.* У нас есть общий враг. *2.* Общий враг. *3.* У нас есть общий друг. *4.* Он нашел общий язык с неверующим. *5.* Общий знаменатель найти было сложно. ● *1.* We have a common enemy. *2.* A common enemy. *3.* We have a friend in common. *4.* He found common ground with the unbeliever. *5.* The common denominator was difficult to find.

**162. слепой** — *blind* — The word 'слепой' is used to describe someone who is unable to see. It can also be used metaphorically to describe someone who is ignorant or unwilling to see the truth.
● *1.* Вы слепой? *2.* Я слепой! *3.* Я не слепой. *4.* Ты слеп. *5.* Он слеп. ● *1.* Are you blind? *2.* I'm blind! *3.* I'm not blind. *4.* You're blind. *5.* He's blind.

**163. немецкий** — *german* — The adjective/adverb 'немецкий' is used to describe something or someone related to Germany or the German language. It can also be used to indicate that something is of German origin or style.
● *1.* Это немецкий. *2.* Отто -- распространенное немецкое имя. *3.* Немецкое пиво было восхитительным. *4.* Он немецкого происхождения. *5.* Где ты выучил немецкий? ● *1.* It's German. *2.* Otto is a common German name. *3.* The German beer was delicious. *4.* He's of German descent. *5.* Where did you learn German?

**164. местный** — *local, aboriginal* — The word 'местный' is used to describe something or someone that is from a specific area or region, typically implying a sense of belonging or familiarity with the local culture or environment.

● *1.* Местный звонок. *2.* Иешива обслуживает местное сообщество. *3.* Она прошла прослушивание в местный театр. *4.* Местный аптекарь очень дружелюбный. *5.* Ей сделали местную анестезию. ● *1.* Local call. *2.* The yeshiva serves the local community. *3.* She auditioned for the local theatre. *4.* The local druggist is very friendly. *5.* She was given a local anaesthetic.

**165. основной** — *main, basic, basal, pivotal* — 'Основной' is used to describe something that is fundamental, essential, or central to a particular concept or idea. It signifies the primary or most important aspect of a subject, emphasizing its significance and importance.

● *1.* Мы теряем основную власть. *2.* В основном просмотрщике. *3.* Все основные системы отключены. *4.* Мы потеряли основную власть. *5.* Основная причина задержки. *6.* Это основные предметы первой необходимости в Chatsworth Estate. ● *1.* We're losing main power. *2.* On main viewer. *3.* All main systems down. *4.* We've lost main power. *5.* The main reason for the delay. *6.* These are Chatsworth Estate's basic essentials.

**166. должный** — *due* — 'Должный' is used to indicate something that is expected, required, or owed. It can refer to obligations, responsibilities, or debts that need to be fulfilled. It is often used in legal, financial, or moral contexts.

● *1.* Отдайте должное там, где это необходимо. *2.* Членские взносы должны были быть уплачены в следующем месяце. *3.* Она получила должное признание. *4.* Когда она должна родить? *5.* Арендная плата должна быть оплачена сегодня. ● *1.* Give credit where it's due. *2.* The membership dues were due next month. *3.* She received the recognition she was due. *4.* When is she due? *5.* The rent is due today.

**167. плотный** — *tight, dense* — The word 'плотный' is used to describe something that is closely packed together or has a high concentration of particles. It can also refer to something that is thick or heavy in texture.

● *1.* Плотно держаться. *2.* Красиво и плотно. *3.* Очень плотно. *4.* У нас плотный график. *5.* Хорошо и плотно. *6.* Он отказался есть плотный фруктовый пирог. *7.* Хвоя савины образовывала плотный полог. *8.* Растительный покров был плотным. • *1.* Sit tight. *2.* Nice and tight. *3.* Very tight. *4.* We're on a tight schedule. *5.* Good and tight. *6.* He refused to eat the dense fruitcake. *7.* The savin needles formed a dense canopy. *8.* The vegetative cover was dense.

**168. национальный** — *national* — 'Национальный' is used to describe something that is related to a specific nation or country. It can refer to cultural, historical, or political aspects that are characteristic of a particular nation.
• *1.* Это вопрос национальной безопасности. *2.* Помните о нашем национальном унижении. *3.* Это национальная безопасность. *4.* Это национальный парк. *5.* Это вопрос национальной безопасности, сэр. • *1.* This is a matter of national security. *2.* Remember our national humiliation. *3.* It's national security. *4.* This is a national park. *5.* It's a matter of national security, sir.

**169. естественный** — *natural* — This word is used to describe something that is in its original state, not artificial or man-made. It can also refer to something that is innate, instinctive, or in accordance with nature.
• *1.* Это естественно. *2.* Ведите себя естественно. *3.* Это не естественно. *4.* Просто веди себя естественно. *5.* Естественные причины. • *1.* It's natural. *2.* Act natural. *3.* It's not natural. *4.* Just act natural. *5.* Natural causes.

**170. мощный** — *powerful, potent* — The word 'мощный' is used to describe something that is strong, forceful, or effective. It can be used to convey the idea of power, intensity, or significance in various contexts.
• *1.* Это мощно. *2.* Мощная штука. *3.* Это очень мощно. *4.* Это слишком мощно. *5.* Это действительно мощно. *6.* Метан – мощный парниковый газ. *7.* Куш -- мощный сорт конопли.
• *1.* It's powerful. *2.* Powerful stuff. *3.* It's very powerful. *4.* It's too powerful. *5.* It's really powerful. *6.* Methane is a potent greenhouse gas. *7.* Kush is a potent strain of cannabis.

**171. уголовный** — *criminal, penal* — 'уголовный' is used to describe something related to crime or punishment. It can refer to criminal activities, penal institutions, or legal matters involving criminal behavior. It is often used in the context of law enforcement and the justice system.

● *1.* Это уголовное преступление. *2.* Работал следователем по уголовным делам. *3.* Изучала уголовное преследование. *4.* Их обвинили в уголовных преступлениях. ● *1.* That's a criminal offense. *2.* He worked as a criminal investigator. *3.* She studied the prosecution of criminal cases. *4.* They were accused of criminal wrongdoing.

**172. громкий** — *loud* — The word 'громкий' is used to describe sounds that are strong and easily heard. It can also be used to describe someone who speaks or laughs loudly.

● *1.* Громко и ясно. *2.* Не так громко. *3.* За то, что громко плакала. *4.* О, за то, что громко плакала. *5.* Это слишком громко. ● *1.* Loud and clear. *2.* Not so loud. *3.* For crying out loud. *4.* Oh, for crying out loud. *5.* It's too loud.

**173. оригинальный** — *original, ingenious* — This word is used to describe something that is unique, creative, or innovative. It implies that the object or idea is not a copy or imitation, but rather a fresh and inventive creation.

● *1.* Как оригинально. *2.* Это оригинально. *3.* Очень оригинально. *4.* Будь оригинальным. *5.* О, это оригинально. ● *1.* How original. *2.* That's original. *3.* Very original. *4.* Be original. *5.* Oh, that's original.

**174. ревнивый** — *jealous* — This word is used to describe someone who feels resentment or suspicion towards others, particularly in relationships. It conveys a sense of possessiveness and insecurity.

● *1.* Я не ревнивый. *2.* Я был ревнив. *3.* Очень ревнивый? *4.* Я так ревнива. *5.* Он очень ревнив. ● *1.* I'm not jealous. *2.* I was jealous. *3.* Jealous much? *4.* I am so jealous. *5.* He's very jealous.

**175. супер** — *super* — Used to emphasize something as being excellent, outstanding, or exceptional. Can be used to describe a person, object, event, or situation in a positive way. Often used informally in casual conversation.

● *1.* Это супер. *2.* Да, супер. *3.* О, супер. *4.* Это было бы супер. *5.* Супергерой обладает сверхспособностями. ● *1.* That's super. *2.* Yeah, super. *3.* Oh, super. *4.* That would be super. *5.* The superhero has super powers.

**176. невероятный** — *incredible, unbelievable, improbable* —

This word is used to describe something that is so extraordinary or unlikely that it is hard to believe. It conveys a sense of amazement or astonishment at the remarkable nature of the subject.

● *1.* Это невероятно. *2.* Это было невероятно. *3.* Ты выглядишь невероятно. *4.* Он невероятный. *5.* Невероятно, не так ли? *6.* Это невероятно. *7.* Ты невероятный. *8.* Это было невероятно. *9.* Это просто невероятно. *10.* Он невероятный. *11.* Казалось невероятным, что они победят. *12.* Невероятная история выживания. *13.* Многие сочли этот план невероятным. *14.* Шансы на успех были невероятными.

● *1.* It's incredible. *2.* It was incredible. *3.* You look incredible. *4.* He's incredible. *5.* Incredible, isn't it? *6.* It's unbelievable. *7.* You're unbelievable. *8.* It was unbelievable. *9.* It's just unbelievable. *10.* He's unbelievable. *11.* It seemed improbable that they would win. *12.* An improbable story of survival. *13.* The plan was considered improbable by many. *14.* The chances of success were improbable.

**177. комфортный** — *comfortable* — 'Комфортный' is used to describe something that provides a sense of ease, convenience, and relaxation. It is often used to refer to physical objects, spaces, or situations that make one feel comfortable and at ease.

● *1.* Не устраивайтесь слишком комфортно. *2.* Мне комфортно. *3.* Очень комфортно. *4.* Мне не комфортно. *5.* Вам здесь комфортно? ● *1.* Don't get too comfortable. *2.* I'm comfortable. *3.* Very comfortable. *4.* I'm not comfortable. *5.* Are you comfortable here?

**178. коричневый** — *brown* — 'Коричневый' is used to describe something that is the color brown. It can be used to describe objects, animals, or even emotions that are associated with the color brown.

● *1.* Коричневые волосы. *2.* Это коричневый. *3.* Код коричневый! *4.* Они коричневые. *5.* Мех полёвки был коричневым и мягким. ● *1.* Brown hair. *2.* It's brown. *3.* Code brown! *4.* They're brown. *5.* The vole's fur was brown and soft.

**179. уродливый** — *ugly, misshapen* — This word is used to describe something that is unattractive or deformed in appearance. It can be used to describe physical features, objects, or even abstract concepts that are considered unpleasant or unsightly.

● *1.* Ты уродлив. *2.* Ты не уродливый. *3.* Он такой уродливый! *4.* Это не уродливо. *5.* Зависть уродлива и уродлива. *6.* Зависть уродлива и уродлива. ● *1.* You're ugly. *2.* You're not ugly. *3.* He's so ugly! *4.* It's not ugly. *5.* Envy is ugly and misshapen. *6.* Envy is ugly and misshapen.

**180. женский** — *female, feminine* — This word is used to describe things or qualities that are typically associated with females or femininity. It can be used to refer to objects, characteristics, or behaviors that are considered feminine in nature.
● *1.* Мужской и женский. *2.* Женская сволочь! *3.* Анима представляла женский аспект. ● *1.* Male and female. *2.* Female scum! *3.* The anima represented the feminine aspect.

**181. мужской** — *male, masculine, virile* — The word 'мужской' is used to describe things that are related to or characteristic of males, masculinity, or virility. It can be used to describe people, objects, or qualities that are traditionally associated with men.
● *1.* Мужской и женский. *2.* Имеет сильное мужское влияние. *3.* Ян – мужской. *4.* Она интересуется мужской модой. *5.* Явно мужской начальник. ● *1.* Male and female. *2.* He has a strong male influence. *3.* The yang is male. *4.* She's interested in male fashion. *5.* A decidedly masculine superior.

**182. социальный** — *social, societal* — This word is used to describe things related to society, social issues, or interactions between people. It can refer to anything from social programs and policies to social norms and behaviors.
● *1.* Я социальный работник. *2.* Социальный работник. *3.* Для продвижения бренда он использовал социальные сети. *4.* И ваш номер социального страхования. *5.* Она ориентировалась по минному полю социальных взаимодействий. ● *1.* I'm a social worker. *2.* A social worker. *3.* He used social media to promote the brand. *4.* And your social security number. *5.* She navigated the minefield of social interactions.

**183. древний** — *ancient* — This word is used to describe something that is very old or ancient in age or origin. It can be used to refer to historical artifacts, buildings, or civilizations that date back to ancient times.
● *1.* Это древняя история. *2.* Это древнее. *3.* Древний Египет. *4.* И вот начинается древнее слово. *5.* Это древнегреческий. ● *1.* It's ancient history. *2.* It's ancient. *3.* Ancient Egypt. *4.* And

now begins the ancient word. *5.* It's ancient Greek.

**184. крошечный** — *tiny, teeny, miniscule, teensy* — 'Крошечный' is used to describe something very small in size. It can be used to emphasize the tiny nature of an object or to convey a sense of cuteness or delicacy.
● *1.* Он крошечный. *2.* Он такой крошечный. *3.* Она такая крошечная. *4.* Она увидела, как мимо пробежала крошечная мышка. *5.* Крошечная саламандра бросилась прочь. *6.* Крошечное насекомое приземлилось на цветок. *7.* Крошечная частица была неразличима. *8.* Крошечную трещину было трудно увидеть. *9.* Ее крошечный почерк производил впечатление. ● *1.* It's tiny. *2.* It's so tiny. *3.* She's so tiny. *4.* She saw a tiny mouse scurry by. *5.* The tiny salamander darted away. *6.* The miniscule insect landed on the flower. *7.* The miniscule particle was indistinguishable. *8.* The miniscule crack was hard to see. *9.* Her miniscule handwriting was impressive.

**185. плоский** — *flat* — This word is used to describe something that is level or smooth, lacking in height or depth. It can also be used to describe something that is dull or lacking in excitement.
● *1.* Это плоско. *2.* Игристое или плоское? *3.* Я плоский. *4.* Плоский как блин. *5.* Плоскостопие. ● *1.* It's flat. *2.* Sparkling or flat? *3.* I'm flat. *4.* Flat as a pancake. *5.* Flat feet.

**186. ненормальный** — *insane, abnormal, anomalous, certifiable* — This word is used to describe something or someone that is not normal or mentally unstable. It can also be used to refer to a situation or behavior that is abnormal or out of the ordinary.
● *1.* Вы ненормальный? *2.* Ненормальная психология. *3.* Ситуация была ненормальной и тревожной. *4.* Животное проявляло ненормальное поведение. *5.* Показания Кельвина были ненормальными. *6.* Его поведение было ненормальным для ребенка. ● *1.* Are you insane? *2.* Abnormal psychology. *3.* The situation was abnormal and unsettling. *4.* The animal exhibited abnormal behavior. *5.* The kelvin readings were abnormal. *6.* His behavior was abnormal for a child.

**187. испанский** — *spanish* — The word 'испанский' is used to describe something or someone related to Spain or the Spanish language. It can also be used as an adverb to describe actions or events that are characteristic of Spain or its culture.

● *1.* Это испанский. *2.* Я немного говорю по-испански. *3.* Как твой испанский? *4.* Испанский танец был прекрасен. *5.* Испанская культура богата. ● *1.* It's Spanish. *2.* I speak a little Spanish. *3.* How's your Spanish? *4.* The Spanish dance was beautiful. *5.* The Spanish culture is rich.

**188. запасной** — *spare* — 'запасной' is used to describe something that is kept in reserve or as a backup. It can also be used to indicate something that is extra or additional, serving as a spare or replacement when needed.

● *1.* Запасная сдача? *2.* У меня есть запасной. *3.* У вас есть запасной? *4.* Боулер взял запасной. *5.* В запасной комнате. ● *1.* Spare change? *2.* I have a spare. *3.* Do you have a spare? *4.* The bowler picked up the spare. *5.* In the spare room.

**189. мокрый** — *wet* — This word is used to describe something that is covered in liquid or moisture. It can also be used to describe the feeling of being wet.

● *1.* Ты весь мокрый. *2.* Мокро. *3.* Ты мокрый. *4.* Я мокрый. *5.* Он все еще мокрый. ● *1.* You're all wet. *2.* It's wet. *3.* You're wet. *4.* I'm wet. *5.* It's still wet.

**190. свободный** — *loose, spare* — This word can be used to describe something that is not tight or constricted, or to indicate that there is extra or unused space or time available. It can also convey a sense of freedom or independence.

● *1.* Оставайся свободным. *2.* Никаких свободных концов. *3.* Это свободно. *4.* Повесьтесь свободно. *5.* Завязываем свободные концы. *6.* Чем ты занимаешься в свободное время? *7.* В свободное время она любит вязать крючком. ● *1.* Stay loose. *2.* No loose ends. *3.* It's loose. *4.* Hang loose. *5.* Tying up loose ends. *6.* What do you do in your spare time? *7.* She enjoys crocheting in her spare time.

**191. яркий** — *bright, vivid, flamboyant* — The word 'яркий' is used to describe something that is colorful, eye-catching, or intense in appearance. It can refer to bright colors, vivid images, or flamboyant personalities.

● *1.* Он яркий. *2.* Свет яркий! *3.* Очень яркий. *4.* Он очень яркий. *5.* Настолько яркий. *6.* Яркий сон казался таким реальным. ● *1.* He's bright. *2.* Light bright! *3.* Very bright. *4.* He's very bright. *5.* So bright. *6.* The vivid dream felt so real.

**192. мягкий** — *soft, gentle, mild, mellow* — 'Мягкий' is used to describe something that is soft, gentle, mild, or mellow in nature. It can refer to textures, flavors, personalities, or actions that are characterized by a sense of gentleness or mildness.

● *1.* Так мягко. *2.* Он такой мягкий. *3.* Он мягкий. *4.* Слишком мягкий. *5.* Ты стал мягким. *6.* Они восхищались мягким характером панды. *7.* Характер у собаки был мягкий. *8.* Она предпочитала мягкую погоду. *9.* Мягкий соус дополнил блюдо. *10.* Мягкая зима была необычной. *11.* Дети получили мягкое наказание. *12.* Карри было слишком мягким. *13.* Альт имеет богатый, мягкий звук. *14.* Мягкая атмосфера всех успокоила. *15.* Ее голос был мягким. *16.* С возрастом он стал более мягким. *17.* Мягкая музыка создавала атмосферу.

● *1.* So soft. *2.* It's so soft. *3.* It's soft. *4.* Too soft. *5.* You've gone soft. *6.* They marveled at the panda's gentle nature. *7.* The dog's temperament was gentle. *8.* She preferred mild weather. *9.* The mild sauce complemented the dish. *10.* The mild winter was unusual. *11.* The kids received a mild punishment. *12.* The curry was too mild. *13.* The viola has a rich, mellow sound. *14.* The mellow atmosphere put everyone at ease. *15.* Her voice had a mellow quality. *16.* He became more mellow as he aged. *17.* The mellow music set the ambiance.

**193. причудливый** — *fancy, quaint, whimsical, freaky* — This word is used to describe something that is unique, unusual, or eccentric in a charming or interesting way. It can refer to a person's behavior, a piece of art, or a design that is fanciful or quirky.

● *1.* Это причудливо. *2.* О, причудливо. *3.* Это место такое причудливое. *4.* Вау, причудливо. *5.* Почему так причудливо? *6.* Она посетила причудливый городок Ли. *7.* Статуя гнома была причудливой. *8.* Довольно причудливо, да? ●

*1.* That's fancy. *2.* Oh, fancy. *3.* This place is so fancy. *4.* Wow, fancy. *5.* Why so fancy? *6.* She visited the quaint town of Leigh. *7.* The gnome statue was whimsical. *8.* Pretty freaky, huh?

**194. дорогие** — *expensive* — This word is used to describe something that is costly or has a high price. It can also be used to express affection or endearment towards someone, similar to calling them "dear" in English.

● *1.* Это дорого. *2.* Очень дорого. *3.* Слишком дорого. *4.*

Это слишком дорого. *5.* Это дорого? ● *1.* It's expensive. *2.* Very expensive. *3.* Too expensive. *4.* It's too expensive. *5.* Is it expensive?

**195. внезапный** — *sudden* — This word is used to describe something that happens unexpectedly or without warning. It is often used to convey a sense of surprise or shock at the suddenness of an event.

● *1.* Откуда такая внезапная перемена в сердце? *2.* Было ли это внезапно? *3.* Почему такая внезапная перемена? *4.* Откуда такой внезапный интерес? *5.* Это так внезапно. ● *1.* Why the sudden change of heart? *2.* Was it sudden? *3.* Why the sudden change? *4.* Why the sudden interest? *5.* This is so sudden.

**196. правовой** — *legal* — 'правовой' is used to describe something that is related to the law or legal matters. It can be used to refer to documents, procedures, rights, obligations, or any other aspect of the legal system.

● *1.* Правовая система сложна. ● *1.* The legal system is complex.

**197. квадратный** — *square* — The word 'квадратный' is used to describe something that has a square shape or is related to a square. It can also be used to indicate something that is squared or raised to the power of two.

● *1.* Мы квадратные. *2.* Ты такой квадратный. ● *1.* We're square. *2.* You're so square.

**198. грубый** — *rough, rude, coarse, gruff* — The word 'грубый' is used to describe something or someone as rough, rude, coarse, or gruff in nature. It can be used to convey a lack of refinement or politeness in behavior or appearance.

● *1.* Это грубо. *2.* Это было грубо. *3.* Не так грубо. *4.* Я люблю грубо. *5.* Хочешь сыграть грубо? *6.* Не грубите. *7.* Как грубо. *8.* Это грубо. *9.* Это было грубо. *10.* Как грубо с моей стороны. *11.* Ткань была грубая и грубая. *12.* Она использовала грубые выражения. *13.* Наждачная бумага была грубой. *14.* Его манеры были грубыми. *15.* Песок под ногами казался грубым. *16.* Он говорил грубым голосом. *17.* Он дал грубый ответ. *18.* Его грубоватая манера поведения меня напугала. *19.* Ее грубое поведение отталкивало ее. *20.*

Грубый менеджер никогда не улыбался. • *1*. That's rough. *2*. It was rough. *3*. Not so rough. *4*. I like it rough. *5*. You wanna play rough? *6*. Don't be rude. *7*. How rude. *8*. That's rude. *9*. That was rude. *10*. How rude of me. *11*. The fabric was rough and coarse. *12*. She used coarse language. *13*. The sandpaper was coarse. *14*. His manners were coarse. *15*. The sand felt coarse under their feet. *16*. He spoke in a gruff voice. *17*. He gave a gruff reply. *18*. His gruff manner intimidated me. *19*. She found his gruff demeanor off-putting. *20*. The gruff manager never smiled.

**199. внизу** — *downstairs* — 'внизу' is used to indicate a location or direction that is below or on a lower level. It is commonly used to describe the position of objects, people, or places in relation to a higher point or level.

• *1*. Я буду внизу. *2*. Я встречу тебя внизу. *3*. Увидимся внизу. *4*. Я буду ждать тебя внизу. *5*. Подожди меня внизу. • *1*. I'll be downstairs. *2*. I'll meet you downstairs. *3*. See you downstairs. *4*. I'll wait for you downstairs. *5*. Wait for me downstairs.

**200. очевидный** — *obvious, apparent, evident, evidentiary* — 'Очевидный' is used to describe something that is clear, easily seen, or apparent without needing further explanation. It is often used to emphasize that something is obvious or evident to anyone who observes it.

• *1*. Разве это не очевидно? *2*. Это очевидно. *3*. Это настолько очевидно? *4*. Это так очевидно. *5*. Это было очевидно. *6*. Безумие ситуации было очевидным. *7*. Бессилие в этом процессе было очевидным. *8*. Острая необходимость перемен была очевидна. *9*. Оплошность комитета была очевидна. *10*. Деградация здания была очевидна. *11*. Раздражительность была очевидна в его тоне. *12*. Дарвиновская эволюция была очевидна. *13*. Расовое разделение было очевидным. • *1*. Isn't it obvious? *2*. It's obvious. *3*. Is it that obvious? *4*. It's so obvious. *5*. It was obvious. *6*. The lunacy of the situation was apparent. *7*. Impotence in the process was apparent. *8*. The dire need for change was apparent. *9*. The committee's oversight was evident. *10*. The degradation of the building was evident. *11*. The irritability was evident in his tone. *12*. Darwinian evolution was evident. *13*. The racial divide was evident.

**201. профессиональный** — *professional, occupational, voca-*

*tional* — This word is used to describe something related to a specific profession or occupation, indicating a high level of skill, expertise, or quality in that particular field.

• *1.* Очень профессиональный. *2.* Вам нужна профессиональная помощь. *3.* Профессиональная вежливость. *4.* Это ваше профессиональное мнение? *5.* Строго профессионально. *6.* Профессиональная опасность. *7.* Это профессиональный риск. *8.* Профессиональные риски значительны. *9.* Он получил профессиональную награду. *10.* Они предлагают профессиональное обучение. *11.* Он выбрал программу профессионального обучения. *12.* Он продолжил профессиональную карьеру. *13.* Они предложили профессиональные курсы в колледже. *14.* Она отличилась в профессиональном училище. *15.* Профессиональная программа ориентирована на практические навыки. • *1.* Very professional. *2.* You need professional help. *3.* Professional courtesy. *4.* Is that your professional opinion? *5.* Strictly professional. *6.* Occupational hazard. *7.* It's an occupational hazard. *8.* The occupational hazards are significant. *9.* He received an occupational award. *10.* They offer occupational training. *11.* He chose a vocational training program. *12.* He pursued a vocational career. *13.* They offered vocational courses at the college. *14.* She excelled in vocational school. *15.* The vocational program focused on practical skills.

**202. серебряный** — *silver* — This word is used to describe something that is the color or material of silver. It can also be used to describe something that is shiny, metallic, or valuable in a similar way to silver.

• *1.* Шпилька была серебряная с замысловатым узором. • *1.* The hairpin was silver with intricate designs.

**203. иностранный** — *foreign* — This word is used to describe something or someone that is from another country or culture, not native to the place where it currently is. It can refer to objects, people, languages, or customs.

• *1.* Он в министерстве иностранных дел. *2.* Она покупала иностранные товары. *3.* Гостиница была заполнена иностранными высокопоставленными лицами. *4.* Том был написан на иностранном языке. *5.* Он говорит на иностранном языке. • *1.* He's in the foreign ministry. *2.* She purchased foreign goods. *3.* The hotel was filled with foreign dignitaries. *4.* The tome was written in a foreign language. *5.* He speaks a foreign language.

**204. романтический** — *romantic* — This word is used to describe something that is related to love, passion, or idealized notions of relationships. It can be used to describe a person, a gesture, a setting, or a situation that evokes feelings of romance or sentimentality.

• *1.* Ужин при свечах был романтическим. *2.* Романтический отдых назрел. *3.* Город идеально подходил для романтических встреч. *4.* Романтический фильм не вызвал никаких эмоций. *5.* Они вместе наслаждались романтическим ужином.
• *1.* The candlelit dinner was romantic. *2.* A romantic getaway is overdue. *3.* The city was perfect for a romantic fling. *4.* The romantic movie failed to arouse any emotions. *5.* They enjoyed a romantic dinner together.

**205. вероятный** — *likely, probable, believable, credible* — This word is used to describe something that is considered to be possible or probable. It is often used to express the likelihood of an event or situation occurring based on available information or evidence.

• *1.* Вероятно. *2.* Вполне вероятная история. *3.* Чертовски маловероятно. *4.* Более чем вероятно. *5.* Это маловероятно. *6.* Вероятный результат – провал. *7.* Это был вероятный исход. *8.* Это вероятно. *9.* Вероятная причина – пренебрежение. *10.* Вероятное объяснение было принято. • *1.* Most likely. *2.* A likely story. *3.* Not bloody likely. *4.* More than likely. *5.* It's not likely. *6.* The probable result is failure. *7.* It was a probable outcome. *8.* It's probable. *9.* The probable cause was neglect. *10.* The probable explanation was accepted.

**206. внимательно** — *carefully, closely* — 'Внимательно' is used to describe the action of paying close attention to something or someone, doing something carefully and thoroughly. It implies a sense of focus and attentiveness in the task being performed.

• *1.* Слушай внимательно. *2.* Слушай меня внимательно. *3.* Слушайте меня очень внимательно. *4.* Теперь слушайте внимательно. *5.* Внимательно следить. *6.* Посмотрите внимательно. *7.* Смотри внимательно. *8.* Слушайте внимательно.

*9.* Следите за ним внимательно. *10.* Теперь смотрите внимательно. • *1.* Listen carefully. *2.* Listen to me carefully. *3.* Listen to me very carefully. *4.* Now listen carefully. *5.* Watch carefully. *6.* Look closely. *7.* Watch closely. *8.* Listen closely. *9.* Watch him closely. *10.* Now watch closely.

**207. надлежащий** — *proper* — 'надлежащий' is used to describe something that is appropriate, fitting, or correct for a particular situation. It implies that something is done in the right way or according to established norms.

• *1.* Ему не хватает надлежащего этикета. *2.* В ее еде не было надлежащего питания. *3.* У них нет надлежащего разрешения. • *1.* He lacks proper etiquette. *2.* Her meals lacked proper nutrition. *3.* They lack proper authorization.

**208. политический** — *political* — 'Политический' is used to describe anything related to politics or government. It can refer to political parties, movements, ideologies, actions, or discussions. It is a versatile term that can be applied to various aspects of the political sphere.

• *1.* Он политический. *2.* Политическая наука. *3.* Они призывали к политической революции. *4.* Он олицетворял худшую политическую подлость. *5.* Политический ландшафт менялся. • *1.* He's political. *2.* Political science. *3.* They called for a political revolution. *4.* He embodied the worst of political sleaze. *5.* The political landscape was in flux.

**209. гигантский** — *giant, gigantic, jumbo* — This word is used to describe something that is very large in size or scale, often emphasizing its impressive or overwhelming nature. It can be used to describe physical objects, creatures, or abstract concepts.

• *1.* Водоворот был похож на гигантский водоворот. *2.* Гигантское чудовище нависло над городом. *3.* Они пошли в поход и увидели гигантского жука. *4.* Он вырастил гигантскую тыкву. *5.* В фильме фигурировали гигантские кайдзю. *6.* Это гигантский! *7.* Его встретила гигантская волна. *8.* Гигантский слон возвышался над деревьями. *9.* Гигантский скелет динозавра доминировал в музее. • *1.* The whirlpool was like a giant eddy. *2.* The giant monstrosity loomed over the city. *3.* They went hiking and saw a giant bug. *4.* He grew a giant pumpkin. *5.* The movie featured giant kaiju. *6.* It's gigantic! *7.* He was met with a gigantic wave. *8.* The gigantic elephant towered over the trees. *9.* The gigantic dinosaur skeleton dominated the museum.

**210. восхитительный** — *delicious, delightful, adorable, admirable* — This word is used to describe something that is extremely pleasing or impressive. It can be used to express admiration for food, people, places, or experiences. It conveys a sense of delight and appreciation.

● *1.* Это выглядит восхитительно. *2.* Они восхитительны. *3.* Они выглядят восхитительно. *4.* Вишня морелло была восхитительной. *5.* Она приготовила восхитительный десерт сабра. *6.* Как восхитительно. *7.* Это восхитительно. *8.* Какой восхитительный сюрприз. *9.* Это было бы восхитительно. *10.* Это было восхитительно. *11.* Это восхитительно. *12.* Она восхитительна. *13.* Разве это не восхитительно? *14.* Это было восхитительно. *15.* Как восхитительно. *16.* Восхитительная женщина. *17.* Как восхитительно. ● *1.* This looks delicious. *2.* They are delicious. *3.* They look delicious. *4.* The morello cherries were delicious. *5.* She made a delicious sabra dessert. *6.* How delightful. *7.* It's delightful. *8.* What a delightful surprise. *9.* That would be delightful. *10.* It's been delightful. *11.* It's adorable. *12.* She's adorable. *13.* Isn't that adorable? *14.* It was adorable. *15.* How adorable. *16.* An admirable woman. *17.* How admirable.

**211. королевский** — *royal, regal* — 'Королевский' is used to describe something that is majestic, grand, or fit for a king or queen. It conveys a sense of luxury, elegance, and importance.

● *1.* Кто-то вне семьи несет в себе королевскую кровь. *2.* Он гордился своим королевским происхождением. *3.* Королевская процессия прошла через город. *4.* Королевская гробница. *5.* Карета ландо была королевской. *6.* Королевские одежды добавляли ему царственного вида. ● *1.* Someone outside the family is carrying royal blood. *2.* He was proud of his royal lineage. *3.* The royal procession passed through the town. *4.* A royal tomb. *5.* The landau carriage was royal. *6.* The kingly robes added to his regal appearance.

**212. конкретный** — *particular, concrete, specific* — This word is used to describe something that is specific or concrete, rather than general or abstract. It is often used to emphasize the exact details or characteristics of a particular thing or situation.

• *1.* Какая-то конкретная причина? *2.* Кто-нибудь конкретно? *3.* Никакого конкретного места. *4.* Вы ищете что-то конкретное? *5.* Ищете что-то конкретное? *6.* Идея не конкретна. *7.* План должен быть конкретным. *8.* Нам нужен конкретный пример. *9.* Вы можете быть более конкретным? *10.* Быть конкретной. *11.* Более конкретно. *12.* Не могли бы вы быть немного более конкретным? *13.* Вам придется быть более конкретным. • *1.* Any particular reason? *2.* Anyone in particular? *3.* No place in particular. *4.* Are you looking for anything in particular? *5.* Looking for anything in particular? *6.* The idea is not concrete. *7.* The plan needs to be concrete. *8.* We need a concrete example. *9.* Can you be more specific? *10.* Be specific. *11.* Be more specific. *12.* Could you be a little more specific? *13.* You'll have to be more specific.

**213. половой** — *sexual, genital* — This word is used to describe things related to sex or genitals. It can be used to talk about gender, sexual orientation, or physical characteristics. It is often used in medical or scientific contexts.

• *1.* Половой акт. *2.* Она изучала историю полового акта. *3.* Область половых органов требует тщательной гигиены. • *1.* Sexual intercourse. *2.* She studied the history of sexual intercourse. *3.* The genital area requires careful hygiene.

**214. золотистый** — *golden* — 'Golden' is used to describe something that has a shiny, yellowish color similar to that of gold. It can be used to describe objects, colors, or even qualities that are reminiscent of the precious metal.

• *1.* Блинчик был золотисто-коричневого цвета. *2.* Курица была золотистой и хрустящей. *3.* Пухлая курица стала золотисто-коричневой. *4.* Золотистый ретривер вилял хвостом. • *1.* The pancake was golden brown. *2.* The chicken was golden and crispy. *3.* The plump chicken turned golden brown. *4.* The golden retriever wagged its tail.

**215. официальный** — *official, formal* — The word 'официальный' is used to describe something that is recognized or authorized by an official authority, or something that is done in a formal manner.

• *1.* Это официально. *2.* Ну это официально. *3.* Официальный бизнес. *4.* Так что это официально. *5.* Это официально?

*6.* Почему так официально? *7.* Они провели официальную оценку. *8.* Он подал официальную жалобу. *9.* Для этого мероприятия она оделась в официальный наряд. *10.* Они присутствовали на официальном балу. • *1.* It's official. *2.* Well, it's official. *3.* Official business. *4.* So it's official. *5.* Is it official? *6.* Why so formal? *7.* They conducted a formal evaluation. *8.* He filed a formal complaint. *9.* She dressed in formal garb for the event. *10.* They attended the formal ball.

**216. положительный** — *positive, affirmative* — This word is used to describe something that is favorable, optimistic, or constructive. It can also be used to indicate agreement or confirmation.
• *1.* Боюсь, тесты положительные. *2.* Положительный идентификатор. *3.* Положительное или отрицательное? *4.* Они почувствовали положительную атмосферу от группы. *5.* Положительный отзыв. • *1.* I'm afraid the tests are positive. *2.* Positive ID. *3.* Positive or negative? *4.* They felt a positive vibe from the group. *5.* Positive review.

**217. желтый** — *yellow* — This word is used to describe objects, substances, or colors that are yellow in color. It can also be used to describe someone's complexion or mood as being yellowish.
• *1.* Желтая тревога. *2.* Перейти к желтой тревоге. *3.* Желтый. *4.* Ты желтый! *5.* Код желтый. • *1.* Yellow alert. *2.* Go to yellow alert. *3.* The yellow one. *4.* You're yellow! *5.* Code yellow.

**218. регулярный** — *regular* — 'Регулярный' is used to describe something that occurs or happens at fixed intervals or in a consistent manner. It can also refer to something that is standard, usual, or normal in terms of frequency or occurrence.
• *1.* Его анемия требовала регулярных анализов крови. *2.* Комбайн нуждался в регулярном обслуживании. *3.* Герань требует регулярной обрезки. *4.* Машина требовала регулярной смазки. *5.* Пневматическая система требует регулярного обслуживания. • *1.* His anemia required regular blood tests. *2.* The tiller needed regular maintenance. *3.* The geranium required regular pruning. *4.* The machine required regular lubrication. *5.* The pneumatic system requires regular maintenance.

**219. здоровый** — *healthy, wholesome, bonny* — The word 'здоровый' is used to describe something that is in good physical or mental condition. It can refer to a person, animal, food, or environment that is healthy, wholesome, or robust.

● *1.* Это вредно для здоровья. *2.* Очень здоровый. *3.* Вы выглядите здоровым. *4.* Я здоров. *5.* Вы здоровы. ● *1.* It's not healthy. *2.* Very healthy. *3.* You look healthy. *4.* I'm healthy. *5.* You're healthy.

**220. физический** — *physical* — 'физический' is used to describe something related to the body or physical activity. It can also be used to emphasize the tangible or material aspects of a situation or object.

● *1.* Это просто физическое. *2.* Они верили в концепцию физического джихада. *3.* Он испытывал физическую боль. *4.* Физический осмотр был тщательным. *5.* Ручной труд требует физической силы. ● *1.* It's just physical. *2.* They believed in the concept of physical jihad. *3.* He suffered physical pain. *4.* The physical exam was thorough. *5.* A manual labor job requires physical strength.

**221. центральный** — *central, focal, pivotal* — The word 'центральный' is used to describe something that is located in the center or is of central importance. It can also refer to something that is pivotal or focal to a particular situation or context.

● *1.* Брачные танцы занимали центральное место в их культуре. *2.* Карн занимал центральное место в деревне. *3.* Троица была центральной верой. ● *1.* Courtship dances were central to their culture. *2.* The karn was central to the village. *3.* The trinity was a central belief.

**222. способный** — *capable, apt* — This word is used to describe someone's ability or skill in doing something. It implies that the person has the necessary qualities or knowledge to successfully perform a task or achieve a goal.

● *1.* Оружие, способное уничтожить вознесенных существ. *2.* Ты знаешь, на что они способны. *3.* Вы понятия не имеете, на что она способна. *4.* Она была чрезвычайно способным лидером. *5.* Вы доказали, что способны. *6.* Студенты были способными учениками. ● *1.* A weapon capable of destroying ascended beings. *2.* You know what they're capable of. *3.* You have no idea what she's capable of. *4.* She was an eminently capable leader. *5.* You have proven yourself capable. *6.* The students were apt learners.

**223. приличный** — *decent* — 'Приличный' is used to describe something that is of good quality or standard, or someone who behaves in a respectable manner. It can also be used to indicate a reasonable amount or size.

● *1.* Это очень прилично с вашей стороны. *2.* Очень прилично с вашей стороны. *3.* Это прилично. *4.* Держите это прилично. *5.* Что-то приличное. ● *1.* That's very decent of you. *2.* Very decent of you. *3.* It's decent. *4.* Keep it decent. *5.* Something decent.

**224. современный** — *modern, contemporary* — This word is used to describe something that is current, up-to-date, or in line with the latest trends and technologies. It can refer to anything from fashion and design to technology and culture.

● *1.* Очень современный. *2.* Это современно. *3.* Он является прародителем современной науки. *4.* Современная архитектура объединяет форму и функцию. *5.* Крематорий был современным и ухоженным. *6.* Она изучала современную литературу. *7.* Дом построен в современном стиле. *8.* Современный дизайн был новаторским. *9.* Современная музыкальная сцена была яркой. *10.* Они наслаждались современным искусством. ● *1.* Very modern. *2.* It's modern. *3.* He is a forefather of modern science. *4.* The modern architecture integrated form and function. *5.* The crematorium was modern and well-kept. *6.* She studied contemporary literature. *7.* The house was built in a contemporary style. *8.* The contemporary design was innovative. *9.* The contemporary music scene was vibrant. *10.* They enjoyed contemporary art.

**225. благодарный** — *grateful, thankful, appreciative* — This word is used to express feelings of gratitude or appreciation towards someone or something. It conveys a sense of thankfulness and acknowledgment for a kind gesture, favor, or act of kindness.

● *1.* Вы должны быть благодарны. *2.* Мы очень благодарны. *3.* Быть благодарным. *4.* Мы благодарны. *5.* Мы бесконечно благодарны. *6.* Быть благодарным. *7.* Вы должны быть благодарны. *8.* Мы должны быть благодарны. *9.* Благодарные улыбки сделали ей день лучше. *10.* Она была благодарна за помощь. *11.* Благодарная публика аплодировала им стоя. ● *1.* You should be grateful. *2.* We're very grateful. *3.* Be grateful. *4.* We are grateful. *5.* We are eternally grateful. *6.* Be thankful. *7.* You should be thankful. *8.* We should be thankful. *9.* The appreciative smiles made her day. *10.* She was appreciative of the help. *11.* The appreciative audience gave them a standing ovation.

**226. доступный** — *available, accessible, affordable* — This word is used to describe something that is easily obtainable or within reach, whether it be in terms of cost, location, or availability. It conveys the idea of something being accessible or affordable.

● *1.* Вы доступны? *2.* Она недоступна. *3.* Эта информация недоступна. *4.* Она доступна. *5.* Она доступна? *6.* Тропа доступна для туристов. *7.* Архивы были доступны исследователям. *8.* Перевод сделал текст доступным. *9.* Информация доступна всем. *10.* Детский сад был доступным. *11.* Платье было сравнительно доступным. *12.* Они предлагают доступные услуги по уходу за детьми. *13.* Проживание было доступным. *14.* Компания предоставила доступные варианты медицинского обслуживания. ● *1.* Are you available? *2.* She's not available. *3.* That information is not available. *4.* She's available. *5.* Is she available? *6.* The trail is accessible to hikers. *7.* The archives were accessible to researchers. *8.* The translation made the text accessible. *9.* The information is accessible to all. *10.* The daycare was affordable. *11.* The dress was comparatively affordable. *12.* They offer affordable childcare services. *13.* The accommodations were affordable. *14.* The company provided affordable healthcare options.

**227. чрезвычайно** — *extremely, immensely, tremendously, grossly* — 'чрезвычайно' is used to emphasize the degree or intensity of something, indicating a high level of extremity or intensity. It is often used to describe emotions, actions, or qualities that are significantly above average.

● *1.* Чрезвычайно опасен. *2.* Это чрезвычайно опасно. *3.* Он чрезвычайно опасен. *4.* Это чрезвычайно важно. *5.* Жидкий азот чрезвычайно холоден. *6.* Задача была чрезвычайно сложной. ● *1.* Extremely dangerous. *2.* It's extremely dangerous. *3.* He's extremely dangerous. *4.* This is extremely important. *5.* Liquid nitrogen is extremely cold. *6.* The task was immensely difficult.

**228. ложный** — *false, untrue, spurious, phoney* — This word is used to describe something that is not genuine or true, often used to refer to fake or misleading information, objects, or people. It can also be used to describe a false impression or appearance.
● *1.* Ложная сигнализация. *2.* Это ложная тревога. *3.* Ложная реклама. *4.* Никакой ложной скромности. *5.* Возможно, это ложная тревога. *6.* Она опасалась ложных предложений. *7.* Ложный слух распространился как лесной пожар. *8.* Он выдвинул ложные обвинения. *9.* Ложные доказательства были отклонены. *10.* Ложные утверждения были быстро опровергнуты. ● *1.* False alarm. *2.* It's a false alarm. *3.* False advertising. *4.* No false modesty. *5.* Maybe it's a false alarm. *6.* She was wary of spurious offers. *7.* The spurious rumor spread like wildfire. *8.* He made spurious accusations. *9.* The spurious evidence was dismissed. *10.* The spurious claims were quickly debunked.

**229. любопытный** — *curious, nosy, nosey* — This word is used to describe someone who is interested in knowing about other people's affairs or who is eager to learn new things. It can also be used to describe something that is intriguing or captivating.
● *1.* Мне любопытно. *2.* Просто любопытно. *3.* Мне было просто любопытно. *4.* Мне было любопытно. *5.* Разве тебе не любопытно? *6.* Не будьте любопытными. *7.* Я любопытный. *8.* Бидди была любопытна. *9.* Любопытная соседка наблюдала из окна. *10.* Люди находят ее любопытное поведение навязчивым. *11.* Она всегда такая любопытная. *12.* Любопытный детектив всех допросил. ● *1.* I'm curious. *2.* Just curious. *3.* I was just curious. *4.* I was curious. *5.* Aren't you curious? *6.* Don't be nosy. *7.* I'm nosy. *8.* The biddy was nosy. *9.* The nosey neighbor watched from her window. *10.* People find her nosey attitude intrusive. *11.* She is always so nosey. *12.* The nosey detective questioned everyone.

**230. молчаливый** — *silent* — The word 'молчаливый' is used to describe someone or something that is quiet or silent. It can be used to characterize a person who speaks very little or a place that is peaceful and devoid of noise.

● *1.* Ты обращаешься со мной молчаливо. *2.* Он был моим молчаливым партнером. *3.* Они погрузились в молчаливое созерцание. *4.* Он выразил молчаливое почтение. ● *1.* You're giving me the silent treatment. *2.* He was my silent partner. *3.* They engaged in silent contemplation. *4.* He offered a silent homage.

**231. незаконный** — *illegal, illegitimate, unlawful, wrongful* — The word 'незаконный' is used to describe something that is not allowed or permitted by law. It can refer to actions, behaviors, or objects that are considered illegal, illegitimate, unlawful, or wrongful.

● *1.* Это незаконно. *2.* Разве это не незаконно? *3.* Это не незаконно. *4.* Это было бы незаконно. *5.* Это незаконно? *6.* Эти дети незаконнорожденные. *7.* Бизнес обвинили в - незаконных действиях. *8.* Они столкнулись с незаконным иском против их собственности. *9.* Она боролась со своим незаконным статусом. *10.* Незаконное проникновение в здание было запрещено. *11.* Его действия были признаны незаконными. *12.* Им предъявлено обвинение в незаконном хранении. *13.* Она подала в суд за незаконное увольнение.
● *1.* It's illegal. *2.* Isn't that illegal? *3.* It's not illegal. *4.* That would be illegal. *5.* Is that illegal? *6.* These children are illegitimate. *7.* The business was accused of illegitimate practices. *8.* They faced an illegitimate claim against their property. *9.* She struggled with her illegitimate status. *10.* Unlawful entry into the building was prohibited. *11.* His actions were deemed unlawful. *12.* They were charged with unlawful possession. *13.* She sued for wrongful termination.

**232. бывший** — *former* — 'Вывший' is used to describe something or someone that was in a previous state or position. It can be used to indicate a past relationship, job, title, or status.

● *1.* Он работал с ее бывшим начальником. *2.* Они остановились у своего бывшего дома. *3.* Он был бывшим президентом. *4.* Предательство бывшего друга ранило его. *5.* Гарриет Джонс, бывший премьер-министр. ● *1.* He worked with her former boss. *2.* They stopped by their former home. *3.* He was a former president. *4.* The treachery of his former friend hurt. *5.* Harriet Jones, former Prime Minister.

**233. мудрый** — *wise* — The word 'мудрый' is used to describe someone who possesses wisdom, knowledge, and good judgment. It can also be used to describe actions, decisions, or advice that are considered wise or thoughtful.

● *1.* Это мудро? *2.* Очень мудрый. *3.* Вы думаете, это мудро? *4.* Мудрый выбор. *5.* Мудрое решение. ● *1.* Is that wise? *2.* Very wise. *3.* Do you think that's wise? *4.* A wise choice. *5.* A wise decision.

**234. отчаянный** — *desperate, foolhardy* — This word is used to describe someone who is in a state of extreme despair or recklessness, often willing to take drastic measures in order to achieve their goals.

● *1.* Ранее в «Отчаянных домохозяйках». *2.* Отчаянные времена требуют отчаянных мер. *3.* Отчаянные времена. *4.* Отчаянные времена, отчаянные меры. *5.* Отчаянные меры. ● *1.* Previously on Desperate Housewives. *2.* Desperate times call for desperate measures. *3.* Desperate times. *4.* Desperate times, desperate measures. *5.* Desperate measures.

**235. популярный** — *popular* — This word is used to describe something that is well-liked or widely known by a large number of people. It can refer to anything from a popular song or movie to a popular tourist destination.

● *1.* Очень популярный. *2.* Это очень популярно. *3.* Они очень популярны. *4.* Тунец -- популярный выбор суши. *5.* Амфитеатр был популярной концертной площадкой. ● *1.* Very popular. *2.* It's very popular. *3.* They're very popular. *4.* Tuna is a popular sushi choice. *5.* The amphitheater was a popular concert venue.

**236. четвертый** — *fourth* — 'четвертый' is used to indicate the position of something in a sequence of four items. It can also be used to describe the order in which something occurs or is ranked.

● *1.* Четвертый этаж. *2.* Где четвертый? *3.* С четвертым июля! *4.* Как зовут четвертого человека? *5.* Четвертый класс. ● *1.* Fourth floor. *2.* Where's the fourth? *3.* Happy Fourth of July! *4.* What is the name of the fourth man? *5.* Fourth grade.

**237. отдельный** — *separate* — This word is used to describe something that is distinct or isolated from others. It can refer to a separate entity or individual, or to something that is distinct or different from the rest.

• *1.* Детская зона была отдельной. *2.* Территория была разделена на отдельные регионы. *3.* Я считаю, что мы должны жить отдельной жизнью. *4.* Двоеженец вел две отдельные жизни. *5.* Отдельные проверки. • *1.* The kiddy area was separate. *2.* The territory was divided into separate regions. *3.* I believe that we should lead separate lives. *4.* The bigamist maintained two separate lives. *5.* Separate checks.

**238. драгоценный** — *precious* — This word is used to describe something that is highly valued or cherished. It can refer to physical objects, emotions, relationships, or moments that hold great significance and importance to someone.

• *1.* Это драгоценно. *2.* Время драгоценно. *3.* Привет, драгоценный. *4.* Жизнь драгоценна. *5.* Разве она не драгоценна? • *1.* That's precious. *2.* Time is precious. *3.* Hello, precious. *4.* Life is precious. *5.* Isn't she precious?

**239. широкий** — *wide, broad* — This word is used to describe something that has a large width or breadth. It can be used to talk about physical objects, spaces, or concepts that are expansive or extensive in size.

• *1.* Откройте широко. *2.* Это широко открыто. *3.* Ты оставил себя широко открытым. *4.* Темба, широко раскинув руки. *5.* Широко откройте рот. *6.* Какой-то широкий. *7.* Компания имеет широкий охват. *8.* У них широкий ассортимент продукции. *9.* Тупая широкая! *10.* Водный путь был широким и глубоким. • *1.* Open wide. *2.* It's wide open. *3.* You left yourself wide open. *4.* Temba, his arms wide. *5.* Open your mouth wide. *6.* Some broad. *7.* The company has a broad reach. *8.* They have a broad range of products. *9.* Dumb broad! *10.* The waterway was broad and deep.

**240. редкий** — *rare, uncommon* — 'Редкий' is used to describe something that is not commonly found or seen. It can refer to objects, events, or characteristics that are unusual or scarce. It is often used to emphasize the uniqueness or infrequency of something.

• *1.* Очень редкий. *2.* Это редкость. *3.* Это очень редко. *4.* Невероятно редкий. *5.* Они очень редки. *6.* Это не редкость. • *1.* Very rare. *2.* It's rare. *3.* It's very rare. *4.* Extremely rare. *5.*

They're very rare. *6.* It's not uncommon.

**241. успешный** — *successful* — 'Успешный' is used to describe someone or something that has achieved a desired outcome or has been prosperous in their endeavors. It conveys a sense of accomplishment and positive results.

● *1.* Очень успешный. *2.* Он стремился стать успешным торговцем. *3.* Подход оказался успешным. *4.* Они оба профессионально успешны. *5.* Благотворительная акция прошла успешно. ● *1.* Very successful. *2.* He aspired to become a successful chapman. *3.* The approach was successful. *4.* They're both professionally successful. *5.* The charity event was successful.

**242. точный** — *exact, precise, accurate* — 'Точный' is used to describe something that is precise or accurate in measurement, time, or description. It is often used to indicate that something is exact or correct in its details or specifications.

● *1.* Это не точная наука. *2.* Каковы были его точные слова? *3.* Это были его точные слова. *4.* Точное изменение. *5.* Это были ее точные слова. *6.* Процесс установки требовал точного выравнивания. *7.* Криогенный процесс требует точного контроля температуры. *8.* Он использовал скальпель, чтобы делать точные разрезы. *9.* Так точно. *10.* Аэрокосмическая техника требовала точных расчетов. *11.* Это точно? *12.* Это точно. *13.* Но точный. *14.* Это не точно. *15.* Транскрипция была точной. ● *1.* It's not an exact science. *2.* What were his exact words? *3.* Those were his exact words. *4.* Exact change. *5.* Those were her exact words. *6.* The insertion process required precise alignment. *7.* The cryogenic process requires precise temperature control. *8.* He used a scalpel to make precise cuts. *9.* So precise. *10.* Aerospace engineering required precise calculations. *11.* Is that accurate? *12.* That's accurate. *13.* But accurate. *14.* That's not accurate. *15.* The transcription was accurate.

**243. чужой** — *alien* — 'Чужой' is used to describe something or someone as foreign, unfamiliar, or belonging to someone else. It can also convey a sense of being strange or different from what is expected or known.

● *1.* Чужой язык звучал как тарабарщина. ● *1.* The alien language sounded like gibberish.

**244. неприятный** — *nasty, unpleasant, grisly, distasteful* — This word is used to describe something that is unpleasant, distasteful, or grisly. It conveys a sense of discomfort or displeasure towards the object or situation being described.

● *1.* Неприятный бизнес. *2.* Неприятная штука. *3.* Неприятный путь. *4.* Это неприятная привычка. *5.* Неприятная привычка. *6.* Очень неприятно. *7.* Запах был неприятным ощущением. *8.* Субпродукты неприятно пахли. *9.* Резиновая текстура была неприятной. *10.* Остаточный запах был неприятным. ● *1.* Nasty business. *2.* Nasty stuff. *3.* Nasty way to go. *4.* It's a nasty habit. *5.* Nasty habit. *6.* Very unpleasant. *7.* The smell was an unpleasant sensation. *8.* The offal smelled unpleasant. *9.* The rubbery texture was unpleasant. *10.* The residual smell was unpleasant.

**245. старший** — *senior* — 'Starshiy' is used to indicate someone or something that is older, higher in rank, or more experienced. It can be used to compare individuals within a group or to show respect towards someone older or in a higher position.

● *1.* Старший Брат! *2.* Старший год. *3.* Да, старший шеф! *4.* Я старший. *5.* Младший или Старший? ● *1.* Senior Brother! *2.* Senior year. *3.* Yes, Senior Chief! *4.* I'm a senior. *5.* Junior or Senior?

**246. необычный** — *unusual* — 'Необычный' is used to describe something that is out of the ordinary or uncommon. It is used to convey the idea of something being unique, strange, or different from what is typically expected.

● *1.* Это необычно. *2.* Ничего необычного. *3.* Это необычно? *4.* Что-нибудь необычное? *5.* Самый необычный. ● *1.* That's unusual. *2.* Nothing unusual. *3.* Is that unusual? *4.* Anything unusual? *5.* Most unusual.

**247. дружественный** — *friendly* — This word is used to describe someone or something that is kind, welcoming, or amicable in nature. It conveys a sense of warmth and openness in interactions and relationships.

● *1.* Дружественный огонь. *2.* Это был дружественный огонь.
● *1.* Friendly fire. *2.* It was friendly fire.

**248. отрицательный** — *negative* — The word 'отрицательный' is used to describe something that is unfavorable, harmful, or lacking in positivity. It can also be used to indicate a pessimistic or cynical attitude towards a situation or person.

● *1.* Отрицательно, сэр. *2.* Это отрицательно. *3.* Отрицательно, капитан. *4.* Это было отрицательно. *5.* Отрицательный, отрицательный. ● *1.* Negative, sir. *2.* It's negative. *3.* Negative, captain. *4.* It was negative. *5.* Negative, negative.

**249. резкий** — *sharp, harsh, abrupt, edgy* — The word 'резкий' is used to describe something that is sharp, harsh, abrupt, or edgy in nature. It is often used to convey a sense of intensity or suddenness in a situation or behavior.

● *1.* Нож имел резкий разрез. *2.* Корабль совершил резкий маневр. *3.* Складка на скатерти была резкой. *4.* Он почувствовал резкий удар. *5.* Автомобильный сигнал издал резкий сигнал. *6.* Она подверглась резкой критике. *7.* Средство для удаления было резким для ее кожи. *8.* Резкий тон только разозлит его. *9.* Резкая критика была жесткой. *10.* Ее мать была резким критиком. *11.* Она ответила резким тоном. *12.* Изменение было резким и неожиданным. *13.* Автомобиль резко остановился. *14.* Изменение цвета было резким. *15.* Он ушел в резкой форме. *16.* Работы художника известны своей резкостью. ● *1.* The knife had a sharp slash. *2.* The ship made a sharp manoeuvre. *3.* The crease in the tablecloth was sharp. *4.* He felt a sharp kick. *5.* The car horn let out a sharp beep. *6.* She received harsh criticism. *7.* The remover was harsh on her skin. *8.* The harsh tone would only antagonize him. *9.* The scathing critique was harsh. *10.* Her mother was a harsh critic. *11.* She answered with an abrupt tone. *12.* The change was abrupt and unexpected. *13.* The car came to an abrupt stop. *14.* The color shift was abrupt. *15.* He left in an abrupt manner. *16.* The artist's work is known for being edgy.

**250. великолепный** — *gorgeous, glorious, magnificent, splendid* — 'Великолепный' is used to describe something that is extremely beautiful, impressive, or magnificent. It is often used to express admiration or awe towards something that is truly exceptional in appearance or quality.

● *1.* Это великолепно. *2.* Ты выглядишь великолепно. *3.* Она великолепна. *4.* Они великолепны. *5.* Вы великолепны. *6.* Это было великолепно. *7.* Разве это не великолепно? *8.* Великолепное произведение искусства вызвало восхищение у многих. *9.* У нее был великолепный голос. *10.* Это великолепно! *11.* Это великолепно. *12.* Великолепно, не так ли? *13.* Она была великолепна. *14.* Это было великолепно. *15.* Ты выглядишь великолепно. *16.* О, великолепно. *17.* Это великолепно. *18.* Великолепно, великолепно. *19.* Великолепная идея. *20.* Ах, великолепно. ● *1.* It's gorgeous. *2.* You look gorgeous. *3.* She's gorgeous. *4.* They're gorgeous. *5.* You are gorgeous. *6.* It was glorious. *7.* Isn't it glorious? *8.* The glorious artwork was admired by many. *9.* She had a glorious voice. *10.* It's glorious! *11.* It's magnificent. *12.* Magnificent, isn't it? *13.* She was magnificent. *14.* It was magnificent. *15.* You look magnificent. *16.* Oh, splendid. *17.* That's splendid. *18.* Splendid, splendid. *19.* Splendid idea. *20.* Ah, splendid.

**251. похожий** — *similar* — 'Похожий' is used to describe things that are alike or resemble each other in some way. It is used to compare similarities between objects, people, or situations.

● *1.* Очень похожий. *2.* Мы похожи. *3.* Герты похожи на ратов. *4.* Наши наряды случайно оказались похожими. *5.* Ткань была похожа на ткань Оксфорд. ● *1.* Very similar. *2.* We're similar. *3.* Herths are similar to raths. *4.* Our outfits were coincidentally similar. *5.* The fabric was similar to Oxford cloth.

**252. международный** — *international* — This word is used to describe something that involves or relates to multiple countries or nations. It can refer to events, organizations, agreements, or any other aspect of global interaction.

● *1.* Они провели международное мероприятие. *2.* В фильме задействован международный актерский состав. *3.* Компания имеет международное присутствие. *4.* Работы художника получили международное признание. *5.* Влияние Тохо распространилось на международные рынки. ● *1.* They hosted an international event. *2.* The movie has an international cast. *3.* The company has an international presence. *4.* The artist's work received international acclaim. *5.* Toho's influence extended to international markets.

**253. федеральный** — *federal* — 'федеральный' is used to describe something that is related to or part of a federal system or government. It can also refer to something that is on a national or country-wide level.

● *1.* Я федеральный агент. *2.* Мы федеральные агенты. *3.* Я федеральный агент Джек Бауэр. *4.* Это федеральное преступление. *5.* Он федеральный агент. ● *1.* I'm a federal agent. *2.* We're federal agents. *3.* I'm Federal Agent Jack Bauer. *4.* It's a federal offense. *5.* He's a federal agent.

**254. умственный** — *mental* — 'Умственный' is used to describe something related to the mind or intellect. It can refer to mental abilities, processes, or conditions. It is often used in contexts discussing intelligence, cognition, or psychological states.
● *1.* Он жаждал умственной стимуляции. ● *1.* He craved mental stimulation.

**255. надежный** — *secure, reliable, trustworthy, dependable* — This word is used to describe something or someone that can be trusted, relied upon, or considered safe and secure. It conveys a sense of dependability and reliability in various contexts.
● *1.* Нитроглицерин хранился в надежном месте. *2.* Замок Чабб был надежным. *3.* Он нашел надежную точку опоры. *4.* Она была надежным арендатором. *5.* Митч был надежным коллегой. *6.* Слуга был прилежным и надежным. *7.* Посредник был надежным и осторожным. *8.* Стивен -- надежный друг. *9.* Я надежный парень. *10.* Брэкетт был надежным к-оллегой. *11.* Коннер был надежным советником. *12.* Для реализации проекта они наняли надежного подрядчика. *13.* Автомобиль показал себя надежным. *14.* Их дружба строилась на надежной поддержке. *15.* Она ценила его надежный характер. ● *1.* The nitroglycerine was stored in a secure location. *2.* The chubb lock was secure. *3.* He found a secure foothold. *4.* She was a reliable tenant. *5.* Mitch was a reliable colleague. *6.* The houseboy was diligent and reliable. *7.* The intermediary was reliable and discreet. *8.* Steven is a reliable friend. *9.* I'm a trustworthy guy. *10.* Brackett was a trustworthy colleague. *11.* The conner was a trustworthy advisor. *12.* They hired a dependable contractor for the project. *13.* The car proved to be dependable. *14.* Their friendship was built on dependable support. *15.* She valued his dependable nature.

**256. эмоциональный** — *emotional* — This word is used to describe someone or something that is highly sensitive, expressive, or prone to strong feelings. It can also refer to actions, reactions, or situations that are driven by emotions rather than logic.

● *1.* Вы эмоциональны. *2.* Вы становитесь эмоциональными. *3.* Сцена на смертном одре была эмоциональной. *4.* Церемония награждения прошла эмоционально. *5.* У нее был эмоциональный интеллект. ● *1.* You're emotional. *2.* You're getting emotional. *3.* The deathbed scene was emotional. *4.* The medal ceremony was emotional. *5.* She had emotional intelligence.

**257. розовый** — *pink, rosy* — This word is used to describe something that is pink or rosy in color. It can be used to describe objects, clothing, or even a person's complexion. It is a versatile word that can be used in various contexts.
● *1.* Он розовый. *2.* Розовые звезды падают. *3.* Розовые звезды падают рядами. *4.* Они розовые. *5.* Розовый. *6.* Розовое сияние восхода солнца. ● *1.* It's pink. *2.* The pink stars are falling. *3.* The pink stars are falling in lines. *4.* They're pink. *5.* The pink one. *6.* The rosy glow of sunrise.

**258. потрясающий** — *terrific, fabulous, breathtaking, fab* — 'Потрясающий' is used to describe something that is amazing, impressive, or awe-inspiring. It is often used to express admiration or excitement about something that is truly exceptional or outstanding.
● *1.* Это потрясающе. *2.* Ты выглядишь потрясающе. *3.* О, потрясающе. *4.* Ты был потрясающим. *5.* Ты потрясающий. *6.* Ты выглядишь потрясающе. *7.* Это потрясающе. *8.* О, потрясающе. *9.* О, это потрясающе. *10.* Разве это не потрясающе? *11.* На ней было потрясающее платье. *12.* Он проделал потрясающую работу над проектом. *13.* У них есть потрясающий новый продукт. ● *1.* That's terrific. *2.* You look terrific. *3.* Oh, terrific. *4.* You were terrific. *5.* You're terrific. *6.* You look fabulous. *7.* It's fabulous. *8.* Oh, fabulous. *9.* Oh, that's fabulous. *10.* Isn't that fabulous? *11.* She wore a breathtaking dress. *12.* He did a fab job on the project. *13.* They have a fab new product.

**259. экстраординарный** — *extraordinary* — This word is used to describe something that is exceptional, remarkable, or out of the ordinary. It is often used to emphasize the uniqueness or special qualities of a person, event, or object.
● *1.* Произошло нечто экстраординарное. *2.* Что-то экстраординарное. *3.* Ничего экстраординарного. ● *1.* Something

extraordinary has happened. *2.* Something extraordinary. *3.* Nothing extraordinary.

**260. тонкий** — *thin, delicate, slender, slim* — 'Тонкий' is used to describe something that is thin, delicate, slender, or slim. It can refer to physical objects, such as a pencil or a thread, as well as to abstract concepts, such as a subtle flavor or a nuanced argument.

• *1.* Тонкий лед. *2.* Это тонко. *3.* Тонкие стены. *4.* Это слишком тонко. *5.* Грань между успехом и неудачей была тонкой. *6.* Ткань была тонкая и тонкая. *7.* Прядильная машина выпустила мягкую, тонкую нить. *8.* Материал был тонким и нежным. *9.* Сложный дизайн отличался тонкими деталями. *10.* Вино соответствовало ее тонкому вкусу. *11.* У нее тонкие пальцы. *12.* Тонкие сборы. • *1.* Thin ice. *2.* That's thin. *3.* Thin walls. *4.* It's too thin. *5.* The line between success and failure was thin. *6.* The fabric was thready and delicate. *7.* The spinner produced a soft, delicate thread. *8.* The material was thin and delicate. *9.* The intricate design featured delicate details. *10.* The wine suited her delicate palate. *11.* She has slender fingers. *12.* Slim pickings.

**261. твердый** — *solid, crusty, steadfast* — 'Твердый' is used to describe something that is solid, firm, or steadfast. It can refer to physical objects, such as food or materials, as well as abstract qualities like beliefs or character traits.

• *1.* Это твердо. *2.* Твердый как скала. *3.* Он твердый. *4.* Это твердо? *5.* Твердое серебро. *6.* Твердая почва затрудняла земледелие. • *1.* It's solid. *2.* Solid as a rock. *3.* He's solid. *4.* Is it solid? *5.* Solid silver. *6.* The crusty soil made farming difficult.

**262. насильственный** — *violent* — The word 'насильственный' is used to describe something that is characterized by force, aggression, or brutality. It can be used to describe actions, behavior, or situations that involve physical or emotional violence.

• *1.* Насильственные преступления с участием простых людей. *2.* Насильственные преступления Здравствуйте? *3.* Бойцы -- это осужденные за насильственные преступления. • *1.* Violent crimes involving ordinary people. *2.* Violent Crimes Hello? *3.* Fighters are convicted violent felons.

**263. фактический** — *actual, factual* — 'Фактический' is used to describe something that is real, true, or existing in fact. It is often used to emphasize the actual state of something, as opposed to what is perceived or assumed.

● *1.* Она фактический владелец дома. ● *1.* She is the actual owner of the house.

**264. ежедневный** — *daily* — This word is used to describe something that happens, is done, or is used every day. It can also be used to describe something that is related to or suitable for daily use or consumption.

● *1.* Она ежедневно тренировалась с Бильбо. *2.* Не ежедневно. *3.* Его пуджа была ежедневной практикой. *4.* Был ежедневный двойной! *5.* Ежедневные дела были сделаны. ● *1.* She trained with the bilbo daily. *2.* Don't daily. *3.* His pooja was a daily practice. *4.* Had the daily double! *5.* The daily chores were done.

**265. застенчивый** — *shy, coy* — This word is used to describe someone who is timid or reserved in social situations, often feeling nervous or uncomfortable when interacting with others. It conveys a sense of modesty and reluctance to draw attention to oneself.

● *1.* Она застенчива. *2.* Он застенчив. *3.* Я застенчив. *4.* Не будь таким застенчивым. *5.* Он просто застенчив. *6.* Не будьте застенчивы. *7.* Не играйте в застенчивость. *8.* Его застенчивое поведение показалось ему интригующим. ● *1.* She's shy. *2.* He's shy. *3.* I'm shy. *4.* Don't be so shy. *5.* He's just shy. *6.* Don't be coy. *7.* Don't play coy. *8.* He found her coy behavior intriguing.

**266. срочный** — *urgent* — This word is used to describe something that requires immediate attention or action. It conveys a sense of urgency and importance, indicating that the matter cannot be delayed or ignored.

● *1.* Это срочно. *2.* Он говорит, что это срочно. *3.* Что такого срочного? *4.* Это очень срочно. *5.* Это срочно? ● *1.* It's urgent. *2.* He says it's urgent. *3.* What's so urgent? *4.* It's very urgent. *5.* Is it urgent?

**267. впечатляющий** — *impressive* — 'Впечатляющий' is used to describe something that leaves a strong and positive impression. It is often used to express admiration or awe towards something that is remarkable or extraordinary.

● *1.* Очень впечатляюще. *2.* Это было впечатляюще. *3.* Наиболее впечатляющим. *4.* Это довольно впечатляюще. *5.* Довольно впечатляюще, да? ● *1.* Very impressive. *2.* That was impressive. *3.* Most impressive. *4.* That's pretty impressive. *5.* Pretty impressive, huh?

**268. уникальный** — *unique* — 'Уникальный' is used to describe something that is one of a kind, unparalleled, or distinct from anything else. It emphasizes the rarity or specialness of the object or concept being described.

● *1.* Вы уникальны. *2.* Это уникально. *3.* Я закупаю уникальные вещи для избранных клиентов. *4.* Она уникальна. *5.* Ореховый вкус был уникальным. ● *1.* You are unique. *2.* It's unique. *3.* I procure unique items for a select clientele. *4.* She's unique. *5.* The nutty flavor was unique.

**269. потенциальный** — *potential* — 'Потенциальный' is used to describe something that has the possibility or capability to become or develop into something else in the future. It implies that there is a latent quality or ability waiting to be realized.

● *1.* Потенциальные убийцы. *2.* Антиматерия обладает потенциальной энергией. *3.* Этот проект представлял собой потенциальное минное поле. *4.* Она могла предвидеть потенциальные проблемы впереди. *5.* Они такие же потенциальные убийцы, как и мы. ● *1.* Potential slayers. *2.* Antimatter has potential energy. *3.* The project was a potential minefield. *4.* She could foresee the potential problems ahead. *5.* They're potential slayers, just like we were.

**270. чувствительный** — *sensitive, susceptible* — This word is used to describe someone who is easily affected by emotions or external factors. It can also refer to something that is delicate or easily damaged.

● *1.* Не будь таким чувствительным. *2.* Очень чувствительный. *3.* Такой чувствительный. *4.* Ты такой чувствительный. *5.* Я не чувствительный. ● *1.* Don't be so sensitive. *2.* Very sensitive. *3.* So sensitive. *4.* You're so sensitive. *5.* I'm not sensitive.

**271. неизвестный** — *unknown* — 'Неизвестный' is used to

describe something or someone that is not known or familiar. It can be used to refer to a person, place, or thing that is unidentified or unfamiliar.

● *1.* Неизвестно, сэр. *2.* Неизвестный абонент. *3.* Неизвестно, капитан. *4.* Объект неизвестного происхождения. *5.* Результаты до сих пор были неизвестны. ● *1.* Unknown, sir. *2.* Unknown caller. *3.* Unknown, captain. *4.* An object of unknown origin. *5.* The results were hitherto unknown.

**272. мобильный** — *mobile* — This word is used to describe something that is able to move easily or is easily transportable. It can also refer to something that is related to or used with mobile devices or technology.

● *1.* Твой мобильный. *2.* Мобильный потерян. *3.* Он специализировался на разработке программного обеспечения для мобильных устройств. *4.* Мы становимся мобильными. *5.* Мобильный принадлежит ей. ● *1.* Your mobile. *2.* The mobile is lost. *3.* He specialized in developing software for mobile devices. *4.* We're going mobile. *5.* The mobile is hers.

**273. устойчивый** — *steady, steadfast* — 'Устойчивый' is used to describe something or someone that is consistent, reliable, and unwavering in their actions or characteristics. It conveys a sense of stability and resilience in various situations.

● *1.* Устойчивый, как она идет. *2.* Устойчиво, устойчиво. *3.* Держите это устойчиво. *4.* Держите его устойчиво. *5.* Теперь устойчив. ● *1.* Steady as she goes. *2.* Steady, steady. *3.* Keep it steady. *4.* Hold it steady. *5.* Steady now.

**274. несчастный** — *miserable, unhappy, unfortunate, wretched* — The word 'несчастный' is used to describe someone or something that is experiencing extreme unhappiness, misfortune, or wretchedness. It conveys a sense of deep sadness or unfortunate circumstances.

● *1.* Она несчастна. *2.* Ты выглядишь несчастным. *3.* Они несчастны. *4.* Ты делаешь меня несчастным. *5.* Не выгляди таким несчастным. *6.* Ты выглядишь несчастным. *7.* Ты делаешь меня несчастным. *8.* Несчастный случай. *9.* Это был несчастный случай. *10.* Это был просто несчастный случай. *11.* После этой новости она почувствовала себя несчастной. *12.* Несчастное здание было осуждено. ● *1.* She's miserable. *2.* You look miserable. *3.* They're miserable. *4.* You make me miserable. *5.* Don't look so miserable. *6.* You seem unhappy. *7.* You make me unhappy. *8.* An unfortunate accident. *9.* It was an unfortunate accident. *10.* It was just an unfortunate incident. *11.* She felt wretched after the news. *12.* The wretched building was condemned.

**275. массивный** — *massive* — 'Массивный' is used to describe something that is very large, heavy, or solid in size or appearance. It can be used to emphasize the impressive or imposing nature of an object or structure.

● *1.* Массивное внутреннее кровотечение. *2.* На нефтяной вышке была массивная вышка. *3.* Скелет мастодонта был массивным. *4.* Корпус корабля был массивным. *5.* Массивный сердечный приступ. ● *1.* Massive internal bleeding. *2.* The oil rig had a massive derrick. *3.* The mastodon's skeleton was massive. *4.* The hulk of the ship was massive. *5.* Massive heart attack.

**276. благородный** — *noble, genteel* — This word is used to describe someone or something that is distinguished, honorable, and possessing high moral qualities. It conveys a sense of elegance, grace, and dignity.

● *1.* Как благородно. *2.* Это благородно. *3.* Это очень благородно с вашей стороны. *4.* Как благородно с твоей стороны. *5.* Очень благородно. *6.* Мероприятие было благородным и изысканным. *7.* Благородное воспитание сформировало ее поведение. *8.* Благородное очарование города впечатляло посетителей. *9.* У нее были благородные манеры. *10.* Он происходил из благородной семьи. ● *1.* How noble. *2.* That's noble. *3.* That's very noble of you. *4.* How noble of you. *5.* Very noble. *6.* The event was genteel and refined. *7.* Her genteel upbringing shaped her behavior. *8.* The genteel charm of the town impressed visitors. *9.* She had a genteel manner about her. *10.* He came from a genteel family.

**277. гражданский** — *civil* — The adjective/adverb 'гражданский' is used to describe things related to civil society, citizenship, or non-military matters. It can refer to things like civil rights, civil duties, or civil infrastructure.

● *1.* Я снимал по гражданскому. *2.* Гражданская служба. *3.* Они праздновали продвижение гражданских прав. *4.* Гражданская война. *5.* Гражданские права или гражданская война! • *1.* I was shooting for civil. *2.* Civil service. *3.* They celebrated the advancement of civil rights. *4.* Civil war. *5.* Civil rights or civil war!

**278. пластиковый** — *plastic* — This word is used to describe something that is made of plastic or has characteristics similar to plastic. It can refer to objects, materials, or even abstract concepts that resemble or are related to plastic in some way.
• *1.* Пластиковая взрывчатка. *2.* Ты принес пластиковых человечков? *3.* Они пластиковые. *4.* Они переработали пластиковые бутылки и бумагу. *5.* Она призвала запретить пластиковые пакеты. • *1.* Plastic explosive. *2.* Did you bring the plastic men? *3.* They're plastic. *4.* They recycled plastic bottles and paper. *5.* She called for a ban on plastic bags.

**279. ядерный** — *nuclear* — The word 'ядерный' is used to describe something related to nuclear energy or weapons. It can also be used to describe something as being powerful, intense, or destructive.
• *1.* Ядерная бомба. *2.* Ядерное оружие. *3.* Дейтерий используется в ядерных реакторах. *4.* Ядерная война. *5.* Плутоний используется в ядерных реакторах. • *1.* A nuclear bomb. *2.* Nuclear weapons. *3.* Deuterium is used in nuclear reactors. *4.* Nuclear war. *5.* Plutonium is used in nuclear reactors.

**280. подозрительный** — *suspicious, fishy, leery* — This word is used to describe something or someone that causes doubt or mistrust. It implies a sense of suspicion or unease, suggesting that there may be something questionable or dishonest about the situation or person.
• *1.* Очень подозрительно. *2.* Он выглядит подозрительно. *3.* Ничего подозрительного. *4.* Не будьте подозрительны. *5.* Что-нибудь подозрительное? *6.* Происходит что-то подозрительное. *7.* Это подозрительно. *8.* Очень подозрительно. *9.* Есть что-то подозрительное в этом парне. *10.* Для меня это звучит подозрительно. • *1.* Very suspicious. *2.* He looks suspicious. *3.* Nothing suspicious. *4.* Don't be suspicious. *5.* Anything suspicious? *6.* There's something fishy going on. *7.* It's fishy. *8.* Very fishy. *9.* There's something fishy about that guy. *10.* Sounds fishy to me.

**281. апельсиновый** — *orange* — This word is used to describe something that is the color or flavor of oranges. It can be used to describe objects, foods, or anything else that is orange in color or taste.

● *1.* Это апельсиновый сок. *2.* Он любит апельсиновый сок. *3.* Детям очень понравился апельсиновый шербет. *4.* Я принес тебе апельсинового сока. ● *1.* It's orange juice. *2.* He loves orange juice. *3.* The children loved the orange sherbet. *4.* I brought you some orange juice.

**282. практически** — *practically* — 'Practically' is used to indicate that something is almost or nearly true, accurate, or applicable. It is often used to suggest that something is very close to being true or accurate, but not entirely.

● *1.* Практически ничего. *2.* Мы практически семья. *3.* Я практически вырос здесь. *4.* Практически нет. *5.* Практически все приходят. ● *1.* Practically nothing. *2.* We're practically family. *3.* I practically grew up here. *4.* Practically none. *5.* Practically everyone is coming.

**283. специфический** — *specific, peculiar* — This word is used to describe something that is unique or particular to a certain situation or group. It implies that the thing being described has distinct characteristics that set it apart from others.

● *1.* Он использовал специфическую терминологию. *2.* Специфический запах было трудно определить. ● *1.* He used specific terminology. *2.* The peculiar smell was hard to identify.

**284. таинственный** — *mysterious* — This word is used to describe something that is difficult to understand or explain, often creating a sense of intrigue or secrecy. It is commonly used to describe places, people, or events that have an air of mystery surrounding them.

● *1.* Господь действует таинственным образом. *2.* Таинственные передачи. *3.* Бог движется таинственным образом. *4.* Ей нравился таинственный воздух бродяги. *5.* Таинственный человек был похож на Гарбо. ● *1.* The Lord works in mysterious ways. *2.* Mysterious Transmissions. *3.* God moves in a mysterious way. *4.* She liked the drifter's mysterious air. *5.* The mysterious man was like Garbo.

**285. эгоистичный** — *selfish* — This word is used to describe someone who is primarily concerned with their own interests and needs, often at the expense of others. It conveys a negative connotation of someone who lacks consideration for others.

● *1.* Ты такой эгоистичный. *2.* Как ты можешь быть таким э-гоистичным? *3.* Ты эгоистичный ублюдок! *4.* Вы эгоистичны. *5.* Не будьте эгоистичны. ● *1.* You're so selfish. *2.* How can you be so selfish? *3.* You selfish bastard! *4.* You're being selfish. *5.* Don't be selfish.

**286. привлекательный** — *attractive, lovable, catchy, likeable* — This word is used to describe something or someone that is visually appealing, charming, or likable. It can refer to physical appearance, personality traits, or qualities that draw attention or admiration.

● *1.* Очень привлекательный. *2.* Она привлекательна. *3.* Он-а очень привлекательна. *4.* Ты очень привлекательный. *5.* Вы очень привлекательная женщина. ● *1.* Very attractive. *2.* She's attractive. *3.* She's very attractive. *4.* You're very attractive. *5.* You're a very attractive woman.

**287. болезненный** — *painful, sickly, morbid* — This word is used to describe something that causes physical or emotional pain, discomfort, or distress. It can also be used to describe something that is unhealthy, sickly, or morbid in nature.

● *1.* Это болезненно? *2.* Это выглядит болезненно. *3.* Выгляд-ит болезненно. *4.* Очень болезненный. *5.* Звучит болезненн-о. *6.* Ее болезненный вид нас беспокоил. *7.* Она выглядела бледной и болезненной. *8.* Это болезненно. *9.* У него было болезненное чувство юмора. *10.* У нее было болезненное о-баяние. ● *1.* Is it painful? *2.* That looks painful. *3.* Looks painful. *4.* Very painful. *5.* Sounds painful. *6.* Her sickly appearance worried us. *7.* She looked pale and sickly. *8.* It's morbid. *9.* He had a morbid sense of humor. *10.* She had a morbid fascination.

**288. стандартный** — *standard* — This word is used to describe something that is considered normal, typical, or average. It is often used to refer to something that meets a certain level of quality or expectation.

● *1.* Это стандартная процедура. *2.* Стандартный вопрос-. *3.* Это стандартно. *4.* Стандартная процедура была ясна. *5.* Стандартным измерением был градус Цельсия. ● *1.* It's standard procedure. *2.* Standard issue. *3.* It's standard. *4.* The standard procedure was clear. *5.* Centigrade was the standard measurement.

**289. классический** — *classic, classical* — 'Классический' is used to describe something that is traditional, timeless, or of high quality. It can refer to anything that is considered to be a classic or follows established standards or conventions.

● *1.* Он заказал классический мартини. *2.* Платье было классического фасона. *3.* Ее любимая книга – классический роман. *4.* Классический вариант был лучше. *5.* Он демонстрировал классические черты нарцисса. *6.* Любишь классическую музыку? *7.* Она была поклонницей классической музыки. *8.* Он стал поклонником классической музыки. *9.* Он сыграл классического Йоханнеса. *10.* Классическая музыка?

● *1.* He ordered a classic martini. *2.* The dress was a classic style. *3.* Her favorite book is a classic novel. *4.* The classic version was better. *5.* He exhibited classic traits of a narcissist. *6.* Do you like classical music? *7.* She was an aficionado of classical music. *8.* He became an admirer of classical music. *9.* He played a classical johannes. *10.* Classical music?

**290. финансовый** — *financial, fiscal* — 'финансовый' is used to describe anything related to finances, money, or fiscal matters. It can be used to talk about financial institutions, transactions, policies, or situations.

● *1.* Она оказалась в затруднительном финансовом положении. *2.* Субстандартное кредитование привело к финансовому краху. *3.* В прошлом году они увидели финансовый рост. *4.* Финансовый консультант был кровопийцей. *5.* Проблема была в основном финансовой. *6.* Финансовый год компании закончился. *7.* Она отвечает за финансовые вопросы. *8.* Они отвечают за финансовое планирование. *9.* Мы обсудили финансовый бюджет. ● *1.* She found herself in a financial strait. *2.* Subprime lending led to financial collapse. *3.* They saw financial growth last year. *4.* The financial advisor was a bloodsucker. *5.* The problem was chiefly financial. *6.* The company's fiscal year ended. *7.* She is responsible for fiscal matters. *8.* They are in charge of fiscal planning. *9.* We discussed the fiscal budget.

**291. откровенно** — *frankly, overtly, candidly* — 'Откровенно' is used to describe when someone is speaking openly and honestly without holding back. It is often used to convey a sense of transparency and sincerity in communication.

- *1.* Могу я говорить откровенно? *2.* Могу ли я говорить откровенно? *3.* Скажи мне откровенно. *4.* Он откровенно признал свою ошибку. *5.* Она сказала ему откровенно. ● *1.* May I speak frankly? *2.* Can I speak frankly? *3.* Tell me frankly. *4.* He frankly admitted his mistake. *5.* She told him frankly.

**292. щедрый** — *generous, prodigal, bountiful* — This word is used to describe someone who is willing to give freely and abundantly, whether it be with their time, money, or resources. It conveys a sense of generosity and openness towards others.

- *1.* Это очень щедро с вашей стороны. *2.* Это очень щедро. *3.* Очень щедро. *4.* Это щедро. *5.* Очень щедро с вашей стороны. ● *1.* That's very generous of you. *2.* That's very generous. *3.* Very generous. *4.* That's generous. *5.* Very generous of you.

**293. недавний** — *recent* — This word is used to describe something that happened or was created not long ago. It can also be used to refer to something that is still fresh in someone's memory or is currently relevant.

- *1.* Насколько недавно? *2.* Это недавняя разработка. *3.* Недавние дожди вызвали наводнение. *4.* Чековая книжка показывала все недавние транзакции. ● *1.* How recent? *2.* It's a recent development. *3.* The recent rainfall caused flooding. *4.* The checkbook showed all the recent transactions.

**294. религиозный** — *religious, devotional* — This word is used to describe something or someone that is related to or characterized by religious beliefs or practices. It can also refer to a devout or pious attitude or behavior.

- *1.* Это религиозная вещь. *2.* Вы религиозный человек? *3.* Религиозная церемония принесла отпущение грехов. *4.* Они жили в соответствии с сильными религиозными убеждениями. *5.* Вы религиозны? ● *1.* It's a religious thing. *2.* Are you a religious man? *3.* The religious ceremony brought absolution. *4.* They lived by a strong religious credo. *5.* You religious?

**295. драматический** — *dramatic* — This word is used to describe situations, events, or people that are intense, emotional, or filled with conflict. It can also be used to convey a sense of theatricality or exaggeration.

- *1.* Ей нравилось драматическое танго. *2.* Она стала свидетельницей драматического выброса из машины. *3.* Мим разыграл драматическую сцену. *4.* У нее было драматическое чутье. *5.* Она сделала драматический выход. • *1.* She loved the dramatic tango. *2.* She witnessed the dramatic ejection from the car. *3.* The mime acted out a dramatic scene. *4.* She had a dramatic flair. *5.* She made a dramatic entrance.

**296. ценный** — *valuable* — This word is used to describe something that is highly prized or important. It can refer to physical objects, qualities, or information that holds significant worth or importance.

• *1.* Это очень ценно. *2.* Что-то ценное. *3.* Это ценно? *4.* Являются ли они ценными? *5.* Вы теряете драгоценное время.

• *1.* It's very valuable. *2.* Something valuable. *3.* Is it valuable? *4.* Are they valuable? *5.* You're wasting valuable time.

**297. далекий** — *distant* — This word is used to describe something that is far away in distance or time. It can also be used to convey a sense of emotional or metaphorical distance between people or ideas.

• *1.* Гудение далекого поезда. *2.* Он услышал далекий лай в ночи. *3.* Пастух услышал далекое баа. *4.* Они могли слышать далекое пение птиц. *5.* Далекие корабли. • *1.* The hummel of a distant train. *2.* He heard a distant bark in the night. *3.* The shepherd heard the distant baa. *4.* They could hear the distant birdsong. *5.* Distant ships.

**298. западный** — *western* — This word is used to describe something or someone that is located, facing, or coming from the west. It can also be used to refer to Western culture or countries.

• *1.* Все западные штаты присоединились к Шайеннам. *2.* Квирт был основным элементом западного снаряжения. • *1.* Western states have all fallen in with Cheyenne. *2.* The quirt was a staple of Western gear.

**299. нежный** — *gentle, delicate* — This word is used to describe something that is soft, tender, or gentle in nature. It can refer to a person's touch, a feeling, or an object that is delicate and requires careful handling.

• *1.* Быть нежным. *2.* Я буду нежным. *3.* Милый и нежный. *4.* Очень нежный. *5.* Будьте с ним нежны. *6.* Шифоновая ткань была нежной. *7.* Цветы были нежного розового оттенка. *8.* Цветок цикория был нежным. *9.* Батистовая блузка была нежной. *10.* Яичная скорлупа была нежной. ● *1.* Be gentle. *2.* I'll be gentle. *3.* Nice and gentle. *4.* Very gentle. *5.* Be gentle with him. *6.* The chiffon fabric was delicate. *7.* The flowers were a delicate shade of pink. *8.* The chicory flower was delicate. *9.* The batiste blouse was delicate. *10.* The eggshell was delicate.

**300. паршивый** — *lousy* — 'Паршивый' is used to describe something of poor quality or low standard. It can be used to express disappointment or dissatisfaction with something or someone.

● *1.* Ты паршивый. *2.* Ты паршивый ублюдок! *3.* Это паршиво. *4.* Ты паршивый лжец. *5.* Он дал паршивое оправдание опозданию. ● *1.* You're lousy. *2.* You lousy bastard! *3.* It's lousy. *4.* You're a lousy liar. *5.* He gave a lousy excuse for being late.

**301. официально** — *officially, formally* — 'Официально' is used to describe something that is done in a formal or official manner. It is often used to indicate that something has been officially confirmed, approved, or recognized by an authority or organization.

● *1.* Не официально. *2.* Мы официально не встречались. *3.* Марди Гра 2006 официально завершилась. *4.* Сторожевая башня официально доступна онлайн. *5.* Официально да. *6.* Нас официально не представили. *7.* Мы не встречались - официально. ● *1.* Not officially. *2.* We haven't officially met. *3.* Mardi Gras 2006 is officially over. *4.* Watchtower is officially online. *5.* Officially, yes. *6.* We haven't been formally introduced. *7.* We haven't formally met.

**302. сложный** — *complex, elaborate, intricate, tricky* — This word is used to describe something that is difficult to understand or solve due to its intricate or complicated nature. It can refer to a complex situation, a challenging task, or a sophisticated piece of work.

● *1.* Это слишком сложно. *2.* Это очень сложно. *3.* Метаболический процесс был сложным. *4.* Принципы экономики сложны. *5.* Взаимосвязь была сложной. *6.* Танцовщица бурлеска носила сложные костюмы. *7.* Он восхищался сложной мускулатурой скульптуры. *8.* Булава была украшена сложной резьбой. *9.* Бивень был украшен сложной резьбой. *10.* Художественное произведение было сложным. *11.* Сари имело сложную вышивку. *12.* Это сложно. *13.* Это немного сложно. *14.* Она сложная. *15.* Это самая сложная часть. *16.* Это может быть сложно. • *1.* It's too complex. *2.* It's very complex. *3.* The metabolic process was complex. *4.* Econ principles are complex. *5.* The inter connections were complex. *6.* The burlesque dancer wore elaborate costumes. *7.* He admired the intricate musculature of the sculpture. *8.* The mace was adorned with intricate carvings. *9.* The tusk was laden with intricate carvings. *10.* The artwork was intricate. *11.* The saree had intricate embroidery. *12.* It's tricky. *13.* It's a little tricky. *14.* She's tricky. *15.* This is the tricky part. *16.* That might be tricky.

**303. базовый** — *basic* — 'Вазовый' is used to describe something fundamental, essential, or primary. It is often used to refer to basic knowledge, skills, or principles. It can also describe something simple or uncomplicated.

• *1.* Зак провалил базовый полет. • *1.* Zak failed basic flight.

**304. невероятно** — *incredibly, unbelievable, unbelievably* — 'невероятно' is used to emphasize the extreme nature of something, indicating that it is beyond belief or highly impressive. It is often used to describe events, situations, or qualities that are remarkable or extraordinary.

• *1.* Фильм невероятно реалистичен. *2.* Бритва была невероятно острой. *3.* Работы живописца были невероятно выразительны. *4.* Торт оказался невероятно вкусным. *5.* Невероятно красивая. *6.* Это невероятно. *7.* Ты невероятный. *8.* Это было невероятно. *9.* Это просто невероятно. *10.* Он невероятный. *11.* Невероятно, но они могли слышать Роджера. *12.* В тот день было невероятно жарко. *13.* Ее выступление было невероятно хорошим. *14.* Новость была невероятно шокирующей. *15.* Вид был невероятно потрясающий. • *1.* The movie was incredibly realistic. *2.* The razer was incredibly sharp. *3.* The painter's work was incredibly expressive. *4.* The cake was incredibly tasty. *5.* Incredibly beautiful. *6.* It's unbelievable. *7.* You're unbelievable. *8.* It was unbelievable. *9.* It's just unbelievable. *10.* He's unbelievable. *11.* Unbelievably, they could hear Roger. *12.* It was unbelievably hot that day. *13.* Her performance was unbelievably good. *14.* The news was unbelievably shocking. *15.* The view was unbelievably stunning.

**305. греческий** — *greek* — This word is used to describe something or someone that is related to Greece or Greek culture. It can be used to talk about Greek food, architecture, history, or people.

● *1.* Это греческий. *2.* По-гречески. *3.* Это древнегреческий. *4.* Греческая мифология. *5.* Агора была центром греческих городов-государств. ● *1.* It's Greek. *2.* In Greek. *3.* It's ancient Greek. *4.* Greek mythology. *5.* The agora was the center of Greek city-states.

**306. гнилой** — *rotten, putrid, unsound* — 'гнилой' is used to describe something that is decaying, spoiled, or in a state of decomposition. It can be used to refer to food, objects, or even abstract concepts that are deteriorating or corrupt.

● *1.* Это гнилое. *2.* Ты гнилой ублюдок! *3.* Ты гнилой. *4.* Гнилая удача. *5.* Гнилой ублюдок. *6.* Мусор имел гнилостный запах. *7.* Гнилое мясо испортилось. *8.* Они утилизировали гнилые отходы. *9.* Гнилая вода заставила ее подавиться. *10.* Она сморщила нос от гнилостного запаха. ● *1.* It's rotten. *2.* You rotten bastard! *3.* You're rotten. *4.* Rotten luck. *5.* Rotten bastard. *6.* The garbage had a putrid smell. *7.* The putrid meat had spoiled. *8.* They disposed of the putrid waste. *9.* The putrid water made her gag. *10.* She wrinkled her nose at the putrid odor.

**307. серый** — *gray, grey* — This word is used to describe something that is a shade between black and white. It can be used to describe objects, animals, or even people's hair or eyes.

● *1.* Он покрасил стены в серый цвет. *2.* День был унылый и серый. *3.* Она покрасила комнату в серый цвет. *4.* Серый кот громко мурлыкал. *5.* Это серый! ● *1.* He painted the walls gray. *2.* The day was dull and gray. *3.* She painted the room grey. *4.* The grey cat purred loudly. *5.* It's grey!

**308. толстый** — *thick, porky* — 'Толстый' is used to describe something that is thick or porky in appearance. It can refer to a person, animal, object, or even a layer of material. It conveys a sense of heaviness or bulkiness.

● *1.* Это слишком толсто. *2.* Толстый лед. *3.* Ты толстый? *4.* Веревка была толстой и прочной. *5.* У дыни была толстая кожура. • *1.* It's too thick. *2.* Thick ice. *3.* Are you thick? *4.* The rope was thick and strong. *5.* The melon had a thick rind.

**309. разумный** — *reasonable, sensible* — 'Разумный' is used to describe someone or something that is logical, practical, and makes sense. It implies that the person or thing is acting in a sensible and rational manner.

• *1.* Звучит разумно. *2.* Это звучит разумно. *3.* Очень разумно. *4.* Это разумно. *5.* Вы не разумны. *6.* Будьте разумны. *7.* Очень разумно. *8.* Он разумный человек. *9.* Это единственный разумный поступок. *10.* Она приняла разумное решение. • *1.* Sounds reasonable. *2.* That sounds reasonable. *3.* Very reasonable. *4.* That's reasonable. *5.* You're not being reasonable. *6.* Be sensible. *7.* Very sensible. *8.* He is a sensible person. *9.* It's the only sensible thing to do. *10.* She made a sensible decision.

**310. глухой** — *deaf, godforsaken, outlandish* — The word 'глухой' is used to describe something that is deaf, isolated, or remote. It can also be used to describe something that is strange or unfamiliar.

• *1.* Вы глухи? *2.* Ты что, глухой? *3.* Он глухой. *4.* Я не глухой. *5.* Ты глухой? • *1.* Are you deaf? *2.* What are you, deaf? *3.* He's deaf. *4.* I'm not deaf. *5.* You deaf?

**311. равный** — *equal* — 'Ravny' is used to describe things that are the same in size, quantity, or quality. It can also be used to indicate that two or more things are equal in value or importance.

• *1.* Мы все равны. *2.* Он верил в равные права. *3.* Я выступаю за равное отношение ко всем людям. *4.* Крестоносец боролся за равные права. *5.* Она хотела, чтобы к ней относились как к равной. • *1.* We're all equal. *2.* He believed in equal rights. *3.* I advocate for equal treatment of all people. *4.* The crusader fought for equal rights. *5.* She wanted to be treated as an equal.

**312. преданный** — *loyal* — 'Преданный' is used to describe someone who is faithful, devoted, and committed to a person, cause, or belief. It conveys a sense of unwavering loyalty and dedication.

• *1.* Сардж был преданным псом. *2.* У дворняжки преданный характер. *3.* Она была преданной поклонницей группы. *4.* Он был преданным последователем. ● *1.* Sarge was a loyal dog. *2.* The mutt has a loyal nature. *3.* She was a loyal groupie of the band. *4.* He was a loyal follower.

**313. электрический** — *electric, electrical* — This word is used to describe things that are related to electricity or powered by electricity. It can be used to talk about electrical appliances, systems, or components.

● *1.* Он электрический. *2.* Мы жили в электрическом мире. *3.* Электрический стул. *4.* Электрический угорь шокировал меня. *5.* Электрический угорь излучает сильный электрический заряд. *6.* Электрический заряд измерялся в фарадах. *7.* Все электрические тайны рая. *8.* Конденсатор хранит электрическую энергию. ● *1.* It's electric. *2.* We lived in an electric world. *3.* The electric chair. *4.* An electric eel shocked me. *5.* The electric eel emits a strong electric charge. *6.* The electrical charge was measured in farads. *7.* All the electrical secrets of heaven. *8.* The capacitor stores electrical energy.

**314. неудобный** — *uncomfortable, awkward, inconvenient* — This word is used to describe situations, objects, or people that cause discomfort, awkwardness, or inconvenience. It is often used to express a feeling of unease or displeasure in various contexts.

● *1.* Это неудобно. *2.* Мне неудобно. *3.* Это очень неудобно. *4.* Вам неудобно? *5.* Ее трусики были неудобными. *6.* Планировка комнаты была неудобной. *7.* Ну это неудобно. *8.* Это неудобно для наших планов. *9.* Расположение неудобное для покупок. *10.* Раскрывается неудобная правда. *11.* Как неудобно. ● *1.* It's uncomfortable. *2.* I'm uncomfortable. *3.* It's very uncomfortable. *4.* Are you uncomfortable? *5.* Her panty was uncomfortable. *6.* The layout of the room was awkward. *7.* Well, that's inconvenient. *8.* This is inconvenient for our plans. *9.* The location is inconvenient for shopping. *10.* An inconvenient truth is revealed. *11.* How inconvenient.

**315. плавный** — *smooth* — The word 'плавный' is used to describe something that is even, gradual, or without sudden changes. It can refer to movements, transitions, or surfaces that are smooth and flowing.

● *1.* Плавное плавание. *2.* Она нарисовала плавную кривую.

*3.* Роскошный лайнер обеспечивал плавный ход. *4.* Плавный ход. *5.* Переход между сценами был плавным. ● *1.* Smooth sailing. *2.* She drew a smooth curve. *3.* The luxury liner offered a smooth ride. *4.* Smooth move. *5.* The segue between scenes was smooth.

**316. индивидуальный** — *individual* — This word is used to describe something that is unique, separate, or distinct from others. It can also be used to emphasize the personal or specific nature of something.
● *1.* Мы ценим индивидуальный вклад. ● *1.* We value individual contributions.

**317. слегка** — *slightly, lightly* — 'Слегка' is used to indicate a small degree or amount of something, suggesting a gentle or subtle quality. It can be used to describe physical sensations, emotions, or actions that are done with a light touch or in a mild manner.
● *1.* Лишь слегка. *2.* Хотите купить слегка подержанные иллюзии? *3.* Упакуйте слегка. *4.* Ткань слегка накинулась на стул. ● *1.* Only slightly. *2.* Want to buy some illusions slightly used? *3.* Pack lightly. *4.* The fabric draped lightly over the chair.

**318. достойный** — *worthy* — 'Достойный' is used to describe something or someone as deserving of respect, admiration, or consideration. It implies that the subject possesses qualities or characteristics that make them suitable or deserving of a particular status or treatment.
● *1.* Вы достойный противник. *2.* Телемарафон собрал средства на достойное дело. ● *1.* You are a worthy adversary. *2.* The telethon raised funds for a worthy cause.

**319. экстремальный** — *extreme* — This word is used to describe something that is very intense, dangerous, or extreme in nature. It can be used to emphasize the severity or intensity of a situation, activity, or experience.
● *1.* Температура по Кельвину может быть экстремальной. *2.* Погода достигла экстремальных температур. *3.* Это немного экстремально, не так ли? *4.* Экстремальное увеличение. *5.* Тигель нагревали до экстремальных температур. ● *1.* Kelvin temperatures can be extreme. *2.* The weather reached extreme temperatures. *3.* That's a bit extreme, isn't it? *4.* Extreme mag-

nification. *5.* The crucible was heated to extreme temperatures.

**320. упрямый** — *stubborn, obstinate, headstrong* — 'Упрямый' is used to describe someone who is unwilling to change their mind or behavior, often in a stubborn or obstinate manner. It can also refer to something that is difficult to move or change.

● *1.* Не будь таким упрямым. *2.* Ты такой упрямый. *3.* Он упрям. *4.* Она упряма. *5.* Не будьте упрямы. ● *1.* Don't be so stubborn. *2.* You're so stubborn. *3.* He's stubborn. *4.* She's stubborn. *5.* Don't be stubborn.

**321. неспособный** — *unable, incapable, inept* — This word is used to describe someone or something that lacks the ability or skill to do a certain task or achieve a certain goal. It implies a sense of incapability or ineptitude.

● *1.* Она чувствовала себя неспособной продолжать. *2.* Он показал себя неспособным к ответственности. *3.* Они неспособны измениться. ● *1.* She felt unable to continue. *2.* He proved himself incapable of responsibility. *3.* They are incapable of change.

**322. стабильный** — *stable* — This word is used to describe something that is steady, consistent, or unchanging. It can refer to a person's emotions, a country's economy, or a relationship. It implies reliability and predictability.

● *1.* Она стабильна. *2.* Жизненные показатели стабильны. *3.* Это стабильно. *4.* Его жизненные показатели стабильны. *5.* Она пока стабильна. ● *1.* She's stable. *2.* Vitals are stable. *3.* It's stable. *4.* His vitals are stable. *5.* She's stable for now.

**323. технически** — *technically* — 'Technically' is used to describe something in a precise or accurate manner, often focusing on the specific details or mechanics of a situation. It is commonly used in discussions or explanations that require a strict adherence to rules or guidelines.

● *1.* Не технически. *2.* Ну, технически. *3.* Ну, технически да. *4.* Только технически. *5.* Задача была технически сложной. ● *1.* Not technically. *2.* Well, technically. *3.* Well, technically, yes. *4.* Only technically. *5.* The issue was technically challenging.

**324. научный** — *scientific* — 'Научный' is used to describe something that is related to or characteristic of science. It can be used to refer to scientific research, methods, theories, or any other aspect of the scientific field.

• *1.* Это научный факт. *2.* Это научно. *3.* Случайное открытие привело к научному прорыву. *4.* Научный журнал является престижным изданием. *5.* Реактор на антиматерии стал научным прорывом. • *1.* It's a scientific fact. *2.* It's scientific. *3.* The accidental discovery led to a scientific breakthrough. *4.* The scientific journal is a prestigious publication. *5.* The antimatter reactor was a scientific breakthrough.

**325. предыдущий** — *previous* — This word is used to refer to something that came before or happened earlier in time or order. It is used to describe something that is immediately before the current one.

• *1.* Он заменил предыдущего менеджера. *2.* Они попытались исправить предыдущую ошибку. *3.* В предыдущие годы фестиваль был масштабнее. *4.* В резюме указан предыдущий опыт работы. *5.* Они последовали прецеденту, созданному предыдущими лидерами. • *1.* He was the replacement for the previous manager. *2.* They attempted to fix the previous mistake. *3.* In previous years, the festival was bigger. *4.* The résumé included previous work experience. *5.* They followed the precedent set by previous leaders.

**326. абсолютный** — *absolute, unmitigated* — The word 'абсолютный' is used to describe something that is complete, total, or without any conditions or limitations. It emphasizes the extreme nature of a situation or quality, indicating that there are no exceptions or compromises.

• *1.* Абсолютная тишина. *2.* Это абсолютное безумие. *3.* Абсолютная сила. *4.* Это абсолютный хаос. *5.* Я абсолютно уверен в тебе. • *1.* Absolute silence. *2.* This is absolute madness. *3.* Absolute power. *4.* It is absolute chaos. *5.* I have absolute confidence in you.

**327. божественный** — *divine, godlike, godly* — This word is used to describe something that is of or related to a divine or godly nature. It can be used to express admiration or awe towards something that is considered to be extraordinary or beyond human understanding.

• *1.* Это божественно. *2.* Божественное вмешательство? *3.* Они верят в божественное провидение. *4.* Она божественна. *5.* Ты божественный. *6.* У нее была божественная аура. *7.*

Он искал божественной мудрости. *8.* Божественный образ благословил деревню. ● *1.* It's divine. *2.* Divine intervention? *3.* They believe in divine providence. *4.* She's divine. *5.* You're divine. *6.* She had a godly aura. *7.* He sought out godly wisdom. *8.* The godly figure blessed the village.

**328. коммерческий** — *commercial, mercantile* — 'Коммерческий' is used to describe something related to business, trade, or commerce. It can refer to products, services, or activities that are done for profit or financial gain.

● *1.* Он специализировался на коммерческих судах. *2.* Коммерческая недвижимость. ● *1.* He specialized in commercial litigation. *2.* Commercial real estate.

**329. жаждущий** — *thirsty, desirous* — 'Жаждущий' is used to describe someone who is eager, thirsty, or desirous of something. It conveys a strong sense of longing or craving for a particular object, experience, or outcome.

● *1.* Ты выглядишь жаждущим. ● *1.* You look thirsty.

**330. типичный** — *typical* — 'Typical' is used to describe something that is characteristic or representative of a particular group or category. It is often used to highlight common traits or behaviors that are expected or usual in a given situation.

● *1.* Это типично. *2.* Это так типично. *3.* Так типично. *4.* Как типично. *5.* Типичный мужчина. ● *1.* That's typical. *2.* This is so typical. *3.* So typical. *4.* How typical. *5.* Typical man.

**331. вечный** — *eternal, perpetual, everlasting* — 'Вечный' is used to describe something that is eternal, perpetual, or everlasting. It conveys the idea of something that will last forever or never come to an end.

● *1.* Вечная жизнь. *2.* Ваш вечный слуга. *3.* Жадность вечна. *4.* Вечный вопрос. *5.* Она искала амриту вечной жизни. *6.* И пусть светит ему вечный свет. *7.* На ее лице сияла вечная улыбка. *8.* Ненавижу вечный дождь. *9.* Его очаровал вечный двигатель. *10.* Их любовь казалась вечной. *11.* Вечная жизнь. *12.* Вечная красота природы вдохновляла ее. *13.* Вечный огонь символизировал надежду. *14.* Она носила вечную улыбку. ● *1.* Eternal life. *2.* Your eternal servant. *3.* Greed is eternal. *4.* The eternal question. *5.* She sought the amrita of eternal life. *6.* And let perpetual light shine upon him. *7.* She had a perpetual smile on her face. *8.* I hate perpetual rain. *9.* The perpetual motion machine fascinated him. *10.* Their love seemed everlasting. *11.* Everlasting life. *12.* The everlasting beauty of nature inspired her. *13.* The everlasting flame symbolized hope. *14.* She wore an everlasting smile.

**332. озорной** — *naughty, mischievous* — 'Озорной' is used to describe someone or something that is playful, mischievous, or naughty in a light-hearted way. It implies a sense of fun and mischief rather than malicious intent.

● *1.* Вы озорной. *2.* В его глазах появился озорной блеск. *3.* Вила могла быть озорной или доброжелательной. *4.* Они рассказывали истории о озорном гоблине. *5.* Озорной негодяй доставил неприятности. *6.* Его племянник очень озорной. ● *1.* You are naughty. *2.* His eyes had a mischievous gleam. *3.* The vila could be mischievous or benevolent. *4.* They told stories of the mischievous goblin. *5.* The mischievous scamp caused trouble. *6.* His nephew is very mischievous.

**333. удаленный** — *remote, outlying* — 'Удаленный' is used to describe something that is far away or distant from a central location. It can refer to physical distance, such as a remote village, or metaphorical distance, such as a remote possibility.

● *1.* Удаленный аванпост был изолирован. *2.* Связь была удаленной. *3.* Они получили доступ к удаленному серверу. ● *1.* The remote outpost was isolated. *2.* The connection was remote. *3.* They accessed the remote server.

**334. моральный** — *moral* — This word is used to describe actions, behaviors, or decisions that are considered ethical, virtuous, or in accordance with principles of right and wrong. It can also refer to a person's character or integrity.

● *1.* Моральная поддержка. *2.* Они рассматривали этот вопрос с моральной точки зрения. *3.* Он обсуждал моральные последствия. *4.* Священное Писание учит моральным ценностям. *5.* Она приняла моральное решение. ● *1.* Moral support. *2.* They considered the issue from a moral standpoint. *3.* He debated the moral implications. *4.* The scripture taught moral values. *5.* She made a moral decision.

**335. песчаный** — *sandy* — This word is used to describe something that is related to or resembles sand in texture, color, or composition. It can be used to describe beaches, soil, or any other surface that is sandy in nature.

- *1.* Пляж был песчаный. *2.* Дорога была песчаной. *3.* Он вытряхнул песчаное полотенце. *4.* Грязь песчаная. *5.* Машина застряла в песчаном грунте. • *1.* The beach was sandy. *2.* The path was sandy. *3.* He shook out the sandy towel. *4.* The dirt is sandy. *5.* The car got stuck in the sandy soil.

**336. жутко** — *creepy* — 'жутко' is used to describe something that is extremely unsettling or frightening. It conveys a sense of horror or dread, often used to emphasize the intensity of a creepy or eerie feeling.

- *1.* Это жутко. *2.* Это было жутко. *3.* Так жутко. *4.* Это немного жутко. *5.* Это место жуткое. • *1.* It's creepy. *2.* It was creepy. *3.* So creepy. *4.* It's kind of creepy. *5.* This place is creepy.

**337. мирный** — *peaceful, pacific* — The word 'мирный' is used to describe something or someone that is peaceful, calm, and non-violent. It conveys a sense of tranquility and harmony, often referring to a situation or environment that is free from conflict or disturbance.

- *1.* Это так мирно. *2.* Так мирно. *3.* Это мирно. *4.* Он выглядит таким мирным. *5.* Здесь мирно. • *1.* It's so peaceful. *2.* So peaceful. *3.* It's peaceful. *4.* He looks so peaceful. *5.* It's peaceful here.

**338. горький** — *bitter* — The word 'горький' is used to describe something with a sharp, unpleasant taste or a feeling of sadness or disappointment. It can be used to describe food, drinks, emotions, or experiences.

- *1.* Это горько. *2.* Я не горький. *3.* Не будьте горькими. *4.* Слишком горько. *5.* Ну же, горькое поведение. • *1.* It's bitter. *2.* I'm not bitter. *3.* Don't be bitter. *4.* Too bitter. *5.* Come, bitter conduct.

**339. южный** — *southern, southerly* — 'южный' is used to describe something that is located in or related to the southern direction. It can refer to a place, region, or direction that is situated in the south or has characteristics associated with the south.

- *1.* Он южный джентльмен. *2.* Еда имела южный вкус. *3.* Южный климат был идеален для земледелия. *4.* Южный ветерок освежал. • *1.* He's a southern gentleman. *2.* The food had a southern flavor. *3.* The southerly climate was ideal for farming. *4.* The southerly breeze was refreshing.

**340. невидимый** — *invisible, unseen* — This word is used to describe something that cannot be seen with the naked eye or is not easily noticed. It implies that the object or person is hidden from view or not easily detectable.

• *1.* Я невидимый. *2.* Это невидимо. *3.* Ты невидим. *4.* Невидимый, неразрушимый и совершенно неизбежный. *5.* Мы н-евидимы. *6.* Она вошла в невидимую тьму. *7.* Он столкнулся с невидимыми препятствиями. *8.* Невидимые силы действовали. *9.* Они открыли невидимую правду. • *1.* I'm invisible. *2.* It's invisible. *3.* You're invisible. *4.* Invisible, indestructible, and completely inescapable. *5.* We're invisible. *6.* She walked into the unseen darkness. *7.* He faced unseen obstacles. *8.* The unseen forces were at work. *9.* They uncovered the unseen truth.

**341. интенсивный** — *intense, intensive* — This word is used to describe something that is strong, powerful, or concentrated in its effect or degree. It can refer to activities, emotions, or situations that are particularly vigorous or demanding.

• *1.* Это было интенсивно. *2.* Это интенсивно. *3.* Это было очень интенсивно. *4.* Это слишком интенсивно. *5.* Очень интенсивно. *6.* Интенсивное обучение принесло свои плоды. *7.* Интенсивная терапия? *8.* У них была интенсивная дискуссия. *9.* Она прошла интенсивный курс. *10.* В отделении интенсивной терапии было многолюдно. • *1.* It was intense. *2.* This is intense. *3.* It was very intense. *4.* It's too intense. *5.* Very intense. *6.* The intensive training paid off. *7.* Intensive care? *8.* They had an intensive discussion. *9.* She took an intensive course. *10.* The intensive care unit was busy.

**342. активный** — *active* — 'Активный' is used to describe something or someone that is lively, energetic, or engaged in action. It can also be used to describe a process or situation that involves a high level of activity or participation.

• *1.* Это активное место преступления. *2.* У вас активное в-оображение. *3.* Поощряйте активное участие в уроке. *4.* В своем возрасте она активна. *5.* Они занимались активным отдыхом. • *1.* This is an active crime scene. *2.* You have an active imagination. *3.* Encourage active participation in the class.

*4.* At her age, she's active. *5.* They engaged in active recreation.

**343. серийный** — *serial* — This word is used to describe something that is produced or occurring in a series or sequence. It can refer to a serial killer, a serial number, or a serialized TV show.

• *1.* Я серийный моногамист. *2.* Он собирал серийные номера. *3.* Серийный номер легко отследить. *4.* Серийные убийцы? • *1.* I'm a serial monogamist. *2.* He collected serial numbers. *3.* The serial number is easily traceable. *4.* Serial killers?

**344. безопасно** — *safely, securely* — This word is used to describe actions or situations that are free from danger or harm. It implies that something is done in a way that minimizes risk and ensures protection. It conveys a sense of security and well-being.

• *1.* Доберитесь домой безопасно. *2.* Путешествуй безопасно. *3.* Он был слишком сонным, чтобы безопасно вести машину. *4.* Они надежно пристегнули ремень безопасности. • *1.* Get home safely. *2.* Travel safely. *3.* He was too sleepy to drive safely. *4.* They fastened the seatbelt securely.

**345. высший** — *upper* — 'высший' is used to describe something that is located at a higher position or level. It can also be used to indicate the highest quality or rank of something.

• *1.* У него был акцент высшего класса. *2.* Высшая кора общества. • *1.* He had an upper class accent. *2.* The upper crust of society.

**346. ленивый** — *lazy, ornery* — The word 'ленивый' is used to describe someone who is unwilling to work or exert effort, or someone who is difficult or uncooperative. It can be used to characterize a person's behavior or attitude.

• *1.* Ленивый ублюдок. *2.* Ленивый мальчик. *3.* Давай, ленивый ублюдок! *4.* Она трудолюбива, а ее брат ленив. *5.* Не будь ленивым дерьмом. • *1.* Lazy bastard. *2.* Lazy boy. *3.* Come on, you lazy bastard! *4.* She is hardworking, whereas her brother is lazy. *5.* Don't be a lazy shitbag.

**347. счастливо** — *happily* — 'Счастливо' is used to describe actions or feelings that are done or experienced in a happy or joyful manner. It can be used to express well-wishes or to describe someone's demeanor or behavior.

• *1.* И жили они долго и счастливо. *2.* Я счастливо женатый человек. *3.* И все они жили долго и счастливо. *4.* Долго и счастливо. *5.* Я счастливо женат. • *1.* And they lived happily ever after. *2.* I'm a happily married man. *3.* And they all lived happily ever after. *4.* Happily ever after. *5.* I'm happily married.

**348. музыкальный** — *musical* — The word 'музыкальный' is used to describe something related to music or possessing musical qualities. It can refer to instruments, compositions, performances, or any other aspect of music.

• *1.* Тюнеры необходимы для музыкальных инструментов. *2.* Его музыкальные способности находились на среднем уровне. *3.* Они исполняли песню под музыкальное сопровождение. *4.* Музыкальный дуэт выступил прекрасно. *5.* Это как музыкальные стулья. • *1.* Tuners are essential for musical instruments. *2.* His musical skills were at an intermediate level. *3.* They sang the song with musical accompaniment. *4.* The musical duo performed beautifully. *5.* It's like musical chairs.

**349. соответствующий** — *appropriate, relevant* — This word is used to describe something that is suitable or fitting for a particular situation or purpose. It indicates that something is in line with expectations or requirements.

• *1.* Он был одет в соответствующую случаю одежду. *2.* Кандидат имел соответствующий опыт. *3.* Копия соответствующих сторон. • *1.* He wore garb appropriate for the occasion. *2.* The candidate had relevant experience. *3.* Cc the relevant parties.

**350. родной** — *native* — 'родной' is used to describe something that is closely related or connected to a person, such as a native language, homeland, or family member. It conveys a sense of familiarity, belonging, and emotional attachment.

• *1.* Броненосец был родным для этого района. *2.* Как родной. *3.* Ты стал родным. • *1.* The armadillo was native to the area. *2.* Like a native. *3.* You've gone native.

**351. критический** — *critical* — 'Критический' is used to describe something that is crucial, essential, or extremely important. It can also refer to a negative or disapproving attitude towards something, or a thorough and detailed analysis or evaluation of a situation.

• *1.* Его состояние критическое. *2.* Он в критическом состоянии. *3.* Ситуация критическая. *4.* Уровень кислорода критический. *5.* Программа обучения направлена на развитие навыков критического мышления. ● *1.* His condition is critical. *2.* He's in critical condition. *3.* The situation is critical. *4.* Oxygen level critical. *5.* The curriculum aimed to develop critical thinking skills.

**352. постоянно** — *constantly, perpetually* — 'Постоянно' is used to describe actions or states that occur without interruption or change. It indicates a continuous or ongoing nature of something, emphasizing the regularity or persistence of the action or state.

● *1.* Малыши постоянно болтают. *2.* Она постоянно повторяла эту фразу. *3.* Финансовая индустрия постоянно меняется. *4.* Я постоянно занят. *5.* Мы постоянно спорим. *6.* Он постоянно жаловался. *7.* Она постоянно улыбалась. *8.* Цветы цвели постоянно. ● *1.* The toddlers babble constantly. *2.* She repeated the phrase constantly. *3.* The finance industry is constantly changing. *4.* I am constantly busy. *5.* We argue constantly. *6.* He perpetually complained. *7.* She perpetually smiled. *8.* The flowers perpetually bloomed.

**353. глобальный** — *global* — 'глобальный' is used to describe something that pertains to or affects the entire world on a large scale. It is often used to emphasize the widespread or universal nature of a particular phenomenon or concept.

● *1.* Глобальное потепление. *2.* Это глобальное потепление. *3.* Угроза дикой природе является глобальной проблемой. ● *1.* Global warming. *2.* It's global warming. *3.* Endangerment of wildlife is a global issue.

**354. смертельный** — *deadly, mortal, fatal, lethal* — This word is used to describe something that has the potential to cause death or is extremely dangerous. It can be used to emphasize the severity of a situation or the consequences of an action.

● *1.* Я смертельно серьезен. *2.* Смертельно серьезно. *3.* Это смертельно. *4.* Бешенство – смертельно опасное заболевание. *5.* Змея была смертельно опасна. *6.* Смертельная рана оказалась смертельной. *7.* Смертельный страх! *8.* Это смертельно? *9.* Окончательный диагноз оказался смертельным. *10.* Укус змеи может оказаться смертельным. *11.* Смертельная рана оказалась смертельной. *12.* Он находился в смертельном состоянии. *13*. Это смертельно. *14*. Вирус оказался смертельным. *15*. Химические вещества представляли собой смертельную комбинацию. *16*. В результате аварии она получила смертельную травму. *17*. Жало скорпиона было смертельным. • *1*. I'm deadly serious. *2*. Deadly serious. *3*. It's deadly. *4*. Rabies is a deadly disease. *5*. The snake was deadly. *6*. The mortal wound was fatal. *7*. Mortal fear! *8*. Is it fatal? *9*. The final diagnosis was fatal. *10*. A snakebite can be fatal. *11*. The mortal wound was fatal. *12*. He was in fatal condition. *13*. It's lethal. *14*. The virus proved to be lethal. *15*. The chemicals were a lethal combination. *16*. She suffered a lethal injury in the accident. *17*. The scorpion's stinger was lethal.

**355. тревожный** — *anxious, worrisome, suspenseful* — 'Тревожный' is used to describe situations, events, or feelings that cause anxiety, worry, or suspense. It conveys a sense of unease or concern, indicating that something is troubling or unsettling. • *1*. Он стал более тревожным. *2*. Она становилась все более тревожной. *3*. Это тревожно. *4*. Результаты биопсии были тревожными. *5*. Очень тревожно. • *1*. He grew more anxious. *2*. She grew increasingly anxious. *3*. That's worrisome. *4*. The biopsy results were worrisome. *5*. Very worrisome.

**356. неудачный** — *unfortunate, unlucky, unsuccessful* — This word is used to describe something that has not turned out well or has been unsuccessful in some way. It conveys a sense of bad luck or lack of success in a situation or outcome. • *1*. Это неудачно. *2*. Самый неудачный. *3*. Неудачное совпадение. *4*. Да, это было неудачно. *5*. Очень неудачно. *6*. Неудачная монета принесла несчастье. *7*. С ней случилась череда неудачных событий. *8*. Охота оказалась неудачной. *9*. Проект с самого начала оказался неудачным. *10*. Он предпринял еще одну неудачную попытку. *11*. Миссия закончилась неудачным спасением. *12*. Его неудачное деловое предприятие оставило его в долгах. • *1*. That's unfortunate. *2*. Most unfortunate. *3*. An unfortunate coincidence. *4*. Yeah, that was unfortunate. *5*. Very unfortunate. *6*. The unlucky coin brought misfortune. *7*. She had a string of unlucky events. *8*. The hunt was unsuccessful. *9*. The project was unsuccessful from the start. *10*. He made another unsuccessful attempt. *11*. The mission ended in an unsuccessful rescue. *12*. His unsuccessful business venture left him in debt.

**357. химический** — *chemical* — 'химический' is used to describe something related to chemistry or chemicals. It can be used to talk about substances, reactions, processes, or properties that are connected to the field of chemistry.

● *1.* Она владела химическим соединением. ● *1.* She owned a chemical compound.

**358. морской** — *marine, naval, nautical* — This word is used to describe things related to the sea or navy, such as marine life, naval vessels, or nautical equipment. It is often used to indicate a connection to the ocean or maritime activities.

● *1.* Морская жизнь была разнообразной. *2.* Она посетила морской музей. *3.* Морские существа жили в морской воде. *4.* Он исследовал морскую среду обитания. *5.* Они изучали морскую биологию. *6.* Он специализировался на морской артиллерийской стрельбе. ● *1.* The marine life was diverse. *2.* She visited the marine museum. *3.* The marine creatures lived in the seawater. *4.* He explored marine habitats. *5.* They studied marine biology. *6.* He specialized in naval gunnery.

**359. советский** — *soviet* — The adjective/adverb 'советский' is used to describe something that is related to or characteristic of the Soviet Union. It can refer to objects, people, events, or ideas that are associated with the former socialist state.

● *1.* Советский цвет. *2.* Советская политика была строгой. *3.* Они изучали советскую историю. *4.* Он жил в советское время. ● *1.* Soviet color. *2.* Soviet policies were strict. *3.* They studied Soviet history. *4.* He lived in Soviet era.

**360. волшебный** — *magical, elvish* — 'волшебный' is used to describe something that is enchanting, mystical, or extraordinary. It conveys a sense of wonder and awe, often associated with fairy tales or fantasy worlds.

● *1.* Это волшебно. *2.* Это волшебное место. *3.* Это было волшебно. *4.* Через калейдоскоп мир выглядел волшебным. *5.* Цирк был волшебным. *6.* Эльфийское королевство волшебно. ● *1.* It's magical. *2.* It's a magical place. *3.* It was magical. *4.* Through the kaleidoscope, the world looked magical. *5.* The cirque was magical. *6.* The elvish kingdom is magical.

**361. временный** — *temporary, transient, interim, transitory* —

This word is used to describe something that is not permanent or lasting, but rather temporary or transient in nature. It can refer to a temporary situation, arrangement, or state of being.

● *1.* Это временно. *2.* Это только временно. *3.* Это просто временно. *4.* Я уверен, что это временно. *5.* Но это только временно. *6.* Его временные перепады настроения беспокоили его друзей. ● *1.* It's temporary. *2.* It's only temporary. *3.* It's just temporary. *4.* I'm sure it's just temporary. *5.* But it's only temporary. *6.* His transitory mood swings worried his friends.

**362. внутренний** — *inner, internal, domestic, inland* — This word is used to describe something that is located or happening inside a particular place or thing, rather than on the outside. It can also refer to something that is domestic or inland.

● *1.* Внутреннее спокойствие. *2.* Детектив обратился к своему внутреннему Шерлоку. *3.* Суровый пейзаж отражал ее внутреннее смятение. *4.* Он исследовал свою внутреннюю сущность. *5.* Он надеялся обрести внутренний покой. *6.* Внутренние весла. *7.* Внутреннее кровотечение. *8.* У нас есть внутренняя угроза. *9.* Массивное внутреннее кровотечение. *10.* У вас может быть внутреннее кровотечение. *11.* Внутренние проблемы требуют внимания. *12.* Внутренний рынок стабилен. *13.* Он предпочитает внутренние путешествия. *14.* Внутренняя пустыня была огромной и пустой. *15.* Она предпочитала спокойствие внутренних вод. ● *1.* Inner peace. *2.* The detective channeled his inner Sherlock. *3.* The dour landscape reflected her inner turmoil. *4.* He explored his inner self. *5.* He hoped to attain inner peace. *6.* Internal paddles. *7.* Internal bleeding. *8.* We have an internal threat. *9.* Massive internal bleeding. *10.* You could have internal bleeding. *11.* Domestic issues require attention. *12.* The domestic market is stable. *13.* He prefers domestic travel. *14.* The inland desert was vast and empty. *15.* She preferred the calm of inland waters.

**363. трагический** — *tragic* — 'Трагический' is used to describe something that is extremely sad, unfortunate, or disastrous. It conveys a sense of deep sorrow or grief, often associated with a dramatic or catastrophic event.

● *1.* Трагическая случайность. *2.* Это было трагическое событие. *3.* Ситуация была трагической. *4.* Они скорбели о трагической утрате. *5.* Холокост был трагическим событием.

• *1.* Tragic accident. *2.* It was a tragic event. *3.* The situation was tragic. *4.* They grieved the tragic loss. *5.* The holocaust was a tragic event.

**364. скалистый** — *rocky, craggy* — The word 'скалистый' is used to describe terrain or landscapes that are characterized by the presence of rocks or cliffs. It conveys a sense of ruggedness and roughness in the natural environment.

• *1.* Лодка ударилась о скалистый берег. *2.* Он поднялся на скалистую вершину. *3.* Альпинисты исследовали скалистую корри. *4.* Она поднялась на скалистый уступ. *5.* Они поднялись на скалистую гору. *6.* Скалистые скалы были опасны. *7.* Она нарисовала скалистый пейзаж. • *1.* The boat hit the rocky shore. *2.* He climbed the rocky peak. *3.* The climbers explored the rocky corrie. *4.* She climbed up to the rocky ledge. *5.* They climbed the craggy mountain. *6.* The craggy cliffs were dangerous. *7.* She painted the craggy landscape.

**365. множественный** — *multiple, plural* — This word is used to describe something that consists of or relates to more than one element or entity. It indicates a quantity that is greater than one, often referring to a group or collection of items.

• *1.* Множественные огнестрельные ранения. *2.* Множественные ножевые ранения. *3.* Множественное убийство. *4.* Множественные переломы ребер. • *1.* Multiple gunshot wounds. *2.* Multiple stab wounds. *3.* Multiple homicide. *4.* Multiple rib fractures.

**366. эффективный** — *effective, efficient* — This word is used to describe something that produces the desired result with minimal waste of time, effort, or resources. It implies that the object or action is successful in achieving its intended purpose.

• *1.* Очень эффективный. *2.* Это очень эффективно. *3.* Добавка CE оказалась эффективной. *4.* Антибиотик оказался эффективным. *5.* Гомеопатические лекарства эффективны. *6.* Очень эффективный. *7.* Это эффективно. *8.* Она очень эффективна. *9.* Новая формула топлива оказалась очень эффективной. *10.* Работники сахарного тростника работали эффективно. • *1.* Very effective. *2.* It's very effective. *3.* The cee supplement was effective. *4.* The antibiotic was effective. *5.* Homeopathic cures are effective. *6.* Very efficient. *7.* It's efficient. *8.* She's very efficient. *9.* The new propellant formula was highly efficient. *10.* The sugarcane workers were efficient.

**367. творческий** — *creative* — 'Творческий' is used to describe someone or something that is imaginative, original, and innovative. It is often used to refer to artistic or inventive qualities, as well as the ability to think outside the box.

● *1.* Проявите творческий подход. *2.* Ведение блога дает возможность творческого самовыражения. *3.* Город создавал творческую среду. *4.* Она выразила свою творческую сторону. *5.* Творческие различия. ● *1.* Get creative. *2.* Blogging allows for creative expression. *3.* The city provided a creative milieu. *4.* She expressed her creative side. *5.* Creative differences.

**368. обязательно** — *necessarily* — 'обязательно' is used to indicate that something is required or must be done. It emphasizes the importance or necessity of a certain action or condition. It is often used to express certainty or obligation.

● *1.* Не обязательно. *2.* Нет, не обязательно. *3.* Ну, не обязательно. *4.* Необязательно в этом порядке. *5.* Это не обязательно так. ● *1.* Not necessarily. *2.* No, not necessarily. *3.* Well, not necessarily. *4.* Not necessarily in that order. *5.* That's not necessarily true.

**369. хромой** — *lame* — The word 'хромой' is used to describe something or someone that is physically impaired or disabled, specifically in terms of having difficulty walking or moving properly.

● *1.* Такой хромой. *2.* Вы хромой. ● *1.* So lame. *2.* You're lame.

**370. деликатный** — *delicate* — 'Delicate' is used to describe something that is subtle, refined, or sensitive. It can refer to physical objects, emotions, or situations that require gentle handling or careful consideration.

● *1.* Это деликатная ситуация. *2.* Очень деликатный. *3.* Это деликатно. *4.* Это очень деликатно. *5.* Такой деликатный. ● *1.* It's a delicate situation. *2.* Very delicate. *3.* It's delicate. *4.* It's very delicate. *5.* So delicate.

**371. обширный** — *vast, extensive, expansive* — 'Обширный' is used to describe something that is large in size, scope, or extent. It conveys the idea of something being vast, extensive, or expansive in nature. It is often used to emphasize the scale or magnitude of something.

● *1.* Сахиб владел обширными поместьями. *2.* Область науки обширна. *3.* Граф владел обширными поместьями и имениями. *4.* У них была обширная коллекция. *5.* Тайга была обширна и дика. *6.* Его познания в физиологии обширны. *7.* Ущерб был обширным. *8.* Книжник имел обширную библиотеку. *9.* Меню было обширным. *10.* Сеть дорог обширна. *11.* Поместье Дауда было обширным. *12.* Они разбили лагерь на обширных лугах. *13.* Космологическая перспектива обширна. ● *1.* The Sahib owned vast estates. *2.* The domain of science is vast. *3.* The earl owned vast estates and properties. *4.* They had a vast collection. *5.* The taiga was vast and wild. *6.* His knowledge of physiology is extensive. *7.* The damage was extensive. *8.* The bookman had an extensive library. *9.* The menu was extensive. *10.* The network of roads is extensive. *11.* The Dowd estate was expansive. *12.* They camped in the expansive grassland. *13.* The cosmological perspective is expansive.

**372. нежно** — *gently* — 'нежно' is used to describe actions or feelings that are done in a gentle, tender, or affectionate manner. It can be used to convey a sense of softness, care, or delicacy in various contexts.

● *1.* Нежно нежно. *2.* Очень нежно. *3.* Красиво и нежно. *4.* Она нежно гладит спящего жеребенка. *5.* Он нежно взял ее за руку. ● *1.* Gently, gently. *2.* Very gently. *3.* Nice and gently. *4.* She gently pet the sleeping foal. *5.* He gently held her hand.

**373. вежливый** — *polite, courteous, suave* — 'Vezhliviy' is used to describe someone who is well-mannered, respectful, and considerate in their interactions with others. It conveys a sense of politeness, courtesy, and sophistication in behavior and speech.

● *1.* Будьте вежливы. *2.* Я просто был вежлив. *3.* Я был вежлив. *4.* Он просто был вежлив. *5.* Просто из вежливости. *6.* Она всегда была вежлива с гостями. *7.* Он вежливо кивнул. ● *1.* Be polite. *2.* I was just being polite. *3.* I was being polite. *4.* He was just being polite. *5.* Just being polite. *6.* She was always courteous to guests. *7.* He gave a courteous nod.

**374. мелочный** — *petty* — The word 'мелочный' is used to describe something as insignificant, trivial, or small in importance. It is often used to refer to minor details, actions, or concerns that are not considered significant or important.

● *1.* Не будь таким мелочным. ● *1.* Don't be so petty.

**375. абсурдный** — *absurd* — This word is used to describe something that is illogical, unreasonable, or ridiculous. It is often used to express disbelief or criticism towards a situation, idea, or behavior that is considered absurd.

● *1.* Это абсурдно. *2.* Как абсурдно. *3.* О, не говорите абсурдно. *4.* Жизнь абсурдна. *5.* Но это абсурдно. ● *1.* It's absurd. *2.* How absurd. *3.* Oh, don't be absurd. *4.* Life is absurd. *5.* But it's absurd.

**376. трезвый** — *sober* — 'Трезвый' is used to describe someone who is not under the influence of alcohol or drugs. It can also be used to describe a clear, rational state of mind or a serious, realistic approach to a situation.

● *1.* Ты трезв? *2.* Я трезв. *3.* Ты трезвый? *4.* Ты мне нужен трезвым. *5.* Он трезв. ● *1.* Are you sober? *2.* I'm sober. *3.* You sober? *4.* I need you sober. *5.* He's sober.

**377. обратный** — *reverse* — 'Обратный' is used to describe something that is opposite or contrary to the usual order or direction. It can also refer to something that is turned around or flipped in the opposite direction.

● *1.* Обратный курс. *2.* Обратная психология? *3.* Обратная мощность. *4.* Это обратная психология. *5.* Она использовала обратную психологию, чтобы психовать его. ● *1.* Reverse course. *2.* Reverse psychology? *3.* Reverse power. *4.* It's reverse psychology. *5.* She used reverse psychology to psych him.

**378. северный** — *northern* — The word 'северный' is used to describe something that is located in or related to the northern direction or region. It is used to indicate a specific geographical location or climate characteristic.

● *1.* Маунт-Вилсон, это Северное сияние. *2.* Операция «Байтмарк», это «Северное сияние», заходите. *3.* Это Северное сияние. ● *1.* Mount Wilson, this is Northern Light. *2.* Operation Bitemark, this is Northern Light, come in. *3.* This is Northern Light.

**379. несправедливый** — *unfair, unjust* — The word 'несправедливый' is used to describe situations, actions, or decisions that are not fair or just. It conveys a sense of inequality or lack of justice in a given context.

● *1.* Это так несправедливо. *2.* Это несправедливо. *3.* Это совершенно несправедливо. *4.* Это было несправедливо. *5.* Ты несправедлив. *6.* Ах, как вы несправедливы, как жестоки! *7.* Она протестовала против несправедливого заключения. *8.* Налогообложение без представительства несправедливо. *9.* Ее задержание казалось несправедливым. ● *1.* It's so unfair. *2.* It's unfair. *3.* This is totally unfair. *4.* It was unfair. *5.* You're unfair. *6.* Ah, how unjust, how cruel you are! *7.* She protested against the unjust imprisonment. *8.* Taxation without representation is unjust. *9.* Her detainment felt unjust.

**380.** **невнятно** — *indistinctly* — 'невнятно' is used to describe something that is unclear or not easily understood. It is often used to refer to unclear speech, writing, or visuals.

**381.** **независимый** — *independent* — This word is used to describe something or someone that is not influenced or controlled by others. It can also be used to describe a state or condition of being self-reliant and free from outside interference.
● *1.* Я независим. *2.* Мы независимы. *3.* Вы независимая женщина. *4.* Я независимый подрядчик. *5.* Вы независимы. ● *1.* I'm independent. *2.* We're independent. *3.* You're an independent woman. *4.* I'm an independent contractor. *5.* You're independent.

**382.** **одинаково** — *alike* — 'одинаково' is used to describe things that are similar or identical in nature, appearance, or quality. It is used to indicate that two or more things are alike in some way.
● *1.* Великие умы думают одинаково. *2.* Делитесь и делитесь одинаково. *3.* Мы думаем одинаково. *4.* Нет двух одинаковых. *5.* Все мужчины одинаковы. ● *1.* Great minds think alike. *2.* Share and share alike. *3.* We think alike. *4.* No two are alike. *5.* All men are alike.

**383.** **традиционный** — *traditional, conventional* — 'Традиционный' is used to describe something that is customary, typical, or in accordance with long-standing practices. It conveys the idea of something being traditional or conventional in nature.
● *1.* Это традиционно. *2.* Постмодернистская архитектура бросила вызов традиционным концепциям. *3.* У нее была

традиционная прическа симада. *4.* Традиционное фанданг-о имело живой ритм. *5.* В традиционном рецепте буйабеса используется шафран. *6.* Он предпочитал традиционные методы. *7.* Дизайн был традиционным и скучным. *8.* Традиционный подход оказался неэффективным. • *1.* It's traditional. *2.* Postmodern architecture challenged traditional concepts. *3.* She wore a traditional shimada hairstyle. *4.* The traditional fandango had a lively rhythm. *5.* The traditional bouillabaisse recipe used saffron. *6.* He preferred conventional methods. *7.* The design was conventional and uninspired. *8.* The conventional approach was ineffective.

**384. напряженный** — *tense, strenuous, stressful* — This word is used to describe situations or environments that are filled with tension, stress, or strain. It can also be used to describe a person who is feeling tense or stressed out.

• *1.* Ты выглядишь напряженным. *2.* Ты выглядишь немного напряженным. *3.* Ты такой напряженный. *4.* Не будь таким напряженным. *5.* Почему ты такой напряженный? *6.* Упражнение было напряженным. *7.* Она нашла этот день напряженным. *8.* Она сказала «уф» после напряженной встречи. • *1.* You seem tense. *2.* You seem a little tense. *3.* You're so tense. *4.* Don't be so tense. *5.* Why are you so tense? *6.* The exercise was strenuous. *7.* She found the day stressful. *8.* She said 'phew' after the stressful meeting.

**385. воспаленный** — *sore* — 'воспаленный' is used to describe something that is experiencing pain or discomfort, typically due to inflammation or irritation. It can be used to describe physical sensations as well as emotional or psychological states.

• *1.* Ему нужен был бальзам для воспаленных мышц. *2.* Взгляд для воспаленных глаз. *3.* Какое зрелище для воспаленных глаз. • *1.* He needed a balm for his sore muscles. *2.* Sight for sore eyes. *3.* What a sight for sore eyes.

**386. без сознания** — *unconscious* — The term 'без сознания' is used to describe a state of being unconscious or lacking awareness. It can refer to both physical unconsciousness and a lack of mental awareness or understanding.

• *1.* Он без сознания. *2.* Она без сознания. *3.* Она все еще без сознания. *4.* Он все еще без сознания. *5.* Все еще без сознания. • *1.* He's unconscious. *2.* She's unconscious. *3.* She's still unconscious. *4.* He's still unconscious. *5.* Still unconscious.

**387. немедленный** — *immediate* — This word is used to describe something that happens or is done without any delay or hesitation. It conveys the sense of urgency and immediacy in a situation or action.

• *1.* Запрашиваю немедленную поддержку. *2.* Распространенные проблемы требуют немедленного внимания. *3.* Эффект был немедленным. *4.* В депеше предписывалось принять немедленные меры. *5.* Они потребовали немедленного перерыва. • *1.* Requesting immediate backup. *2.* Prevalent issues need immediate attention. *3.* The effect was immediate. *4.* The dispatch ordered immediate action. *5.* They called for an immediate adjournment.

**388. комический** — *comic, comical* — 'комический' is used to describe something that is funny, humorous, or amusing in a light-hearted way. It is often used to characterize situations, events, or people that provoke laughter or amusement.

• *1.* Она любила читать комические романы. *2.* Произошло комическое недоразумение. *3.* Лицо ее имело комическое выражение. • *1.* She enjoyed reading comic novels. *2.* There was a comical misunderstanding. *3.* Her face had a comical expression.

**389. относительный** — *relative* — This word is used to describe something in comparison to something else, indicating that it is not absolute or fixed. It conveys the idea of being dependent on or influenced by other factors.

• *1.* Это все относительно. *2.* У меня будут основания более относительные, чем эти. • *1.* It's all relative. *2.* I'll have grounds more relative than this.

**390. духовный** — *spiritual, clerical, ecclesiastical* — This word is used to describe things related to religion, spirituality, or the church. It can refer to beliefs, practices, or objects that are connected to the spiritual or religious realm.

• *1.* Символ аум имел духовное значение. *2.* Она встретила духовного свами. *3.* Духовный лидер поделился эзотерическими учениями. *4.* Слово «ом» имеет духовное значение. *5.* Она испытала духовное пробуждение с помощью аяуаски. • *1.* The aum symbol held spiritual significance. *2.* She met a spiritual swami. *3.* The spiritual leader shared esoteric teachings. *4.* The word 'om' is of spiritual significance. *5.* She experienced a spiritual awakening with ayahuasca.

**391. тесно** — *closely, intimately* — 'Tesno' is used to describe a close or intimate relationship or connection between people or things. It can also be used to describe a tight or cramped space or feeling.

● *1.* Не тесно. *2.* Они тесно сотрудничали. *3.* Она тесно сотрудничала с опытным подрядчиком. *4.* Эти две идеи тесно связаны. *5.* Два художника тесно сотрудничали. ● *1.* Not closely. *2.* They worked closely together. *3.* She worked closely with a skilled contractor. *4.* The two ideas are closely related. *5.* The two artists collaborated intimately.

**392. жизненно важный** — *vital* — This word is used to describe something that is crucial, essential, or extremely important for the well-being, survival, or success of a person, organization, or situation. It emphasizes the significance and necessity of the subject.

● *1.* Это жизненно важно. *2.* Раствор был жизненно важным компонентом в строительстве. *3.* Продолговатый мозг регулирует жизненно важные функции. *4.* Они оказали жизненно важную поддержку. *5.* Информация была жизненно важной. ● *1.* It's vital. *2.* The mortar was a vital component in construction. *3.* The medulla regulates vital functions. *4.* They provided vital support. *5.* The information was vital.

**393. солнечный** — *sunny, solar* — The word 'солнечный' is used to describe something that is related to the sun or has characteristics of the sun. It can be used to describe weather, a place, or a person's disposition.

● *1.* Прогноз обещал солнечную погоду. *2.* Погода была теплая и солнечная. *3.* Светлая и солнечная комната подняла ей настроение. *4.* Они прогулялись солнечным днем. *5.* Сегодня солнечный день. *6.* Она установила солнечную панель Пико. ● *1.* The forecast called for sunny skies. *2.* The weather was warm and sunny. *3.* The bright and sunny room lifted her spirits. *4.* They took a walk on a sunny afternoon. *5.* It's a sunny day. *6.* She installed a pico solar panel.

**394. физически** — *physically* — 'физически' is used to describe actions or states that pertain to the physical body or world. It is used to emphasize the physical aspect of something, rather than the mental or emotional.

● *1.* Не физически. *2.* Я имею в виду физически. *3.* Физически, да. *4.* Физически ты в порядке. *5.* Это физически невозможно. ● *1.* Not physically. *2.* I mean, physically. *3.* Physically, yeah. *4.* Physically, you're fine. *5.* That's physically impossible.

**395. ржавый** — *rusty* — This word is used to describe something that has rust on it, typically metal objects that have been exposed to moisture for a long period of time. It can also be used figuratively to describe something old or outdated.

● *1.* Я немного заржавел. *2.* Ты ржавый. *3.* Вилы были ржавые и старые. *4.* Они миновали ржавый указатель. *5.* На старом сундуке был ржавый замок. ● *1.* I'm a little rusty. *2.* You're rusty. *3.* The pitchfork was rusty and old. *4.* They passed a rusty signpost. *5.* The old chest had a rusty padlock.

**396. практический** — *practical* — 'Практический' is used to describe something that is useful, functional, or efficient in a real-life situation. It implies that the object or action serves a practical purpose and is not just theoretical or abstract.

● *1.* Профессиональная программа ориентирована на практические навыки. ● *1.* The vocational program focused on practical skills.

**397. задний** — *rear, posterior* — 'Задний' is used to describe something located at the back or rear of an object or person. It can also be used to indicate a position or direction that is behind or after something else.

● *1.* Заднее колесо имело прокол. *2.* Задний вход закрыт. *3.* Правый задний карман. *4.* У заднего входа было меньше людей. *5.* Она прислонилась к задней стене. *6.* Задний конец лодки. ● *1.* The rear tire had a puncture. *2.* The rear entrance is closed. *3.* Right rear pocket. *4.* The posterior entrance was less crowded. *5.* She leaned against the posterior wall. *6.* The posterior end of the boat.

**398. обожаемый** — *adorable* — 'Adorable' is used to describe something or someone that is extremely lovable, charming, or delightful. It conveys a sense of affection and admiration towards the object or person being described.

● *1.* Он обожаемый. ● *1.* He is adorable.

**399. уязвимый** — *vulnerable* — 'Уязвимый' is used to describe someone or something that is susceptible to harm, attack, or criticism. It conveys a sense of fragility or weakness, highlighting the need for protection or care.
● *1.* Они уязвимы. *2.* Она уязвима. *3.* Он уязвим. *4.* Ты уязвим. *5.* Я уязвим. ● *1.* They're vulnerable. *2.* She's vulnerable. *3.* He's vulnerable. *4.* You're vulnerable. *5.* I'm vulnerable.

**400. конкретно** — *specifically* — 'конкретно' is used to emphasize specificity or precision in a statement. It is often used to highlight a particular detail or point in a conversation or argument.
● *1.* Не конкретно. *2.* Что конкретно? *3.* Она хочет знать конкретно, что произошло. *4.* Более конкретно? ● *1.* Not specifically. *2.* What specifically? *3.* She wants to know specifically what happened. *4.* More specifically?

**401. бледный** — *pale* — The word 'бледный' is used to describe something that lacks color or is light in complexion. It can be used to describe a person's skin tone, a color, or a general lack of vibrancy in something.
● *1.* Вы выглядите бледным. *2.* Ты бледный. *3.* Ты выглядишь таким бледным. *4.* Ты выглядишь немного бледным. *5.* Ты очень бледный. ● *1.* You look pale. *2.* You're pale. *3.* You look so pale. *4.* You look a bit pale. *5.* You're very pale.

**402. анонимный** — *anonymous* — This word is used to describe something or someone that is unidentified or unknown. It is often used in reference to online profiles, surveys, or sources of information where the identity of the person or thing is not revealed.
● *1.* Анонимный совет. *2.* Это анонимно. *3.* Это было анонимно. *4.* Анонимный источник. *5.* Донор спермы остался анонимным. ● *1.* Anonymous tip. *2.* It's anonymous. *3.* It was anonymous. *4.* An anonymous source. *5.* The semen donor remained anonymous.

**403. фиолетовый** — *purple* — 'фиолетовый' is used to describe objects, colors, or emotions that are similar to the color purple. It can be used to convey a sense of royalty, mystery, or creativity.

• *1.* Это фиолетовый. *2.* Небо постепенно меняло цвет с оранжевого на фиолетовый. *3.* У Эгги были яркие фиолетовые цветы. *4.* Петуния была ярко-фиолетового цвета. *5.* Баклажаны были темно-фиолетового цвета. • *1.* It's purple. *2.* The sky turned gradually from orange to purple. *3.* The aggie had vibrant purple flowers. *4.* The petunia was a vibrant purple. *5.* The aubergine was a deep purple color.

**404. визуальный** — *visual* — 'визуальный' is used to describe something that is related to sight or vision. It is used to indicate that something is visually appealing or stimulating, or that it is perceived through the sense of sight.

• *1.* У нас есть визуальный. *2.* Визуальный контакт. *3.* Дайте мне визуальное представление. *4.* У меня есть визуальный контакт. *5.* Я получил визуальное представление. • *1.* We have visual. *2.* Visual contact. *3.* Give me a visual. *4.* I have visual contact. *5.* I got a visual.

**405. суровый** — *harsh, stern, severe, dour* — The word 'суровый' is used to describe someone or something that is strict, severe, or unforgiving in nature. It can also be used to convey a sense of seriousness or severity in a situation or environment.

• *1.* Антарктическая зима сурова. *2.* Тюрьма славилась своими суровыми условиями. *3.* Дерево способно переносить суровые погодные условия. *4.* Зима на Аляске суровая. *5.* Автомобиль не испытан в суровых условиях. *6.* Он повернулся к суровому интервьюеру. *7.* Констебль был суров. *8.* Сержант был шомполом суров. *9.* Суровая погода. *10.* В сообщении говорилось о суровой погоде. *11.* Наказание было суровым. *12.* Ее суровый тон. *13.* Им грозило суровое наказание. *14.* Суровый пейзаж отражал ее внутреннее смятение. *15.* Суровая погода соответствовала его настроению. *16.* Его суровое отношение повлияло на всю команду. *17.* Суровое выражение его лица осталось неизменным. *18.* Его суровый взгляд на жизнь вызывал беспокойство. • *1.* The Antarctic winter is harsh. *2.* The jailhouse was notorious for its harsh conditions. *3.* The tree can endure harsh weather. *4.* Winter in Alaska is harsh. *5.* The car is untested in harsh conditions. *6.* He faced the stern interviewer. *7.* The constable was stern. *8.* The sergeant was ramrod stern. *9.*

The severe weather. *10*. The advisory warned of severe weather. *11*. The punishment was severe. *12*. Her severe tone. *13*. They faced a severe penalty. *14*. The dour landscape reflected her inner turmoil. *15*. The dour weather matched his mood. *16*. His dour attitude affected the entire team. *17*. The dour expression on his face remained unchanged. *18*. His dour outlook on life was concerning.

**406. агрессивный** — *aggressive, invasive* — This word is used to describe someone or something that is forceful, hostile, or assertive in behavior. It can also be used to describe actions or behaviors that are intrusive or overly assertive.

● *1*. Будьте агрессивны! *2*. Очень агрессивный. *3*. Это слишком агрессивно. *4*. Его поведение было агрессивным. *5*. Нуги может быть игривым или агрессивным. ● *1*. Be aggressive! *2*. Very aggressive. *3*. It's too aggressive. *4*. His demeanor was aggressive. *5*. A noogie can be playful or aggressive.

**407. коммунистический** — *communist* — 'Коммунистический' is used to describe something that is related to or characteristic of communism. It can be used to describe political ideologies, movements, parties, or anything else associated with the principles of communism.

● *1*. В стране правил коммунистический режим. *2*. Он верил в коммунистические принципы. *3*. Они были преданы коммунистической партии. *4*. Коммунистическая революция стала поворотным моментом. ● *1*. The country was ruled by a communist regime. *2*. He believed in communist principles. *3*. They were devoted to the communist party. *4*. The communist revolution was a turning point.

**408. первичный** — *primary* — 'Первичный' is used to describe something that is first in importance, order, or time. It can also refer to something original, fundamental, or essential. It is often used to emphasize the main or most important aspect of something.

● *1*. Начать первичное зажигание. *2*. Обнаружено вторжение в ядро первичных данных. ● *1*. Commence primary ignition. *2*. Incursion detected in primary data core.

**409. жидкий** — *liquid, runny, soupy* — 'Жидкий' is used to describe substances that are in a liquid or runny state, such as water, soup, or milk. It can also be used to describe the consistency of certain foods or materials.

• *1.* Жидкость для мытья посуды пахла свежестью. *2.* Жидкий соус, впитавшийся в макароны. *3.* Жидкая консистенция была неаппетитной. *4.* Она вытерла жидкую тушь. *5.* Его жидкие яйца были переварены. *6.* Кесо было слишком жидким.
• *1.* The dishwashing liquid smelled fresh. *2.* The runny sauce soaked into the pasta. *3.* The runny consistency was unappetizing. *4.* She wiped away her runny mascara. *5.* His runny eggs were overcooked. *6.* The queso was too runny.

**410. унылый** — *dull, godforsaken, despondent, dumpy* — 'Унылый' is used to describe something or someone that is lacking in excitement, energy, or interest. It conveys a sense of gloominess, sadness, or boredom. It can also be used to describe a place that is unattractive or depressing.

• *1.* В комнате царила унылая атмосфера. *2.* День был унылый и серый. *3.* Его унылое выражение лица беспокоило меня. *4.* Унылая атмосфера висела тяжело. • *1.* The room had a dull atmosphere. *2.* The day was dull and gray. *3.* His despondent expression worried me. *4.* The despondent atmosphere hung heavy.

**411. альтернативный** — *alternative* — This word is used to describe something that serves as a different option or choice from the usual or traditional. It implies a different approach or solution to a problem or situation.

• *1.* Они сочли альтернативный подход предпочтительным. *2.* В тезаурусе перечислено несколько альтернативных слов. • *1.* They considered the alternative approach preferable. *2.* The thesaurus listed several alternative words.

**412. узкий** — *narrow, parochial* — This word is used to describe something that is limited in scope or width. It can refer to physical objects like roads or hallways, as well as abstract concepts like viewpoints or perspectives.

• *1.* Они прошли через узкий пролив. *2.* Маленькая лодка прошла через узкий залив. *3.* Узкий мост покачнулся. *4.* Она протиснулась через узкий коридор. • *1.* They navigated through the narrow strait. *2.* The small boat navigated the narrow inlet. *3.* The narrow bridge swayed. *4.* She squeezed through the narrow hallway.

**413. значительный** — *significant, considerable, substantial, sizeable* — This word is used to describe something that is important, large, or has a noticeable impact. It is often used to emphasize the significance or size of something in comparison to other things.

• *1.* Что-то значительное. *2.* Психологическое воздействие этого события было значительным. *3.* Средства массовой информации имеют значительное влияние. *4.* Слияние привело к значительным увольнениям. *5.* Она добилась значительного успеха. *6.* Погода демонстрирует значительные колебания. *7.* Он пользовался значительным влиянием. *8.* В торте было значительное количество сахара. • *1.* Something significant. *2.* The psychological impact of the event was significant. *3.* The media has significant influence. *4.* The merger resulted in significant layoffs. *5.* She made a significant gain. *6.* The weather exhibits considerable variance. *7.* He wielded considerable influence. *8.* The cake had a substantial amount of sugar.

**414. корпоративный** — *corporate* — This word is used to describe something related to a corporation or business. It can refer to events, culture, policies, or anything else associated with a corporate entity.

• *1.* Корпоративная кредиторская задолженность. *2.* Корпоративный шпионаж. *3.* Его считали корпоративным создателем дождя. *4.* Команда искала корпоративное спонсорство. *5.* Он боролся с корпоративным языком. • *1.* Corporate accounts payable. *2.* Corporate espionage. *3.* He was considered a corporate rainmaker. *4.* The team sought corporate sponsorship. *5.* He struggled with corporate parlance.

**415. увлеченный** — *keen* — 'Keen' is used to describe someone who is enthusiastic, passionate, or deeply interested in something. It can also be used to describe an activity or interest that someone is very dedicated to or enjoys greatly.

• *1.* Персиковый увлеченный. *2.* Увлеченный студент задавал вопросы. • *1.* Peachy keen. *2.* The keen student asked questions.

**416. тщеславный** — *vain, conceited* — 'Тщеславный' is used to describe someone who is excessively proud of their appearance or achievements, often to the point of being arrogant or self-centered. It conveys a negative connotation of vanity and self-importance.

• *1.* Он такой тщеславный. *2.* Она стала тщеславной. *3.* Не будь таким тщеславным. *4.* Тщеславный человек прихорашился. *5.* Она проявляла тщеславное поведение. • *1.* He's so vain. *2.* She's become vain. *3.* Don't be so vain. *4.* The vain man preened. *5.* She displayed conceited behavior.

**417. аккуратный** — *neat, tidy, natty* — 'Akkyratny' is used to describe something that is well-organized, clean, and carefully arranged. It can refer to a person's appearance, a room, or any object that is neat and tidy.

• *1.* Разве это не аккуратно? *2.* Аккуратно, да? *3.* Довольно аккуратно, да? *4.* Очень аккуратный. *5.* Это аккуратно. *6.* Очень аккуратно. *7.* Постоялец оказался тихим и аккуратным арендатором. • *1.* Isn't that neat? *2.* Neat, huh? *3.* Pretty neat, huh? *4.* Very neat. *5.* It's neat. *6.* Very tidy. *7.* The lodger was a quiet and tidy tenant.

**418. случайно** — *accidentally, coincidentally, perchance* — This word is used to describe something that happens by chance or without intention. It can be used to explain a coincidence or an accidental occurrence.

• *1.* Она случайно уронила трубку телефона. *2.* Компания случайно переплатила заработную плату. *3.* Он случайно проглотил зубочистку. *4.* Она случайно наступила на какашку. *5.* Спичечный коробок случайно загорелся. *6.* Наши наряды случайно оказались похожими. *7.* Они случайно прибыли в одно и то же время. *8.* Со своим старым другом она познакомилась случайно. • *1.* She accidentally dropped the handset of the phone. *2.* The company accidentally overpaid the payroll. *3.* He accidentally swallowed a toothpick. *4.* She accidentally stepped in a turd. *5.* The matchbox caught fire accidentally. *6.* Our outfits were coincidentally similar. *7.* They coincidentally arrived at the same time. *8.* She met her old friend coincidentally.

**419. миролюбивый** — *pacific* — The word 'миролюбивый' is used to describe someone or something that is peaceful, calm, and non-aggressive. It conveys a sense of harmony and tranquility, suggesting a preference for peaceful resolutions and a dislike for conflict.

**420. любезно** — *kindly, graciously* — 'Любезно' is used to describe actions or behaviors that are done in a kind and gracious manner. It is often used when asking for a favor or making a polite request.

● *1.* Спасибо, любезно. *2.* Спасибо вам очень любезно. *3.* Она любезно предложила помощь. *4.* Я любезно благодарю вас. *5.* Он любезно принял благодарность. *6.* Она любезно приняла его извинения. *7.* Он любезно впустил меня. *8.* Он любезно принял это признание. ● *1.* Thank you kindly. *2.* Thank you very kindly. *3.* She kindly offered to help. *4.* I graciously thank you. *5.* He received the thankyou graciously. *6.* She accepted his apology graciously. *7.* He graciously allowed me in. *8.* He accepted the acknowledgement graciously.

**421. электронный** — *electronic* — The word 'электронный' is used to describe things that are related to or operated by electricity, particularly in the context of technology and devices. It can also refer to digital or online forms of communication and information.

● *1.* Электронный глушитель заблокировал систему наблюдения. ● *1.* The electronic jammer blocked the surveillance system.

**422. слабый** — *faint, weak, mild* — This word is used to describe something that lacks strength or intensity, whether it be a physical sensation, emotion, or quality. It can also be used to indicate a subtle or slight degree of something.

● *1.* Я чувствую слабость. *2.* Это слабо. *3.* Это очень слабо. *4.* Не для слабонервных. *5.* Оно слабое, но оно есть. *6.* Ты слабый. *7.* Я слаб. *8.* Он слабый. *9.* Я был слаб. *10.* Я слишком слаб. *11.* Расслабляющее лекарство имело легкие побочные эффекты. ● *1.* I feel faint. *2.* It's faint. *3.* It's very faint. *4.* Not for the faint of heart. *5.* It's faint, but it's there. *6.* You're weak. *7.* I'm weak. *8.* He's weak. *9.* I was weak. *10.* I'm too weak. *11.* The relaxant medication had mild side effects.

**423. славный** — *glorious* — 'Славный' is used to describe something or someone as magnificent, splendid, or excellent. It conveys a sense of grandeur and admiration, highlighting the impressive or praiseworthy qualities of the subject.

● *1.* Надежда в виде славного боя. *2.* Какой славный день. *3.* Команда одержала славную победу. ● *1.* Hope in the form of glorious combat. *2.* What a glorious day. *3.* The team won a glorious victory.

**424. подлинный** — *genuine, authentic* — This word is used to describe something that is real, true, or original. It is often used to emphasize the authenticity or genuineness of a person, object, or experience.

• *1.* Подлинная статья. *2.* Это подлинно. *3.* Они не смогли проверить подлинность подписи. *4.* Картина была подлинной. *5.* Эксперт смог отличить подлинное искусство. • *1.* The genuine article. *2.* It is genuine. *3.* They could not verify the authentic signature. *4.* The painting was authentic. *5.* The expert could distinguish authentic art.

**425. строго** — *strictly, rigorously* — 'Строго' is used to describe a strict or rigorous approach to something. It implies a high level of discipline, adherence to rules, or precision in following instructions. It can also convey a sense of seriousness or severity.

• *1.* Строго бизнес. *2.* Это строго бизнес. *3.* Строго профессионально. *4.* Строго запрещено! *5.* Наши отношения строго профессиональные. *6.* Она строго следовала диете. *7.* Они строго соблюдали правила. • *1.* Strictly business. *2.* It's strictly business. *3.* Strictly professional. *4.* Strictly forbidden! *5.* Our relationship is strictly professional. *6.* She followed the diet plan rigorously. *7.* They enforced the rules rigorously.

**426. смелый** — *bold, courageous, audacious* — The word 'смелый' is used to describe someone who is brave, daring, or fearless in their actions or decisions. It conveys a sense of confidence and willingness to take risks in order to achieve a goal.

• *1.* Смелый шаг. *2.* Быть смелым. *3.* Очень смело. *4.* Удача благоволит смелым. *5.* Это смело. *6.* Очень смелый. *7.* Ты смелый. • *1.* Bold move. *2.* Be bold. *3.* Very bold. *4.* Fortune favors the bold. *5.* It's bold. *6.* Very courageous. *7.* You're courageous.

**427. формальный** — *formal* — 'Formal' is used to describe something that is official, proper, or following established rules or conventions. It can refer to behavior, language, attire, or procedures that are appropriate for formal settings or occasions.

• *1.* Не будьте так формальны. *2.* Так формально. *3.* На

мероприятии действует формальный дресс-код. *4.* Знаете, формальных правил нет. *5.* Это формальное дело. ● *1.* Don't be so formal. *2.* So formal. *3.* The event has a formal dress code. *4.* There are no formal rules, you know. *5.* It's a formal affair.

**428. рискованный** — *risky, touchy, dicey* — The word 'рискованный' is used to describe situations or actions that involve a high level of risk or uncertainty. It can also be used to describe something that is delicate or sensitive in nature.

● *1.* Это слишком рискованно. *2.* Слишком рискованно. *3.* Это рискованно. *4.* Нет, это слишком рискованно. *5.* Разве это не рискованно? *6.* Будущее выглядело рискованным. *7.* Ситуация была рискованная. *8.* Она предпочла избежать рискованного варианта. ● *1.* It's too risky. *2.* Too risky. *3.* It's risky. *4.* No, it's too risky. *5.* Isn't that risky? *6.* The future looked dicey. *7.* The situation was dicey. *8.* She chose to avoid the dicey option.

**429. до некоторой степени** — *somewhat* — This term is used to indicate a moderate or limited degree of something. It suggests that a certain quality or characteristic is present, but not to a significant extent. It conveys a sense of partiality or incompleteness.

● *1.* Да, в некоторой степени. *2.* Она в некоторой степени счастлива. ● *1.* Yeah, somewhat. *2.* She is somewhat happy.

**430. незначительный** — *slight* — 'незначительный' is used to describe something that is small or insignificant in amount, degree, or importance. It can be used to indicate a slight difference, impact, or effect.

● *1.* Боль незначительная. *2.* Насколько незначительно? ● *1.* The pain is only slight. *2.* How slight?

**431. лесбийский** — *lesbian* — This word is used to describe something or someone related to lesbianism or homosexuality between women. It can be used to refer to relationships, behaviors, or characteristics associated with lesbians.

● *1.* В фильме рассказывается о лесбийской паре. ● *1.* The film features a lesbian couple.

**432. к счастью** — *fortunately, luckily, mercifully* — 'к счастью' is used to express relief or gratitude for a positive outcome or situation. It is often used to highlight a fortunate event or circumstance that has occurred, bringing a sense of relief or happiness.

● *1.* К счастью, нет. *2.* К счастью, он нашел ключи. *3.* К - счастью, они прибыли вовремя. *4.* К счастью, она осталась невредимой. *5.* К счастью, они решили проблему. *6.* К счастью, она оказалась в нужном месте. *7.* К счастью, у него был зонтик. *8.* К счастью, никто не пострадал. *9.* К счастью, у нее был запасной ключ. *10.* К счастью, Флетчер схватил меня. *11.* К счастью, короткая встреча оставила время для обеда. *12.* Дождь, к счастью, прекратился. ● *1.* Fortunately not. *2.* He found the keys fortunately. *3.* Fortunately, they arrived on time. *4.* She was fortunately unharmed. *5.* They resolved the issue fortunately. *6.* She was luckily at the right place. *7.* Luckily, he had an umbrella. *8.* Luckily, no one was hurt. *9.* Luckily, she had a spare key. *10.* Luckily, Fletcher grabbed me. *11.* The mercifully short meeting left time for lunch. *12.* The rain stopped, mercifully.

**433. наивный** — *naive, unsophisticated* — 'Наивный' is used to describe someone who lacks experience, wisdom, or sophistication, often resulting in a tendency to trust others easily or believe things without questioning. It can also refer to something that is simplistic or overly idealistic.

● *1.* Не будьте наивными. *2.* Не будь таким наивным. *3.* Ты такой наивный. *4.* Я не наивный. *5.* Ты наивный. ● *1.* Don't be naive. *2.* Don't be so naive. *3.* You're so naive. *4.* I'm not naive. *5.* You're naive.

**434. лысый** — *bald* — This word is used to describe someone or something that is lacking hair on their head. It can also be used to describe a surface that is smooth and without any protrusions.

● *1.* Ты лысый. *2.* Он лысый. *3.* Лысый – это красиво. *4.* Я лысый. *5.* Мой дядя лысый. ● *1.* You're bald. *2.* He's bald. *3.* Bald is beautiful. *4.* I'm bald. *5.* My uncle is bald.

**435. нацистский** — *nazi* — This word is used to describe something or someone related to the Nazi party or ideology. It can be used to refer to actions, beliefs, symbols, or individuals associated with the Nazi regime during World War II.

● *1.* Нацистский режим был репрессивным. ● *1.* The nazi regime was oppressive.

**436. генетический** — *genetic* — 'Генетический' is used to describe something related to genetics or inherited traits. It can be used to talk about genetic diseases, traits passed down through generations, or anything else related to the study of genes.

● *1.* Это генетическое. *2.* Должно быть, генетическое. *3.* Это генетическое заболевание. *4.* У вас такое же генетическое заболевание. *5.* Исследование изучало генетическую предрасположенность. ● *1.* It's genetic. *2.* Must be genetic. *3.* It's a genetic disease. *4.* You have the same genetic disease. *5.* The study explored the genetic predisposition.

**437. технический** — *technical* — 'Технический' is used to describe something related to technology, engineering, or mechanics. It is often used to refer to things that are practical, functional, or involving specific skills or knowledge in a technical field.

● *1.* Она технический писатель. *2.* Это технический термин? *3.* Терминология в книге была технической. *4.* Она изо всех сил пыталась понять технический жаргон. *5.* Нам нужно техническое решение. ● *1.* She's a technical writer. *2.* Is that a technical term? *3.* The terminology in the book was technical. *4.* She struggled to understand the technical jargon. *5.* We need a technical solution.

**438. императорский** — *imperial* — 'Императорский' is used to describe something that is related to or characteristic of an empire or emperor. It conveys a sense of grandeur, power, and authority.

● *1.* Его Превосходительство, императорский посол. ● *1.* His Excellency, the imperial ambassador.

**439. изумительный** — *marvelous, stupendous, marvellous* — 'Iзумительный' is used to describe something that is extraordinary, amazing, or impressive. It is often used to express admiration or awe towards something that is truly remarkable or outstanding.

● *1.* Ты выглядишь изумительно. *2.* Ты изумительный. *3.* Ее выступление было изумительным. *4.* Ты изумительный. ● *1.* You look marvelous. *2.* You're marvelous. *3.* Her performance was marvellous. *4.* You're marvellous.

**440. максимальный** — *maximum* — 'Максимальный' is used to describe the highest possible level or amount of something. It can also be used to emphasize the extreme nature of a situation or action.

● *1.* Он достиг максимальной скорости. *2.* Перейти на максимальный варп. *3.* Машина была разработана для максимальной эффективности. ● *1.* He reached the maximum speed. *2.* Go to maximum warp. *3.* The machine was designed for maximum efficiency.

**441. тайно** — *secretly* — 'Тайно' is used to describe actions or information that are kept hidden or concealed from others. It implies that something is done in a discreet or covert manner, without others knowing about it.

● *1.* Члены синдиката встречались тайно. *2.* Лидеры конфедерации встречались тайно. *3.* Он действовал тайно. *4.* Он тайно жаждал ее таланта. *5.* План был разработан тайно. ● *1.* Members of the syndicate met secretly. *2.* The leaders of the confederacy met secretly. *3.* He acted secretly. *4.* He secretly coveted her talent. *5.* The plan was hatched secretly.

**442. всемогущий** — *almighty, omnipotent* — 'Всемогущий' is used to describe someone or something as having unlimited power and authority, capable of achieving anything. It conveys a sense of ultimate strength and control.

● *1.* Всемогущая сила природы. *2.* Всемогущая сила была подавляющей. *3.* Она чувствовала себя всемогущей в своих знаниях. *4.* Ощущение всемогущего контроля опьяняло. *5.* Волшебник обладал всемогущей магией. *6.* Царя считали всемогущим. *7.* Всемогущий обладает великой властью. ● *1.* The almighty power of nature. *2.* The almighty force was overwhelming. *3.* She felt omnipotent in her knowledge. *4.* The feeling of omnipotent control was intoxicating. *5.* The wizard possessed omnipotent magic. *6.* The king was considered omnipotent. *7.* The omnipotent being held great power.

**443. фатальный** — *fatal* — 'Фатальный' is used to describe something that is deadly, disastrous, or has serious consequences. It is often used to emphasize the severity or finality of a situation or outcome.

● *1.* Он совершил фатальную ошибку. *2.* Обескровливание может оказаться фатальным. *3.* Авария оказалась фатальной. ● *1.* He made a fatal mistake. *2.* Exsanguination can be fatal. *3.* The accident was fatal.

**444. сонный** — *sleepy* — This word is used to describe someone who is feeling tired and ready to fall asleep, or something that makes you feel drowsy or relaxed. It can also be used to describe a sleepy atmosphere.

● *1.* Я сонный. *2.* Я не сонный. *3.* Ты сонный? *4.* Я такой сонный. *5.* Просыпайся, сонная голова. ● *1.* I'm sleepy. *2.* I'm not sleepy. *3.* Are you sleepy? *4.* I'm so sleepy. *5.* Wake up, sleepy head.

**445. древесный** — *woody* — This word is used to describe something that is related to or made of wood. It can be used to describe objects, materials, or even certain characteristics or qualities.

**446. смертный** — *mortal* — The word 'смертный' is used to describe something or someone that is subject to death or has a limited lifespan. It can be used to emphasize the temporary nature of life or the vulnerability of living beings.

● *1.* Это смертный грех. *2.* Их любовь была смертной и страстной. *3.* Мир смертных полон страданий. *4.* Смертный грех. *5.* Он боялся своей смертной слабости. ● *1.* It's a mortal sin. *2.* Their love was mortal and passionate. *3.* The mortal world is full of suffering. *4.* A mortal sin. *5.* He feared his own mortal frailty.

**447. каверзный** — *tricky* — 'Каверзный' is used to describe something or someone that is difficult to understand or deal with, often in a deceptive or sly manner. It implies a sense of complexity or trickiness in a situation or person.

● *1.* Репортер задавал каверзные вопросы. *2.* Она задала мне каверзный вопрос. ● *1.* The reporter asked tricky questions. *2.* She gave me a tricky question.

**448. удачный** — *fortunate* — 'Удачный' is used to describe something that brings good luck or success. It can refer to a person, event, or outcome that is favorable or fortunate. It is often used to express positive outcomes or circumstances.

● *1.* Удачный поворот событий спас их. *2.* Это очень удачно для тебя. ● *1.* The fortunate turn of events saved them. *2.* That's very fortunate for you.

**449. инструментальный** — *instrumental* — The word 'инструментальный' is used to describe something that is related to or serves as a tool or means to achieve a particular goal or outcome. It can also refer to something that is essential or crucial in a process or situation.

● *1.* Инструментальная музыка успокаивала ее. *2.* Флейта была инструментальной. *3.* Инструментальное сопровождение было прекрасным. ● *1.* The instrumental music soothed her. *2.* The flute was instrumental. *3.* The instrumental accompaniment was beautiful.

**450. экономический** — *economic, economical* — This word is used to describe something related to finances, money, or resources. It can refer to something being cost-effective, efficient, or related to the economy.

● *1.* Они обсудили экономическую политику. *2.* Во время экономического спада бродяжничество возросло. *3.* Легализация азартных игр принесла экономическую выгоду. *4.* Она изучала экономическую теорию. *5.* Страна приняла капиталистическую экономическую систему. ● *1.* They discussed economic policy. *2.* Vagrancy increased during the economic downturn. *3.* The legalization of gambling brought economic benefits. *4.* She studied economic theory. *5.* The country embraced a capitalistic economic system.

**451. интимный** — *intimate* — This word is used to describe close personal relationships or private moments. It can refer to emotional connections, physical closeness, or private settings. It conveys a sense of personal connection and vulnerability.

● *1.* Это очень интимно. *2.* Это интимно. ● *1.* It's very intimate. *2.* It's intimate.

**452. деревянный** — *wooden* — This word is used to describe something that is made of wood or has the characteristics of wood. It can also be used metaphorically to describe something as stiff, rigid, or lacking in emotion or warmth.

● *1.* Она покрасила деревянные стулья. *2.* Эпплджек выдерживался в деревянных бочках. *3.* Он вырезал деревянную скульптуру. *4.* Линейка была деревянной. *5.* Хрупкие предметы они упаковали в деревянный ящик. ● *1.* She painted the wooden chairs. *2.* The applejack was aged in wooden barrels. *3.* He carved a wooden sculpture. *4.* The ruler was wooden. *5.* They packed fragile items in a wooden crate.

**453. высокомерный** — *arrogant, haughty, snooty, upstage* — This word is used to describe someone who behaves in a superior or condescending manner, often looking down on others and displaying a sense of entitlement or superiority.

● *1.* Такой высокомерный! *2.* У нее высокомерное отношение. *3.* Ты такой высокомерный. *4.* Высокомерный ублюдок. *5.* Президент компании был самовлюбленным и высокомерным. *6.* Их высокомерное отношение оттолкнуло людей. *7.* Он выставлял напоказ свое высокомерное поведение. *8.* Она высокомерно посмотрела на него. *9.* Не будь таким высокомерным. *10.* Она вела себя высокомерно по отношению к своим сверстникам. *11.* Высокомерное отношение оттолкнуло. *12.* Его высокомерное поведение было неуместным. ● *1.* So arrogant! *2.* She has an arrogant attitude. *3.* You're so arrogant. *4.* Arrogant bastard. *5.* The company president was narcissistic and arrogant. *6.* Their haughty attitude turned people away. *7.* He flaunted his haughty demeanor. *8.* She gave him a haughty look. *9.* Don't be so snooty about it. *10.* She acted snooty towards her peers. *11.* The snooty attitude was off-putting. *12.* His snooty behavior was uncalled for.

**454. жадный** — *greedy, avid, insatiable, voracious* — This word is used to describe someone who has an excessive desire for something, usually money or possessions. It implies a selfish and insatiable craving for more, often at the expense of others.

● *1.* Я не жадная. *2.* Не будьте жадными. *3.* Не жадничайте. *4.* Ты жадный. *5.* Не будь таким жадным. ● *1.* I'm not greedy. *2.* Don't be greedy. *3.* Don't get greedy. *4.* You're greedy. *5.* Don't be so greedy.

**455. эксклюзивный** — *exclusive* — This word is used to describe something that is unique, limited, or restricted to a select group of people. It conveys a sense of luxury, prestige, or special treatment.

● *1.* Очень эксклюзивный. *2.* Зона у ринга была эксклюзивной. *3.* Специальное издание включало эксклюзивный контент. *4.* Показ мод Chichi был эксклюзивным. ● *1.* Very exclusive. *2.* The ringside area was exclusive. *3.* The special edition included exclusive content. *4.* The chichi fashion show was exclusive.

**456. страстный** — *passionate, ardent, impassioned* — This word is used to describe intense emotions or actions that are driven by strong feelings. It conveys a sense of fervor and enthusiasm in a particular activity or relationship.

• *1.* Их любовь была смертной и страстной. *2.* Я страстный. *3.* Он был известен как страстный звонарь. *4.* Она страстный защитник прав человека. *5.* Они наслаждались страстной интрижкой. *6.* Он написал страстное любовное письмо. *7.* Его страстная просьба была трогательной. *8.* Ее страстная защита выиграла дело. *9.* Она произнесла страстную речь. *10.* Страстное выступление вызвало слезы. • *1.* Their love was mortal and passionate. *2.* I'm passionate. *3.* He was known as a passionate beller. *4.* She is a passionate advocate for human rights. *5.* They enjoyed a passionate fling. *6.* He wrote an impassioned love letter. *7.* His impassioned plea was moving. *8.* Her impassioned defense won the case. *9.* She gave an impassioned speech. *10.* The impassioned performance brought tears.

**457. порочный** — *vicious* — The word 'порочный' is used to describe something or someone that is morally corrupt or evil. It conveys the idea of being harmful, wicked, or malicious in nature.

• *1.* Это порочный круг. *2.* Порочный круг. *3.* Они порочные. *4.* Это порочно. • *1.* It's a vicious circle. *2.* Vicious circle. *3.* They're vicious. *4.* It's vicious.

**458. элегантный** — *elegant, genteel* — This word is used to describe something or someone as stylish, sophisticated, and refined in appearance or behavior. It conveys a sense of grace, class, and tastefulness.

• *1.* Очень элегантно. *2.* Так элегантно. *3.* Это элегантно. *4.* Мантуя представляла собой элегантное платье. *5.* Ты очень элегантный. • *1.* Very elegant. *2.* So elegant. *3.* It's elegant. *4.* The mantua was an elegant gown. *5.* You're very elegant.

**459. статический** — *static* — The word 'статический' is used to describe something that is unchanging, stable, or stationary. It can refer to objects, situations, or conditions that remain constant or motionless over a period of time.

• *1.* Статическое электричество. *2.* Статическое электричество поразило ее. *3.* Воздух был настолько сухим, что вызывал статический заряд. • *1.* Static electricity. *2.* The static electricity shocked her. *3.* The air was so dry, causing static.

**460. тройной** — *triple, triplicate* — 'Тройной' is used to describe something that is three times the usual amount or size. It can also be used to indicate that something is made up of three parts or components.

• *1.* Тройная угроза. *2.* Тройной Шпигель. • *1.* Triple threat. *2.* Triple Spiegel.

**461. племенной** — *tribal* — The word 'племенной' is used to describe something that is related to or characteristic of a tribe or group of people with a common ancestry or culture. It can refer to customs, traditions, or relationships within a tribal community.

• *1.* Он носил племенную маску. *2.* Племенной язык находился под угрозой исчезновения. *3.* Племенные люди жили дружно. *4.* Она изучала племенные культуры. • *1.* He wore a tribal mask. *2.* The tribal language was endangered. *3.* The tribal people lived in harmony. *4.* She studied tribal cultures.

**462. маловероятный** — *unlikely* — This word is used to describe something that is not likely to happen or be true. It conveys a sense of improbability or unlikelihood in a situation or event.

• *1.* Это маловероятно. *2.* Маловероятно. *3.* Это кажется маловероятным. *4.* Кажется маловероятным. *5.* Это крайне маловероятно. • *1.* That's unlikely. *2.* Very unlikely. *3.* That seems unlikely. *4.* Seems unlikely. *5.* It's highly unlikely.

**463. логический** — *logical* — 'логический' is used to describe something that is based on reason, sound judgment, or clear thinking. It is used to indicate that something follows a logical sequence or is in accordance with the principles of logic.

• *1.* Должно быть логическое объяснение. *2.* Логический вывод был достигнут. *3.* Ее логический подход решил проблему. • *1.* There must be a logical explanation. *2.* The logical conclusion was reached. *3.* Her logical approach solved the problem.

**464. подходящий** — *suitable, eligible, propitious* — This word is used to describe something that is appropriate or fitting for a particular purpose or situation. It can also indicate that something is well-suited or advantageous in a given context.

• *1.* Темперамент, подходящий для лидерства. *2.* Подходящих кандидатов пригласили на собеседование. • *1.* A temperament suitable for leadership. *2.* The eligible candidates were called for interviews.

**465. взаимный** — *mutual* — 'Взаимный' is used to describe a relationship or action that is reciprocal or shared between two or more parties. It implies a sense of mutual understanding, cooperation, or benefit.
• *1.* Чувство взаимно. *2.* Это чувство взаимно. *3.* Это было взаимно. *4.* Это взаимно. *5.* Это не взаимно. • *1.* The feeling is mutual. *2.* The feeling's mutual. *3.* It was mutual. *4.* It's mutual. *5.* It's not mutual.

**466. эффектный** — *spectacular* — This word is used to describe something that is visually striking or impressive, often in a dramatic or eye-catching way. It is typically used to emphasize the impact or appeal of something.
• *1.* Ты выглядишь эффектно. • *1.* You look spectacular.

**467. белокурый** — *blond* — This word is used to describe someone with light-colored hair, typically ranging from pale yellow to golden. It can also be used to describe objects or animals with a similar light color.
• *1.* Белокурые волосы. • *1.* Blond hair.

**468. революционный** — *revolutionary* — 'Revolutionary' is used to describe something that is innovative, groundbreaking, or causing a significant change or upheaval. It can refer to ideas, movements, technologies, or any other aspect of society that brings about a major shift.
• *1.* Идеи теоретика были революционными. *2.* Ультразвуковая технология была революционной. *3.* Революционное движение имело целью захват власти. *4.* Новое лечение было революционным. *5.* Бионическая технология была революционной. • *1.* The theorist's ideas were revolutionary. *2.* The ultrasonic technology was revolutionary. *3.* The revolutionary movement aimed to seize power. *4.* The new treatment was revolutionary. *5.* The bionic technology was revolutionary.

**469. враждебный** — *hostile* — 'Враждебный' is used to describe someone or something that is unfriendly, antagonistic, or opposed to another. It conveys a sense of hostility or animosity towards a person or group.

• *1.* Не будьте враждебны. *2.* Почему ты такой враждебный? *3.* Враждебное поглощение. *4.* Враждебный вниз! *5.* Поглощение было враждебным. • *1.* Don't be hostile. *2.* Why are you being so hostile? *3.* Hostile takeover. *4.* Hostile down! *5.* The takeover was hostile.

**470. ежегодный** — *annual, yearly* — This word is used to describe events, occurrences, or activities that happen once a year. It emphasizes the regularity and consistency of something happening on an annual basis.

• *1.* Он организовал ежегодный бизнес-пау-вау. *2.* Она завершила ежегодную оценку. *3.* Они посетили девятый ежегодный фестиваль. *4.* Ежегодный доход увеличивается. *5.* Она организовала ежегодный банкет. • *1.* He organized the annual business powwow. *2.* She completed the annual evaluation. *3.* They attended the ninth annual festival. *4.* The annual income is increasing. *5.* She organized the annual banquet.

**471. почетный** — *honorable, honorary, honourable* — 'почетный' is used to describe someone or something that is deserving of respect or recognition for their achievements or qualities. It can also be used to indicate a position or title that is given as an honor or privilege.

• *1.* Очень почетно. *2.* У нее почетная профессия. *3.* Почетное упоминание было вполне заслуженным. *4.* Почетное увольнение. *5.* Он получил почетное упоминание. • *1.* Very honorable. *2.* She has an honorable profession. *3.* The honorable mention was well-deserved. *4.* Honorable discharge. *5.* He received an honorable mention.

**472. хрупкий** — *fragile, frail, brittle* — This word is used to describe something that is delicate, easily broken, or weak. It can refer to physical objects, emotions, or situations that are vulnerable or easily damaged.

• *1.* Это хрупкое. *2.* Она хрупкая. *3.* Это очень хрупко. *4.* Он хрупкий. *5.* Будьте осторожны, он хрупкий. *6.* Ее костлявое телосложение делало ее хрупкой. *7.* Она выглядела истощенной и хрупкой. *8.* Хрупкое печенье рассыпалось у нее в руке. *9.* Хрупкий снежный покров был коварным. *10.* Ее хрупкое поведение смягчилось в солнечном свете. *11.* Хрупкие ветки трещали на ветру. • *1.* It's fragile. *2.* She's fragile. *3.* It's very fragile. *4.* He's fragile. *5.* Be careful, it's fragile. *6.* Her bony frame made her look frail. *7.* She looked malnourished and frail. *8.* The brittle cookie crumbled in her hand. *9.* The brittle snow cover was treacherous. *10.* Her brittle demeanor softened in the sunlight. *11.* The brittle branches snapped in the wind.

**473. искренний** — *sincere, heartfelt, candid* — This word is used to describe something that is genuine and honest, without any hidden motives or deception. It conveys a sense of authenticity and openness in communication or emotions.

• *1.* Мои искренние извинения. *2.* Мои искренние соболезнования. *3.* Он выразил искреннюю благодарность. *4.* Она принесла искренние извинения. *5.* Извиняющийся тон был искренним. *6.* Благодарности были искренними. *7.* Ее признание было искренним. *8.* Искреннее выражение эмоций было трогательным. *9.* Они принесли искренние извинения. *10.* Тексты баллады были искренними. • *1.* My sincere apologies. *2.* My sincere condolences. *3.* He gave a sincere thankyou. *4.* She made a sincere apology. *5.* The apologetic tone was sincere. *6.* The acknowledgements were heartfelt. *7.* Her confession was heartfelt. *8.* The heartfelt expression of emotion was moving. *9.* They offered a heartfelt apologise. *10.* The ballad lyrics were heartfelt.

**474. бессмертный** — *immortal, undying* — The word 'бессмертный' is used to describe something or someone that is immortal or undying, suggesting that they will live forever or never be forgotten. It conveys a sense of eternal existence or lasting significance.

• *1.* Ты сделаешь меня бессмертным другом. *2.* Творчество художника стало бессмертным. *3.* Мы бессмертны. *4.* Она стремилась создать бессмертное наследие. *5.* Он добился бессмертной славы. *6.* Она спела песню бессмертной надежды. *7.* Она заявляет о своей бессмертной любви. *8.* Наследие бессмертного героя продолжает жить. *9.* Бессмертная история любви покорила сердца. • *1.* You will make me an immortal mate. *2.* The artist's work became immortal. *3.* We are immortal. *4.* She aimed to create an immortal legacy. *5.* He achieved immortal fame. *6.* She sang a song of undying hope. *7.* She proclaims her undying love. *8.* The legacy of the undying hero lives on. *9.* The undying love story captured hearts.

**475. решающий** — *crucial, decisive, conclusive* — This word is used to describe something that is crucial, decisive, or conclusive in a situation. It emphasizes the importance of a particular action, event, or decision in determining the outcome or result.

● *1.* Своевременное представление доклада имело решающее значение. *2.* Полузащитник сделал решающий пас. *3.* Отдых имеет решающее значение для заживления сухожилий. *4.* Настройка диафрагмы имела решающее значение. *5.* Поддержка лиц, осуществляющих уход, имела решающее значение для их выздоровления. *6.* Она сыграла решающую роль. *7.* Кайо – решающая победа в боксе. ● *1.* The punctual submission of the report was crucial. *2.* The midfield player made a crucial pass. *3.* Rest is crucial for tendon healing. *4.* The aperture setting was crucial. *5.* Caregiver support was crucial for their recovery. *6.* She played a decisive role. *7.* A kayo is a decisive victory in boxing.

**476. единственный** — *sole, unopposed* — This word is used to describe something that is the only one of its kind or that has no equal. It emphasizes uniqueness and exclusivity in a situation where there is only one option or possibility.

● *1.* Это моя единственная цель. *2.* Он был единственным владельцем ключа. *3.* Он был единственным жильцом. ● *1.* It is my sole purpose. *2.* He was the sole possessor of the key. *3.* He was the sole occupant.

**477. биологический** — *biological* — This word is used to describe things related to biology or living organisms. It can be used to talk about biological processes, characteristics, or substances. It is often used in scientific contexts.

● *1.* Это биологическое. *2.* Ваши биологические часы тикают. *3.* Мой биологический отец. ● *1.* It's biological. *2.* Your biological clock is ticking. *3.* My biological father.

**478. невежественный** — *ignorant* — The word 'невежественный' is used to describe someone who lacks knowledge or understanding in a particular subject or area. It is often used to criticize someone for being uninformed or ignorant about a topic.

● *1.* Ты такой невежественный. *2.* Вы невежественны. *3.* Невежественные комментарии оскорбили ее. *4.* Ты невежественный дурак! *5.* Он говорил с позиции невежественных предположений. • *1.* You're so ignorant. *2.* You're ignorant. *3.* The ignorant comments offended her. *4.* You ignorant fool! *5.* He spoke from a place of ignorant assumptions.

**479. последовательный** — *consistent, coherent, successive, consecutive* — This word is used to describe something that follows a logical order or sequence without deviation. It can refer to actions, decisions, or arguments that are connected and make sense in relation to each other.

• *1.* По крайней мере, вы последовательны. *2.* Нам нужно было представить последовательные аргументы. *3.* Ее мысли были последовательными и организованными. *4.* В рассказе не было последовательного развития сюжета. *5.* Он представил последовательный план действий. *6.* Он предпринял несколько последовательных попыток. *7.* Они провели ряд последовательных встреч. *8.* Последовательные числа образовывали последовательность. • *1.* At least you're consistent. *2.* We needed to present a coherent argument. *3.* Her thoughts were coherent and organized. *4.* The story lacked coherent plot development. *5.* He presented a coherent plan of action. *6.* He made several successive attempts. *7.* They held a series of successive meetings. *8.* The consecutive numbers formed a sequence.

**480. грустно** — *sadly* — 'грустно' is used to describe a feeling of sadness or sorrow in a situation or towards a person. It conveys a sense of melancholy or disappointment.

• *1.* Он грустно покачал головой. *2.* Она грустно покачала головой. *3.* Он грустно посмотрел на нее. • *1.* He shook his head sadly. *2.* She shook her head sadly. *3.* He looked at her sadly.

**481. блестящий** — *shiny, brilliant, lustrous* — This word is used to describe something that is shiny, brilliant, or lustrous. It is often used to describe objects that reflect light or have a polished appearance.

• *1.* Он блестящий. *2.* Новое блестящее кольцо блестело. *3.* Сорока собирала блестящие предметы. *4.* Мундштук был отполированным и блестящим. *5.* Металлическое стремя было полированным и блестящим. *6.* Это блестяще. *7.* Это было блестяще. *8.* Это блестящая идея. *9.* Абсолютно блестящий. *10.* Блестящий, блестящий. • *1.* It's shiny. *2.* The shiny new ring glittered. *3.* The magpie gathered shiny objects. *4.* The mouthpiece was polished and shiny. *5.* The metal stirrup was polished and shiny. *6.* That's brilliant. *7.* It was brilliant. *8.* That's a brilliant idea. *9.* Absolutely brilliant. *10.* Brilliant, brilliant.

**482. культурный** — *cultural* — This word is used to describe something or someone that is related to culture, refinement, or education. It can refer to manners, behavior, or activities that are considered sophisticated or intellectual.

● *1.* Культурные различия. *2.* Программа культурного обмена прошла успешно. *3.* Она с гордостью относилась к своему культурному наследию. *4.* Она изучала культурные традиции. *5.* Культурные различия очаровывали ее. ● *1.* Cultural differences. *2.* The cultural exchange program was a success. *3.* She embraced her cultural heritage with pride. *4.* She studied the cultural traditions. *5.* The cultural differences fascinated her.

**483. психологический** — *psychological* — This word is used to describe something related to the mind, emotions, or behavior of a person. It is often used in the context of psychology, therapy, or mental health.

● *1.* Психологическая война. *2.* Психологические последствия были разрушительными. *3.* Психологическое воздействие этого события было значительным. *4.* Психологическую травму было трудно преодолеть. *5.* Ее психологическая оценка была очень тщательной. ● *1.* Psychological warfare. *2.* The psychological effects were devastating. *3.* The psychological impact of the event was significant. *4.* The psychological trauma was difficult to overcome. *5.* Her psychological evaluation was very thorough.

**484. расистский** — *racist* — This word is used to describe attitudes, actions, or beliefs that discriminate against or show prejudice towards people of different races. It is often used to criticize behavior that is discriminatory or offensive.

● *1.* Она столкнулась с расистским фанатиком. *2.* Расистские комментарии вызвали большое возмущение. *3.* Владельца магазина обвинили в расистском поведении. *4.* Группа протестовала против расистской политики. *5.* Расистским настроениям нет места в обществе. ● *1.* She encountered a racist bigot. *2.* The racist comments caused a lot of outrage. *3.*

The store owner was accused of racist behavior. *4.* The group protested against racist policies. *5.* Racist attitudes have no place in society.

**485. поровну** — *equally* — 'Equally' is used to indicate that something is divided or distributed evenly among multiple parties or individuals. It can also be used to describe actions or qualities that are shared or balanced between different entities.
• *1.* Он разделил деньги поровну. • *1.* He divided the money equally.

**486. сознательный** — *conscious, conscientious* — This word is used to describe someone who is aware of their actions and takes responsibility for them. It can also refer to someone who is diligent, careful, and thorough in their work.
• *1.* Она предприняла сознательное усилие по переработке отходов. • *1.* She made a conscious effort to recycle.

**487. идентичный** — *identical* — This word is used to describe two or more things that are exactly the same in every way. It is often used to emphasize the similarity or exactness of something in comparison to another.
• *1.* Они идентичны. *2.* Это идентично. *3.* Идентичные близнецы. *4.* Отпечатки пальцев были почти идентичны. *5.* Двойник выглядел почти идентично. • *1.* They're identical. *2.* It's identical. *3.* Identical twins. *4.* The fingerprints were nearly identical. *5.* The doppelganger looked almost identical.

**488. конфиденциальный** — *confidential* — This word is used to describe information or communication that is meant to be kept private or secret. It implies a level of trust and discretion in handling sensitive or classified material.
• *1.* Это конфиденциально. *2.* Это конфиденциальная информация. *3.* Она поделилась конфиденциальным разговором со своей подругой. *4.* Документ был помечен как конфиденциальный. *5.* Информация строго конфиденциальна. • *1.* It's confidential. *2.* That's confidential information. *3.* She shared a confidential conversation with her friend. *4.* The document was marked as confidential. *5.* The information is highly confidential.

**489. умственно** — *mentally* — 'Умственно' is used to describe actions, processes, or states that pertain to the mind or intellect.

It indicates that something is related to mental activity or cognitive functions.

● *1.* Ее любимыми были умственно стимулирующие головоломки. ● *1.* The mentally stimulating puzzles were her favorite.

**490. сентиментальный** — *sentimental, maudlin, slushy, hokey* — This word is used to describe something that is overly emotional, nostalgic, or melodramatic. It often refers to sentimental or cheesy expressions of emotion that may be seen as insincere or exaggerated.

● *1.* Не будьте сентиментальны. *2.* Сентиментальное значение. *3.* Оно имеет сентиментальную ценность. *4.* Давайте не будем сентиментальными. *5.* Старая Веста имела сентиментальную ценность. *6.* Она находит сентиментальные фильмы трогательными. *7.* С ее сентиментальными вспышками становилось трудно справляться. *8.* Он был в сентиментальном настроении. *9.* Его сентиментальное поведение меня раздражало. *10.* После расставания она стала сентиментальной.
● *1.* Don't get sentimental. *2.* Sentimental value. *3.* It has sentimental value. *4.* Let's not get sentimental. *5.* The old vesta held sentimental value. *6.* She finds maudlin movies touching. *7.* Her maudlin outbursts were becoming difficult to handle. *8.* He was in a maudlin mood. *9.* His maudlin behavior was wearing on me. *10.* She became maudlin after the breakup.

**491. органический** — *organic* — This word is used to describe something that is natural, free from synthetic chemicals or additives. It is often used in reference to food, farming practices, or materials that are environmentally friendly and sustainable.

● *1.* Он изучал разложение органических веществ. *2.* Криогенная заморозка используется для сохранения органических веществ. *3.* Она предпочитала есть органическую пищу неорганической. *4.* Она ела только органические продукты. *5.* Он успешный производитель органических фруктов. ● *1.* He studied the decomp of organic matter. *2.* Cryogenic freezing is used to preserve organic matter. *3.* She preferred to eat organic food over inorganic. *4.* She ate only organic produce. *5.* He's a successful grower of organic fruits.

**492. неуместный** — *inappropriate* — 'Неуместный' is used to describe something that is not suitable or proper for a particular situation. It conveys the idea of being out of place or unsuitable in a given context.

● *1.* Это неуместно. *2.* Это было неуместно. *3.* Это действительно неуместно. *4.* Это совершенно неуместно. *5.* Он вел себя отвратительно неуместно. ● *1.* It's inappropriate. *2.* That was inappropriate. *3.* This is really inappropriate. *4.* This is totally inappropriate. *5.* He acted disgustingly inappropriate.

**493. соответствующие** — *relevant* — This word is used to describe something that is appropriate or fitting for a particular situation or context. It indicates that something is directly related or applicable to a specific topic or circumstance.

● *1.* Кандидат имел соответствующий опыт. *2.* Копия соответствующих сторон. ● *1.* The candidate had relevant experience. *2.* Cc the relevant parties.

**494. объективный** — *objective* — This word is used to describe something that is unbiased, fair, and based on facts rather than personal opinions or feelings. It is often used in discussions, debates, and analysis to emphasize the importance of being impartial and neutral.

● *1.* Их целью было оставаться объективными. *2.* Вы не объективны. *3.* Нам нужна объективная оценка. *4.* Ему нужно было объективное мнение. *5.* Она оставалась объективной на протяжении всего процесса. ● *1.* Their goal was to stay objective. *2.* You're not objective. *3.* We need an objective assessment. *4.* He needed an objective opinion. *5.* She remained objective throughout the trial.

**495. скромный** — *modest, humble, lowly, coy* — This word is used to describe someone who is not boastful or arrogant, but rather humble and unassuming. It can also be used to describe something that is simple or unpretentious.

● *1.* Не будьте скромными. *2.* Не будь таким скромным. *3.* Ох, не скромничайте. *4.* Она скромна. *5.* Вы скромны. *6.* Добро пожаловать в мою скромную обитель. *7.* Добро пожаловать в нашу скромную обитель. *8.* Будь он таким скромным. *9.* Она скромно рассказывала о своих достижениях. *10.* Он был скромным человеком. *11.* Она называла его скромным дворнягой. *12.* Он работал скромным стажером. *13.* Он прожил скромную жизнь. *14.* Скромный слуга старательно убирался. *15.* Скромный ответ возбудил его любопытство. ● *1.* Don't be modest. *2.* Don't be so modest. *3.*

Oh, don't be modest. *4.* She's being modest. *5.* You're being modest. *6.* Welcome to my humble abode. *7.* Welcome to our humble abode. *8.* Be it ever so humble. *9.* She was humble about her achievements. *10.* He was a humble person. *11.* She called him a lowly cur. *12.* He worked as a lowly intern. *13.* He lived a lowly life. *14.* The lowly servant cleaned diligently. *15.* The coy response piqued his curiosity.

**496. автоматический** — *automatic* — This word is used to describe something that operates or functions without the need for human intervention. It can also be used to describe actions or processes that occur automatically or spontaneously.

● *1.* Это автоматически. *2.* В доме есть автоматические гаражные ворота. *3.* Автомобиль имеет автоматическую коробку передач. *4.* Все автоматически. *5.* У нее автоматическая реакция на критику. ● *1.* It's automatic. *2.* The house has an automatic garage door. *3.* The car has automatic transmission. *4.* Everything's automatic. *5.* She has an automatic reaction to criticism.

**497. законный** — *legitimate, rightful, lawful, justifiable* — This word is used to describe something that is in accordance with the law, rightful, or justifiable. It implies that the action or object is legitimate and conforms to legal or moral standards.

● *1.* Это законный вопрос. *2.* Это законно. *3.* Она проверила законные источники. *4.* Это законное беспокойство. *5.* Законный наследник унаследовал имение. *6.* Она стала законным обладателем. *7.* Они искали законного владельца. *8.* В договоре прописаны законные права и обязанности. *9.* Соблюдена законная процедура получения разрешений. *10.* Действия не были признаны законными. *11.* Она всегда соблюдала законные нормы. ● *1.* It's a legitimate question. *2.* It's legitimate. *3.* She checked for legitimate sources. *4.* It's a legitimate concern. *5.* The legitimate heir inherited the estate. *6.* She became the rightful possessor. *7.* They sought the rightful possessor. *8.* The contract outlined the lawful rights and responsibilities. *9.* The lawful process was followed for obtaining permits. *10.* The action was not deemed lawful. *11.* She always abided by lawful standards.

**498. взрывной** — *explosive* — 'Explosive' is used to describe something that is sudden, intense, and powerful. It can refer to physical explosions or metaphorical situations that are dynamic and impactful. It conveys a sense of energy and force.

● *1.* Встреча переросла в взрывной спор. *2.* Фейерверк был взрывным. ● *1.* The meeting turned into an explosive argument. *2.* The fireworks display was explosive.

**499. цифровой** — *digital* — This word is used to describe something that is related to or involves digital technology, such as digital devices, digital content, or digital communication. It can also refer to something that is represented or stored in numerical form.

● *1.* Это цифровой. *2.* Она предпочитала аналоговый, а не цифровой. *3.* Биткойн -- это цифровая валюта. *4.* Цифровые часы оправдали ее ожидания. *5.* Компания вела цифровой реестр. ● *1.* It's digital. *2.* She preferred analog over digital. *3.* Bitcoin is a digital currency. *4.* The digital clock met her expectation. *5.* The company maintained a digital ledger.

**500. алкогольный** — *alcoholic* — This word is used to describe something that is related to or contains alcohol. It can refer to beverages, substances, or even behaviors that involve the consumption of alcohol.

● *1.* На вечеринке подавали алкогольные напитки. *2.* Абсент – крепкий алкогольный напиток. *3.* Алкогольный напиток был крепким. ● *1.* Alcoholic drinks were served at the party. *2.* Absinthe is a strong alcoholic drink. *3.* The alcoholic beverage was strong.

**501. токсичный** — *toxic* — 'Токсичный' is used to describe something that is harmful, damaging, or poisonous. It can refer to physical substances, relationships, behaviors, or environments that have a negative impact on one's well-being.

● *1.* Это токсично? *2.* Она токсична. *3.* Мусоросжигательный завод выделял токсичные пары. *4.* Плутоний -- высокотоксичный элемент. *5.* Жидкость токсична. ● *1.* Is it toxic? *2.* She's toxic. *3.* The incinerator emitted toxic fumes. *4.* Plutonium is a highly toxic element. *5.* The fluid is toxic.

**502. ненужный** — *unnecessary, unwanted, superfluous* — This word is used to describe something that is not needed or desired, something that is excessive or surplus to requirements. It conveys the idea of being unnecessary or unwanted in a particular context.

• *1.* Это совершенно ненужно. *2.* Никаких ненужных рисков. *3.* Так ненужно. *4.* Это было совершенно ненужно. *5.* Постарайтесь избегать ненужного стресса. *6.* Она чувствовала себя ненужной в группе. • *1.* This is completely unnecessary. *2.* No unnecessary risks. *3.* So unnecessary. *4.* That was totally unnecessary. *5.* Try to avoid unnecessary stress. *6.* She felt unwanted in the group.

**503. красиво** — *beautifully, handsomely* — 'Красиво' is used to describe something that is aesthetically pleasing or attractive. It can be used to describe physical appearance, actions, or objects in a positive way.

• *1.* Красиво сделано. *2.* Она красиво украсила торт. *3.* Шторы красиво драпируются на окне. *4.* Змея была красивого цвета. *5.* Закуска была красиво представлена. *6.* Она была красиво одета. • *1.* Beautifully done. *2.* She decorated the cake beautifully. *3.* The curtains drape beautifully over the window. *4.* The serpent was beautifully colored. *5.* The appetizer was beautifully presented. *6.* She was handsomely dressed.

**504. исторический** — *historical, historic* — 'Iсторический' is used to describe something that is related to history or has historical significance. It can refer to events, places, objects, or people that are important in the past and have had an impact on the present.

• *1.* Эксгумация исторического деятеля вызвала споры. *2.* В книге описан исторический период. *3.* Историческая личность была неизвестна. *4.* Диорама изображала историческую сцену. *5.* Фракия – историческая область. *6.* Это исторический момент. *7.* Это историческое событие. *8.* Они посетили исторический город. *9.* Они посетили историческую Кордову. *10.* Исторический документ бережно сохранялся. • *1.* The historical figure's exhumation was controversial. *2.* The book described the historical period. *3.* The historical figure was unknown. *4.* The diorama depicted a historical scene. *5.* Thrace is a historical region. *6.* This is a historic moment. *7.* It's historic. *8.* They visited the historic burg. *9.* They visited the historic Cordoba. *10.* The historic document was carefully preserved.

**505. эмоционально** — *emotionally* — 'Эмоционально' is used to describe something that is related to or influenced by emotions. It can be used to convey how someone feels or reacts in a particular situation.

● *1.* Она начала эмоционально выздоравливать. ● *1.* She began to recover emotionally.

**506. видимый** — *visible* — 'Visible' is used to describe something that can be seen or perceived easily. It indicates that the object or phenomenon is not hidden or obscured from view, and is able to be observed by the naked eye.

● *1.* Есть видимое оружие? ● *1.* Any visible weapons?

**507. подводный** — *underwater, undersea* — 'подводный' is used to describe something that is located or occurring beneath the surface of water. It can refer to underwater creatures, activities, or environments.

● *1.* Лодка была построена для подводных исследований. *2.* Они исследовали подводные пещеры. *3.* Она любила фотографировать подводные сцены. *4.* Миссия заключалась в изучении подводной жизни. ● *1.* The boat was built for underwater exploration. *2.* They explored the underwater caves. *3.* She loved to photograph underwater scenes. *4.* The mission was to study underwater life.

**508. выдающийся** — *outstanding, eminent* — 'Выдающийся' is used to describe someone or something that is exceptional, remarkable, or distinguished in a particular field. It signifies a high level of achievement or talent that sets the individual or object apart from others.

● *1.* О, выдающийся. *2.* Выдающийся поэт получил престижную награду. *3.* Выдающийся учёный сделал революционное открытие. ● *1.* Oh, outstanding. *2.* The eminent poet received a prestigious award. *3.* The eminent scientist made a groundbreaking discovery.

**509. неизбежный** — *inevitable, imminent, unavoidable, inescapable* — This word is used to describe something that is bound to happen, cannot be avoided, or is certain to occur in the near future. It conveys a sense of inevitability and impending occurrence.

● *1.* Это неизбежно. *2.* Это было неизбежно. *3.* Думаю, это было неизбежно. *4.* Ты просто оттягиваешь неизбежное. *5.* Падение было неизбежным. *6.* Расторжение контракта было неизбежным. *7.* Нарушение ядра неизбежно. *8.* Восхождение на престол было неизбежным. *9.* Это неизбежно. *10.* Это было неизбежно. *11.* Тропа войны была неизбежна. *12.* Но это неизбежно. *13.* Невидимый, неразрушимый и совершенно неизбежный. *14.* Невидимый, нерушимый, неизбежный. *15.* Трясина была неизбежна. • *1.* It's inevitable. *2.* It was inevitable. *3.* I guess it was inevitable. *4.* You're just delaying the inevitable. *5.* The decline was inevitable. *6.* The termination of the contract was imminent. *7.* Core breach is imminent. *8.* The ascension to the throne was imminent. *9.* It's unavoidable. *10.* It was unavoidable. *11.* The warpath was unavoidable. *12.* But it's unavoidable. *13.* Invisible, indestructible, and completely inescapable. *14.* Invisible, indestructible, inescapable. *15.* The mire was inescapable.

**510. элитный** — *elite* — This word is used to describe something or someone as being of the highest quality, exclusive, or superior in a particular group or category. It conveys a sense of prestige, sophistication, and excellence.
• *1.* Мэм, мы элитная боевая сила. • *1.* Ma'am, we are an elite fighting force.

**511. кислый** — *sour* — This word is used to describe something that has a sharp, acidic taste. It can be used to describe foods like lemons or vinegar, as well as emotions or expressions that are bitter or unpleasant.
• *1.* Виски кислый. *2.* Кислый виноград. *3.* Тамариндовая паста была кислой. *4.* Квашеная капуста была кислой и вкусной. *5.* Краут был кислым. • *1.* Whiskey sour. *2.* Sour grapes. *3.* The tamarind paste was sour. *4.* The sauerkraut was sour and delicious. *5.* The kraut was sour.

**512. жестокий** — *fierce, cruel, brutal, brutish* — 'Жестокий' is used to describe something or someone that is characterized by a lack of mercy or compassion, often displaying harsh or brutal behavior. It conveys a sense of cruelty, fierceness, or brutality.
• *1.* Ее осуждение было жестоким. *2.* Конкуренция была жестокой. *3.* Росомаха – жестокое животное. *4.* У нее была жестокая решимость. *5.* Он был известен как жестокий риммер. *6.* Вы жестоки. *7.* Это жестоко. *8.* Не будьте жестокими. *9.* Почему ты такой жестокий? *10.* Как ты можешь быть таким жестоким? *11.* Это жестоко. *12.* Это было ж-

естоко. *13.* Довольно жестоко. *14.* Будьте жестокими. *15.* Девушка стала жертвой жестокого убийства! *16.* Они столкнулись с группой жестоких мужчин. *17.* Жестокий поступок был встречен неодобрительно. *18.* Жестокое отношение ее смутило. ● *1.* Her condemnation was fierce. *2.* The competition was fierce. *3.* The wolverine is a fierce animal. *4.* She had a fierce determination. *5.* He was known as a fierce rimmer. *6.* You're cruel. *7.* That's cruel. *8.* Don't be cruel. *9.* Why are you so cruel? *10.* How can you be so cruel? *11.* It's brutal. *12.* It was brutal. *13.* Pretty brutal. *14.* Be brutal. *15.* Girl victim in brutal slaying! *16.* They encountered a group of brutish men. *17.* The brutish act was met with disapproval. *18.* The brutish attitude unsettled her.

**513. небесный** — *heavenly* — The word 'небесный' is used to describe something that is related to or resembles heaven in a positive way. It can be used to describe things like beauty, peace, or happiness.

● *1.* Небесные солдаты! *2.* Небесный Боже! ● *1.* Heavenly Soldiers! *2.* Heavenly God!

**514. респектабельный** — *respectable* — 'Респектабельный' is used to describe someone or something that is worthy of respect, admiration, or esteem. It implies a sense of dignity, honor, and good reputation. It is often used to describe a person's appearance, behavior, or social status.

● *1.* Даже в поражении она оставалась респектабельной. *2.* На мероприятие она пришла в респектабельном наряде. ● *1.* Even in defeat, she remained respectable. *2.* She wore a respectable outfit to the event.

**515. случайный** — *casual, random, accidental, incidental* — This word is used to describe something that happens by chance or without a specific reason. It can refer to a random event, an accidental occurrence, or something that is incidental or casual in nature.

● *1.* Это случайно. *2.* Он открыл дверь случайным сообщением. *3.* Она попрощалась со случайной сией. *4.* Это так случайно. *5.* Это случайно. *6.* Не случайно. *7.* Насколько это случайно? *8.* Это совершенно случайно. *9.* Случайное открытие привело к научному прорыву. *10.* Разбитая ваза была случайностью. *11.* Автокатастрофа произошла в

результате случайного столкновения. *12.* Механизм блоки-
ровки предотвращает случайное открытие. *13.* Травма ребенка была чисто случайной. *14.* Шум был просто случайным. *15.* Они внесли небольшие, случайные изменения. • *1.*
It's casual. *2.* He answered the door with a casual whassup. *3.*
She bid farewell with a casual seeya. *4.* That's so random. *5.*
It's random. *6.* Not random. *7.* How random is that? *8.* It's
totally random. *9.* The accidental discovery led to a scientific
breakthrough. *10.* The broken vase was an accidental mishap.
*11.* The car crash was an accidental collision. *12.* The interlock
mechanism prevents accidental opening. *13.* The child's injury
was purely accidental. *14.* The noise was merely incidental. *15.*
They made small, incidental changes.

**516. радикальный** — *radical, drastic* — The word 'радикальный' is used to describe something that is extreme,
fundamental, or revolutionary in nature. It implies a significant
and often dramatic change or action that goes beyond the
usual or conventional.

• *1.* Левая точка зрения была радикальной. *2.* Изгнание
было радикальной мерой. • *1.* The leftist view was radical. *2.*
The expulsion was a drastic measure.

**517. защитный** — *protective, defensive* — 'Защитный' is
used to describe something that provides protection or defense
against potential harm or danger. It can refer to physical objects,
actions, or measures taken to ensure safety and security.

• *1.* Защитная опека. *2.* Она носила защитный головной
убор. *3.* На ней было защитное снаряжение от серных
паров. *4.* Во время строительства он носил защитную маску.
*5.* Сварщик был в защитном снаряжении. *6.* Никаких защи-
тных ран. • *1.* Protective custody. *2.* She wore a protective
headgear. *3.* She wore protective gear for the sulfuric fumes.
*4.* He wore a protective mask during the construction. *5.* The
welder wore protective gear. *6.* No defensive wounds.

**518. возмутительный** — *outrageous, ungodly* — 'Возмутительный' is used to describe something that is shocking, offensive,
or morally wrong. It conveys a sense of outrage or disbelief at
the behavior or situation being described.

• *1.* Это возмутительно. *2.* Его поведение было возмутите-
льным. *3.* Цены были возмутительными. *4.* Это возмутит-

ельное обвинение. *5.* Она носила возмутительный наряд. ●
*1.* This is outrageous. *2.* His behavior was outrageous. *3.* The prices were outrageous. *4.* That's an outrageous accusation. *5.* She wore an outrageous outfit.

**519. волосатый** — *hairy* — 'Волосатый' is used to describe something or someone that has a lot of hair. It can refer to animals, people, or objects that have a hairy or furry appearance.
● *1.* Монстр был волосатый. *2.* У него была волосатая грудь. *3.* И волосатый. ● *1.* The monster was hairy. *2.* He had a hairy chest. *3.* And hairy.

**520. милостивый** — *gracious, merciful* — The word 'милостивый' is used to describe someone who shows kindness, compassion, and forgiveness towards others. It conveys a sense of mercy and generosity in their actions and behavior.
● *1.* Боже милостивый! *2.* О, боже мой, милостивый. *3.* Боже мой, милостивый. *4.* О, милостивый. *5.* Милостивый я! *6.* Бог милостив. *7.* Справедливость, милостивое небо! *8.* Господь милостив. ● *1.* Goodness gracious! *2.* Oh, my goodness gracious. *3.* Good gracious me. *4.* Oh, gracious. *5.* Gracious me! *6.* God is merciful. *7.* Justice, merciful heaven! *8.* The Lord is merciful.

**521. искусственный** — *artificial* — This word is used to describe something that is not natural or real, but instead made by humans. It can refer to objects, materials, or even behaviors that are not genuine or authentic.
● *1.* Подсластитель был изготовлен из искусственных ингредиентов. *2.* Сперму использовали для искусственного оплодотворения. *3.* Цветы выглядели искусственными, но были настоящими. *4.* Технологии искусственного интеллекта стремительно развиваются. *5.* Искусственный интеллект был развит. ● *1.* The sweetener was made from artificial ingredients. *2.* The semen was used for artificial insemination. *3.* The flowers looked artificial but were real. *4.* The artificial intelligence technology is advancing rapidly. *5.* The artificial intelligence was advanced.

**522. пьяный** — *drunken, boozy, tipsy, woozy* — This word is used to describe someone who has consumed alcohol and is intoxicated. It can also be used to describe a feeling of dizziness or disorientation.

● *1.* Пьяный смех заполнил бар. *2.* Ее пьяная болтовня была чистой тарабарщиной. *3.* Пьяный мужчина споткнулся по улице. *4.* Пьяный ублюдок выставил себя дураком. *5.* Ночь была наполнена пьяным разгулом. *6.* Она почувствовала эффект пьяного коктейля. *7.* Вечеринка стала немного пьяной. *8.* Он слишком пьян. *9.* На ее лице появилась пьяная улыбка. *10.* После одной порции она почувствовала себя - немного пьяной. ● *1.* The drunken laughter filled the bar. *2.* Her drunken ramblings were pure gibberish. *3.* The drunken man stumbled down the street. *4.* The drunken gobshite made a fool of himself. *5.* The night was filled with boozy revelry. *6.* She felt the effects of the boozy cocktail. *7.* The party got a little boozy. *8.* He's a bit too boozy. *9.* A tipsy smile appeared on her face. *10.* She felt a little tipsy after one drink.

**523. полый** — *hollow* — This word is used to describe something that is empty or has a space inside. It can refer to objects like a hollow tree trunk or a hollow chocolate bunny, as well as abstract concepts like hollow promises or hollow victories.

● *1.* У старого дерева был полый ствол. ● *1.* The old tree had a hollow trunk.

**524. детский** — *childish, childlike, infantile* — This word is used to describe something that is characteristic of or suitable for children, or something that is immature or lacking in sophistication. It can also refer to something that is innocent or pure in a childlike way.

● *1.* Его отругали за детскую шалость. *2.* Ты ведешь себя по-детски. *3.* Ее детское поведение раздражало родителей. *4.* Художник запечатлел радость детской невинности. *5.* Детский спор был быстро разрешен. *6.* Они участвовали в детских играх. *7.* У него был детский энтузиазм. *8.* Ее детское удивление никогда не угасало. *9.* Детский рисунок поразил их воображение. *10.* Ее детская невинность была очаровательна. ● *1.* He was scolded for his childish prank. *2.* You're being childish. *3.* Her childish behavior annoyed her parents. *4.* The artist captured the joy of childish innocence. *5.* The childish argument was quickly resolved. *6.* They engaged in childlike play. *7.* He had a childlike enthusiasm. *8.* Her childlike wonder never faded. *9.* The childlike drawing captured their imagination. *10.*

Her childlike innocence was endearing.

**525. неустойчивый** — *unstable, erratic, woozy, unsustainable* — This word is used to describe something that is not steady or reliable, often changing or fluctuating unpredictably. It can refer to physical objects, emotions, or situations that are not sustainable or secure.

• *1.* Стол был неустойчив. *2.* Он был психологически неустойчив. *3.* Шатающийся стул был неустойчив. *4.* Пол был неустойчив. *5.* Его пульс неустойчивый. *6.* Они столкнулись с последствиями неустойчивых решений. *7.* Он протестовал против неустойчивого развития. *8.* Она беспокоилась о неустойчивой жизни. *9.* Компания столкнулась с неустойчивым долговым кризисом. *10.* Их деловая практика была неустойчивой. • *1.* The table was unstable. *2.* He was psychologically unstable. *3.* The wobbly chair was unstable. *4.* The floor was unstable. *5.* His pulse is erratic. *6.* They faced the consequences of unsustainable decisions. *7.* He protested against unsustainable development. *8.* She worried about unsustainable living. *9.* The company faced an unsustainable debt crisis. *10.* Their business practices were unsustainable.

**526. экзотический** — *exotic* — The word 'экзотический' is used to describe something that is foreign, unusual, or strikingly different from what is familiar or typical. It is often used to refer to things such as food, animals, or travel destinations.

• *1.* Что-то экзотическое. *2.* Она собрала целый зверинец экзотических питомцев. *3.* Аромат был экзотическим. *4.* Ее вкус наслаждался экзотическими вкусами. *5.* Он попробовал экзотический деликатес. • *1.* Something exotic. *2.* She collected a menagerie of exotic pets. *3.* The scent was exotic. *4.* Her palate savored the exotic flavors. *5.* He sampled the exotic delicacy.

**527. эффективное** — *efficient* — The word 'эффективное' is used to describe something that is able to produce desired results with minimal waste of time, effort, or resources. It implies that the object or action is successful in achieving its intended purpose.

• *1.* Очень эффективный. *2.* Это эффективно. *3.* Она очень эффективна. *4.* Новая формула топлива оказалась очень эффективной. *5.* Работники сахарного тростника работали эффективно. • *1.* Very efficient. *2.* It's efficient. *3.* She's very efficient. *4.* The new propellant formula was highly efficient. *5.* The sugarcane workers were efficient.

**528. шумный** — *noisy, rowdy, tumultuous* — This word is used to describe something or someone that is loud, boisterous, or causing a lot of noise or commotion. It can refer to a noisy environment, a rowdy crowd, or a tumultuous event.

• *1.* Слишком шумно. *2.* Она шшшшшшшшшшшилась шумной толпе. *3.* В ресторане было шумно и многолюдно. *4.* В ночном клубе было многолюдно и шумно. *5.* В литейном цехе было жарко и шумно. *6.* В баре шумно. • *1.* Too noisy. *2.* She shhhh'd the noisy crowd. *3.* The restaurant was noisy and crowded. *4.* The nightclub was crowded and noisy. *5.* The foundry was hot and noisy. *6.* The barroom is rowdy.

**529. легендарный** — *legendary, storied* — This word is used to describe something that is famous, well-known, or iconic. It implies that the subject has a significant and lasting impact, often with a sense of awe or admiration attached to it.

• *1.* Легендарное сокровище осталось спрятанным. *2.* Он рассказал легендарную историю. *3.* Истории этого компьютерщика были легендарными. *4.* Легендарный герой храбро сражался. *5.* Левиафан был легендарным морским существом. • *1.* The legendary treasure remained hidden. *2.* He told a legendary tale. *3.* The stories of that geek were legendary. *4.* The legendary hero fought bravely. *5.* The leviathan was a legendary sea creature.

**530. мелкий** — *shallow, potty* — The word 'мелкий' is used to describe something that is shallow or insignificant in depth or size. It can also be used to describe someone who is petty or small-minded.

• *1.* Это слишком мелко. *2.* Барракуда охотится на мелководье. *3.* У берега было мелко. *4.* Цапля пробиралась по мелководью. • *1.* It's too shallow. *2.* The barracuda hunts in shallow waters. *3.* The water was shallow near the shore. *4.* The heron waded through the shallow water.

**531. несчастливый** — *unlucky* — The word 'несчастливый' is used to describe someone or something that is unfortunate or unlucky. It can be used to express feelings of sadness, disappointment, or bad luck in various situations.

- *1.* Несчастливое число 13. • *1.* The unlucky number 13.

**532. входящий** — *incoming, inbound* — 'входящий' is used to describe something that is coming in or arriving. It is often used to refer to incoming calls, messages, or information.

- *1.* Входящее сообщение. *2.* Входящий звонок. *3.* У нас есть входящие. *4.* Входящая передача. *5.* Мы получили входящие. • *1.* Incoming message. *2.* Incoming call. *3.* We have incoming. *4.* Incoming transmission. *5.* We got incoming.

**533. настоящим** — *hereby, herewith* — 'Настоящим' is used to indicate that something is being done or stated officially or formally. It is often used in legal documents, contracts, or official announcements to emphasize the seriousness or importance of the information being presented.

- *1.* Настоящим она отказалась от своих претензий. *2.* Настоящим он назначается менеджером. *3.* Настоящим мы подтверждаем соглашение. *4.* Настоящим я заявляю о своей поддержке. *5.* Настоящим контракт связывает их. • *1.* She hereby relinquished her claim. *2.* He is hereby appointed manager. *3.* We hereby confirm the agreement. *4.* I hereby declare my support. *5.* The contract hereby binds them.

**534. вдумчивый** — *thoughtful* — 'Вдумчивый' is used to describe someone who is deep in thought, reflective, and attentive. It conveys the idea of someone who carefully considers their actions and decisions, showing a high level of mindfulness and consideration for others.

- *1.* Очень вдумчиво. *2.* Это вдумчиво. *3.* Такой вдумчивый. *4.* У них состоялся вдумчивый разговор. *5.* Ты очень вдумчивый. • *1.* Very thoughtful. *2.* That's thoughtful. *3.* So thoughtful. *4.* They had a thoughtful conversation. *5.* You're very thoughtful.

**535. судебный** — *forensic, judicial* — This word is used to describe things related to the legal system, such as court cases, judges, or evidence. It can also refer to anything involving the process of law or the administration of justice.

- *1.* Я судебный антрополог. *2.* Его увлекало судебно-медицинское расследование. *3.* Она работала в судебно-медицинской экспертизе. *4.* Она специализировалась в области судебной токсикологии. *5.* Они проанализировали заключение судебно-медицинской экспертизы. *6.* Он работает в судебной коллегии. *7.* Судебная система сложна. *8.* Ее судебная карьера заслуживает уважения. *9.* Она вынесла судебное постановление. • *1.* I'm a forensic anthropologist. *2.* He had a fascination with forensic investigation. *3.* She worked in forensic science. *4.* She specialized in forensic toxicology. *5.* They analyzed the forensic report. *6.* He serves on a judicial panel. *7.* The judicial system is complex. *8.* Her judicial career is esteemed. *9.* She issued a judicial decree.

**536. универсальный** — *universal* — This word is used to describe something that is applicable or suitable for all purposes, situations, or people. It conveys the idea of being versatile, all-encompassing, or widely applicable.

• *1.* Понятие смертности универсально. *2.* Концепция была универсальной. *3.* Универсальным языком была музыка. *4.* Истина была универсальной. • *1.* The concept of mortality is universal. *2.* The concept was universal. *3.* The universal language was music. *4.* The truth was universal.

**537. фальшивый** — *phony, phoney, pseudo, hokey* — This word is used to describe something that is fake, counterfeit, or not genuine. It can be used to describe objects, people, or situations that are not authentic or true to their nature.

• *1.* Фальшивый бриллиант был раскрыт. *2.* Фальшивая картина всех обманула. *3.* У него фальшивая улыбка. *4.* Он использовал фальшивое оправдание. *5.* Она фальшивый друг. *6.* Он фальшивый. • *1.* The phony diamond was exposed. *2.* The phony painting fooled everyone. *3.* He has a phony smile. *4.* He used a phony excuse. *5.* She's a phony friend. *6.* He's a phoney.

**538. неуклюжий** — *clumsy, uncouth, gauche* — 'Неуклюжий' is used to describe someone who is awkward, clumsy, or lacking grace in their movements or actions. It can also refer to someone who is socially awkward or lacks finesse in their behavior.

• *1.* Как неуклюже с моей стороны. *2.* Я такой неуклюжий. *3.* Неуклюжий я. *4.* Неуклюже с моей стороны. *5.* Очень неуклюже. *6.* Его комментарий был неуклюжим. • *1.* How clumsy of me. *2.* I'm so clumsy. *3.* Clumsy me. *4.* Clumsy of me. *5.* Very clumsy. *6.* His comment was gauche.

**539. механический** — *mechanical* — The word 'механический' is used to describe something that is related to or characteristic of machinery or mechanics. It can also be used to describe something that is done in a mechanical or automatic way.

● *1.* Хэппи, механическое вундеркинд. *2.* Механическая поломка. *3.* Мехавоин сражался с механической точностью. *4.* Механические системы были самыми современными. *5.* Ее увлекало все механическое. ● *1.* Happy, a mechanical prodigy. *2.* Mechanical failure. *3.* The mecha warrior fought with mechanical precision. *4.* The mechanical systems were state-of-the-art. *5.* She was fascinated with all things mechanical.

**540. оборонительный** — *defensive* — 'Оборонительный' is used to describe something that is related to defense or protection. It can be used to describe tactics, strategies, equipment, or actions that are intended to defend against an attack or threat.

● *1.* Оборонительные позиции. *2.* Оборонительные раны. *3.* Команда представляет собой мощную оборонительную машину. *4.* Не занимай такую оборонительную позицию. *5.* Он занял оборонительную позицию. ● *1.* Defensive positions. *2.* Defensive wounds. *3.* The team is a defensive powerhouse. *4.* Don't be so defensive. *5.* He took a defensive stance.

**541. примитивный** — *primitive* — The word 'примитивный' is used to describe something that is simple, basic, or undeveloped. It can refer to a person, object, idea, or situation that lacks complexity or sophistication.

● *1.* Неолитические орудия были примитивными. *2.* Это примитивно. ● *1.* Neolithic tools were primitive. *2.* It's primitive.

**542. военно морской** — *naval* — 'военно морской' is used to describe something related to the navy or naval forces. It is often used to refer to ships, personnel, operations, or anything else connected to the naval branch of the military.

● *1.* Он специализировался на морской артиллерийской стрельбе. ● *1.* He specialized in naval gunnery.

**543. дерьмовый** — *crappy* — This word is used to describe something of very poor quality or extremely unpleasant. It is often used informally to express strong disapproval or disappointment.

**544. чудный** — *marvellous* — 'Чудный' is used to describe something that is wonderful, amazing, or extraordinary. It is often used to express admiration or awe towards something that is considered to be truly remarkable or exceptional.

**545. демократический** — *democratic* — This word is used to describe something that is related to or characteristic of democracy, such as a political system, government, society, or process. It conveys the idea of equality, freedom, and participation in decision-making.
● *1.* Она верила в демократические принципы. *2.* Он выступал за демократические ценности. *3.* Решение было принято демократическим путем. *4.* Демократическое общество способствует равенству. ● *1.* She believed in democratic principles. *2.* He advocated for democratic values. *3.* The decision was made through democratic process. *4.* A democratic society promotes equality.

**546. обнаженный** — *nude* — This word is used to describe something or someone that is without clothing or covering, exposed or bare. It can be used to refer to a person, object, or landscape that is completely uncovered.
● *1.* Обнаженные женщины! *2.* Обнаженное искусство. ● *1.* Nude women! *2.* Nude art.

**547. художественный** — *artistic* — This word is used to describe something related to art or creativity, often indicating a high level of skill or aesthetic value. It can refer to anything from paintings and sculptures to literature and performances.
● *1.* Они оценили художественный стиль. *2.* Лоскутная стена представляла собой художественное произведение. *3.* Собралось художественное сообщество. *4.* Дом был наполнен художественным декором. *5.* Художественные различия? ● *1.* They appreciated the artistic style. *2.* The patchwork wall was an artistic display. *3.* The artistic community gathered. *4.* The home was filled with artistic decor. *5.* Artistic differences?

**548. достаточный** — *sufficient, ample, adequate* — This word is used to describe a quantity or amount that is enough or satisfactory for a particular purpose or need. It indicates that there is an adequate or sufficient amount of something.

● *1.* Этого достаточно? *2.* Этого достаточно. *3.* Недостаточно для выборов. *4.* Пространство предоставляло достаточно места для деятельности. *5.* У противника было достаточно боеприпасов. *6.* Вяз давал достаточно тени. *7.* Он предоставил достаточное количество доказательств. *8.* Луга предоставляли достаточно места для выпаса скота. *9.* Припасов было недостаточно. ● *1.* Is that sufficient? *2.* That's sufficient. *3.* Not sufficient for election. *4.* The space provided ample room for activities. *5.* The enemy had ample ammunition. *6.* The elm tree provided ample shade. *7.* He provided an ample amount of evidence. *8.* The grassland provided ample grazing space. *9.* The supplies weren't adequate.

**549. интеллектуальный** — *intellectual* — This word is used to describe someone or something that is related to or involves intellect, intelligence, or knowledge. It can be used to describe a person, a conversation, a book, or any other intellectual activity or product.

● *1.* Она искала интеллектуальную стимуляцию. *2.* У него был интеллектуальный разговор. *3.* Они преуспели в интеллектуальных репликах. *4.* Она интеллектуальный человек. *5.* Книга была полна интеллектуальных идей. ● *1.* She sought out intellectual stimulation. *2.* He had an intellectual conversation. *3.* They excelled in intellectual repartee. *4.* She's an intellectual person. *5.* The book was full of intellectual insights.

**550. своеобразный** — *peculiar* — 'Своеобразный' is used to describe something that is unique, distinctive, or peculiar in a way that sets it apart from others. It implies a sense of individuality or unconventional characteristics.

● *1.* Самый своеобразный. *2.* Как своеобразно. *3.* Очень своеобразно. *4.* В своеобразном магазине хранился целый зверинец странностей. *5.* Это своеобразный выбор. ● *1.* Most peculiar. *2.* How peculiar. *3.* Very peculiar. *4.* The peculiar shop housed a menagerie of oddities. *5.* That's a peculiar choice.

**551. истерический** — *hysterical* — This word is used to describe someone or something that is overly emotional, irrational, or out of control. It can refer to a person's behavior or to a situation that is chaotic or frenzied.

● *1.* Ситуация приобретала истерический характер. ● *1.* The situation was getting hysterical.

**552. жировой** — *fatty* — 'Жировой' is used to describe something that is high in fat content or related to fat. It can be used to describe food, substances, or even body types.

**553. липкий** — *sticky, tacky, gooey, gummy* — This word is used to describe something that is adhesive or has a sticky texture, often used to refer to substances like glue, honey, or certain foods. It can also be used metaphorically to describe a situation or person.

● *1.* Он липкий. *2.* Клавиатура была липкой. *3.* Рис был - липким. *4.* Ириска была липкой и сладкой. *5.* Счетчик был липким. *6.* В гостиничном номере был липкий ковер. ● *1.* It's sticky. *2.* The keypad was sticky. *3.* The rice was sticky. *4.* The taffy was sticky and sweet. *5.* The counter was sticky. *6.* The hotel room had a tacky carpet.

**554. классный** — *classy, groovy, crackerjack* — 'Классный' is used to describe something as stylish, excellent, or impressive. It can be used to compliment a person, object, or situation. It conveys a sense of high quality or coolness.

● *1.* Очень классно. *2.* Это классно. *3.* У нее классный стиль. *4.* Действительно классный. *5.* Классный ход. *6.* Очень классно. ● *1.* Very classy. *2.* That's classy. *3.* She has a classy style. *4.* Really classy. *5.* Classy move. *6.* Very groovy.

**555. городской** — *urban* — 'Urban' is used to describe things related to cities or city life. It can refer to buildings, infrastructure, culture, or anything else associated with urban areas.

● *1.* Это городская легенда. *2.* Городские беспорядки длились несколько дней. *3.* Он талантливый городской художник. *4.* Они исследовали городской пейзаж. *5.* Городские джунгли могут быть опасными. ● *1.* It's an urban legend. *2.* The urban riot lasted for days. *3.* He's a talented urban artist. *4.* They explored the urban landscape. *5.* The urban jungle can be dangerous.

**556. эпический** — *epic* — 'Эпический' is used to describe something grand, heroic, or monumental in scale. It conveys a sense of awe and admiration for something that is larger than life or has a significant impact.

**557. тщательный** — *thorough, meticulous, rigorous, scrupulous* — 'Тщательный' is used to describe someone or something that pays close attention to detail, is careful and precise in their work, and ensures that everything is done thoroughly and accurately. • *1.* Очень тщательно. *2.* Будьте тщательны. *3.* Просто т-щательно. *4.* Я тщательный. *5.* Он очень тщательный. *6.* Интервьюер делал тщательные записи. *7.* Интендант вел - тщательный учет. *8.* Бухгалтерия велась тщательно. *9.* Был проявлен тщательный уход. *10.* Она провела тщательное р-асследование. • *1.* Very thorough. *2.* Be thorough. *3.* Just being thorough. *4.* I'm thorough. *5.* He's very thorough. *6.* The interviewer took meticulous notes. *7.* The quartermaster kept meticulous records. *8.* The bookkeeping was meticulous. *9.* Meticulous care was taken. *10.* She conducted a scrupulous investigation.

**558. героический** — *heroic* — The word 'героический' is used to describe actions, behavior, or qualities that are brave, coura-geous, or noble in a way that is reminiscent of a hero. It conveys a sense of valor and selflessness.

• *1.* Памятник изображал героическую фигуру. *2.* Она пр-инесла героическую жертву. *3.* Она восхищалась его геро-ическим поступком. *4.* Он совершил героический поступок. *5.* Героические усилия спасли жизни. • *1.* The monument depicted a heroic figure. *2.* She made a heroic sacrifice. *3.* She admired his heroic act. *4.* He performed a heroic deed. *5.* The heroic effort saved lives.

**559. атомный** — *atomic* — The word 'атомный' is used to describe something related to atoms or atomic energy. It can also be used to emphasize the extreme power or intensity of something.

• *1.* Модель Бора изображала атомную структуру. *2.* Атом-ный номер был 14. *3.* Бомба имела атомный взрыв. *4.* Атом-ный локоть! *5.* Атомная структура была сложной. • *1.* The Bohr model depicted atomic structure. *2.* The atomic number was 14. *3.* The bomb had an atomic explosion. *4.* Atomic elbow! *5.* The atomic structure was complex.

**560. космический** — *cosmic* — 'Космический' is used to de-scribe something that is related to outer space, the universe, or something that is vast, immense, or extraordinary in scale. It can also convey a sense of awe, wonder, or grandeur.

• *1.* Она смотрела на космическое зрелище. *2.* Космическое событие было завораживающим. *3.* Космическая энергия была ошеломляющей. *4.* Космические силы эффектно столкнулись. *5.* Они восхищались космическими чудесами. • *1.* She gazed at the cosmic display. *2.* The cosmic event was mesmerizing. *3.* The cosmic energy was overwhelming. *4.* The cosmic forces collided spectacularly. *5.* They marveled at the cosmic wonders.

**561. веселый** — *cheerful, merry, jolly, hilarious* — 'Веселый' is used to describe someone or something that is happy, joyful, or full of laughter. It can also be used to describe an event or atmosphere that is lively and fun.

• *1.* Они весело помахали на прощание. *2.* Тэмми всегда была веселой. *3.* Она приветствовала его веселым приветом. *4.* Ее необъяснимо веселое настроение подняло всем настроение. *5.* Чего ты такой веселый? *6.* Что должен делать человек, как не веселиться? *7.* Веселый приход весны. *8.* Вы веселы, милорд. *9.* Веселый шутник. *10.* У него была веселая, дородная фигура. *11.* Корсар управлял «Веселым Роджером». *12.* Привет, Веселый Роджер. *13.* Это весело. *14.* Ты веселый. *15.* Это было весело. *16.* Он веселый. *17.* Да, весело. • *1.* They waved goodbye with a cheerful seeya. *2.* Tammy was always cheerful. *3.* She greeted him with a cheerful hullo. *4.* Her inexplicably cheerful mood lifted everyone's spirits. *5.* What are you so cheerful about? *6.* What should a man do but be merry? *7.* The merry arrival of spring. *8.* You are merry, my lord. *9.* Jolly joker. *10.* He had a jolly, portly figure. *11.* The corsair flew the Jolly Roger. *12.* Hello, Jolly Roger. *13.* It's hilarious. *14.* You're hilarious. *15.* That was hilarious. *16.* He's hilarious. *17.* Yeah, hilarious.

**562. сдержанный** — *discreet, reticent* — This word is used to describe someone who is reserved and cautious in their actions and speech, often keeping their thoughts and emotions to themselves. It conveys a sense of restraint and modesty.

• *1.* Очень сдержанный. *2.* Она оценила его сдержанный подход. *3.* Он разрешил ситуацию с помощью сдержанной дипломатии. *4.* Его сдержанные жесты остались незамеченными. *5.* Она очень сдержанно рассказывает о своем прошлом. *6.* Сдержанный студент редко высказывался. *7.* На протяжении всей встречи она оставалась сдержанной. • *1.*

Very discreet. *2.* She appreciated his discreet approach. *3.* He handled the situation with discreet diplomacy. *4.* His discreet gestures went unnoticed. *5.* She's very reticent about her past. *6.* The reticent student rarely spoke up. *7.* She remained reticent throughout the meeting.

**563. хирургический** — *surgical* — This word is used to describe anything related to surgery or the surgical process. It can refer to tools, procedures, techniques, or anything else that is specifically related to the field of surgery.

● *1.* Стерильность хирургических инструментов имела решающее значение. *2.* Хирургическая бригада провела лечение тампонады. ● *1.* The sterility of the surgical tools was crucial. *2.* The surgical team treated the tamponade.

**564. зубной** — *dental* — 'Зубной' is used to describe things related to teeth or dental care. It can refer to objects, procedures, or products that are used for maintaining oral health or treating dental issues.

● *1.* Стоматолог посоветовал установить зубной имплантат. *2.* Зубная паста содержит фтор, необходимый для здоровья зубов. ● *1.* The dentist recommended a dental implant. *2.* The toothpaste contained fluoride for dental health.

**565. оживленный** — *lively, brisk, upbeat, vivacious* — This word is used to describe something or someone that is full of energy, enthusiasm, and liveliness. It conveys a sense of vibrancy and excitement, suggesting a lively and upbeat atmosphere or personality.

● *1.* Шагайте оживленно. *2.* Выглядите оживленно! *3.* Бубен добавил оживленного ритма. *4.* В парикмахерской царили оживленные разговоры. *5.* Агора была оживленным и шумным местом. *6.* Он говорил оживленным тоном. *7.* Оживленная музыка наполняла воздух. *8.* Ему нравилась ее оживленная беседа. ● *1.* Step lively. *2.* Look lively! *3.* The tambourine added a lively rhythm. *4.* The barbershop was filled with lively conversation. *5.* The agora was a lively and bustling place. *6.* He spoke in a brisk tone. *7.* The vivacious music filled the air. *8.* He enjoyed her vivacious conversation.

**566. праведный** — *righteous* — 'Righteous' is used to describe someone who is morally upright, virtuous, and just in their actions and beliefs. It conveys a sense of goodness and integrity in a person's character.

● *1.* Праведник отказался идти на компромисс. *2.* Она прожила праведную жизнь. *3.* Он сражался за праведный путь. *4.* Праведное дело привлекло сторонников. ● *1.* The righteous man refused to compromise. *2.* She lived a righteous life. *3.* He fought for the righteous path. *4.* The righteous cause attracted supporters.

**567.** **отвратительный** — *hideous, crummy, loathsome, atrocious* — This word is used to describe something that is extremely unpleasant, disgusting, or repulsive. It conveys a strong sense of disgust or revulsion towards the object or situation being described.

● *1.* Я отвратительный. *2.* Они отвратительны. *3.* Она была шокирована его отвратительным поведением. *4.* Он отвратительный. *5.* Ты выглядишь отвратительно. *6.* Отвратительный запах заставил ее поперхнуться. *7.* Вкус ей показался отвратительным. *8.* Отвратительный акт предательства преследовал его. *9.* Он сделал отвратительный комментарий. *10.* Отвратительное существо ускользнуло.
● *1.* I'm hideous. *2.* They're hideous. *3.* She was shocked by his hideous behavior. *4.* He's hideous. *5.* You look hideous. *6.* The loathsome smell made her gag. *7.* She found the taste loathsome. *8.* The loathsome act of betrayal haunted him. *9.* He made a loathsome comment. *10.* The loathsome creature slithered away.

**568. пряный** — *spicy* — 'пряный' is used to describe food or drinks that have a strong, pungent flavor due to the presence of spices. It can also be used to describe a strong, intense aroma or taste.

● *1.* Имбирный перец имел теплый и пряный вкус. *2.* Пряный ролл из скумбрии был восхитительным. *3.* Попурри включало пряные ароматы. ● *1.* The gingersnap had a warm and spicy flavor. *2.* The spicy bonito roll was delicious. *3.* The potpourri included spicy aromas.

**569. рациональный** — *rational* — This word is used to describe something or someone that is logical, reasonable, and based on sound judgment. It is often used to refer to decisions, arguments, or behavior that is sensible and well-thought-out.

• *1.* Это не рационально. *2.* Она ценила рациональное мышление. *3.* Рациональное решение было очевидным. *4.* Он был известен своим рациональным умом. *5.* Я уверен, что этому есть рациональное объяснение. • *1.* It's not rational. *2.* She valued rational thought. *3.* The rational decision was obvious. *4.* He was known for his rational mind. *5.* I'm sure there's a rational explanation.

**570. бесконечный** — *infinite, unending* — This word is used to describe something that has no end or limit, conveying the idea of endlessness or eternity. It is often used to emphasize the vastness or boundlessness of a concept or object.

• *1.* Любовь была бесконечной. *2.* Водная гладь казалась бесконечной. *3.* Он чувствовал бесконечную благодарность. *4.* У нее было бесконечное терпение. *5.* Круг был бесконечным. *6.* Она чувствовала себя перегруженной бесконечными задачами. *7.* Линия как бесконечный горизонт. *8.* Его бесконечный оптимизм вдохновлял других. • *1.* The love was infinite. *2.* The expanse of water seemed infinite. *3.* He felt infinite gratitude. *4.* She had infinite patience. *5.* The circle was infinite. *6.* She felt overwhelmed by the unending tasks. *7.* A line as the unending horizon. *8.* His unending optimism inspired others.

**571. реалистичный** — *realistic* — The word 'реалистичный' is used to describe something that closely resembles reality or is based on practicality and common sense. It is often used to describe art, literature, or situations that are believable and true to life.

• *1.* Быть реалистичным. *2.* Это очень реалистично. *3.* Перестрелка была реалистичной. *4.* Ей нужно было реалистичное решение. *5.* У нее был реалистичный взгляд на ситуацию. • *1.* Be realistic. *2.* It's very realistic. *3.* The gunplay was realistic. *4.* She needed a realistic solution. *5.* She had a realistic outlook.

**572. безответственный** — *irresponsible* — This word describes someone who lacks accountability and does not take their duties or obligations seriously. It can also refer to actions or behavior that show a disregard for consequences or the well-being of others.

• *1.* Это безответственно. *2.* Как ты мог быть таким безответственным? *3.* Решение было признано безответственным. *4.*

Он проявил безответственное поведение на работе. *5.* Так безответственно. ● *1.* It's irresponsible. *2.* How could you be so irresponsible? *3.* The decision was deemed irresponsible. *4.* He showed irresponsible behavior at work. *5.* So irresponsible.

**573. значительно** — *greatly, vastly* — 'Значительно' is used to emphasize a significant difference or increase in something. It indicates a large degree of change or impact, often implying a noticeable and substantial difference compared to a previous state or situation.

● *1.* Погода значительно улучшилась. *2.* Его талант значительно улучшился. *3.* Его богатство значительно возросло. ●
*1.* The weather greatly improved. *2.* His talent improved vastly.
*3.* His wealth increased vastly.

**574. небрежный** — *sloppy, negligent* — The word 'небрежный' is used to describe someone or something that is careless, untidy, or negligent in their actions or appearance. It conveys a sense of sloppiness or lack of attention to detail.

● *1.* Они небрежные. *2.* Медсестра была небрежна в уходе.
● *1.* They're sloppy. *2.* The nurse was negligent in her care.

**575. иммунный** — *immune* — This word is used to describe something that is resistant to a particular disease or harmful influence. It can also be used to describe a person or organism that has a strong defense against infections.

● *1.* Си полезен для иммунной системы. ● *1.* Cee is good for the immune system.

**576. аутентичный** — *authentic* — This word is used to describe something that is genuine, original, or true to its origins. It is often used to refer to objects, experiences, or people that are considered to be real or legitimate.

● *1.* Очень аутентично. *2.* Это аутентично. *3.* Это аутентично? ● *1.* Very authentic. *2.* It's authentic. *3.* Is it authentic?

**577. ядовитый** — *poisonous, noxious, venomous, virulent* — This word is used to describe something that is harmful or toxic, such as a poisonous plant or venomous snake. It can also be used figuratively to describe something that is extremely harmful or dangerous.

● *1.* Это не ядовито. *2.* Это ядовито. *3.* Это ядовито? *4.* Они ядовиты. *5.* Листья шиповника были ядовиты. *6.* Ядовитая шпора присуща только утконосу. *7.* Укус медянки ядовит. *8.* Они избегали ядовитой змеи. *9.* Змея была ядовитой. *10.* Кожа жабы выделяла ядовитое вещество. • *1.* It's not poisonous. *2.* It's poisonous. *3.* Is it poisonous? *4.* They're poisonous. *5.* The briony leaves were poisonous. *6.* The venomous spur is unique to the platypus. *7.* The copperhead's bite is venomous. *8.* They avoided the venomous snake. *9.* The snake was venomous. *10.* The toad's skin secreted a venomous substance.

**578. потный** — *sweaty* — This word is used to describe someone or something that is covered in sweat. It can be used to talk about physical exertion, hot weather, or intense emotions.

• *1.* Ты потный. *2.* Почему ты такой потный? *3.* Я потный. *4.* Ты такой потный. *5.* У тебя руки потные. • *1.* You're sweaty. *2.* Why are you so sweaty? *3.* I'm sweaty. *4.* You're so sweaty. *5.* Your hands are sweaty.

**579. пожилой** — *elderly* — 'пожилой' is used to describe someone who is older in age, typically referring to someone who is advanced in years or elderly. It can also be used to describe things that are old or mature.

• *1.* Она работает над проектом для пожилых людей. *2.* Пожилая пара наслаждалась прогулкой. *3.* Мошенник нацелился на пожилых жертв. *4.* Они с состраданием заботились о пожилых людях. *5.* Он известен тем, что помогает пожилым людям. • *1.* She's working on a project for the elderly. *2.* The elderly couple enjoyed a walk. *3.* The conman targeted elderly victims. *4.* They cared for the elderly with compassion. *5.* He's known for helping the elderly.

**580. постепенно** — *gradually* — 'Постепенно' is used to describe a process or change that happens slowly over time, in small increments. It indicates a gradual progression or development of something, without sudden or abrupt changes.

• *1.* Синяк постепенно исчез. *2.* В саду постепенно расцвели цветы. *3.* Небо постепенно меняло цвет с оранжевого на фиолетовый. *4.* Цвета постепенно менялись от светлых к темным. *5.* Я постепенно узнаю, кто эти женщины. • *1.* The bruise gradually faded away. *2.* The flowers bloomed gradually in the garden. *3.* The sky turned gradually from orange to purple. *4.* The colors changed gradually from light to dark. *5.* I'm gradually learning who these women are.

**581.** **фундаментальный** — *fundamental* — 'Фундаментальный' is used to describe something that is essential, basic, or foundational. It is often used to emphasize the importance or significance of a particular concept, idea, or principle.

● *1.* Кварк -- фундаментальная частица в физике. *2.* Это фундаментально. *3.* Бозон был фундаментальной частицей. *4.* Равенство является фундаментальным правом человека. *5.* Вебер – это фундаментальная единица. ● *1.* Quark is a fundamental particle in physics. *2.* It's fundamental. *3.* The boson was a fundamental particle. *4.* Equality is a fundamental human right. *5.* The weber is a fundamental unit.

**582.** **временно** — *temporarily* — 'Временно' is used to describe something that is only for a short period of time or temporarily. It indicates that a situation, condition, or action is not permanent and will change in the future.

● *1.* Только временно. *2.* Просто временно. *3.* Она решила временно приостановить проект. *4.* Временно, да. *5.* Они временно находились в убежище. ● *1.* Only temporarily. *2.* Just temporarily. *3.* She chose to suspend the project temporarily. *4.* Temporarily, yes. *5.* They stayed at a safehouse temporarily.

**583.** **неблагодарный** — *ungrateful* — This word is used to describe someone who does not show appreciation or gratitude for something that has been done for them. It conveys a sense of disappointment or disapproval towards the ungrateful person.

● *1.* Ты неблагодарный ублюдок! *2.* Не будьте неблагодарными. *3.* Неблагодарный ублюдок. *4.* Неблагодарный ребенок отказался сказать спасибо. *5.* Я не хочу показаться неблагодарным. ● *1.* You ungrateful bastard! *2.* Don't be ungrateful. *3.* Ungrateful bastard. *4.* The ungrateful child refused to say thank you. *5.* I don't mean to sound ungrateful.

**584.** **регулярно** — *regularly* — This word is used to describe actions or events that occur consistently and at fixed intervals. It indicates that something is done regularly or routinely, without any significant deviations or interruptions.

● *1.* В лаборатории регулярно проводятся эксперименты. *2.* Чистоту воды проверяли регулярно. *3.* Он регулярно употреблял нюхательный табак. *4.* Ракетбольный клуб собирается регулярно. *5.* Они регулярно играли в лото. ● *1.* The lab conducts experimentation regularly. *2.* The water purity was tested regularly. *3.* He used snuff regularly. *4.* The racquetball club meets regularly. *5.* They played the lotto regularly.

**585. странно** — *strangely* — 'Strangely' is used to describe something that is unusual or out of the ordinary. It can be used to express surprise, confusion, or curiosity about a situation or behavior.

• *1.* Очень странно, говорят они. *2.* Он ведет себя очень странно. *3.* Ты ведешь себя странно. *4.* Храп собаки странно успокаивал. *5.* Как странно? • *1.* Very strangely, they say. *2.* He's acting very strangely. *3.* You're acting strangely. *4.* The dog's snore was strangely comforting. *5.* How strangely?

**586. конкурентоспособный** — *competitive* — This word is used to describe something that is able to compete effectively with others in terms of quality, price, or other factors. It implies that the object or entity has the ability to succeed in a competitive environment.

• *1.* Швейная промышленность конкурентоспособна. *2.* Индустрия шоу-бизнеса конкурентоспособна. *3.* Их вознаграждение было конкурентоспособным. *4.* Поставщик предложил конкурентоспособные цены. *5.* Индустрия развлечений конкурентоспособна. • *1.* The apparel industry is competitive. *2.* The showbiz industry is competitive. *3.* Their remuneration package was competitive. *4.* The supplier offered competitive prices. *5.* The entertainment industry is competitive.

**587. специально** — *specially, expressly* — This word is used to indicate that something is done with a specific purpose or intention in mind, often implying that it was done deliberately or intentionally. It can also be used to emphasize that something was done for a particular reason.

• *1.* Я сделал это специально для тебя. • *1.* I made it specially for you.

**588. элементарный** — *elementary, rudimentary* — This word is used to describe something that is basic, simple, or easy to understand. It can refer to a fundamental concept, a straightforward task, or a basic level of knowledge or skill.

• *1.* Элементарно, мой дорогой Ватсон. *2.* Он решил элементарную математическую задачу. *3.* Проект был элементарным. *4.* Они изучали элементарную науку. ● *1.* Elementary, my dear Watson. *2.* He solved the elementary math problem. *3.* The project was elementary. *4.* They studied elementary science.

**589. частичный** — *partial* — 'частичный' is used to describe something that is incomplete or only covers a portion of a whole. It indicates that something is not total or complete, but rather only a part or fraction of the whole.

● *1.* Она почувствовала лишь частичное облегчение. *2.* Он проявил частичное понимание. *3.* У нее был частичный вид на сцену. *4.* Сделали частичную реконструкцию. ● *1.* She felt only partial relief. *2.* He showed partial understanding. *3.* She had a partial view of the stage. *4.* They did a partial remodel.

**590. нейтральный** — *neutral* — 'нейтральный' is used to describe something that is impartial, unbiased, or not favoring one side over another. It can also refer to something that is not strongly positive or negative in nature.

● *1.* Нейтральный угол. *2.* Нейтральная земля. *3.* Поставьте его в нейтральное положение. *4.* У них было нейтральное мнение. *5.* Комната была окрашена в нейтральный цвет. ● *1.* Neutral corner. *2.* Neutral ground. *3.* Put it in neutral. *4.* They had a neutral opinion. *5.* The room was painted a neutral color.

**591. республиканский** — *republican* — 'Республиканский' is used to describe something related to a republic or republicanism. It can refer to political parties, government systems, or ideologies that support the idea of a republic as a form of government.

● *1.* Она голосовала за кандидата от республиканской партии. *2.* Они были членами Республиканской партии. *3.* Он поддержал республиканскую платформу. ● *1.* She voted for the Republican candidate. *2.* They were members of the Republican party. *3.* He supported the Republican platform.

**592. психиатрический** — *psychiatric* — This word is used to describe things related to mental health and the treatment of mental disorders. It can refer to hospitals, treatments, medications, or any other aspect of psychiatric care.

● *1.* Это психиатрическая больница. *2.* Его поместили в психиатрическую больницу. *3.* Психиатрическая больница? *4.* В фильме изображена психиатрическая больница. *5.* Больница предлагает психиатрические услуги. • *1.* It's a psychiatric hospital. *2.* He was admitted to a psychiatric facility. *3.* A psychiatric hospital? *4.* The movie portrays a psychiatric hospital. *5.* The hospital offers psychiatric services.

**593. строгий** — *stern, strict, rigorous, stringent* — This word is used to describe someone or something that is firm, severe, or exacting in their behavior or standards. It conveys a sense of seriousness and discipline in a situation or relationship.

• *1.* Строгий взгляд учителя заставил учеников вздрогнуть. *2.* Она успокоила шум строгим взглядом. *3.* Политика возврата является строгой. *4.* Он сидит на строгой диете. *5.* Сёгунат сохранял строгий контроль. *6.* Его мать строгая. *7.* Новый шериф был очень строгим. *8.* Она прошла строгую подготовку. *9.* Он следовал строгому режиму тренировок. *10.* Строгий процесс занял месяцы. *11.* В компании проводится строгий отбор. *12.* У нее был строгий режим тренировок. *13.* Рекомендации были строгими. *14.* Они внедрили строгие санитарные протоколы. *15.* В компании были приняты строгие меры безопасности. *16.* К ней предъявлялись строгие требования на этой должности. *17.* В школе действовали строгие правила. • *1.* The teacher's stern gaze made the students flinch. *2.* She quieted the ruckus with a stern look. *3.* The refund policy is strict. *4.* He is on a strict diet. *5.* The shogunate maintained strict control. *6.* His mother is strict. *7.* The new sheriff was very strict. *8.* She underwent rigorous training. *9.* He followed a rigorous workout routine. *10.* The rigorous process took months. *11.* The company has a rigorous selection process. *12.* She had a rigorous workout routine. *13.* The guidelines were stringent. *14.* They implemented stringent sanitation protocols. *15.* The company had stringent security measures. *16.* She faced stringent requirements for the job. *17.* The school enforced stringent rules.

**594. воображаемый** — *imaginary* — 'воображаемый' is used to describe something that exists only in the imagination or is not real. It is often used to refer to things that are created or perceived in the mind rather than in reality.

• *1.* Сказочная страна была воображаемой. • *1.* Fairyland was imaginary.

**595. еженедельно** — *weekly* — This word is used to describe something that occurs or is done once every week. It is often used to indicate the frequency of events, tasks, or activities that happen on a weekly basis.

● *1.* Он получал еженедельное пособие. *2.* Еженедельное собрание было обязательным. *3.* Она читала еженедельный информационный бюллетень. *4.* Они проводили еженедельные мероприятия. ● *1.* He received a weekly allowance. *2.* The weekly meeting was mandatory. *3.* She read the weekly newsletter. *4.* They held weekly events.

**596. пыльный** — *dusty* — The word 'пыльный' is used to describe something covered in dust or producing dust. It can refer to objects, surfaces, or environments that have not been cleaned or maintained properly.

● *1.* Здесь пыльно. *2.* В комнате было пыльно. *3.* Старый чердак был темным и пыльным. *4.* Пыльная книга лежала много лет. *5.* Он чихнул в пыльном воздухе. ● *1.* It's dusty. *2.* The room was dusty. *3.* The old attic was dark and dusty. *4.* The dusty book had been sitting for years. *5.* He sneezed from the dusty air.

**597. уединенный** — *solitary* — This word is used to describe something or someone that is isolated or alone, often in a peaceful or remote setting. It conveys a sense of being separate from others and enjoying solitude.

● *1.* Он жил уединенной жизнью. *2.* Они отправились в уединенную пустыню. ● *1.* He lived a solitary life. *2.* They ventured into the solitary wilderness.

**598. дипломатический** — *diplomatic* — The word 'дипломатический' is used to describe actions, behaviors, or statements that are tactful, strategic, and aimed at maintaining good relations between individuals, groups, or countries. It is often associated with diplomacy and negotiation.

● *1.* Дипломатический иммунитет. *2.* У меня есть дипломатический иммунитет. *3.* Он занимал должность дипломатического атташе. *4.* Страна столкнулась с дипломатической трясиной. *5.* Дипломатическая инициатива была хорошо принята. ● *1.* Diplomatic immunity. *2.* I have diplomatic immunity. *3.* He served as a diplomatic attache. *4.* The country faced a diplomatic quagmire. *5.* The diplomatic overture was well-received.

**599. успешно** — *successfully* — 'Успешно' is used to describe the outcome of an action or event that has been accomplished with a positive result. It indicates that something has been done effectively and without any major issues.

● *1.* Штрих-код успешно отсканирован. *2.* Контрмера успешно нейтрализовала атаку. *3.* Орбитальный аппарат успешно вернулся на Землю. *4.* Они успешно осуществили ограбление. *5.* Космический корабль успешно стартовал. ● *1.* The barcode scanned successfully. *2.* The countermeasure successfully neutralized the attack. *3.* The orbiter successfully returned to Earth. *4.* They pulled off the heist successfully. *5.* The spacecraft launched successfully.

**600. звуковой** — *audio, sonic, acoustic* — 'Звуковой' is used to describe things related to sound, such as audio equipment, sonic waves, or acoustic properties. It is often used in the context of music, technology, or physics.

● *1.* Эквалайзер сбалансировал звуковые частоты. *2.* Звуковая отвертка. ● *1.* The equalizer balanced the audio frequencies. *2.* Sonic screwdriver.

**601. невыносимый** — *unbearable, intolerable, insufferable* — This word is used to describe something that is extremely difficult or impossible to endure or tolerate. It conveys a sense of extreme discomfort, annoyance, or pain.

● *1.* Это невыносимо. *2.* Это было невыносимо. *3.* Пытка была невыносимой. *4.* Боль в животе была невыносимой. *5.* Тропическая погода была невыносимой. *6.* Это невыносимо. *7.* Она безропотно переносила невыносимые условия. *8.* Оскорбление ее достоинства было невыносимым. *9.* Ситуация стала невыносимой. *10.* Он нашел уровень шума невыносимым. *11.* Он невыносим. ● *1.* It's unbearable. *2.* It was unbearable. *3.* The torture was unbearable. *4.* His bellyache was unbearable. *5.* The tropic weather was unbearable. *6.* This is intolerable. *7.* She endured the intolerable conditions without complaint. *8.* The affront to her dignity was intolerable. *9.* The situation had become intolerable. *10.* He found the noise level intolerable. *11.* He's insufferable.

**602. непобедимый** — *invincible, unbeatable, undefeated* — This word is used to describe something or someone that cannot be defeated or overcome, emphasizing their strength, power, or

resilience in the face of challenges or opposition.
● *1.* Я непобедим. *2.* Супергерой был непобедим. *3.* Мы непобедимы! *4.* Они играли так, будто были непобедимы. *5.* Непобедимая армия шла вперед. *6.* Я непобедим. *7.* Непобедимый чемпион праздновал победу. ● *1.* I'm invincible. *2.* The superhero was invincible. *3.* We're invincible! *4.* They played like they were invincible. *5.* The invincible army marched forward. *6.* I'm unbeatable. *7.* The undefeated champion celebrated.

**603. дорого** — *dearly, costly* — The word 'дорого' is used to describe something that is expensive or highly valued. It can be used to express the idea of something being costly or cherished.
● *1.* Это фиаско им дорого обошлось. *2.* Она очень дорожила своей свободой. *3.* Билеты на концерт стоили дорого. *4.* Ошибка обошлась дорого. *5.* Ремонт оказался дорогостоящим. *6.* Дорогая ваза разбилась на куски. *7.* Утилизация осадка стоила дорого. *8.* Развод стоил дорого. ● *1.* The fiasco cost them dearly. *2.* She cherished her freedom dearly. *3.* The concert tickets were dearly priced. *4.* The mistake turned out to be costly. *5.* The repairs proved to be costly. *6.* The costly vase shattered into pieces. *7.* The sludge disposal was costly. *8.* The divorce was a costly affair.

**604. мирно** — *peacefully* — 'Мирно' is used to describe actions or situations that are calm, tranquil, and free from disturbance or conflict. It conveys a sense of peace and harmony in various contexts, such as nature, relationships, or environments.
● *1.* Они мирно шли по лесу. *2.* Овца мирно паслась. *3.* Бамбино мирно спал. *4.* Река Колорадо текла мирно. *5.* Лось мирно пасся. ● *1.* They walked peacefully through the forest. *2.* The ewe grazed peacefully. *3.* The bambino slept peacefully. *4.* The Colorado River flowed peacefully. *5.* The moose was grazing peacefully.

**605. нетерпеливый** — *impatient* — 'нетерпеливый' describes someone who struggles to wait or be patient in various situations. It conveys a sense of restlessness and eagerness for things to happen quickly.
● *1.* Не будьте нетерпеливы. *2.* Не будь таким нетерпеливым. *3.* Ты такой нетерпеливый. *4.* Почему ты такой нетерпеливый? *5.* Вы нетерпеливы. ● *1.* Don't be impatient. *2.* Don't be so impatient. *3.* You're so impatient. *4.* Why are

you so impatient? *5.* You're impatient.

**606. грубо** — *roughly, crudely, grossly* — 'Грубо' is used to describe something that is done in a rough, crude, or gross manner. It can be used to indicate a lack of refinement or precision in an action or statement.

● *1.* Здание было построено грубо. *2.* Его поведение было грубо оскорбительным. *3.* Картина выполнена грубо. *4.* Письмо было написано грубо. *5.* Она грубо залатала дыру. *6.* Шутка была воспринята грубо. ● *1.* The building was roughly constructed. *2.* His behavior was crudely offensive. *3.* The painting was crudely done. *4.* The letter was crudely written. *5.* She crudely patched the hole. *6.* The joke was received crudely.

**607. удивительно** — *surprisingly, amazingly, astonishingly* — 'Удивительно' is used to describe something that is surprising, amazing, or astonishing. It conveys a sense of wonder or disbelief at the unexpected nature of a situation or event.

● *1.* Удивительно, но нет. *2.* Они вели игру удивительно умело. *3.* Он удивительно свободно говорил по-испански. ● *1.* Surprisingly, no. *2.* They played the game amazingly skillfully. *3.* He spoke amazingly fluent Spanish.

**608. вегетарианский** — *vegetarian, vegan* — This word is used to describe food, dishes, or people who do not consume meat or animal products. It is commonly used in menus, recipes, and discussions about dietary choices.

● *1.* Это вегетарианское. *2.* В ресторане было вегетарианское меню. *3.* Они ели вегетарианскую еду. *4.* Они наслаждались вегетарианской едой. *5.* В основном она ела вегетарианские блюда. ● *1.* It's vegetarian. *2.* The restaurant had a vegetarian menu. *3.* They ate a vegetarian meal. *4.* They enjoyed a vegetarian meal. *5.* She mainly ate vegetarian dishes.

**609. самый старший** — *eldest* — 'Самый старший' is used to indicate the oldest person or thing in a group. It is used to compare age or seniority within a specific context.

● *1.* Мой старший. *2.* Рикко старший сын Риты. *3.* Я старший!
● *1.* My eldest. *2.* Ricco eldest son of Rita. *3.* I'm the eldest!

**610. гнусный** — *vile, heinous, abominable, nefarious* — 'гнусный' is used to describe something extremely unpleasant, disgusting, or morally reprehensible. It conveys a sense of deep revulsion or disgust towards the object or action being described.

• *1.* Он изрыгал гнусные оскорбления. *2.* Гнусные комментарии расстроили ее. *3.* Она раскрыла гнусную деятельность группы. *4.* Он был известен своими гнусными поступками. *5.* Гнусный персонаж встретил свою кончину. • *1.* He spewed vile insults. *2.* The vile comments upset her. *3.* She uncovered the group's nefarious activities. *4.* He was known for his nefarious deeds. *5.* The nefarious character met his demise.

**611. несовершеннолетний** — *juvenile, underage* — This word is used to describe someone who is not of legal age, typically under 18 years old. It is often used in legal contexts or when discussing individuals who are not yet considered adults.

• *1.* Его арестовали по обвинению в преступлении несовершеннолетних. *2.* Она несовершеннолетняя. *3.* Ты несовершеннолетний. • *1.* He was arrested for juvenile delinquency. *2.* She's underage. *3.* You're underage.

**612. скользкий** — *slippery* — This word is used to describe surfaces or objects that are smooth and difficult to walk on without slipping. It can also be used metaphorically to describe situations that are unpredictable or dangerous.

• *1.* Это скользкий путь. *2.* Это скользко. *3.* Осторожно, здесь скользко. *4.* Частый дождь сделал дорогу скользкой. *5.* Земля была морозной и скользкой. • *1.* It's a slippery slope. *2.* It's slippery. *3.* Careful, it's slippery. *4.* The frequent rain made the road slippery. *5.* The ground was frosty and slippery.

**613. параллельный** — *parallel* — This word is used to describe two or more lines, objects, or events that are side by side and will never meet. It can also be used to describe things that are similar or happening at the same time.

• *1.* Они двигались по параллельным путям. *2.* Она шла по параллельному пути. *3.* Их цели были параллельны. *4.* Параллельная вселенная. *5.* Параллельная вселенная? • *1.* They moved along parallel tracks. *2.* She walked along a parallel path. *3.* Their goals were parallel. *4.* A parallel universe. *5.* Parallel universe?

**614. исключительный** — *exceptional* — This word is used to describe something or someone that is outstanding, extraordinary, or unique in a positive way. It signifies a high level of quality or distinction that sets it apart from others.

• *1.* Она исключительная. *2.* Она исключительная молодая женщина. *3.* Вид был исключительным. *4.* Еда была исключительной. *5.* Я признаю себя исключительным. • *1.* She's exceptional. *2.* She's an exceptional young woman. *3.* The view was exceptional. *4.* The food was exceptional. *5.* I recognize myself as exceptional.

**615. потенциально** — *potentially* — 'Potentially' is used to describe something that has the possibility of happening in the future. It indicates that there is a chance or likelihood of a certain outcome occurring, without guaranteeing it.

• *1.* Потенциально, да. *2.* Падение потенциально могло его покалечить. • *1.* Potentially, yes. *2.* The fall could potentially maim him.

**616. неприемлемый** — *unacceptable* — This word is used to describe something that is not suitable or appropriate, and is not able to be accepted or tolerated. It conveys a strong sense of disapproval or rejection towards a certain action, behavior, or situation.

• *1.* Это неприемлемо. *2.* Это совершенно неприемлемо. *3.* Совершенно неприемлемо. *4.* Нет, это неприемлемо. *5.* Неуважительное отношение было неприемлемо. • *1.* This is unacceptable. *2.* This is totally unacceptable. *3.* Completely unacceptable. *4.* No, that's unacceptable. *5.* The disrespectful attitude was unacceptable.

**617. сверхъестественный** — *supernatural, uncanny* — This word is used to describe something that is beyond the natural or normal realm, often referring to supernatural or uncanny occurrences or beings. It conveys a sense of mystery and awe.

• *1.* На протяжении веков среди нас жили сверхъестественные существа. *2.* Ничего сверхъестественного. *3.* Это сверхъестественная материнская жила. *4.* Это было сверхъестественно. *5.* Ясновидение было сверхъестественным. • *1.* For centuries, supernatural creatures have lived among us. *2.* Nothing supernatural. *3.* It is the supernatural mother lode. *4.* It was uncanny. *5.* The clairvoyance was uncanny.

**618. автоматически** — *automatically* — This word is used to describe actions or processes that are done without manual intervention or control. It implies that something is done automatically, without the need for human input or direction.

• *1.* Сигнализация может отключаться автоматически. *2.* Пробег рассчитывается автоматически. *3.* Спринклеры настроены на автоматическое включение. *4.* Он отключается автоматически. *5.* Резервный генератор включился автоматически. • *1.* The alarm system can deactivate automatically. *2.* The mileage is calculated automatically. *3.* The sprinklers are set to switch on automatically. *4.* It shuts off automatically. *5.* The backup generator kicked in automatically.

**619. вульгарный** — *vulgar* — 'вульгарный' is used to describe something that is crude, offensive, or lacking in good taste. It is often used to refer to language, behavior, or objects that are considered inappropriate or offensive.

• *1.* Не будьте вульгарными. *2.* Слово «придурок» считается вульгарным. *3.* Это вульгарно. *4.* Будь фамильярным, но ни в коем случае не вульгарным. • *1.* Don't be vulgar. *2.* The word twat is considered vulgar. *3.* It's vulgar. *4.* Be thou familiar, but by no means vulgar.

**620. всемирный** — *worldwide* — 'Всемирный' is used to describe something that is present or happening all over the world. It indicates a global scale or reach, emphasizing the widespread nature of the subject it is describing.

**621. действительный** — *valid* — This word is used to describe something that is considered to be true, real, or legitimate. It can be used to emphasize the authenticity or accuracy of something.

• *1.* Это действительно так. • *1.* That's valid.

**622. сочный** — *juicy, succulent* — This word is used to describe food that is full of flavor and moisture, often implying that it is delicious and satisfying to eat. It can also be used to describe something that is visually appealing and vibrant.

• *1.* Она съела сочный арбуз. *2.* Я съел сочный фрукт сабра. *3.* Ему очень хотелось сочного чизбургера. *4.* Стейк был сочным и нежным. *5.* Он наслаждался сочной грушей. *6.* Сочный аромат наполнил комнату. *7.* Она подала тарелку сочных фруктов. *8.* Сочные листья сохраняли воду. *9.* Они приготовили сочный обед. • *1.* She ate a juicy watermelon. *2.*

I ate a juicy sabra fruit. *3.* He craved a juicy cheeseburger. *4.* The steak was juicy and tender. *5.* He enjoyed a juicy pear. *6.* The succulent aroma filled the room. *7.* She served a plate of succulent fruit. *8.* The succulent leaves retained water. *9.* They cooked a succulent meal.

**623. отсутствующий** — *absent* — This word is used to describe something that is missing or not present. It can refer to physical objects, people, or abstract concepts. It indicates a lack or absence of something.

● *1.* Отсутствующим друзьям. *2.* Отсутствующие друзья. *3.* Учитель принял участие отсутствующих учеников. *4.* Он остался отсутствующим на работе. *5.* Отсутствующий ученик пропустил урок. ● *1.* To absent friends. *2.* Absent friends. *3.* The teacher took attendance of the absent students. *4.* He remained absent from work. *5.* The absent student missed the lesson.

**624. динамический** — *dynamic* — This word is used to describe something that is characterized by constant change, activity, or progress. It is often used to convey a sense of energy, movement, or innovation in a particular situation or context.

**625. понятный** — *understandable, foolproof* — The word 'понятный' is used to describe something that is easy to understand or comprehend. It implies that the information or concept is clear, straightforward, and easily grasped by others.

● *1.* Это понятно. *2.* Это совершенно понятно. *3.* Ну это понятно. *4.* Совершенно понятно. *5.* Он нашел ее точку зрения понятной. ● *1.* That's understandable. *2.* It's perfectly understandable. *3.* Well, that's understandable. *4.* Totally understandable. *5.* He found her point of view understandable.

**626. вторичный** — *secondary* — 'вторичный' is used to describe something that is of lesser importance or significance compared to something else. It can also refer to something that is derived from or dependent on something else.

● *1.* Все остальное вторично. ● *1.* Everything else is secondary.

**627. онемелый** — *numb* — The word 'онемелый' is used to describe a lack of sensation or feeling in a specific body part or emotionally. It can also be used to describe a lack of reaction or response to a situation or stimulus.

● *1.* Они онемели. *2.* Я онемела. *3.* Мое лицо онемело. *4.* Он онемел. *5.* Моя рука онемела. ● *1.* They're numb. *2.* I'm numb. *3.* My face is numb. *4.* It's numb. *5.* My hand is numb.

**628. предварительный** — *preliminary* — This word is used to describe something that is done or prepared in advance, before the main event or action. It can also refer to something that is not final or definitive, but rather serves as an initial step or stage.
● *1.* Она дала предварительный отчет. *2.* Предварительные результаты были многообещающими. *3.* Это всего лишь предварительный этап. *4.* Предварительное исследование оказалось безрезультатным. *5.* Команда составила предварительные планы. ● *1.* She gave a preliminary report. *2.* The preliminary results were promising. *3.* It's just the preliminary stage. *4.* The preliminary study was inconclusive. *5.* The team made preliminary plans.

**629. спелый** — *ripe* — 'Спелый' is used to describe fruits or vegetables that are fully developed and ready to eat. It can also be used to describe a person who is mature or experienced in a certain area.
● *1.* Сад был полон спелых фруктов. *2.* Дерево кумкват принесло спелые плоды. *3.* Летние ягоды были спелыми и сочными. *4.* Она надкусила спелый персик. *5.* Он собрал спелый урожай сои. ● *1.* The orchard was full of ripe fruits. *2.* The kumquat tree bore ripe fruit. *3.* The summer berries were ripe and juicy. *4.* She bit into the ripe peach. *5.* He harvested the ripe soybean crops.

**630. консервативный** — *conservative* — The word 'консервативный' is used to describe someone or something that is traditional, resistant to change, or holding onto traditional values. It can also refer to policies or beliefs that advocate for maintaining existing social, political, or economic structures.
● *1.* У нее консервативные ценности. *2.* Он консервативный инвестор. *3.* Они наняли консервативного архитектора. *4.* Консервативный подход победил. ● *1.* She has conservative values. *2.* He's a conservative investor. *3.* They hired a conservative architect. *4.* The conservative approach won out.

**631. мрачный** — *grim, gloomy, somber, glum* — This word is used to describe something that is dark, depressing, or lacking in brightness. It conveys a sense of sadness, seriousness, or heaviness in mood or atmosphere.

● *1.* Выражение ее лица было низким и мрачным. *2.* Выражение ее лица стало мрачным. *3.* Ситуация выглядела мрачной. *4.* Прогноз на выходные был мрачным. *5.* Их будущее казалось мрачным. *6.* Почему так мрачно? *7.* Мрачные звуки. *8.* Он был в мрачном настроении. *9.* Это так мрачно. *10.* Будущее выглядело мрачным и неопределённым. *11.* На мероприятии он был одет в мрачные цвета. *12.* Небо имело мрачный вид. *13.* После аварии настроение было мрачным. *14.* Похороны прошли мрачно. *15.* Ее голос приобрел мрачный тон. *16.* Не смотри так мрачно. *17.* Почему такой мрачный, приятель? *18.* Несмотря на их усилия, она оставалась мрачной. ● *1.* Her expression was lowery and grim. *2.* Her expression turned grim. *3.* The situation looked grim. *4.* The forecast was grim for the weekend. *5.* Their future appeared grim. *6.* Why so gloomy? *7.* Gloomy sounds. *8.* He was in a gloomy mood. *9.* It's so gloomy. *10.* The future looked gloomy and uncertain. *11.* He wore somber colors to the event. *12.* The sky had a somber look. *13.* The mood was somber after the accident. *14.* The funeral was a somber affair. *15.* Her voice took on a somber tone. *16.* Don't look so glum. *17.* Why so glum, chum? *18.* She remained glum despite their efforts.

**632. коллективный** — *collective* — This word is used to describe something that involves or is shared by a group of people. It emphasizes the idea of working together or belonging to a group. It can also refer to something that is done or owned by a group.

● *1.* Коллективная реакция была ошеломляющей. *2.* Коллективные усилия принесли свои плоды. *3.* Коллективное решение было принято. *4.* Коллектив боргов обладал коллективным разумом. *5.* Мы коллективная команда. ● *1.* The collective response was overwhelming. *2.* The collective effort paid off. *3.* The collective decision was made. *4.* The borg collective had a hive mind. *5.* We are a collective team.

**633. датский** — *danish* — This word is used to describe something or someone related to Denmark or Danish culture. It can refer to anything from Danish food and design to people or traditions from Denmark.

● *1.* Датская мразь! ● *1.* Danish scum!

**634. относительно** — *relatively, comparatively* — 'Относительно' is used to compare or contrast one thing with another, indicating that something is not absolute but rather relative or comparative in nature. It is often used to show a degree of difference or similarity between two things.

● *1.* Его травма была относительно легкой. *2.* Цена была - относительно низкой. *3.* Проект был относительно простым. *4.* Она была относительно новичком в компании. *5.* Он был относительно спокоен под давлением. ● *1.* His injury was relatively minor. *2.* The price was relatively low. *3.* The project was relatively easy. *4.* She was relatively new to the company. *5.* He was relatively calm under pressure.

**635. непредсказуемый** — *unpredictable* — This word is used to describe something that cannot be foreseen or anticipated. It implies that the outcome or behavior of the subject is uncertain and cannot be easily predicted.

● *1.* Он непредсказуем. *2.* Жизнь непредсказуема. *3.* Погода была капризной и непредсказуемой. *4.* Аномальная погода была непредсказуемой. *5.* Эксперимент дал непредсказуемые результаты. ● *1.* He's unpredictable. *2.* Life is unpredictable. *3.* The weather was moody and unpredictable. *4.* The anomalous weather was unpredictable. *5.* The experiment yielded unpredictable results.

**636. холодно** — *chilly, coldly* — 'Холодно' is used to describe a low temperature or a lack of warmth. It can also be used to describe someone's demeanor or actions as cold or indifferent.

● *1.* Холодно. *2.* Здесь холодно. *3.* Мне немного холодно. *4.* Холодный ветер прорезал ее пальто. *5.* Холодная погода была неожиданностью. *6.* Она холодно смотрела, как он уходит. *7.* Они холодно приветствовали друг друга. *8.* Холодно донесенная новость шокировала их. *9.* Она холодно отвернулась. *10.* Он холодно разговаривал со своими коллегами. ● *1.* It's chilly. *2.* It's chilly in here. *3.* I'm a little chilly. *4.* The chilly wind cut through her coat. *5.* The chilly weather was unexpected. *6.* She watched coldly as he left. *7.* They greeted each other coldly. *8.* The coldly delivered news shocked them. *9.* She turned away coldly. *10.* He spoke coldly to his colleagues.

**637. академический** — *academic* — The word 'академический' is used to describe something that is related to or characteristic of academia, scholarly work, or educational institutions. It can also refer to a formal, traditional, or theoretical approach to a subject.

● *1.* Ешива способствует академическому успеху. *2.* Он выполнил свою академическую норму. *3.* Это была строгая академическая программа. ● *1.* The yeshiva promotes academic excellence. *2.* He met his academic quota. *3.* It was a rigorous academic program.

**638. полярный** — *polar* — 'Полярный' is used to describe something that is related to or characteristic of the North or South Pole. It can also be used to emphasize extreme differences or contrasts between two things.

● *1.* Полярные условия были суровыми. *2.* Он изучал полярные регионы. *3.* Полярные льды таяли. *4.* Она восхищалась полярным пейзажем. ● *1.* The polar conditions were harsh. *2.* He studied the polar regions. *3.* The polar ice caps were melting. *4.* She marveled at the polar landscape.

**639. милосердный** — *merciful* — This word describes someone who shows compassion and forgiveness towards others, especially those who are suffering or in need. It conveys a sense of kindness and understanding in their actions and behavior.

● *1.* Милосердные небеса! *2.* Будьте милосердны. *3.* Милосердный Боже! ● *1.* Merciful heavens! *2.* Be merciful. *3.* Merciful God!

**640. средневековый** — *medieval* — This word is used to describe something that is related to or characteristic of the Middle Ages, particularly in terms of architecture, art, culture, or historical events.

● *1.* Они продемонстрировали средневековое оружие, в том числе булаву. *2.* Он выступал на средневековой ярмарке. *3.* Мой дворец огромен даже по средневековым меркам. ● *1.* They displayed medieval weapons, including a mace. *2.* He performed at a medieval faire. *3.* My palace is vast, even by medieval standards.

**641. безоружный** — *unarmed* — The word 'безоружный' is used to describe someone or something that is not carrying any weapons or defenses. It can also be used figuratively to describe someone who is defenseless or vulnerable.

● *1.* Мы безоружны. *2.* Они безоружны. *3.* Нападавший сбил безоружного мужчину. *4.* Он подошел к медведю безоружным. *5.* Солдаты шли в бой безоружными. ● *1.* We're unarmed. *2.* They're unarmed. *3.* The unarmed man was overpowered by the attacker. *4.* He approached the bear unarmed. *5.* The soldiers went into battle unarmed.

**642. фашистский** — *fascist* — The word 'фашистский' is used to describe something or someone that is related to or resembles fascism. It is often used in a negative context to criticize authoritarian or oppressive behavior.

● *1.* Фашистская свинья! *2.* Фашистский лидер угнетал свой народ. *3.* Фашистская идеология была опасной и радикальной. *4.* Фашистский режим подавлял любое инакомыслие. *5.* Фашистские порнографии! ● *1.* Fascist pig! *2.* The fascist leader oppressed his people. *3.* The fascist ideology was dangerous and extreme. *4.* The fascist regime suppressed all dissent. *5.* Fascist pornographers!

**643. тропический** — *tropical* — This word is used to describe something that is characteristic of or related to the tropics, such as tropical climate, plants, or animals. It can also be used to describe a feeling or atmosphere reminiscent of the tropics.

● *1.* Тропический остров напоминал Эдем. *2.* Экваториальная область имела тропический климат. *3.* Атолл был тропическим раем. *4.* Киви добавил тропический оттенок. *5.* Вечеринка была оформлена в тропической тематике. ● *1.* The tropical island felt like Eden. *2.* The equatorial region had a tropical climate. *3.* The atoll was a tropical paradise. *4.* The kiwi added a tropical touch. *5.* The party had a tropical theme.

**644. расплывчатый** — *vague, muzzy* — The word 'расплывчатый' is used to describe something that is unclear, blurry, or lacking in distinctness. It is often used to characterize vague or muddled ideas, images, or descriptions.

● *1.* Это расплывчато. *2.* Слишком расплывчато. *3.* Он дал расплывчатое описание подозреваемого. *4.* Инструкции были удручающе расплывчатыми. ● *1.* It's vague. *2.* Too vague. *3.* He gave a vague description of the suspect. *4.* The instructions were frustratingly vague.

**645. положительно** — *positively* — This word is used to describe a positive or favorable attitude, opinion, or outcome. It can also be used to indicate that something is confirmed or approved.

● *1.* Результат был положительно идеальным. *2.* Нейтрон был заряжен положительно. *3.* Новость была воспринята положительно. *4.* Его отношение было положительно сияющим. ● *1.* The outcome was positively perfect. *2.* The neutron was positively charged. *3.* The news was received positively. *4.* His attitude was positively radiant.

**646. изысканный** — *exquisite, dainty* — 'Изысканный' is used to describe something that is elegant, refined, and of high quality. It is often used to refer to food, clothing, or art that is delicate and sophisticated in nature.

● *1.* Это изысканно. *2.* Вы изысканны. *3.* Коллекция Зины была изысканной. *4.* На ней было изысканное платье. *5.* Вино было изысканным. *6.* Подали изысканные бутерброды. *7.* Изящные украшения были изысканными. *8.* Торт получился изысканным и элегантным. *9.* Изысканный фарфор был хрупким. ● *1.* It's exquisite. *2.* You are exquisite. *3.* The zina collection was exquisite. *4.* She wore an exquisite gown. *5.* The vino was exquisite. *6.* They served dainty sandwiches. *7.* The dainty jewelry was exquisite. *8.* The cake was dainty and elegant. *9.* The dainty china was fragile.

**647. вокальный** — *vocal* — 'вокальный' is used to describe something related to or involving the voice or singing. It can refer to vocal music, vocal techniques, or anything else that pertains to the voice or singing.

● *1.* Певице пришлось напрячь свой вокальный диапазон. *2.* Битбоксинг – это разновидность вокальной перкуссии. ● *1.* The singer had to exert her vocal range. *2.* Beatboxing is a form of vocal percussion.

**648. женственный** — *feminine, womanly* — This word is used to describe qualities, characteristics, or behaviors that are traditionally associated with femininity or womanhood. It can be used to describe a person, object, or action that embodies these qualities.

● *1.* Очень женственно. *2.* Я стала довольно женственной. *3.* Я становлюсь женственным существом. *4.* Я рано повзрослела и стала женственной. • *1.* Very feminine. *2.* I've grown quite womanly. *3.* I emerge as a womanly creature. *4.* I ripened early and became womanly.

**649. неоднократно** — *repeatedly* — This word is used to describe something that has happened multiple times or on several occasions. It indicates a repeated action or event without specifying the exact number of times it has occurred.

• *1.* Сигнализация сработала неоднократно. *2.* Она неоднократно просила его остановиться. *3.* В дверь звонили неоднократно. *4.* Их неоднократно предупреждали об опасности. • *1.* The alarm went off repeatedly. *2.* She asked him repeatedly to stop. *3.* The doorbell rang repeatedly. *4.* They were warned repeatedly about the dangers.

**650. мужеподобная** — *butch* — The word 'мужеподобная' is used to describe someone or something that is masculine or has qualities typically associated with men. It is often used to describe women who exhibit traditionally masculine traits or behaviors.

**651. частично** — *partly, partially* — 'частично' is used to indicate that something is only partially true, complete, or done. It implies that there is still some aspect that is missing or incomplete.

• *1.* На это решение частично повлияли внешние факторы. *2.* Она была частично ответственна за успех проекта. *3.* Ваза была частично скрыта за занавеской. *4.* Листья улуна частично окисляются. • *1.* The decision was partly influenced by external factors. *2.* She was partly responsible for the project's success. *3.* The vase was partly hidden behind the curtain. *4.* The oolong leaves are partially oxidized.

**652. месячный** — *monthly* — This word is used to describe something that occurs or is done once a month. It can refer to a regular occurrence, payment, or subscription that happens on a monthly basis.

• *1.* Информационный бюллетень выходит ежемесячно. *2.* Они отслеживали свои ежемесячные расходы. *3.* Он получает ежемесячную пенсию. *4.* Она получала ежемесячную стипендию. *5.* Они достигли месячной квоты продаж. • *1.* The newsletter comes out monthly. *2.* They tracked their monthly expenditure. *3.* He receives a monthly pension. *4.* She received a monthly stipend. *5.* They reached their monthly sales quota.

**653. праздный** — *idle, gossipy* — The word 'праздный' is used to describe someone or something that is idle or gossipy. It can be used to convey a sense of laziness or unproductiveness, as well as a tendency to engage in frivolous or meaningless chatter.

• *1.* Праздные руки – мастерская дьявола. *2.* Они занимались праздной болтовней. • *1.* Idle hands are the devil's workshop. *2.* They engaged in idle palaver.

**654. сурово** — *severely* — The word 'сурово' is used to describe something that is done in a strict or harsh manner. It can also be used to convey a sense of severity or seriousness in a situation or action.

• *1.* Военные сурово наказывали за неповиновение. • *1.* The military punished insubordination severely.

**655. публично** — *publicly* — 'Публично' is used to describe actions or events that are done or occur in a public setting or are meant to be seen or heard by a large group of people. It indicates that something is done openly or in a way that is visible to others.

• *1.* Компания опубликовала это публично. *2.* Она собирается публично обвинить моего сына в убийстве. *3.* Новость была объявлена публично. *4.* Он публично заявил о своей любви. *5.* Она публично извинилась. • *1.* The company published it publicly. *2.* She's gonna publicly accuse my son of murder. *3.* The news was announced publicly. *4.* He declared his love publicly. *5.* She apologized publicly.

**656. неслышный** — *inaudible* — The word 'неслышный' is used to describe something that cannot be heard or is barely audible. It is often used to refer to sounds that are very quiet or faint, making them difficult to perceive or distinguish.

**657. экспериментальный** — *experimental* — This word is used to describe something that is done or created in order to test new ideas or methods, often in a scientific or artistic context. It implies a sense of innovation and exploration.

• *1.* Криогенный резервуар содержал экспериментальный

материал. *2.* Очень экспериментально. *3.* Результаты экспериментального исследования. *4.* Экспериментальный кварк столкнулся на высоких скоростях. *5.* Они провели экспериментальное испытание. • *1.* The cryogenic tank held the experimental material. *2.* Very experimental. *3.* The results of the experimental study. *4.* The experimental quark collided at high speeds. *5.* They conducted an experimental trial.

**658. открыто** — *openly, overtly* — 'Открыто' is used to describe actions or behaviors that are done in a transparent and straightforward manner, without any attempt to conceal or hide them. It conveys the idea of being honest and upfront about something.
• *1.* Он был открытым гомофобом. *2.* Троица открыто поделилась своим мнением. *3.* Они открыто обсуждают этот вопрос. *4.* Они открыто обсуждали тему менструации. *5.* Она открыто плакала. • *1.* He was openly homophobic. *2.* The threesome shared their opinions openly. *3.* They are openly discussing the issue. *4.* They discussed the topic of menstruation openly. *5.* She was openly weeping.

**659. либеральный** — *liberal* — The word 'liberal' is used to describe someone or something that is open-minded, tolerant, and progressive in their beliefs or actions. It can also refer to policies or systems that prioritize individual freedoms and rights.
• *1.* У нее было либеральное отношение к жизни. *2.* Его либеральный подход к преподаванию оказался эффективным. *3.* Либеральная интерпретация закона вызвала споры. *4.* Либеральная политика допускала гибкость. • *1.* She had a liberal attitude towards life. *2.* His liberal approach to teaching was effective. *3.* The liberal interpretation of the law was controversial. *4.* The liberal policy allowed for flexibility.

**660. эквивалентный** — *equivalent* — 'Эквивалентный' is used to describe something that is equal in value, meaning, or function to something else. It is often used in mathematics, science, and language to indicate a comparable or interchangeable relationship between two things.
• *1.* Заслужить их доверие эквивалентно успеху. *2.* Оба эквивалентны по ценности. *3.* Условия были эквивалентны сортире. • *1.* Earning their trust is equivalent to success. *2.* The two are equivalent in value. *3.* The conditions were equivalent

to a shithouse.

**661. кратко** — *briefly* — 'Кратко' is used to indicate that something is being done or explained in a concise and succinct manner. It is often used to summarize information or provide a brief overview of a topic.

● *1.* Вкратце, да. *2.* Кратко, давайте обсудим. ● *1.* Briefly, yes. *2.* Briefly, let's discuss.

**662. незаконченный** — *unfinished* — This word is used to describe something that has not been completed or finished. It can refer to a task, project, or any other work that is still in progress and not yet finalized.

● *1.* Незаконченное дело. *2.* У нас с тобой есть незаконченные дела. ● *1.* Unfinished business. *2.* You and I have unfinished business.

**663. утвердительный** — *affirmative* — This word is used to describe statements or actions that confirm or assert something as true or valid. It is often used in discussions, debates, or when expressing agreement with a particular idea or opinion.

● *1.* Это утвердительно. *2.* Утвердительно, сэр. *3.* Это утвердительно, сэр. *4.* Утвердительно, капитан. *5.* Утвердительно, Михаил. ● *1.* That's affirmative. *2.* Affirmative, sir. *3.* That's affirmative, sir. *4.* Affirmative, Captain. *5.* Affirmative, Michael.

**664. дерзкий** — *cocky, brash, insolent, pert* — The word 'дерзкий' is used to describe someone who is bold, confident, and sometimes disrespectful in their actions or words. It conveys a sense of arrogance and lack of regard for authority or social norms.

● *1.* Не будьте дерзкими. *2.* Не будь дерзким. *3.* Дерзкий спортсмен похвастался своим мастерством. *4.* Дерзкая манера поведения раздражала людей. *5.* Ты дерзкий. *6.* Дерзкое поведение может отпугнуть. *7.* У нее был дерзкий стиль речи. *8.* Их дерзкое поведение не нравилось другим. *9.* Дерзкие замечания оскорбили ее. *10.* У него дерзкий характер. *11.* Дерзкое отношение было освежающим. *12.* Ее дерзкий ответ удивил его. *13.* Она дерзкая. *14.* Дерзкий подросток обладал сообразительностью. *15.* Он нашел ее дерзкие замечания забавными. ● *1.* Don't get cocky. *2.* Don't be cocky. *3.* The cocky athlete bragged about his skills. *4.* The cocky demeanor rubbed people the wrong way. *5.* You're cocky. *6.* Brash behavior can be off-putting. *7.* She had a brash style of speaking. *8.* Their brash attitude didn't sit well with others. *9.* The brash remarks offended her. *10.* He has a brash personality. *11.* The pert attitude was refreshing. *12.* Her pert response surprised him. *13.* She is pert. *14.* The pert teenager had a quick wit. *15.* He found her pert remarks entertaining.

**665. утомленный** — *weary* — 'утомленный' is used to describe someone who is physically or mentally exhausted. It can also be used to describe something that looks tired or worn out.
● *1.* Нищий выглядел утомленным. *2.* Утомленные путники разыскали Джейков. ● *1.* The beggar looked weary. *2.* The weary travelers sought out the jakes.

**666. психотический** — *psychotic* — The word 'психотический' is used to describe behaviors, thoughts, or experiences that are characteristic of psychosis, a severe mental disorder. It can also be used to describe something that is extremely irrational or disconnected from reality.
● *1.* Он страдал от психотических эпизодов. *2.* В фильме фигурирует психотический антагонист. *3.* Психотическое поведение вызывало тревогу. ● *1.* He suffered from psychotic episodes. *2.* The movie featured a psychotic antagonist. *3.* The psychotic behavior was alarming.

**667. хитрый** — *sly, cunning, shifty, devious* — The word 'хитрый' is used to describe someone who is clever and deceitful, often using cunning tactics to achieve their goals. It can also refer to something that is tricky or deceptive in nature.
● *1.* Ты хитрая собака. *2.* На его лице появилась хитрая ухмылка. *3.* Он хитрый, как Рейнард. *4.* Иезавель была хитра. *5.* С виду невинная, она была хитрой. *6.* Он хитрый. *7.* Хитрый инквизитор разгадал правду. *8.* Он исполнил роль хитрого сыщика. *9.* Коварные люди известны своей хитростью. ● *1.* You sly dog. *2.* A sly grin appeared on his face. *3.* He's as sly as a reynard. *4.* The jezebel was cunning. *5.* Seemingly innocent, she was cunning. *6.* He's cunning. *7.* The cunning inquisitor unraveled the truth. *8.* He played the role of a cunning sleuth. *9.* The devious are renowned for their cunning.

**668. выносливый** — *hardy* — 'выносливый' describes someone or something that is able to endure difficult conditions or situations without easily becoming tired or weak. It implies strength, resilience, and the ability to withstand challenges.

● *1.* Факел оказался выносливым. *2.* Выносливый скот пасся в поле. *3.* Коровяка была выносливым растением. *4.* Савинское дерево было выносливым. *5.* Выносливое растение пережило зиму. ● *1.* The torchwood was hardy. *2.* The hardy cattle grazed in the field. *3.* The mullen was a hardy plant. *4.* The savin tree was hardy. *5.* The hardy plant survived the winter.

**669. дождливый** — *rainy* — This word is used to describe weather conditions when it is raining or when there is a lot of rain. It can also be used to describe a place or season that is characterized by frequent rainfall.

● *1.* День был дождливый. *2.* Их пикник выдался дождливым. *3.* Он любил дождливые дни. *4.* Погода была дождливая. ● *1.* The day was rainy. *2.* Their picnic was rainy. *3.* He loved rainy days. *4.* The weather was rainy.

**670. позорный** — *shameful, disreputable, disgraceful, dishonorable* — This word is used to describe something that brings shame or disgrace. It is often used to criticize actions or behavior that are considered dishonorable or disreputable.

● *1.* Это позорно. *2.* Позорное поведение привело к последствиям. *3.* Позорный поступок потребовал извинений. *4.* Нарушить клятву было позорно. *5.* Действия политика были позорными. *6.* Это позорно. *7.* Их поведение было позорным развратом. *8.* Позорное увольнение. ● *1.* That's shameful. *2.* The shameful behavior led to consequences. *3.* The shameful act warranted an apology. *4.* Breaking one's troth was shameful. *5.* The politician's actions were shameful. *6.* It's disgraceful. *7.* Their behavior was a disgraceful debauchery. *8.* Dishonorable discharge.

**671. оперативный** — *operational, operative* — 'Оперативный' is used to describe something that is efficient, effective, and able to be put into immediate action. It can refer to a person, process, or system that is capable of quickly achieving desired results.

● *1.* Они провели оперативный аудит. *2.* Она решала

повседневные оперативные задачи. • *1.* They conducted an operational audit. *2.* She managed the day-to-day operational tasks.

**672. соленый** — *salty, briny* — This word is used to describe food or water that has a salty or briny taste. It can also be used metaphorically to describe something as being bitter or harsh.
• *1.* Слишком соленый. *2.* Это соленое. *3.* Сладкий и соленый. *4.* Сардина была соленой. *5.* Соленый привкус остался во рту. *6.* Он почувствовал вкус соленой воды. *7.* Соленый океан был полон жизни. *8.* В воздухе пахло соленостью. *9.* Морепродукты имели соленый вкус. • *1.* Too salty. *2.* It's salty. *3.* Sweet and salty. *4.* The sardine was salty. *5.* The salty taste lingered in his mouth. *6.* He tasted the briny water. *7.* The briny ocean was full of life. *8.* The air had a briny smell. *9.* The seafood had a briny flavor.

**673. рыбный** — *fishy* — The word 'рыбный' is used to describe something that seems suspicious or questionable, often implying deceit or dishonesty. It can also refer to something that has a strong smell or taste of fish.

**674. стратегический** — *strategic* — This word is used to describe something that is related to long-term planning or important decisions that are made to achieve a specific goal or outcome. It is often used in military, business, and political contexts.
• *1.* Они приняли стратегическое решение подождать. *2.* Он руководил военно-стратегическим планом. *3.* Решение было чисто стратегическим. *4.* Варкрафт требует стратегического мышления. *5.* Генерал обладал стратегическим умом. • *1.* They made a strategic decision to wait. *2.* He led the militarily strategic plan. *3.* The decision was purely strategic. *4.* Warcraft requires strategic thinking. *5.* The general had a strategic mind.

**675. искусный** — *skilled, skillful, natty, skilful* — The word 'искусный' is used to describe someone who is highly skilled or talented in a particular area, or something that is well-made or cleverly designed. It can also refer to someone who is stylish or natty in appearance.
• *1.* Шарп был искусным мастером. *2.* Он был известен как искусный фокусник. *3.* Он был искусным фехтовальщиком. *4.*

Он был искусным собеседником. *5.* Сондерс был искусным мастером. *6.* Со временем она стала искусной танцовщицей. *7.* Искусный художник написал прекрасный портрет. *8.* В мебели было видно искусное мастерство. *9.* Они были искусными танцорами. ● *1.* Sharpe was a skilled artisan. *2.* He was known as a skilled conjurer. *3.* He was a skilled swordsman. *4.* He was a skilled conversationalist. *5.* Saunders was a skilled craftsman. *6.* She became a skillful dancer over time. *7.* The skillful artist painted a beautiful portrait. *8.* The skilful craftsmanship was evident in the furniture. *9.* They were skilful dancers.

**676. кардиальный** — *cardiac* — The adjective/adverb 'кардиальный' is used to describe something related to the heart or cardiovascular system. It can be used to refer to medical conditions, treatments, or procedures that involve the heart.

**677. оптимистичный** — *optimistic* — This word is used to describe a positive outlook or attitude towards the future. It conveys a sense of hopefulness and confidence in the face of challenges or uncertainties.
● *1.* Я настроен оптимистично. *2.* Прогнозы по доходам были оптимистичными. *3.* Это оптимистично. *4.* Он был настроен решительно оптимистично. *5.* Они представили оптимистичный план на будущее. ● *1.* I'm optimistic. *2.* The revenue projections were optimistic. *3.* That's optimistic. *4.* He was decidedly optimistic. *5.* They presented an optimistic plan for the future.

**678. лохматый** — *shaggy* — The word 'лохматый' is used to describe something or someone with long, unkempt hair or fur. It conveys a sense of untidiness or wildness in appearance.
● *1.* Она восхищалась лохматой гривой льва. *2.* Лохматую собаку нужно было искупать. *3.* В фильме он сыграл лохматого персонажа. ● *1.* She admired the shaggy mane of the lion. *2.* The shaggy dog needed a bath. *3.* He played a shaggy character in the movie.

**679. региональный** — *regional* — 'Regional' is used to describe something that pertains to a specific region or area within a country. It can refer to anything from local government policies to cultural traditions and events that are specific to a particular region.

● *1.* Он обратился за советом к региональному шерифу. ● *1.* He sought advice from the regional sharif.

**680. пушистый** — *fuzzy, furry, fluffy, bushy* — This word is used to describe something that is soft, fluffy, or covered in fur. It can refer to animals, fabrics, or even hairstyles that have a fuzzy or bushy texture.

● *1.* Она погладила пушистую шерсть кота. *2.* У щенка была пушистая шерсть. *3.* Они нашли в саду пушистую гусеницу. *4.* Пушистый кролик отпрыгнул. *5.* Пушистое одеяло было мягким. *6.* Пушистый зверек был игрив. *7.* Пышка имела пушистую текстуру. *8.* У собаки пушистая шея. *9.* Шерсть колли была мягкой и пушистой. *10.* Пушистое одеяло согревало ее. *11.* На завтрак она съела пушистый блин. *12.* У куницы пушистый хвост. ● *1.* She petted the cat's fuzzy coat. *2.* The puppy had a fuzzy coat. *3.* They found a fuzzy caterpillar in the garden. *4.* The furry rabbit hopped away. *5.* The furry blanket was soft. *6.* The furry animal was playful. *7.* The crumpet had a fluffy texture. *8.* The dog has a fluffy neck. *9.* The collie's fur was soft and fluffy. *10.* The fluffy comforter kept her warm. *11.* She ate a fluffy pancake for breakfast. *12.* The marten has a bushy tail.

**681. плавно** — *smoothly, fluently* — 'Плавно' is used to describe actions or movements that are done in a smooth and fluent manner, without any sudden or jerky movements. It implies a sense of grace and ease in the way something is done.

● *1.* Глобус плавно вращался. *2.* Лунный корабль приземлился плавно. *3.* Новая бритва плавно скользила по его коже. *4.* Сани плавно скользили по снегу. *5.* Самолет плавно взлетел. ● *1.* The globe rotated smoothly. *2.* The lunar lander touched down smoothly. *3.* The new razor glided smoothly over his skin. *4.* The sledge glided smoothly over the snow. *5.* The airplane took off smoothly.

**682. мужественный** — *manly, virile, spunky* — This word is used to describe someone or something that embodies qualities typically associated with masculinity, such as strength, courage, and vigor. It can be used to praise someone's bravery or toughness.

● *1.* Очень мужественный. *2.* Лекарство заставило его почувствовать себя мужественным. *3.* Она ценит его мужественную силу. *4.* Он известен своей мужественной энергией. *5.* Считается, что растение обладает мужественными свойствами. *6.* Он все еще очень мужественный. • *1.* Very manly. *2.* The medicine made him feel virile. *3.* She appreciates his virile strength. *4.* He's known for his virile energy. *5.* The plant is believed to have virile properties. *6.* He's still very virile.

**683. необоснованный** — *unreasonable, unfounded, unwarranted, unjustified* — This word is used to describe something that lacks a valid reason or justification. It implies that the action or belief is not based on logic or evidence. It conveys a sense of irrationality or unfairness.

• *1.* Требования были необоснованными. *2.* Необоснованные ожидания вызвали стресс. *3.* Необоснованная просьба была отклонена. *4.* Презумпция оказалась необоснованной. *5.* Подозрение оказалось необоснованным. *6.* Решение было необоснованным и внезапным. *7.* Обвинения были необоснованными. • *1.* The demands were unreasonable. *2.* The unreasonable expectations caused stress. *3.* The unreasonable request was denied. *4.* The presumption was unfounded. *5.* The suspicion was unfounded. *6.* The decision was unjustified and abrupt. *7.* The accusations were unjustified.

**684. заразительный** — *contagious* — This word is used to describe something that has the ability to spread easily from one person to another, whether it be a physical illness or a feeling or emotion. It implies a strong influence or impact on others.

• *1.* Его сперма заразительна. *2.* Улыбка Мина была заразительной. *3.* Эякуляция радости была заразительной. *4.* У Кэролайн заразительный смех. *5.* Ее беспечное отношение заразительно. • *1.* His spunk is contagious. *2.* Ming's smile was contagious. *3.* The ejaculation of joy was contagious. *4.* Caroline has a contagious laugh. *5.* Her blythe attitude is contagious.

**685. чрезмерный** — *excessive, undue, inordinate* — 'чрезмерный' is used to describe something that is beyond what is considered normal or appropriate, often implying that it is too much or unnecessary. It conveys a sense of excessiveness or imbalance in a negative way.

• *1.* Кажется чрезмерным. *2.* Это чрезмерно. *3.* Дискреционные расходы были чрезмерными. *4.* Синдром вызывает чрезмерный страх. *5.* Никакого чрезмерного применения насилия. • *1.* Seems excessive. *2.* That's excessive. *3.* The discretionary spending was excessive. *4.* The syndrome causes excessive fear. *5.* No excessive use of violence.

**686. спинной** — *spinal* — This word is used to describe something related to the spine or spinal cord. It can be used to refer to medical conditions, treatments, or anatomical structures that are connected to the spine.
• *1.* Спинной мозг – хрупкая структура. *2.* Грудные позвонки защищают спинной мозг. *3.* Ей сделали спинномозговую пункцию. • *1.* The spinal cord is a delicate structure. *2.* The thoracic vertebrae protect the spinal cord. *3.* She had a spinal tap.

**687. социалистический** — *socialist* — This word is used to describe something that is related to or characteristic of socialism, a political and economic system based on collective ownership and control of the means of production.
• *1.* Страна приняла социалистические идеалы. *2.* Социалистическая политика в действии. • *1.* The country embraced socialist ideals. *2.* Socialist policies in action.

**688. тусклый** — *dim, fishy* — 'Тусклый' is used to describe something that is lacking brightness or clarity, often implying a sense of dullness or suspicion. It can refer to both physical objects and abstract concepts, suggesting a lack of vibrancy or transparency.
• *1.* Его зрение было тусклым. *2.* Тусклый свет замерцал. *3.* Тусклая лампочка едва освещала комнату. • *1.* His eyesight was dim. *2.* The dim light flickered. *3.* The dim lightbulb barely illuminated the room.

**689. небезопасный** — *insecure* — This word is used to describe something that is not safe or secure, posing a potential risk or danger. It can refer to physical environments, situations, or relationships that are unstable or unreliable.
• *1.* Небезопасный стиль привязанности. • *1.* An insecure attachment style.

**690. спонтанный** — *spontaneous* — This word is used to describe something that happens or is done in a natural, impulsive, or unplanned way, without much thought or preparation beforehand.

• *1.* Будьте спонтанны. *2.* Они спонтанно поцеловались п- од дождем. *3.* Ее смех был заразительным и спонтанным. *4.* Спонтанное решение привело к приключению. *5.* Толпа разразилась спонтанными аплодисментами. • *1.* Be sponta- neous. *2.* They shared a spontaneous kiss in the rain. *3.* Her laughter was infectious and spontaneous. *4.* The spontaneous decision led to an adventure. *5.* The crowd burst into sponta- neous applause.

**691. развязный** — *cheeky* — 'Развязный' is used to describe someone who is bold, daring, or impudent in their actions or be- havior. It conveys a sense of cheekiness or audacity in a playful or mischievous way.

**692. неопознанный** — *unidentified* — This word is used to describe something that is not recognized or known. It is often used in reference to unidentified objects, people, or phenom- ena.

• *1.* Неопознанный Ликантант. *2.* Неопознанная жертва - осталась загадкой. *3.* Неопознанный летающий объект. *4.* Неопознанный самолет пролетел над головой. • *1.* Uniden- tified Lycantant. *2.* The unidentified victim remained a mystery. *3.* An unidentified flying object. *4.* The unidentified aircraft flew overhead.

**693. стрессовый** — *stressful* — This word is used to describe situations, events, or experiences that cause feelings of pressure, tension, or anxiety. It is often used to convey the idea of some- thing being difficult or challenging to deal with.

• *1.* Это звучит стрессово. *2.* Они пережили стрессовые ус- ловия. *3.* Он склонен к чрезмерной реакции в стрессовых ситуациях. *4.* Ситуация стала стрессовой. *5.* У него была ст- рессовая работа. • *1.* That sounds stressful. *2.* They endured the stressful conditions. *3.* He tends to overreaction in stressful situations. *4.* The situation became stressful. *5.* He was in a stressful job.

**694. виртуальный** — *virtual* — This word is used to describe something that exists or occurs in a computerized or online en- vironment rather than in the physical world. It can also refer to something that is simulated or imitated.

• *1.* Ты аватар, виртуальное представление Зои. *2.* Игра в виртуальной реальности была захватывающей. *3.* Она исследовала виртуальный мир. *4.* Он присутствовал на виртуальной встрече. *5.* Он создал виртуальный тур. • *1.* You're an avatar, a virtual representation of Zoe. *2.* The virtual reality game was immersive. *3.* She explored a virtual world. *4.* He attended a virtual meeting. *5.* He created a virtual tour.

**695. вонючий** — *smelly, stinky* — This word is used to describe something that has a strong and unpleasant smell. It is often used to refer to things like garbage, dirty clothes, or spoiled food.

• *1.* И вонючий. *2.* Вонючие носки нужно было постирать. *3.* Мусор был вонючий. *4.* Кухня была наполнена вонючим дымом. *5.* Он вынес вонючий мусор. *6.* Вонючий тофу! • *1.* And smelly. *2.* The smelly socks needed to be washed. *3.* The garbage was smelly. *4.* The kitchen was filled with smelly fumes. *5.* He took out the smelly trash. *6.* Stinky tofu!

**696. некомпетентный** — *incompetent* — This word is used to describe someone who lacks the necessary skills, knowledge, or ability to perform a task effectively or competently. It implies a lack of expertise or capability in a particular area.

• *1.* Отчет выявил крайне некомпетентное поведение. *2.* Ты некомпетентный дурак! *3.* Адвоката признали некомпетентным. *4.* Компания пострадала из-за некомпетентного руководства. *5.* Некомпетентный сотрудник создал проблемы. • *1.* The report revealed grossly incompetent behavior. *2.* You incompetent fool! *3.* The lawyer was found to be incompetent. *4.* The company suffered due to incompetent leadership. *5.* The incompetent employee caused problems.

**697. спортивный** — *athletic, sporty* — This word is used to describe someone or something that is related to sports or physical activities. It can be used to talk about a person's appearance, abilities, or interests in sports.

• *1.* Спортивный клуб предлагает различные спортивные - программы. *2.* Он был известен своим спортивным мастерством. *3.* У нее есть природные спортивные способности. *4.* Очень спортивный. *5.* Спортивная стипендия покрыла ее обучение. *6.* Он был одет в спортивный костюм. *7.* Новые кроссовки выглядят спортивно. *8.* Она водит спортивную машину. *9.* Этот мотоцикл очень спортивный. *10.* Дизайн реглана спортивный. • *1*. The athletic club offers various sports programs. *2*. He was notorious for his athletic prowess. *3*. She has a natural athletic ability. *4*. Very athletic. *5*. The athletic scholarship covered her tuition. *6*. He wore a sporty outfit. *7*. The new sneakers look sporty. *8*. She drives a sporty car. *9*. This bike is very sporty. *10*. The raglan design is sporty.

**698. стоящий** — *worthwhile* — Used to describe something that is valuable, deserving of attention, or worth the effort. It implies that the object or action is beneficial or rewarding in some way.

• *1*. Ничего стоящего никогда не бывает. • *1*. Nothing worthwhile ever is.

**699. тенистый** — *shady* — 'Тенистый' is used to describe a place that is shaded or shadowy, typically due to the presence of trees or buildings blocking the sunlight. It can also be used to describe a person or situation that is suspicious or untrustworthy.

• *1*. Они отдыхали под тенистым деревом. *2*. На улице было темно и тенисто. *3*. Он сидел в тенистом углу. • *1*. They rested under the shady tree. *2*. The street was dark and shady. *3*. He sat in the shady corner.

**700. аномальный** — *abnormal, anomalous* — The word 'аномальный' is used to describe something that is abnormal or deviates from the norm. It is often used to refer to unusual or unexpected occurrences, behaviors, or characteristics.

• *1*. Железистая ткань демонстрировала аномальный рост. *2*. Результаты теста были аномальными. *3*. Аномальная погода была непредсказуемой. *4*. Она столкнулась с аномальной ситуацией. *5*. Результаты были аномальными. *6*. Аномальное событие озадачило учёных. *7*. Аномальное поведение вызвало подозрения. • *1*. The glandular tissue showed abnormal growth. *2*. The results of the test were abnormal. *3*. The anomalous weather was unpredictable. *4*. She faced an anomalous situation. *5*. The results were anomalous. *6*. The anomalous event puzzled scientists. *7*. The anomalous behavior raised suspicions.

**701. упорядоченный** — *orderly* — 'Упорядоченный' is used to describe something that is neat, organized, and well--

arranged. It implies a sense of structure and tidiness in the way things are arranged or done.

● *1.* Общество было мирным и упорядоченным. *2.* Упорядоченное расположение облегчило поиск. ● *1.* The society was peaceful and orderly. *2.* The orderly arrangement made it easy to find.

**702. клинический** — *clinical* — 'Клинический' is used to describe something that is very precise, objective, and based on scientific evidence, often in a medical or scientific context. It implies a detached and analytical approach, focusing on facts rather than emotions.

● *1.* Она прошла обучение на клинического психолога. *2.* Его карьера вращалась вокруг клинической токсикологии. ● *1.* She trained to become a clinical psychologist. *2.* His career revolved around clinical toxicology.

**703. сенсационный** — *sensational* — This word is used to describe something that causes a strong reaction or excitement, often due to being surprising, scandalous, or extraordinary. It is commonly used in journalism, entertainment, and marketing to grab attention.

● *1.* Она сенсационная. *2.* Вы были сенсационны. *3.* Ты выглядишь сенсационно. *4.* Фильм получил сенсационные отзывы. *5.* Его фокус был сенсационным. ● *1.* She's sensational. *2.* You were sensational. *3.* You look sensational. *4.* The movie received sensational reviews. *5.* His magic trick was sensational.

**704. радиоактивный** — *radioactive* — This word is used to describe substances or materials that emit radiation or are contaminated with radiation. It is commonly used in the context of nuclear energy, radioactive waste, and environmental contamination.

● *1.* Берегись, Радиоактивный Человек! *2.* Изотоп был радиоактивным. ● *1.* Watch out, Radioactive Man! *2.* The isotope was radioactive.

**705. трусливый** — *cowardly, craven, dastardly* — 'Трусливый' is used to describe someone who lacks courage or bravery, often showing fear or timidity in the face of danger or difficulty. It can also be used to describe actions or behavior that are cowardly or dastardly.

● *1.* Это был подлый и трусливый поступок. *2.* Это трусливо. *3.* Его называли трусливым солдатом. *4.* Трусливый лев нашел в себе смелость. *5.* Она презирала его трусливое - поведение. ● *1.* It was a despicable and cowardly act. *2.* It's cowardly. *3.* He was labeled a cowardly soldier. *4.* The cowardly lion found his courage. *5.* She despised his cowardly behavior.

**706. незаконно** — *illegally, unlawful, unlawfully* — The word 'незаконно' is used to describe actions or behaviors that are against the law or not permitted by legal regulations. It conveys the idea of something being done in a way that is not authorized or lawful.

● *1.* Незаконное проникновение в здание было запрещено. *2.* Его действия были признаны незаконными. *3.* Им предъявлено обвинение в незаконном хранении. ● *1.* Unlawful entry into the building was prohibited. *2.* His actions were deemed unlawful. *3.* They were charged with unlawful possession.

**707. циничный** — *cynical, bitchy* — The word 'циничный' is used to describe someone who is distrustful of human sincerity and motivated by self-interest. It can also refer to behavior that is contemptuous or scornful.

● *1.* Не будьте таким циничным. *2.* Ты такой циничный. *3.* Когда ты успел стать таким циничным? *4.* Почему ты такой циничный? ● *1.* Don't be so cynical. *2.* You're so cynical. *3.* When did you get so cynical? *4.* Why are you so cynical?

**708. внеземной** — *extraterrestrial* — This word is used to describe something or someone that is not from Earth, typically referring to beings, objects, or phenomena originating from outer space or beyond our planet.

● *1.* Был замечен внеземной космический корабль. *2.* Они верят во внеземные формы жизни. ● *1.* An extraterrestrial spacecraft was spotted. *2.* They believe in extraterrestrial life forms.

**709. молочный** — *milky* — This word is used to describe something that is related to or resembles milk in color, taste, or texture. It can be used to describe food, drinks, or other items that have a milky quality.

● *1.* Молочный кофе был слишком сладким. *2.* Ее молочный цвет лица был поразительным. *3.* Напиток имел молочный

вид. *4.* В рецепте указана консистенция молочного цвета. •
*1.* The milky coffee was too sweet. *2.* Her milky complexion was striking. *3.* The drink had a milky appearance. *4.* The recipe called for milky consistency.

**710. титанический** — *titanic* — 'Титанический' is used to describe something of immense size, strength, or power, often in a metaphorical sense. It conveys the idea of something monumental, colossal, or extraordinary in scale or impact.

**711. отчетливый** — *distinct* — The word 'distinct' is used to describe something that is clear, easily recognizable, or sharply defined. It is often used to emphasize the clarity or sharpness of a particular quality or characteristic.
• *1.* Они услышали отчетливый шум. *2.* Он говорил с отчетливым южным акцентом. *3.* Она почувствовала отчетливый запах пропана. *4.* Запах был отчетливый. • *1.* They heard a distinct noise. *2.* He spoke with a distinct southerner accent. *3.* She smelled the distinct scent of propane. *4.* The smell was distinct.

**712. крутой** — *steep, drastic* — 'Крутой' is used to describe something that is intense, extreme, or impressive. It can refer to a steep slope, a drastic change, or a cool and impressive person or thing.
• *1.* Склон был слишком крут, чтобы подняться наверх. *2.* Край холма был крутым. *3.* Беговая дорожка была установлена на крутой уклон. *4.* Это слишком круто. *5.* Холм имел крутой уклон. • *1.* The slope was too steep to climb. *2.* The brow of the hill was steep. *3.* The treadmill was set to a steep incline. *4.* It's too steep. *5.* The hill had a steep incline.

**713. разрушительный** — *destructive, disruptive* — This word is used to describe something that causes destruction or disruption. It is often used to emphasize the negative impact of a particular action or event.
• *1.* Он стал свидетелем разрушительного лесного пожара. *2.* Гнев может быть разрушительным. *3.* Гомофобия разрушительна и вредна. • *1.* He witnessed the destructive wildfire. *2.* Anger can be destructive. *3.* Homophobia is destructive and harmful.

**714. литературный** — *literary* — This word is used to describe something that is related to literature or has qualities typically found in literature, such as being well-written, artistic, or intellectual.

● *1.* Я хочу совершить литературное паломничество. ● *1.* I want to make a literary pilgrimage.

**715. сварливый** — *grumpy, contentious, cantankerous, quarrelsome* — This word is used to describe someone who is easily irritated, argumentative, and prone to starting conflicts or disagreements with others. It conveys a negative attitude and a tendency to be confrontational in interactions.

● *1.* Я не сварливый. *2.* Почему ты такой сварливый? *3.* Он сварливый старый чудак. *4.* Почему такой сварливый? *5.* Сварливая собака залаяла. *6.* Сварливый кот почесался. *7.* Их сварливый спор продолжался. *8.* Он всегда сварливый. *9.* Проворчал сварливый старик. *10.* Они избегали сварливого коллегу. *11.* Она оказалась в сварливом настроении. *12.* У него был сварливый характер. ● *1.* I'm not grumpy. *2.* Why are you so grumpy? *3.* He's a grumpy old codger. *4.* Why so grumpy? *5.* The cantankerous dog barked. *6.* The cantankerous cat scratched. *7.* Their cantankerous arguing continued. *8.* He's always cantankerous. *9.* The cantankerous old man grumbled. *10.* They avoided the quarrelsome colleague. *11.* She found herself in a quarrelsome mood. *12.* He had a quarrelsome nature.

**716. зудящий** — *itchy* — This word is used to describe a sensation on the skin that causes a desire to scratch. It can also be used metaphorically to describe a strong desire or urge for something.

● *1.* Чесоточная сыпь была зудящей. *2.* Экзема вызывает зудящие высыпания. ● *1.* The scabies rash was itchy. *2.* Eczema causes itchy rashes.

**717. плотно** — *tightly, densely* — 'Плотно' is used to describe something that is tightly packed or closely spaced together. It can refer to physical objects being close together or to something being tightly secured or fitting snugly.

● *1.* Плунжер плотно присосался к сливу. *2.* Марлевая повязка была плотно замотана. *3.* Плотно намотайте пряжу. *4.* Упаковщик плотно запечатал коробки. *5.* Флакон был плотно закрыт. ● *1.* The plunger suctioned tightly to the drain. *2.* The gauze bandage was wrapped tightly. *3.* Wind the yarn tightly.

*4.* The packer sealed the boxes tightly. *5.* The vial was sealed tightly.

**718. предсказуемый** — *predictable* — This word is used to describe something that is easy to foresee or anticipate, lacking surprises or unexpected elements. It is often used to describe people, events, or situations that follow a pattern or are easily understood.

● *1.* Я настолько предсказуем? *2.* Так предсказуемо. *3.* Ты такой предсказуемый. *4.* Ты предсказуем. *5.* Как предсказуемо. ● *1.* Am I that predictable? *2.* So predictable. *3.* You're so predictable. *4.* You're predictable. *5.* How predictable.

**719. безумно** — *madly, crazily, insanely* — This word is used to intensify emotions or actions, indicating a high level of intensity or extremity. It conveys a sense of extreme passion, enthusiasm, or irrationality in a situation or behavior.

● *1.* Я безумно люблю тебя. *2.* Я безумно в тебя влюблен. *3.* Я был безумно влюблен в нее. *4.* Она танцевала безумно. *5.* Он безумно крутился. *6.* Они безумно смеялись вместе. ● *1.* I love you madly. *2.* I'm madly in love with you. *3.* I was madly in love with her. *4.* She danced crazily. *5.* He spun around crazily. *6.* They laughed crazily together.

**720. вымерший** — *extinct* — 'вымерший' is used to describe something that no longer exists or is no longer in use. It is often used in reference to animals, plants, languages, or customs that have disappeared over time.

● *1.* Вид был объявлен вымершим. *2.* Додо -- вымершая птица. *3.* Додо -- культовый вымерший вид. ● *1.* The species was declared extinct. *2.* The dodo is an extinct bird. *3.* The dodo is an iconic extinct species.

**721. образовательный** — *educational* — This word is used to describe something that is related to or intended to provide education or knowledge. It can refer to materials, programs, activities, or experiences that are designed to teach or inform.

● *1.* Неграмотному населению необходимо больше образовательных ресурсов. ● *1.* The illiterate population needs more educational resources.

**722. хронический** — *chronic* — 'Хронический' is used to describe a condition or situation that is long-lasting, persistent, or recurring. It implies that the issue has been ongoing for a significant period of time and is unlikely to be resolved quickly.

● *1.* Хроническая усталость может изнурить. *2.* Он страдал хроническим запором. *3.* Он получил лечение кетамином от хронической боли. *4.* У него было хроническое заболевание бронхов. *5.* Она была хроническим беспокойным человеком. ● *1.* Chronic fatigue can be debilitating. *2.* He suffered from chronic constipation. *3.* He received ketamine treatments for chronic pain. *4.* He had a chronic bronchial condition. *5.* She was a chronic worrier.

**723. эффективно** — *effectively* — This word is used to describe something that is done in a way that produces the desired result or outcome. It indicates that a task or action is carried out successfully and efficiently.

● *1.* Лекарство не подействовало эффективно. *2.* Как мы можем эффективно использовать свое время? *3.* Она эффективно управляла проектом. *4.* Она эффективно играла на фортепиано. *5.* Он эффективно разговаривал с толпой. ● *1.* The medicine was not working effectively. *2.* How can we leverage our time effectively? *3.* She managed the project effectively. *4.* She played the piano effectively. *5.* He spoke effectively to the crowd.

**724. незрелый** — *immature* — 'незрелый' is used to describe something or someone that is not fully developed or mature. It can refer to physical, emotional, or intellectual immaturity. It implies a lack of readiness or completeness in a particular aspect.

● *1.* Ребята, вы такие незрелые. *2.* Ты незрелый. *3.* Ты такой незрелый. *4.* И вы, ребята, называете меня незрелым? ● *1.* You guys are so immature. *2.* You're immature. *3.* You're so immature. *4.* And you guys call me immature?

**725. удаленно** — *remotely* — 'Удаленно' is used to describe something that is far away in distance or time, or to indicate that something is being done from a distance, such as remote work or remote learning.

● *1.* Не удаленно. ● *1.* Not remotely.

**726. поспешный** — *hasty* — The word 'поспешный' is used to describe actions or decisions that are done quickly or without proper consideration. It conveys a sense of urgency or haste in a negative context.

● *1.* Давайте не будем слишком поспешными. *2.* Я сожалею о своем поспешном ответе. *3.* Она поспешно отступила. *4.* Поспешные действия вызвали проблемы. *5.* Его нетерпение привело к поспешным решениям. ● *1.* Let's not be too hasty. *2.* I regret my hasty response. *3.* She made a hasty retreat. *4.* The hasty action caused problems. *5.* His impatience led to hasty decisions.

**727. зловещий** — *ominous, sinister, inauspicious* — 'Зловещий' is used to describe something that gives off a sense of foreboding or danger. It conveys a feeling of unease or dread, suggesting that something bad or threatening may happen.

● *1.* Это звучит зловеще. *2.* Звучит зловеще. *3.* Это совсем не звучит зловеще. *4.* Небо казалось мрачно-зловещим. *5.* Пещера была темной и зловещей. *6.* Зловещая правда была раскрыта. *7.* От зловещего смеха у нее по спине пробежал озноб. *8.* Зловещая фигура скрывалась в тени. *9.* Зловещий заговор наконец был раскрыт. *10.* Он проигнорировал зловещие предупредительные знаки. ● *1.* That sounds ominous. *2.* Sounds ominous. *3.* That doesn't sound ominous at all. *4.* The sky appeared darkly ominous. *5.* The cavern was dark and ominous. *6.* The sinister truth was exposed. *7.* The sinister laugh sent chills down her spine. *8.* The sinister figure lurked in the shadows. *9.* The sinister plot was finally revealed. *10.* He ignored the inauspicious warning signs.

**728. тактичный** — *considerate* — 'Тактичный' is used to describe someone who is thoughtful and considerate in their actions and words, especially in sensitive or delicate situations. It implies a level of tact and diplomacy in dealing with others.

● *1.* Это тактично. ● *1.* That's considerate.

**729. боком** — *sideways* — 'Воком' is used to describe something positioned or moving sideways in relation to a reference point. It can also be used to describe a situation where something is not in its usual or expected position.

● *1.* Повернитесь боком. *2.* Идите боком. ● *1.* Turn sideways. *2.* Go sideways.

**730. неполный** — *incomplete* — The word 'неполный' is used to describe something that is lacking or unfinished. It implies that there is a missing or incomplete aspect to the object or situation being described.

• *1.* Это неполно. *2.* Синтетическая калибровка неполная. *3.* Нотный лист был неполным. *4.* В неполной головоломке не хватало нескольких частей. *5.* Она сдала неполное задание.
• *1.* It's incomplete. *2.* Synthetic calibration incomplete. *3.* The music sheet was incomplete. *4.* The incomplete puzzle was missing a few pieces. *5.* She submitted the incomplete assignment.

**731. буржуазный** — *bourgeois* — 'Burzhuzny' is used to describe something or someone as being characteristic of the bourgeoisie, typically implying a focus on material wealth, social status, and conventional values. It can also refer to something that is perceived as being overly capitalist or elitist.

• *1.* Они жили в буржуазном районе. *2.* Буржуазный образ жизни был комфортным. • *1.* They lived in a bourgeois neighborhood. *2.* The bourgeois lifestyle was comfortable.

**732. частый** — *frequent* — This word is used to describe something that happens often or occurs with regularity. It can be used to indicate a high frequency of events or actions.

• *1.* У пекарни был частый клиент. *2.* Частый дождь сделал дорогу скользкой. *3.* Раньше у них были частые половые отношения. *4.* Постановление требовало частых проверок. *5.* Вы можете найти частые автобусы в город. • *1.* The bakery had a frequent customer. *2.* The frequent rain made the road slippery. *3.* They had frequent intercourse in the past. *4.* The regulation required frequent inspections. *5.* You can find frequent buses to the city.

**733. нервно** — *nervously* — 'нервно' is used to describe actions or behaviors that are done in a nervous or anxious manner. It can be used to convey a sense of tension or unease in a situation.

• *1.* Он нервно коснулся бритвы. *2.* Жених нервно ждал. *3.* Она нервно заломила руки. *4.* Они нервно и тревожно ходили. *5.* Она нервно ждала результатов дебатов. • *1.* He nervously touched the razer. *2.* The bridegroom waited nervously. *3.* She wrung her hands nervously. *4.* They nervously and anxiously paced. *5.* She waited nervously for the deb results.

**734. бесшабашный** — *daft* — The word 'бесшабашный' is

used to describe someone or something as reckless, wild, or unruly. It implies a lack of restraint or control, often in a carefree or foolish manner.

**735. поэтический** — *poetic* — The word 'поэтический' is used to describe something that is related to or characteristic of poetry. It is often used to convey a sense of beauty, creativity, or emotional depth in a non-literal way.

• *1.* Поэтический стих покорил публику. *2.* Он восхищался ее поэтическим талантом. *3.* Поэтический язык рисовал картину. *4.* Поэтические образы вызвали слезы. *5.* Ее поэтическая душа текла через ее письмо. • *1.* The poetic verse captivated the audience. *2.* He admired her poetic talent. *3.* The poetic language painted a picture. *4.* The poetic imagery brought tears. *5.* Her poetic soul flowed through her writing.

**736. ледяной** — *icy, glacial* — The word 'ледяной' is used to describe something that is icy or glacial in nature. It can be used to convey a sense of coldness, harshness, or a lack of warmth in a situation or environment.

• *1.* Вода во фьорде была ледяной. • *1.* The fjord's water was icy cold.

**737. гибкий** — *flexible, supple, limber, versatile* — This word describes something or someone that is able to bend, adapt, or change easily. It can refer to physical flexibility or versatility in terms of skills, ideas, or plans.

• *1.* Я гибкий. *2.* График работы няни был гибким. *3.* Стебель растения был гибким. *4.* График был гибким. *5.* Это гибко. *6.* Его мышцы оставались гибкими благодаря упражнениям. *7.* Во время танца у нее были гибкие движения. *8.* Растения были гибкими после дождя. • *1.* I'm flexible. *2.* The babysitting schedule was flexible. *3.* The plant stem was flexible. *4.* The schedule was flexible. *5.* It's flexible. *6.* His muscles remained supple with exercise. *7.* She had supple movements during the dance. *8.* The plants were supple after the rain.

**738. четкий** — *crisp, legible* — The word 'четкий' is used to describe something that is clear, sharp, and easy to read or understand. It can refer to writing, images, or any other form of communication that is well-defined and easily comprehensible.

• *1.* Почерк у нее был аккуратный и четкий. *2.* Его речь была ясной и четкой. • *1.* Her handwriting was neat and crisp. *2.* His speech was clear and crisp.

**739. восторженный** — *enthusiastic, ecstatic* — This word is used to describe someone who is extremely excited or thrilled about something. It conveys a sense of enthusiasm and joy, often indicating a high level of excitement or happiness.

• *1.* Вы не выглядите очень восторженно. *2.* Ты не кажешься восторженным. *3.* Поведение толпы было восторженным. *4.* Это заявление вызвало восторженную реакцию. • *1.* You don't sound very enthusiastic. *2.* You don't sound enthusiastic. *3.* The demeanour of the crowd was enthusiastic. *4.* The announcement elicited an ecstatic response.

**740. травматический** — *traumatic* — 'Травматический' is used to describe something that causes emotional or physical trauma. It can refer to events, experiences, or situations that are distressing or harmful in nature.

**741. красочный** — *colorful, colourful* — 'Красочный' is used to describe something that is vibrant, vivid, and full of color. It is often used to describe artwork, scenery, or descriptions that are visually striking and lively.

• *1.* Фестиваль Кали – красочный праздник. *2.* Фейерверк произвел красочный грохот. *3.* Костюм шута был красочным. *4.* Красочная птица привлекла мое внимание. *5.* Рыбы в соленой воде были красочными. *6.* Книга имела красочную обложку. *7.* На ней был красочный шарф. *8.* Парад представлял собой красочное зрелище. *9.* Художник нарисовал красочную фреску. • *1.* The Kali festival is a colorful celebration. *2.* The fireworks made a colorful boom. *3.* The jester's costume was colorful. *4.* The colorful bird caught my eye. *5.* The fish in the salina were colorful. *6.* The book had a colourful cover. *7.* She wore a colourful scarf. *8.* The parade was a colourful spectacle. *9.* The artist painted a colourful mural.

**742. нечувствительный** — *insensitive* — This word is used to describe someone who lacks empathy or is indifferent to the feelings of others. It can also be used to describe something that does not respond to stimuli or is not affected by external influences.

• *1.* Он говорил расово-нечувствительные слова. • *1.* Не

spoke racially insensitive words.

**743. политически** — *politically* — This word is used to describe something related to politics or government. It can be used to talk about political events, decisions, beliefs, or actions. It is often used to discuss the impact of politics on society.
● *1.* Он был политически подкованным и хорошо информированным. ● *1.* He was politically savvy and well-informed.

**744. лунный** — *lunar* — This word is used to describe things that are related to or characteristic of the moon. It can be used to talk about the moon itself, moonlight, or anything else that is connected to the moon.
● *1.* Лунный корабль приземлился плавно. ● *1.* The lunar lander touched down smoothly.

**745. чудовищный** — *monstrous, prodigious, whopping* — 'Чудовищный' is used to describe something that is extremely large, impressive, or overwhelming in size or scale. It conveys a sense of astonishment or awe at the magnitude or intensity of the object or situation being described.
● *1.* Это чудовищно. *2.* Он рассказал историю о чудовищном звере. *3.* Чудовищная буря бушевала. *4.* Она нарисовала чудовищного дракона. *5.* Чудовищное существо взревело.
● *1.* It's monstrous. *2.* He told a story of a monstrous beast. *3.* The monstrous storm raged on. *4.* She drew a monstrous dragon. *5.* The monstrous creature roared.

**746. суверенный** — *sovereign* — The word 'суверенный' is used to describe something or someone that possesses supreme power, authority, or independence. It conveys a sense of autonomy and control over one's own affairs.

**747. гибридный** — *hybrid* — 'гибридный' is used to describe something that is a combination of two different things or has characteristics of two different things. It is often used in the context of technology, culture, or organisms that are a mix of different elements.

**748. видный** — *prominent, eminent* — 'Видный' is used to describe someone or something that is distinguished, notable, or prominent in a particular field or context. It conveys a sense of importance or significance.

● *1.* Знаменитая достопримечательность была видна за несколько миль. *2.* Вергилий был видной фигурой в античной литературе. *3.* Она занимала видное положение в компании. ● *1.* The prominent landmark was visible from miles away. *2.* Virgil was a prominent figure in ancient literature. *3.* She held a prominent position in the company.

**749. жуткий** — *eerie, spooky* — 'Жуткий' is used to describe something that is eerie, spooky, or unsettling. It is often used to convey a sense of fear or unease in a situation, place, or person.
● *1.* Тишина толпы была жуткой. *2.* Она шла через жуткую деревню. *3.* Это жутко. *4.* В могиле было жутко и тихо. *5.* В морге было холодно и жутко. *6.* Это жутко. *7.* Он рассказывал жуткие истории о привидениях у костра. *8.* Они исследовали жуткую деревню. *9.* В старом доме царила жуткая атмосфера. *10.* Гх был жутким. ● *1.* The hush of the crowd was eerie. *2.* She walked through the eerie vill. *3.* It's eerie. *4.* The sepulchre was eerie and silent. *5.* The morgue was cold and eerie. *6.* It's spooky. *7.* He told spooky ghost stories around the campfire. *8.* They explored the spooky vill. *9.* The old house had a spooky atmosphere. *10.* The gh was spooky.

**750. ветреный** — *windy, flighty, harebrained* — This word is used to describe someone or something that is unpredictable, unreliable, or easily changing their mind. It can also refer to a situation or behavior that is characterized by sudden shifts or lack of stability.
● *1.* Ветрено. *2.* Это был ветреный день. *3.* Ветер был сильный и ветреный. *4.* Воздушный змей летел высоко в ветреную погоду. *5.* Ей было трудно идти в ветреную погоду. ● *1.* It's windy. *2.* It was a windy day. *3.* The wind was strong and windy. *4.* The kite flew high in the windy. *5.* She struggled to walk in the windy weather.

**751. умышленно** — *intentionally, willfully* — 'Умышленно' is used to describe actions or behaviors that are done with deliberate intent or purpose. It implies that the action was not accidental or unintentional, but rather done with full awareness and intention.
● *1.* Не умышленно. *2.* Она умышленно нарушила закон. *3.* Ребенок умышленно не подчинялся родителям. ● *1.* Not intentionally. *2.* She willfully broke the law. *3.* The child willfully

disobeyed his parents.

**752. цвета буйволовой кожи** — *buff* — This term is used to describe a color that is a pale yellowish-brown, similar to the color of buffalo leather. It is often used to describe clothing, furniture, or other items that have a similar hue.

**753. вероломный** — *unfaithful, perfidious* — This word is used to describe someone or something that is untrustworthy, deceitful, or treacherous. It implies a lack of loyalty or honesty, often in a sneaky or underhanded manner.
● *1.* Его вероломные действия предали их доверие. ● *1.* His perfidious actions betrayed their trust.

**754. неопределенный** — *uncertain, indeterminate, indefinite, iffy* — This word is used to describe something that is not clearly defined or decided, lacking a specific or precise nature. It conveys a sense of ambiguity or uncertainty in regards to a particular situation or concept.
● *1.* Ее прогноз был неопределенным. *2.* Это неопределенно. *3.* Его будущее неопределенно. *4.* Прогноз погоды неопределенный. *5.* Время полета было неопределенным. *6.* Он представил неопределенный график. *7.* Будущее казалось неопределенным. *8.* Ответ был неопределенным. *9.* Она почувствовала неопределенное беспокойство. *10.* Они столкнулись с неопределенными задержками. *11.* Сомнительный прогноз вызвал неопределенность. ● *1.* Her prognosis was uncertain. *2.* It's uncertain. *3.* His future is uncertain. *4.* The weather forecast is uncertain. *5.* The flight's eta was uncertain. *6.* He presented an indefinite timeline. *7.* The future seemed indefinite. *8.* The answer was indefinite. *9.* She felt an indefinite unease. *10.* They faced indefinite delays. *11.* The iffy forecast caused uncertainty.

**755. меньший** — *lesser* — 'Меньший' is used to compare two or more things, indicating that one is smaller, lesser, or inferior in some way. It is often used to describe quantities, sizes, or qualities in a negative or diminishing context.
● *1.* Меньшее зло все еще оставалось вариантом. *2.* Они остановились на меньшем варианте. ● *1.* The lesser evil was still an option. *2.* They settled for the lesser option.

**756. поддельный** — *bogus, counterfeit, spurious* — This word is used to describe something that is fake or not genuine. It can refer to counterfeit money, fake documents, or anything that is not authentic. It is often used to warn others about fraudulent items.

● *1.* Его полномочия были поддельными. *2.* Продавались поддельные товары. ● *1.* His credentials were bogus. *2.* Bogus merchandise was being sold.

**757.  свадебный** — *bridal, nuptial* — This word is used to describe things that are related to weddings or marriage ceremonies. It can be used to talk about items, events, or traditions that are associated with getting married.

● *1.* Свадебная вечеринка позировала для фотографий. *2.* Она примеряла свадебные платья. *3.* Свадебный вечер был радостным событием. *4.* Она представляла себе свой свадебный выход. ● *1.* The bridal party posed for photos. *2.* She tried on bridal gowns. *3.* The bridal shower was a joyous occasion. *4.* She envisioned her bridal entrance.

**758.  аморальный** — *immoral, amoral* — This word is used to describe actions, behaviors, or attitudes that are considered unethical, lacking moral principles, or not conforming to societal standards of right and wrong.

● *1.* Это аморально. ● *1.* It's immoral.

**759.  преждевременный** — *premature, precocious* — This word is used to describe something that happens or develops earlier than expected or appropriate. It can refer to physical, mental, or emotional traits that are advanced for a person's age or stage of development.

● *1.* Она почувствовала преждевременную вину. *2.* Это было преждевременное суждение. *3.* Его преждевременные действия вызвали проблемы. *4.* Решение было преждевременным. ● *1.* She felt premature guilt. *2.* It was a premature judgment. *3.* His premature action caused problems. *4.* The decision was premature.

**760.  торжественный** — *solemn, ceremonial* — 'Торжественный' is used to describe events, ceremonies, or occasions that are serious, formal, and dignified. It conveys a sense of importance and reverence, often associated with rituals, celebrations, or official functions.

• *1.* Крематорий был торжественным местом. *2.* Церемония кремации прошла торжественно. *3.* Церемония причастия была торжественной. *4.* Обряд был торжественным событием. *5.* Они организовали торжественную похоронную процессию. *6.* Это событие потребовало торжественного приема. *7.* Они приняли участие в торжественном ритуале. *8.* Платье имело торжественный вид. • *1.* The crematorium was a solemn place. *2.* The cremation ceremony was solemn. *3.* The communion ceremony was solemn. *4.* The rite was a solemn occasion. *5.* They organized a solemn funeral procession. *6.* The occasion called for a ceremonial welcome. *7.* They took part in the ceremonial ritual. *8.* The dress had a ceremonial feel.

**761. коварный** — *treacherous, insidious, crafty, underhand* — 'Коварный' is used to describe someone or something that is deceitful, sneaky, or manipulative in a way that is not immediately obvious. It implies a sense of danger or betrayal lurking beneath the surface.

• *1.* Путь через болото был коварным. *2.* Хрупкий снежный покров был коварным. *3.* Безжалостный, коварный, развратный, бессердечный злодей! *4.* Логово гидры представляло собой коварное болото. *5.* Форд оказался коварным. *6.* У него был коварный мотив. *7.* Коварный план был раскрыт. *8.* Коварная болезнь быстро распространилась. *9.* Они столкнулись с коварным врагом. *10.* Помните о коварной опасности. • *1.* The path through the bog was treacherous. *2.* The brittle snow cover was treacherous. *3.* Remorseless, treacherous, lecherous, kindless villain! *4.* The hydra's lair was a treacherous swamp. *5.* The Ford was treacherous. *6.* He had an insidious motive. *7.* The insidious plan was revealed. *8.* The insidious disease spread quickly. *9.* They faced an insidious enemy. *10.* Be aware of the insidious danger.

**762. бронированный** — *armored* — The word 'бронированный' is used to describe something that is protected by armor or made of armored material. It can also be used to describe a vehicle or building that has been reinforced for protection.

• *1.* Бронированная кожа броненосца защищала его. *2.* Они следовали по пути бронированной голгофы. *3.* Танк был бронированным. • *1.* The armadillo's armored skin protected it. *2.* They followed the path of the armored calvary. *3.* The tank was armored.

**763. эксцентричный** — *eccentric* — This word is used to describe someone or something that is unconventional, quirky, or unusual in behavior or appearance. It implies a sense of uniqueness and individuality that sets the person or thing apart from the norm.

• *1.* Эксцентричный сосед был кнатом. • *1.* The eccentric neighbor was a knut.

**764. неотразимый** — *irresistible* — 'Неотразимый' is used to describe something or someone that is impossible to resist or ignore, often due to their charm, attractiveness, or appeal. It conveys a sense of being overwhelmingly captivating or alluring.

• *1.* Ты неотразим. *2.* Сладкая булочка с корицей была неотразима. *3.* Обаяние куртизанки было неотразимым. *4.* Она неотразима. *5.* Наживка была неотразима. • *1.* You're irresistible. *2.* The sweet cinnamon bun was irresistible. *3.* The courtesan's charm was irresistible. *4.* She's irresistible. *5.* The bait was irresistible.

**765. спорный** — *controversial, moot, contentious, argumentative* — This word is used to describe something that is the subject of disagreement or debate, often sparking controversy or differing opinions. It implies that there is no clear consensus on the matter and that it is open to interpretation or dispute.

• *1.* Решение трибунала было спорным. *2.* Легализация наркотиков – спорная тема. *3.* Мандат был спорным. *4.* Как спорно. *5.* Спорная статья вызовет дискуссию. *6.* Вопрос спорный. *7.* Теперь этот вопрос является спорным. *8.* Это спорный вопрос. *9.* Вопрос стал спорным. *10.* Он старался избегать спорных тем. *11.* Спорный вопрос разделил группу. *12.* Она оказалась в спорном споре. *13.* Спорные дебаты продолжались несколько часов. *14.* У него был спорный характер. *15.* Спорный тон быстро нарастал. *16.* Они старались избегать спорных тем. *17.* В стрессе он становился спорным.
• *1.* The tribunal's ruling was controversial. *2.* The legalization of drugs is a controversial topic. *3.* The mandate was controversial. *4.* How controversial. *5.* The controversial article would provoke discussion. *6.* The question is moot. *7.* The issue is now moot. *8.* That's a moot point. *9.* The issue has become contentious.

*10.* He tried to avoid contentious topics. *11.* The contentious issue divided the group. *12.* She found herself in a contentious argument. *13.* The contentious debate continued for hours. *14.* He had an argumentative personality. *15.* The argumentative tone escalated quickly. *16.* They tried to avoid argumentative topics. *17.* He became argumentative when stressed.

**766. вулканический** — *volcanic* — 'вулканический' is used to describe something that is related to or resembles a volcano. It can be used to describe the characteristics, properties, or behavior of something that is similar to a volcano.

● *1.* Город был построен на вулканической скале. *2.* Отложения серы свидетельствовали о вулканической активности. *3.* Вулканическая порода была наполнена пемзой. *4.* Вулканический ландшафт был бесплодным. *5.* Вулканический остров был прекрасен. ● *1.* The town was built on volcanic rock. *2.* The brimstone deposits indicated volcanic activity. *3.* The volcanic rock was filled with pumice. *4.* The volcanic landscape was barren. *5.* The volcanic island was beautiful.

**767. иррациональный** — *irrational* — 'Irrational' is used to describe something that lacks logic or reason. It can refer to actions, beliefs, or decisions that are not based on sound judgment or clear thinking.

● *1.* Ты ведешь себя иррационально. *2.* Паранойя привела к иррациональному поведению. *3.* Иррациональная вера - вызвала проблемы. *4.* Его фобия была иррациональной. *5.* Они отреагировали с иррациональным гневом. ● *1.* You're being irrational. *2.* The paranoia led to irrational behavior. *3.* The irrational belief caused problems. *4.* His phobia was irrational. *5.* They reacted with irrational anger.

**768. грозный** — *formidable, fearsome* — The word 'грозный' is used to describe something or someone that is intimidating, powerful, or impressive. It conveys a sense of fear or respect towards the subject being described.

● *1.* Она столкнулась с грозным противником. *2.* Армия - представляла собой грозную силу. *3.* Заклятый враг был грозным противником. *4.* Грозный противник был грозным. *5.* Герой сражался с грозной мантикорой. *6.* Левиафан был огромным и грозным. *7.* Она унаследовала грозную репутацию. *8.* Грозный киномонстр напугал детей. *9.* Трог был грозным воином. • *1.* She faced a formidable opponent. *2.* The army presented a formidable force. *3.* The archenemy was a formidable foe. *4.* The fearsome opponent was formidable. *5.* The hero fought a fearsome manticore. *6.* The leviathan was huge and fearsome. *7.* She inherited a fearsome reputation. *8.* The fearsome movie monster scared the children. *9.* The trog was a fearsome warrior.

**769. саркастический** — *sarcastic* — This word is used to describe someone or something that uses irony, mockery, or satire to convey contempt or ridicule. It is often used to characterize a tone of speech or writing that is meant to be humorous but critical.

• *1.* Она издала саркастический пффффф. • *1.* She let out a sarcastic pfff.

**770. обязательный** — *mandatory, obligatory, compulsory* — This word is used to describe something that is required or necessary to be done, without any choice or option to avoid it. It indicates that a certain action or condition is mandatory and cannot be skipped or ignored.

• *1.* Эссе является обязательным заданием. *2.* Вводный - курс был обязательным. *3.* Обязательно носить защитное снаряжение. *4.* Еженедельное собрание было обязательным. *5.* Это было обязательно. *6.* Курс был обязательным для всех студентов. *7.* Она прошла обязательную военную службу. *8.* Политика обязательного посещения была строгой. *9.* Он сдал обязательный экзамен. *10.* Собрание стало обязательным для всех сотрудников. • *1.* The essay is a mandatory assignment. *2.* The introductory course was mandatory. *3.* It's mandatory to wear safety gear. *4.* The weekly meeting was mandatory. *5.* It was mandatory. *6.* The course was compulsory for all students. *7.* She completed her compulsory military service. *8.* The compulsory attendance policy was strict. *9.* He took the compulsory exam. *10.* The meeting was made compulsory for all employees.

**771. прибыльный** — *profitable, lucrative* — This word is used to describe something that brings in a profit or is financially beneficial. It is often used in business contexts to refer to investments, ventures, or opportunities that have the potential to generate income.

• *1.* Дочерняя компания была прибыльной. *2.* Предпринимательское предприятие было прибыльным. *3.* Контрабандная торговля была очень прибыльной. • *1.* The subsidiary was profitable. *2.* The entrepreneurial venture was profitable. *3.* The contraband trade was highly lucrative.

**772. неестественный** — *unnatural* — This word is used to describe something that is not natural or normal, often referring to behavior, appearance, or characteristics that are artificial, contrived, or abnormal.
• *1.* Это неестественно. *2.* Причудливая погода казалась - неестественной. • *1.* It's unnatural. *2.* The freakish weather seemed unnatural.

**773. компетентный** — *competent* — 'Компетентный' is used to describe someone who has the necessary knowledge, skills, and abilities to perform a task effectively and efficiently. It implies that the person is capable, qualified, and reliable in their area of expertise.
• *1.* Они считали ее компетентной. *2.* Она показала себя компетентной. *3.* Она компетентный руководитель. • *1.* They deemed her competent. *2.* She proved herself competent. *3.* She's a competent leader.

**774. слышный** — *audible* — This word is used to describe something that can be heard or is loud enough to be heard. It is often used to indicate that a sound is noticeable or easily heard.
• *1.* Музыку было отчетливо слышно. *2.* Крадущаяся змея была едва слышна. *3.* Его «мммм» было едва слышно. *4.* Хрипло произнесенные слова были едва слышны. *5.* Слова были едва слышны из-за шума. • *1.* The music was clearly audible. *2.* The slink of the snake was barely audible. *3.* His mmhmm was barely audible. *4.* The hoarsely spoken words were barely audible. *5.* The words were barely audible over the noise.

**775. символический** — *symbolic* — This word is used to describe something that represents or signifies something else, often in a metaphorical or abstract way. It can also imply that something is done as a gesture or token rather than having a practical effect.
• *1.* Он сделал символический жест. *2.* Символический смысл был ясен. *3.* Символические действия говорят громко.

*4. Символический язык обладает силой.* ● *1.* He made a symbolic gesture. *2.* The symbolic meaning was clear. *3.* Symbolic actions speak loudly. *4.* Symbolic language is powerful.

**776. земной** — *earthly, terrestrial, earthbound* — 'Земной' is used to describe things that are related to or characteristic of the Earth. It can refer to physical objects, beings, or qualities that are connected to the planet or limited to earthly existence.
● *1.* У меня нет земной идеи. *2.* Люди – земные существа. *3.* Земной ландшафт простирался на многие мили. *4.* Земная среда была разнообразной. *5.* Наземные животные были очаровательны. *6.* Наземная среда обитания оказалась под угрозой. ● *1.* I have no earthly idea. *2.* Humans are terrestrial beings. *3.* The terrestrial landscape stretched for miles. *4.* The terrestrial environment was diverse. *5.* The terrestrial animals were fascinating. *6.* The terrestrial habitat was under threat.

**777. шикарный** — *chic, posh, swanky* — This word is used to describe something luxurious, stylish, or elegant. It is often used to compliment someone's appearance or to describe a high-end item or place.
● *1.* Очень шикарный. *2.* Ее будуар был элегантным и шикарным. *3.* Они сделали покупки в шикарном бутике в центре города. *4.* Очень шикарно. *5.* Очень шикарно. *6.* Вечеринка прошла в шикарном месте. *7.* Он водил шикарную спортивную машину. *8.* В шикарном ресторане подают изысканные блюда. *9.* В отеле был шикарный бар на крыше. ● *1.* Very chic. *2.* Her boudoir was elegant and chic. *3.* They shopped at a chic boutique downtown. *4.* Très chic. *5.* Very posh. *6.* The party was at a swanky venue. *7.* He drove a swanky sports car. *8.* The swanky restaurant served gourmet meals. *9.* The hotel had a swanky rooftop bar.

**778. металлический** — *metallic* — This word is used to describe something that is related to or resembles metal in some way, such as its appearance, texture, or sound. It can be used to describe objects, colors, or even tastes.
● *1.* Топ имел металлический запах. ● *1.* The toph had a metallic scent.

**779. преднамеренный** — *deliberate, judgmental* — This word is used to describe actions or decisions that are done intentionally and with purpose. It implies that the person has thought carefully about their actions and made a conscious choice.

● *1.* Нанесение увечий было преднамеренным. ● *1.* The mutilation was deliberate.

**780. неограниченный** — *unlimited, indefinite* — This word is used to describe something that has no limits or boundaries, something that is endless or infinite. It can be used to convey the idea of something being unrestricted or boundless.

● *1.* В парке имеется неограниченное количество аттракционов. *2.* Интернет-план предлагает неограниченный объем данных. *3.* У него неограниченный потенциал. *4.* У него неограниченный запас терпения. *5.* Возможности неограниченны. ● *1.* The park features unlimited attractions. *2.* The internet plan offers unlimited data. *3.* He has unlimited potential. *4.* He has an unlimited supply of patience. *5.* The possibilities are unlimited.

**781. капризный** — *cranky, whimsical, capricious, freakish* — The word 'капризный' is used to describe someone or something that is unpredictable, moody, or easily irritated. It implies a tendency to change one's mind frequently or act in a whimsical or fickle manner.

● *1.* Я не капризный. *2.* Кто-то капризный. *3.* Погода была капризная. *4.* Настроение ее было капризным. *5.* Капризные решения вызвали хаос. *6.* Его капризное поведение было непредсказуемым. *7.* Капризный ветер затруднял плавание. ● *1.* I'm not cranky. *2.* Someone's cranky. *3.* The weather was capricious. *4.* Her mood was capricious. *5.* The capricious decisions caused chaos. *6.* His capricious behavior was unpredictable. *7.* The capricious winds made sailing challenging.

**782. бесплодный** — *barren, infertile* — This word is used to describe something that is unable to produce offspring or results. It can refer to land that is unable to grow crops, animals that cannot reproduce, or situations that do not lead to any positive outcomes.

● *1.* Бесплодный ландшафт лишен растительности. *2.* Двор был бесплодным. *3.* Пустынный ландшафт был бесплодным. *4.* Вулканический ландшафт был бесплодным. ● *1.* The barren landscape lacked vegetation. *2.* The yard was barren. *3.* The desert landscape was barren. *4.* The volcanic landscape was barren.

**783. суеверный** — *superstitious* — The word 'суеверный' is used to describe someone who believes in superstitions or has irrational beliefs in supernatural forces. It is often used to characterize individuals who rely on luck or rituals to avoid bad luck or bring good fortune.

• *1.* Она носила свой талисман, как всегда суеверная. *2.* Она была суеверна по отношению к черным кошкам. • *1.* She wore her lucky charm, superstitious as ever. *2.* She was superstitious about black cats.

**784. вирусный** — *viral* — 'вирусный' is used to describe something that is related to or characteristic of a virus, typically in the context of spreading rapidly and widely, often through the internet or social media.

• *1.* Песня стала вирусным хитом. *2.* Вирусный мем был веселым. *3.* Мем стал вирусным. *4.* Видео стало вирусным. *5.* Отфотошопленное изображение стало вирусным. • *1.* The song was a viral hit. *2.* The viral meme was hilarious. *3.* The meme went viral. *4.* The video went viral. *5.* The photoshopped image went viral.

**785. расовый** — *racial* — This word is used to describe something related to race or ethnicity. It can be used to talk about racial discrimination, racial identity, or anything else that pertains to different racial groups.

• *1.* Расовая напряженность была высокой. *2.* Расовое разделение было очевидным. *3.* Расовая дискриминация является серьезной проблемой. *4.* Нападение имело расовый подтекст. *5.* Расовые оскорбления были оскорбительными. • *1.* The racial tensions were high. *2.* The racial divide was evident. *3.* Racial discrimination was a serious issue. *4.* The attack had racial undertones. *5.* The racial slurs were offensive.

**786. портативный** — *portable* — This word is used to describe something that is easy to carry or move from one place to another. It is often used to refer to electronic devices, tools, or equipment that can be easily transported.

• *1.* Портативный компьютер. *2.* У нее было портативное зарядное устройство. *3.* Портативные музыкальные плееры пользуются популярностью. *4.* Портативный генератор был

жизненно необходим. *5.* У него есть портативный телефон.
● *1.* A portable computer. *2.* She carried a portable charger. *3.* Portable music players are popular. *4.* A portable generator was vital. *5.* He has a portable phone.

**787. почтительный** — *respectful, dutiful* — The word 'почтительный' is used to describe someone who shows respect and obedience towards others, especially those in authority. It conveys a sense of politeness and consideration in one's actions and behavior.
● *1.* Быть почтительным. *2.* Он дал почтительное намасте. ● *1.* Be respectful. *2.* He gave a respectful namaste.

**788. продуктивный** — *productive* — The word 'продуктивный' is used to describe something that is efficient, effective, or yielding positive results. It is often used to refer to a person, process, or activity that is able to achieve a lot in a short amount of time.
● *1.* Собрание акционеров прошло продуктивно. *2.* Направьте свою энергию на что-то продуктивное. *3.* Двусторонние переговоры прошли продуктивно. *4.* Очень продуктивно. *5.* Дискуссия была продуктивной. ● *1.* The stockholder meeting was productive. *2.* Channel your energy into something productive. *3.* The bilateral talks were productive. *4.* Very productive. *5.* The discussion was productive.

**789. непочтительный** — *disrespectful* — The word 'непочтительный' is used to describe behavior or actions that show a lack of respect or consideration for others. It can be used to criticize someone for being rude, impolite, or disrespectful in their interactions with others.

**790. феноменальный** — *phenomenal* — 'Феноменальный' is used to describe something extraordinary, exceptional, or outstanding. It is often used to emphasize the impressive or remarkable nature of a person, event, or object.
● *1.* Это феноменально. ● *1.* That's phenomenal.

**791. синтетический** — *synthetic* — This word is used to describe something that is made by combining different elements or materials, rather than being natural or organic. It can refer to materials, substances, or products that are artificially created.
● *1.* Синтетическая калибровка неполная. ● *1.* Synthetic cali-

bration incomplete.

**792. изобретательный** — *ingenious, resourceful, inventive* — This word describes someone who is creative and able to come up with innovative solutions to problems. It can also be used to describe something that is cleverly designed or thought out.

• *1.* Очень изобретательно. *2.* Вы изобретательны. *3.* Ее кулинария была изобретательной. *4.* Устройство было очень изобретательным. *5.* Их подход был изобретательным. *6.* Он был изобретательным мыслителем. *7.* План был весьма изобретательным. • *1.* Very ingenious. *2.* You are ingenious. *3.* Her cooking was inventive. *4.* The device was very inventive. *5.* Their approach was inventive. *6.* He was an inventive thinker. *7.* The plan was quite inventive.

**793. доминирующий** — *dominant* — This word is used to describe something or someone that has power, influence, or control over others. It signifies a position of authority or superiority in a particular situation or context.

• *1.* На протяжении веков человечество было доминирующим видом. • *1.* For centuries, mankind has been the dominant species.

**794. импульсивный** — *impulsive* — The word 'импульсивный' describes someone who acts or makes decisions suddenly, without thinking carefully beforehand. It is used to characterize behavior that is driven by emotions or impulses rather than rational thought.

• *1.* Она приняла импульсивное решение. • *1.* She made an impulsive decision.

**795. сырный** — *cheesy* — This word is used to describe something that is overly sentimental, exaggerated, or lacking in sophistication. It can also refer to something that is overly dramatic or cliché.

**796. плодородный** — *fertile* — The word 'плодородный' is used to describe land or soil that is capable of producing abundant crops. It can also be used to describe a person or animal that is capable of producing offspring.

• *1.* Коричневая почва была плодородной. *2.* Почва богато плодородна. *3.* Регион известен своими плодородными землями. *4.* Сельскохозяйственные угодья были плодородн-

ыми и ухоженными. *5.* Земля была богатой и плодородной.
● *1.* The brownish soil was fertile. *2.* The soil is richly fertile.
*3.* The region is known for its fertile land. *4.* The farmland was
fertile and well-maintained. *5.* The terra was rich and fertile.

**797. самодовольный** — *smug, complacent, conceited, huffy*
— This word is used to describe someone who is overly pleased
with themselves, often to the point of being arrogant or self--
satisfied. It conveys a sense of superiority and lack of humility.
● *1.* Самодовольный ублюдок. *2.* Не будьте самодовольны.
*3.* Он оказался самодовольным невеждой. *4.* Его самодово-
льное злорадство. *5.* Они были самодовольны, Ширли. ● *1.*
Smug bastard. *2.* Don't be smug. *3.* He proved to be a smug
ignoramus. *4.* His smug gloat. *5.* They've been complacent,
Shirley.

**798. формально** — *formally* — 'Formally' is used to describe
something that is done in accordance with established rules or
conventions, often without considering the actual intent or spirit
behind the action. It can also indicate a superficial or insincere
adherence to regulations.
● *1.* Нет, не формально. ● *1.* No, not formally.

**799. тепловой** — *thermal* — 'Тепловой' is used to describe
something related to heat or temperature. It can refer to objects,
materials, or processes that involve the transfer or generation of
heat. It is commonly used in scientific and technical contexts.
● *1.* Тепловизор зафиксировал движение. *2.* Тепловые с-
лои сохраняли тепло. *3.* Тепловое одеяло было уютным. *4.*
Тепловая энергия обогревала дом. ● *1.* The thermal scope
detected movement. *2.* The thermal layers kept them warm. *3.*
The thermal blanket was cozy. *4.* The thermal energy warmed
the house.

**800. жизнеспособный** — *viable* — 'Жизнеспособный' is
used to describe something that is capable of surviving and
thriving in a given situation or environment. It implies that the
subject has the necessary qualities or resources to be successful
or effective.

**801. нереальный** — *unreal, unrealistic* — 'нереальный' is
used to describe something that is impossible or highly unlikely
to happen in reality. It can also be used to express disbelief or

astonishment at a situation or event.

● *1.* Это нереально. *2.* Это было нереально. *3.* Нереально ожидать столького. *4.* Это нереально для любого бизнеса. *5.* Это все нереально. *6.* «Это совершенно нереально», -- пробормотал он. *7.* Сцена фелляции была нереальной. ● *1.* This is unreal. *2.* It was unreal. *3.* It's unrealistic to expect so much. *4.* That's unrealistic for any business. *5.* This is all unrealistic. *6.* That's totally unrealistic, he muttered. *7.* The fellatio scene was unrealistic.

**802. анальный** — *anal* — This word is used to describe something related to or resembling the anus or anal region. It can also be used figuratively to describe something overly detailed or focused on minor aspects.

**803. шаткий** — *shaky, wobbly, wonky* — The word 'шаткий' is used to describe something that is unstable, unsteady, or insecure. It can refer to physical objects that are shaky or wobbly, as well as to situations or plans that are uncertain or unreliable.

● *1.* Немного шатко. *2.* Он провел шаткую линию. *3.* Мост выглядел шатким. *4.* Ее шаткие очки нуждались в поправке. *5.* На шатком стуле сидеть было неудобно. *6.* Его шаткая походка произошла из-за травмы. ● *1.* A little shaky. *2.* He drew a wobbly line. *3.* The bridge looked wobbly. *4.* Her wonky glasses needed adjusting. *5.* The wonky chair was uncomfortable to sit in. *6.* His wonky walk was due to an injury.

**804. континентальный** — *continental* — 'Континентальный' is used to describe something that is characteristic of or related to continents. It can refer to climate, cuisine, or any other aspect that is typical of the large landmasses on Earth.

● *1.* Отель был континентального типа. *2.* Континентальный водораздел прошёл через всю страну. *3.* Были использованы континентальные плиты. *4.* Это был континентальный климат. *5.* Они подавали континентальный завтрак. ● *1.* The hotel was continental style. *2.* The continental divide traversed the country. *3.* The continental plates were used. *4.* It was a continental climate. *5.* They served a continental breakfast.

**805. поверхностный** — *superficial, cursory, sketchy* — This word is used to describe something that is shallow or lacking in depth. It can refer to a person's understanding, a conversation, or a piece of work that is not thorough or detailed.

● *1.* Это поверхностно. *2.* Ее поверхностная уборка оставляла желать лучшего. ● *1.* It's superficial. *2.* Her cursory cleaning left much to be desired.

**806. добровольно** — *voluntarily* — This word is used to describe actions or decisions made willingly and without coercion. It implies that the person acted out of their own free will, without being forced or obligated to do so.

● *1.* Я здесь добровольно. ● *1.* I'm here voluntarily.

**807. патриотический** — *patriotic* — The word 'патриотический' is used to describe something that is related to or characteristic of love and devotion to one's country. It is often used to describe actions, feelings, or symbols that show loyalty and pride towards one's nation.

● *1.* Патриотическое шоу сопровождалось фейерверком. *2.* Город украшен патриотическими флагами. *3.* Праздник стал временем патриотического торжества. *4.* Он проявил патриотический пыл. *5.* В речи были подчеркнуты патриотические ценности страны. ● *1.* The patriotic display included a fireworks show. *2.* The town decorated with patriotic bunting. *3.* The holiday was a time for patriotic celebration. *4.* He displayed a patriotic fervor. *5.* The speech emphasized the country's patriotic values.

**808. исламский** — *islamic* — This word is used to describe something related to the religion of Islam, such as beliefs, practices, or cultural aspects. It is commonly used to refer to mosques, holidays, traditions, and other aspects of Islamic culture.

● *1.* Исламская община собралась на молитву. *2.* Исламское право основывалось на религиозных принципах. *3.* Исламский праздник отметили весело. *4.* Исламское искусство известно своей красотой. ● *1.* The Islamic community gathered for prayers. *2.* The Islamic law was based on religious principles. *3.* The Islamic holiday was celebrated joyfully. *4.* Islamic art is known for its beauty.

**809. неохотный** — *reluctant, loath, averse* — The word 'неохотный' is used to describe someone who is unwilling or hesitant to do something, expressing a feeling of reluctance or aversion towards a particular action or situation.

• *1.* Она была неохотным участником. *2.* Его тон был неохотным. • *1.* She was a reluctant participant. *2.* His tone was reluctant.

**810. решительный** — *decisive, resolute, drastic* — This word is used to describe someone or something that is firm, determined, and takes strong and quick actions to achieve a goal or solve a problem. It implies a sense of decisiveness and resolve in decision-making.

• *1.* Они пришли к решительному выводу. *2.* Реакция была быстрой и решительной. *3.* Он сделал решительный шаг. *4.* Встреча привела к решительным действиям. *5.* Она одержала решительную победу. *6.* Решительный взгляд в ее глазах пугал. *7.* Он говорил с решительной решимостью. *8.* Решительный отказ был неожиданным. *9.* Их решительная позиция привела к победе. • *1.* They reached a decisive conclusion. *2.* The reaction was swift and decisive. *3.* He made a decisive move. *4.* The meeting led to a decisive action. *5.* She had a decisive victory. *6.* The resolute look in her eyes was intimidating. *7.* He spoke with resolute determination. *8.* The resolute refusal was unexpected. *9.* Their resolute stance led to victory.

**811. влиятельный** — *influential* — 'Влиятельный' is used to describe someone or something that has a significant impact or influence on others. It is often used to refer to powerful individuals, organizations, or ideas that hold sway over others.

**812. одновременно** — *simultaneously* — 'одновременно' is used to describe actions or events that occur at the same time. It indicates that two or more things are happening simultaneously, without any delay or interruption.

• *1.* Часто одновременно. • *1.* Often simultaneously.

**813. сельский** — *rural, arcadian* — The word 'сельский' is used to describe things related to the countryside or rural areas. It conveys a sense of simplicity, natural beauty, and a slower pace of life often associated with rural settings.

• *1.* Сельский пейзаж был усеян фермами. *2.* Были предприняты усилия по заселению сельского региона. *3.* Они наслаждались мирной сельской жизнью. *4.* В сельской местности не хватало современных удобств. *5.* В сельском городке была дружная община. *6.* Они искали убежища в сельской местности Аркадии. • *1.* The rural landscape was dotted with farms. *2.* Efforts were made to populate the rural region. *3.* They enjoyed the peaceful rural life. *4.* The rural area lacked modern amenities. *5.* The rural town had a tight-knit community. *6.* They sought refuge in the arcadian countryside.

**814. заслуживающий доверия** — *trustworthy, credible* — This word is used to describe someone or something that is reliable and can be trusted. It implies that the person or thing has earned trust through their actions or behavior.

**815. мистический** — *mystical, mystic* — The word 'мистический' is used to describe something that is mysterious, spiritual, or otherworldly in nature. It conveys a sense of magic, enchantment, or a connection to the supernatural.
• *1.* Мистический ритуал был проведен. *2.* У нее был мистический опыт. *3.* Эфир – мистическая стихия. *4.* Моли обладала мистическим свойством. *5.* Это место имело мистическую ауру. • *1.* The mystical ritual was performed. *2.* She had a mystical experience. *3.* The aether is a mystical element. *4.* The moly had a mystical quality. *5.* The place had a mystical aura.

**816. заранее** — *beforehand* — 'Заранее' is used to indicate that something is done in advance or beforehand. It is often used to describe actions or preparations that are made prior to a specific event or situation.
• *1.* Инструкции были даны заранее. *2.* Она подготовилась заранее. *3.* Я хотел знать заранее. *4.* Он закончил заранее. *5.* Решение было принято заранее. • *1.* The instructions were given beforehand. *2.* She prepared beforehand. *3.* I wanted to know beforehand. *4.* He finished beforehand. *5.* The decision was made beforehand.

**817. незабываемый** — *memorable, unforgettable* — 'незабываемый' is used to describe something that leaves a lasting impression, something that is unforgettable or memorable. It is often used to describe experiences, events, or moments that are particularly special or significant.
• *1.* Они вместе совершили незабываемое путешествие. *2.* Их студенческие годы были наполнены незабываемыми

событиями. *3.* Величественные пейзажи сделали поездку незабываемой. *4.* Этот выдающийся момент был незабываемым. *5.* Звездное событие было незабываемым. *6.* Он произнес незабываемую речь. *7.* Поездка в Боливию была незабываемой. *8.* На ней было незабываемое платье. • *1.* They shared a memorable trip together. *2.* Their undergrad years were filled with memorable experiences. *3.* The majestic scenery made for a memorable trip. *4.* The standout moment was unforgettable. *5.* The stellar event was unforgettable. *6.* He delivered an unforgettable speech. *7.* The Bolivia trip was unforgettable. *8.* She wore an unforgettable dress.

**818. профессионально** — *professionally* — The word 'профессионально' is used to describe actions or behaviors that are done in a skilled, competent, or expert manner, typically in a work or professional setting. It conveys a sense of professionalism and expertise.

• *1.* Они оба профессионально успешны. *2.* Он профессионально играл в хоккей. *3.* Для интервью он оделся профессионально. *4.* Только профессионально. *5.* Компания управляется профессионально. • *1.* They're both professionally successful. *2.* He played hockey professionally. *3.* He dressed professionally for the interview. *4.* Only professionally. *5.* The company is run professionally.

**819. беспрецедентный** — *unprecedented, uneventful* — This word is used to describe something that has never happened before or is completely new and unique. It is often used to emphasize the extraordinary nature of a situation or event.

• *1.* Это беспрецедентно. *2.* Странное событие было беспрецедентным. • *1.* It's unprecedented. *2.* The freakish event was unprecedented.

**820. молекулярный** — *molecular* — This word is used to describe something related to molecules or molecular structure. It is often used in scientific contexts to refer to the properties or characteristics of substances at a molecular level.

• *1.* Молекулярный биолог сделал важное открытие. *2.* Молекулярная структура была сложной. *3.* Она изучила молекулярный состав вещества. *4.* Молекулярный уровень анализа был новаторским. *5.* Молекулярные связи были прочными. • *1.* The molecular biologist made a significant discovery. *2.* The molecular structure was complex. *3.* She studied the molecular composition of the substance. *4.* The molecular level of analysis was groundbreaking. *5.* The molecular bonds were strong.

**821. запоздалый** — *overdue, belated, tardy* — The word 'запоздалый' is used to describe something that is late or delayed. It can refer to a person being tardy or something being overdue. It implies that the action or event should have happened earlier.

• *1.* Визит запоздал. *2.* Встреча одноклассников запоздала. *3.* Она отправила запоздалую поздравительную открытку. *4.* Запоздалое извинение было встречено скептически. *5.* Запоздалое заявление вызвало недоумение. *6.* Они получили запоздалый свадебный подарок. *7.* Он дал запоздалое объяснение. *8.* Они проводили запоздалую политику. *9.* Она извинилась за запоздалый ответ. • *1.* The visit was overdue. *2.* The schoolmate reunion was overdue. *3.* She sent a belated birthday card. *4.* The belated apology was met with skepticism. *5.* The belated announcement caused confusion. *6.* They received a belated wedding gift. *7.* He offered a belated explanation. *8.* They implemented a tardy policy. *9.* She apologized for the tardy response.

**822. исключительно** — *exclusively* — This word is used to emphasize that something is limited to a specific group or category, indicating that it is the only option or choice available. It conveys the idea of exclusivity or uniqueness in a given context.

• *1.* Не исключительно. • *1.* Not exclusively.

**823. воздушный** — *aerial* — The word 'воздушный' is used to describe something that is related to the air or sky, such as aerial views, aerial photography, or aerial acrobatics. It can also refer to something that is light, airy, or ethereal in nature.

• *1.* Они выполнили воздушный трюк. *2.* Воздушный дрон сделал потрясающие кадры. *3.* Воздушная акробатика была впечатляющей. • *1.* They performed an aerial stunt. *2.* The aerial drone captured stunning footage. *3.* The aerial acrobatics were impressive.

**824. этический** — *ethical* — This word is used to describe actions, decisions, or beliefs that are morally right or conform to ethical principles. It is often used in discussions about behavior, values, and responsibilities in various contexts.

● *1*. История подняла вопросы этической морали. ● *1*. The story raised ethical morality issues.

**825. прозрачный** — *transparent* — This word is used to describe something that is clear, see-through, or easily understood. It can refer to physical objects like glass or water, as well as abstract concepts like intentions or communication.

● *1*. Ты такой прозрачный. *2*. Управление компанией было прозрачным. *3*. Тактика соблазнителя была прозрачна. ● *1*. You're so transparent. *2*. The governance of the company was transparent. *3*. The seducer's tactics were transparent.

**826. чудесно** — *wonderfully, marvelously* — 'Чудесно' is used to describe something that is done in a wonderful or marvelous way. It can be used to express admiration or approval for a particular action, event, or situation.

● *1*. Цветы пахли чудесно сладко. *2*. Вода чудесно отражала свет. ● *1*. The flowers smelled wonderfully sweet. *2*. The water was wonderfully reflective.

**827. предпочтительно** — *preferably* — This word is used to indicate a preference for one option over another. It suggests that something is the preferred choice, but not necessarily required. It is often used when giving instructions or recommendations.

● *1*. Предпочтительно нет. *2*. Предпочтительно оба. ● *1*. Preferably not. *2*. Preferably both.

**828. бессильный** — *impotent* — This word is used to describe someone or something that lacks power, strength, or effectiveness. It can be used to convey a sense of helplessness or incapacity in various situations.

● *1*. Бессильный ответ сделал их уязвимыми. *2*. Бессильный правитель не смог остановить восстание. *3*. Он чувствовал себя бессильным перед лицом несправедливости. ● *1*. The impotent response left them vulnerable. *2*. The impotent ruler could not stop the rebellion. *3*. He felt impotent in the face of injustice.

**829. остроумный** — *witty, ingenious, facetious* — This word is used to describe someone who is clever, quick-witted, and humorous in their remarks or actions. It implies a sharp intellect and the ability to make clever and amusing observations.

● *1.* Очень остроумно. *2.* Ты остроумный. *3.* Она известна своими остроумными высказываниями. *4.* Они оценили его остроумный юмор. *5.* От ее остроумного замечания последовал смех. ● *1.* Very witty. *2.* You're witty. *3.* She's known for her witty remarks. *4.* They appreciated his witty humor. *5.* Laughter ensued from her witty remark.

**830. электромагнитный** — *electromagnetic* — This word is used to describe something that is related to or produced by electricity and magnetism. It is commonly used in the fields of physics, engineering, and technology to refer to devices or phenomena that involve electromagnetic forces.

● *1.* Электромагнитный импульс. *2.* Электромагнитный спектр включает радиоволны. *3.* В устройстве используется электромагнитная технология. *4.* Она специализировалась в области электромагнитной техники. *5.* Он изучал электромагнитные поля. ● *1.* Electromagnetic pulse. *2.* The electromagnetic spectrum includes radio waves. *3.* The device uses electromagnetic technology. *4.* She specialized in electromagnetic engineering. *5.* He studied electromagnetic fields.

**831. смутный** — *obscure, hazy* — The word 'смутный' is used to describe something that is unclear, vague, or difficult to understand. It can refer to a situation, a feeling, or a piece of information that lacks clarity or definition.

● *1.* Она почувствовала смутное чувство беспокойства. *2.* Ее воспоминания об этом событии были смутными. ● *1.* She felt an obscure sense of unease. *2.* Her recollection of the event was hazy.

**832. заскорузлый** — *corny* — 'Заскорузлый' is used to describe something that is outdated, cliché, or lacking originality. It is often used to criticize something as being unoriginal or overly sentimental.

**833. миниатюрный** — *miniature* — This word is used to describe something that is very small in size or scale, often used to refer to models, artwork, or objects that are much smaller than the original version.

● *1.* Она собирала миниатюрные фигурки. *2.* Миниатюрный автомобиль был подарком. *3.* Он нарисовал миниатюрный пейзаж. *4.* Диорама демонстрировала миниатюрный мир.

*5.* Дом представлял собой миниатюрную копию. • *1.* She collected miniature figurines. *2.* The miniature car was a gift. *3.* He painted a miniature landscape. *4.* The diorama showcased a miniature world. *5.* The house was a miniature replica.

**834. графический** — *graphic* — The word 'графический' is used to describe something related to visual representation or design. It can refer to images, charts, diagrams, or any other visual elements that convey information or enhance communication.

• *1.* В колледже она изучала графический дизайн. *2.* Графический дизайн лайнера был смелым. *3.* Они наняли внештатного графического дизайнера. *4.* Это графический роман.
• *1.* She studied graphic design in college. *2.* The graphic liner design was bold. *3.* They hired a freelance graphic designer. *4.* It's a graphic novel.

**835. прогрессивный** — *progressive* — The word 'прогрессивный' is used to describe something or someone that is forward-thinking, innovative, or open to change. It is often used to refer to ideas, policies, or individuals that promote social, political, or technological progress.

• *1.* Это прогрессивно. *2.* Компания придерживалась прогрессивного подхода. *3.* Она придерживалась прогрессивных взглядов по социальным вопросам. *4.* В стране существовала прогрессивная система образования. *5.* Прогрессивная политика привела к положительным изменениям.
• *1.* It's progressive. *2.* The company embraced a progressive approach. *3.* She held progressive views on social issues. *4.* The country had a progressive education system. *5.* The progressive policies led to positive changes.

**836. библейский** — *biblical* — The word 'библейский' is used to describe something that is related to or reminiscent of the Bible. It can be used to refer to religious texts, stories, or themes that are found in the Bible.

• *1.* Аврам -- библейское имя. • *1.* Abram is a biblical name.

**837. душный** — *stuffy* — The word 'душный' is used to describe a feeling of being confined or lacking fresh air. It can also refer to a place that is poorly ventilated or oppressive. It is often used to describe a room or atmosphere.

● *1.* Здесь немного душно. *2.* Душно. *3.* В комнате было душно и жарко. *4.* Здесь душно? *5.* По телефону он говорил душно. ● *1.* It's a bit stuffy in here. *2.* It's stuffy. *3.* The room felt stuffy and hot. *4.* Is it stuffy in here? *5.* He sounded stuffy on the phone.

**838. хаотичный** — *chaotic* — 'Хаотичный' is used to describe something that is disorganized, unpredictable, and lacking order. It conveys a sense of confusion and disorder, often referring to situations, environments, or behaviors that are chaotic in nature.

● *1.* Улицы города были хаотичны из-за движения транспорта. *2.* Это хаотично. *3.* Хаотичная сцена развернулась в прямом эфире. *4.* Сцена была хаотичной. *5.* Столпотворение на улицах было хаотичным. ● *1.* The city streets were chaotic with traffic. *2.* It's chaotic. *3.* The chaotic scene unfolded on live TV. *4.* The scene was chaotic. *5.* The pandemonium in the streets was chaotic.

**839. гордо** — *proudly* — 'гордо' is used to describe actions or behaviors that are done with a sense of pride or dignity. It conveys a feeling of confidence and self-assurance in one's actions or accomplishments.

● *1.* Она с гордостью выставила свой трофей на полке. *2.* Она носила медаль с гордостью. *3.* Он с гордостью представлял Баму на конкурсе. *4.* Он с гордостью называл себя ботаном. *5.* Она с гордостью продемонстрировала флаг Ганы. ● *1.* She proudly displayed her trophy on the shelf. *2.* She wore the medal proudly. *3.* He proudly represented Bama in the competition. *4.* He proudly declared himself a nerd. *5.* She proudly displayed the Ghana flag.

**840. офшорный** — *offshore* — The term 'офшорный' is used to describe something that is related to or located in an offshore location, typically referring to businesses, accounts, or activities that are conducted in a foreign country for financial or legal purposes.

**841. галантный** — *gallant* — 'галантный' is used to describe someone who is courteous, chivalrous, and polite in their actions towards others. It is often used to compliment someone's behavior or manners in a formal or romantic context.

• *1.* Очень галантный. • *1.* Very gallant.

**842. бесполезный** — *futile, unhelpful* — This word is used to describe something that is pointless, ineffective, or not providing any benefit or assistance. It conveys the idea of being futile or unhelpful in achieving a desired outcome.

• *1.* Сопротивление бесполезно. *2.* Сопротивление было бесполезным. *3.* Ее бесполезное отношение раздражало всех. *4.* Бесполезный ответ расстроил. *5.* Он вел себя бесполезно, когда она нуждалась в нем. *6.* Бесполезный сервис привел к негативным отзывам. *7.* Бесполезный совет только усугубил ситуацию. • *1.* Resistance is futile. *2.* The resistance was futile. *3.* Her unhelpful attitude annoyed everyone. *4.* The unhelpful response was frustrating. *5.* He acted unhelpful when she needed him. *6.* The unhelpful service led to negative reviews. *7.* The unhelpful advice only made things worse.

**843. непристойный** — *obscene, lewd, indecent, bawdy* — This word is used to describe something that is inappropriate, offensive, or vulgar in a sexual manner. It is often used to criticize behavior, language, or content that is considered indecent or offensive.

• *1.* Это непристойно. *2.* Это непристойно! *3.* Его арестовали за непристойное поведение. *4.* Шутки комика были признаны непристойными. *5.* Ее оскорбил непристойный жест. *6.* Непристойное обнажение. • *1.* It's obscene. *2.* This is obscene! *3.* He was arrested for obscene behavior. *4.* The comedian's jokes were deemed obscene. *5.* She was offended by the obscene gesture. *6.* Indecent exposure.

**844. несвежий** — *stale* — The word 'несвежий' is used to describe something that is no longer fresh or has lost its original quality. It is often used to refer to food that has gone bad or is past its expiration date.

• *1.* Они несвежие. *2.* Хлеб был несвежим. *3.* Сигарета пахла несвежим. • *1.* They're stale. *2.* The bread was stale. *3.* The cigarette smelled stale.

**845. пуленепробиваемый** — *bulletproof* — This word is used to describe something that is resistant to bullets or other projectiles. It implies that the object is extremely durable and cannot be easily penetrated or damaged by gunfire.

● *1.* Он пуленепробиваемый. *2.* Пуленепробиваемые стекла. *3.* Материал пуленепробиваемый. *4.* Пуленепробиваемая машина стоит дорого. *5.* Стекло пуленепробиваемое. ● *1.* It's bulletproof. *2.* Bulletproof glass. *3.* The material is bulletproof. *4.* A bulletproof car is expensive. *5.* The glass is bulletproof.

**846. гравитационный** — *gravitational* — This word is used to describe things related to gravity or gravitational forces. It can be used to talk about objects, phenomena, or theories that involve the force of gravity.

● *1.* Гравитационная сила планеты была сильной. *2.* Гравитационное воздействие Луны на Землю хорошо документировано. *3.* Гравитационное поле становилось сильнее. ● *1.* The planet's gravitational force was strong. *2.* The moon's gravitational effect on Earth is well-documented. *3.* The gravitational field was growing stronger.

**847. фармацевтический** — *pharmaceutical* — This word is used to describe things related to the field of pharmacy or the production of drugs. It can be used to talk about pharmaceutical companies, products, research, or practices.

● *1.* Новый фармацевтический продукт одобрен. *2.* Она занимается фармацевтическими исследованиями. *3.* Фармацевтическая отрасль строго регулируется. ● *1.* The new pharmaceutical product has been approved. *2.* She works in pharmaceutical research. *3.* The pharmaceutical industry is highly regulated.

**848. валлийский** — *welsh* — 'Welsh' is used to describe something or someone related to Wales, its people, language, or culture. It can also be used as an adverb to describe actions or characteristics that are typical of Wales or its people.

● *1.* Валлийский торт был восхитительным. *2.* Валлийский язык имеет долгую историю. ● *1.* The welsh cake was delicious. *2.* The welsh language has a long history.

**849. катастрофический** — *catastrophic, cataclysmic* — This word is used to describe something that is extremely disastrous or catastrophic in nature. It conveys a sense of extreme severity and often implies a situation that is beyond repair or redemption.

• *1.* Наводнение было катастрофическим. *2.* Пожар нанес катастрофический ущерб. *3.* Пандемия имела катастрофические последствия. *4.* Удар астероида был катастрофическим. *5.* Шторм имел катастрофические последствия. *6.* Шторм был катастрофическим. *7.* Катастрофическое событие разрушило город. *8.* Битва была катастрофической. *9.* Землетрясение имело катастрофический характер. *10.* Взрыв был катастрофическим. • *1.* The flood was catastrophic. *2.* The fire caused catastrophic damage. *3.* The pandemic had a catastrophic impact. *4.* The impact of the asteroid was catastrophic. *5.* The storm had a catastrophic effect. *6.* The storm was cataclysmic. *7.* The cataclysmic event destroyed the city. *8.* The battle was cataclysmic. *9.* The earthquake was cataclysmic. *10.* The explosion was cataclysmic.

**850. модный** — *fashionable, trendy* — This word is used to describe something that is currently popular or stylish in fashion or culture. It can refer to clothing, accessories, music, or any other trend that is considered fashionable at the moment.

• *1.* Они следовали за модной толпой. *2.* Она всегда носила самую модную одежду. *3.* Он восхищался ее модным чувством стиля. *4.* Одежда Сулу была модной. *5.* Дизайн был одновременно функциональным и модным. *6.* Магазины в верхней части города были модными. *7.* Необычные прически – это модно. *8.* Его стиль очень модный. • *1.* They followed the fashionable crowd. *2.* She always wore the most fashionable clothes. *3.* He admired her fashionable sense of style. *4.* Sulu clothing was fashionable. *5.* The design was both functional and fashionable. *6.* The uptown shops were trendy. *7.* Funky hairstyles are trendy. *8.* His style is very trendy.

**851. дефицитный** — *scarce* — 'Дефицитный' is used to describe something that is in short supply or lacking in quantity. It is often used to indicate scarcity or a shortage of a particular resource, product, or item.

• *1.* Сделайте себя дефицитным. • *1.* Make yourself scarce.

**852. минимальный** — *minimal* — 'Минимальный' is used to describe something that is at the lowest possible level or amount. It can also be used to indicate something that is very small or insignificant in comparison to others.

• *1.* Минимальный ущерб. *2.* Участие в проекте было минимальным. *3.* Набедренная повязка обеспечивала минимальную защиту. *4.* Это минимально. ● *1.* Minimal damage. *2.* The involvement in the project was minimal. *3.* The loincloth provided minimal protection. *4.* It's minimal.

**853. соответственно** — *accordingly, suitably* — 'Soootvetstvenno' is used to indicate that something is in accordance with or appropriate to a particular situation or context. It is often used to show a logical or causal relationship between two ideas or actions.
● *1.* Действуй соответственно. ● *1.* Act accordingly.

**854. придирчивый** — *picky, cantankerous* — This word is used to describe someone who is overly critical or difficult to please. It can be used to refer to someone who is picky or finds fault with small details.
● *1.* Я не придирчив. *2.* Она придирчива в еде. *3.* Она была придирчивой в еде. *4.* Придирчивый клиент имел высокие стандарты. *5.* Не будьте такими придирчивыми. ● *1.* I'm not picky. *2.* She's a picky eater. *3.* She was a picky eater. *4.* The picky customer had high standards. *5.* Don't be so picky.

**855. справедливо** — *rightly, rightfully* — 'Справедливо' is used to indicate that something is done in a fair and just manner, in accordance with what is morally or ethically right. It is often used to express agreement or approval of a decision or action.
● *1.* Справедливо так. ● *1.* Rightly so.

**856. удобно** — *comfortably, conveniently* — 'Удобно' is used to describe something that is easy to use or comfortable to do. It indicates that a situation or object is convenient and suitable for the person using it.
● *1.* Вы сидите удобно? *2.* Она удобно села в кресло. *3.* Лайкра удобно тянется. *4.* Она удобно вписалась в свои старые джинсы. *5.* Они удобно проигнорировали эту проблему. *6.* Магазин был удобно расположен. *7.* Она прибыла удобно вовремя. *8.* Он удобно забыл о встрече. *9.* Система отключилась удобно. ● *1.* Are you sitting comfortably? *2.* She sat comfortably in the armchair. *3.* The lycra stretched comfortably. *4.* She comfortably fit into her old jeans. *5.* They conveniently ignored the issue. *6.* The store was conveniently located. *7.* She arrived conveniently on time. *8.* He conveniently forgot about

the meeting. *9.* The system shut down conveniently.

**857. удовлетворительный** — *satisfactory* — This word is used to describe something that meets expectations or requirements, but may not be exceptional. It indicates that something is adequate or acceptable, but not necessarily outstanding.

● *1.* Это было бы удовлетворительно. ● *1.* That would be satisfactory.

**858. почтительно** — *respectfully* — 'Почтительно' is used to show respect or politeness towards someone or something. It is often used in formal or professional settings to convey a sense of courtesy and consideration for others.

● *1.* Она почтительно выслушала. *2.* Он почтительно поприветствовал сеньора. *3.* Они почтительно не согласились. *4.* Придворный почтительно приветствовал короля. *5.* Я почтительно отказываюсь. ● *1.* She listened respectfully. *2.* He greeted the senor respectfully. *3.* They disagreed respectfully. *4.* The courtier greeted the king respectfully. *5.* I respectfully decline.

**859. дико** — *wildly* — The word 'дико' is used to describe something that is done in a wild or untamed manner. It can also be used to convey a sense of extreme or intense behavior or emotions.

● *1.* Бронк дико дернулся. *2.* Она пела дико. *3.* Он дико аплодировал. *4.* Они дико танцевали. ● *1.* The bronc bucked wildly. *2.* She sang wildly. *3.* He cheered wildly. *4.* They danced wildly.

**860. на открытом воздухе** — *outdoor* — This word is used to describe activities or events that take place outside, in the open air. It can refer to anything from outdoor dining to outdoor concerts or sports.

● *1.* Они выступили в открытом амфитеатре. *2.* В бистро есть места на открытом воздухе. *3.* В Колорадо есть множество развлечений на свежем воздухе. *4.* Активный отдых на свежем воздухе полезен для физического здоровья. ● *1.* They performed at the outdoor amphitheater. *2.* The bistro has outdoor seating. *3.* Colorado has many outdoor activities. *4.* Outdoor activity is good for physical health.

**861. в значительной степени** — *largely* — 'В значительной степени' is used to describe something that is mostly or predominantly true or present. It emphasizes the extent or degree to which something is true or present.

- *1.* Группа была в значительной степени конформистской.
- *1.* The group was largely conformist.

**862. клеточный** — *cellular* — 'Клеточный' is used to describe something that is related to cells or has a cellular structure. It can refer to biological cells, as well as other structures that are made up of smaller units or compartments.

- *1.* Клеточная структура была сложной. *2.* Она изучала клеточный метаболизм. *3.* Клеточная биология была его страстью. • *1.* The cellular structure was complex. *2.* She studied cellular metabolism. *3.* Cellular biology was his passion.

**863. церебральный** — *cerebral* — This word is used to describe something that is related to the brain or intellect, often implying a high level of intelligence or thoughtfulness. It can also refer to something that is complex or intellectual in nature.

**864. вслух** — *aloud* — 'вслух' is used to describe something that is spoken or read out loud, rather than silently. It indicates that the action is meant to be heard by others, rather than kept private.

- *1.* Прочитайте это вслух. *2.* Он прочитал некролог вслух. *3.* Она прочитала заголовок вслух. *4.* Прокламация была зачитана вслух толпе. • *1.* Read it aloud. *2.* He read the obituary aloud. *3.* She read the headline aloud. *4.* The proclamation was read aloud to the crowd.

**865. гипотетически** — *theoretically, hypothetically* — 'гипотетически' is used to describe something that is based on a hypothesis or theory rather than actual facts or evidence. It is often used to discuss possibilities or scenarios that may not be currently true or proven.

- *1.* Гипотетически говоря. *2.* Гипотетически, конечно. *3.* Она предположила гипотетически. *4.* Гипотетически это могло бы сработать. *5.* Он попытался ответить гипотетически.
- *1.* Hypothetically speaking. *2.* Hypothetically speaking, of course. *3.* She hypothesized hypothetically. *4.* Hypothetically, it could work. *5.* He tried to answer hypothetically.

**866. инфракрасный** — *infrared* — This word is used to describe something that emits or is sensitive to infrared radiation, which is a type of electromagnetic radiation with longer wavelengths than visible light. It is commonly used in technology, such as infrared cameras and sensors.

• *1.* Инфракрасные камеры зафиксировали злоумышленника. *2.* Инфракрасный датчик обнаружил движение. *3.* Инфракрасный свет не виден человеку. *4.* Система безопасности использует инфракрасную технологию. • *1.* The infrared cameras captured the intruder. *2.* The infrared sensor detected motion. *3.* Infrared light is not visible to humans. *4.* The security system uses infrared technology.

**867. с разбитым сердцем** — *heartbroken* — This term is used to describe a feeling of deep sadness and emotional pain due to a significant loss or disappointment. It conveys a sense of shattered emotions and profound sorrow.

**868. отличительный** — *distinctive* — 'Отличительный' is used to describe something that is unique or easily recognizable because of its distinguishing characteristics. It is often used to highlight the special qualities that set something apart from others.

• *1.* Униформа бидла была отличительной. • *1.* The beadle's uniform was distinctive.

**869. завистливый** — *envious* — This word is used to describe someone who feels resentment or discontent towards another person's possessions, qualities, or achievements. It conveys a sense of jealousy or covetousness.

• *1.* Завистливые мысли поглотили ее. *2.* Завистливые комментарии были обидны. *3.* Завистливые взгляды были очевидны. • *1.* Envious thoughts consumed her. *2.* The envious comments were hurtful. *3.* The envious glances were obvious.

**870. слизистый** — *slimy* — This word is used to describe something that is covered in a slippery, viscous substance. It is often used to describe things like slime, mucus, or other substances that have a slimy texture.

• *1.* Пруд был полон слизистых водорослей. *2.* Рыба была покрыта слизистой оболочкой. *3.* Слизистая текстура лягушки. *4.* Он неохотно прикоснулся к слизистой субстанции. *5.* Пол был покрыт слизистой водой. • *1.* The pond was full of slimy algae. *2.* The fish had a slimy coating. *3.* The slimy texture of the frog. *4.* He reluctantly touched the slimy substance. *5.* The floor was covered in slimy water.

**871. адекватный** — *adequate* — This word is used to describe something that is appropriate, reasonable, or suitable for a particular situation. It implies that the object or person in question meets the necessary standards or requirements.

● *1.* Работа была в лучшем случае адекватной. *2.* Им нужно было адекватное решение. *3.* Мне нужна адекватная сумма. ● *1.* The work was adequate at best. *2.* They needed an adequate solution. *3.* I need an adequate amount.

**872. тошнотворный** — *nauseous* — This word is used to describe something that causes a feeling of nausea or disgust. It is often used to describe smells, tastes, or situations that make someone feel sick or uncomfortable.

**873. неостанавливаемый** — *unstoppable* — This word is used to describe something that cannot be stopped or prevented, indicating a continuous and relentless nature. It conveys a sense of power, strength, and determination in the subject it is describing.

**874. супружеский** — *marital, matrimonial, conjugal, spousal* — This word is used to describe things or actions related to marriage or spouses. It can refer to relationships, activities, or items that are connected to the institution of marriage.

● *1.* Супружеские узы стали крепче. *2.* Песня прославляла супружескую любовь. *3.* Супружеские обязательства подверглись испытанию. *4.* Супружеские узы были крепкими. *5.* Супружеский визит сблизил их. *6.* Супружеская связь была нерушимой. *7.* Они обратились за супружеской консультацией к терапевту. *8.* Пара отпраздновала свой супружеский союз. *9.* Она заключила супружеские объятия. ● *1.* The marital bond grew stronger. *2.* The song celebrated marital love. *3.* The marital commitment was tested. *4.* The matrimonial bond was strong. *5.* The conjugal visit brought them closer. *6.* The conjugal bond was unbreakable. *7.* They sought conjugal advice from a therapist. *8.* The couple celebrated their conjugal union. *9.* She gave a conjugal hug.

**875. стерильный** — *sterile* — This word is used to describe something that is free from bacteria or other microorganisms. It can also be used to describe something that is very clean and devoid of any contaminants.

● *1.* Это стерильно. *2.* Марлевый тампон был стерильным. *3.* Солевой раствор был стерильным. ● *1.* It's sterile. *2.* The gauze pad was sterile. *3.* The saline solution was sterile.

**876. словесный** — *verbal, wordy* — The word 'словесный' is used to describe something that is related to words or language, often implying that it is verbose or wordy in nature. It can be used to characterize written or spoken communication.

● *1.* Они использовали словесный подстрекатель. *2.* Он начал неспровоцированную словесную атаку. ● *1.* They used a verbal goad. *2.* He launched an unprovoked verbal assault.

**877. грешный** — *sinful* — The word 'грешный' is used to describe someone or something that is sinful or has committed a wrongdoing. It conveys a sense of moral fault or guilt.

● *1.* Торт был грешным и вкусным. ● *1.* The cake was sinful and delicious.

**878. заблудившись** — *astray* — 'Заблудившись' is used to describe someone who is lost or confused, either physically or mentally. It conveys a sense of being off course or disoriented.

**879. равнодушный** — *indifferent, unconcerned, apathetic* — This word describes someone who shows no interest, emotion, or concern towards a particular situation or person. It conveys a sense of detachment and lack of involvement in what is happening around them.

● *1.* Ее равнодушное отношение озадачивало. *2.* Она была равнодушна к их жалобам. *3.* Он оставался равнодушным, несмотря на обстоятельства. *4.* Равнодушный ответ расстроил. *5.* Как равнодушные дети земли. *6.* Несмотря на хаос, она оставалась равнодушной. ● *1.* Her indifferent attitude was puzzling. *2.* She was indifferent to their complaints. *3.* He remained indifferent despite the circumstances. *4.* The indifferent response was frustrating. *5.* As the indifferent children of the earth. *6.* She remained unconcerned despite the chaos.

**880. мудро** — *wisely* — 'Мудро' is used to describe actions or decisions made with wisdom and intelligence. It implies a thoughtful and careful approach to solving problems or making choices. It suggests a deep understanding of the situation and the ability to make sound judgments.

- *1.* Использовать его мудро. *2.* Она будет управлять мудро.
- *1.* Use it wisely. *2.* She will govern wisely.

**881. абстрактный** — *abstract* — This word is used to describe something that is conceptual or theoretical in nature, rather than concrete or physical. It is often used in discussions about art, philosophy, and academic subjects to refer to ideas that are not based on specific, tangible objects.

- *1.* Стиль художника можно охарактеризовать как абстрактный. *2.* Работы Миро были абстрактными. *3.* Волнистый узор был абстрактным. *4.* Художник работает в абстрактном жанре. ● *1.* The artist's style can be characterized as abstract. *2.* Miro's work was abstract. *3.* The squiggly pattern was abstract. *4.* The artist works in the abstract genre.

**882. оскорбительный** — *abusive* — This word is used to describe language or behavior that is offensive, insulting, or disrespectful towards someone. It conveys a sense of harm or hurt caused by the abusive actions or words.

- *1.* Отношения стали оскорбительными. *2.* Оскорбительное поведение продолжалось. ● *1.* The relationship turned abusive. *2.* The abusive behavior continued.

**883. скупой** — *stingy* — The word 'скупой' is used to describe someone who is unwilling to spend money or share resources. It conveys a sense of being frugal or miserly in their actions and behavior.

- *1.* Не скупитесь. *2.* Не будь таким скупым. ● *1.* Don't be stingy. *2.* Don't be so stingy.

**884. румяный** — *rosy, ruddy* — This word is used to describe someone's complexion or cheeks as having a healthy, pinkish color. It can also be used to describe something that is a rosy or reddish color.

- *1.* Румяные щеки свидетельствовали о здоровье. *2.* Румяные щеки свидетельствовали о лихорадке. *3.* Румяный цвет поразил. ● *1.* The rosy cheeks showed health. *2.* The ruddy cheeks indicated fever. *3.* The ruddy color was striking.

**885. функциональный** — *functional* — This word is used to describe something that is designed or intended to be practical, useful, or efficient in its purpose. It is often used to highlight the functionality or effectiveness of an object, system, or process.

● *1.* Планировка нового офиса была функциональной. *2.* Машина была функциональной, но не кричащей. *3.* Дизайн был одновременно функциональным и модным. *4.* Машина была функциональной, но громкой. ● *1.* The new office layout was functional. *2.* The car was functional but not flashy. *3.* The design was both functional and fashionable. *4.* The machine was functional but loud.

**886. изящный** — *graceful, dainty, dinky, nifty* — 'Izyschny' is used to describe something that is elegant, delicate, or skillfully made. It can refer to objects, movements, or even ideas that possess a certain charm or finesse.

● *1.* Ты знаешь, что ты очень изящная? *2.* Очень изящно. *3.* Уклонение было быстрым и изящным. *4.* Она такая изящная. *5.* Балерина исполнила изящный пируэт. *6.* Изящные украшения были изысканными. *7.* Она совершила изящную прогулку. ● *1.* You know that you're very graceful? *2.* Very graceful. *3.* The dodge was swift and graceful. *4.* She is so graceful. *5.* The ballerina executed a graceful pirouette. *6.* The dainty jewelry was exquisite. *7.* She had a dainty walk.

**887. правдивый** — *truthful* — This word is used to describe something or someone that is honest, accurate, and tells the truth. It can be used to describe statements, stories, or people who are known for their honesty and integrity.

● *1.* Она говорила холодные, жесткие, правдивые факты. *2.* Правдивое признание принесло облегчение. *3.* Он всегда был правдив. *4.* Ее взгляд был честным и правдивым. *5.* Они требовали правдивого ответа. ● *1.* She spoke the cold, hard, truthful facts. *2.* The truthful confession was a relief. *3.* He was always truthful. *4.* Her gaze was honest and truthful. *5.* They demanded a truthful answer.

**888. нерегулярный** — *irregular* — This word is used to describe something that does not occur at regular intervals or in a predictable pattern. It can also refer to something that is not conforming to established rules or norms.

● *1.* Это крайне нерегулярно. *2.* Аритмия вызвала нерегулярное сердцебиение. *3.* Крайне нерегулярный. ● *1.* This is most irregular. *2.* The arrhythmia caused irregular heartbeats. *3.*

Highly irregular.

**889. невиданный** — *unseen* — 'невиданный' is used to describe something that has never been seen before or is unprecedented. It conveys the idea of something being completely new, unexpected, or extraordinary.

● *1.* Появился ранее невиданный объект. *2.* Невиданная красота сада. ● *1.* The heretofore unseen object appeared. *2.* The unseen beauty of the garden.

**890. травяной** — *herbal* — 'Травяной' is used to describe something that is related to or made from herbs. It is often used to refer to herbal teas, remedies, or products.

● *1.* Это травяное. *2.* Он предпочитал травяные добавки традиционной медицине. *3.* Она использовала травяные средства от простуды. *4.* Травяной аромат наполнил комнату. *5.* Травяное лекарство помогло ей справиться с простудой. ● *1.* It's herbal. *2.* He preferred herbal supplements over traditional medicine. *3.* She used herbal remedies for colds. *4.* The herbal scent filled the room. *5.* The herbal remedy helped with her cold.

**891. почтовый** — *postal* — 'Почтовый' is used to describe things related to the postal service, such as mail, letters, packages, or post offices. It indicates that something is connected to or used for sending or receiving mail.

● *1.* Перед отправкой проверьте почтовый индекс. *2.* Это служба почтовой доставки. *3.* Это почтовый адрес. *4.* Почтовая служба потеряла мою посылку. *5.* Почтовый чувак. ● *1.* Check the postal code before sending. *2.* It's a postal delivery service. *3.* This is a postal address. *4.* The postal service lost my package. *5.* Postal Dude .

**892. недостойный** — *unworthy* — 'Недостойный' is used to describe something or someone as not deserving of respect, honor, or consideration. It conveys a sense of unworthiness or lack of merit.

● *1.* Недостойному противнику не было равных. *2.* Недостойного кандидата быстро отсеяли. *3.* Недостойное предложение было отклонено. *4.* Соперницы назвали ее недостойной. *5.* Он чувствовал себя недостойным ее любви. ● *1.* The unworthy opponent was no match. *2.* The unworthy candidate was quickly eliminated. *3.* The unworthy proposal was rejected. *4.* She was labeled unworthy by her rivals. *5.* He felt unworthy of her affection.

**893. морально** — *morally* — 'Morally' is used to describe actions, decisions, or situations in terms of their ethical or moral implications. It can indicate whether something is right or wrong based on principles of morality or ethics.

● *1.* Эта история подняла моральные вопросы. *2.* Он руководствовался моральными принципами. *3.* Решение было морально сложным. *4.* Она поступала в соответствии со своими моральными убеждениями. *5.* Спор вращался вокруг моральных вопросов. ● *1.* The story raised morally questions. *2.* He was guided by morally principles. *3.* The decision was a morally complex one. *4.* She acted in accordance with her morally beliefs. *5.* The argument revolved around morally issues.

**894. неприличный** — *indecent, unbecoming* — This word is used to describe something that is inappropriate or offensive, often in a social or moral context. It implies behavior or language that is not suitable for a particular situation or setting.

● *1.* Это неприлично. ● *1.* It's indecent.

**895. вежливо** — *politely* — 'вежливо' is used to describe actions or behavior that are courteous, respectful, and considerate towards others. It is often used to indicate polite communication or interactions in various social situations.

● *1.* Он попытался вежливо не согласиться. ● *1.* He tried to disagree politely.

**896. туманный** — *misty, hazy, foggy* — 'Туманный' is used to describe something that is unclear, vague, or indistinct, often referring to physical objects or abstract concepts. It conveys a sense of mystery or obscurity, suggesting a lack of clarity or definition.

● *1.* Туманный туман поглотил все. *2.* Она смотрела на туманные горы. *3.* Утро было туманным и прохладным. *4.* Он любил гулять под туманным дождём. *5.* Туманный воздух освежал. *6.* Западный горизонт был туманным. *7.* Туманное утро мешало видеть. *8.* Туманная погода задержала их поездку. *9.* Туманный день затмил обзор. *10.* Туманная атмосфера создавала таинственное ощущение. • *1.* The misty fog engulfed everything. *2.* She gazed at the misty mountains. *3.* The morning was misty and cool. *4.* He loved walking in the misty rain. *5.* The misty air was refreshing. *6.* The westen horizon was hazy. *7.* The foggy morning made it hard to see. *8.* The foggy weather delayed their trip. *9.* The foggy day obscured the view. *10.* The foggy atmosphere created a mysterious feeling.

**897. подотчетный** — *accountable, answerable* — This word is used to describe someone who is responsible for their actions and can be held accountable for their decisions or behavior. It implies that the person can be asked to explain or justify their actions.

• *1.* Компания подотчетна своим акционерам. • *1.* The business is accountable to its shareholders.

**898. облачный** — *cloudy* — 'Облачный' is used to describe weather conditions or skies that are filled with clouds. It can also be used to describe something that has a cloudy or hazy appearance.

• *1.* Небо выглядит облачным. • *1.* The sky looks cloudy.

**899. некорректный** — *incorrect* — 'некорректный' is used to describe something that is not accurate or appropriate. It can refer to actions, statements, or behavior that is not in line with accepted norms or standards.

**900. нежелательный** — *unwanted, unwelcome, undesirable, objectionable* — This word is used to describe something that is not wanted or not desired. It conveys a sense of negativity or disapproval towards the object or situation being described.

• *1.* Она почувствовала вторжение нежелательных мыслей. *2.* Внимание было нежелательным. *3.* Нежелательные письма заполнили мой почтовый ящик. *4.* Незваное присутствие было нежелательным. *5.* Вмешательство было нежелательным. *6.* Ее дерзость была нежелательна. *7.* Он получил нежелательную критику. *8.* Ее присутствие было нежелательным. *9.* Погода создала нежелательные условия. *10.* Она сочла эту работу нежелательной. *11.* Он столкнулся с нежелательными последствиями. *12.* Гости вечеринки были нежелательны. • *1.* She felt the intrusion of unwanted thoughts. *2.* The attention was unwanted. *3.* Unwanted emails filled my inbox. *4.* The uninvited presence was unwelcome. *5.* The interference was unwelcome. *6.* Her impertinence was unwelcome. *7.* He received unwelcome criticism. *8.* Her presence was unwelcome. *9.* The weather resulted in undesirable conditions. *10.* She found the job undesirable. *11.* He faced undesirable consequences. *12.* The party guests were undesirable.

**901. брюшной** — *abdominal* — The word 'брюшной' is used to describe something related to the abdomen or stomach area. It can be used to refer to abdominal pain, abdominal muscles, or any other aspect of the abdomen.
● *1.* Брюшная броня. ● *1.* Abdominal armour.

**902. недействительный** — *invalid, unavailable* — This word is used to describe something that is not valid or functioning properly. It can refer to documents, contracts, or any other item that is not legally or practically effective.
● *1.* Его лицензия недействительна. *2.* Авторизация недействительна. ● *1.* His license is invalid. *2.* Authorization invalid.

**903. смиренно** — *humbly* — 'Смиренно' is used to describe someone who behaves in a modest and unassuming manner, showing humility and respect towards others. It conveys a sense of quiet confidence and a lack of arrogance.
● *1.* Я смиренно благодарю вас, сэр. *2.* Я смиренно принимаю. *3.* Она смиренно просила о помощи. *4.* Она смиренно приняла награду. *5.* Просьба была сделана смиренно. ● *1.* I humbly thank you, sir. *2.* I humbly accept. *3.* She humbly asked for help. *4.* She accepted the award humbly. *5.* The request was made humbly.

**904. доблестный** — *valiant* — The word 'доблестный' is used to describe someone who shows courage, bravery, and heroism in the face of danger or adversity. It is often used to praise individuals who demonstrate exceptional valor and bravery.

**905. скрытный** — *secretive, reticent, cagey* — This word is used to describe someone who is secretive, reserved, or cautious in revealing information. It implies a sense of mystery or hidden motives.
● *1.* У него скрытный характер. ● *1.* He has a secretive nature.

**906. добровольный** — *voluntary* — This word describes actions or decisions made willingly, without being forced or obligated. It implies a sense of choice and willingness in the action or decision being made.

● *1.* Решение является добровольным. *2.* Она сделала добровольное пожертвование. *3.* Это чисто добровольно. *4.* Это не добровольно. ● *1.* The decision is voluntary. *2.* She made a voluntary donation. *3.* It's purely voluntary. *4.* It's not voluntary.

**907. административный** — *administrative* — This word is used to describe things related to the organization and management of a system or institution. It can refer to tasks, processes, or structures that are involved in the administration of a business, government, or other organization.

● *1.* Интендант выполнял административные обязанности. ● *1.* The intendant handled administrative duties.

**908. кавказский** — *caucasian* — The adjective/adverb 'кавказский' is used to describe something or someone that is related to the Caucasus region, including its people, culture, or geography. It can also refer to the Caucasian race.

● *1.* Они изучали кавказские языки. *2.* Кавказская культура имеет богатую историю. ● *1.* They studied Caucasian languages. *2.* Caucasian culture has a rich history.

**909. бредовый** — *delirious, delusional, freaky* — The word 'бредовый' is used to describe something that is irrational, absurd, or bizarre. It conveys a sense of delirium or delusion, often used to describe ideas, stories, or behavior that are outlandish or fantastical.

● *1.* Бредовое состояние длилось несколько часов. *2.* Она бредовая ● *1.* The delirious state lasted for hours. *2.* She's delusional.

**910. совместимый** — *compatible* — This word is used to describe things that work well together or can be used together without causing problems. It is often used in the context of technology, software, or relationships.

● *1.* Мы совместимы. *2.* Они совместимы по вкусам. *3.* Они искали совместимого компаньона. *4.* Эти две системы были несовместимы. *5.* Пара обнаружила, что они совместимы. ● *1.* We're compatible. *2.* They are compatible in their tastes. *3.* They searched for a compatible companion. *4.* The two systems were not compatible. *5.* The couple found that they were compatible.

**911. стильный** — *stylish, nifty* — This word is used to describe something that is fashionable, elegant, or well-designed. It is often used to compliment someone's appearance or taste in clothing, accessories, or home decor.

● *1.* Очень стильно. *2.* Пирсинг ее перегородки выглядел стильно. *3.* На ней был стильный шерстяной свитер. *4.* Ее туника была стильной. *5.* Водолазка – это стильно. ● *1.* Very stylish. *2.* Her septum piercing looked stylish. *3.* She wore a stylish wooly sweater. *4.* Her tunic was stylish. *5.* The turtleneck is stylish.

**912. яростно** — *violently, ferociously* — 'яростно' is used to describe actions or emotions that are intense, aggressive, or passionate. It conveys a sense of violence or ferocity in the way something is done or felt.

● *1.* Он яростно тряс дверью. *2.* Волны яростно разбились. *3.* Фонтан яростно хлынул наружу. *4.* Их яростный дух соперничества впечатлял многих. *5.* Он яростно спорил. *6.* Собака яростно залаяла. *7.* Он рисовал яростно, широкими мазками. *8.* Она яростно отстаивала свою позицию. ● *1.* He shook the door violently. *2.* The waves crashed violently. *3.* The gusher spurted out violently. *4.* Their ferociously competitive spirit impressed many. *5.* He argued ferociously. *6.* The dog barked ferociously. *7.* He painted ferociously with broad strokes. *8.* She defended her position ferociously.

**913. колоссальный** — *colossal, stupendous* — This word is used to describe something extremely large or impressive in size or scale. It conveys a sense of awe or astonishment at the sheer magnitude or grandeur of the object or situation being described.

● *1.* Он столкнулся с колоссальным противником. *2.* Они столкнулись с колоссальным испытанием. *3.* Здание представляло собой колоссальное сооружение. *4.* Это колоссально. *5.* Задача была колоссальной. *6.* Ее колоссальный талант был неоспорим. *7.* Он добился колоссального достижения. ● *1.* He faced a colossal opponent. *2.* They faced a colossal challenge. *3.* The building was a colossal structure. *4.* It's colossal. *5.* The task was a colossal undertaking. *6.* Her stupendous talent was undeniable. *7.* He made a stupendous achievement.

**914.   сострадательный** — *compassionate* — This word describes someone who shows empathy and understanding towards others who are suffering or in need.   It conveys a sense of kindness and a willingness to help alleviate the pain or difficulties of others.

● *1.* Он говорил сострадательным голосом. *2.* Им была оказана сострадательная забота. *3.* Он был известен своим сострадательным характером. *4.* Этот сострадательный жест тронул ее сердце. *5.* У нее было сострадательное сердце к грешнику.   ● *1.* He spoke with a compassionate voice. *2.* They received compassionate care. *3.* He was known for his compassionate nature. *4.* The compassionate gesture touched her heart. *5.* She had a compassionate heart for the sinner.

**915. разумно** — *reasonably, sensibly* — 'Разумно' is used to describe actions or decisions that are logical, practical, and based on sound judgment. It implies that something is done in a sensible and reasonable manner.

● *1.* Это было по разумной цене. *2.* Она старалась быть разумно понимающей. *3.* В чрезвычайной ситуации он действовал разумно. *4.* Она разумно выбрала более здоровый вариант. *5.* Команда разумно поработала над решением - проблемы. *6.* Она подошла к проекту разумно. ● *1.* It was reasonably priced. *2.* She tried to be reasonably understanding. *3.* He acted sensibly in the emergency. *4.* She sensibly chose the healthier option. *5.* The team worked sensibly to solve the problem. *6.* She approached the project sensibly.

**916.   волнующий** — *groovy* — 'волнующий' is used to describe something that is exciting, thrilling, or captivating. It conveys a sense of energy and enthusiasm, often used to describe music, events, or experiences that are enjoyable and engaging.

**917.   распутная** — *slutty* — The word 'распутная' is used to describe someone who is promiscuous or behaves in a sexually provocative manner. It is often used in a derogatory way to criticize someone's behavior or character.

**918.   энергичный** — *energetic, snappy, feisty, punchy* — This word is used to describe someone or something that is full of energy, lively, and dynamic.   It can also convey a sense of determi-

nation, enthusiasm, and vigor in a person's actions or behavior.
● *1.* Она очень энергичная. *2.* Атмосфера ночного клуба - была энергичной. *3.* Ее собака была худой и энергичной. *4.* Полька – энергичный танец. ● *1.* She's very energetic. *2.* The ambiance of the nightclub was energetic. *3.* Her dog was skinny and energetic. *4.* The polka is an energetic dance.

**919. телесный** — *bodily, corporeal* — 'Телесный' is used to describe something related to the physical body or material world. It can refer to physical sensations, bodily functions, or anything pertaining to the physical aspect of existence.
● *1.* Телесное повреждение было серьезным. *2.* Телесные ощущения были ошеломляющими. *3.* Они установили телесный контакт. *4.* Ему были причинены телесные повреждения. *5.* Она почувствовала телесную боль. ● *1.* The bodily injury was serious. *2.* The bodily sensations were overwhelming. *3.* They made bodily contact. *4.* He suffered bodily harm. *5.* She felt bodily pain.

**920. протестантский** — *protestant* — This word is used to describe something related to Protestantism, such as beliefs, practices, or traditions. It can also be used to describe individuals or groups who adhere to Protestant beliefs.

**921. афганский** — *afghan* — This word is used to describe something or someone related to Afghanistan. It can refer to the country itself, its people, culture, language, or anything else associated with Afghanistan.

**922. непрерывно** — *continuously* — 'непрерывно' is used to describe actions or processes that occur without interruption or pause. It indicates that something is happening continuously, without any breaks or gaps.
● *1.* Дождь шел непрерывно в течение нескольких часов. *2.* Он работал непрерывно, без перерыва. *3.* Машина непрерывно пищала. *4.* Она говорила непрерывно, не останавливаясь. ● *1.* The rain fell continuously for hours. *2.* He worked continuously without a break. *3.* The machine beeped continuously. *4.* She spoke continuously without pausing.

**923. театральный** — *theatrical* — 'Teatralny' is used to describe someone or something that is overly dramatic, exaggerated, or flamboyant in behavior or appearance. It can also refer to something related to or characteristic of the theater.

• *1.* Театральная труппа развлекала публику. • *1.* The theatrical troupe entertained the audience.

**924. респираторный** — *respiratory* — This word is used to describe something related to the respiratory system or the act of breathing. It is often used in medical contexts to refer to conditions, treatments, or equipment that are specifically designed for the respiratory system.

**925. обстоятельный** — *circumstantial* — The word 'обстоятельный' is used to describe something that is detailed, thorough, or comprehensive. It implies that the subject is characterized by a significant amount of information or circumstances.

**926. беззаботный** — *carefree, unconcerned* — The word 'беззаботный' is used to describe someone who is carefree and unconcerned about problems or responsibilities. It conveys a sense of freedom from worry or stress.

• *1.* Она смеялась весело и беззаботно. *2.* Они наслаждались беззаботным днем на пляже. *3.* Дети беззаботно играли в саду. *4.* Она беззаботна, она снобистская звезда. *5.* Жить беззаботно - ее цель. *6.* Беззаботное отношение удивило всех. • *1.* She laughed blythe and carefree. *2.* They enjoyed a carefree day at the beach. *3.* The children played carefree in the garden. *4.* She's carefree, she's a snobbish star. *5.* Livin carefree is her goal. *6.* The unconcerned attitude surprised everyone.

**927. конституционный** — *constitutional* — This word is used to describe something that is related to or in accordance with a constitution. It is often used in legal and political contexts to refer to laws, rights, or principles that are established by a constitution.

**928. неуловимый** — *elusive* — 'Elusive' describes something that is difficult to catch, grasp, or understand. It is often used to describe something that is fleeting, evasive, or hard to pin down.

• *1.* Он сфотографировал неуловимую рысь. *2.* Реализация была неуловимой. *3.* Неуловимая пищуха осталась скрытой. *4.* Тар может быть неуловимым. *5.* Народ фейри был неуловим. • *1.* He photographed the elusive bobcat. *2.* Fulfilment was elusive. *3.* The elusive pika remained hidden. *4.* The thar can be elusive. *5.* The fey folk were elusive.

**929. притязательный** — *pretentious* — This word is used to describe someone or something that tries to impress others by pretending to be more important, intelligent, or cultured than they really are. It can also refer to something that is overly elaborate or showy.

**930. сияющий** — *radiant* — 'Сияющий' is used to describe something or someone that is shining brightly, glowing, or exuding a radiant light or energy. It conveys a sense of brightness, brilliance, and positivity.

• *1.* Ты выглядишь сияющим. *2.* У нее был сияющий цвет лица. *3.* Его отношение было положительно сияющим. •
*1.* You look radiant. *2.* She had a radiant complexion. *3.* His attitude was positively radiant.

**931. капиталистический** — *capitalist, capitalistic* — This word is used to describe something related to capitalism or characteristic of a capitalist system. It can refer to economic practices, ideologies, or societal structures that are based on private ownership and the pursuit of profit.

• *1.* Она критиковала недостатки капиталистического общества. *2.* Страна приняла капиталистическую экономическую систему. *3.* Бизнес процветал в капиталистической среде. •
*1.* She criticized the flaws of a capitalistic society. *2.* The country embraced a capitalistic economic system. *3.* The business thrived in a capitalistic environment.

**932. кудрявый** — *crispy* — 'Кудрявый' is used to describe something that is crispy or crunchy in texture. It can be used to describe food, such as fried chicken or potato chips, or other items that have a crispy texture.

**933. нетронутый** — *untouched, pristine, untapped* — 'Нетронутый' is used to describe something that has not been touched, altered, or disturbed in any way. It conveys a sense of purity, untouched beauty, and pristine condition.

• *1.* Первозданный лес был нетронут человеком. *2.* Нетронутое сокровище наконец было обнаружено. *3.* Целина осталась нетронутой. *4.* Пляж был девственно чистым и нетронутым. *5.* Нетронутая земля была объявлена национальным парком. *6.* Нетронутый пляж был девственно чистым. *7.* Нетронутый снег блестел на солнце. *8.* Пляж был девственно чистым и нетронутым. • *1.* The primordial forest was untouched by man. *2.* The untouched treasure was finally discovered. *3.* The virgin land was untouched. *4.* The beach was pristine and untouched. *5.* The untouched land was declared a national park. *6.* The unspoiled beach was pristine. *7.* The pristine snow glistened in the sun. *8.* The beach was pristine and untouched.

**934. убедительный** — *persuasive, conclusive* — 'Убедительный' is used to describe something that is convincing or conclusive in a way that leaves little room for doubt or argument. It is often used to describe arguments, evidence, or presentations that are particularly compelling.

• *1.* Вы очень убедительны. *2.* Я могу быть очень убедительным. *3.* Он может быть очень убедительным. *4.* Телемаркетинговая реклама оказалась убедительной. *5.* Она очень убедительна. *6.* Ничего убедительного. *7.* Результаты испытаний были убедительными. *8.* Результаты исследования оказались убедительными. *9.* Вряд ли убедительно. *10.* Доказательства убедительны. • *1.* You're very persuasive. *2.* I can be very persuasive. *3.* He can be very persuasive. *4.* The telemarketing pitch was persuasive. *5.* She's very persuasive. *6.* Nothing conclusive. *7.* The test results were conclusive. *8.* The study was conclusive in its findings. *9.* Hardly conclusive. *10.* The evidence is conclusive.

**935. штормовой** — *stormy* — The word 'штормовой' is used to describe something that is related to or characteristic of a storm. It can be used to describe weather conditions, emotions, or situations that are turbulent, intense, or unpredictable.

• *1.* Бомбардир шел в штормовую погоду. • *1.* The bombardier navigated through stormy weather.

**936. домашний** — *homey* — 'Домашний' is used to describe something that is cozy, comfortable, or familiar, often associated with being at home. It can refer to physical spaces, activities, or feelings that evoke a sense of warmth and security.

• *1.* Эй, домашний. *2.* Это очень по-домашнему. • *1.* Hey, homey. *2.* It's very homey.

**937. храбро** — *bravely, gallantly* — 'Храбро' is used to describe someone acting with courage and bravery in the face of danger or adversity. It conveys a sense of fearlessness and determination in the way a person approaches challenges.

- *1.* Вы храбро сражались. *2.* Риттер храбро сражался в бою. *3.* Он храбро сражался. *4.* Они храбро сражались за свободу. *5.* Легендарный герой храбро сражался. • *1.* You fought bravely. *2.* The ritter fought bravely in battle. *3.* He fought bravely. *4.* They fought for freedom bravely. *5.* The legendary hero fought bravely.

**938. незабвенный** — *unforgettable* — 'Unforgettable' is used to describe something that leaves a lasting impression or memory. It is often used to emphasize the significance or impact of a person, event, or experience.

**939. старческий** — *senile* — This word is used to describe someone or something that is showing signs of old age, particularly in terms of mental or physical deterioration. It implies a lack of clarity, coherence, or strength typically associated with aging.

- *1.* Он старческий. • *1.* He's senile.

**940. приятным** — *enjoyable* — 'Приятным' is used to describe something that brings pleasure or satisfaction. It is often used to express enjoyment of an experience, such as a pleasant conversation, a delicious meal, or a relaxing day.

- *1.* Его компания была приятной. • *1.* His company was enjoyable.

**941. съедобный** — *edible* — This word is used to describe food or substances that are safe and suitable for consumption by humans. It indicates that something is fit to be eaten without causing harm or discomfort.

- *1.* Он отказывался есть все несъедобное. *2.* Съедобные растения поддерживали их. *3.* Они не могли отличить, что съедобно. *4.* Цветы были съедобны и использовались в салатах. *5.* Это отвратительно, но съедобно. • *1.* He refused to eat anything that wasn't edible. *2.* The edible plants sustained them. *3.* They couldn't distinguish what was edible. *4.* The flowers were edible and used in salads. *5.* It's grosse but edible.

**942. потертый** — *shabby* — 'Потертый' is used to describe something that is worn out, old, or in poor condition. It can refer to physical objects, clothing, or even a person's appearance.

● *1.* Не слишком потертый. ● *1.* Not too shabby.

**943. утомительный** — *tedious* — 'утомительный' is used to describe something that is boring, tiresome, or monotonous. It conveys a sense of tedium and can be used to express feelings of exhaustion or frustration towards a particular task or situation.
● *1.* Он назвал встречу утомительной. *2.* Утомительный процесс требовал терпения. *3.* Лишние слова сделали отрывок утомительным. *4.* Они трудились в течение утомительных часов. *5.* Эта работа показалась ей утомительной. ● *1.* He described the meeting as tedious. *2.* The tedious process required patience. *3.* The redundant words made the passage tedious. *4.* They toiled through the tedious hours. *5.* She found the work tedious.

**944. доисторический** — *prehistoric* — This word is used to describe something that existed or occurred before recorded history, typically referring to ancient times or events that took place long before written records were kept.
● *1.* Доисторические скальные образования остаются загадкой. *2.* Они изучали доисторические цивилизации. *3.* Доисторическая эпоха была полна неизведанного. *4.* Были обнаружены доисторические кости. *5.* Доисторические существа бродили по земле. ● *1.* Prehistoric rock formations remain a mystery. *2.* They studied prehistoric civilizations. *3.* The prehistoric era was filled with unknowns. *4.* The prehistoric bones were discovered. *5.* Prehistoric creatures roamed the earth.

**945. навязчивый** — *obsessive, intrusive* — This word is used to describe something or someone that is persistent, intrusive, or overly insistent. It conveys the idea of something that is difficult to ignore or get rid of, often causing discomfort or annoyance.
● *1.* У детектива была навязчивая сосредоточенность. *2.* У него была навязчивая потребность во контроле. *3.* Ее навязчивое поведение обеспокоило ее друзей. *4.* Они искали помощи в борьбе со своими навязчивыми мыслями. *5.* У него был навязчивый характер. *6.* Навязчивые мысли не уходили. *7.* Люди находят ее любопытное поведение навязчивым. *8.* Телефонный звонок был навязчивым. *9.* Камера показалась мне навязчивой. ● *1.* The detective had an obsessive focus. *2.* He had an obsessive need for control. *3.* Her obsessive behavior worried her friends. *4.* They sought help

for their obsessive thoughts. *5.* He had an intrusive personality. *6.* The intrusive thoughts wouldn't go away. *7.* People find her nosey attitude intrusive. *8.* The phone call was intrusive. *9.* The camera felt intrusive.

**946. солевой** — *saline* — The word 'солевой' is used to describe something that contains or is related to salt. It can refer to a salty taste, a saline solution, or anything else that is connected to salt or saltiness.

**947. с завязанными глазами** — *blindfold* — This term describes a situation where someone's eyes are covered with a cloth or bandage, preventing them from seeing. It is often used in games, challenges, or situations where someone must rely on their other senses.

**948. ритмичный** — *rhythmic* — This word is used to describe something that has a regular and consistent pattern or beat, often in music or movement. It implies a sense of flow and harmony in the way something is structured or performed.
● *1.* Ритмичный звук галопа. *2.* Он танцевал под ритмичный дум. ● *1.* The rhythmic sound of gallop. *2.* He danced to the rhythmic dum.

**949. материнский** — *maternal* — The word 'материнский' is used to describe something related to or characteristic of a mother or motherhood. It can be used to refer to qualities, actions, or objects associated with the maternal role.
● *1.* В ней сработал материнский инстинкт. *2.* Он оказал - материнскую помощь раненой птице. *3.* Материнская связь была сильной. *4.* Она получила материнский совет от своей матери. *5.* Она проявила к сироте материнскую привязанность. ● *1.* Her maternal instincts kicked in. *2.* He provided maternal care to the injured bird. *3.* The maternal bond was strong. *4.* She received maternal advice from her mother. *5.* She displayed maternal affection toward the orphan.

**950. праздничный** — *festive, celebratory* — This word is used to describe something that is related to a celebration or holiday, conveying a sense of festivity and joy. It is often used to describe decorations, clothing, food, or atmosphere that is festive in nature.
● *1.* Очень празднично. *2.* Это празднично. *3.* Поездка -

на сене была праздничной традицией. *4.* Фестиваль в Гане был праздничным. *5.* Праздничный галстук был красно-зеленым. *6.* Это было праздничное событие. *7.* Они произнесли праздничный тост. *8.* Она организовала праздничное мероприятие. *9.* Команда разразилась праздничными аплодисментами. *10.* Торт был праздничным жестом. ● *1.* Very festive. *2.* That's festive. *3.* The hayride was a festive tradition. *4.* The Ghana festival was festive. *5.* The festive necktie was red and green. *6.* This was a celebratory occasion. *7.* They had a celebratory toast. *8.* She organized a celebratory event. *9.* The team engaged in celebratory cheers. *10.* The cake was a celebratory gesture.

**951. сельскохозяйственный** — *agricultural* — This word is used to describe things related to agriculture, such as farms, crops, or equipment. It is commonly used in discussions about rural areas, farming practices, and agricultural policies.

● *1.* Они осмотрели сельскохозяйственный музей. *2.* Район в основном сельскохозяйственный. *3.* Сельскохозяйственный рынок процветает. ● *1.* They toured the agricultural museum. *2.* The area is mostly agricultural. *3.* The agricultural market is thriving.

**952. паранормальный** — *paranormal* — This word is used to describe phenomena or experiences that are beyond the scope of scientific understanding or explanation, often associated with the supernatural or unexplained.

**953. теоретический** — *theoretical* — 'Теоретический' is used to describe something based on theory rather than practical experience or actual facts. It is often used to discuss hypothetical situations, abstract concepts, or academic discussions.

● *1.* Она сосредоточена на теоретических аспектах. *2.* Теоретическая физика увлекательна. *3.* Теоретический подход ошибочен. *4.* Это только теоретически. *5.* Они обсудили теоретические последствия. ● *1.* She's focused on the theoretical aspects. *2.* The theoretical physics is fascinating. *3.* The theoretical approach is flawed. *4.* It's only theoretical. *5.* They discussed the theoretical implications.

**954. редакционный** — *editorial* — 'Редакционный' is used to describe something related to editing or editorial work. It can refer to content, opinions, or decisions made by editors. It is commonly used in the context of newspapers, magazines, and other media outlets.

**955. фронтальный** — *frontal* — 'Фронтальный' is used to describe something that is located at the front or facing forward. It can also refer to actions or processes that involve direct confrontation or interaction with someone or something.

**956. непростительный** — *unforgivable, inexcusable, unpardonable* — This word is used to describe actions or behavior that are considered to be morally wrong or unacceptable, to the point where they cannot be forgiven or excused under any circumstances.

• *1.* Это непростительно. *2.* Это было бы непростительно. *3.* Непростительные вещи. *4.* Предательство доверия было непростительно. *5.* Это непростительно. *6.* То, что я сделал, было непростительно. • *1.* It's unforgivable. *2.* That would be unforgivable. *3.* Unforgivable things. *4.* The betrayal of trust was unforgivable. *5.* It's inexcusable. *6.* What I did was inexcusable.

**957. невредимый** — *unharmed, unscathed* — This word is used to describe something or someone that has not been harmed or damaged in any way. It implies that the object or person is in perfect condition and has not suffered any negative effects.

• *1.* Она невредима. *2.* К счастью, она осталась невредимой. *3.* Им повезло, что они остались невредимыми. *4.* Здание осталось невредимым. *5.* Невредимый выживший рассказал эту историю. *6.* Из места крушения она вышла чудом невредимой. *7.* Сокровище осталось невредимым. • *1.* She's unharmed. *2.* She was fortunately unharmed. *3.* They were lucky to be unscathed. *4.* The building remained unscathed. *5.* The unscathed survivor told the story. *6.* She emerged from the crash miraculously unscathed. *7.* The treasure was unscathed.

**958. широко** — *widely, extensively* — This word is used to describe something that is done or spread out over a large area or range. It can also be used to indicate that something is done in a comprehensive or thorough manner.

• *1.* Преследование меньшинств было широко осуждено. *2.*

Книга получила широкое признание. *3.* Аббревиатура получила широкое распространение. *4.* Теория получила широкое признание. *5.* Творчество драматурга получило широкое признание. *6.* Он широко изучал меловую эпоху. • *1.* The persecution of minorities was widely condemned. *2.* The book was widely acclaimed. *3.* The acronym was widely used. *4.* The theory was widely accepted. *5.* The playwright's work was widely acclaimed. *6.* He studied the cretaceous era extensively.

**959. дисциплинарный** — *disciplinary* — This word is used to describe something related to discipline, punishment, or control within a specific context, such as a disciplinary action, measure, or procedure. It is often used in professional, educational, or organizational settings.
• *1.* Неподчинение повлекло за собой дисциплинарное взыскание. • *1.* The insubordination was met with disciplinary action.

**960. напористый** — *pushy, feisty, ballsy* — 'Напористый' is used to describe someone who is assertive, determined, and not afraid to speak their mind or take charge in a situation. It conveys a sense of confidence and boldness in their actions.
• *1.* У нее напористый настрой. • *1.* She has a ballsy attitude.

**961. тоскующий по дому** — *homesick* — The term 'тоскующий по дому' describes a feeling of longing or nostalgia for one's home or homeland. It conveys a sense of emotional distress or sadness that comes from being separated from familiar surroundings and loved ones.

**962. единодушный** — *unanimous* — 'Unanimous' describes a situation where everyone involved agrees or feels the same way about something. It indicates a complete agreement or unity of opinion among a group of people.
• *1.* Мы единодушны в этом вопросе. • *1.* We are unanimous on that point.

**963. мимолетный** — *fleeting* — The word 'мимолетный' is used to describe something that is brief, passing quickly, or fleeting in nature. It conveys the idea of something that is temporary or short-lived.
• *1.* Мимолетная мысль пришла ей в голову. *2.* Между ними пробежал мимолетный взгляд. *3.* Преходящая природа

славы мимолетна. *4.* Солнце отбрасывало мимолетные тени. *5.* Ощущение превосходства было мимолетным. • *1.* A fleeting thought crossed her mind. *2.* A fleeting glance passed between them. *3.* The transitory nature of fame is fleeting. *4.* The sun cast fleeting shadows. *5.* The feeling of transcendence was fleeting.

**964. малиновый** — *crimson* — This word is used to describe something that is a deep red color, similar to the color of ripe raspberries. It can be used to describe objects, clothing, or even emotions.

• *1.* Я нашел малиновый кленовый лист. *2.* Закат имел малиновый оттенок. *3.* На ней было малиновое платье. • *1.* I found a crimson maple leaf. *2.* The sunset was a crimson hue. *3.* She wore a crimson dress.

**965. убийственный** — *murderous, homicidal* — This word is used to describe something that is extremely dangerous, deadly, or destructive. It conveys a sense of imminent threat or harm, often implying a high level of violence or aggression.

• *1.* В романе был убийственный сюжет. *2.* Она отшатнулась от его убийственного намерения. *3.* В его глазах был убийственный взгляд. *4.* Его действия были поистине убийственными. *5.* Убийственное насилие потрясло город. • *1.* The novel featured a murderous plot. *2.* She recoiled from his murderous intent. *3.* He had a murderous look in his eyes. *4.* His actions were truly murderous. *5.* The murderous rampage shocked the town.

**966. безостановочно** — *nonstop* — This word is used to describe something that continues without stopping or pausing. It is often used to emphasize the continuous and uninterrupted nature of an action or process.

• *1.* Это безостановочно. • *1.* It's nonstop.

**967. рехнувшийся** — *nutty, dippy* — 'Рехнувшийся' is used to describe someone or something as eccentric, crazy, or silly. It conveys a sense of being out of touch with reality or behaving in a bizarre manner.

**968. диабетический** — *diabetic* — This word is used to describe something that is related to or characteristic of diabetes. It can be used to refer to food, products, or conditions that are

specifically designed for or associated with individuals who have diabetes.
● *1.* Она тщательно контролировала свое диабетическое состояние. ● *1.* She managed her diabetic condition carefully.

**969. сильнодействующий** — *potent* — This word is used to describe something that is powerful, strong, or effective in producing a particular result. It is often used in reference to medications, chemicals, or other substances that have a strong impact.
● *1.* Экстракт кураре был сильнодействующим. ● *1.* The curare extract was potent.

**970. робкий** — *timid* — The word 'робкий' is used to describe someone who is shy, hesitant, or lacking in confidence. It can also be used to describe actions or behaviors that are cautious or timid in nature.
● *1.* Они предприняли робкую попытку принять вызов. *2.* Робкий ребенок цеплялся за своего родителя. *3.* Она чувствовала себя робкой в новой обстановке. *4.* Робкий кот спрятался под кроватью. *5.* Он говорил робким голосом. ● *1.* They made a timid attempt at the challenge. *2.* The timid child clung to their parent. *3.* She felt timid in the new environment. *4.* The timid cat hid under the bed. *5.* He spoke in a timid voice.

**971. исследовательский** — *investigative, exploratory* — This word is used to describe something that is related to investigation or exploration, often in a scientific or academic context. It implies a sense of curiosity and a desire to uncover new information or knowledge.
● *1.* Исследовательская миссия обнаружила новые виды. *2.* Исследовательское путешествие привело их в неизведанные воды. *3.* Их исследовательские усилия привели к новым открытиям. ● *1.* The exploratory mission found new species. *2.* The exploratory voyage took them to uncharted waters. *3.* Their exploratory efforts led to new discoveries.

**972. неграмотный** — *illiterate* — The word 'неграмотный' is used to describe someone who lacks basic literacy skills or knowledge in a particular subject. It can also be used to describe something that is poorly written or executed.
● *1.* Многие взрослые жители деревни неграмотны. *2.* Неграмотные люди могут испытывать трудности с трудоустро-

йством. *3.* Неграмотному населению необходимо больше образовательных ресурсов. *4.* Несмотря на обучение в школе, она оставалась неграмотной. *5.* Неграмотный человек с трудом мог читать. • *1.* Many adults in the village are illiterate. *2.* Illiterate people may struggle with job opportunities. *3.* The illiterate population needs more educational resources. *4.* She remained illiterate despite schooling. *5.* The illiterate man struggled to read.

**973. провинциальный** — *provincial* — The word 'провинциальный' is used to describe something or someone as having characteristics or qualities that are typical of a province or rural area, often implying a lack of sophistication or refinement.
• *1.* Провинциальные законы устарели. *2.* У него был провинциальный акцент. *3.* Провинциальный образ жизни был прост. *4.* Она жила в провинциальном городке. • *1.* The provincial laws were outdated. *2.* He had a provincial accent. *3.* The provincial lifestyle was simple. *4.* She lived in a provincial town.

**974. гуманный** — *humane* — The word 'гуманный' is used to describe actions, behavior, or treatment that is compassionate, kind, and considerate towards others. It conveys a sense of empathy and understanding in various situations.
• *1.* Гуманным поступком было помочь. *2.* Гуманное общество работало на защиту животных. *3.* Она выступала за более гуманную политику. *4.* Ее действия были гуманными и сострадательными. • *1.* The humane thing to do was to help. *2.* The humane society worked to protect animals. *3.* She advocated for a more humane policy. *4.* Her actions were humane and compassionate.

**975. галактический** — *galactic* — 'Galactic' is used to describe something that is related to or resembles a galaxy. It can be used to emphasize the vastness, scale, or otherworldly nature of something.
• *1.* Галактический привет! *2.* Галактический совет собрался на экстренное заседание. *3.* Он имел глубокое увлечение галактическими явлениями. *4.* Космический корабль вошел в галактическую туманность. *5.* Галактическая империя охватывала несколько звездных систем. • *1.* Galactic greetings! *2.* The galactic council convened for an emergency meeting. *3.*

He had a deep fascination with galactic phenomena. *4.* The spaceship entered the galactic nebula. *5.* The galactic empire spanned multiple star systems.

**976. неопределенно** — *indefinitely* — 'Неопределенно' is used to describe something that is not clearly defined or specified, lacking a definite end or limit. It conveys a sense of uncertainty or vagueness in regards to time, quantity, or quality.

• *1.* Она останется в городе на неопределенный срок. *2.* Вопрос останется нерешенным на неопределенный срок. *3.* Вечеринка будет перенесена на неопределенный срок. *4.* Заседание было перенесено на неопределенный срок. *5.* Сроки реализации проекта продлены на неопределенный срок. • *1.* She is staying in the city indefinitely. *2.* The issue will remain unresolved indefinitely. *3.* The party will be postponed indefinitely. *4.* The meeting was postponed indefinitely. *5.* The project's timeline is indefinitely extended.

**977. посредственный** — *mediocre, middling* — This word is used to describe something that is average or ordinary in quality, not particularly good or bad. It is often used to express a lack of excellence or distinction in something.

• *1.* У него были посредственные писательские способности. *2.* Они остановились на посредственном решении. *3.* Она получила посредственную оценку производительности. *4.* Еда была посредственной. *5.* Команда показала посредственный результат. *6.* Команда показала посредственный результат. *7.* Посредственные результаты разочаровали. *8.* Посредственное качество продукта его разочаровало. • *1.* He had mediocre writing skills. *2.* They settled for a mediocre solution. *3.* She received a mediocre performance review. *4.* The meal was mediocre. *5.* The team delivered a mediocre performance. *6.* The team delivered a middling performance. *7.* The middling results were a letdown. *8.* The middling quality of the product disappointed him.

**978. бесчеловечный** — *inhuman* — The word 'бесчеловечный' is used to describe actions, behavior, or situations that lack compassion, empathy, or humanity. It conveys a sense of cruelty, brutality, or indifference towards others.

• *1.* Это бесчеловечно. • *1.* It's inhuman.

**979. легкомысленный** — *giddy, frivolous, flippant, hare-brained* — This word is used to describe someone who is thoughtless, lacking seriousness or depth in their actions or decisions. It conveys a sense of being carefree and not taking things seriously.

• *1.* Легкомысленный до! *2.* О, моя легкомысленная тетушка. *3.* Ее легкомысленное поведение раздражало коллег. *4.* Она отвергла эту легкомысленную идею. *5.* Легкомысленные сплетни ей наскучили. *6.* Она ответила легкомысленным «не знаю». *7.* Легкомысленный тон ее голоса расстроил его. *8.* Она сделала легкомысленное замечание, которое вызвало напряжение. *9.* Его легкомысленное отношение раздражало окружающих. *10.* Это все просто легкомысленная шутка.
• *1.* Giddy up! *2.* Oh, my giddy aunt. *3.* Her frivolous behavior annoyed her colleagues. *4.* She dismissed the frivolous idea. *5.* The frivolous gossip bored her. *6.* She replied with a flippant dunno. *7.* The flippant tone of her voice upset him. *8.* She made a flippant remark that caused tension. *9.* His flippant attitude annoyed others. *10.* It's all just something flippant quip.

**980. гуманитарный** — *humanitarian* — This word is used to describe actions, organizations, or individuals that are focused on promoting human welfare and addressing social issues. It conveys a sense of compassion, empathy, and a commitment to helping others in need.

• *1.* Они поддерживают гуманитарные цели. *2.* Свою жизнь он посвятил гуманитарной деятельности. *3.* Группа оказывает гуманитарную помощь. *4.* Организация является гуманитарной некоммерческой организацией. *5.* Ее усилия носили гуманитарный характер. • *1.* They support humanitarian causes. *2.* He devoted his life to humanitarian work. *3.* The group provides humanitarian aid. *4.* The organization is a humanitarian nonprofit. *5.* Her efforts were humanitarian.

**981. эволюционный** — *evolutionary, developmental* — This word is used to describe something that is related to evolution or development. It can be used to talk about processes, theories, or changes that involve growth and progress over time.

• *1.* Она изучала эволюционную биологию. *2.* Он восхищался эволюционным процессом. *3.* Эволюционную тенденцию было невозможно остановить. *4.* Они обсуждали эволюционные теории. *5.* Теория эволюционных изменений. • *1.* She studied evolutionary biology. *2.* He admired the evolutionary process. *3.* The evolutionary trend was unstoppable. *4.* They discussed evolutionary theories. *5.* The theory of evolutionary change.

**982. неразрешенный** — *unauthorized, unresolved* — The word 'неразрешенный' is used to describe something that is not authorized or resolved. It implies that there is a lack of permission or a lack of resolution in a particular situation.

• *1.* Разногласия остались неразрешенными. • *1.* The disagreement remained unresolved.

**983. вспомогательный** — *auxiliary, subsidiary, ancillary* — This word is used to describe something that provides additional support or assistance to something else, often playing a secondary or supporting role. It is used to indicate something that is not primary or essential, but still important.

• *1.* Генератор обеспечивал вспомогательное электричество. *2.* В организации имелось вспомогательное подразделение на случай чрезвычайных ситуаций. *3.* Вспомогательное питание активировано. *4.* Вспомогательная мощность. *5.* Во время отключения было активировано вспомогательное питание. *6.* Поддержку оказал вспомогательный персонал. *7.* Она взяла на себя вспомогательные задачи. *8.* Вспомогательное оборудование было самым современным. *9.* Он руководил вспомогательными операциями. *10.* Вспомогательные услуги были необходимы. • *1.* The generator provided auxiliary electricity. *2.* The organization had an auxiliary unit for emergencies. *3.* Auxiliary power activated. *4.* Auxiliary power. *5.* The auxiliary power was activated during the outage. *6.* The ancillary staff provided support. *7.* She took care of ancillary tasks. *8.* The ancillary equipment was state-of-the-art. *9.* He managed the ancillary operations. *10.* The ancillary services were essential.

**984. неважный** — *unimportant* — This word is used to describe something that is not significant or crucial. It conveys the idea that the thing in question does not hold much importance or relevance in a given situation.

• *1.* Это неважно. *2.* Неважные дела могут подождать. *3.* Он отмахнулся от неважных вопросов. • *1.* It's unimportant. *2.* Unimportant tasks can wait. *3.* He dismissed the unimportant matters.

**985. игривый** — *playful, frisky* — 'Ігривый' is used to describe someone or something that is lively, mischievous, or full of playful energy. It conveys a sense of fun and excitement, often associated with a carefree and spirited attitude.

• *1.* Порода папийон маленькая и игривая. *2.* Они смеялись над игривым мимом. *3.* Он игривым тоном назвал ее любопытной. *4.* Братья и сестры затеяли игривую драку. *5.* Котик игривый. *6.* Ей нравилось его игривое поведение. • *1.* The papillon breed is small and playful. *2.* They laughed at the playful mime. *3.* He called her nosey in a playful tone. *4.* The siblings engaged in a playful fight. *5.* The kitty is playful. *6.* She found his frisky behavior endearing.

**986. нездоровый** — *unhealthy, unwell, unsound* — 'нездоровый' is used to describe something that is not in good health or condition. It can refer to physical health, mental health, or the overall state of something being unsound or unhealthy.

• *1.* Она ела ужасно нездоровую пищу. *2.* Фиксация была нездоровой. *3.* Его одержимость фитнесом стала нездоровой. *4.* Вы нездоровы? *5.* Нездоровый пациент нуждался в уходе. *6.* Он выглядел нездоровым. • *1.* She ate morbidly unhealthy food. *2.* The fixation was unhealthy. *3.* His obsession with fitness became unhealthy. *4.* Are you unwell? *5.* The unwell patient needed care. *6.* He appeared unwell.

**987. правдоподобный** — *plausible* — 'Plausible' is used to describe something that seems believable or likely to be true. It is often used to refer to a story, explanation, or excuse that appears to be reasonable or convincing.

• *1.* Правдоподобное отрицание. *2.* Звучит правдоподобно. *3.* Теория была правдоподобной. *4.* Это было правдоподобное предложение. *5.* Объяснение казалось правдоподобным. • *1.* Plausible deniability. *2.* Sounds plausible. *3.* The theory was plausible. *4.* That was a plausible suggestion. *5.* The explanation seemed plausible.

**988. отталкивающий** — *repulsive, repellent* — This word is used to describe something that causes a strong feeling of disgust or aversion. It is often used to express a strong negative reaction to a person, object, or situation.

● *1.* Это отталкивающе. *2.* Ты отталкивающий. *3.* Сама мысль об этом была отталкивающей. *4.* Я нахожу это отталкивающим. *5.* Запах был отталкивающим. ● *1.* It's repulsive. *2.* You're repulsive. *3.* The idea of it was repulsive. *4.* I find that repulsive. *5.* The smell was repulsive.

**989. хитроумный** — *dodgy* — The word 'хитроумный' is used to describe something or someone as sly, cunning, or deceitful. It implies a sense of trickery or dishonesty in a subtle or clever way.

**990. суррогатный** — *surrogate* — The word 'суррогатный' is used to describe something that serves as a substitute or replacement for something else, typically in a negative or inferior way. It can refer to a surrogate mother, product, or solution.

**991. мускулистый** — *muscular, beefy* — This word is used to describe someone or something that is strong, well-built, and has a lot of muscle mass. It can be used to talk about a person's physique or the appearance of an object.

● *1.* Мускулистая лошадь натянула поводья. *2.* У него были мускулистые руки от поднятия тяжестей. *3.* Мускулистая собака дернула поводок. *4.* Она восхищалась его мускулистым телосложением. *5.* Мускулистый мужчина устрашал своих противников. *6.* В комнату вошел мускулистый мужчина. *7.* Линейный судья был мускулистым и сильным. ● *1.* The muscular horse strained against the reins. *2.* He had muscular arms from lifting weights. *3.* The muscular dog pulled at the leash. *4.* She admired his muscular physique. *5.* The muscular man intimidated his opponents. *6.* A beefy man entered the room. *7.* The lineman was beefy and strong.

**992. престижный** — *prestigious* — 'престижный' is used to describe something that is highly respected, esteemed, or honored. It is often used to refer to prestigious schools, events, awards, or positions.

● *1.* Должность легата была престижной. *2.* Научный журнал является престижным изданием. *3.* Школа Уэйкфилда была престижной. *4.* «Ритц» был престижным местом проведения. *5.* Йель – престижная школа. ● *1.* The legate's position was prestigious. *2.* The scientific journal is a prestigious publication. *3.* The Wakefield school was prestigious. *4.* The Ritz was a prestigious venue. *5.* Yale is a prestigious school.

**993. гипотетический** — *hypothetical* — This word is used to describe something that is based on a hypothesis or assumption rather than proven fact. It is often used in discussions or arguments to consider possibilities or scenarios that may not be true.
● *1.* Это гипотетически. ● *1.* It's a hypothetical.

**994. чувственный** — *sensual, voluptuous, sensuous, carnal* — This word is used to describe something that is related to physical pleasure, desire, or sensuality. It conveys a sense of indulgence, passion, and intensity in a way that appeals to the senses.
● *1.* Аромат был чувственным. *2.* Она одарила меня чувственным взглядом. *3.* В книге описан чувственный опыт. *4.* Ее танцевальные движения были стройными и чувственными. *5.* Шоколад был чувственным. *6.* Работа была чувственной. *7.* Его прикосновения были чувственными. *8.* Чувственная музыка наполнила комнату. *9.* Ее танец был чувственным. *10.* Духи имели чувственный аромат. ● *1.* The perfume was sensual. *2.* She gave me a sensual look. *3.* The book described a sensual experience. *4.* Her dance moves were slinky and sensual. *5.* The chocolate was sensual. *6.* The artwork was sensuous. *7.* His touch was sensuous. *8.* The sensuous music filled the room. *9.* Her dance was sensuous. *10.* The perfume had a sensuous aroma.

**995. сердечный** — *hearty, cordial, cardiac* — The word 'сердечный' is used to describe something that is warm, sincere, and heartfelt. It can also refer to something related to the heart or cardiac system.
● *1.* Они уехали с сердечным головокружением. *2.* Она издала сердечный хёк. *3.* Он сделал сердечное приглашение. *4.* Встреча была сердечной. *5.* Она приветствовала его сердечной улыбкой. *6.* Этот сердечный разговор успокоил их. ● *1.* They rode off with a hearty giddap. *2.* She let out a hearty hyuk. *3.* He made a cordial invitation. *4.* The meeting was cordial. *5.* She greeted him with a cordial smile. *6.* The cordial exchange put them at ease.

**996. ненавистный** — *hateful, odious* — This word is used to describe something or someone that is intensely disliked or detested. It conveys a strong sense of disgust or aversion towards the object or person being described.

● *1.* Ненавистные граффити возмутили общественность. *2.* Она не могла вынести ненавистной атмосферы. *3.* Он извергал ненавистную риторику. *4.* Ненавистные комментарии были неприемлемы. *5.* Жидкое оскорбление было ненавистным. ● *1.* The hateful graffiti upset the community. *2.* She couldn't stand the hateful atmosphere. *3.* He spewed hateful rhetoric. *4.* The hateful comments were unacceptable. *5.* The kike slur was hateful.

**997. дорогостоящий** — *costly* — This word is used to describe something that is expensive or has a high cost associated with it. It is often used to emphasize the significant amount of money required to obtain or maintain the item or service.

● *1.* Ремонт оказался дорогостоящим. *2.* Эта чушь оказалась дорогостоящей ошибкой. ● *1.* The repairs proved to be costly. *2.* The bollock was a costly mistake.

**998. непрофессиональный** — *unprofessional* — This word is used to describe someone or something that lacks the skills, knowledge, or behavior expected in a professional setting. It implies a lack of competence, reliability, or professionalism in a given situation.

● *1.* Это непрофессионально. *2.* Это было непрофессионально. *3.* Это так непрофессионально. *4.* Это было бы непрофессионально. *5.* Так непрофессионально. ● *1.* It's unprofessional. *2.* It was unprofessional. *3.* It's so unprofessional. *4.* That would be unprofessional. *5.* So unprofessional.

**999. кулинарный** — *culinary* — This word is used to describe anything related to cooking, food preparation, or culinary arts. It can be used to talk about dishes, recipes, techniques, or anything else related to the world of cooking and food.

● *1.* Его кулинарное мастерство поразило всех. *2.* Она исследовала кулинарную расу. *3.* Он создал шедевр кулинарного изыска. *4.* Он изучает французскую кухню в кулинарной школе. ● *1.* His culinary artistry impressed everyone. *2.* She explored the culinary rasa. *3.* He created a masterpiece of culinary delicacy. *4.* He's studying French cuisine in culinary school.

**1000. незнакомый** — *unfamiliar* — 'незнакомый' is used to describe something or someone that is unfamiliar or unknown. It can be used to express a lack of recognition or knowledge about a person, place, or thing.

● *1.* Гортанный язык был им незнаком. *2.* Слово «оцу» было незнакомым. ● *1.* The guttural language was unfamiliar to them. *2.* The word 'otsu' was unfamiliar.

**1001. суетливый** — *fussy, fidgety* — The word 'суетливый' is used to describe someone who is overly concerned with trivial matters, restless, or easily agitated. It conveys a sense of busyness and nervous energy.

● *1.* Она была суетлива в деталях. *2.* Не будь таким суетливым. ● *1.* She was fussy about the details. *2.* Don't be so fussy.

**1002. роскошный** — *luxurious, deluxe, princely* — 'роскошный' is used to describe something that is very luxurious, deluxe, or princely in nature. It is often used to convey a sense of opulence, extravagance, and high quality.

● *1.* Они наслаждались роскошным отдыхом. *2.* Номер в отеле был роскошным. *3.* Их образ жизни был роскошным. *4.* Шелковые простыни были роскошными. *5.* Вечеринка была роскошной. *6.* Роскошное издание имело дополнительные функции. *7.* В роскошном автомобиле были кожаные сиденья. ● *1.* They enjoyed a luxurious vacation. *2.* The hotel room was luxurious. *3.* Their lifestyle was luxurious. *4.* The silken sheets were luxurious. *5.* The party was luxurious. *6.* The deluxe edition had extra features. *7.* The deluxe car had leather seats.

**1003. негодный** — *unfit, unqualified* — The word 'негодный' is used to describe something or someone as unfit or unqualified for a particular purpose or task. It implies that the object or person is not suitable or capable of meeting certain standards or requirements.

● *1.* Его признали негодным к военной службе. ● *1.* He was deemed unfit for military service.

**1004. невротический** — *neurotic* — The word 'невротический' is used to describe someone or something that is characterized by excessive anxiety, irrational fears, and emotional instability. It is often used to refer to behaviors or traits associated with neurosis.

● *1.* Они находили его невротические наклонности милыми. *2.* Она невротически относилась к чистоте. *3.* Она боролась со своими невротическими мыслями. *4.* Их беспокоило невротическое поведение. *5.* Он вел себя невротически. ● *1.* They found his neurotic tendencies endearing. *2.* She was neurotic about cleanliness. *3.* She struggled with her neurotic thoughts. *4.* The neurotic behavior worried them. *5.* He acted neurotic.

**1005. авантюрный** — *adventurous* — This word is used to describe someone who is daring, bold, and willing to take risks. It can also be used to describe actions or situations that involve excitement, unpredictability, and a sense of adventure.

● *1.* Авантюрное путешествие было захватывающим. *2.* Авантюрные люди ищут новых впечатлений. *3.* Адреналин подогревал их авантюрный дух. *4.* Она восхищалась авантюрным духом купца. *5.* Они отправились в авантюрное путешествие. ● *1.* The adventurous trip was thrilling. *2.* Adventurous people seek new experiences. *3.* Adrenalin fueled their adventurous spirit. *4.* She admired the chapman's adventurous spirit. *5.* They embarked on an adventurous journey.

**1006. неоценимый** — *invaluable* — 'Неоценимый' is used to describe something that is extremely valuable or precious, often emphasizing that its worth cannot be measured or fully appreciated. It conveys the idea of something being highly important or indispensable.

● *1.* Руководство было неоценимым. *2.* Руководство наставника было неоценимо. *3.* Она внесла неоценимый вклад в проект. ● *1.* The guidance was invaluable. *2.* The mentor's guidance was invaluable. *3.* She made invaluable contributions to the project.

**1007. философский** — *philosophical* — 'Философский' is used to describe something that is related to or characteristic of philosophy, deep thinking, or contemplation. It can also refer to a calm and thoughtful attitude towards life's challenges.

● *1.* Смертность является темой философских дебатов. ● *1.* Mortality is a topic of philosophical debate.

**1008. окольный** — *devious, roundabout* — The word 'окольный' is used to describe something that is devious or roundabout in nature. It implies a sense of indirectness or cunning in the way something is done or achieved.

- *1.* Окольным путем. • *1.* In a roundabout way.

**1009. выпуклый** — *bossy* — The word 'выпуклый' is used to describe someone who is domineering, controlling, or authoritative in a negative way. It is often used to characterize individuals who exhibit bossy behavior or have a tendency to assert their authority over others.

**1010. структурный** — *structural* — This word is used to describe something related to the structure or organization of a system, object, or concept. It implies a focus on the underlying framework or arrangement of elements.

- *1.* Структурных аномалий нет. *2.* Компания внесла некоторые структурные изменения. *3.* Необходимо было устранить структурные дефекты. *4.* Предплюсна обеспечивает структурную поддержку. *5.* Мы теряем структурную целостность.
- *1.* No structural abnormalities. *2.* The company made some structural changes. *3.* The structural defects needed to be addressed. *4.* The tarsus provides structural support. *5.* We're losing structural integrity.

**1011. немыслимый** — *unthinkable* — 'Unthinkable' is used to describe something that is beyond belief or impossible to imagine. It conveys the idea that a situation or concept is so extreme or outrageous that it cannot be comprehended or considered as a possibility.

- *1.* Это немыслимо. *2.* Он сделал немыслимое. *3.* Потеря немыслима. *4.* Мысль немыслимая. *5.* Последствия немыслимы. • *1.* It's unthinkable. *2.* He did the unthinkable. *3.* The loss is unthinkable. *4.* The thought is unthinkable. *5.* The consequences are unthinkable.

**1012. неполноценный** — *defective* — The word 'неполноценный' is used to describe something that is lacking in quality or completeness, often implying that it is not up to standard or is inferior in some way.

**1013. скандальный** — *scandalous* — This word is used to describe something that is shocking, controversial, or likely to cause a scandal. It is often used to refer to behavior, events, or situations that are considered inappropriate or disgraceful.

● *1.* Это скандально! *2.* Скандальное дело попало в заголовки газет. *3.* Скандальный слух быстро распространился. *4.* Скандальное разоблачение вызвало возмущение. *5.* Она была в скандальном наряде. ● *1.* It's scandalous! *2.* The scandalous affair made headlines. *3.* The scandalous rumor spread quickly. *4.* The scandalous revelation led to outrage. *5.* She wore a scandalous outfit.

**1014. скептический** — *skeptical* — The word 'скептический' is used to describe someone who doubts or questions the validity of something. It is often used to convey a sense of skepticism or disbelief towards a particular idea or claim.

● *1.* Я настроен скептически. *2.* Вы настроены скептически. *3.* Она скептически отнеслась к последней моде. *4.* Она была настроена скептически. *5.* Они отнеслись к этому предложению со скептической осторожностью. ● *1.* I'm skeptical. *2.* You're skeptical. *3.* She was skeptical of the latest fad. *4.* She had a skeptical attitude. *5.* They approached the offer with skeptical caution.

**1015. незаконнорожденный** — *illegitimate* — The term 'незаконнорожденный' is used to describe something or someone that is considered illegitimate or born out of wedlock. It carries a negative connotation and is often used in a derogatory manner.

● *1.* Эти дети незаконнорожденные. ● *1.* These children are illegitimate.

**1016. находчивый** — *resourceful* — 'Находчивый' describes someone who is clever and quick to find solutions to problems, often using whatever resources are available to them. It implies a knack for thinking creatively and being able to adapt to different situations.

● *1.* Очень находчивый. *2.* Вы находчивы. *3.* Он находчив. *4.* Я находчивый. *5.* Находчивая команда справилась с этой задачей. ● *1.* Very resourceful. *2.* You're resourceful. *3.* He's resourceful. *4.* I'm resourceful. *5.* The resourceful team overcame the challenge.

**1017. женоненавистнический** — *sexist* — This word is used to describe attitudes, behaviors, or beliefs that discriminate against or show prejudice towards women based on their gender. It is often used to criticize individuals or institutions for perpetuating gender inequality.

**1018. экстравагантный** — *extravagant* — This word is used to describe something that is excessive, luxurious, or over-the-top in a way that is showy or wasteful. It is often used to describe people, events, or objects that are flamboyant or extravagant.

• *1.* В рекламе содержались экстравагантные заявления. *2.* Шичи-мероприятие было экстравагантным. *3.* Пышная демонстрация богатства была экстравагантной. *4.* Особняк Гэтсби был экстравагантным. • *1.* The advertisement made extravagant claims. *2.* The chichi event was extravagant. *3.* The opulent display of wealth was extravagant. *4.* Gatsby's mansion was extravagant.

**1019. летучий** — *volatile* — 'летучий' is used to describe something that is easily evaporated or changes rapidly. It can also refer to something that is fleeting or transient in nature.

• *1.* Летучее химическое вещество требовало осторожного обращения. • *1.* The volatile chemical required careful handling.

**1020. пунктуальный** — *punctual* — The word 'пунктуальный' is used to describe someone who is always on time and respects deadlines. It is often used to praise individuals who are reliable and organized in their time management.

• *1.* Вы пунктуальны. *2.* Пунктуальное прибытие было оценено по достоинству. *3.* Мне нравится быть пунктуальным. *4.* Она была известна своей пунктуальностью. *5.* Быть пунктуальным. • *1.* You're punctual. *2.* The punctual arrival was appreciated. *3.* I like to be punctual. *4.* She was known for her punctual nature. *5.* Be punctual.

**1021. незамеченный** — *unnoticed* — This word is used to describe something that has not been noticed or paid attention to. It can refer to physical objects, actions, or events that have gone unnoticed by others.

• *1.* Его ничем не примечательная внешность осталась незамеченной. *2.* Он пытался ускользнуть незамеченным. *3.* Его сдержанные жесты остались незамеченными. *4.* Незначительная ошибка осталась незамеченной. *5.* Трусливый поступок не остался незамеченным. • *1.* His unremarkable appearance went unnoticed. *2.* He tried to slink away unnoticed. *3.* His discreet gestures went unnoticed. *4.* The minor mistake went unnoticed. *5.* The cowardly act did not go unnoticed.

**1022. пухленький** — *crummy* — 'Пухленький' is used to describe something as being of poor quality, shabby, or crummy. It can also be used to describe something as being chubby or plump in a cute or endearing way.

**1023. выгодный** — *lucrative, beneficial* — 'выгодный' is used to describe something that is advantageous or profitable. It implies that the subject will bring benefits or advantages to the person or situation it is associated with.
• *1.* Уиллер и дилер заключили выгодную сделку. *2.* Обмен был взаимовыгодным. *3.* Проект будет выгодным. • *1.* The wheeler and dealer struck a lucrative deal. *2.* The swap was mutually beneficial. *3.* The project will be beneficial.

**1024. крепкий** — *sturdy, robust* — 'Крепкий' is used to describe something that is strong, durable, and able to withstand pressure or force. It can refer to physical objects, materials, or even a person's health or constitution.
• *1.* Дерево было высоким и крепким. *2.* Они построили крепкую колыбель. *3.* Каменщик построил крепкую стену. *4.* Дерево гикори было высоким и крепким. *5.* Дом был крепким, несмотря на бурю. *6.* У нее крепкий иммунитет. *7.* Его крепкое здоровье впечатляет. *8.* Крепкое дерево стояло высоко. • *1.* The tree was tall and sturdy. *2.* They built a sturdy cradle. *3.* The bricklayer built a sturdy wall. *4.* The hickory tree was tall and sturdy. *5.* The house was sturdy despite the storm. *6.* She has a robust immune system. *7.* His robust health is impressive. *8.* The robust tree stood tall.

**1025. бесконечно** — *endlessly, indefinitely* — This word is used to describe something that goes on without limit or end, continuing indefinitely. It conveys the idea of something being boundless, infinite, or never-ending.
• *1.* Горизонт простирался бесконечно. *2.* На заднем плане бесконечно играла музыка. *3.* Вечеринка, казалось, продолжалась бесконечно. *4.* Она бесконечно искала потерянные

ключи. *5.* Он бесконечно рассказывал о своей новой машине. *6.* Проблема будет существовать бесконечно. • *1.* The horizon stretched out endlessly. *2.* The music played endlessly in the background. *3.* The party seemed to continue endlessly. *4.* She searched endlessly for her lost keys. *5.* He talked endlessly about his new car. *6.* The problem will exist indefinitely.

**1026. варварский** — *barbaric, barbarous* — 'варварский' is used to describe something as barbaric or uncivilized. It conveys a sense of brutality or lack of refinement. It is often used to criticize actions, behaviors, or customs that are considered primitive or cruel.

• *1.* Варварский обычай был объявлен вне закона. *2.* Варварский акт потряс мир. *3.* Варварское племя совершило набег на деревню. *4.* Варварское нападение имело долгосрочные последствия. *5.* Они осудили варварское поведение. *6.* Варварский поступок потряс общество. *7.* Варварское вторжение привело к разрушениям. *8.* Она живо описала варварскую сцену. • *1.* The barbaric custom was outlawed. *2.* The barbaric act shocked the world. *3.* The barbaric tribe raided the village. *4.* The barbarous attack had lasting effects. *5.* They condemned the barbarous behavior. *6.* The barbarous act shocked the community. *7.* The barbarous invasion led to destruction. *8.* She vividly described the barbarous scene.

**1027. неистовый** — *frantic, rabid, boisterous, amok* — 'Неистовый' is used to describe something that is extremely intense, uncontrollable, and wild. It conveys a sense of frenzy or chaos, often implying a lack of restraint or moderation in behavior or emotions.

• *1.* Неистовая толпа разошлась. • *1.* The frantic crowd dispersed.

**1028. диагностический** — *diagnostic* — This word is used to describe something that is related to or used for the purpose of diagnosis or identifying a problem or disease. It is often used in medical, technical, or scientific contexts.

• *1.* Диагностический отчет был неубедительным. *2.* Диагностическое оборудование вышло из строя. *3.* Диагностический процесс выявил проблему. *4.* Врач сделал диагностическое заключение. • *1.* The diagnostic report was inconclusive. *2.* The diagnostic equipment malfunctioned. *3.* The diagnostic process revealed the issue. *4.* The doctor made a diagnostic conclusion.

**1029. фотографический** — *photographic* — This word is used to describe something that is related to or resembles a photograph. It can be used to describe the quality of an image, the accuracy of a representation, or the visual nature of a memory.
● *1.* Фотографическая память. *2.* У меня фотографическая память. *3.* Она сделала фотографический портрет. *4.* У него была фотографическая память. ● *1.* Photographic memory. *2.* I have a photographic memory. *3.* She took a photographic portrait. *4.* He had a photographic memory.

**1030. правдоподобно** — *believable* — 'Believable' is used to describe something that seems realistic or plausible. It is often used to express that something is likely to be true or accurate based on the information or evidence available.
● *1.* Это неправдоподобно. *2.* Очень правдоподобно. *3.* Это было правдоподобное объяснение. *4.* Ее оправдания были едва ли правдоподобными. *5.* Игра актера была абсолютно правдоподобной. ● *1.* It's not believable. *2.* Very believable. *3.* It was a believable explanation. *4.* Her excuse was barely believable. *5.* The actor's performance was perfectly believable.

**1031. терпеливо** — *patiently* — 'Терпеливо' is used to describe the manner in which someone is behaving or acting with patience and tolerance. It conveys the idea of calmly enduring difficulties or delays without becoming frustrated or agitated.
● *1.* Учитель терпеливо объяснял. *2.* Терпеливо ждите своей очереди. *3.* Она терпеливо выслушивала его напыщенную речь. *4.* Он терпеливо ждал ее ответа. ● *1.* The teacher explained patiently. *2.* Patiently wait for your turn. *3.* She listened to his rant patiently. *4.* He waited patiently for her reply.

**1032. геологический** — *geological* — 'Геологический' is used to describe something related to the study of the Earth's structure, history, and processes. It is commonly used in scientific contexts to refer to geological formations, processes, or studies.
● *1.* Они исследовали геологический образец. ● *1.* They examined the geological specimen.

**1033. одноразовый** — *disposable* — This word is used to describe items or products that are intended to be used once and then thrown away. It can also refer to actions or events that are temporary or short-lived.

● *1.* Тарелки одноразовые. *2.* Он использовал одноразовую камеру. *3.* Они предпочитают одноразовые подгузники. *4.* В наличии одноразовые перчатки. ● *1.* The plates are disposable. *2.* He used a disposable camera. *3.* They prefer disposable diapers. *4.* Disposable gloves are available.

**1034. уклончивый** — *evasive* — 'Уклончивый' is used to describe someone who avoids giving direct answers or responses, often in order to evade a question or responsibility. It implies a sense of being elusive or indirect in communication.

● *1.* Вы уклончивы. ● *1.* You're being evasive.

**1035. несоответствующий** — *untrue* — The word 'несоответствующий' is used to describe something that does not correspond or match with reality or expectations. It is often used to indicate that something is false or incorrect.

**1036. волшебно** — *magically* — 'волшебно' is used to describe something that is done or happens in a magical or enchanting way. It can be used to convey a sense of wonder or awe towards a particular event or experience.

● *1.* Корабли не появляются волшебным образом из ниоткуда. *2.* Это волшебно вкусно. ● *1.* Ships don't just magically appear out of nowhere. *2.* It's magically delicious.

**1037. устарелый** — *obsolete, antiquated, passe* — This word is used to describe something that is outdated, no longer in use, or considered old-fashioned. It implies that the object or idea is no longer relevant or current in modern society.

● *1.* Его навыки устарели. *2.* Технология устарела. *3.* Это устарело. *4.* Этот стиль настолько устарел. ● *1.* His skills were rendered obsolete. *2.* The technology became obsolete. *3.* It's obsolete. *4.* That style is so passe.

**1038. пышный** — *lush, opulent* — The word 'пышный' is used to describe something that is luxurious, extravagant, or rich in a way that is visually appealing. It is often used to describe lavish decorations, elaborate feasts, or opulent surroundings.

● *1.* Газон был зеленым и пышным. *2.* Поле тимофеевки было зеленым и пышным. *3.* Дальнее поле было пышным и зеленым. *4.* Они исследовали пышную растительность. *5.* Виноградник был пышным и зеленым. 6. Пышная демонстрация богатства была экстравагантной. • 1. The turf was green and lush. 2. The timothy field was green and lush. 3. The outfield was lush and green. 4. They explored the lush vegetation. 5. The vineyard was lush and green. 6. The opulent display of wealth was extravagant.

**1039. намеренный** — *intentional* — 'намеренный' is used to describe actions or decisions that are done with a specific purpose or goal in mind. It implies that the action was deliberate and planned, rather than accidental or spontaneous.
• 1. Это было не намеренно. 2. Это было намеренно. 3. Изменение стиля художника намеренно. 4. Вялый темп фильма был намеренным. 5. Нарушение рисунка было намеренным. • 1. It wasn't intentional. 2. It was intentional. 3. The artist's variance in style is intentional. 4. The languid pace of the film was intentional. 5. The irregularity in the pattern was intentional.

**1040. превратно** — *wrongly* — 'превратно' is used to describe something that is done incorrectly or in a mistaken manner. It indicates that an action or situation is not as it should be, or is not in accordance with the correct way of doing things.

**1041. исходящий** — *outgoing* — The word 'исходящий' is used to describe something or someone that is moving away from a central point or source. It can also be used to describe a person who is sociable and extroverted.
• 1. Они обрабатывали исходящую почту в почтовом отделении. • 1. They processed outgoing mail in the mailroom.

**1042. научно** — *scientifically* — 'Научно' is used to describe something that is done in a scientific manner or based on scientific principles. It is often used to indicate that something is backed by research, evidence, or logical reasoning.
• 1. Теория имеет научное обоснование. 2. Он доказал это научно. 3. Она подошла к этому с научной точки зрения. 4. Процесс научно доказан. 5. Это научно обосновано. • 1. The theory holds scientifically. 2. He proved it scientifically. 3. She approached it scientifically. 4. The process is scientifically proven. 5. It's scientifically sound.

**1043. баллистический** — *ballistic* — The word 'баллистический' is used to describe something related to the science or technology of projectiles, such as missiles or rockets. It can also be used to describe something that moves very quickly or uncontrollably.

**1044. морозный** — *frosty* — This word is used to describe something that is very cold, icy, or covered in frost. It can be used to describe weather, objects, or even a person's demeanor.
● *1.* Оставайся морозным. *2.* Земля была морозной и скользкой. *3.* Ночью погода стала морозной. *4.* Морозный воздух щипал ее щеки. ● *1.* Stay frosty. *2.* The ground was frosty and slippery. *3.* The weather turned frosty overnight. *4.* The frosty air nipped at her cheeks.

**1045. безмятежный** — *serene* — This word is used to describe a state of calmness and tranquility, often in the face of challenges or stressful situations. It conveys a sense of peace and composure, suggesting a serene and undisturbed demeanor.
● *1.* Безмятежный вечер успокоил ее. *2.* Бай был безмятежным местом для отдыха. *3.* На берегу реки было тихо и безмятежно. *4.* В заливе было безмятежно. *5.* Тарн открывал безмятежный вид. ● *1.* The serene evening calmed her. *2.* The bai was a serene spot for rest. *3.* The riverside was peaceful and serene. *4.* The bay was serene. *5.* The tarn provided a serene view.

**1046. прославленный** — *illustrious* — 'прославленный' is used to describe someone or something that is famous, well--known, or highly esteemed for their achievements or qualities. It conveys a sense of honor and recognition.

**1047. родовой** — *ancestral* — The word 'родовой' is used to describe something that is related to or inherited from one's ancestors. It can refer to traits, traditions, or possessions that have been passed down through generations.
● *1.* Он проследил свои родовые корни. *2.* Они посещают свое родовое кладбище. ● *1.* He traced his ancestral roots. *2.* They visit their ancestral cemetery.

**1048. извращенный** — *perverse* — The word 'извращенный' is used to describe something or someone that deviates from what is considered normal or acceptable, often in a morally or sexually inappropriate way.
● *1.* Это извращенно. ● *1.* It's perverse.

**1049. буквальный** — *literal* — 'Вуквальный' is used to describe something that is exact, precise, or true to the original meaning. It is often used to emphasize that something is being interpreted or understood in a strictly literal sense.

● *1.* Буквальный смысл был ясен. *2.* Он боролся с буквальными интерпретациями. *3.* Ее ответ был буквальным переводом. *4.* Она восприняла его слова как буквальную истину. *5.* Инструкции были буквальными. ● *1.* The literal meaning was clear. *2.* He struggled with literal interpretations. *3.* Her response was a literal translation. *4.* She took his words as a literal truth. *5.* The instructions were literal.

**1050. церемониальный** — *ceremonial* — This word is used to describe something that is formal, ritualistic, or related to ceremonies. It is often used to refer to events, clothing, or behavior that is characterized by elaborate or traditional customs.

● *1.* Церемониальная музыка наполняла воздух. *2.* Она несла церемониальный кинжал. *3.* Он выполнял церемониальные обязанности. ● *1.* Ceremonial music filled the air. *2.* She carried a ceremonial dagger. *3.* He carried out the ceremonial duties.

**1051. первобытный** — *primal, primordial* — The word 'первобытный' is used to describe something that is ancient, original, or existing from the earliest times. It is often used to refer to primitive or elemental aspects of nature, culture, or society.

● *1.* Что-то первобытное. *2.* Их первобытные инстинкты сработали. *3.* Бой был первобытным и напряженным. *4.* Она издала первобытный крик. *5.* Картина обладала первобытной энергетикой. *6.* Она чувствовала первобытную связь с землей. *7.* Они изучали первобытные истоки жизни. *8.* Сработал первобытный инстинкт выживания. ● *1.* Something primal. *2.* Their primal instincts kicked in. *3.* The fight was primal and intense. *4.* She released a primal scream. *5.* The painting had a primal energy. *6.* She felt a primordial connection to the land. *7.* They studied the primordial origins of life. *8.* The primordial instinct for survival kicked in.

**1052. относящийся к конгрессу** — *congressional* — This term is used to describe something that is related to or associated with a congress or legislative body. It is often used to refer to laws, committees, or events that pertain to the functioning of a congress.

**1053. гротескный** — *grotesque* — 'Гротескный' is used to describe something that is strange, distorted, or absurd in a way that is both disturbing and exaggerated. It is often used to characterize art, literature, or situations that are bizarre or unsettling.
● *1.* Они носили гротескные маски. *2.* Его работы были гротескными. *3.* Это была гротескная скульптура. *4.* Сцена была гротескной. *5.* История имела гротескный конец. ● *1.* They wore grotesque masks. *2.* His artwork was grotesque. *3.* It was a grotesque sculpture. *4.* The scene was grotesque. *5.* The story had a grotesque ending.

**1054. склонный** — *apt* — 'Склонный' is used to describe someone who is inclined or likely to do something. It indicates a tendency or predisposition towards a certain behavior or action.
● *1.* Они были склонны к ссоре. ● *1.* They were apt to quarrel.

**1055. компактный** — *compact* — 'Компактный' is used to describe something that is small, closely packed, and efficiently designed to take up minimal space. It is often used to refer to objects or devices that are portable and easy to carry.
● *1.* Компактная камера маленькая. *2.* Автомобиль компактный. *3.* Диск компактный. *4.* Компактная косметичка для путешествий. ● *1.* A compact camera is small. *2.* The car is compact. *3.* The disk is compact. *4.* Compact makeup for travel.

**1056. весело** — *merrily, gaily* — 'Весело' is used to describe actions or events that are done in a cheerful and joyful manner. It conveys a sense of happiness and lightheartedness in the way something is being done or experienced.
● *1.* Бубенчики на санях весело звенели. *2.* Дети весело играли в парке. *3.* Праздник отметили весело. *4.* Завсегдатаи вечеринки весело смеялись и пели. *5.* Они весело танцевали под звездами. ● *1.* The sleigh bells jingled merrily. *2.* The children played gaily in the park. *3.* The festival was celebrated gaily. *4.* The partygoers laughed and sang gaily. *5.* They danced gaily under the stars.

**1057. троянский** — *trojan* — 'Троянский' is used to describe something related to the ancient city of Troy or the Trojan War. It can also be used metaphorically to describe something deceptive or hidden, similar to the Trojan Horse.

• *1.* Троянские шпионы собирали информацию. *2.* Он защитил свой компьютер от троянских вирусов. *3.* Троянская программа была установлена. *4.* Троянский конь содержал солдат. *5.* Они защищали от троянских атак. • *1.* The trojan spies gathered information. *2.* He protected his computer from trojan viruses. *3.* The trojan program was installed. *4.* The trojan horse contained soldiers. *5.* They defended against trojan attacks.

**1058. трагически** — *tragically* — 'Трагически' is used to describe something that is related to or characterized by tragedy. It conveys a sense of sadness, sorrow, or disaster in a situation or event. It emphasizes the seriousness and gravity of the circumstances.

• *1.* Несчастный случай трагически повлиял на семью. *2.* История закончилась трагически. *3.* Она трагически потеряла родителей. *4.* Ситуация развивалась трагически. • *1.* The accident impacted the family tragically. *2.* The story ended tragically. *3.* She lost her parents tragically. *4.* The situation unfolded tragically.

**1059. оккультный** — *occult* — This word is used to describe something related to supernatural practices, beliefs, or phenomena that are beyond the realm of conventional understanding. It is often associated with mysterious or hidden knowledge.

• *1.* Она изучает оккультные практики. • *1.* She studies occult practices.

**1060. манипулятивный** — *manipulative* — This word describes someone or something that is skilled at influencing or controlling others in a deceptive or unfair way. It implies a tendency to use manipulation for personal gain or to achieve a desired outcome.

• *1.* Манипулятивное поведение было деструктивным. *2.* Манипулятивная тактика была шокирующей. • *1.* The manipulative behavior was destructive. *2.* The manipulative tactics were shocking.

**1061. размыто** — *blurry* — 'Размыто' is used to describe something that is not clear or distinct, often appearing fuzzy or out of focus. It can refer to physical objects, images, or ideas that lack sharpness or definition.

● *1.* Все размыто. *2.* Это размыто. *3.* Фотокопия была размытой. *4.* Видео было дрожащим и размытым. ● *1.* Everything's blurry. *2.* It's blurry. *3.* The photocopy was blurry. *4.* The footage was shaky and blurry.

**1062. лисий** — *foxy* — The word 'лисий' is used to describe someone or something as cunning, sly, or clever in a way that is reminiscent of a fox. It can also refer to physical characteristics resembling those of a fox.

**1063. мифический** — *mythical* — 'Мифический' is used to describe something that is related to or characteristic of myths or legends. It can also be used to describe something that is imaginary, unreal, or existing only in stories or folklore.
● *1.* В книге фигурируют мифические звери. *2.* Гарпия – мифическое существо. *3.* Нага -- мифическая змея. *4.* Пегас – мифическое существо. *5.* Тэнгу был мифическим существом. ● *1.* The book featured mythical beasts. *2.* The harpy is a mythical creature. *3.* The naga is a mythical serpent. *4.* The pegasus is a mythical creature. *5.* The tengu was a mythical creature.

**1064. неэтично** — *unethical* — 'Неэтично' is used to describe actions, behaviors, or decisions that are morally wrong or not in line with accepted principles of right and wrong. It conveys a sense of impropriety or lack of ethical standards.
● *1.* Это было бы неэтично. *2.* Это неэтично. *3.* Обманная тактика неэтична. *4.* Их обвинили в неэтичном поведении. *5.* Эксплуатация животных неэтична. ● *1.* That would be unethical. *2.* It's unethical. *3.* Deceitful tactics are unethical. *4.* They were accused of unethical behavior. *5.* The exploitation of animals is unethical.

**1065. несвязанный** — *unrelated* — The word 'несвязанный' is used to describe things that are not connected or related to each other. It can be used to indicate a lack of correlation or association between different elements or ideas.
● *1.* Он обсуждал несвязанные вопросы. ● *1.* He discussed unrelated matters.

**1066. неопытный** — *inexperienced* — 'Неопытный' is used to describe someone who lacks experience or skill in a particular area. It can be used to refer to a person who is new to a job, task, or activity and has not yet gained the necessary knowledge or expertise.

● *1.* Команда была неопытна в игре. *2.* Ее считали неопытной. *3.* Они наняли неопытный персонал. *4.* Она чувствовала себя неопытной в этой роли. ● *1.* The team was inexperienced in the game. *2.* She was seen as inexperienced. *3.* They hired inexperienced staff. *4.* She felt inexperienced in the role.

**1067. озлобленный** — *bitchy* — 'Озлобленный' is used to describe someone who is irritable, easily angered, and prone to snapping at others. It conveys a sense of bitterness and hostility in their behavior or attitude.

**1068. дремлющий** — *dormant* — This word is used to describe something that is currently inactive or not in use, but has the potential to become active or in use in the future. It implies a state of temporary rest or inactivity.

● *1.* Битва пробудила его дремлющую жажду крови. ● *1.* The battle awakened his dormant bloodlust.

**1069. недостаточный** — *inadequate, insufficient* — This word is used to describe something that is not enough or not sufficient for a particular purpose or need. It indicates a lack or insufficiency in quantity, quality, or degree.

● *1.* Имеющихся ресурсов было недостаточно для выполнения этой задачи. *2.* Инфраструктура недостаточна для роста. *3.* Его извинений было недостаточно, чтобы исправить ситуацию. *4.* В ее обзоре производительности отмечался недостаточный прогресс. *5.* Вознаграждение было недостаточным. *6.* Недостаточные данные. *7.* Недостаточно средств. *8.* Недостаточно доказательств. *9.* Бюджета было недостаточно для их нужд. *10.* Она получила недостаточную подготовку. ● *1.* The resources available were inadequate for the task. *2.* The infrastructure is inadequate for growth. *3.* His apology was inadequate to mend the situation. *4.* Her performance review cited inadequate progress. *5.* The recompense was inadequate. *6.* Insufficient data. *7.* Insufficient funds. *8.* Insufficient evidence. *9.* The budget was insufficient for their needs. *10.* She received insufficient training.

**1070. неврологический** — *neurological* — The word 'неврологический' is used to describe something related to the nervous system or neurology. It is commonly used in medical contexts to refer to conditions, treatments, or examinations involving the brain, spinal cord, and nerves.

● *1.* Неисправность синапса вызвала неврологические проблемы. *2.* Его неврологическое состояние не очень хорошее. *3.* Неврологическое исследование выявило серьезные проблемы. *4.* Мальчику необходимо неврологическое обследование. *5.* У него серьезные неврологические проблемы. ●
*1.* The malfunctioning synapse caused neurological issues. *2.* His neurological state isn't good. *3.* A neurological study uncovered profound issues. *4.* The boy needs a neurological examination. *5.* He has severe neurological problems.

**1071. слабо** — *weakly* — 'Слабо' is used to describe something that is done with little strength or intensity. It can also be used to express a lack of conviction or effort in a particular action or behavior.

● *1.* После операции он говорил слабо. *2.* Он слабо протестовал против этого решения. *3.* Она слабо помахала рукой, когда они ушли. *4.* Она слабо улыбнулась этой новости. ●
*1.* He spoke weakly after the surgery. *2.* He protested weakly against the decision. *3.* She waved weakly as they left. *4.* She smiled weakly at the news.

**1072. садистский** — *sadistic* — The word 'садистский' is used to describe behavior or actions that involve deriving pleasure from inflicting pain or suffering on others. It conveys a sense of cruelty and enjoyment in causing harm or humiliation.

● *1.* Она была известна своими садистскими наклонностями. *2.* Его садистская натура делала его опасным. *3.* Его садистское поведение вызывало беспокойство. *4.* Садистский персонаж смеялся над болью других. ● *1.* She was known for her sadistic tendencies. *2.* His sadistic nature made him dangerous. *3.* His sadistic behavior was disturbing. *4.* The sadistic character laughed at others' pain.

**1073. доступной** — *accessible* — The word 'доступной' is used to describe something that is easily reached, used, or understood. It indicates that something is available or within reach for use or participation.

● *1.* Тропа доступна для туристов. *2.* Архивы были доступны исследователям. *3.* Перевод сделал текст доступным. *4.* Информация доступна всем. • *1.* The trail is accessible to hikers. *2.* The archives were accessible to researchers. *3.* The translation made the text accessible. *4.* The information is accessible to all.

**1074. конструктивный** — *constructive* — The word 'конструктивный' is used to describe something that is helpful, positive, and aimed at finding solutions or improving a situation. It is often used in discussions or debates to encourage productive and constructive dialogue.
• *1.* Они дали конструктивную обратную связь. • *1.* They gave constructive feedback.

**1075. беспокойный** — *hectic, worrisome, fidgety* — The word 'беспокойный' is used to describe situations or people that are characterized by a sense of restlessness, anxiety, or unease. It conveys a feeling of being unsettled, agitated, or constantly on edge.
• *1.* Это было беспокойно. *2.* Она беспокойно постучала ногой. *3.* Беспокойная собака скулила и ходила по комнате. *4.* Его беспокойное поведение раздражало окружающих. •
*1.* It's been hectic. *2.* She tapped her foot in a fidgety manner. *3.* The fidgety dog whined and paced. *4.* His fidgety behavior annoyed those around him.

**1076. активно** — *actively* — 'Активно' is used to describe actions that are done with energy, enthusiasm, or intensity. It indicates that something is being done in a proactive and vigorous manner.
• *1.* Команда активно взаимодействует с сообществом. *2.* Она активно добивалась своих целей. *3.* Он активно искал возможности. *4.* Они активно выступали за перемены. *5.* Они активно участвовали в дискуссии. • *1.* The team actively engaged with the community. *2.* She actively pursued her goals. *3.* He actively sought out opportunities. *4.* They actively advocated for change. *5.* They actively participated in the debate.

**1077. недостаточное** — *insufficient* — This word is used to describe something that is not enough or lacking in quantity, quality, or degree. It indicates that there is a deficiency or inadequacy in a particular aspect or area.
• *1.* Недостаточные данные. *2.* Недостаточно средств. *3.* Не-

достаточно доказательств. *4.* Бюджета было недостаточно для их нужд. *5.* Она получила недостаточную подготовку. ● *1.* Insufficient data. *2.* Insufficient funds. *3.* Insufficient evidence. *4.* The budget was insufficient for their needs. *5.* She received insufficient training.

**1078.  нерушимый** — *indestructible, ironclad* — The word 'нерушимый' is used to describe something that is unbreakable, impervious to damage, or extremely strong. It conveys the idea of being solid, sturdy, and resistant to any kind of destruction or harm.

● *1.* Невидимый, нерушимый, неизбежный. *2.* Я нерушим. *3.* Она верила в нерушимую любовь. *4.* Ты нерушим. ● *1.* Invisible, indestructible, inescapable. *2.* I'm indestructible. *3.* She believed in indestructible love. *4.* You're indestructible.

**1079. заковыристый** — *catchy* — 'Заковыристый' is used to describe something that is difficult to understand or solve, often in a tricky or complex way. It can also refer to something that is catchy or memorable in a unique or intriguing way.

**1080. умеренный** — *moderate, temperate* — 'Умеренный' is used to describe something that is not extreme or excessive, but rather balanced and moderate in nature. It can refer to anything from weather conditions to political views.

● *1.* Умеренный подход казался лучшим. *2.* Температура была умеренной - 72 градуса. *3.* Они пользовались умеренным успехом. *4.* Его взгляды были умеренными. *5.* Она хотела найти умеренное решение. ● *1.* The moderate approach seemed best. *2.* The temperature was a moderate 72 degrees. *3.* They enjoyed a moderate success. *4.* His views were moderate. *5.* She wanted to find a moderate solution.

**1081.  наследственный** — *hereditary* — This word is used to describe traits, characteristics, or conditions that are passed down from one generation to another within a family. It refers to something that is inherited or genetic in nature.

● *1.* Это наследственное. *2.* Она унаследовала наследственный титул. *3.* Наследственная предрасположенность играет роль в заболевании. *4.* Этот ген является наследственным. *5.* Расстройство является наследственным. ● *1.* It's hereditary. *2.* She inherited the hereditary title. *3.* Hereditary predisposition plays a role in the condition. *4.* That gene is hereditary. *5.* The disorder is hereditary.

**1082. аккуратно** — *neatly* — 'Akkuatno' is used to describe something that is done with care and precision, in a tidy and organized manner. It can refer to physical actions, such as cleaning or arranging objects, as well as to behaviors or attitudes.

• *1.* Ее униформа была аккуратно выглажена. *2.* Она аккуратно сложила нижнее белье в ящик. *3.* Она аккуратно сложила трусы. *4.* Он аккуратно сложил футон. *5.* Горничная аккуратно сложила полотенца. • *1.* Her uniform was neatly pressed. *2.* She folded the underwear neatly in the drawer. *3.* She folded the underpants neatly. *4.* He folded the futon neatly. *5.* The maid folded the towels neatly.

**1083. обезумевший** — *distraught* — 'Обезумевший' is used to describe someone who is in a state of extreme emotional distress or agitation. It conveys a sense of being overwhelmed by emotions to the point of losing control.

• *1.* Обезумевшая мать лихорадочно искала. • *1.* The distraught mother searched frantically.

**1084. кричащий** — *flashy, technicolor* — 'Кричащий' is used to describe something that is bright, bold, and attention-grabbing. It is often used to describe colors, patterns, or designs that are vibrant and eye-catching.

• *1.* Машина была функциональной, но не кричащей. • *1.* The car was functional but not flashy.

**1085. пограничный** — *borderline* — 'пограничный' is used to describe something that is on the border or boundary of something else, often implying that it is at the edge or limit of a certain quality or characteristic.

• *1.* У больного была пограничная температура. • *1.* The patient had a borderline temperature.

**1086. разнообразный** — *diverse, miscellaneous* — This word is used to describe a wide variety of things that are different from each other in some way. It can be used to talk about a range of options, choices, or characteristics that are diverse or varied.

• *1.* Луга были домом для разнообразной дикой природы. *2.* Репертуар хора был разнообразным. *3.* Этническая принадлежность района разнообразна. *4.* Список кандидатов был

разнообразным. *5.* Морская жизнь была разнообразной. ●
*1.* The grassland was home to diverse wildlife. *2.* The choir had a diverse repertoire. *3.* The ethnicity of the neighborhood is diverse. *4.* The slate of candidates was diverse. *5.* The marine life was diverse.

**1087.** **неоплаченный** — *unpaid, unrequited* — 'Неоплаченный' is used to describe something that has not been paid for or reciprocated. It conveys the idea of something lacking compensation or acknowledgment.

**1088. общенациональный** — *nationwide* — This word is used to describe something that is applicable or relevant to the entire nation or country, rather than just a specific region or group. It indicates that something is widespread or affects the entire population.

**1089. сюрреалистичный** — *surreal* — This word is used to describe something that is strange, dreamlike, or bizarre in a way that is not typical of reality. It is often used to convey a sense of the uncanny or fantastical.
● *1.* Это сюрреалистично. *2.* Это так сюрреалистично. *3.* Это было сюрреалистично. *4.* Опыт был захватывающим и сюрреалистичным. ● *1.* This is surreal. *2.* This is so surreal. *3.* That was surreal. *4.* The experience was breathtaking and surreal.

**1090.** **акустический** — *acoustic* — This word is used to describe something related to sound or the sense of hearing, specifically in terms of how sound is produced, transmitted, or heard without the use of electronic amplification.
● *1.* Она оценила акустическое исполнение. *2.* Он изучил акустические свойства помещения. *3.* В комнате было отличное акустическое оформление. *4.* Акустическая гитара заполнила зал. *5.* Акустическая плитка улучшила качество звука. ● *1.* She appreciated the acoustic performance. *2.* He studied the acoustic properties of the room. *3.* The room had excellent acoustic design. *4.* The acoustic guitar filled the auditorium. *5.* The acoustic tiles improved the sound quality.

**1091. косметический** — *cosmetic* — 'Косметический' is used to describe something related to beauty products or procedures that enhance or improve a person's appearance. It can also refer to something superficial or minor in nature, such as a cosmetic

change.
● *1.* Тальк используется во многих косметических продуктах. *2.* Ей сделали косметическое улучшение. ● *1.* Talc is used in many cosmetic products. *2.* She underwent a cosmetic enhancement.

**1092. всесторонний** — *comprehensive* — 'Comprehensive' describes something that covers all aspects or angles of a subject, providing a thorough and detailed understanding. It implies a thorough examination or consideration of all relevant factors.
● *1.* Он получил всестороннее образование. *2.* В докладе представлен всесторонний анализ. ● *1.* He received a comprehensive education. *2.* The report provided a comprehensive analysis.

**1093. невыразимый** — *unspeakable* — 'Unspeakable' is used to describe something that is too intense, extreme, or overwhelming to be expressed in words. It conveys a sense of awe, astonishment, or disbelief at the magnitude or impact of a particular experience or emotion.
● *1.* Невыразимые вещи. *2.* Тайна была слишком невыразимой, чтобы делиться ею. *3.* Ее горе было невыразимо. *4.* Это невыразимо. *5.* Невыразимое преступление потрясло город. ● *1.* Unspeakable things. *2.* The secret was too unspeakable to share. *3.* Her grief was unspeakable. *4.* It's unspeakable. *5.* The unspeakable crime shocked the town.

**1094. примерный** — *exemplary, approximate* — 'Примерный' is used to describe something that is either exemplary or approximate in nature. It can refer to something that serves as a good example or is close to the actual value or amount without being exact.
● *1.* Она всегда демонстрировала примерное поведение. *2.* Примерное расстояние 5 миль. *3.* Назовите мне примерные сроки. ● *1.* She showed exemplary behavior at all times. *2.* The approximate distance is 5 miles. *3.* Give me an approximate time frame.

**1095. провокационный** — *provocative* — This word is used to describe something that is intended to provoke a reaction or stir controversy. It is often used to describe behavior, art, or statements that are meant to challenge or incite a response.

● *1.* Очень провокационный. ● *1.* Very provocative.

**1096. прочувствованный** — *heartfelt* — This word is used to describe something that is deeply felt or experienced with great emotion and sincerity. It conveys a sense of genuine and heartfelt sentiment or expression.

● *1.* На надгробии была прочувствованная надпись. ● *1.* The headstone bore a heartfelt inscription.

**1097. внимательный** — *attentive, considerate, mindful* — This word is used to describe someone who pays close attention to details, shows care and consideration towards others, and is mindful of their surroundings. It conveys the idea of being attentive and thoughtful in one's actions and interactions.

● *1.* Он такой внимательный. *2.* Студенты были вежливы и внимательны. *3.* Какой внимательный. *4.* Это очень внимательно с вашей стороны. *5.* Это очень внимательно. *6.* Очень внимательный. *7.* Как внимательно с твоей стороны. *8.* Она призвала своих учеников быть внимательными. *9.* Он внимательно следил за своими потребительскими привычками. ● *1.* He's so attentive. *2.* The students were polite and attentive. *3.* How considerate. *4.* That's very considerate of you. *5.* That's very considerate. *6.* Very considerate. *7.* How considerate of you. *8.* She encouraged her students to be mindful. *9.* He was mindful of his spending habits.

**1098. психологически** — *psychologically* — 'Психологически' is used to describe something related to the mind or emotions. It is used to indicate a psychological or emotional aspect of a situation, behavior, or experience.

● *1.* Он был психологически неустойчив. ● *1.* He was psychologically unstable.

**1099. невообразимый** — *unimaginable* — This word is used to describe something that is beyond what can be imagined or believed. It conveys a sense of astonishment or disbelief at the magnitude or extent of something.

● *1.* Зрелища были невообразимыми. *2.* Ситуация казалась невообразимой. *3.* Боль была невообразимой. *4.* Это невообразимо. *5.* Красота пейзажа была невообразимой. ● *1.* The sights were unimaginable. *2.* The situation seemed unimaginable. *3.* The pain was unimaginable. *4.* It's unimaginable. *5.*

The beauty of the landscape was unimaginable.

**1100. захватывающий** — *breathtaking, groovy* — 'Захватывающий' is used to describe something that is extremely exciting, impressive, or captivating. It conveys a sense of awe and wonder, often used to describe experiences, events, or performances that leave a strong impression.

● *1.* Со склона холма открывался захватывающий вид. *2.* Вид с вершины горы был захватывающий. *3.* Опыт был захватывающим и сюрреалистичным. *4.* Дрон сделал захватывающие кадры с воздуха. *5.* Акробатическое представление было захватывающим. ● *1.* The hillside offered a breathtaking view. *2.* The view from the mountaintop was breathtaking. *3.* The experience was breathtaking and surreal. *4.* The drone captured breathtaking aerial footage. *5.* The acrobatic performance was breathtaking.

# 2. Index of Words

абсолютный (326) — absolute, unmitigated

абстрактный (881) — abstract

абсурдный (375) — absurd

авантюрный (1005) — adventurous

автоматически (618) — automatically

автоматический (496) — automatic

агрессивный (406) — aggressive, invasive

адекватный (871) — adequate

административный (907) — administrative

академический (637) — academic

аккуратно (1082) — neatly

аккуратный (417) — neat, tidy, natty

активно (1076) — actively

активный (342) — active

акустический (1090) — acoustic

алкогольный (500) — alcoholic

альтернативный (411) — alternative

аморальный (758) — immoral, amoral

анальный (802) — anal

английский (120) — english

аномальный (700) — abnormal, anomalous

анонимный (402) — anonymous

апельсиновый (281) — orange

атомный (559) — atomic

аутентичный (576) — authentic

афганский (921) — afghan

базовый (303) — basic

баллистический (1043) — ballistic

без сознания (386) — unconscious

беззаботный (926) — carefree, unconcerned

| безмятежный (1045) | serene |
| безопасно (344) | safely, securely |
| безопасный (73) | safe, secure |
| безоружный (641) | unarmed |
| безостановочно (966) | nonstop |
| безответственный (572) | irresponsible |
| безумно (719) | madly, crazily, insanely |
| безумный (88) | mad, insane, certifiable |
| белокурый (467) | blond |
| белый (70) | white |
| беременная (144) | pregnant |
| бесконечно (1025) | endlessly, indefinitely |
| бесконечный (570) | infinite, unending |
| бесплатно (58) | free |
| бесплодный (782) | barren, infertile |
| беспокойный (1075) | hectic, worrisome, fidgety |
| бесполезный (842) | futile, unhelpful |
| беспрецедентный (819) | unprecedented, uneventful |
| бессильный (828) | impotent |
| бессмертный (474) | immortal, undying |
| бесчеловечный (978) | inhuman |
| бесшабашный (734) | daft |
| библейский (836) | biblical |
| биологический (477) | biological |
| благодарный (225) | grateful, thankful, appreciative |
| благородный (276) | noble, genteel |
| бледный (401) | pale |
| блестящий (481) | shiny, brilliant, lustrous |
| близко (50) | close |
| богатый (115) | rich, wealthy, plentiful, opulent |
| божественный (327) | divine, godlike, godly |

| | |
|---|---|
| боком (729) | sideways |
| более (6) | more |
| болезненный (287) | painful, sickly, morbid |
| больной (72) | sick, ill, sore |
| больше не (54) | anymore |
| большой (17) | big, great, high, large |
| бредовый (909) | delirious, delusional, freaky |
| бронированный (762) | armored |
| брюшной (901) | abdominal |
| буквальный (1049) | literal |
| буржуазный (731) | bourgeois |
| бывший (232) | former |
| быстро (109) | quickly, fast, quick |
| быстрый (81) | fast, quick, swift, rapid |
| в значительной степени (861) | largely |
| в состоянии (57) | able |
| важный (53) | important, newsworthy |
| валлийский (848) | welsh |
| варварский (1026) | barbaric, barbarous |
| вдумчивый (534) | thoughtful |
| вегетарианский (608) | vegetarian, vegan |
| вежливо (895) | politely |
| вежливый (373) | polite, courteous, suave |
| великий (12) | great, grand |
| великолепный (250) | gorgeous, glorious, magnificent, splendid |
| верно (3) | right |
| верный (10) | sure, correct, loyal, faithful |
| вероломный (753) | unfaithful, perfidious |
| вероятно (40) | probably |
| вероятный (205) | likely, probable, believable, credible |

| | |
|---|---|
| верхний (78) | top, upper, overhead |
| весело (1056) | merrily, gaily |
| веселый (561) | cheerful, merry, jolly, hilarious |
| ветреный (750) | windy, flighty, harebrained |
| вечный (331) | eternal, perpetual, everlasting |
| взаимный (465) | mutual |
| взрывной (498) | explosive |
| видимый (506) | visible |
| видный (748) | prominent, eminent |
| визуальный (404) | visual |
| виновный (145) | guilty, culpable |
| виртуальный (694) | virtual |
| вирусный (784) | viral |
| влиятельный (811) | influential |
| внезапный (195) | sudden |
| внеземной (708) | extraterrestrial |
| внизу (199) | downstairs |
| внимательно (206) | carefully, closely |
| внимательный (1097) | attentive, considerate, mindful |
| внутренний (362) | inner, internal, domestic, inland |
| внутри (47) | inside |
| военно морской (542) | naval |
| воздушный (823) | aerial |
| возможный (77) | possible |
| возмутительный (518) | outrageous, ungodly |
| вокальный (647) | vocal |
| волнующий (916) | groovy |
| волосатый (519) | hairy |
| волшебно (1036) | magically |
| волшебный (360) | magical, elvish |
| вонючий (695) | smelly, stinky |

| | |
|---|---|
| воображаемый (594) | imaginary |
| воспаленный (385) | sore |
| восторженный (739) | enthusiastic, ecstatic |
| восхитительный (210) | delicious, delightful, adorable, admirable |
| впечатляющий (267) | impressive |
| вполне (52) | quite |
| враждебный (469) | hostile |
| временно (582) | temporarily |
| временный (361) | temporary, transient, interim, transitory |
| всемирный (620) | worldwide |
| всемогущий (442) | almighty, omnipotent |
| всесторонний (1092) | comprehensive |
| вслух (864) | aloud |
| вспомогательный (983) | auxiliary, subsidiary, ancillary |
| вторичный (626) | secondary |
| второй (43) | second |
| вулканический (766) | volcanic |
| вульгарный (619) | vulgar |
| входящий (532) | incoming, inbound |
| выгодный (1023) | lucrative, beneficial |
| выдающийся (508) | outstanding, eminent |
| вымерший (720) | extinct |
| выносливый (668) | hardy |
| выпуклый (1009) | bossy |
| высокомерный (453) | arrogant, haughty, snooty, upstage |
| высший (345) | upper |
| выше (4) | up, above |
| галактический (975) | galactic |
| галантный (841) | gallant |
| генетический (436) | genetic |

| | |
|---|---|
| геологический (1032) | geological |
| героический (558) | heroic |
| гибкий (737) | flexible, supple, limber, versatile |
| гибридный (747) | hybrid |
| гигантский (209) | giant, gigantic, jumbo |
| гипотетически (865) | theoretically, hypothetically |
| гипотетический (993) | hypothetical |
| глобальный (353) | global |
| глубоко (111) | deep, deeply |
| глупый (59) | stupid, silly, foolish |
| глухой (310) | deaf, godforsaken, outlandish |
| гнилой (306) | rotten, putrid, unsound |
| гнусный (610) | vile, heinous, abominable, nefarious |
| голодный (121) | hungry |
| гордо (839) | proudly |
| гордый (117) | proud, prideful |
| городской (555) | urban |
| горький (338) | bitter |
| готовый (30) | ready |
| гравитационный (846) | gravitational |
| гражданский (277) | civil |
| грандиозный (139) | grand, grandiose |
| графический (834) | graphic |
| греческий (305) | greek |
| грешный (877) | sinful |
| грозный (768) | formidable, fearsome |
| громкий (172) | loud |
| гротескный (1053) | grotesque |
| грубо (606) | roughly, crudely, grossly |
| грубый (198) | rough, rude, coarse, gruff |

| | |
|---|---|
| грустно (480) | sadly |
| грязный (136) | dirty, muddy, filthy, messy |
| гуманитарный (980) | humanitarian |
| гуманный (974) | humane |
| далекий (297) | distant |
| дальний (46) | far, distant |
| датский (633) | danish |
| двойной (150) | double, dual, binary |
| действительно (5) | really, actually, indeed |
| действительный (621) | valid |
| деликатный (370) | delicate |
| демократический (545) | democratic |
| деревянный (452) | wooden |
| дерзкий (664) | cocky, brash, insolent, pert |
| дерьмовый (543) | crappy |
| детский (524) | childish, childlike, infantile |
| дефицитный (851) | scarce |
| диабетический (968) | diabetic |
| диагностический (1028) | diagnostic |
| дикий (158) | wild |
| дико (859) | wildly |
| динамический (624) | dynamic |
| дипломатический (598) | diplomatic |
| дисциплинарный (959) | disciplinary |
| до некоторой степени (429) | somewhat |
| доблестный (904) | valiant |
| добровольно (806) | voluntarily |
| добровольный (906) | voluntary |
| добрый (19) | kind |
| дождливый (669) | rainy |
| доисторический (944) | prehistoric |
| должный (166) | due |

| | |
|---|---|
| домашний (936) | homey |
| доминирующий (793) | dominant |
| дополнительный (155) | extra, additional, auxiliary, supplementary |
| дорогие (194) | expensive |
| дорого (603) | dearly, costly |
| дорогой (49) | dear, expensive |
| дорогостоящий (997) | costly |
| достаточно (21) | enough, sufficient |
| достаточный (548) | sufficient, ample, adequate |
| достойный (318) | worthy |
| доступной (1073) | accessible |
| доступный (226) | available, accessible, affordable |
| драгоценный (238) | precious |
| драматический (295) | dramatic |
| древесный (445) | woody |
| древний (183) | ancient |
| дремлющий (1068) | dormant |
| дружественный (247) | friendly |
| духовный (390) | spiritual, clerical, ecclesiastical |
| душный (837) | stuffy |
| единодушный (962) | unanimous |
| единственный (476) | sole, unopposed |
| ежегодный (470) | annual, yearly |
| ежедневный (264) | daily |
| еженедельно (595) | weekly |
| естественный (169) | natural |
| жадный (454) | greedy, avid, insatiable, voracious |
| жаждущий (329) | thirsty, desirous |
| жалкий (9) | sorry, miserable, pathetic, wretched |

| | |
|---|---|
| жаркий (66) | hot |
| желтый (217) | yellow |
| женоненавистнический (1017) | sexist |
| женский (180) | female, feminine |
| женственный (648) | feminine, womanly |
| жесткий (35) | hard, tough, stiff |
| жестокий (512) | fierce, cruel, brutal, brutish |
| живой (29) | live, lively |
| жидкий (409) | liquid, runny, soupy |
| жизненно важный (392) | vital |
| жизнеспособный (800) | viable |
| жировой (552) | fatty |
| жуткий (749) | eerie, spooky |
| жутко (336) | creepy |
| заблудившись (878) | astray |
| завистливый (869) | envious |
| задний (397) | rear, posterior |
| заковыристый (1079) | catchy |
| законный (497) | legitimate, rightful, lawful, justifiable |
| замечательный (89) | wonderful, remarkable, admirable |
| занятой (94) | busy |
| западный (298) | western |
| запасной (188) | spare |
| запоздалый (821) | overdue, belated, tardy |
| заразительный (684) | contagious |
| заранее (816) | beforehand |
| заскорузлый (832) | corny |
| заслуживающий доверия (814) | trustworthy, credible |
| застенчивый (265) | shy, coy |

| захватывающий (1100) | breathtaking, groovy |
| защитный (517) | protective, defensive |
| звуковой (600) | audio, sonic, acoustic |
| здоровый (219) | healthy, wholesome, bonny |
| зеленый (130) | green |
| земной (776) | earthly, terrestrial, earthbound |
| зловещий (727) | ominous, sinister, inauspicious |
| злой (133) | evil, wicked |
| знаменитый (157) | famous, renowned, illustrious |
| значительно (573) | greatly, vastly |
| значительный (413) | significant, considerable, substantial, sizeable |
| золотистый (214) | golden |
| золотой (116) | gold, golden |
| зубной (564) | dental |
| зудящий (716) | itchy |
| игривый (985) | playful, frisky |
| идентичный (487) | identical |
| извращенный (1048) | perverse |
| изобретательный (792) | ingenious, resourceful, inventive |
| изумительный (439) | marvelous, stupendous, marvellous |
| изысканный (646) | exquisite, dainty |
| изящный (886) | graceful, dainty, dinky, nifty |
| иммунный (575) | immune |
| императорский (438) | imperial |
| импульсивный (794) | impulsive |
| индивидуальный (316) | individual |
| иногда (63) | sometimes, occasionally |
| иностранный (203) | foreign |

| | |
|---|---|
| инструментальный (449) | instrumental |
| интеллектуальный (549) | intellectual |
| интенсивный (341) | intense, intensive |
| интимный (451) | intimate |
| инфракрасный (866) | infrared |
| иррациональный (767) | irrational |
| исключительно (822) | exclusively |
| исключительный (614) | exceptional |
| искренний (473) | sincere, heartfelt, candid |
| искусный (675) | skilled, skillful, natty, skilful |
| искусственный (521) | artificial |
| исламский (808) | islamic |
| испанский (187) | spanish |
| исследовательский (971) | investigative, exploratory |
| истерический (551) | hysterical |
| истинный (38) | true |
| исторический (504) | historical, historic |
| исходящий (1041) | outgoing |
| к счастью (432) | fortunately, luckily, mercifully |
| каверзный (447) | tricky |
| кавказский (908) | caucasian |
| капиталистический (931) | capitalist, capitalistic |
| капризный (781) | cranky, whimsical, capricious, freakish |
| кардиальный (676) | cardiac |
| катастрофический (849) | catastrophic, cataclysmic |
| квадратный (197) | square |
| кислый (511) | sour |
| классический (289) | classic, classical |
| классно (146) | awesome |
| классный (554) | classy, groovy, crackerjack |
| клеточный (862) | cellular |

| | |
|---|---|
| клинический (702) | clinical |
| ключевой (108) | key |
| коварный (761) | treacherous, insidious, crafty, underhand |
| коллективный (632) | collective |
| колоссальный (913) | colossal, stupendous |
| комический (388) | comic, comical |
| коммерческий (328) | commercial, mercantile |
| коммунистический (407) | communist |
| компактный (1055) | compact |
| компетентный (773) | competent |
| комфортный (177) | comfortable |
| конкретно (400) | specifically |
| конкретный (212) | particular, concrete, specific |
| конкурентоспособный (586) | competitive |
| консервативный (630) | conservative |
| конституционный (927) | constitutional |
| конструктивный (1074) | constructive |
| континентальный (804) | continental |
| конфиденциальный (488) | confidential |
| коричневый (178) | brown |
| королевский (211) | royal, regal |
| короткий (105) | short, brief |
| корпоративный (414) | corporate |
| косметический (1091) | cosmetic |
| космический (560) | cosmic |
| красиво (503) | beautifully, handsomely |
| красный (76) | red |
| красочный (741) | colorful, colourful |
| кратко (661) | briefly |
| крепкий (1024) | sturdy, robust |
| критический (351) | critical |

| | |
|---|---|
| кричащий (1084) | flashy, technicolor |
| кровавый (125) | bloody |
| крошечный (184) | tiny, teeny, miniscule, teensy |
| круглый (96) | round |
| крутой (712) | steep, drastic |
| кудрявый (932) | crispy |
| кулинарный (999) | culinary |
| культурный (482) | cultural |
| левый (20) | left |
| легендарный (529) | legendary, storied |
| легкомысленный (979) | giddy, frivolous, flippant, harebrained |
| ледяной (736) | icy, glacial |
| ленивый (346) | lazy, ornery |
| лесбийский (431) | lesbian |
| летучий (1019) | volatile |
| либеральный (659) | liberal |
| липкий (553) | sticky, tacky, gooey, gummy |
| лисий (1062) | foxy |
| литературный (714) | literary |
| личный (110) | personal |
| логический (463) | logical |
| ложный (228) | false, untrue, spurious, phoney |
| лохматый (678) | shaggy |
| лунный (744) | lunar |
| лучше (14) | better |
| лучший (27) | best |
| лысый (434) | bald |
| любезно (420) | kindly, graciously |
| любимый (149) | favorite, favourite |
| любопытный (229) | curious, nosy, nosey |

| | |
|---|---|
| максимальный (440) | maximum |
| малиновый (964) | crimson |
| маловероятный (462) | unlikely |
| малый (71) | small |
| манипулятивный (1060) | manipulative |
| массивный (275) | massive |
| материнский (949) | maternal |
| медицинский (153) | medical, medicinal |
| медленный (134) | slow |
| международный (252) | international |
| мелкий (530) | shallow, potty |
| мелочный (374) | petty |
| меньший (755) | lesser |
| местный (164) | local, aboriginal |
| месячный (652) | monthly |
| металлический (778) | metallic |
| механический (539) | mechanical |
| милосердный (639) | merciful |
| милостивый (520) | gracious, merciful |
| милый (131) | cute, lovable, likeable, cutesy |
| мимолетный (963) | fleeting |
| миниатюрный (833) | miniature |
| минимальный (852) | minimal |
| мирно (604) | peacefully |
| мирный (337) | peaceful, pacific |
| миролюбивый (419) | pacific |
| мистический (815) | mystical, mystic |
| мифический (1063) | mythical |
| многие (26) | many |
| множественный (365) | multiple, plural |
| мобильный (272) | mobile |
| модный (850) | fashionable, trendy |

| | |
|---|---|
| мокрый (189) | wet |
| молекулярный (820) | molecular |
| молодой (42) | young |
| молочный (709) | milky |
| молчаливый (230) | silent |
| морально (893) | morally |
| моральный (334) | moral |
| морозный (1044) | frosty |
| морской (358) | marine, naval, nautical |
| мощный (170) | powerful, potent |
| мрачный (631) | grim, gloomy, somber, glum |
| мудро (880) | wisely |
| мудрый (233) | wise |
| мужеподобная (650) | butch |
| мужественный (682) | manly, virile, spunky |
| мужской (181) | male, masculine, virile |
| музыкальный (348) | musical |
| мускулистый (991) | muscular, beefy |
| мягкий (192) | soft, gentle, mild, mellow |
| на открытом воздухе (860) | outdoor |
| навсегда (100) | forever |
| навязчивый (945) | obsessive, intrusive |
| надежный (255) | secure, reliable, trustworthy, dependable |
| надлежащий (207) | proper |
| наивный (433) | naive, unsophisticated |
| наименее (51) | least |
| наихудший (140) | worst |
| намеренный (1039) | intentional |
| напористый (960) | pushy, feisty, ballsy |
| напряженный (384) | tense, strenuous, stressful |
| насильственный (262) | violent |

| наследственный (1081) | hereditary |
| настоящим (533) | hereby, herewith |
| научно (1042) | scientifically |
| научный (324) | scientific |
| находчивый (1016) | resourceful |
| национальный (168) | national |
| нацистский (435) | nazi |
| небезопасный (689) | insecure |
| небесный (513) | heavenly |
| неблагодарный (583) | ungrateful |
| небрежный (574) | sloppy, negligent |
| неважный (984) | unimportant |
| невежественный (478) | ignorant |
| невероятно (304) | incredibly, unbelievable, unbelievably |
| невероятный (176) | incredible, unbelievable, improbable |
| невиданный (889) | unseen |
| невидимый (340) | invisible, unseen |
| невинный (143) | innocent |
| невнятно (380) | indistinctly |
| невозможно (127) | impossible |
| невообразимый (1099) | unimaginable |
| невредимый (957) | unharmed, unscathed |
| неврологический (1070) | neurological |
| невротический (1004) | neurotic |
| невыносимый (601) | unbearable, intolerable, insufferable |
| невыразимый (1093) | unspeakable |
| негодный (1003) | unfit, unqualified |
| неграмотный (972) | illiterate |
| недавний (293) | recent |
| недействительный (902) | invalid, unavailable |

| | |
|---|---|
| недостаточное (1077) | insufficient |
| недостаточный (1069) | inadequate, insufficient |
| недостойный (892) | unworthy |
| неестественный (772) | unnatural |
| нежелательный (900) | unwanted, unwelcome, undesirable, objectionable |
| нежно (372) | gently |
| нежный (299) | gentle, delicate |
| незабвенный (938) | unforgettable |
| незабываемый (817) | memorable, unforgettable |
| независимый (381) | independent |
| незаконно (706) | illegally, unlawful, unlawfully |
| незаконнорожденный (1015) | illegitimate |
| незаконный (231) | illegal, illegitimate, unlawful, wrongful |
| незаконченный (662) | unfinished |
| незамеченный (1021) | unnoticed |
| нездоровый (986) | unhealthy, unwell, unsound |
| незнакомый (1000) | unfamiliar |
| незначительный (430) | slight |
| незрелый (724) | immature |
| неизбежный (509) | inevitable, imminent, unavoidable, inescapable |
| неизвестный (271) | unknown |
| неистовый (1027) | frantic, rabid, boisterous, amok |
| нейтральный (590) | neutral |
| некомпетентный (696) | incompetent |
| некорректный (899) | incorrect |
| нелепый (152) | ridiculous, preposterous, ungodly |
| немедленно (137) | immediately, forthwith |
| немедленный (387) | immediate |

| | |
|---|---|
| немецкий (163) | german |
| немногие (37) | few |
| немного (8) | little, slightly |
| немыслимый (1011) | unthinkable |
| ненавистный (996) | hateful, odious |
| ненормальный (186) | insane, abnormal, anomalous, certifiable |
| ненужный (502) | unnecessary, unwanted, superfluous |
| необоснованный (683) | unreasonable, unfounded, unwarranted, unjustified |
| необычный (246) | unusual |
| неограниченный (780) | unlimited, indefinite |
| неоднократно (649) | repeatedly |
| неоплаченный (1087) | unpaid, unrequited |
| неопознанный (692) | unidentified |
| неопределенно (976) | indefinitely |
| неопределенный (754) | uncertain, indeterminate, indefinite, iffy |
| неопытный (1066) | inexperienced |
| неостанавливаемый (873) | unstoppable |
| неотразимый (764) | irresistible |
| неохотный (809) | reluctant, loath, averse |
| неоценимый (1006) | invaluable |
| непобедимый (602) | invincible, unbeatable, undefeated |
| неполноценный (1012) | defective |
| неполный (730) | incomplete |
| непочтительный (789) | disrespectful |
| неправильный (22) | wrong |
| непредсказуемый (635) | unpredictable |
| непрерывно (922) | continuously |
| неприемлемый (616) | unacceptable |

| | |
|---|---|
| неприличный (894) | indecent, unbecoming |
| непристойный (843) | obscene, lewd, indecent, bawdy |
| неприятный (244) | nasty, unpleasant, grisly, distasteful |
| непростительный (956) | unforgivable, inexcusable, unpardonable |
| непрофессиональный (998) | unprofessional |
| неразрешенный (982) | unauthorized, unresolved |
| нервно (733) | nervously |
| нервный (141) | nervous, neural, jumpy |
| нереальный (801) | unreal, unrealistic |
| нерегулярный (888) | irregular |
| нерушимый (1078) | indestructible, ironclad |
| несвежий (844) | stale |
| несвязанный (1065) | unrelated |
| неслышный (656) | inaudible |
| несовершеннолетний (611) | juvenile, underage |
| несоответствующий (1035) | untrue |
| неспособный (321) | unable, incapable, inept |
| несправедливый (379) | unfair, unjust |
| несчастливый (531) | unlucky |
| несчастный (274) | miserable, unhappy, unfortunate, wretched |
| нетерпеливый (605) | impatient |
| нетронутый (933) | untouched, pristine, untapped |
| неудачный (356) | unfortunate, unlucky, unsuccessful |
| неудобный (314) | uncomfortable, awkward, inconvenient |
| неуклюжий (538) | clumsy, uncouth, gauche |
| неуловимый (928) | elusive |
| неуместный (492) | inappropriate |

| | |
|---|---|
| неустойчивый (525) | unstable, erratic, woozy, unsustainable |
| нечувствительный (742) | insensitive |
| неэтично (1064) | unethical |
| новый (15) | new, fresh |
| нормальный (107) | normal |
| обезумевший (1083) | distraught |
| облачный (898) | cloudy |
| обнаженный (546) | nude |
| обожаемый (398) | adorable |
| оборонительный (540) | defensive |
| образовательный (721) | educational |
| обратный (377) | reverse |
| обстоятельный (925) | circumstantial |
| обширный (371) | vast, extensive, expansive |
| общая (93) | general |
| общенациональный (1088) | nationwide |
| общественный (118) | public, societal |
| общий (161) | common |
| объективный (494) | objective |
| обычно (138) | usually, normally, generally, ordinarily |
| обязательно (368) | necessarily |
| обязательный (770) | mandatory, obligatory, compulsory |
| огромный (135) | huge, enormous, vast, massive |
| одинаково (382) | alike |
| одинокий (106) | single, lonely, lone |
| одновременно (812) | simultaneously |
| одноразовый (1033) | disposable |
| оживленный (565) | lively, brisk, upbeat, vivacious |
| озлобленный (1067) | bitchy |
| озорной (332) | naughty, mischievous |

| | |
|---|---|
| оккультный (1059) | occult |
| окольный (1008) | devious, roundabout |

| | |
|---|---|
| окончательный (142) | final, definitive, irrevocable, conclusive |
| онемелый (627) | numb |
| оперативный (671) | operational, operative |
| определенно (99) | definitely |
| определенный (112) | certain, specific, definite |
| оптимистичный (677) | optimistic |
| органический (491) | organic |
| оригинальный (173) | original, ingenious |
| оскорбительный (882) | abusive |
| основной (165) | main, basic, basal, pivotal |
| особенно (128) | especially, particularly, notably, singularly |
| осторожный (85) | careful, wary, cautious, discreet |
| остроумный (829) | witty, ingenious, facetious |
| ответственный (160) | responsible, liable, answerable |
| отвратительный (567) | hideous, crummy, loathsome, atrocious |
| отдельный (237) | separate |
| откровенно (291) | frankly, overtly, candidly |
| откровенный (101) | frank, outspoken |
| открыто (658) | openly, overtly |
| открытый (36) | open |
| отличительный (868) | distinctive |
| относительно (634) | relatively, comparatively |
| относительный (389) | relative |
| относящийся к конгрессу (1052) | congressional |

| | |
|---|---|
| отрицательный (248) | negative |
| отсутствующий (623) | absent |
| отталкивающий (988) | repulsive, repellent |
| отчаянный (234) | desperate, foolhardy |
| отчетливый (711) | distinct |
| официально (301) | officially, formally |
| официальный (215) | official, formal |
| офшорный (840) | offshore |
| очевидный (200) | obvious, apparent, evident, evidentiary |
| очень (7) | very, extremely, highly, awfully |
| параллельный (613) | parallel |
| паранормальный (952) | paranormal |
| паршивый (300) | lousy |
| патриотический (807) | patriotic |
| первичный (408) | primary |
| первобытный (1051) | primal, primordial |
| первый (11) | first |
| передний (60) | front |
| песчаный (335) | sandy |
| печальный (119) | sad, grievous, lamentable |
| плавно (681) | smoothly, fluently |
| плавный (315) | smooth |
| пластиковый (278) | plastic |
| племенной (461) | tribal |
| плодородный (796) | fertile |
| плоский (185) | flat |
| плотно (717) | tightly, densely |
| плотный (167) | tight, dense |
| плохой (23) | bad, poor |
| поверхностный (805) | superficial, cursory, sketchy |
| пограничный (1085) | borderline |

| | |
|---|---|
| подводный (507) | underwater, undersea |
| поддельный (756) | bogus, counterfeit, spurious |
| подлинный (424) | genuine, authentic |
| подозрительный (280) | suspicious, fishy, leery |
| подотчетный (897) | accountable, answerable |
| подходящий (464) | suitable, eligible, propitious |
| пожилой (579) | elderly |
| позади (55) | behind |
| поздно (41) | late |
| позорный (670) | shameful, disreputable, disgraceful, dishonorable |
| политически (743) | politically |
| политический (208) | political |
| полностью (95) | completely, entirely, fully, totally |
| полный (62) | full, complete, total, thorough |
| половой (213) | sexual, genital |
| положительно (645) | positively |
| положительный (216) | positive, affirmative |
| полый (523) | hollow |
| полярный (638) | polar |
| понятный (625) | understandable, foolproof |
| популярный (235) | popular |
| поровну (485) | equally |
| порочный (457) | vicious |
| портативный (786) | portable |
| последний (13) | last, final |
| последовательный (479) | consistent, coherent, successive, consecutive |
| поспешный (726) | hasty |
| посредственный (977) | mediocre, middling |
| постепенно (580) | gradually |
| постоянно (352) | constantly, perpetually |

| | |
|---|---|
| потенциально (615) | potentially |
| потенциальный (269) | potential |
| потертый (942) | shabby |
| потный (578) | sweaty |
| потрясающий (258) | terrific, fabulous, breathtaking, fab |
| похожий (251) | similar |
| почетный (471) | honorable, honorary, honourable |
| почти (56) | almost, nearly |
| почтительно (858) | respectfully |
| почтительный (787) | respectful, dutiful |
| почтовый (891) | postal |
| поэтический (735) | poetic |
| правдивый (887) | truthful |
| правдоподобно (1030) | believable |
| правдоподобный (987) | plausible |
| праведный (566) | righteous |
| правовой (196) | legal |
| праздничный (950) | festive, celebratory |
| праздный (653) | idle, gossipy |
| практически (282) | practically |
| практический (396) | practical |
| превосходный (159) | excellent, superb, tiptop |
| превратно (1040) | wrongly |
| преданный (312) | loyal |
| предварительный (628) | preliminary |
| преднамеренный (779) | deliberate, judgmental |
| предпочтительно (827) | preferably |
| предсказуемый (718) | predictable |
| предыдущий (325) | previous |
| преждевременный (759) | premature, precocious |

| | |
|---|---|
| прекрасный (39) | beautiful, lovely |
| престижный (992) | prestigious |
| прибыльный (771) | profitable, lucrative |
| привлекательный (286) | attractive, lovable, catchy, likeable |
| придирчивый (854) | picky, cantankerous |
| приличный (223) | decent |
| примерный (1094) | exemplary, approximate |
| примитивный (541) | primitive |
| притязательный (929) | pretentious |
| причудливый (193) | fancy, quaint, whimsical, freaky |
| приятный (18) | nice, pleasant |
| приятным (940) | enjoyable |
| провинциальный (973) | provincial |
| провокационный (1095) | provocative |
| прогрессивный (835) | progressive |
| продуктивный (788) | productive |
| прозрачный (825) | transparent |
| проклятый (151) | goddamn, damnedest, accursed |
| прославленный (1046) | illustrious |
| просто (2) | just, simply, merely |
| простой (103) | simple, plain, mere, idle |
| протестантский (920) | protestant |
| профессионально (818) | professionally |
| профессиональный (201) | professional, occupational, vocational |
| прохладный (61) | cool |
| прочувствованный (1096) | heartfelt |
| прямой (87) | straight, direct, straightforward |
| пряный (568) | spicy |

| | |
|---|---|
| психиатрический (592) | psychiatric |
| психологически (1098) | psychologically |
| психологический (483) | psychological |
| психотический (666) | psychotic |
| публично (655) | publicly |
| пуленепробиваемый (845) | bulletproof |
| пунктуальный (1020) | punctual |
| пустой (147) | empty, blank, null |
| пухленький (1022) | crummy |
| пушистый (680) | fuzzy, furry, fluffy, bushy |
| пыльный (596) | dusty |
| пышный (1038) | lush, opulent |
| пьяный (522) | drunken, boozy, tipsy, woozy |
| равнодушный (879) | indifferent, unconcerned, apathetic |
| равный (311) | equal |
| радикальный (516) | radical, drastic |
| радиоактивный (704) | radioactive |
| радостный (79) | glad, joyful, joyous |
| развязный (691) | cheeky |
| различный (48) | different, various |
| размыто (1061) | blurry |
| разнообразный (1086) | diverse, miscellaneous |
| разрушительный (713) | destructive, disruptive |
| разумно (915) | reasonably, sensibly |
| разумный (309) | reasonable, sensible |
| расистский (484) | racist |
| расовый (785) | racial |
| расплывчатый (644) | vague, muzzy |
| распутная (917) | slutty |
| рациональный (569) | rational |
| реалистичный (571) | realistic |

| | |
|---|---|
| реальный (28) | real |
| ревнивый (174) | jealous |
| революционный (468) | revolutionary |
| региональный (679) | regional |
| регулярно (584) | regularly |
| регулярный (218) | regular |
| редакционный (954) | editorial |
| редкий (240) | rare, uncommon |
| резкий (249) | sharp, harsh, abrupt, edgy |
| религиозный (294) | religious, devotional |
| респектабельный (514) | respectable |
| респираторный (924) | respiratory |
| республиканский (591) | republican |
| рехнувшийся (967) | nutty, dippy |
| решающий (475) | crucial, decisive, conclusive |
| решительный (810) | decisive, resolute, drastic |
| ржавый (395) | rusty |
| рискованный (428) | risky, touchy, dicey |
| ритмичный (948) | rhythmic |
| робкий (970) | timid |
| ровно (45) | exactly |
| родной (350) | native |
| родовой (1047) | ancestral |
| розовый (257) | pink, rosy |
| романтический (204) | romantic |
| роскошный (1002) | luxurious, deluxe, princely |
| румяный (884) | rosy, ruddy |
| рыбный (673) | fishy |
| с завязанными глазами (947) | blindfold |
| с разбитым сердцем (867) | heartbroken |
| садистский (1072) | sadistic |

| | |
|---|---|
| самодовольный (797) | smug, complacent, conceited, huffy |
| самый старший (609) | eldest |
| саркастический (769) | sarcastic |
| свадебный (757) | bridal, nuptial |
| сварливый (715) | grumpy, contentious, cantankerous, quarrelsome |
| свежий (148) | fresh, crisp, breezy |
| сверхъестественный (617) | supernatural, uncanny |
| световой (65) | light |
| свободный (190) | loose, spare |
| своеобразный (550) | peculiar |
| святой (132) | holy, saintly, sainted |
| сдержанный (562) | discreet, reticent |
| северный (378) | northern |
| секретный (86) | secret |
| сельский (813) | rural, arcadian |
| сельскохозяйственный (951) | agricultural |
| сенсационный (703) | sensational |
| сентиментальный (490) | sentimental, maudlin, slushy, hokey |
| сердечный (995) | hearty, cordial, cardiac |
| сердитый (114) | angry |
| серебряный (202) | silver |
| серийный (343) | serial |
| серый (307) | gray, grey |
| серьезно (102) | seriously, gravely |
| серьезный (75) | serious, grave, severe |
| сильнодействующий (969) | potent |
| сильный (92) | strong, intense, severe, potent |
| символический (775) | symbolic |
| синий (97) | blue |

| | |
|---|---|
| синтетический (791) | synthetic |
| сияющий (930) | radiant |
| скалистый (364) | rocky, craggy |
| скандальный (1013) | scandalous |
| скептический (1014) | skeptical |
| склонный (1054) | apt |
| скользкий (612) | slippery |
| скромный (495) | modest, humble, lowly, coy |
| скрытный (905) | secretive, reticent, cagey |
| скупой (883) | stingy |
| слабо (1071) | weakly |
| слабый (422) | faint, weak, mild |
| славный (423) | glorious |
| сладкий (82) | sweet, sugary |
| слегка (317) | slightly, lightly |
| следующий (25) | next |
| слепой (162) | blind |
| слизистый (870) | slimy |
| словесный (876) | verbal, wordy |
| сложный (302) | complex, elaborate, intricate, tricky |
| случайно (418) | accidentally, coincidentally, perchance |
| случайный (515) | casual, random, accidental, incidental |
| слышный (774) | audible |
| смелый (426) | bold, courageous, audacious |
| смертельный (354) | deadly, mortal, fatal, lethal |
| смертный (446) | mortal |
| смешной (67) | funny, ridiculous |
| смиренно (903) | humbly |
| смутный (831) | obscure, hazy |
| снаружи (64) | outside |

| | |
|---|---|
| собственный (24) | own |
| советский (359) | soviet |
| совместимый (910) | compatible |
| современный (224) | modern, contemporary |
| сознательный (486) | conscious, conscientious |
| солевой (946) | saline |
| соленый (672) | salty, briny |
| солнечный (393) | sunny, solar |
| сонный (444) | sleepy |
| соответственно (853) | accordingly, suitably |
| соответствующие (493) | relevant |
| соответствующий (349) | appropriate, relevant |
| сострадательный (914) | compassionate |
| социалистический (687) | socialist |
| социальный (182) | social, societal |
| сочный (622) | juicy, succulent |
| спелый (629) | ripe |
| специально (587) | specially, expressly |
| специальный (74) | special |
| специфический (283) | specific, peculiar |
| спинной (686) | spinal |
| спонтанный (690) | spontaneous |
| спорный (765) | controversial, moot, contentious, argumentative |
| спортивный (697) | athletic, sporty |
| способный (222) | capable, apt |
| справедливо (855) | rightly, rightfully |
| спящий (154) | asleep, dormant |
| средневековый (640) | medieval |
| средний (104) | middle, average, intermediate, middling |
| срочный (266) | urgent |

| | |
|---|---|
| стабильный (322) | stable |
| стандартный (288) | standard |
| старческий (939) | senile |
| старший (245) | senior |
| старый (16) | old |
| статический (459) | static |

| | |
|---|---|
| стерильный (875) | sterile |
| стильный (911) | stylish, nifty |
| стоящий (698) | worthwhile |
| странно (585) | strangely |
| странный (91) | strange, odd, weird, bizarre |
| страстный (456) | passionate, ardent, impassioned |
| стратегический (674) | strategic |
| страшный (98) | terrible, scary, fearsome, grisly |
| стрессовый (693) | stressful |
| строгий (593) | stern, strict, rigorous, stringent |
| строго (425) | strictly, rigorously |
| структурный (1010) | structural |
| суверенный (746) | sovereign |
| судебный (535) | forensic, judicial |
| суеверный (783) | superstitious |
| суетливый (1001) | fussy, fidgety |
| сумасшедший (44) | crazy, mad |
| супер (175) | super |
| супружеский (874) | marital, matrimonial, conjugal, spousal |
| сурово (654) | severely |
| суровый (405) | harsh, stern, severe, dour |

| | |
|---|---|
| суррогатный (990) | surrogate |
| счастливо (347) | happily |
| счастливый (31) | happy, lucky |
| съедобный (941) | edible |
| сырный (795) | cheesy |
| сюрреалистичный (1089) | surreal |
| таинственный (284) | mysterious |
| тайно (441) | secretly |
| так (1) | so |
| такой (32) | such |
| тактичный (728) | considerate |
| твердый (261) | solid, crusty, steadfast |
| творческий (367) | creative |
| театральный (923) | theatrical |
| телесный (919) | bodily, corporeal |
| тенистый (699) | shady |
| теоретический (953) | theoretical |
| тепловой (799) | thermal |
| терпеливо (1031) | patiently |
| тесно (391) | closely, intimately |
| технически (323) | technically |
| технический (437) | technical |
| типичный (330) | typical |
| титанический (710) | titanic |
| тихий (84) | quiet, silent, pacific |
| токсичный (501) | toxic |
| толстый (308) | thick, porky |
| тонкий (260) | thin, delicate, slender, slim |
| торжественный (760) | solemn, ceremonial |
| тоскующий по дому (961) | homesick |
| точный (242) | exact, precise, accurate |
| тошнотворный (872) | nauseous |

| | |
|---|---|
| травматический (740) | traumatic |
| травяной (890) | herbal |
| трагически (1058) | tragically |
| трагический (363) | tragic |
| традиционный (383) | traditional, conventional |
| тревожный (355) | anxious, worrisome, suspenseful |
| трезвый (376) | sober |
| третий (122) | third |
| тройной (460) | triple, triplicate |
| тропический (643) | tropical |
| троянский (1057) | trojan |
| трусливый (705) | cowardly, craven, dastardly |
| туманный (896) | misty, hazy, foggy |
| тусклый (688) | dim, fishy |
| тщательный (557) | thorough, meticulous, rigorous, scrupulous |
| тщеславный (416) | vain, conceited |
| тяжелый (156) | heavy, severe, grievous |
| убедительный (934) | persuasive, conclusive |
| убийственный (965) | murderous, homicidal |
| увлеченный (415) | keen |
| уголовный (171) | criminal, penal |
| удаленно (725) | remotely |
| удаленный (333) | remote, outlying |
| удачливый (83) | lucky, weirdly |
| удачный (448) | fortunate |
| удивительно (607) | surprisingly, amazingly, astonishingly |
| удобно (856) | comfortably, conveniently |
| удовлетворительный (857) | satisfactory |
| уединенный (597) | solitary |

| | |
|---|---|
| узкий (412) | narrow, parochial |
| уклончивый (1034) | evasive |
| умеренный (1080) | moderate, temperate |
| умный (113) | smart, clever, intelligent |
| умственно (489) | mentally |
| умственный (254) | mental |
| умышленно (751) | intentionally, willfully |
| универсальный (536) | universal |
| уникальный (268) | unique |
| унылый (410) | dull, godforsaken, despondent, dumpy |
| упорядоченный (701) | orderly |
| упрямый (320) | stubborn, obstinate, headstrong |
| уродливый (179) | ugly, misshapen |
| успешно (599) | successfully |
| успешный (241) | successful |
| устарелый (1037) | obsolete, antiquated, passe |
| устойчивый (273) | steady, steadfast |
| утвердительный (663) | affirmative |
| утомительный (943) | tedious |
| утомленный (665) | weary |
| уязвимый (399) | vulnerable |
| фактический (263) | actual, factual |
| фальшивый (537) | phony, phoney, pseudo, hokey |
| фармацевтический (847) | pharmaceutical |
| фатальный (443) | fatal |
| фашистский (642) | fascist |
| федеральный (253) | federal |
| феноменальный (790) | phenomenal |
| физически (394) | physically |

| | |
|---|---|
| физический (220) | physical |
| философский (1007) | philosophical |
| финансовый (290) | financial, fiscal |
| фиолетовый (403) | purple |
| формально (798) | formally |
| формальный (427) | formal |
| фотографический (1029) | photographic |
| французский (129) | french |
| фронтальный (955) | frontal |
| фундаментальный (581) | fundamental |
| функциональный (885) | functional |
| хаотичный (838) | chaotic |
| химический (357) | chemical |
| хирургический (563) | surgical |
| хитроумный (989) | dodgy |
| хитрый (667) | sly, cunning, shifty, devious |
| холодно (636) | chilly, coldly |
| холодный (80) | cold, chilly |
| хорошенький (33) | pretty |
| храбро (937) | bravely, gallantly |
| хромой (369) | lame |
| хронический (722) | chronic |
| хрупкий (472) | fragile, frail, brittle |
| художественный (547) | artistic |
| цвета буйволовой кожи (752) | buff |
| целый (34) | whole |
| ценный (296) | valuable |
| центральный (221) | central, focal, pivotal |
| церебральный (863) | cerebral |
| церемониальный (1050) | ceremonial |
| циничный (707) | cynical, bitchy |

| | |
|---|---|
| цифровой (499) | digital |
| частично (651) | partly, partially |
| частичный (589) | partial |
| частный (126) | private, proprietary |
| часто (123) | often, frequently, oft |
| частый (732) | frequent |
| черный (69) | black |
| честный (124) | honest |
| четвертый (236) | fourth |
| четкий (738) | crisp, legible |
| чистый (90) | clean, pure, neat, sheer |
| чрезвычайно (227) | extremely, immensely, tremendously, grossly |
| чрезмерный (685) | excessive, undue, inordinate |
| чувственный (994) | sensual, voluptuous, sensuous, carnal |
| чувствительный (270) | sensitive, susceptible |
| чудесно (826) | wonderfully, marvelously |
| чудный (544) | marvellous |
| чудовищный (745) | monstrous, prodigious, whopping |
| чужой (243) | alien |
| шаткий (803) | shaky, wobbly, wonky |
| шикарный (777) | chic, posh, swanky |
| широкий (239) | wide, broad |
| широко (958) | widely, extensively |
| штормовой (935) | stormy |
| шумный (528) | noisy, rowdy, tumultuous |
| щедрый (292) | generous, prodigal, bountiful |
| эволюционный (981) | evolutionary, developmental |
| эгоистичный (285) | selfish |
| эквивалентный (660) | equivalent |
| экзотический (526) | exotic |

| | |
|---|---|
| экономический (450) | economic, economical |
| эксклюзивный (455) | exclusive |
| экспериментальный (657) | experimental |
| экстравагантный (1018) | extravagant |
| экстраординарный (259) | extraordinary |
| экстремальный (319) | extreme |
| эксцентричный (763) | eccentric |
| элегантный (458) | elegant, genteel |
| электрический (313) | electric, electrical |
| электромагнитный (830) | electromagnetic |
| электронный (421) | electronic |
| элементарный (588) | elementary, rudimentary |
| элитный (510) | elite |
| эмоционально (505) | emotionally |
| эмоциональный (256) | emotional |
| энергичный (918) | energetic, snappy, feisty, punchy |
| эпический (556) | epic |
| этический (824) | ethical |
| эффективно (723) | effectively |
| эффективное (527) | efficient |
| эффективный (366) | effective, efficient |
| эффектный (466) | spectacular |
| южный (339) | southern, southerly |
| ядерный (279) | nuclear |
| ядовитый (577) | poisonous, noxious, venomous, virulent |
| яркий (191) | bright, vivid, flamboyant |
| яростно (912) | violently, ferociously |
| ясный (68) | clear |

# 3. Index of Words (English)

| | |
|---|---|
| abdominal | 901. брюшной |
| able | 57. в состоянии |
| abnormal | 700. аномальный, 186. ненормальный |
| abominable | 610. гнусный |
| aboriginal | 164. местный |
| above | 4. выше |
| abrupt | 249. резкий |
| absent | 623. отсутствующий |
| absolute | 326. абсолютный |
| abstract | 881. абстрактный |
| absurd | 375. абсурдный |
| abusive | 882. оскорбительный |
| academic | 637. академический |
| accessible | 1073. доступной, 226. доступный |
| accidental | 515. случайный |
| accidentally | 418. случайно |
| accordingly | 853. соответственно |
| accountable | 897. подотчетный |
| accurate | 242. точный |
| accursed | 151. проклятый |
| acoustic | 1090. акустический, 600. звуковой |
| active | 342. активный |
| actively | 1076. активно |
| actual | 263. фактический |
| actually | 5. действительно |
| additional | 155. дополнительный |
| adequate | 871. адекватный, 548. достаточный |

| | |
|---|---|
| administrative | 907. административный |
| admirable | 210. восхитительный, 89. замечательный |
| adorable | 210. восхитительный, 398. обожаемый |
| adventurous | 1005. авантюрный |
| aerial | 823. воздушный |
| affirmative | 216. положительный, 663. утвердительный |
| affordable | 226. доступный |
| afghan | 921. афганский |
| aggressive | 406. агрессивный |
| agricultural | 951. сельскохозяйственный |
| alcoholic | 500. алкогольный |
| alien | 243. чужой |
| alike | 382. одинаково |
| almighty | 442. всемогущий |
| almost | 56. почти |
| aloud | 864. вслух |
| alternative | 411. альтернативный |
| amazingly | 607. удивительно |
| amok | 1027. неистовый |
| amoral | 758. аморальный |
| ample | 548. достаточный |
| anal | 802. анальный |
| ancestral | 1047. родовой |
| ancient | 183. древний |
| ancillary | 983. вспомогательный |
| angry | 114. сердитый |
| annual | 470. ежегодный |
| anomalous | 700. аномальный, 186. ненормальный |
| anonymous | 402. анонимный |

| | |
|---|---|
| answerable | 160. ответственный, 897. подотчетный |
| antiquated | 1037. устарелый |
| anxious | 355. тревожный |
| anymore | 54. больше не |
| apathetic | 879. равнодушный |
| apparent | 200. очевидный |
| appreciative | 225. благодарный |
| appropriate | 349. соответствующий |
| approximate | 1094. примерный |
| apt | 1054. склонный, 222. способный |
| arcadian | 813. сельский |
| ardent | 456. страстный |
| argumentative | 765. спорный |
| armored | 762. бронированный |
| arrogant | 453. высокомерный |
| artificial | 521. искусственный |
| artistic | 547. художественный |
| asleep | 154. спящий |
| astonishingly | 607. удивительно |
| astray | 878. заблудившись |
| athletic | 697. спортивный |
| atomic | 559. атомный |
| atrocious | 567. отвратительный |
| attentive | 1097. внимательный |
| attractive | 286. привлекательный |
| audacious | 426. смелый |
| audible | 774. слышный |
| audio | 600. звуковой |
| authentic | 576. аутентичный, 424. подлинный |
| automatic | 496. автоматический |

| | |
|---|---|
| automatically | 618. автоматически |
| auxiliary | 983. вспомогательный, 155. дополнительный |
| available | 226. доступный |
| average | 104. средний |
| averse | 809. неохотный |
| avid | 454. жадный |
| awesome | 146. классно |
| awfully | 7. очень |
| awkward | 314. неудобный |
| bad | 23. плохой |
| bald | 434. лысый |
| ballistic | 1043. баллистический |
| ballsy | 960. напористый |
| barbaric | 1026. варварский |
| barbarous | 1026. варварский |
| barren | 782. бесплодный |
| basal | 165. основной |
| basic | 303. базовый, 165. основной |
| bawdy | 843. непристойный |
| beautiful | 39. прекрасный |
| beautifully | 503. красиво |
| beefy | 991. мускулистый |
| beforehand | 816. заранее |
| behind | 55. позади |
| belated | 821. запоздалый |
| believable | 205. вероятный, 1030. правдоподобно |
| beneficial | 1023. выгодный |
| best | 27. лучший |
| better | 14. лучше |
| biblical | 836. библейский |

| | |
|---|---|
| big | 17. большой |
| binary | 150. двойной |
| biological | 477. биологический |
| bitchy | 1067. озлобленный, 707. циничный |
| bitter | 338. горький |
| bizarre | 91. странный |
| black | 69. черный |
| blank | 147. пустой |
| blind | 162. слепой |
| blindfold | 947. с завязанными глазами |
| blond | 467. белокурый |
| bloody | 125. кровавый |
| blue | 97. синий |
| blurry | 1061. размыто |
| bodily | 919. телесный |
| bogus | 756. поддельный |
| boisterous | 1027. неистовый |
| bold | 426. смелый |
| bonny | 219. здоровый |
| boozy | 522. пьяный |
| borderline | 1085. пограничный |
| bossy | 1009. выпуклый |
| bountiful | 292. щедрый |
| bourgeois | 731. буржуазный |
| brash | 664. дерзкий |
| bravely | 937. храбро |
| breathtaking | 1100. захватывающий, 258. потрясающий |
| breezy | 148. свежий |
| bridal | 757. свадебный |
| brief | 105. короткий |

| | |
|---|---|
| briefly | 661. кратко |
| bright | 191. яркий |
| brilliant | 481. блестящий |
| briny | 672. соленый |
| brisk | 565. оживленный |
| brittle | 472. хрупкий |
| broad | 239. широкий |
| brown | 178. коричневый |
| brutal | 512. жестокий |
| brutish | 512. жестокий |
| buff | 752. цвета буйволовой кожи |
| bulletproof | 845. пуленепробиваемый |
| bushy | 680. пушистый |
| busy | 94. занятой |
| butch | 650. мужеподобная |
| cagey | 905. скрытный |
| candid | 473. искренний |
| candidly | 291. откровенно |
| cantankerous | 854. придирчивый, 715. сварливый |
| capable | 222. способный |
| capitalist | 931. капиталистический |
| capitalistic | 931. капиталистический |
| capricious | 781. капризный |
| cardiac | 676. кардиальный, 995. сердечный |
| carefree | 926. беззаботный |
| careful | 85. осторожный |
| carefully | 206. внимательно |
| carnal | 994. чувственный |
| casual | 515. случайный |
| cataclysmic | 849. катастрофический |

| | |
|---|---|
| catastrophic | 849. катастрофический |
| catchy | 1079. заковыристый, 286. привлекательный |
| caucasian | 908. кавказский |
| cautious | 85. осторожный |
| celebratory | 950. праздничный |
| cellular | 862. клеточный |
| central | 221. центральный |
| cerebral | 863. церебральный |
| ceremonial | 760. торжественный, 1050. церемониальный |
| certain | 112. определенный |
| certifiable | 88. безумный, 186. ненормальный |
| chaotic | 838. хаотичный |
| cheeky | 691. развязный |
| cheerful | 561. веселый |
| cheesy | 795. сырный |
| chemical | 357. химический |
| chic | 777. шикарный |
| childish | 524. детский |
| childlike | 524. детский |
| chilly | 636. холодно, 80. холодный |
| chronic | 722. хронический |
| circumstantial | 925. обстоятельный |
| civil | 277. гражданский |
| classic | 289. классический |
| classical | 289. классический |
| classy | 554. классный |
| clean | 90. чистый |
| clear | 68. ясный |
| clerical | 390. духовный |

| | |
|---|---|
| clever | 113. умный |
| clinical | 702. клинический |
| close | 50. близко |
| closely | 206. внимательно, 391. тесно |
| cloudy | 898. облачный |
| clumsy | 538. неуклюжий |
| coarse | 198. грубый |
| cocky | 664. дерзкий |
| coherent | 479. последовательный |
| coincidentally | 418. случайно |
| cold | 80. холодный |
| coldly | 636. холодно |
| collective | 632. коллективный |
| colorful | 741. красочный |
| colossal | 913. колоссальный |
| colourful | 741. красочный |
| comfortable | 177. комфортный |
| comfortably | 856. удобно |
| comic | 388. комический |
| comical | 388. комический |
| commercial | 328. коммерческий |
| common | 161. общий |
| communist | 407. коммунистический |
| compact | 1055. компактный |
| comparatively | 634. относительно |
| compassionate | 914. сострадательный |
| compatible | 910. совместимый |
| competent | 773. компетентный |
| competitive | 586. конкурентоспособный |
| complacent | 797. самодовольный |
| complete | 62. полный |

| | |
|---|---|
| completely | 95. полностью |
| complex | 302. сложный |
| comprehensive | 1092. всесторонний |
| compulsory | 770. обязательный |
| conceited | 797. самодовольный, 416. тщеславный |
| conclusive | 142. окончательный, 475. решающий, 934. убедительный |
| concrete | 212. конкретный |
| confidential | 488. конфиденциальный |
| congressional | 1052. относящийся к конгрессу |
| conjugal | 874. супружеский |
| conscientious | 486. сознательный |
| conscious | 486. сознательный |
| consecutive | 479. последовательный |
| conservative | 630. консервативный |
| considerable | 413. значительный |
| considerate | 1097. внимательный, 728. тактичный |
| consistent | 479. последовательный |
| constantly | 352. постоянно |
| constitutional | 927. конституционный |
| constructive | 1074. конструктивный |
| contagious | 684. заразительный |
| contemporary | 224. современный |
| contentious | 715. сварливый, 765. спорный |
| continental | 804. континентальный |
| continuously | 922. непрерывно |
| controversial | 765. спорный |
| conveniently | 856. удобно |

| | |
|---|---|
| conventional | 383. традиционный |
| cool | 61. прохладный |
| cordial | 995. сердечный |
| corny | 832. заскорузлый |
| corporate | 414. корпоративный |
| corporeal | 919. телесный |
| correct | 10. верный |
| cosmetic | 1091. косметический |
| cosmic | 560. космический |
| costly | 603. дорого, 997. дорогостоящий |
| counterfeit | 756. поддельный |
| courageous | 426. смелый |
| courteous | 373. вежливый |
| cowardly | 705. трусливый |
| coy | 265. застенчивый, 495. скромный |
| crackerjack | 554. классный |
| crafty | 761. коварный |
| craggy | 364. скалистый |
| cranky | 781. капризный |
| crappy | 543. дерьмовый |
| craven | 705. трусливый |
| crazily | 719. безумно |
| crazy | 44. сумасшедший |
| creative | 367. творческий |
| credible | 205. вероятный, 814. заслуживающий доверия |
| creepy | 336. жутко |
| criminal | 171. уголовный |
| crimson | 964. малиновый |
| crisp | 148. свежий, 738. четкий |

| | |
|---|---|
| crispy | 932. кудрявый |
| critical | 351. критический |
| crucial | 475. решающий |
| crudely | 606. грубо |
| cruel | 512. жестокий |
| crummy | 567. отвратительный, 1022. пухленький |
| crusty | 261. твердый |
| culinary | 999. кулинарный |

| | |
|---|---|
| culpable | 145. виновный |
| cultural | 482. культурный |
| cunning | 667. хитрый |
| curious | 229. любопытный |
| cursory | 805. поверхностный |
| cute | 131. милый |
| cutesy | 131. милый |
| cynical | 707. циничный |
| daft | 734. бесшабашный |
| daily | 264. ежедневный |
| dainty | 646. изысканный, 886. изящный |
| damnedest | 151. проклятый |
| danish | 633. датский |
| dastardly | 705. трусливый |
| deadly | 354. смертельный |
| deaf | 310. глухой |
| dear | 49. дорогой |
| dearly | 603. дорого |
| decent | 223. приличный |
| decisive | 475. решающий, 810. решительный |

| | |
|---|---|
| deep | 111. глубоко |
| deeply | 111. глубоко |
| defective | 1012. неполноценный |
| defensive | 517. защитный, 540. оборонительный |
| definite | 112. определенный |
| definitely | 99. определенно |
| definitive | 142. окончательный |
| deliberate | 779. преднамеренный |
| delicate | 370. деликатный, 299. нежный, 260. тонкий |
| delicious | 210. восхитительный |
| delightful | 210. восхитительный |
| delirious | 909. бредовый |
| delusional | 909. бредовый |
| deluxe | 1002. роскошный |
| democratic | 545. демократический |
| dense | 167. плотный |
| densely | 717. плотно |
| dental | 564. зубной |
| dependable | 255. надежный |
| desirous | 329. жаждущий |
| desperate | 234. отчаянный |
| despondent | 410. унылый |
| destructive | 713. разрушительный |
| developmental | 981. эволюционный |
| devious | 1008. окольный, 667. хитрый |
| devotional | 294. религиозный |
| diabetic | 968. диабетический |
| diagnostic | 1028. диагностический |
| dicey | 428. рискованный |
| different | 48. различный |

| | |
|---|---|
| digital | 499. цифровой |
| dim | 688. тусклый |
| dinky | 886. изящный |
| diplomatic | 598. дипломатический |
| dippy | 967. рехнувшийся |
| direct | 87. прямой |
| dirty | 136. грязный |
| disciplinary | 959. дисциплинарный |
| discreet | 85. осторожный, 562. сдержанный |
| disgraceful | 670. позорный |
| dishonorable | 670. позорный |
| disposable | 1033. одноразовый |
| disreputable | 670. позорный |
| disrespectful | 789. непочтительный |
| disruptive | 713. разрушительный |
| distant | 297. далекий, 46. дальний |
| distasteful | 244. неприятный |
| distinct | 711. отчетливый |
| distinctive | 868. отличительный |
| distraught | 1083. обезумевший |
| diverse | 1086. разнообразный |
| divine | 327. божественный |
| dodgy | 989. хитроумный |
| domestic | 362. внутренний |
| dominant | 793. доминирующий |
| dormant | 1068. дремлющий, 154. спящий |
| double | 150. двойной |
| dour | 405. суровый |
| downstairs | 199. внизу |
| dramatic | 295. драматический |

| | |
|---|---|
| drastic | 712. крутой, 516. радикальный, 810. решительный |
| drunken | 522. пьяный |
| dual | 150. двойной |
| due | 166. должный |
| dull | 410. унылый |
| dumpy | 410. унылый |
| dusty | 596. пыльный |
| dutiful | 787. почтительный |
| dynamic | 624. динамический |
| earthbound | 776. земной |
| earthly | 776. земной |
| eccentric | 763. эксцентричный |
| ecclesiastical | 390. духовный |
| economic | 450. экономический |
| economical | 450. экономический |
| ecstatic | 739. восторженный |
| edgy | 249. резкий |
| edible | 941. съедобный |
| editorial | 954. редакционный |
| educational | 721. образовательный |
| eerie | 749. жуткий |
| effective | 366. эффективный |
| effectively | 723. эффективно |
| efficient | 527. эффективное, 366. эффективный |
| elaborate | 302. сложный |
| elderly | 579. пожилой |
| eldest | 609. самый старший |
| electric | 313. электрический |
| electrical | 313. электрический |

| | |
|---|---|
| electromagnetic | 830. электромагнитный |
| electronic | 421. электронный |
| elegant | 458. элегантный |
| elementary | 588. элементарный |
| eligible | 464. подходящий |
| elite | 510. элитный |
| elusive | 928. неуловимый |
| elvish | 360. волшебный |
| eminent | 748. видный, 508. выдающийся |
| emotional | 256. эмоциональный |
| emotionally | 505. эмоционально |
| empty | 147. пустой |
| endlessly | 1025. бесконечно |
| energetic | 918. энергичный |
| english | 120. английский |
| enjoyable | 940. приятным |
| enormous | 135. огромный |
| enough | 21. достаточно |
| enthusiastic | 739. восторженный |
| entirely | 95. полностью |
| envious | 869. завистливый |
| epic | 556. эпический |
| equal | 311. равный |
| equally | 485. поровну |
| equivalent | 660. эквивалентный |
| erratic | 525. неустойчивый |
| especially | 128. особенно |
| eternal | 331. вечный |
| ethical | 824. этический |
| evasive | 1034. уклончивый |
| everlasting | 331. вечный |

| | |
|---|---|
| evident | 200. очевидный |
| evidentiary | 200. очевидный |
| evil | 133. злой |
| evolutionary | 981. эволюционный |
| exact | 242. точный |
| exactly | 45. ровно |
| excellent | 159. превосходный |
| exceptional | 614. исключительный |
| excessive | 685. чрезмерный |
| exclusive | 455. эксклюзивный |
| exclusively | 822. исключительно |
| exemplary | 1094. примерный |
| exotic | 526. экзотический |
| expansive | 371. обширный |
| expensive | 194. дорогие, 49. дорогой |
| experimental | 657. экспериментальный |
| exploratory | 971. исследовательский |
| explosive | 498. взрывной |
| expressly | 587. специально |
| exquisite | 646. изысканный |
| extensive | 371. обширный |
| extensively | 958. широко |
| extinct | 720. вымерший |
| extra | 155. дополнительный |
| extraordinary | 259. экстраординарный |
| extraterrestrial | 708. внеземной |
| extravagant | 1018. экстравагантный |
| extreme | 319. экстремальный |
| extremely | 7. очень, 227. чрезвычайно |
| fab | 258. потрясающий |
| fabulous | 258. потрясающий |
| facetious | 829. остроумный |

| | |
|---|---|
| factual | 263. фактический |
| faint | 422. слабый |
| faithful | 10. верный |
| false | 228. ложный |
| famous | 157. знаменитый |
| fancy | 193. причудливый |
| far | 46. дальний |
| fascist | 642. фашистский |
| fashionable | 850. модный |
| fast | 109. быстро, 81. быстрый |
| fatal | 354. смертельный, 443. фатальный |
| fatty | 552. жировой |
| favorite | 149. любимый |
| favourite | 149. любимый |
| fearsome | 768. грозный, 98. страшный |
| federal | 253. федеральный |
| feisty | 960. напористый, 918. энергичный |
| female | 180. женский |
| feminine | 180. женский, 648. женственный |
| ferociously | 912. яростно |
| fertile | 796. плодородный |
| festive | 950. праздничный |
| few | 37. немногие |
| fidgety | 1075. беспокойный, 1001. суетливый |
| fierce | 512. жестокий |
| filthy | 136. грязный |
| final | 142. окончательный, 13. последний |
| financial | 290. финансовый |

| first | 11. первый |
|---|---|
| fiscal | 290. финансовый |
| fishy | 280. подозрительный, 673. рыбный, 688. тусклый |
| flamboyant | 191. яркий |
| flashy | 1084. кричащий |
| flat | 185. плоский |
| fleeting | 963. мимолетный |
| flexible | 737. гибкий |
| flighty | 750. ветреный |
| flippant | 979. легкомысленный |
| fluently | 681. плавно |
| fluffy | 680. пушистый |
| focal | 221. центральный |
| foggy | 896. туманный |
| foolhardy | 234. отчаянный |
| foolish | 59. глупый |
| foolproof | 625. понятный |
| foreign | 203. иностранный |
| forensic | 535. судебный |
| forever | 100. навсегда |
| formal | 215. официальный, 427. формальный |
| formally | 301. официально, 798. формально |
| former | 232. бывший |
| formidable | 768. грозный |
| forthwith | 137. немедленно |
| fortunate | 448. удачный |
| fortunately | 432. к счастью |
| fourth | 236. четвертый |
| foxy | 1062. лисий |

| | |
|---|---|
| fragile | 472. хрупкий |
| frail | 472. хрупкий |
| frank | 101. откровенный |
| frankly | 291. откровенно |
| frantic | 1027. неистовый |
| freakish | 781. капризный |
| freaky | 909. бредовый, 193. причудливый |
| free | 58. бесплатно |
| french | 129. французский |
| frequent | 732. частый |
| frequently | 123. часто |
| fresh | 15. новый, 148. свежий |
| friendly | 247. дружественный |
| frisky | 985. игривый |
| frivolous | 979. легкомысленный |
| front | 60. передний |
| frontal | 955. фронтальный |
| frosty | 1044. морозный |
| full | 62. полный |
| fully | 95. полностью |
| functional | 885. функциональный |
| fundamental | 581. фундаментальный |
| funny | 67. смешной |
| furry | 680. пушистый |
| fussy | 1001. суетливый |
| futile | 842. бесполезный |
| fuzzy | 680. пушистый |
| gaily | 1056. весело |
| galactic | 975. галактический |
| gallant | 841. галантный |
| gallantly | 937. храбро |

| | |
|---|---|
| gauche | 538. неуклюжий |
| general | 93. общая |
| generally | 138. обычно |
| generous | 292. щедрый |
| genetic | 436. генетический |
| genital | 213. половой |
| genteel | 276. благородный, 458. элегантный |
| gentle | 192. мягкий, 299. нежный |
| gently | 372. нежно |
| genuine | 424. подлинный |
| geological | 1032. геологический |
| german | 163. немецкий |
| giant | 209. гигантский |
| giddy | 979. легкомысленный |
| gigantic | 209. гигантский |
| glacial | 736. ледяной |
| glad | 79. радостный |
| global | 353. глобальный |
| gloomy | 631. мрачный |
| glorious | 250. великолепный, 423. славный |
| glum | 631. мрачный |
| goddamn | 151. проклятый |
| godforsaken | 310. глухой, 410. унылый |
| godlike | 327. божественный |
| godly | 327. божественный |
| gold | 116. золотой |
| golden | 214. золотистый, 116. золотой |
| gooey | 553. липкий |
| gorgeous | 250. великолепный |
| gossipy | 653. праздный |

| | |
|---|---|
| graceful | 886. изящный |
| gracious | 520. милостивый |
| graciously | 420. любезно |
| gradually | 580. постепенно |
| grand | 12. великий, 139. грандиозный |
| grandiose | 139. грандиозный |
| graphic | 834. графический |
| grateful | 225. благодарный |
| grave | 75. серьезный |
| gravely | 102. серьезно |

| | |
|---|---|
| gravitational | 846. гравитационный |
| gray | 307. серый |
| great | 17. большой, 12. великий |
| greatly | 573. значительно |
| greedy | 454. жадный |
| greek | 305. греческий |
| green | 130. зеленый |
| grey | 307. серый |
| grievous | 119. печальный, 156. тяжелый |
| grlm | 631. мрачный |
| grisly | 244. неприятный, 98. страшный |
| groovy | 916. волнующий, 1100. захватывающий, 554. классный |
| grossly | 606. грубо, 227. чрезвычайно |
| grotesque | 1053. гротескный |
| gruff | 198. грубый |

| | |
|---|---|
| grumpy | 715. сварливый |
| guilty | 145. виновный |
| gummy | 553. липкий |
| hairy | 519. волосатый |
| handsomely | 503. красиво |
| happily | 347. счастливо |
| happy | 31. счастливый |
| hard | 35. жесткий |
| hardy | 668. выносливый |
| harebrained | 750. ветреный, 979. легкомысленный |
| harsh | 249. резкий, 405. суровый |
| hasty | 726. поспешный |
| hateful | 996. ненавистный |
| haughty | 453. высокомерный |
| hazy | 831. смутный, 896. туманный |
| headstrong | 320. упрямый |
| healthy | 219. здоровый |
| heartbroken | 867. с разбитым сердцем |
| heartfelt | 473. искренний, 1096. прочувствованный |
| hearty | 995. сердечный |
| heavenly | 513. небесный |
| heavy | 156. тяжелый |
| hectic | 1075. беспокойный |
| heinous | 610. гнусный |
| herbal | 890. травяной |
| hereby | 533. настоящим |
| hereditary | 1081. наследственный |
| herewith | 533. настоящим |
| heroic | 558. героический |
| hideous | 567. отвратительный |

| | |
|---|---|
| high | 17. большой |
| highly | 7. очень |
| hilarious | 561. веселый |
| historic | 504. исторический |
| historical | 504. исторический |
| hokey | 490. сентиментальный, 537. фальшивый |
| hollow | 523. полый |
| holy | 132. святой |
| homesick | 961. тоскующий по дому |
| homey | 936. домашний |
| homicidal | 965. убийственный |
| honest | 124. честный |
| honorable | 471. почетный |
| honorary | 471. почетный |
| honourable | 471. почетный |
| hostile | 469. враждебный |
| hot | 66. жаркий |
| huffy | 797. самодовольный |
| huge | 135. огромный |
| humane | 974. гуманный |
| humanitarian | 980. гуманитарный |
| humble | 495. скромный |
| humbly | 903. смиренно |
| hungry | 121. голодный |
| hybrid | 747. гибридный |
| hypothetical | 993. гипотетический |
| hypothetically | 865. гипотетически |
| hysterical | 551. истерический |
| icy | 736. ледяной |
| identical | 487. идентичный |
| idle | 653. праздный, 103. простой |

| iffy | 754. неопределенный |
| ignorant | 478. невежественный |
| ill | 72. больной |
| illegal | 231. незаконный |
| illegally | 706. незаконно |
| illegitimate | 1015. незаконнорожденный, 231. незаконный |
| illiterate | 972. неграмотный |
| illustrious | 157. знаменитый, 1046. прославленный |
| imaginary | 594. воображаемый |
| immature | 724. незрелый |
| immediate | 387. немедленный |
| immediately | 137. немедленно |
| immensely | 227. чрезвычайно |
| imminent | 509. неизбежный |
| immoral | 758. аморальный |
| immortal | 474. бессмертный |
| immune | 575. иммунный |
| impassioned | 456. страстный |
| impatient | 605. нетерпеливый |
| imperial | 438. императорский |
| important | 53. важный |
| impossible | 127. невозможно |
| impotent | 828. бессильный |
| impressive | 267. впечатляющий |
| improbable | 176. невероятный |
| impulsive | 794. импульсивный |
| inadequate | 1069. недостаточный |
| inappropriate | 492. неуместный |
| inaudible | 656. неслышный |
| inauspicious | 727. зловещий |

| | |
|---|---|
| inbound | 532. входящий |
| incapable | 321. неспособный |
| incidental | 515. случайный |
| incoming | 532. входящий |
| incompetent | 696. некомпетентный |
| incomplete | 730. неполный |
| inconvenient | 314. неудобный |
| incorrect | 899. некорректный |
| incredible | 176. невероятный |
| incredibly | 304. невероятно |
| indecent | 894. неприличный, 843. непристойный |
| indeed | 5. действительно |
| indefinite | 780. неограниченный, 754. неопределенный |
| indefinitely | 1025. бесконечно, 976. неопределенно |
| independent | 381. независимый |
| indestructible | 1078. нерушимый |
| indeterminate | 754. неопределенный |
| indifferent | 879. равнодушный |
| indistinctly | 380. невнятно |
| individual | 316. индивидуальный |
| inept | 321. неспособный |
| inescapable | 509. неизбежный |
| inevitable | 509. неизбежный |
| inexcusable | 956. непростительный |
| inexperienced | 1066. неопытный |
| infantile | 524. детский |
| infertile | 782. бесплодный |
| infinite | 570. бесконечный |
| influential | 811. влиятельный |

| | |
|---|---|
| infrared | 866. инфракрасный |
| ingenious | 792. изобретательный, 173. оригинальный, 829. остроумный |
| inhuman | 978. бесчеловечный |
| inland | 362. внутренний |
| inner | 362. внутренний |
| innocent | 143. невинный |
| inordinate | 685. чрезмерный |
| insane | 88. безумный, 186. ненормальный |
| insanely | 719. безумно |
| insatiable | 454. жадный |
| insecure | 689. небезопасный |
| insensitive | 742. нечувствительный |
| inside | 47. внутри |
| insidious | 761. коварный |
| insolent | 664. дерзкий |
| instrumental | 449. инструментальный |
| insufferable | 601. невыносимый |
| insufficient | 1077. недостаточное, 1069. недостаточный |
| intellectual | 549. интеллектуальный |
| intelligent | 113. умный |
| intense | 341. интенсивный, 92. сильный |
| intensive | 341. интенсивный |
| intentional | 1039. намеренный |
| intentionally | 751. умышленно |
| interim | 361. временный |
| intermediate | 104. средний |
| internal | 362. внутренний |
| international | 252. международный |

| | |
|---|---|
| intimate | 451. интимный |
| intimately | 391. тесно |
| intolerable | 601. невыносимый |
| intricate | 302. сложный |
| intrusive | 945. навязчивый |
| invalid | 902. недействительный |
| invaluable | 1006. неоценимый |
| invasive | 406. агрессивный |
| inventive | 792. изобретательный |
| investigative | 971. исследовательский |
| invincible | 602. непобедимый |
| invisible | 340. невидимый |
| ironclad | 1078. нерушимый |
| irrational | 767. иррациональный |
| irregular | 888. нерегулярный |
| irresistible | 764. неотразимый |
| irresponsible | 572. безответственный |
| irrevocable | 142. окончательный |
| islamic | 808. исламский |
| itchy | 716. зудящий |
| jealous | 174. ревнивый |
| jolly | 561. веселый |
| joyful | 79. радостный |
| joyous | 79. радостный |
| judgmental | 779. преднамеренный |
| judicial | 535. судебный |
| juicy | 622. сочный |
| jumbo | 209. гигантский |
| jumpy | 141. нервный |
| just | 2. просто |
| justifiable | 497. законный |
| juvenile | 611. несовершеннолетний |

| | |
|---|---|
| keen | 415. увлеченный |
| key | 108. ключевой |
| kind | 19. добрый |
| kindly | 420. любезно |
| lame | 369. хромой |
| lamentable | 119. печальный |
| large | 17. большой |
| largely | 861. в значительной степени |
| last | 13. последний |
| late | 41. поздно |
| lawful | 497. законный |
| lazy | 346. ленивый |
| least | 51. наименее |
| leery | 280. подозрительный |
| left | 20. левый |
| legal | 196. правовой |
| legendary | 529. легендарный |
| legible | 738. четкий |
| legitimate | 497. законный |
| lesbian | 431. лесбийский |
| lesser | 755. меньший |
| lethal | 354. смертельный |
| lewd | 843. непристойный |
| liable | 160. ответственный |
| liberal | 659. либеральный |
| light | 65. световой |
| lightly | 317. слегка |
| likeable | 131. милый, 286. привлекательный |
| likely | 205. вероятный |
| limber | 737. гибкий |
| liquid | 409. жидкий |

| | |
|---|---|
| literal | 1049. буквальный |
| literary | 714. литературный |
| little | 8. немного |
| live | 29. живой |
| lively | 29. живой, 565. оживленный |
| loath | 809. неохотный |
| loathsome | 567. отвратительный |
| local | 164. местный |
| logical | 463. логический |
| lone | 106. одинокий |
| lonely | 106. одинокий |
| loose | 190. свободный |
| loud | 172. громкий |
| lousy | 300. паршивый |
| lovable | 131. милый, 286. привлекательный |
| lovely | 39. прекрасный |
| lowly | 495. скромный |
| loyal | 10. верный, 312. преданный |
| luckily | 432. к счастью |
| lucky | 31. счастливый, 83. удачливый |
| lucrative | 1023. выгодный, 771. прибыльный |
| lunar | 744. лунный |
| lush | 1038. пышный |
| lustrous | 481. блестящий |
| luxurious | 1002. роскошный |
| mad | 88. безумный, 44. сумасшедший |
| madly | 719. безумно |
| magical | 360. волшебный |
| magically | 1036. волшебно |

| | |
|---|---|
| magnificent | 250. великолепный |
| main | 165. основной |
| male | 181. мужской |
| mandatory | 770. обязательный |
| manipulative | 1060. манипулятивный |
| manly | 682. мужественный |
| many | 26. многие |
| marine | 358. морской |
| marital | 874. супружеский |
| marvellous | 439. изумительный, 544. чудный |
| marvelous | 439. изумительный |
| marvelously | 826. чудесно |
| masculine | 181. мужской |
| massive | 275. массивный, 135. огромный |
| maternal | 949. материнский |
| matrimonial | 874. супружеский |
| maudlin | 490. сентиментальный |
| maximum | 440. максимальный |
| mechanical | 539. механический |
| medical | 153. медицинский |
| medicinal | 153. медицинский |
| medieval | 640. средневековый |
| mediocre | 977. посредственный |
| mellow | 192. мягкий |
| memorable | 817. незабываемый |
| mental | 254. умственный |
| mentally | 489. умственно |
| mercantile | 328. коммерческий |
| merciful | 639. милосердный, 520. милостивый |
| mercifully | 432. к счастью |

| | |
|---|---|
| mere | 103. простой |
| merely | 2. просто |
| merrily | 1056. весело |
| merry | 561. веселый |
| messy | 136. грязный |
| metallic | 778. металлический |
| meticulous | 557. тщательный |
| middle | 104. средний |
| middling | 977. посредственный, 104. средний |
| mild | 192. мягкий, 422. слабый |
| milky | 709. молочный |
| mindful | 1097. внимательный |
| miniature | 833. миниатюрный |
| minimal | 852. минимальный |
| miniscule | 184. крошечный |

| | |
|---|---|
| miscellaneous | 1086. разнообразный |
| mischievous | 332. озорной |
| miserable | 9. жалкий, 274. несчастный |
| misshapen | 179. уродливый |
| misty | 896. туманный |
| mobile | 272. мобильный |
| moderate | 1080. умеренный |
| modern | 224. современный |
| modest | 495. скромный |
| molecular | 820. молекулярный |
| monstrous | 745. чудовищный |
| monthly | 652. месячный |
| moot | 765. спорный |
| moral | 334. моральный |

| | |
|---|---|
| morally | 893. морально |
| morbid | 287. болезненный |
| more | 6. более |
| mortal | 354. смертельный, 446. смертный |
| muddy | 136. грязный |
| multiple | 365. множественный |
| murderous | 965. убийственный |
| muscular | 991. мускулистый |
| musical | 348. музыкальный |
| mutual | 465. взаимный |
| muzzy | 644. расплывчатый |
| mysterious | 284. таинственный |
| mystic | 815. мистический |
| mystical | 815. мистический |
| mythical | 1063. мифический |
| naive | 433. наивный |
| narrow | 412. узкий |
| nasty | 244. неприятный |
| national | 168. национальный |
| nationwide | 1088. общенациональный |
| native | 350. родной |
| natty | 417. аккуратный, 675. искусный |
| natural | 169. естественный |
| naughty | 332. озорной |
| nauseous | 872. тошнотворный |
| nautical | 358. морской |
| naval | 542. военно морской, 358. морской |
| nazi | 435. нацистский |
| nearly | 56. почти |

| | |
|---|---|
| neat | 417. аккуратный, 90. чистый |
| neatly | 1082. аккуратно |
| necessarily | 368. обязательно |
| nefarious | 610. гнусный |
| negative | 248. отрицательный |
| negligent | 574. небрежный |
| nervous | 141. нервный |
| nervously | 733. нервно |
| neural | 141. нервный |
| neurological | 1070. неврологический |
| neurotic | 1004. невротический |
| neutral | 590. нейтральный |
| new | 15. новый |
| newsworthy | 53. важный |
| next | 25. следующий |
| nice | 18. приятный |
| nifty | 886. изящный, 911. стильный |
| noble | 276. благородный |
| noisy | 528. шумный |
| nonstop | 966. безостановочно |
| normal | 107. нормальный |
| normally | 138. обычно |
| northern | 378. северный |
| nosey | 229. любопытный |
| nosy | 229. любопытный |
| notably | 128. особенно |
| noxious | 577. ядовитый |
| nuclear | 279. ядерный |
| nude | 546. обнаженный |
| null | 147. пустой |
| numb | 627. онемелый |

| | |
|---|---|
| nuptial | 757. свадебный |
| nutty | 967. рехнувшийся |
| objectionable | 900. нежелательный |
| objective | 494. объективный |
| obligatory | 770. обязательный |
| obscene | 843. непристойный |
| obscure | 831. смутный |
| obsessive | 945. навязчивый |
| obsolete | 1037. устарелый |
| obstinate | 320. упрямый |
| obvious | 200. очевидный |
| occasionally | 63. иногда |
| occult | 1059. оккультный |
| occupational | 201. профессиональный |
| odd | 91. странный |
| odious | 996. ненавистный |
| official | 215. официальный |
| officially | 301. официально |
| offshore | 840. офшорный |
| oft | 123. часто |
| often | 123. часто |
| old | 16. старый |
| ominous | 727. зловещий |
| omnipotent | 442. всемогущий |
| open | 36. открытый |
| openly | 658. открыто |
| operational | 671. оперативный |
| operative | 671. оперативный |
| optimistic | 677. оптимистичный |
| opulent | 115. богатый, 1038. пышный |
| orange | 281. апельсиновый |
| orderly | 701. упорядоченный |

| | |
|---|---|
| ordinarily | 138. обычно |
| organic | 491. органический |
| original | 173. оригинальный |
| ornery | 346. ленивый |
| outdoor | 860. на открытом воздухе |
| outgoing | 1041. исходящий |
| outlandish | 310. глухой |
| outlying | 333. удаленный |
| outrageous | 518. возмутительный |
| outside | 64. снаружи |
| outspoken | 101. откровенный |
| outstanding | 508. выдающийся |
| overdue | 821. запоздалый |
| overhead | 78. верхний |
| overtly | 291. откровенно, 658. открыто |
| own | 24. собственный |
| pacific | 337. мирный, 419. миролюбивый, 84. тихий |
| painful | 287. болезненный |
| pale | 401. бледный |
| parallel | 613. параллельный |
| paranormal | 952. паранормальный |
| parochial | 412. узкий |
| partial | 589. частичный |
| partially | 651. частично |
| particular | 212. конкретный |
| particularly | 128. особенно |
| partly | 651. частично |
| passe | 1037. устарелый |
| passionate | 456. страстный |
| pathetic | 9. жалкий |

| | |
|---|---|
| patiently | 1031. терпеливо |
| patriotic | 807. патриотический |
| peaceful | 337. мирный |
| peacefully | 604. мирно |
| peculiar | 550. своеобразный, 283. специфический |
| penal | 171. уголовный |
| perchance | 418. случайно |
| perfidious | 753. вероломный |
| perpetual | 331. вечный |
| perpetually | 352. постоянно |
| personal | 110. личный |
| persuasive | 934. убедительный |
| pert | 664. дерзкий |
| perverse | 1048. извращенный |
| petty | 374. мелочный |
| pharmaceutical | 847. фармацевтический |
| phenomenal | 790. феноменальный |
| philosophical | 1007. философский |
| phoney | 228. ложный, 537. фальшивый |
| phony | 537. фальшивый |
| photographic | 1029. фотографический |
| physical | 220. физический |
| physically | 394. физически |
| picky | 854. придирчивый |
| pink | 257. розовый |
| pivotal | 165. основной, 221. центральный |
| plain | 103. простой |
| plastic | 278. пластиковый |
| plausible | 987. правдоподобный |

| | |
|---|---|
| playful | 985. игривый |
| pleasant | 18. приятный |
| plentiful | 115. богатый |
| plural | 365. множественный |
| poetic | 735. поэтический |
| poisonous | 577. ядовитый |
| polar | 638. полярный |
| polite | 373. вежливый |
| politely | 895. вежливо |
| political | 208. политический |
| politically | 743. политически |
| poor | 23. плохой |
| popular | 235. популярный |
| porky | 308. толстый |
| portable | 786. портативный |
| posh | 777. шикарный |
| positive | 216. положительный |
| positively | 645. положительно |
| possible | 77. возможный |
| postal | 891. почтовый |
| posterior | 397. задний |
| potent | 170. мощный, 969. сильнодействующий, 92. сильный |
| potential | 269. потенциальный |
| potentially | 615. потенциально |
| potty | 530. мелкий |
| powerful | 170. мощный |
| practical | 396. практический |
| practically | 282. практически |
| precious | 238. драгоценный |
| precise | 242. точный |

| precocious | 759. преждевременный |
|---|---|
| predictable | 718. предсказуемый |
| preferably | 827. предпочтительно |
| pregnant | 144. беременная |
| prehistoric | 944. доисторический |
| preliminary | 628. предварительный |
| premature | 759. преждевременный |
| preposterous | 152. нелепый |
| prestigious | 992. престижный |
| pretentious | 929. притязательный |
| pretty | 33. хорошенький |
| previous | 325. предыдущий |
| prideful | 117. гордый |
| primal | 1051. первобытный |
| primary | 408. первичный |
| primitive | 541. примитивный |
| primordial | 1051. первобытный |
| princely | 1002. роскошный |
| pristine | 933. нетронутый |
| private | 126. частный |
| probable | 205. вероятный |
| probably | 40. вероятно |
| prodigal | 292. щедрый |
| prodigious | 745. чудовищный |
| productive | 788. продуктивный |
| professional | 201. профессиональный |
| professionally | 818. профессионально |
| profitable | 771. прибыльный |
| progressive | 835. прогрессивный |
| prominent | 748. видный |
| proper | 207. надлежащий |
| propitious | 464. подходящий |

| proprietary | 126. частный |
| protective | 517. защитный |
| protestant | 920. протестантский |
| proud | 117. гордый |
| proudly | 839. гордо |
| provincial | 973. провинциальный |
| provocative | 1095. провокационный |
| pseudo | 537. фальшивый |
| psychiatric | 592. психиатрический |
| psychological | 483. психологический |
| psychologically | 1098. психологически |
| psychotic | 666. психотический |
| public | 118. общественный |
| publicly | 655. публично |
| punchy | 918. энергичный |
| punctual | 1020. пунктуальный |
| pure | 90. чистый |
| purple | 403. фиолетовый |
| pushy | 960. напористый |
| putrid | 306. гнилой |
| quaint | 193. причудливый |
| quarrelsome | 715. сварливый |
| quick | 109. быстро, 81. быстрый |
| quickly | 109. быстро |
| quiet | 84. тихий |
| quite | 52. вполне |
| rabid | 1027. неистовый |
| racial | 785. расовый |
| racist | 484. расистский |
| radiant | 930. сияющий |
| radical | 516. радикальный |
| radioactive | 704. радиоактивный |

| | |
|---|---|
| rainy | 669. дождливый |
| random | 515. случайный |
| rapid | 81. быстрый |
| rare | 240. редкий |
| rational | 569. рациональный |
| ready | 30. готовый |
| real | 28. реальный |
| realistic | 571. реалистичный |
| really | 5. действительно |
| rear | 397. задний |
| reasonable | 309. разумный |
| reasonably | 915. разумно |
| recent | 293. недавний |
| red | 76. красный |
| regal | 211. королевский |
| regional | 679. региональный |
| regular | 218. регулярный |
| regularly | 584. регулярно |
| relative | 389. относительный |
| relatively | 634. относительно |
| relevant | 493. соответствующие, 349. соответствующий |
| reliable | 255. надежный |
| religious | 294. религиозный |
| reluctant | 809. неохотный |
| remarkable | 89. замечательный |
| remote | 333. удаленный |
| remotely | 725. удаленно |
| renowned | 157. знаменитый |
| repeatedly | 649. неоднократно |
| repellent | 988. отталкивающий |
| republican | 591. республиканский |

| | |
|---|---|
| repulsive | 988. отталкивающий |
| resolute | 810. решительный |
| resourceful | 792. изобретательный, 1016. находчивый |
| respectable | 514. респектабельный |
| respectful | 787. почтительный |
| respectfully | 858. почтительно |
| respiratory | 924. респираторный |
| responsible | 160. ответственный |
| reticent | 562. сдержанный, 905. скрытный |
| reverse | 377. обратный |

| | |
|---|---|
| revolutionary | 468. революционный |
| rhythmic | 948. ритмичный |
| rich | 115. богатый |
| ridiculous | 152. нелепый, 67. смешной |
| right | 3. верно |
| righteous | 566. праведный |
| rightful | 497. законный |
| rightfully | 855. справедливо |
| rightly | 855. справедливо |
| rigorous | 593. строгий, 557. тщательный |
| rigorously | 425. строго |
| ripe | 629. спелый |
| risky | 428. рискованный |
| robust | 1024. крепкий |
| rocky | 364. скалистый |
| romantic | 204. романтический |
| rosy | 257. розовый, 884. румяный |

| | |
|---|---|
| rotten | 306. гнилой |
| rough | 198. грубый |
| roughly | 606. грубо |
| round | 96. круглый |
| roundabout | 1008. окольный |
| rowdy | 528. шумный |
| royal | 211. королевский |
| ruddy | 884. румяный |
| rude | 198. грубый |
| rudimentary | 588. элементарный |
| runny | 409. жидкий |
| rural | 813. сельский |
| rusty | 395. ржавый |
| sad | 119. печальный |
| sadistic | 1072. садистский |
| sadly | 480. грустно |
| safe | 73. безопасный |
| safely | 344. безопасно |
| sainted | 132. святой |
| saintly | 132. святой |
| saline | 946. солевой |
| salty | 672. соленый |
| sandy | 335. песчаный |
| sarcastic | 769. саркастический |
| satisfactory | 857. удовлетворительный |
| scandalous | 1013. скандальный |
| scarce | 851. дефицитный |
| scary | 98. страшный |
| scientific | 324. научный |
| scientifically | 1042. научно |
| scrupulous | 557. тщательный |
| second | 43. второй |

| | |
|---|---|
| secondary | 626. вторичный |
| secret | 86. секретный |
| secretive | 905. скрытный |
| secretly | 441. тайно |
| secure | 73. безопасный, 255. надежный |
| securely | 344. безопасно |
| selfish | 285. эгоистичный |
| senile | 939. старческий |
| senior | 245. старший |
| sensational | 703. сенсационный |
| sensible | 309. разумный |
| sensibly | 915. разумно |
| sensitive | 270. чувствительный |
| sensual | 994. чувственный |
| sensuous | 994. чувственный |
| sentimental | 490. сентиментальный |
| separate | 237. отдельный |
| serene | 1045. безмятежный |
| serial | 343. серийный |
| serious | 75. серьезный |
| seriously | 102. серьезно |
| severe | 75. серьезный, 92. сильный, 105. суровый, 156. тяжелый |
| severely | 654. сурово |
| sexist | 1017. женоненавистнический |
| sexual | 213. половой |
| shabby | 942. потертый |
| shady | 699. тенистый |
| shaggy | 678. лохматый |
| shaky | 803. шаткий |
| shallow | 530. мелкий |

| | |
|---|---|
| shameful | 670. позорный |
| sharp | 249. резкий |
| sheer | 90. чистый |
| shifty | 667. хитрый |
| shiny | 481. блестящий |
| short | 105. короткий |
| shy | 265. застенчивый |
| sick | 72. больной |
| sickly | 287. болезненный |
| sideways | 729. боком |
| significant | 413. значительный |
| silent | 230. молчаливый, 84. тихий |
| silly | 59. глупый |
| silver | 202. серебряный |
| similar | 251. похожий |
| simple | 103. простой |
| simply | 2. просто |
| simultaneously | 812. одновременно |
| sincere | 473. искренний |
| sinful | 877. грешный |
| single | 106. одинокий |
| singularly | 128. особенно |
| sinister | 727. зловещий |
| sizeable | 413. значительный |
| skeptical | 1014. скептический |
| sketchy | 805. поверхностный |
| skilful | 675. искусный |
| skilled | 675. искусный |
| skillful | 675. искусный |
| sleepy | 444. сонный |
| slender | 260. тонкий |
| slight | 430. незначительный |

| | |
|---|---|
| slightly | 8. немного, 317. слегка |
| slim | 260. тонкий |
| slimy | 870. слизистый |
| slippery | 612. скользкий |
| sloppy | 574. небрежный |
| slow | 134. медленный |
| slushy | 490. сентиментальный |
| slutty | 917. распутная |
| sly | 667. хитрый |
| small | 71. малый |
| smart | 113. умный |
| smelly | 695. вонючий |
| smooth | 315. плавный |
| smoothly | 681. плавно |
| smug | 797. самодовольный |
| snappy | 918. энергичный |
| snooty | 453. высокомерный |
| so | 1. так |
| sober | 376. трезвый |
| social | 182. социальный |
| socialist | 687. социалистический |
| societal | 118. общественный, 182. социальный |
| soft | 192. мягкий |
| solar | 393. солнечный |
| sole | 476. единственный |
| solemn | 760. торжественный |
| solid | 261. твердый |
| solitary | 597. уединенный |
| somber | 631. мрачный |
| sometimes | 63. иногда |
| somewhat | 429. до некоторой степени |

| | |
|---|---|
| sonic | 600. звуковой |
| sore | 72. больной, 385. воспаленный |
| sorry | 9. жалкий |
| soupy | 409. жидкий |
| sour | 511. кислый |
| southerly | 339. южный |
| southern | 339. южный |
| sovereign | 746. суверенный |
| soviet | 359. советский |
| spanish | 187. испанский |
| spare | 188. запасной, 190. свободный |
| special | 74. специальный |
| specially | 587. специально |
| specific | 212. конкретный, 112. определенный, 283. специфический |
| specifically | 400. конкретно |
| spectacular | 466. эффектный |
| spicy | 568. пряный |
| spinal | 686. спинной |
| spiritual | 390. духовный |
| splendid | 250. великолепный |
| spontaneous | 690. спонтанный |
| spooky | 749. жуткий |
| sporty | 697. спортивный |
| spousal | 874. супружеский |
| spunky | 682. мужественный |
| spurious | 228. ложный, 756. поддельный |
| square | 197. квадратный |
| stable | 322. стабильный |

| | |
|---|---|
| stale | 844. несвежий |
| standard | 288. стандартный |
| static | 459. статический |
| steadfast | 261. твердый, 273. устойчивый |
| steady | 273. устойчивый |
| steep | 712. крутой |
| sterile | 875. стерильный |
| stern | 593. строгий, 405. суровый |
| sticky | 553. липкий |
| stiff | 35. жесткий |
| stingy | 883. скупой |
| stinky | 695. вонючий |
| storied | 529. легендарный |
| stormy | 935. штормовой |
| straight | 87. прямой |
| straightforward | 87. прямой |
| strange | 91. странный |
| strangely | 585. странно |
| strategic | 674. стратегический |
| strenuous | 384. напряженный |
| stressful | 384. напряженный, 693. стрессовый |
| strict | 593. строгий |
| strictly | 425. строго |
| stringent | 593. строгий |
| strong | 92. сильный |
| structural | 1010. структурный |
| stubborn | 320. упрямый |
| stuffy | 837. душный |
| stupendous | 439. изумительный, 913. колоссальный |
| stupid | 59. глупый |

| | |
|---|---|
| sturdy | 1024. крепкий |
| stylish | 911. стильный |
| suave | 373. вежливый |
| subsidiary | 983. вспомогательный |
| substantial | 413. значительный |
| successful | 241. успешный |
| successfully | 599. успешно |
| successive | 479. последовательный |
| succulent | 622. сочный |
| such | 32. такой |
| sudden | 195. внезапный |
| sufficient | 21. достаточно, 548. достаточный |
| sugary | 82. сладкий |
| suitable | 464. подходящий |
| suitably | 853. соответственно |
| sunny | 393. солнечный |
| super | 175. супер |
| superb | 159. превосходный |
| superficial | 805. поверхностный |
| superfluous | 502. ненужный |
| supernatural | 617. сверхъестественный |
| superstitious | 783. суеверный |
| supple | 737. гибкий |
| supplementary | 155. дополнительный |
| sure | 10. верный |
| surgical | 563. хирургический |
| surprisingly | 607. удивительно |
| surreal | 1089. сюрреалистичный |
| surrogate | 990. суррогатный |
| susceptible | 270. чувствительный |
| suspenseful | 355. тревожный |

| | |
|---|---|
| suspicious | 280. подозрительный |
| swanky | 777. шикарный |
| sweaty | 578. потный |
| sweet | 82. сладкий |
| swift | 81. быстрый |
| symbolic | 775. символический |
| synthetic | 791. синтетический |
| tacky | 553. липкий |
| tardy | 821. запоздалый |
| technical | 437. технический |
| technically | 323. технически |
| technicolor | 1084. кричащий |
| tedious | 943. утомительный |
| teensy | 184. крошечный |
| teeny | 184. крошечный |
| temperate | 1080. умеренный |
| temporarily | 582. временно |
| temporary | 361. временный |
| tense | 384. напряженный |
| terrestrial | 776. земной |
| terrible | 98. страшный |
| terrific | 258. потрясающий |
| thankful | 225. благодарный |
| theatrical | 923. театральный |
| theoretical | 953. теоретический |
| theoretically | 865. гипотетически |
| thermal | 799. тепловой |
| thick | 308. толстый |
| thin | 260. тонкий |
| third | 122. третий |
| thirsty | 329. жаждущий |

| | |
|---|---|
| thorough | 62. полный, 557. тщательный |
| thoughtful | 534. вдумчивый |
| tidy | 417. аккуратный |
| tight | 167. плотный |
| tightly | 717. плотно |
| timid | 970. робкий |
| tiny | 184. крошечный |
| tipsy | 522. пьяный |
| tiptop | 159. превосходный |
| titanic | 710. титанический |
| top | 78. верхний |
| total | 62. полный |
| totally | 95. полностью |
| touchy | 428. рискованный |
| tough | 35. жесткий |
| toxic | 501. токсичный |
| traditional | 383. традиционный |
| tragic | 363. трагический |
| tragically | 1058. трагически |
| transient | 361. временный |
| transitory | 361. временный |
| transparent | 825. прозрачный |
| traumatic | 740. травматический |
| treacherous | 761. коварный |
| tremendously | 227. чрезвычайно |
| trendy | 850. модный |
| tribal | 461. племенной |
| tricky | 447. каверзный, 302. сложный |
| triple | 460. тройной |
| triplicate | 460. тройной |

| | |
|---|---|
| trojan | 1057. троянский |
| tropical | 643. тропический |
| true | 38. истинный |
| trustworthy | 814. заслуживающий доверия, 255. надежный |
| truthful | 887. правдивый |
| tumultuous | 528. шумный |
| typical | 330. типичный |
| ugly | 179. уродливый |

| | |
|---|---|
| unable | 321. неспособный |
| unacceptable | 616. неприемлемый |
| unanimous | 962. единодушный |
| unarmed | 641. безоружный |
| unauthorized | 982. неразрешенный |
| unavailable | 902. недействительный |
| unavoidable | 509. неизбежный |
| unbearable | 601. невыносимый |
| unbeatable | 602. непобедимый |
| unbecoming | 894. неприличный |
| unbelievable | 304. невероятно, 176. невероятный |
| unbelievably | 304. невероятно |
| uncanny | 617. сверхъестественный |
| uncertain | 754. неопределенный |
| uncomfortable | 314. неудобный |
| uncommon | 240. редкий |
| unconcerned | 926. беззаботный, 879. равнодушный |
| unconscious | 386. без сознания |
| uncouth | 538. неуклюжий |

| | |
|---|---|
| undefeated | 602. непобедимый |
| underage | 611. несовершеннолетний |
| underhand | 761. коварный |
| undersea | 507. подводный |
| understandable | 625. понятный |
| underwater | 507. подводный |
| undesirable | 900. нежелательный |
| undue | 685. чрезмерный |
| undying | 474. бессмертный |
| unending | 570. бесконечный |
| unethical | 1064. неэтично |
| uneventful | 819. беспрецедентный |
| unfair | 379. несправедливый |
| unfaithful | 753. вероломный |
| unfamiliar | 1000. незнакомый |
| unfinished | 662. незаконченный |
| unfit | 1003. негодный |
| unforgettable | 938. незабвенный, 817. незабываемый |
| unforgivable | 956. непростительный |
| unfortunate | 274. несчастный, 356. неудачный |
| unfounded | 683. необоснованный |
| ungodly | 518. возмутительный, 152. нелепый |
| ungrateful | 583. неблагодарный |
| unhappy | 274. несчастный |
| unharmed | 957. невредимый |
| unhealthy | 986. нездоровый |
| unhelpful | 842. бесполезный |
| unidentified | 692. неопознанный |
| unimaginable | 1099. невообразимый |
| unimportant | 984. неважный |

| | |
|---|---|
| unique | 268. уникальный |
| universal | 536. универсальный |
| unjust | 379. несправедливый |
| unjustified | 683. необоснованный |
| unknown | 271. неизвестный |
| unlawful | 706. незаконно, 231. незаконный |
| unlawfully | 706. незаконно |
| unlikely | 462. маловероятный |
| unlimited | 780. неограниченный |
| unlucky | 531. несчастливый, 356. неудачный |
| unmitigated | 326. абсолютный |
| unnatural | 772. неестественный |
| unnecessary | 502. ненужный |
| unnoticed | 1021. незамеченный |
| unopposed | 476. единственный |
| unpaid | 1087. неоплаченный |
| unpardonable | 956. непростительный |
| unpleasant | 244. неприятный |
| unprecedented | 819. беспрецедентный |
| unpredictable | 635. непредсказуемый |
| unprofessional | 998. непрофессиональный |
| unqualified | 1003. негодный |
| unreal | 801. нереальный |
| unrealistic | 801. нереальный |
| unreasonable | 683. необоснованный |
| unrelated | 1065. несвязанный |
| unrequited | 1087. неоплаченный |
| unresolved | 982. неразрешенный |
| unscathed | 957. невредимый |
| unseen | 889. невиданный, 340. невидимый |

| | |
|---|---|
| unsophisticated | 433. наивный |
| unsound | 306. гнилой, 986. нездоровый |
| unspeakable | 1093. невыразимый |
| unstable | 525. неустойчивый |
| unstoppable | 873. неостанавливаемый |
| unsuccessful | 356. неудачный |
| unsustainable | 525. неустойчивый |
| untapped | 933. нетронутый |
| unthinkable | 1011. немыслимый |
| untouched | 933. нетронутый |
| untrue | 228. ложный, 1035. несоответствующий |
| unusual | 246. необычный |
| unwanted | 900. нежелательный, 502. ненужный |
| unwarranted | 683. необоснованный |
| unwelcome | 900. нежелательный |
| unwell | 986. нездоровый |
| unworthy | 892. недостойный |
| up | 4. выше |
| upbeat | 565. оживленный |
| upper | 78. верхний, 345. высший |
| upstage | 453. высокомерный |
| urban | 555. городской |
| urgent | 266. срочный |
| usually | 138. обычно |
| vague | 644. расплывчатый |
| vain | 416. тщеславный |
| valiant | 904. доблестный |
| valid | 621. действительный |
| valuable | 296. ценный |

| | |
|---|---|
| various | 48. различный |
| vast | 371. обширный, 135. огромный |
| vastly | 573. значительно |
| vegan | 608. вегетарианский |
| vegetarian | 608. вегетарианский |
| venomous | 577. ядовитый |
| verbal | 876. словесный |
| versatile | 737. гибкий |
| very | 7. очень |
| viable | 800. жизнеспособный |
| vicious | 457. порочный |
| vile | 610. гнусный |
| violent | 262. насильственный |
| violently | 912. яростно |
| viral | 784. вирусный |
| virile | 682. мужественный, 181. мужской |
| virtual | 694. виртуальный |
| virulent | 577. ядовитый |
| visible | 506. видимый |
| visual | 404. визуальный |
| vital | 392. жизненно важный |
| vivacious | 565. оживленный |
| vivid | 191. яркий |
| vocal | 647. вокальный |
| vocational | 201. профессиональный |
| volatile | 1019. летучий |
| volcanic | 766. вулканический |
| voluntarily | 806. добровольно |
| voluntary | 906. добровольный |
| voluptuous | 994. чувственный |

| | |
|---|---|
| voracious | 454. жадный |
| vulgar | 619. вульгарный |
| vulnerable | 399. уязвимый |
| wary | 85. осторожный |
| weak | 422. слабый |
| weakly | 1071. слабо |
| wealthy | 115. богатый |
| weary | 665. утомленный |
| weekly | 595. еженедельно |
| weird | 91. странный |
| weirdly | 83. удачливый |
| welsh | 848. валлийский |
| western | 298. западный |
| wet | 189. мокрый |
| whimsical | 781. капризный, 193. причудливый |
| white | 70. белый |
| whole | 34. целый |
| wholesome | 219. здоровый |
| whopping | 745. чудовищный |
| wicked | 133. злой |
| wide | 239. широкий |
| widely | 958. широко |
| wild | 158. дикий |
| wildly | 859. дико |
| willfully | 751. умышленно |
| windy | 750. ветреный |
| wise | 233. мудрый |
| wisely | 880. мудро |
| witty | 829. остроумный |
| wobbly | 803. шаткий |
| womanly | 648. женственный |

| | |
|---|---|
| wonderful | 89. замечательный |
| wonderfully | 826. чудесно |
| wonky | 803. шаткий |
| wooden | 452. деревянный |
| woody | 445. древесный |
| woozy | 525. неустойчивый, 522. пьяный |
| wordy | 876. словесный |
| worldwide | 620. всемирный |
| worrisome | 1075. беспокойный, 355. тревожный |
| worst | 140. наихудший |
| worthwhile | 698. стоящий |
| worthy | 318. достойный |
| wretched | 9. жалкий, 274. несчастный |
| wrong | 22. неправильный |
| wrongful | 231. незаконный |
| wrongly | 1040. превратно |
| yearly | 470. ежегодный |
| yellow | 217. желтый |
| young | 42. молодой |

# Appendix: Phrase Practice Drills

This appendix contains phrases for practice. Each phrase includes at least one **adjective/adverb**.

You can use this appendix for practice in two ways:

- **Read practice:** Read the original phrases, try to guess the English translation, and then check your guess against the provided translation.
- **Speak practice:** Read the English translations, and try to recall and say the original phrases.

To facilitate this, the English translations are provided separately from the original phrases.

The phrases are organized into several groups. They start with the easiest and shortest phrases, gradually increasing in complexity as you progress through the groups.

In the initial groups, the phrases are deliberately repetitive to reinforce beginner vocabulary.

We hope you enjoy this appendix and find it helpful in your language learning journey.

## Difficulty Level: 1

**[1]** *1.* Не. *2.* Не я. *3.* Я не! *4.* Это не? *5.* Не это. *6.* Ты что? *7.* Он не? *8.* Это так? *9.* Так ты. *10.* Не так. *11.* Так? *12.* Она не. *13.* Не она. *14.* Как это? *15.* Как он?

• *1.* Did not. *2.* Not me. *3.* I don't! *4.* It's not? *5.* Not this. *6.* You just what? *7.* He isn't? *8.* Is that so? *9.* So are you. *10.* Not that way. *11.* So? *12.* She's not. *13.* She is not. *14.* How's that? *15.* How is he?

**[2]** *1.* Как она? *2.* Как так? *3.* Как я? *4.* Как? *5.* Как ты? *6.* Как вы? *7.* Не вы. *8.* Вы не! *9.* Я здесь. *10.* Здесь. *11.* Он здесь. *12.* Она здесь.

• *1.* How is she? *2.* How is that? *3.* How am I? *4.* How? *5.* How did you? *6.* How are you? *7.* Not you. *8.* You're not! *9.* I'm here. *10.* Over here. *11.* He's here. *12.* She's here.

**[3]** *1.* Это здесь. *2.* Вы здесь? *3.* Ты здесь? *4.* Что здесь? *5.*

Не здесь. 6. Здесь, здесь! 7. Мы здесь. 8. Не все. 9. Как все? 10. Все это. 11. Все здесь. 12. Нет, нет.

• 1. It's here. 2. Are you here? 3. You're here? 4. What's in here? 5. Not in here. 6. Here, here! 7. Here we are. 8. Not everyone. 9. How's everything? 10. The whole thing. 11. Everybody's here. 12. No, you don't.

[4] 1. Я нет. 2. Он - нет? 3. Что нет? 4. Просто так. 5. Это просто. 6. Просто это. 7. Просто здесь. 8. Не просто. 9. И что? 10. И я. 11. И здесь. 12. И так?

• 1. I haven't. 2. He's not? 3. What isn't? 4. Just like that. 5. It's easy. 6. Just this. 7. Just here. 8. Not easy. 9. Then what? 10. So was I. 11. And here. 12. And so?

[5] 1. И как? 2. Не было. 3. Они здесь. 4. Как они? 5. Не они. 6. Они не. 7. Где ты? 8. Где он? 9. Где она? 10. Где это? 11. Где они? 12. Где мы?

• 1. And how? 2. Was not. 3. They're here. 4. How are they? 5. Not them. 6. They do not. 7. Where are you? 8. Where is he? 9. Where is she? 10. Where is it? 11. Where are they? 12. Where are we?

[6] 1. Где я? 2. Где все? 3. Где что? 4. Как где? 5. Где? 6. И где? 7. Где в? 8. Очень. 9. Очень просто. 10. Да так? 11. Это да? 12. Да очень.

• 1. Where am I? 2. Where is everyone? 3. Where's what? 4. Like where? 5. Where? 6. And where? 7. Where at? 8. Very much. 9. Very simple. 10. Yeah, so? 11. Is that a yes? 12. Yes, very.

[7] 1. Да нет. 2. Да, здесь. 3. Да, да? 4. Это хорошо. 5. Очень хорошо. 6. Хорошо хорошо. 7. Не хорошо. 8. Все хорошо? 9. Просто хорошо. 10. Да, хорошо. 11. Хорошо что? 12. Так хорошо.

• 1. Yes, now. 2. Yeah, here. 3. Yeah, huh? 4. That's good. 5. Very well. 6. Good, good. 7. Not good. 8. Is that okay? 9. Just fine. 10. Yeah, good. 11. Well, what? 12. So good.

[8] 1. Хорошо. 2. Хорошо, да? 3. Хорошо, здесь. 4. Как хорошо? 5. Мне хорошо. 6. Ну, да. 7. Ну ну. 8. Ну я. 9. Ну, нет. 10. Что еще? 11. Еще нет! 12. Где еще?

• 1. OK, good. 2. Good, huh? 3. All right, here. 4. How good? 5. I'm very good. 6. Well, yeah. 7. Well, well. 8. Well, I am. 9.

Well, you don't. *10.* What else? *11.* Not yet! *12.* Where else?

**[9]** *1.* Еще что? *2.* Все еще. *3.* Почему это? *4.* Почему? *5.* Нет почему? *6.* Да почему? *7.* И почему? *8.* Почему ты? *9.* Что почему? *10.* Почему да. *11.* Почему он? *12.* Почему она?
● *1.* More what? *2.* Still is. *3.* Why is that? *4.* How come? *5.* No, why? *6.* Yeah, why? *7.* And why? *8.* Why you? *9.* Why what? *10.* Why, yes. *11.* Why him? *12.* Why her?

**[10]** *1.* Почему еще? *2.* Почему нет? *3.* Так почему? *4.* Почему так? *5.* О, хорошо. *6.* О, да. *7.* О, здесь. *8.* О, нет! *9.* И сейчас? *10.* Почему сейчас? *11.* Не сейчас! *12.* Сейчас.
● *1.* Why else? *2.* Why not? *3.* So why? *4.* Why that? *5.* Oh, good. *6.* Uh, yeah. *7.* Oh, here. *8.* Uh, no! *9.* And now? *10.* Why now? *11.* Not now! *12.* It is now.

**[11]** *1.* Сейчас сейчас. *2.* Я сейчас. *3.* Хорошо, сейчас. *4.* Где сейчас? *5.* Да, сейчас. *6.* Как сейчас. *7.* Вы сейчас? *8.* Ты сейчас. *9.* Это - сейчас. *10.* Сейчас мы. *11.* Не могу? *12.* Вот так.
● *1.* Now, now. *2.* I am now. *3.* Okay, now. *4.* Where to now? *5.* Yeah, now. *6.* Like now. *7.* Are you now? *8.* You are now. *9.* This is now. *10.* We are now. *11.* Can't I? *12.* Here we go.

**[12]** *1.* Ну вот. *2.* Вот. *3.* Вот они. *4.* Вот почему. *5.* Вот она. *6.* Хорошо, вот. *7.* Что теперь? *8.* Ну теперь. *9.* Теперь да. *10.* Теперь ты. *11.* Теперь здесь. *12.* Не знаю.
● *1.* Here you go. *2.* Here it is. *3.* Here they are. *4.* That's why. *5.* Here she is. *6.* All right, here you go. *7.* Now what? *8.* Well, now. *9.* Now I do. *10.* Now you do. *11.* Now, here. *12.* Don't know.

**[13]** *1.* Знаю, почему? *2.* Нет никогда. *3.* Никогда. *4.* Сейчас есть. *5.* Да, есть. *6.* Есть еще? *7.* Там. *8.* Там там. *9.* Вы там. *10.* Он там. *11.* Это там. *12.* Я там.
● *1.* Know why? *2.* No, never. *3.* Never ever. *4.* There is now. *5.* Yes there is. *6.* Are there more? *7.* In there. *8.* There, there. *9.* You there? *10.* He's in there. *11.* It's over there. *12.* I'm there.

**[14]** *1.* Она там. *2.* Был там. *3.* Там сейчас. *4.* И там. *5.* Они там. *6.* Что там? *7.* Просто там. *8.* Ты там? *9.* Но почему? *10.* Но как? *11.* Но где? *12.* Но сейчас?
● *1.* She's in there. *2.* Been there. *3.* There now. *4.* And there. *5.*

They're in there. *6.* What's out there? *7.* Just there. *8.* Are you out there? *9.* But why? *10.* But how? *11.* But where? *12.* But now?

**[15]** *1.* Есть больше. *2.* Больше? *3.* Больше никогда. *4.* Больше, больше. *5.* Не больше. *6.* Больше ничего. *7.* Еще ничего. *8.* Нет, ничего. *9.* Только я. *10.* Только ты. *11.* Только мы. *12.* Только то.

● *1.* There's more. *2.* Any more? *3.* No longer. *4.* More, more. *5.* Not any longer. *6.* Nothing more. *7.* Still nothing. *8.* No, not a thing. *9.* Just me. *10.* Just you. *11.* Just us. *12.* Just that.

**[16]** *1.* Только он. *2.* Только что? *3.* Для тебя. *4.* Когда это? *5.* Но когда? *6.* Сейчас, когда. *7.* Когда что? *8.* И когда? *9.* Что тогда? *10.* Ну тогда. *11.* Хорошо, тогда. *12.* Тогда я.

● *1.* Just him. *2.* Only what? *3.* Just for you. *4.* When is it? *5.* But when? *6.* Now, then. *7.* When what? *8.* And when? *9.* What then? *10.* Well, then. *11.* OK, then. *12.* Then I will.

**[17]** *1.* Почему тогда? *2.* Где тогда? *3.* Тогда что? *4.* Тогда где? *5.* Тогда нет. *6.* Тогда да. *7.* Тогда как? *8.* Тогда ничего. *9.* Действительно хорошо. *10.* Да, действительно. *11.* Действительно? *12.* Ты действительно?

● *1.* Why then? *2.* Where then? *3.* Then what is? *4.* Then where? *5.* Then no. *6.* Then, yes. *7.* Then how? *8.* Then nothing. *9.* Really good. *10.* Yeah, really. *11.* Really? *12.* Do you really?

**[18]** *1.* Вы действительно? *2.* Нет, действительно. *3.* Действительно, я. *4.* О, действительно. *5.* Не были. *6.* Были здесь! *7.* Были там. *8.* Хочу еще? *9.* Не хочу.

● *1.* Are you really? *2.* No, indeed. *3.* Really, I am. *4.* Oh, indeed. *5.* We're not. *6.* We're here! *7.* We're there. *8.* Want some more? *9.* Don't want to.

**[19]** *1.* Хочу больше? *2.* Это лучше? *3.* Ты лучше. *4.* Лучше. *5.* Так лучше. *6.* Мне лучше. *7.* Тебе лучше? *8.* Теперь лучше. *9.* Все лучше. *10.* Было лучше. *11.* Вам лучше? *12.* Лучше тебя.

● *1.* Want more? *2.* Is that better? *3.* You better. *4.* It's better. *5.* It's better this way. *6.* I feel better. *7.* Do you feel better? *8.* Better now. *9.* All better. *10.* Been better. *11.* Are you better? *12.* Better than you.

**[20]** *1.* Он лучше. *2.* Лучше бы. *3.* Она лучше. *4.* Я тоже. *5.* Ты тоже. *6.* Вы тоже. *7.* Это тоже. *8.* Мы тоже. *9.* Он тоже. *10.* Она тоже. *11.* Тоже. *12.* Думаю, да.

● *1.* He's better. *2.* Better be. *3.* She's better. *4.* Me, too. *5.* You too. *6.* So do you. *7.* That, too. *8.* So did we. *9.* Him too. *10.* So is she. *11.* Are too. *12.* Yeah, I think so.

**[21]** *1.* Просто думаю. *2.* Может больше. *3.* Может что? *4.* Не нам. *5.* Тоже сделал. *6.* Слишком. *7.* Слишком хорошо. *8.* Их нет. *9.* Мне жаль. *10.* Очень жаль. *11.* Да жаль. *12.* Как жаль.

● *1.* Just thinking. *2.* Maybe more. *3.* Maybe what? *4.* Not us. *5.* Did too. *6.* Too much. *7.* Too good. *8.* There aren't any. *9.* I'm sorry. *10.* Too bad. *11.* Yeah, sorry. *12.* How unfortunate.

**[22]** *1.* Тебе жаль. *2.* За нас. *3.* Кто еще? *4.* Кто нет? *5.* Кто здесь? *6.* Тогда кто? *7.* Кто там? *8.* Кто тогда? *9.* Где кто? *10.* Ну, кто? *11.* Как всегда. *12.* Всегда есть.

● *1.* You're sorry. *2.* Here's to us. *3.* Who else? *4.* Who doesn't? *5.* Who's here? *6.* Then who? *7.* Who's out there? *8.* Who then? *9.* Where's who? *10.* Well, who? *11.* As always. *12.* Always have.

**[23]** *1.* Всегда были. *2.* Так всегда. *3.* Всегда будет. *4.* Ладно ладно. *5.* Ладно, хорошо. *6.* Тогда ладно. *7.* Ну ладно. *8.* Ладно. *9.* Просто ладно? *10.* Нет, ладно? *11.* Уже нет. *12.* Уже сделал.

● *1.* Always have been. *2.* Since always. *3.* Always will be. *4.* Okay, okay. *5.* Okay, good. *6.* Okay, then. *7.* Well, okay. *8.* Alright, then. *9.* Just okay? *10.* No, okay? *11.* Not anymore. *12.* Already did.

**[24]** *1.* Я уже. *2.* Ладно, уже. *3.* Еще раз. *4.* Только раз. *5.* Куда? *6.* Как делать? *7.* Пожалуйста. *8.* Вот, пожалуйста. *9.* Всегда пожалуйста. *10.* Сейчас, пожалуйста. *11.* О, пожалуйста. *12.* И пожалуйста.

● *1.* I already am. *2.* All right, already. *3.* One more time. *4.* Just once. *5.* Where to? *6.* How do? *7.* You're welcome. *8.* Here you are. *9.* You're very welcome. *10.* Now, please. *11.* Oh, you're welcome. *12.* And you're welcome.

**[25]** *1.* Да, пожалуйста. *2.* Здесь пожалуйста. *3.* Сюда, пожалуйста. *4.* Очень много. *5.* Много раз. *6.* Так много. *7.* Не много. *8.* Прямо здесь. *9.* Прямо там.

● *1.* Yeah, you're welcome. *2.* Here, please. *3.* Over here, please. *4.* Too many. *5.* Many times. *6.* So much. *7.* Not a lot. *8.* Right here. *9.* Right there.

**[26]** *1.* Прямо сейчас. *2.* Прямо тогда. *3.* Я уверен. *4.* Ты уверен? *5.* Не уверен. *6.* Очень уверен. *7.* А ты? *8.* А, хорошо. *9.* А жаль. *10.* Не снова. *11.* Снова ты? *12.* Снова.
● *1.* Right now. *2.* Right, then. *3.* I'm sure. *4.* You're sure? *5.* Not sure. *6.* Very sure. *7.* How about you? *8.* Ah, good. *9.* Well, sorry. *10.* Not again. *11.* You again? *12.* Once again.

**[27]** *1.* Это снова? *2.* Да, снова. *3.* Итак, почему? *4.* Все время? *5.* Не мой. *6.* Мой тоже. *7.* Он мой! *8.* Ты мой! *9.* Да, конечно. *10.* Конечно. *11.* Конечно, нет! *12.* Конечно, да.
● *1.* This again? *2.* Yes, again. *3.* Now, why is that? *4.* The whole time? *5.* Not mine. *6.* Mine, too. *7.* He's mine! *8.* You're mine! *9.* Yeah, sure. *10.* Sure thing. *11.* Of course not! *12.* Sure you do.

**[28]** *1.* Конечно, сделал. *2.* Почему конечно. *3.* О, конечно. *4.* Конечно, хорошо. *5.* Конечно ты. *6.* Конечно, есть. *7.* Конечно, знаю. *8.* Конечно же. *9.* Конечно, может.
● *1.* Sure did. *2.* Why, of course. *3.* Oh, certainly. *4.* Sure, fine. *5.* Sure, you are. *6.* Sure there is. *7.* Indeed I do. *8.* Sure enough. *9.* Sure can.

**[29]** *1.* Конечно, было. *2.* Конечно, будет. *3.* Хорошо, конечно. *4.* Ну, конечно. *5.* Как дела? *6.* Только один. *7.* Ты один? *8.* Еще один. *9.* Не один. *10.* Вот один. *11.* Вы один. *12.* Он один.
● *1.* Sure was. *2.* Sure will. *3.* All right, sure. *4.* Well, certainly. *5.* How you doing? *6.* Just one. *7.* Are you alone? *8.* One more. *9.* Not one. *10.* Here's one. *11.* You're alone. *12.* He's alone.

**[30]** *1.* Я один. *2.* Один здесь. *3.* Такой как? *4.* Я такой. *5.* Возможно, нет. *6.* Возможно. *7.* Это возможно? *8.* Ну, возможно. *9.* Все возможно. *10.* Да, возможно. *11.* О, возможно. *12.* Эй, сейчас.
● *1.* I am alone. *2.* This one here. *3.* Such as? *4.* That's how I am. *5.* Maybe not. *6.* It's possible. *7.* Is that possible? *8.* Well, maybe. *9.* Anything's possible. *10.* Yes, perhaps. *11.* Oh, maybe. *12.* Hey, now.

**[31]** *1.* Эй, сюда! *2.* Ну, эй. *3.* Эй, эй. *4.* Эй, там! *5.* Немного. *6.* Немного больше. *7.* Только немного. *8.* Да, немного. *9.* Еще немного. *10.* Ну, немного. *11.* Немного, да. *12.* Очень хороший.

● *1.* Hey, over here! *2.* Well, hey. *3.* Uh, hey. *4.* Ahoy there! *5.* A little bit. *6.* A little more. *7.* Just a little bit. *8.* Yeah, a little. *9.* A bit more. *10.* Well, a little bit. *11.* A little bit, yeah. *12.* Very good.

**[32]** *1.* Хороший. *2.* Ты хороший. *3.* Он хороший? *4.* Это хороший. *5.* Ему лучше. *6.* Ему жаль. *7.* Сколько? *8.* За сколько? *9.* Сколько это? *10.* Сколько они? *11.* Сколько там? *12.* Сколько еще?

● *1.* Nice one. *2.* You are good. *3.* Is he good? *4.* This is a good one. *5.* He'd better. *6.* He's sorry. *7.* How much? *8.* For how much? *9.* How many is that? *10.* How much are they? *11.* How much is there? *12.* How many others?

**[33]** *1.* Это правда. *2.* Не правда. *3.* Нет, правда? *4.* Ты правда? *5.* Правда правда. *6.* Правда что. *7.* Только правда. *8.* Что, правда? *9.* Вот правда. *10.* Быстро, быстро! *11.* Как быстро? *12.* Слишком быстро.

● *1.* It's true. *2.* Not true. *3.* No, really? *4.* Did you really? *5.* True, true. *6.* True that. *7.* Just the truth. *8.* What, really? *9.* Here's the truth. *10.* Quick, quick! *11.* How fast? *12.* Too fast.

**[34]** *1.* Очень быстро. *2.* И быстро. *3.* Это быстро. *4.* Приятно, да? *5.* Это приятно. *6.* Очень приятно. *7.* Всегда приятно. *8.* Приятно. *9.* Да, приятно. *10.* Приятно, приятно. *11.* Приятно, правда? *12.* Она моя!

● *1.* Very fast. *2.* And fast. *3.* That's fast. *4.* Nice, huh? *5.* It feels good. *6.* Real nice. *7.* Always a pleasure. *8.* Feels good. *9.* Yeah, nice. *10.* Nice, nice. *11.* Nice, right? *12.* She's mine!

**[35]** *1.* Давай же. *2.* Теперь давай. *3.* Ну, давай. *4.* Да, давай. *5.* Хорошо, давай. *6.* Давай сюда. *7.* Давай, быстро. *8.* Просто давай. *9.* О, давай. *10.* Давай, сейчас. *11.* Давай, пожалуйста. *12.* Давай, давай.

● *1.* Come on now. *2.* Now, come on. *3.* Well, come on. *4.* Yeah, go ahead. *5.* All right, go ahead. *6.* Come on over here. *7.* Come on, quick. *8.* Just come on. *9.* Oh, go ahead. *10.* Come, now. *11.* Go ahead, please. *12.* Go ahead, go ahead.

**[36]** *1.* Тогда давай! *2.* Конечно, давай. *3.* Спасибо. *4.* Почему, спасибо. *5.* Хорошо, спасибо. *6.* Конечно, спасибо. *7.* Лучше, спасибо. *8.* Не можем? *9.* Я рад.

● *1.* Go on, then! *2.* Sure, come on. *3.* Thanks so much. *4.* Why, thank you. *5.* Good, thanks. *6.* Sure, thanks. *7.* Better, thanks. *8.* Can't we? *9.* I'm pleased.

**[37]** *1.* Идти куда? *2.* Приятно идти. *3.* Быстро идти. *4.* Даже лучше. *5.* Даже очень. *6.* Даже вы. *7.* Даже я. *8.* Даже не. *9.* Хорошо ей. *10.* Хочешь еще? *11.* Просто иди. *12.* Иди сюда.

● *1.* Go where? *2.* Nice going. *3.* Go quickly. *4.* Even better. *5.* Very much so. *6.* Even you. *7.* Even me. *8.* Not even. *9.* Good for her. *10.* Do you want some more? *11.* Just go. *12.* Come over here.

**[38]** *1.* Теперь иди. *2.* Иди сейчас. *3.* Тогда иди. *4.* Вот оно. *5.* Как оно? *6.* Возможно, позже. *7.* Да, позже. *8.* Если только. *9.* Конечно, сэр. *10.* Да сэр! *11.* Пожалуйста, сэр. *12.* Хорошо, сэр.

● *1.* Now go. *2.* Go now. *3.* Go then. *4.* Here it comes. *5.* How's it? *6.* Perhaps later. *7.* Yeah, later. *8.* If only. *9.* Certainly, sir. *10.* Yes sir! *11.* You're welcome, sir. *12.* Good, sir.

**[39]** *1.* Откуда ты? *2.* Откуда? *3.* Откуда вы? *4.* Откуда это? *5.* Откуда они? *6.* Откуда он? *7.* Ты прав. *8.* Он прав. *9.* Я прав? *10.* Иди туда. *11.* Хороший человек. *12.* Я человек.

● *1.* Where are you from? *2.* From where? *3.* Where you from? *4.* Where did it come from? *5.* Where are they from? *6.* Where's he from? *7.* You're right. *8.* He's right. *9.* Am I right? *10.* Get over there. *11.* Good man. *12.* I'm human.

**[40]** *1.* Ты человек. *2.* Он человек. *3.* Сколько чего? *4.* Много времени. *5.* Сколько времени? *6.* Нет времени. *7.* Мы вместе. *8.* Все вместе. *9.* Конечно дорогая.

● *1.* You're human. *2.* He's human. *3.* How much what? *4.* Long time. *5.* How much time? *6.* There isn't time. *7.* We're together. *8.* All together. *9.* Of course, dear.

**[41]** *1.* Хорошо, дорогая. *2.* Вот, дорогая. *3.* Нет, чувак. *4.* Позже, чувак. *5.* Где твой? *6.* Вот твой. *7.* Вот, возьми. *8.* Давай, возьми. *9.* Тогда возьми.

● *1.* All right, dear. *2.* Here, darling. *3.* Nah, man. *4.* Later, man. *5.* Where's yours? *6.* Here's yours. *7.* Here, take it. *8.* Go ahead, take it. *9.* Then take it.

**[42]** *1.* Просто друг. *2.* Назад туда. *3.* Назад куда? *4.* Назад откуда? *5.* Назад назад! *6.* Назад. *7.* Давайте снова. *8.* Давайте тогда. *9.* Извините извините.
● *1.* Just a friend. *2.* Back there. *3.* Back where? *4.* Back from where? *5.* Back, back! *6.* Out back. *7.* Let's go again. *8.* Let's go, then. *9.* Excuse me, sorry.

**[43]** *1.* Извините, кто? *2.* Как долго? *3.* Не долго. *4.* Долго. *5.* Это долго. *6.* Так долго? *7.* Не сегодня. *8.* Ни один. *9.* Зачем мне? *10.* Ну зачем? *11.* Зачем ты? *12.* Не происходит.
● *1.* I'm sorry, who? *2.* For how long? *3.* Not for long. *4.* A long time. *5.* That's a long time. *6.* That long? *7.* Not today. *8.* Not a one. *9.* Why would I? *10.* Well, why? *11.* Why did you? *12.* Not happening.

**[44]** *1.* Э, что? *2.* Э, почему? *3.* Это здорово. *4.* Было здорово. *5.* Да, здорово. *6.* Здорово-здорово. *7.* Как здорово. *8.* Все здорово. *9.* Действительно здорово.
● *1.* Uh, what? *2.* Uh, why? *3.* It's great. *4.* It was great. *5.* Yeah, great. *6.* Great, great. *7.* How exciting. *8.* Everything's great. *9.* Really great.

**[45]** *1.* Так здорово. *2.* Черт возьми. *3.* О черт. *4.* Не этот. *5.* Извините ребята. *6.* Э, ребята? *7.* Вот, ребята. *8.* Достаточно. *9.* Достаточно хорошо. *10.* Этого достаточно? *11.* Достаточно уверен. *12.* Уже достаточно.
● *1.* So great. *2.* God damn. *3.* Oh, darn. *4.* Not that one. *5.* Sorry, guys. *6.* Uh, guys? *7.* Here you go, guys. *8.* That's enough. *9.* Good enough. *10.* Is that enough? *11.* Pretty sure. *12.* Enough already.

**[46]** *1.* Хорошо, достаточно. *2.* Это достаточно? *3.* Достаточно много. *4.* Отсюда? *5.* Ты отсюда? *6.* Выглядишь хорошо. *7.* Хорошая идея. *8.* Вот идея. *9.* Просто идея.
● *1.* Okay, enough. *2.* Is it enough? *3.* Quite a lot. *4.* From here? *5.* Are you from around here? *6.* Lookin' good. *7.* Good idea. *8.* Here's an idea. *9.* Just an idea.

**[47]** *1.* Спокойной ночи. *2.* Очень скоро. *3.* Как скоро? *4.* Достаточно скоро. *5.* Хорошо знать. *6.* Не знать. *7.* Именно так. *8.* Что именно? *9.* Где именно? *10.* Вот именно. *11.*

Несколько раз. *12.* Это плохо?

● *1.* Good night. *2.* Very soon. *3.* How soon? *4.* Soon enough. *5.* Good to know. *6.* Do not know. *7.* Quite so. *8.* Just what? *9.* Where exactly? *10.* That's it exactly. *11.* Several times. *12.* That bad?

**[48]** *1.* Очень плохо. *2.* Действительно плохо. *3.* Ну, почти. *4.* Почти все. *5.* Почти ничего. *6.* Да, почти. *7.* Хорошо пойти. *8.* Большой. *9.* Большой день. *10.* Очень большой. *11.* Он большой. *12.* Хорошая работа.

● *1.* Real bad. *2.* Really bad. *3.* Well, almost. *4.* Almost everything. *5.* Almost nothing. *6.* Yeah, almost. *7.* Good to go. *8.* A big one. *9.* Big day. *10.* Very big. *11.* He's big. *12.* Good job.

**[49]** *1.* Хороший парень. *2.* Большой парень. *3.* Скажи когда. *4.* Звучит здорово. *5.* Звучит хорошо. *6.* Это мило. *7.* Мило. *8.* Как мило. *9.* Действительно мило.

● *1.* Nice guy. *2.* Big guy. *3.* Say when. *4.* Sounds great. *5.* It sounds good. *6.* That's nice. *7.* It's nice. *8.* How nice. *9.* Really nice.

**[50]** *1.* Так мило. *2.* Очень мило. *3.* О, мило. *4.* Рад помочь. *5.* Увидимся позже. *6.* Увидимся. *7.* Увидимся скоро. *8.* Тогда увидимся. *9.* Еще увидимся. *10.* Увидимся там. *11.* Это красиво. *12.* Так красиво.

● *1.* So sweet. *2.* Very cute. *3.* Oh, lovely. *4.* Glad to be of service. *5.* See you later. *6.* I'll see you later. *7.* I'll see you soon. *8.* See you then. *9.* See you again. *10.* See you out there. *11.* It's beautiful. *12.* So beautiful.

**[51]** *1.* Как красиво. *2.* Здесь красиво. *3.* О, красиво. *4.* Красиво, да? *5.* Будь там. *6.* Я готов. *7.* Готов идти? *8.* Хорошо, готов? *9.* Он готов. *10.* Будь готов. *11.* Ты готов. *12.* Один готов.

● *1.* How beautiful. *2.* It's beautiful here. *3.* Oh, beautiful. *4.* Beautiful, huh? *5.* Be right there. *6.* I'm ready. *7.* Ready to go? *8.* Okay, ready? *9.* He's ready. *10.* Be ready. *11.* You're ready. *12.* One down.

**[52]** *1.* Почти готов. *2.* Довольно хорошо. *3.* Довольно много. *4.* Хороший вопрос. *5.* Выглядит хорошо. *6.* Или нет. *7.* Или еще? *8.* Не совсем? *9.* О, совсем.

● *1.* Almost ready. *2.* Pretty good. *3.* Pretty much. *4.* Good question. *5.* It looks good. *6.* Or not. *7.* Or else? *8.* Not really? *9.* Oh, totally.

**[53]** *1.* Сколько лет? *2.* О верно. *3.* Это верно! *4.* Верно-верно. *5.* Верно, сэр. *6.* Верно, да. *7.* Да, верно. *8.* Верно, конечно. *9.* Очень верно. *10.* Верно, ребята? *11.* Хорошо, верно. *12.* Верно.

● *1.* How old? *2.* Oh, right. *3.* That's right! *4.* Right, right. *5.* Right, sir. *6.* Right, yeah. *7.* Yes, right. *8.* Right, of course. *9.* Very true. *10.* Right, guys? *11.* Okay, right. *12.* True dat.

**[54]** *1.* Верно, именно. *2.* Все верно. *3.* Как новый. *4.* Это новый. *5.* Он новый. *6.* Доброе утро. *7.* Вы готовы? *8.* Мы готовы. *9.* Все готовы? *10.* Они готовы. *11.* Это странно. *12.* Странно.

● *1.* Right, exactly. *2.* All true. *3.* Good as new. *4.* That's a new one. *5.* He's new. *6.* Good morning. *7.* You ready? *8.* We're ready. *9.* Everybody ready? *10.* They're ready. *11.* That's strange. *12.* That's odd.

**[55]** *1.* Как странно. *2.* Очень странно. *3.* Странно, да? *4.* Так странно. *5.* Странно как? *6.* Странно, правда? *7.* Вернуться сюда! *8.* Хорошо вернуться. *9.* Вернуться позже.

● *1.* How strange. *2.* Very strange. *3.* Weird, huh? *4.* So weird. *5.* Weird how? *6.* Weird, right? *7.* Come back here! *8.* It's good to be back. *9.* Come back later.

**[56]** *1.* Вернуться! *2.* То самое. *3.* Да правильно. *4.* Правильно. *5.* Это правильно. *6.* Звучит правильно. *7.* Правильно, чувак. *8.* Подожди здесь. *9.* Теперь подожди.

● *1.* Turn back! *2.* The very same. *3.* Yeah, right. *4.* That's correct. *5.* It's the right thing to do. *6.* Sounds about right. *7.* That's right, man. *8.* Wait right here. *9.* Now, hold on.

**[57]** *1.* Просто подожди! *2.* Подожди, почему? *3.* Подожди там. *4.* Подожди, правда? *5.* Подожди сейчас. *6.* Надеюсь нет. *7.* Пока. *8.* Пока ничего. *9.* Да, пока.

● *1.* Just wait! *2.* Wait, why? *3.* Wait right there. *4.* Wait, really? *5.* Hold on now. *6.* I hope not. *7.* So long. *8.* Nothing yet. *9.* Yeah, for now.

**[58]** *1.* Ну, пока. *2.* Пока-пока. *3.* Тогда пока. *4.* Легко, легко. *5.* Это легко. *6.* Теперь легко. *7.* Легко, сейчас. *8.* Слишком легко. *9.* Эй, легко. *10.* Там легко. *11.* Ладно, легко. *12.* О, легко.

● *1.* Well, so long. *2.* Bye-bye now. *3.* Goodbye then. *4.* Easy, easy. *5.* That's easy. *6.* Easy now. *7.* Easy, now. *8.* Too easy. *9.* Hey, easy. *10.* Easy there. *11.* All right, easy. *12.* Oh, easy.

**[59]** *1.* Очень смешно. *2.* Это смешно? *3.* Смешно, да? *4.* Так смешно. *5.* Хотите еще? *6.* Хороший мальчик. *7.* Где мальчик? *8.* Вот, мальчик. *9.* Большой мальчик.

● *1.* Very funny. *2.* Is that funny? *3.* Funny, huh? *4.* So funny. *5.* Would you like some more? *6.* Good boy. *7.* Where's the boy? *8.* Here, boy. *9.* Big boy.

**[60]** *1.* Иди домой. *2.* Домой. *3.* Всегда делаю. *4.* Где мама? *5.* Мама здесь. *6.* Как мама? *7.* Слишком поздно. *8.* Уже поздно. *9.* Было поздно. *10.* Так поздно? *11.* Поздно. *12.* Увидимся вечером.

● *1.* Go home now. *2.* Back home. *3.* Always do. *4.* Where's Mom? *5.* Mommy's here. *6.* How's Mom? *7.* Too late. *8.* It's late. *9.* It was late. *10.* This late? *11.* It is late. *12.* See you tonight.

**[61]** *1.* Это ясно? *2.* Ясно. *3.* Все ясно. *4.* Нам ясно! *5.* Очень ясно. *6.* Мне ясно. *7.* Они хорошие? *8.* Просто поговорить. *9.* Совершенно верно. *10.* Совершенно уверен. *11.* Совершенно новый. *12.* Куда собираешься?

● *1.* Is that clear? *2.* It's clear. *3.* It's all clear. *4.* We're clear! *5.* Very clear. *6.* I'm clear. *7.* Are they good? *8.* Just to talk. *9.* Quite right. *10.* Quite sure. *11.* Brand new. *12.* Where are you going now?

**[62]** *1.* Большое спасибо. *2.* Большое дело. *3.* Все нормально. *4.* Это нормально. *5.* Совершенно нормально. *6.* Кажется, так. *7.* Так себе. *8.* Как далеко? *9.* Далеко.

● *1.* Thank you very much. *2.* Big deal. *3.* It's okay. *4.* That's okay. *5.* Perfectly normal. *6.* Seems so. *7.* So, so. *8.* How far? *9.* Far away.

**[63]** *1.* Это далеко? *2.* Очень далеко. *3.* Достаточно далеко. *4.* Это ужасно! *5.* Как ужасно. *6.* Другой. *7.* Он другой. *8.* Я другой. *9.* А другой? *10.* Этот другой. *11.* Нет, другой. *12.* Ты другой.

● *1.* Is it far? *2.* Too far. *3.* Far enough. *4.* That's terrible! *5.* How terrible. *6.* The other one. *7.* He's different. *8.* I'm different. *9.*

And the other one? *10.* This one's different. *11.* No, the other one. *12.* You are different.

**[64]** *1.* Теперь другой. *2.* Насколько плохо? *3.* Насколько правильно. *4.* Подожди секунду. *5.* Всего секунду. *6.* Извините, секунду. *7.* Через секунду. *8.* Как жизнь? *9.* Какой еще?

• *1.* Now the other one. *2.* How bad is it? *3.* How true. *4.* Wait a second. *5.* Just a second. *6.* Excuse me a second. *7.* In a second. *8.* How's life? *9.* What other one?

**[65]** *1.* Ох, ладно. *2.* Ох, спасибо. *3.* Ох, хорошо. *4.* Ох, пожалуйста. *5.* Ох, здорово. *6.* Не работает. *7.* Это интересно. *8.* Очень интересно. *9.* Интересно, почему.

• *1.* Oh, okay. *2.* Uh, thank you. *3.* Uh, good. *4.* Uh, please. *5.* Uh, great. *6.* Doesn't work. *7.* That's interesting. *8.* Very interesting. *9.* I wonder why.

**[66]** *1.* Как интересно. *2.* Вам интересно? *3.* Звучит интересно. *4.* Было интересно. *5.* Я вернусь. *6.* Это прекрасно. *7.* Просто прекрасно. *8.* Я боюсь. *9.* Боюсь.

• *1.* How interesting. *2.* Are you interested? *3.* Sounds interesting. *4.* It was interesting. *5.* I'll be back. *6.* That's wonderful. *7.* Just beautiful. *8.* I'm scared. *9.* I'm afraid.

**[67]** *1.* Не боюсь. *2.* Боюсь, нет. *3.* Боюсь, да. *4.* Это важно. *5.* Очень важно. *6.* О, круто. *7.* Это круто. *8.* Очень круто. *9.* Да, круто. *10.* Круто, да? *11.* Не круто. *12.* Так круто.

• *1.* Afraid not. *2.* I'm afraid I don't. *3.* I'm afraid I do. *4.* It's important. *5.* Very important. *6.* Oh, great. *7.* It's cool. *8.* Very cool. *9.* Yeah, cool. *10.* Cool, huh? *11.* Not cool. *12.* So cool.

**[68]** *1.* Совершенно круто. *2.* Круто, правда? *3.* Где ребенок? *4.* Как ребенок? *5.* Хороший ребенок. *6.* Я вернулся. *7.* Он вернулся. *8.* Ты вернулся. *9.* Уже вернулся?

• *1.* Totally cool. *2.* Cool, right? *3.* Where's the kid? *4.* How's the baby? *5.* Nice kid. *6.* I'm back. *7.* He's back. *8.* You came back. *9.* Back already?

**[69]** *1.* Хорошо обязательно. *2.* Не обязательно. *3.* Ты серьезно? *4.* Я серьезно. *5.* Серьезно? *6.* Вы серьезно? *7.* Это серьезно. *8.* Нет, серьезно. *9.* Он серьезно?

• *1.* Well, sure. *2.* Don't have to. *3.* Are you serious? *4.* I'm serious. *5.* For real? *6.* You serious? *7.* This is serious. *8.* No, seriously. *9.* Is he serious?

**[70]** *1.* Очень серьезно. *2.* Звучит серьезно. *3.* Да, серьезно. *4.* Насколько серьезно? *5.* Она серьезно? *6.* Чувак, серьезно? *7.* Не волнуйся. *8.* Доброе имя. *9.* Точно нет.
● *1.* Very serious. *2.* Sounds serious. *3.* Yeah, seriously. *4.* How serious? *5.* Is she serious? *6.* Dude, seriously? *7.* Don't worry. *8.* Good name. *9.* Absolutely not.

**[71]** *1.* Это точно. *2.* Да, точно. *3.* Ну, точно. *4.* Хорошая вещь. *5.* Возможно маленький. *6.* Слишком маленький. *7.* Маленький. *8.* Хорошие люди. *9.* Последний.
● *1.* That's for sure. *2.* Yes, exactly. *3.* Well, exactly. *4.* Good stuff. *5.* Maybe a little. *6.* Too small. *7.* A small one. *8.* Good people. *9.* Last one.

**[72]** *1.* Это последний. *2.* О, Боже. *3.* Боже! *4.* Боже мой! *5.* Ну посмотрите. *6.* Посмотрите сюда. *7.* Хорошие новости. *8.* Прости мама. *9.* Прости, дорогая.
● *1.* This is the last one. *2.* Oh, dear. *3.* Good God! *4.* Good heavens! *5.* Well, look. *6.* Looky here. *7.* Good news. *8.* Sorry, Mom. *9.* Sorry, sweetheart.

**[73]** *1.* Просто говорю'. *2.* Ты дома? *3.* Мы дома! *4.* Это потрясающе. *5.* Выглядишь потрясающе. *6.* О, потрясающе. *7.* Не проблема. *8.* Такое большое. *9.* Не говори.
● *1.* Just sayin'. *2.* You home? *3.* We're home! *4.* It's amazing. *5.* You look amazing. *6.* Oh, terrific. *7.* Not a problem. *8.* It's so big. *9.* Don't speak.

**[74]** *1.* Так говори. *2.* Просто говори. *3.* Говори быстро. *4.* Удачи. *5.* Удачи тебе. *6.* Ну удачи. *7.* И удачи. *8.* Удачи, сэр. *9.* Удачи чувак. *10.* Хорошо удачи. *11.* Удачи сегодня. *12.* Удачи, ребята.
● *1.* So talk. *2.* Just talk. *3.* Talk fast. *4.* Good luck. *5.* Good luck to you. *6.* Well, good luck. *7.* And good luck. *8.* Good luck, sir. *9.* Good luck, man. *10.* Okay, good luck. *11.* Good luck today. *12.* Good luck, guys.

**[75]** *1.* Эй, удачи. *2.* Удачи там. *3.* Хорошее место. *4.* Хорошее время. *5.* Где папа? *6.* Прости, папа. *7.* Папа здесь. *8.* Верно, папа? *9.* Как папа? *10.* Добрый день. *11.* Очень добрый. *12.* Звучит отлично.

● *1.* Hey, good luck. *2.* Good luck out there. *3.* Nice place. *4.* Good timing. *5.* Where's Dad? *6.* Sorry, Dad. *7.* Daddy's here. *8.* Right, Dad? *9.* How's Dad? *10.* Good day. *11.* Very kind. *12.* Sounds good.

**[76]** *1.* Отлично. *2.* Хорошо, отлично. *3.* Выглядит отлично. *4.* Это отлично. *5.* О, отлично. *6.* Отлично, отлично. *7.* Да, отлично. *8.* Эй, отлично. *9.* Где дом?

● *1.* This is great. *2.* Okay, great. *3.* Looks great. *4.* This is fine. *5.* Oh, excellent. *6.* Excellent, excellent. *7.* Yes, great. *8.* Hey, great. *9.* Where's home?

**[77]** *1.* Только тот. *2.* Это мои. *3.* Они мои! *4.* Он милый. *5.* Ты милый. *6.* Вот, милый. *7.* Милый дом. *8.* Милый парень. *9.* Я пойду. *10.* Прости, приятель. *11.* Вот, приятель. *12.* Удачи, приятель.

● *1.* Just the one. *2.* Those are mine. *3.* They're mine! *4.* He's cute. *5.* You're sweet. *6.* Here, honey. *7.* Nice house. *8.* Cute kid. *9.* I'll be off. *10.* Sorry, pal. *11.* Here you go, buddy. *12.* Good luck, buddy.

**[78]** *1.* Конечно, приятель. *2.* Как давно? *3.* Давно. *4.* Давно здесь? *5.* Это мое! *6.* Где мое? *7.* Она красивая. *8.* И красивая. *9.* Хорошая ночь. *10.* Тогда вперед. *11.* Извините, Отец. *12.* Никто другой.

● *1.* Sure, buddy. *2.* How long ago? *3.* Long time ago. *4.* Been here long? *5.* It's mine! *6.* Where's mine? *7.* She is beautiful. *8.* And beautiful. *9.* Nice night. *10.* Then let's go. *11.* Sorry, Father. *12.* No one else.

**[79]** *1.* Сложно сказать. *2.* Это сложно. *3.* Сложно поверить. *4.* Теперь слушай. *5.* Ну, слушай. *6.* Только держись. *7.* Просто держись. *8.* Держись, приятель. *9.* Держись, пожалуйста.

● *1.* It's hard to say. *2.* It's hard. *3.* Hard to believe. *4.* Now listen. *5.* Well, listen. *6.* Just hold on. *7.* Just hang on. *8.* Hang in there, buddy. *9.* Hold still, please.

**[80]** *1.* Теперь держись. *2.* А привет. *3.* Ну привет. *4.* Привет. *5.* И более. *6.* Хорошо идет. *7.* Теперь пойдем. *8.* Пойдем сейчас. *9.* Пойдем туда. *10.* Мы пойдем. *11.* Пойдем вместе. *12.* Пойдем сюда.

• 1. Now hold on. 2. Well, hello. 3. Well, hello there. 4. Uh, hi. 5. And more. 6. Good going. 7. Now, let's go. 8. Come along now. 9. Let's go over there. 10. Well, go. 11. Let's go together. 12. Let's go in here.

**[81]** 1. Ты сумасшедший. 2. Он сумасшедший. 3. Я сумасшедший? 4. Я счастлив. 5. Ты счастлив? 6. Счастлив теперь? 7. Будь счастлив. 8. Очень счастлив. 9. Счастлив.

• 1. You're insane. 2. He's crazy. 3. Am I crazy? 4. I'm happy. 5. You happy? 6. Happy now? 7. Be happy. 8. Very happy. 9. Happy to.

**[82]** 1. Так счастлив. 2. Он счастлив. 3. Кто следующий? 4. Следующий вопрос. 5. Следующий, пожалуйста. 6. Я следующий. 7. Ты следующий! 8. Следующий. 9. Хорошо, следующий.

• 1. So happy. 2. He's happy. 3. Who's next? 4. Next question. 5. Next, please. 6. I'm next. 7. You're next! 8. Next one. 9. Okay, next.

**[83]** 1. Где деньги? 2. Как прошло? 3. Правильно, детка. 4. Прости, детка. 5. Вот, детка. 6. Это весело. 7. Как весело. 8. Это сильно. 9. Насколько сильно?

• 1. Where is the money? 2. How did it go? 3. That's right, baby. 4. Sorry, babe. 5. Here, baby. 6. It's hilarious. 7. How funny. 8. It's strong. 9. How badly?

**[84]** 1. Это трудно. 2. Трудно сказать. 3. Это великолепно. 4. О, великолепно. 5. Идеально. 6. О, идеально. 7. Хорошо, идеально. 8. Просто идеально. 9. Все идеально.

• 1. This is hard. 2. It's difficult to say. 3. It's brilliant. 4. Oh, splendid. 5. It's perfect. 6. Oh, perfect. 7. Okay, perfect. 8. Just perfect. 9. Everything's perfect.

**[85]** 1. Да, идеально. 2. Сейчас сделаю. 3. Ты хорош? 4. Он хорош. 5. Это неправильно. 6. Вы рано. 7. Так рано? 8. Еще рано. 9. Слишком рано? 10. Я рано? 11. Как рано? 12. Ты лучший.

• 1. Yes, perfect. 2. I do now. 3. You good? 4. He's good. 5. This isn't right. 6. You're early. 7. So soon? 8. It's early. 9. Too soon? 10. Am I early? 11. How early? 12. You're the best.

**[86]** 1. Он лучший. 2. Повезло тебе. 3. Мне повезло. 4. Тебе повезло. *5.* Нам повезло. *6.* Вам повезло. *7.* Ей повезло. *8.* Ему повезло. *9.* Отличная работа.

● *1.* He's the best. *2.* Good for you. *3.* Lucky me. *4.* You got lucky. *5.* We got lucky. *6.* Lucky for you. *7.* She's lucky. *8.* He was lucky. *9.* Well done.

**[87]** *1.* Отличная идея. *2.* Старый друг. *3.* Вы старый. *4.* Очень старый. *5.* Тогда завтра. *6.* Удачи завтра. *7.* Еще два. *8.* Где вещи? *9.* Хорошие вещи. *10.* Смотри сюда. *11.* Вот, смотри. *12.* Теперь смотри.

● *1.* Great idea. *2.* An old friend. *3.* You're old. *4.* Very old. *5.* Tomorrow, then. *6.* Good luck tomorrow. *7.* Two more. *8.* Where's the stuff? *9.* The good stuff. *10.* Look here. *11.* Here, look. *12.* Now, look.

**[88]** *1.* Не смотри! *2.* Другой путь. *3.* Отличная история. *4.* Хорошая девочка. *5.* Как девочка? *6.* Оставайся здесь. *7.* Оставайся там. *8.* Тогда оставайся. *9.* Хороший план.

● *1.* Don't look! *2.* Other way. *3.* Great story. *4.* Good girl. *5.* How's the girl? *6.* Stay here. *7.* Stay there. *8.* Then stay. *9.* Good plan.

**[89]** *1.* Вот план. *2.* Тихо, пожалуйста. *3.* Тихо. *4.* Тихо, тихо. *5.* Слишком тихо. *6.* Теперь тихо. *7.* Тихо, ты. *8.* Это другое. *9.* Вы первый. *10.* Первый раз? *11.* Ты первый. *12.* Первый вопрос.

● *1.* Here's the plan. *2.* Quiet, please. *3.* It's quiet. *4.* Quiet, quiet. *5.* Too quiet. *6.* Quiet now. *7.* Quiet, you. *8.* This is different. *9.* You go first. *10.* First time? *11.* You're the first. *12.* First question.

**[90]** *1.* Где дети? *2.* Как дети? *3.* Достаточно близко. *4.* Мы близко. *5.* Так близко. *6.* Как близко? *7.* Очень близко. *8.* Слишком близко. *9.* Это близко. *10.* Они близко. *11.* Я близко. *12.* Довольно близко.

● *1.* Where are the kids? *2.* How are the kids? *3.* Close enough. *4.* We're close. *5.* So close. *6.* How close? *7.* Very close. *8.* Too close. *9.* It's close. *10.* They're close. *11.* I'm close. *12.* Pretty close.

**[91]** *1.* Он близко. *2.* Ты близко. *3.* Большая мама? *4.* Я настоящий. *5.* Ты настоящий? *6.* Он настоящий. *7.* Настоящий. *8.* Приятно познакомиться. *9.* Все вниз!

• *1.* He's close. *2.* You're close. *3.* Big Momma? *4.* I'm real. *5.* Are you real? *6.* He's real. *7.* The real one. *8.* It's nice to meet you. *9.* Everybody down!

**[92]** *1.* Давай вниз. *2.* Два вниз. *3.* Вниз, мальчик. *4.* Вы уверены? *5.* Я занят. *6.* Ты занят? *7.* Как часто? *8.* Не часто. *9.* Это тяжело. *10.* Что дальше? *11.* Сколько дальше? *12.* Насколько дальше?

• *1.* Come on down. *2.* Two down. *3.* Down, boy. *4.* Are you sure? *5.* I'm busy. *6.* You busy? *7.* How often? *8.* Not often. *9.* It's heavy. *10.* What's next? *11.* How much further? *12.* How much farther?

**[93]** *1.* Немного дальше. *2.* Куда дальше? *3.* А потом? *4.* Потом. *5.* Это хуже. *6.* Хуже того. *7.* Почти понял. *8.* Я одна. *9.* Она одна. *10.* Где машина? *11.* Добрый вечер. *12.* Глаза вниз.

• *1.* A little further. *2.* Where to next? *3.* And then? *4.* Then come. *5.* It's worse. *6.* Worse than that. *7.* Almost got it. *8.* I'm alone. *9.* She's alone. *10.* Where's the car? *11.* Good evening. *12.* Eyes down.

**[94]** *1.* Ах, да. *2.* Ах хорошо. *3.* Ах, отлично. *4.* Ах, конечно. *5.* Он ушел. *6.* Ушел куда? *7.* Я ушел. *8.* О, можно? *9.* Это невозможно. *10.* Невозможно. *11.* Ты единственный. *12.* Единственный.

• *1.* Oh yeah. *2.* Ah, well. *3.* Ah, great. *4.* Ah, sure. *5.* He got away. *6.* Gone where? *7.* I got away. *8.* Uh, may I? *9.* That's impossible. *10.* Not possible. *11.* You're the only one. *12.* The only one.

**[95]** *1.* Он единственный. *2.* Несколько минут. *3.* Я голоден. *4.* Кто голоден? *5.* Он голоден. *6.* Ты голоден. *7.* Извини чувак. *8.* Извини, что? *9.* Извини, приятель.

• *1.* He's the only one. *2.* A few minutes. *3.* I'm hungry. *4.* Who's hungry? *5.* He's hungry. *6.* You're hungry. *7.* Sorry, man. *8.* Sorry, what? *9.* Sorry, buddy.

**[96]** *1.* Ой, извини! *2.* Извини друг. *3.* Эй, извини. *4.* Извини, детка. *5.* Верно, извини. *6.* Извини, дорогая. *7.* Э, извини? *8.* Ох, извини. *9.* Ах, извини.

• *1.* Oh, sorry! *2.* Sorry, mate. *3.* Hey, sorry. *4.* Sorry, baby. *5.* Right, sorry. *6.* Sorry, darling. *7.* Uh, excuse me? *8.* Ooh, sorry.

*9.* Ah, sorry.

**[97]** *1.* Абсолютно ничего. *2.* Да, абсолютно. *3.* О, абсолютно. *4.* Абсолютно верно. *5.* Абсолютно да. *6.* Абсолютно уверен. *7.* Отличный вопрос. *8.* Отличный парень. *9.* Ладно, хватит.

• *1.* Absolutely nothing. *2.* Yeah, absolutely. *3.* Oh, absolutely. *4.* Exactly right. *5.* Absolutely, yes. *6.* Absolutely sure. *7.* Excellent question. *8.* Great guy. *9.* All right, that's enough.

**[98]** *1.* Хватит этого. *2.* Хватит, хватит. *3.* Хватит уже! *4.* Эй, хватит. *5.* Ты плохой. *6.* Извини брат. *7.* Прости, брат. *8.* Не ваш. *9.* Это глупо. *10.* Момент. *11.* Хороший ответ. *12.* Ответ: да.

• *1.* That's enough of that. *2.* Enough, enough. *3.* That's enough now! *4.* Hey, that's enough. *5.* You're bad. *6.* Sorry, bro. *7.* Sorry, brother. *8.* Not yours. *9.* That's silly. *10.* Just a moment. *11.* Good answer. *12.* The answer is yes.

**[99]** *1.* Осторожно, осторожно. *2.* Теперь осторожно. *3.* Осторожно. *4.* Очень осторожно. *5.* Там осторожно. *6.* О, осторожно. *7.* Слушай внимательно. *8.* Посмотрите внимательно. *9.* Смотри внимательно.

• *1.* Careful, careful. *2.* Careful now. *3.* Careful, now. *4.* Very carefully. *5.* Careful there. *6.* Oh, careful. *7.* Listen carefully. *8.* Look closely. *9.* Look carefully.

**[100]** *1.* Чертовски верно. *2.* Ты милая. *3.* Она милая. *4.* Милая машина. *5.* Извини милая. *6.* Вот, милая. *7.* Держись подальше! *8.* Наконец. *9.* Приятно слышать.

• *1.* Damn right. *2.* You're cute. *3.* She's cute. *4.* Nice car. *5.* Sorry, honey. *6.* Here you go, honey. *7.* Stay back! *8.* At last. *9.* That's good to hear.

**[101]** *1.* Рад слышать. *2.* Минуту, пожалуйста. *3.* Да, наверное. *4.* Наверное, ничего. *5.* Просто успокойся. *6.* Эй, успокойся. *7.* Успокойся! *8.* Ладно, успокойся. *9.* Успокойся, чувак.

• *1.* Glad to hear that. *2.* Just a moment, please. *3.* Yeah, probably. *4.* Probably nothing. *5.* Just calm down. *6.* Hey, take it easy. *7.* Stay calm! *8.* All right, take it easy. *9.* Take it easy, man.

**[102]** *1.* Успокойся, сейчас. *2.* Успокойся, успокойся. *3.* Успокойся, ладно? *4.* Успокойся, приятель. *5.* Теперь успокойся. *6.* Он красивый. *7.* Ты красивый. *8.* Очень красивый. *9.* Красивый день.

● *1.* Take it easy, now. *2.* Take it easy, take it easy. *3.* Take it easy, will you? *4.* Take it easy, pal. *5.* Now, calm down. *6.* He's beautiful. *7.* You are beautiful. *8.* Very beautiful. *9.* Beautiful day.

**[103]** *1.* Красивый вид. *2.* Такой красивый. *3.* Действительно красивый. *4.* Похоже так. *5.* Хорошая собака. *6.* Где собака? *7.* Маленькая девочка. *8.* Маленькая помощь? *9.* Уходи.

● *1.* Nice view. *2.* So handsome. *3.* Really beautiful. *4.* It appears so. *5.* Good dog. *6.* Where's the dog? *7.* A little girl. *8.* Little help? *9.* Walk away.

**[104]** *1.* Уходи пожалуйста. *2.* Тогда уходи. *3.* Прости, малыш. *4.* Эй, малыш. *5.* Удачи, малыш. *6.* Успокойся, малыш. *7.* Хороший выбор. *8.* Просто остаться. *9.* Как чудесно.

● *1.* Go away, please. *2.* Then leave. *3.* Sorry, kid. *4.* Hey, little guy. *5.* Good luck, kid. *6.* Take it easy, kid. *7.* Good choice. *8.* Just stay. *9.* How wonderful.

**[105]** *1.* О, чудесно. *2.* Это чудесно. *3.* Звучит чудесно. *4.* Просто друзья. *5.* Хорошие друзья. *6.* Жарко. *7.* Мне жарко. *8.* Так жарко. *9.* Здесь жарко? *10.* Осторожно, жарко. *11.* Очень жарко. *12.* Тебе жарко?

● *1.* Oh, wonderful. *2.* That's marvelous. *3.* It sounds wonderful. *4.* Just friends. *5.* Good friends. *6.* It's hot. *7.* I'm hot. *8.* It's so hot. *9.* Is it hot in here? *10.* Careful, it's hot. *11.* It's very hot. *12.* Are you hot?

**[106]** *1.* Как семья? *2.* Здесь больно? *3.* Когда начать? *4.* Да, дорогой. *5.* Спасибо, дорогой. *6.* Привет, дорогой. *7.* Нет, дорогой. *8.* Мой дорогой. *9.* Он рядом?

● *1.* How's the family? *2.* Does it hurt here? *3.* Where to start? *4.* Yes, dear. *5.* Thank you, dear. *6.* Hello, dear. *7.* No, dear. *8.* My dear. *9.* Is he around?

**[107]** *1.* Становится поздно. *2.* Становится лучше. *3.* Да, полностью. *4.* Не полностью. *5.* Глупый вопрос. *6.* Ты глупый. *7.* Ваша тоже. *8.* Недостаточно быстро. *9.* Недостаточно времени.

● *1.* It's getting late. *2.* It gets better. *3.* Yeah, totally. *4.* Not completely. *5.* Stupid question. *6.* You're silly. *7.* Yours too. *8.* Not fast enough. *9.* Not enough time.

**[108]** *1.* Это новое. *2.* Последний шанс. *3.* Намного лучше. *4.* Давай вернемся. *5.* Где девушка? *6.* Красивая девушка. *7.* Милая девушка. *8.* Тебе холодно. *9.* Здесь холодно.
● *1.* That's new. *2.* Last chance. *3.* Much better. *4.* Let's go back. *5.* Where's the girl? *6.* Nice girl. *7.* Sweet girl. *8.* You're cold. *9.* It's freezing in here.

**[109]** *1.* Там холодно. *2.* Руки вверх! *3.* Все вверх! *4.* Вверх вверх. *5.* Да, мэм. *6.* Привет, мэм. *7.* Спасибо, мэм. *8.* Вот, мэм. *9.* Вчера вечером. *10.* Вы правы. *11.* Они правы. *12.* Посмотри туда.
● *1.* It's cold out there. *2.* Hands up! *3.* Everybody up! *4.* Up, up. *5.* Yes, ma'am. *6.* Hi, ma'am. *7.* Thanks, ma'am. *8.* Here you go, ma'am. *9.* Last night. *10.* Right you are. *11.* They're right. *12.* Look over there.

**[110]** *1.* Просто посмотри. *2.* Посмотри снова. *3.* Посмотри сюда. *4.* Очень медленно. *5.* Это безумие. *6.* Сколько людей? *7.* Он умный. *8.* Умный человек. *9.* Я умный.
● *1.* Just watch. *2.* Look again. *3.* Lookie here. *4.* Very slowly. *5.* This is crazy. *6.* How many people? *7.* He's smart. *8.* Smart man. *9.* I'm smart.

**[111]** *1.* Умный мальчик. *2.* Тут жарко. *3.* Просто оставить. *4.* Маленький мир. *5.* Мир. *6.* Она права. *7.* Хорошая речь. *8.* Он вернется. *9.* Она вернется. *10.* Оно вернется. *11.* Оставь его! *12.* Это последнее.
● *1.* Clever boy. *2.* It's hot in here. *3.* Just leave. *4.* Small world. *5.* Peace out. *6.* She's right. *7.* Nice speech. *8.* He'll be back. *9.* She'll be back. *10.* It'll come back. *11.* Leave him alone! *12.* That's the last of it.

**[112]** *1.* Делаем добро. *2.* Это лучшее. *3.* Только лучшее. *4.* Ох, посмотрим. *5.* Посмотрим сейчас. *6.* Тогда посмотрим. *7.* Молодец, молодец. *8.* Молодец, чувак. *9.* Молодец, ты.
● *1.* Doing good. *2.* It's the best. *3.* Only the best. *4.* Uh, let's see. *5.* Let's see now. *6.* Then we'll see. *7.* Well done, well done. *8.* Good for you, man. *9.* Well done, you.

**[113]** *1.* Подожди минутку. *2.* Хорошая игра. *3.* О сладкий. *4.* Прости, сладкий. *5.* Конечно, сладкий. *6.* Больше одного. *7.* Удачи, сынок. *8.* Прости, сынок. *9.* Молодец, сынок.

● *1.* Wait just a minute. *2.* Good game. *3.* Oh, sweet. *4.* Sorry, sweetie. *5.* Sure, sweetie. *6.* More than one. *7.* Good luck, son. *8.* Sorry, son. *9.* Well done, son.

**[114]** *1.* Самый лучший. *2.* Нет никакого. *3.* Это новая. *4.* Она новая. *5.* Да, иногда. *6.* Ну, иногда. *7.* Иногда да. *8.* Это подарок. *9.* Больше кофе? *10.* Просто кофе. *11.* Иду где? *12.* Он наш.

● *1.* The very best. *2.* There isn't any. *3.* This is new. *4.* She's new. *5.* Yeah, sometimes. *6.* Well, sometimes. *7.* Sometimes, yes. *8.* It's a present. *9.* More coffee? *10.* Just coffee. *11.* Going where? *12.* He's ours.

**[115]** *1.* Не лицо! *2.* Это невероятно. *3.* Держи его! *4.* Держи её! *5.* Быстрее быстрее! *6.* Быстрее! *7.* Быстрее пожалуйста. *8.* Несколько часов. *9.* Оставаться вместе.

● *1.* Not the face! *2.* It's incredible. *3.* Hold him down! *4.* Hold her down! *5.* Faster, faster! *6.* Go faster! *7.* Quickly, please. *8.* A few hours. *9.* Stay together.

**[116]** *1.* Вот, видишь? *2.* Видишь там? *3.* Как еда? *4.* Где еда? *5.* Не волнуйтесь. *6.* Хорошего дня. *7.* Ничего хорошего. *8.* Всего хорошего. *9.* Что хорошего?

● *1.* There, you see? *2.* See there? *3.* How's the food? *4.* Where's the food? *5.* Don't sweat it. *6.* Have a nice day. *7.* Nothing good. *8.* Be well. *9.* What's good?

**[117]** *1.* Еще три. *2.* Подожди снаружи. *3.* Они снаружи. *4.* Это снаружи. *5.* Посмотрите снаружи. *6.* Где доктор? *7.* Что нового? *8.* Ничего нового. *9.* Будь хорошим.

● *1.* Three more. *2.* Wait outside. *3.* They're outside. *4.* It's outside. *5.* Look outside. *6.* Where's the doctor? *7.* What's new? *8.* Nothing new. *9.* Be good.

**[118]** *1.* Добро пожаловать. *2.* Возвращайся. *3.* Возвращайся туда. *4.* Не навсегда. *5.* Навсегда. *6.* Идите сюда. *7.* Идите вверх. *8.* Просто идите. *9.* Идите вперед.

● *1.* Welcome back. *2.* Get back. *3.* Get back there. *4.* Not forever. *5.* For ever. *6.* Come here. *7.* Go on up. *8.* Just walk. *9.* Go on ahead.

**[119]** *1.* Увидимся ночью. *2.* Поздно ночью? *3.* Да, окей. *4.* Ох, окей. *5.* Конечно, окей. *6.* Нет, окей. *7.* Отлично, окей. *8.* Вернись! *9.* Пожалуйста вернись.

● *1.* I'll see you tonight. *2.* Late night? *3.* Yeah, okay. *4.* Uh, okay. *5.* Sure, okay. *6.* No, okay. *7.* Great, okay. *8.* Come back! *9.* Please come back.

**[120]** *1.* Эй, вернись! *2.* Вернись, вернись! *3.* Прийти сюда. *4.* Просто прийти. *5.* Неплохо. *6.* Выглядит неплохо. *7.* Звучит неплохо. *8.* Неплохо, да? *9.* О, неплохо.

● *1.* Hey, come back! *2.* Get back, get back! *3.* Come up here. *4.* Just come. *5.* Good one. *6.* Looks good. *7.* Sounds good to me. *8.* Pretty good, huh? *9.* Oh, not bad.

**[121]** *1.* Прекрасный день. *2.* Прекрасный выбор. *3.* Слово вверх. *4.* Быстро думать. *5.* Сначала ты. *6.* Сначала. *7.* Сначала я. *8.* Поговорим позже. *9.* Скоро поговорим.

● *1.* It's a beautiful day. *2.* Excellent choice. *3.* Word up. *4.* Think fast. *5.* You first. *6.* At first. *7.* Me first. *8.* I'll talk to you later. *9.* Talk soon.

**[122]** *1.* Теперь поговорим. *2.* Это опасно. *3.* И опасно. *4.* Звучит опасно. *5.* Вернитесь сюда! *6.* Вернитесь внутрь. *7.* Вернитесь туда! *8.* Будь осторожен. *9.* Как фильм?

● *1.* Now talk. *2.* It's dangerous. *3.* And dangerous. *4.* Sounds dangerous. *5.* Get back here! *6.* Go back inside. *7.* Get back in there! *8.* Be careful. *9.* How was the movie?

**[123]** *1.* Простите, мэм. *2.* Ой, простите! *3.* Простите всех. *4.* Двигаться вперед. *5.* Где пистолет? *6.* Я спал. *7.* Ты спал? *8.* Он сильный. *9.* Очень сильный.

● *1.* Sorry, ma'am. *2.* Oh, I'm sorry! *3.* Sorry, everyone. *4.* Move forward. *5.* Where's the gun? *6.* I was asleep. *7.* Were you asleep? *8.* He's strong. *9.* Very strong.

**[124]** *1.* Ты сильный. *2.* Это реально. *3.* Извините, капитан. *4.* Где капитан? *5.* Где угодно. *6.* Они старые. *7.* Старые друзья. *8.* Он полон. *9.* Едва. *10.* Тогда продолжайте. *11.* Продолжайте, сейчас. *12.* Продолжайте.

● *1.* You are strong. *2.* It's real. *3.* Sorry, Captain. *4.* Where's the captain? *5.* Anywhere you want. *6.* They're old. *7.* Old friends. *8.* It's full. *9.* Just barely. *10.* Go on, then. *11.* Go on, now. *12.* Go on now.

**[125]** *1.* Теперь продолжайте. *2.* Продолжайте, сэр. *3.* Продолжайте, капитан. *4.* Просто продолжайте. *5.* Да, вполне. *6.* Вполне нормально. *7.* Вполне возможно. *8.* Как обычно. *9.* Очень мало.

● *1.* Now go on. *2.* Go ahead, sir. *3.* Go ahead, Captain. *4.* Just get on with it. *5.* Yes, quite. *6.* Quite all right. *7.* Quite possibly. *8.* Same as usual. *9.* Very little.

**[126]** *1.* Как мало? *2.* Это необходимо? *3.* Если необходимо. *4.* Необходимо. *5.* Хорошая комната. *6.* Несколько дней. *7.* Как вода? *8.* Меня устраивает. *9.* Остановить сейчас!

● *1.* How little? *2.* Is that necessary? *3.* If necessary. *4.* It's necessary. *5.* Nice room. *6.* A few days. *7.* How's the water? *8.* Fine by me. *9.* Stop now!

**[127]** *1.* Все кончено. *2.* Почти готово. *3.* Готово. *4.* Все готово. *5.* Готово, капитан. *6.* Дайте сюда! *7.* Хорошие времена. *8.* Он великолепен. *9.* Ты великолепен.

● *1.* It's over. *2.* Almost there. *3.* It's ready. *4.* Everything is ready. *5.* Ready, Captain. *6.* Give it here! *7.* Good times. *8.* He's great. *9.* You are amazing.

**[128]** *1.* Где телефон? *2.* Ты болен? *3.* Он болен? *4.* Просто шутка. *5.* Ничего плохого? *6.* Извините, босс. *7.* Где босс? *8.* Конечно, босс. *9.* Это неловко. *10.* Как неловко. *11.* Не поэтому. *12.* Он придет.

● *1.* Where's the phone? *2.* Are you ill? *3.* Is he sick? *4.* Just joking. *5.* Anything wrong? *6.* Sorry, boss. *7.* Where's the boss? *8.* Sure, boss. *9.* It's embarrassing. *10.* How embarrassing. *11.* That's not why. *12.* He'll come around.

**[129]** *1.* Она придет. *2.* Ты пьян? *3.* Он пьян. *4.* Я пьян. *5.* Это вкусно. *6.* Звучит вкусно. *7.* Очень вкусно. *8.* Выглядит вкусно. *9.* Отойди. *10.* Отойди назад! *11.* Отойди, чувак. *12.* Почти забыл.

● *1.* She'll come around. *2.* Are you drunk? *3.* He's drunk. *4.* I'm drunk. *5.* It's delicious. *6.* Sounds delicious. *7.* Very tasty. *8.* Looks delicious. *9.* Stand back. *10.* Move back! *11.* Back off, man. *12.* Almost forgot.

**[130]** *1.* Это очевидно. *2.* Очевидно нет. *3.* Ну, очевидно. *4.* Да, очевидно. *5.* Вы знали? *6.* Они повсюду. *7.* Это повсюду. *8.* Глубоко вниз. *9.* Это глубоко.

● *1.* It's obvious. *2.* Obviously not. *3.* Well, obviously. *4.* Yeah, obviously. *5.* Did you now? *6.* They're everywhere. *7.* It's every-where. *8.* Down, down. *9.* That's deep.

**[131]** *1.* Как глубоко? *2.* Неважно. *3.* Не, неважно. *4.* Ну, неважно. *5.* Неважно сейчас. *6.* Ужин готов. *7.* Вау, действительно? *8.* Вау, окей. *9.* Красивое имя.
● *1.* How deep? *2.* Never mind that. *3.* No, never mind. *4.* Well, no matter. *5.* Never mind that now. *6.* Dinner's ready. *7.* Wow, really? *8.* Wow, okay. *9.* That's a pretty name.

**[132]** *1.* Не беспокоиться. *2.* Я старик. *3.* Где старик? *4.* Он старик. *5.* Эй, старик. *6.* Стоит попробовать. *7.* Ты странный. *8.* Так грустно. *9.* Как грустно.
● *1.* Not to worry. *2.* I'm an old man. *3.* Where's the old man? *4.* He's an old man. *5.* Hey, old man. *6.* It's worth a try. *7.* You're weird. *8.* So sad. *9.* How sad.

**[133]** *1.* Забавно. *2.* Это забавно. *3.* Очень забавно. *4.* Это страшно. *5.* Он внутри. *6.* Она внутри. *7.* Оставаться внутри. *8.* Увидимся внутри. *9.* Они внутри.
● *1.* That's funny. *2.* It's funny. *3.* Very amusing. *4.* It's scary. *5.* He's inside. *6.* She's inside. *7.* Stay inside. *8.* I'll see you inside. *9.* They're inside.

**[134]** *1.* Это неправда. *2.* Оставайся внизу! *3.* Где внизу? *4.* Отличная вечеринка. *5.* Хорошая вечеринка. *6.* Ты опоздал. *7.* Я опоздал. *8.* Ты вернешься? *9.* Шаг назад.
● *1.* That isn't true. *2.* Stay down! *3.* Down where? *4.* Great party. *5.* Nice party. *6.* You're late. *7.* I was late. *8.* Are you coming back? *9.* Step back.

**[135]** *1.* Шаг вперед. *2.* Чертовски стыдно. *3.* Немного ближе. *4.* Тем лучше. *5.* Вот номер. *6.* Он черный. *7.* Хорошее начало. *8.* Новое начало. *9.* Каждый из.
● *1.* Step forward. *2.* Damn shame. *3.* A little closer. *4.* All the better. *5.* Here's the number. *6.* He's black. *7.* Good start. *8.* A new beginning. *9.* Every single one.

**[136]** *1.* Полный вперед. *2.* И опять. *3.* Опять неправильно. *4.* Опять правильно. *5.* Что опять? *6.* Имеет смысл. *7.* Где мальчики? *8.* Простите, мальчики. *9.* Как мальчики?
● *1.* Full speed ahead. *2.* And again. *3.* Wrong again. *4.* Right

again. *5.* What, again? *6.* Makes perfect sense. *7.* Where are the boys? *8.* Sorry, boys. *9.* How are the boys?

**[137]** *1.* Теперь садись. *2.* Садись там. *3.* Садись сюда. *4.* Это нехорошо. *5.* Час назад. *6.* Время час. *7.* Это грубо. *8.* Как грубо. *9.* Настоящее оружие! *10.* Хорошо, поехали. *11.* Ну, поехали. *12.* Теперь поехали.
- *1.* Now sit down. *2.* Sit over there. *3.* Sit over here. *4.* This isn't good. *5.* An hour ago. *6.* One o'clock. *7.* That's gross. *8.* How rude. *9.* Present arms! *10.* All right, here we go. *11.* Well, here we go. *12.* Now let's go.

**[138]** *1.* Давай, поехали. *2.* Ты свободен. *3.* Я свободен. *4.* Это безопасно. *5.* Дай пять. *6.* Вы другие. *7.* И другие? *8.* Было темно. *9.* Темно. *10.* Здесь темно. *11.* Другие вопросы? *12.* Молодой человек.
- *1.* Come on, here we go. *2.* You're free. *3.* I'm free. *4.* It's safe. *5.* High five. *6.* You're different. *7.* And the other? *8.* It was dark. *9.* It's dark. *10.* It's dark in here. *11.* Any other questions? *12.* Young man.

**[139]** *1.* Ты боишься? *2.* Большой сюрприз. *3.* Убери это. *4.* Убери пистолет. *5.* Плохая собака! *6.* Мой любимый. *7.* Ваш любимый. *8.* Вы счастливы? *9.* Были счастливы.
- *1.* Are you afraid? *2.* Big surprise. *3.* Put it away. *4.* Put the gun away. *5.* Bad dog! *6.* My favorite. *7.* Your favorite. *8.* Are you happy? *9.* We're happy.

**[140]** *1.* Все счастливы. *2.* Другой способ. *3.* Это честно. *4.* Нет, честно. *5.* Настоящая любовь. *6.* Она настоящая. *7.* Всё хорошо. *8.* Выходи. *9.* Выходи вперед.
- *1.* Everybody's happy. *2.* The other way. *3.* That's fair. *4.* No, honestly. *5.* True love. *6.* She's real. *7.* Everything is fine. *8.* Come on out. *9.* Come forward.

**[141]** *1.* Выходи сюда. *2.* Я горжусь. *3.* Хороший звонок. *4.* Последний звонок. *5.* Справедливо. *6.* Это справедливо. *7.* Сразу. *8.* Да, сразу. *9.* Бедный малыш.
- *1.* Come out here. *2.* I'm proud. *3.* Good call. *4.* Last call. *5.* Fair enough. *6.* It's only fair. *7.* Right away. *8.* Yes, right away. *9.* Poor little guy.

**[142]** *1.* Бедный человек. *2.* Бедный ребенок. *3.* Твоя очередь. *4.* Как бизнес? *5.* Просто бизнес. *6.* Бизнес хороший. *7.* Большие. *8.* Большие новости. *9.* Большие деньги.

● *1.* You poor man. *2.* You poor child. *3.* Your turn now. *4.* How's business? *5.* Just business. *6.* Business is good. *7.* Big ones. *8.* Big news. *9.* Big money.

**[143]** *1.* Он спит. *2.* Она спит. *3.* Будь сильным. *4.* Оставайся сильным. *5.* Ну, заходите. *6.* Конечно, заходите. *7.* Итак, начнем. *8.* Как поездка? *9.* Хорошая поездка.

● *1.* He's asleep. *2.* She's asleep. *3.* Be strong. *4.* Stay strong. *5.* Well, come on in. *6.* Sure, come on in. *7.* So let's go. *8.* How was your trip? *9.* Nice ride.

## Difficulty Level: 2

**[1]** *1.* Это не я. *2.* Это не ты. *3.* Это не он. *4.* Это не так. *5.* Я как ты. *6.* Я не здесь. *7.* Вы не здесь. *8.* Как ты здесь? *9.* Что это здесь? *10.* Это все здесь. *11.* Мы все здесь. *12.* Так это все?

● *1.* This isn't me. *2.* This isn't you. *3.* It's not him. *4.* It wasn't. *5.* I'm just like you. *6.* I'm outta here. *7.* You're not here. *8.* How are you here? *9.* What's this here? *10.* It's all here. *11.* We're all here. *12.* So is that it?

**[2]** *1.* Нет я не. *2.* Нет, мы не. *3.* Нет, она не. *4.* Нет, не здесь. *5.* Нет, ты не. *6.* Так что нет. *7.* Нет, он не! *8.* Нет не так. *9.* Нет, он здесь. *10.* Нет, не ты! *11.* Нет, не это! *12.* Это просто я.

● *1.* No, I'm not. *2.* No, we're not. *3.* No, she's not. *4.* No, not here. *5.* No, you are not. *6.* So, no. *7.* No, he's not! *8.* No, not like this. *9.* No, he's here. *10.* No, not you! *11.* No, not that! *12.* It's just me.

**[3]** *1.* Это так просто. *2.* Это просто так. *3.* Это просто что? *4.* Я не был. *5.* Он был здесь. *6.* Я был здесь. *7.* Здесь и здесь. *8.* Так и это. *9.* И как это?

● *1.* It's that simple. *2.* It just is. *3.* It's just what? *4.* I wasn't. *5.* He was here. *6.* I've been there. *7.* Here and here. *8.* So is this. *9.* And how's that?

**[4]** *1.* И что это? *2.* И я не? *3.* И я здесь. *4.* Как и ты. *5.* Как это было? *6.* Это было здесь. *7.* Меня не было. *8.* Не на мне. *9.* Они все здесь. *10.* Это не они. *11.* Где ты был? *12.* Где был я?

● *1.* So, what is this? *2.* And I'm not? *3.* And I'm here. *4.* As are you. *5.* How was it? *6.* It was here. *7.* I was out. *8.* Not on me. *9.* They're all here. *10.* It's not them. *11.* Where have you been? *12.* Where was I?

**[5]** *1.* Так где он? *2.* Где он был? *3.* Где это было? *4.* И где он? *5.* И где это? *6.* Так где она? *7.* Где я был? *8.* И где она? *9.* И где ты? *10.* Так где они? *11.* Это очень просто. *12.* Да, я здесь.

● *1.* So where is he? *2.* Where was he? *3.* Where was that? *4.* And where is he? *5.* And where is that? *6.* So where is she? *7.* Where have I been? *8.* And where is she? *9.* And where are you? *10.* So where are they? *11.* It's very simple. *12.* Yeah, I'm here.

**[6]** *1.* Да, и что? *2.* Да, он здесь. *3.* Да просто так. *4.* Так что да. *5.* Просто так, да? *6.* Да, она здесь. *7.* Это ты, да? *8.* Да, мы здесь. *9.* Нет, все хорошо.

● *1.* Yeah, so what? *2.* Yes, he's here. *3.* Just because. *4.* So, yeah. *5.* Just like that, huh? *6.* Yeah, she's here. *7.* That's you, right? *8.* Yeah, we're here. *9.* No, it's fine.

**[7]** *1.* Это было хорошо. *2.* Это очень хорошо. *3.* Это не хорошо. *4.* Да, это хорошо. *5.* Хорошо у тебя. *6.* Нет, это хорошо. *7.* Да очень хорошо. *8.* Хорошо очень хорошо. *9.* Хорошо, ты здесь.

● *1.* It was good. *2.* That's very good. *3.* It's no good. *4.* Yeah, that's good. *5.* It's nice here. *6.* No, it's good. *7.* Yes, very good. *8.* Good, very good. *9.* Good, you're here.

**[8]** *1.* Очень очень хорошо. *2.* Хорошо, как ты? *3.* Это хорошо, да? *4.* Это так хорошо. *5.* Хорошо, я здесь. *6.* Мне здесь хорошо. *7.* Хорошо, мы здесь. *8.* Хорошо, это хорошо. *9.* Да, хорошо, хорошо.

● *1.* Very, very good. *2.* Good, how are you? *3.* It's good, huh? *4.* That's so good. *5.* Okay, I'm here. *6.* I'm fine here. *7.* Okay, here we are. *8.* All right, that's good. *9.* Yeah, all right, all right.

**[9]** *1.* У меня хорошо? *2.* И это хорошо. *3.* Ну и что? *4.* Ну, это так. *5.* Ну, как ты? *6.* Ну, я был. *7.* Ну и как? *8.* Ну, я нет. *9.* Ну, что это? *10.* Ну, это я. *11.* Ну, мы здесь. *12.* Ну, это

просто.
- *1.* Am I good? *2.* And that's good. *3.* So what? *4.* Well, it is. *5.* Well, how are you? *6.* Well, I was. *7.* Well, how? *8.* Well, I haven't. *9.* Well, which is it? *10.* Well, this is me. *11.* Well, we're here. *12.* Well, it's simple.

**[10]** *1.* Ну, он был. *2.* Его здесь нет. *3.* И что еще? *4.* Все еще здесь? *5.* Хорошо, что еще? *6.* Почему ты здесь? *7.* И почему так? *8.* Почему он здесь? *9.* И почему это?
- *1.* Well, he was. *2.* He isn't here. *3.* And what else? *4.* Still here? *5.* Okay, what else? *6.* Why are you here? *7.* And why is that? *8.* Why is he here? *9.* And why's that?

**[11]** *1.* Почему это было? *2.* Почему ты нет? *3.* Почему ты так? *4.* Почему это так? *5.* О, да, да. *6.* О, это хорошо. *7.* О, все хорошо. *8.* О, это так? *9.* О, хорошо, хорошо.
- *1.* Why was that? *2.* Why aren't you? *3.* Why are you being like this? *4.* Why would that be? *5.* Oh, yeah, yeah. *6.* Oh, that's good. *7.* Oh, it's okay. *8.* Oh, is that so? *9.* Oh, good, good.

**[12]** *1.* О, очень хорошо. *2.* О, ты здесь. *3.* О да, это. *4.* О, я нет. *5.* Как тебе это? *6.* Она была здесь. *7.* Где она была? *8.* Она не была. *9.* Где он сейчас?
- *1.* Oh, very well. *2.* Oh, you're here. *3.* Oh, yeah, that. *4.* Oh, I'm not. *5.* How do you like that? *6.* She was here. *7.* Where was she? *8.* She wasn't. *9.* Where is he now?

**[13]** *1.* Где она сейчас? *2.* Где вы сейчас? *3.* Где они сейчас? *4.* Нет, не сейчас. *5.* Где это сейчас? *6.* Где ты сейчас? *7.* Где мы сейчас? *8.* Ты сейчас здесь. *9.* Здесь и сейчас.
- *1.* Where is she now? *2.* Where are you now? *3.* Where are they now? *4.* No, not now. *5.* Where is it now? *6.* Where are you right now? *7.* Where are we now? *8.* You're here now. *9.* Right here, right now.

**[14]** *1.* Что это сейчас? *2.* Мы сейчас здесь. *3.* Ну, не сейчас. *4.* Он сейчас здесь. *5.* Ну, это сейчас. *6.* Ты в порядке? *7.* Я в порядке. *8.* Все в порядке. *9.* Он в порядке.
- *1.* What's that now? *2.* We're here now. *3.* Well, not now. *4.* He's here now. *5.* Well, it is now. *6.* Are you okay? *7.* I'm fine. *8.* It's all right. *9.* He's fine.

**[15]** *1.* Она в порядке. *2.* Они в порядке. *3.* Вы в порядке?

*4.* В порядке Хорошо! *5.* Не то, что? *6.* Я не могу. *7.* Как я могу? *8.* Не могу что? *9.* Ну вот хорошо.

● *1.* She's fine. *2.* They're fine. *3.* You alright? *4.* Okay, fine! *5.* Not what? *6.* I can't. *7.* How can I? *8.* Can't what? *9.* Well, that's good.

**[16]** *1.* Вот и она. *2.* Вот и все. *3.* Вот так вот. *4.* Вот и я. *5.* И вот еще. *6.* Вот что-то. *7.* О, вот он. *8.* Вот и мы. *9.* О, вот она. *10.* Почему бы это? *11.* И что теперь? *12.* Ну что теперь?

● *1.* Here she comes. *2.* That's just it. *3.* That's how it is. *4.* Here I come. *5.* And one more thing. *6.* Here's something. *7.* Oh, here he is. *8.* Here we come. *9.* Oh, here she is. *10.* Why would it? *11.* So what now? *12.* So now what?

**[17]** *1.* Теперь я здесь. *2.* Хорошо, что теперь? *3.* Теперь этого нет. *4.* Теперь его нет. *5.* Я не знаю. *6.* Я просто знаю. *7.* Я знаю почему. *8.* Теперь я знаю. *9.* Я знаю это.

● *1.* I'm here now. *2.* Okay, now what? *3.* Now it's gone. *4.* Now he's gone. *5.* I don't know. *6.* I just know. *7.* I know why. *8.* Now I know. *9.* I know so.

**[18]** *1.* Не знаю его. *2.* Ну, я знаю. *3.* Я знаю как. *4.* Я это знаю. *5.* Это я знаю. *6.* Я хорошо знаю. *7.* Я знаю где. *8.* Не так ли? *9.* Не знаю ее. *10.* Нет, не ее. *11.* Никогда не было. *12.* Я бы никогда.

● *1.* Don't know him. *2.* Well, I know. *3.* I know how. *4.* I know that much. *5.* That much I know. *6.* I'm well aware. *7.* I know where. *8.* Isn't it? *9.* Don't know her. *10.* No, not her. *11.* Never happened. *12.* I would never.

**[19]** *1.* Ну я никогда! *2.* Ну, он есть. *3.* Есть ли еще? *4.* Он есть сейчас. *5.* Все еще есть. *6.* Я был там. *7.* Ты еще там? *8.* Что еще там? *9.* Это не там. *10.* Здесь и там. *11.* Ее там нет. *12.* Она была там.

● *1.* Well, I never! *2.* Well, he is. *3.* Is there more? *4.* He is now. *5.* Still am. *6.* I was there. *7.* Are you still there? *8.* What else is there? *9.* It's not there. *10.* Here and there. *11.* She's not there. *12.* She was there.

**[20]** *1.* Ты был там? *2.* Это все там. *3.* Где-то там. *4.* Это было там. *5.* Нет, не там. *6.* Все еще там. *7.* Они все там. *8.* Но не сейчас. *9.* Но почему я? *10.* Да, но почему? *11.* Но почему сейчас? *12.* Да, но как?

● *1.* Have you been there? *2.* It's all in there. *3.* Nearly there. *4.* It was there. *5.* No, not there. *6.* Still there. *7.* They're all there. *8.* But not now. *9.* But why me? *10.* Yeah, but why? *11.* But why now? *12.* Yeah, but how?

**[21]** *1.* Но ты здесь. *2.* Но где он? *3.* Но это все. *4.* Нет, больше нет. *5.* Но не больше. *6.* Ну, больше нет. *7.* Здесь ничего нет. *8.* Там ничего нет. *9.* Больше ничего нет.
● *1.* But you're here. *2.* But where is he? *3.* But that's just it. *4.* No, not anymore. *5.* But not anymore. *6.* Well, not anymore. *7.* There's nothing in here. *8.* There's nothing out there. *9.* There's nothing else.

**[22]** *1.* Это только мы. *2.* Это только я. *3.* Это только ты. *4.* Нет, только я. *5.* Не только ты. *6.* Это только что. *7.* Не только сейчас. *8.* Только не сейчас. *9.* Не для меня.
● *1.* It's just us. *2.* It's only me. *3.* It's just you. *4.* No, just me. *5.* Not just you. *6.* This just in. *7.* Not just now. *8.* Just not now. *9.* Not to me.

**[23]** *1.* Не для тебя. *2.* Больше для меня. *3.* Хорошо для меня. *4.* Только для меня. *5.* Когда это было? *6.* Где и когда? *7.* Тогда что это? *8.* Тогда очень хорошо. *9.* Тогда где он?
● *1.* Not for you. *2.* More for me. *3.* Good for me. *4.* Just for me. *5.* When was that? *6.* Where and when? *7.* Then what is it? *8.* Very well, then. *9.* Then where is he?

**[24]** *1.* Что было тогда. *2.* И что тогда? *3.* Тогда где это? *4.* Но что тогда? *5.* Что это тогда? *6.* Тогда где она? *7.* Все будет хорошо. *8.* Вам будет хорошо. *9.* Будет все хорошо.
● *1.* That was then. *2.* And what then? *3.* Then where is it? *4.* But then what? *5.* What's this then? *6.* Then where is she? *7.* I'll be fine. *8.* You'll be fine. *9.* It's gonna be all right.

**[25]** *1.* Он будет здесь. *2.* Нет, не будет. *3.* Она не будет. *4.* Она будет здесь. *5.* Он будет там. *6.* Она будет там. *7.* Это будет хорошо. *8.* Это не будет. *9.* Это действительно хорошо.
● *1.* He'll be here. *2.* No, it won't. *3.* She won't. *4.* She'll be here. *5.* He'll be there. *6.* She'll be there. *7.* This is gonna be good. *8.* It won't be. *9.* It's really good.

**[26]** *1.* Это действительно так. *2.* Это действительно ты? *3.*

О да, действительно. *4.* Я действительно хорошо. *5.* Он действительно есть. *6.* Ты действительно здесь. *7.* Где вы были? *8.* Где были мы? *9.* Они были здесь.

● *1.* It really is. *2.* Is it really you? *3.* Oh, yes, indeed. *4.* I'm really good. *5.* He really is. *6.* You're really here. *7.* Where were you? *8.* Where were we? *9.* They were here.

**[27]** *1.* Вы не были. *2.* Где они были? *3.* Вы были здесь. *4.* Где мы были? *5.* Вы были там? *6.* Я хочу больше. *7.* Я не хочу. *8.* Я хочу сейчас. *9.* Так-то лучше.

● *1.* You weren't. *2.* Where were they? *3.* You were here. *4.* Now where were we? *5.* You've been there? *6.* I want more. *7.* I don't wanna. *8.* I want it now. *9.* That's better.

**[28]** *1.* Лучше бы так. *2.* Вы бы лучше. *3.* Мне сейчас лучше. *4.* Ты лучше этого. *5.* Да, так лучше. *6.* Вот так лучше. *7.* О, так лучше. *8.* Я могу лучше. *9.* Я знаю лучше.

● *1.* It better be. *2.* You'd better. *3.* I'm better now. *4.* You're better than this. *5.* Yeah, that's better. *6.* There, that's better. *7.* Oh, that's better. *8.* I can do better. *9.* I know better.

**[29]** *1.* Это было лучше. *2.* Ну, это лучше. *3.* Да, я тоже. *4.* Да, ты тоже. *5.* И я тоже. *6.* Я тоже нет. *7.* И мы тоже. *8.* И ты тоже. *9.* Я бы тоже. *10.* И вы тоже. *11.* Для меня тоже. *12.* Я тоже могу.

● *1.* That was better. *2.* Well, that's better. *3.* Yeah, me, too. *4.* Yeah, you too. *5.* So have I. *6.* I don't either. *7.* So are we. *8.* And so are you. *9.* So would I. *10.* And so do you. *11.* For me too. *12.* So can I.

**[30]** *1.* Ну, я тоже. *2.* О, я тоже. *3.* Да, это тоже. *4.* О, ты тоже. *5.* Как же так? *6.* Все так же. *7.* Больше чем это. *8.* Лучше, чем это. *9.* Лучше, чем что?

● *1.* Well, so do I. *2.* Oh, me, too. *3.* Yeah, that too. *4.* Oh, you too. *5.* How so? *6.* All the same. *7.* More than that. *8.* Better than that. *9.* Better than what?

**[31]** *1.* Лучше чем ничего. *2.* Я так думаю. *3.* Я не думаю. *4.* Я просто думаю. *5.* Да, думаю, да. *6.* Может быть, я. *7.* Она не может. *8.* Может быть это. *9.* Да, может быть.

● *1.* Better than nothing. *2.* I think so. *3.* I don't think. *4.* I'm just thinking. *5.* Yeah, guess so. *6.* Maybe I am. *7.* She can't. *8.* Maybe it is. *9.* Yes, maybe.

**[32]** *1.* Может для тебя. *2.* Может быть, да. *3.* Может быть, ничего. *4.* Не может быть. *5.* Может быть, есть. *6.* Может быть вы. *7.* Может быть, никогда. *8.* Может быть ты. *9.* Как он может?

● *1.* Maybe for you. *2.* Maybe, yeah. *3.* Maybe nothing. *4.* It cannot be. *5.* Maybe there is. *6.* Maybe you are. *7.* Maybe never. *8.* Maybe you. *9.* How can he?

**[33]** *1.* Может быть, нет. *2.* Мне нужно больше. *3.* Не слишком хорошо. *4.* Все слишком хорошо. *5.* Это слишком просто. *6.* Их там нет. *7.* Мне тоже жаль. *8.* Я-мне жаль. *9.* Мне очень жаль.

● *1.* Maybe you don't. *2.* I need more. *3.* Not too good. *4.* All too well. *5.* This is too easy. *6.* They're not there. *7.* I'm sorry, too. *8.* I-I'm sorry. *9.* I really am sorry.

**[34]** *1.* Мне-мне жаль. *2.* Нам очень жаль. *3.* Мне жаль ее. *4.* У нас нет. *5.* Не для нас. *6.* Никогда не знаешь. *7.* Ты знаешь почему? *8.* Ну, знаешь что? *9.* И знаешь почему?

● *1.* I'm-I'm sorry. *2.* We're really sorry. *3.* I feel sorry for her. *4.* We haven't. *5.* Not for us. *6.* You never know. *7.* Do you know why? *8.* Well, you know what? *9.* And you know why?

**[35]** *1.* Теперь ты знаешь. *2.* Знаешь что еще? *3.* Знаешь, где это? *4.* Ты знаешь как? *5.* Ты знаешь где. *6.* Ты знаешь лучше. *7.* Знаешь ли ты? *8.* Кто-то там? *9.* Есть кто там?

● *1.* Now you know. *2.* You know what else? *3.* You know where it is? *4.* Do you know how? *5.* You know where. *6.* You know better. *7.* Do you now? *8.* Is anyone there? *9.* Anybody there?

**[36]** *1.* Кто-то здесь. *2.* Тогда кто ты? *3.* Так кто он? *4.* Кто еще здесь? *5.* Кто ты тогда? *6.* Ну, кто это? *7.* Кто был здесь? *8.* Тогда кто это? *9.* Ну кто ты?

● *1.* Someone's here. *2.* Then what are you? *3.* So who is he? *4.* Who else is there? *5.* Who are you, then? *6.* Well, who is it? *7.* Who was here? *8.* Then who is it? *9.* Well, who are you?

**[37]** *1.* Так кто она? *2.* Это всегда так. *3.* Так было всегда. *4.* Я всегда был. *5.* Всегда ли так? *6.* Я всегда здесь. *7.* Вы всегда есть. *8.* Ладно это хорошо. *9.* Ну, ладно, тогда.

● *1.* So who is she? *2.* It always is. *3.* It always has been. *4.* I always have been. *5.* Is it always like this? *6.* I'm always here. *7.* You always are. *8.* Okay, that's good. *9.* Well, all right, then.

**[38]** *1.* Я знаю, ладно? *2.* Что-нибудь еще? *3.* Кто-нибудь еще? *4.* Кто-нибудь здесь? *5.* Где-нибудь еще. *6.* Кто-нибудь там? *7.* Есть что-нибудь? *8.* Я уже сделал. *9.* Уже на этом.

● *1.* I know, okay? *2.* Anything else? *3.* Anyone else? *4.* Anybody here? *5.* Somewhere else. *6.* Somebody there? *7.* Anything there? *8.* I already did. *9.* Already on it.

**[39]** *1.* Мне уже лучше. *2.* Я уже знаю. *3.* Уже все хорошо. *4.* Ты уже сделал. *5.* Его уже нет. *6.* Вы уже есть. *7.* Он уже здесь. *8.* Ты уже знаешь. *9.* Они уже здесь.

● *1.* I feel better already. *2.* I already know. *3.* It's all right now. *4.* You already did. *5.* He's gone now. *6.* You already are. *7.* He's already here. *8.* You already know. *9.* They're already here.

**[40]** *1.* Они уже есть. *2.* Мы уже здесь. *3.* Мне еще раз. *4.* Здесь для вас. *5.* Не делать что? *6.* Вот сюда, пожалуйста. *7.* Не сейчас, пожалуйста. *8.* Пожалуйста, не сейчас. *9.* Не так много.

● *1.* They already have. *2.* We're already here. *3.* Me again. *4.* Here, for you. *5.* Don't do what? *6.* Right this way, please. *7.* Not now, please. *8.* Please, not now. *9.* Not so much.

**[41]** *1.* Это слишком много. *2.* Ты слишком много. *3.* Их слишком много. *4.* Он сказал почему? *5.* Кто сказал так? *6.* Сказал Вам так. *7.* Я сказал сейчас! *8.* Я не сказал. *9.* Ты так сказал.

● *1.* That's too much. *2.* You're too much. *3.* There's too many of them. *4.* Did he say why? *5.* Who said so? *6.* Told you so. *7.* I said now! *8.* I didn't say. *9.* You said so.

**[42]** *1.* От куда это? *2.* Не прямо сейчас. *3.* Это прямо здесь. *4.* Прямо как ты. *5.* Прямо за тобой. *6.* Прямо как я. *7.* Да, прямо здесь. *8.* Прямо на тебя. *9.* Это прямо там.

● *1.* Where does it come from? *2.* Not right now. *3.* It's right here. *4.* Just like you. *5.* Right behind you. *6.* Just like me. *7.* Yeah, right here. *8.* Right back at you. *9.* It's right over there.

**[43]** *1.* Он прямо там. *2.* Да прямо сейчас. *3.* Она прямо там. *4.* Они прямо здесь. *5.* Да, я уверен. *6.* Я не уверен. *7.* О, я уверен. *8.* Уверен в чем? *9.* Ну, а ты?

● *1.* He's right over there. *2.* Yes, right now. *3.* She's right over there. *4.* They're right here. *5.* Yeah, I'm sure. *6.* I'm not certain. *7.* Oh, I'm sure. *8.* Sure of what? *9.* Well, do you?

**[44]** *1.* А ты куда? *2.* А теперь это. *3.* А теперь ты. *4.* А что здесь? *5.* Ну а когда? *6.* Хорошо, а Вы? *7.* Это снова мы. *8.* Это снова я. *9.* Вот и снова. *10.* Снова и снова. *11.* Это снова ты. *12.* Вот она снова.

● *1.* And where are you going? *2.* And now this. *3.* And now you. *4.* What about here? *5.* Well, when? *6.* Good, and you? *7.* Here we go again. *8.* It's me again. *9.* There you go again. *10.* Over and over again. *11.* It's you again. *12.* There she goes again.

**[45]** *1.* Он снова там. *2.* Итак, мы здесь. *3.* Итак, это все? *4.* Итак, где он? *5.* Итак, где это? *6.* Итак, вы здесь. *7.* Итак, где она? *8.* Итак, кто вы? *9.* Как ты можешь?

● *1.* He's back there. *2.* So here we are. *3.* So, that's it? *4.* So, where is he? *5.* Now, where is it? *6.* So here you are. *7.* So, where is she? *8.* Now, who are you? *9.* How can you?

**[46]** *1.* Ты можешь лучше. *2.* Еще есть время. *3.* Сейчас не время. *4.* Как и мой. *5.* Теперь ты мой. *6.* О да, конечно. *7.* Конечно, я уверен. *8.* Да, да, конечно. *9.* Ну, конечно нет.

● *1.* You can do better. *2.* There's still time. *3.* This isn't the time. *4.* So is mine. *5.* You're mine now. *6.* Oh, yeah, sure. *7.* Of course I'm sure. *8.* Yeah, yeah, sure. *9.* Well, of course not.

**[47]** *1.* О, конечно, конечно. *2.* Конечно я могу. *3.* Я, конечно, сделал. *4.* Я, конечно, да. *5.* Да, конечно, конечно. *6.* Нет, конечно, нет. *7.* Конечно, я думаю. *8.* Ну да, конечно. *9.* Конечно, он есть.

● *1.* Oh, sure, sure. *2.* Sure I can. *3.* I certainly did. *4.* I certainly am. *5.* Yeah, sure, sure. *6.* No, of course you don't. *7.* Sure, I guess. *8.* Well, yes, of course. *9.* Sure he is.

**[48]** *1.* Конечно, ты был. *2.* Конечно, они есть. *3.* Почему да, конечно. *4.* Он, конечно, есть. *5.* Она, конечно, есть. *6.* Ну, конечно, да. *7.* О, конечно, да. *8.* Так как дела? *9.* Как там дела?

● *1.* Sure you were. *2.* Sure they are. *3.* Why, yes, of course. *4.* He certainly is. *5.* She certainly is. *6.* Well, of course you do. *7.* Oh, sure, yeah. *8.* So how's it going? *9.* How's it going in there?

**[49]** *1.* Итак, как дела? *2.* Как дела здесь? *3.* Ну, как дела? *4.* Только один раз. *5.* Вот еще один. *6.* Где еще один? *7.* Я был один. *8.* Здесь только один. *9.* Еще один раз.

● *1.* So, how's it going? *2.* How's it going in here? *3.* Well, how do you do? *4.* Just this once. *5.* Here's another one. *6.* Where's the other one? *7.* I was alone. *8.* There's only one. *9.* Just one more time.

**[50]** *1.* Да, один раз. *2.* Есть еще один. *3.* Еще один, пожалуйста. *4.* Он был один. *5.* Действительно, я такой. *6.* Он всегда такой? *7.* Как это возможно? *8.* Возможно когда-нибудь. *9.* Да, это возможно.
● *1.* Yeah, once. *2.* There's one more. *3.* One more, please. *4.* He was alone. *5.* Indeed I am. *6.* Is he always like that? *7.* How is that possible? *8.* Maybe someday. *9.* Yeah, it's possible.

**[51]** *1.* Я не буду. *2.* Я буду там. *3.* Я буду здесь. *4.* Ну, я буду. *5.* Я сейчас буду. *6.* Я всегда буду. *7.* Конечно я буду. *8.* Эй, ты как? *9.* Эй, как дела?
● *1.* I won't. *2.* I'll be there. *3.* I'll be here. *4.* Well, I'll be. *5.* I'll be right up. *6.* I always will. *7.* Sure I will. *8.* Hey, how are you? *9.* Hey, how's it going?

**[52]** *1.* Эй где вы? *2.* Эй, ты там! *3.* И еще немного. *4.* Ты очень хороший. *5.* Я всегда хороший. *6.* Сколько их там? *7.* Сколько их было? *8.* Сколько вас здесь? *9.* На сколько больше?
● *1.* Hey, where are you? *2.* Hey, you there! *3.* And then some. *4.* You're very good. *5.* I'm always nice. *6.* How many are there? *7.* How many were there? *8.* How many of you are there? *9.* How many more?

**[53]** *1.* Да, это правда. *2.* Но это правда. *3.* Ну, это правда. *4.* Это хорошо, правда? *5.* Это все правда. *6.* Это правда ты? *7.* Нет, это правда. *8.* Так это правда? *9.* Не правда ли?
● *1.* Yes, that's true. *2.* But it's true. *3.* Well, it's true. *4.* That's good, right? *5.* It's all true. *6.* Is that really you? *7.* No, that's true. *8.* So it's true? *9.* Isn't it true?

**[54]** *1.* Нет, нет, правда. *2.* И это правда. *3.* Это действительно правда? *4.* Тогда это правда. *5.* О, это правда! *6.* Не так быстро. *7.* Это было быстро. *8.* Ну, ты должен. *9.* Возможно я должен.
● *1.* No, no, really. *2.* And it's true. *3.* Is it really true? *4.* Then it's true. *5.* Oh, that's right! *6.* Not so fast. *7.* That was fast. *8.* Well, you should. *9.* Maybe I should.

**[55]** *1.* Просто сказать это. *2.* Сказать еще раз? *3.* Не могу сказать. *4.* Просто сказать да. *5.* Это действительно приятно. *6.* Это было приятно. *7.* Да, это приятно. *8.* О, очень приятно. *9.* Это так приятно.

● *1.* Just say it. *2.* Say again? *3.* Can't say. *4.* Just say yes. *5.* It's really nice. *6.* It felt good. *7.* Yeah, it's nice. *8.* Oh, very nice. *9.* It's so nice.

**[56]** *1.* Ну, это приятно. *2.* Мне так приятно. *3.* О, это приятно. *4.* Нет, это приятно. *5.* Это приятно, правда? *6.* Это очень приятно. *7.* Действительно очень приятно. *8.* О, давай, сейчас. *9.* Ну, давай тогда.

● *1.* Well, this is nice. *2.* I'm so pleased. *3.* Oh, that feels good. *4.* No, it's nice. *5.* It's nice, right? *6.* That's real nice. *7.* Very nice indeed. *8.* Oh, come on, now. *9.* Well, come on, then.

**[57]** *1.* Не со мной. *2.* Как ты мог? *3.* Как я мог? *4.* Как он мог? *5.* Я не мог! *6.* Еще раз спасибо. *7.* Очень хорошо, спасибо. *8.* Я хорошо, спасибо. *9.* О, ну, спасибо.

● *1.* Not with me. *2.* How could you? *3.* How could I? *4.* How could he? *5.* I couldn't! *6.* Thanks again. *7.* Very well, thank you. *8.* I'm fine, thanks. *9.* Oh, well, thank you.

**[58]** *1.* О, нет, спасибо. *2.* Я так рад. *3.* Я очень рад. *4.* Я буду рад. *5.* Еще один день. *6.* И идти куда? *7.* Я должен идти. *8.* Куда нам идти? *9.* Мне лучше идти.

● *1.* Uh, no, thank you. *2.* I'm so relieved. *3.* I'm very excited. *4.* I'd be glad to. *5.* One more day. *6.* And go where? *7.* I must go now. *8.* Where shall we go? *9.* I better get going.

**[59]** *1.* Куда мне идти? *2.* Тебе лучше идти. *3.* Нам лучше идти. *4.* Ну что ж. *5.* Что ж, пожалуйста. *6.* Это даже лучше. *7.* Даже не немного. *8.* Даже для тебя. *9.* Сколько ты хочешь?

● *1.* Where should I go? *2.* You better get going. *3.* We better get going. *4.* Oh, well. *5.* Well, you're welcome. *6.* That's even better. *7.* Not even a little bit. *8.* Even for you. *9.* How much do you want?

**[60]** *1.* Ты хочешь больше? *2.* Ты хочешь еще? *3.* Эй, иди сюда. *4.* Иди сюда, ты. *5.* Иди сейчас же! *6.* Так что иди. *7.* О, иди сюда. *8.* Хорошо, иди сюда. *9.* Ты, иди сюда.

● *1.* You want more? *2.* You want some more? *3.* Hey, come here. *4.* Come here, you. *5.* Go now! *6.* So go. *7.* Oh, come here. *8.* Okay, come here. *9.* You, come here.

**[61]** *1.* Пожалуйста, просто иди. *2.* Теперь иди сюда. *3.* Вот, иди сюда. *4.* Да, иди сюда. *5.* Просто иди сюда. *6.* Иди сюда быстро. *7.* Где оно было? *8.* О, вот оно. *9.* Вот оно снова.
● *1.* Please, just go. *2.* Now come here. *3.* Here, come here. *4.* Yeah, come here. *5.* Just get over here. *6.* Come here now. *7.* Where was it? *8.* Oh, here it is. *9.* There it is again.

**[62]** *1.* Так вот оно? *2.* Хорошо, вот оно. *3.* Ну, вот оно. *4.* И вот оно. *5.* Да, вот оно. *6.* Итак, вот оно. *7.* Хорошо для него. *8.* Может быть позже. *9.* А если нет?
● *1.* So this is it? *2.* Okay, here it is. *3.* Well, there it is. *4.* And here it is. *5.* Yes, here it is. *6.* So, this is it. *7.* Good for him. *8.* Maybe later. *9.* And if it doesn't?

**[63]** *1.* Очень хорошо, сэр. *2.* Это так, сэр. *3.* Как вы, сэр? *4.* Вот сюда, сэр. *5.* О да, сэр. *6.* Это все, сэр? *7.* Откуда ты знаешь? *8.* Итак, откуда ты? *9.* Ты был прав.
● *1.* Very good, sir. *2.* That's right, sir. *3.* How are you, sir? *4.* Right this way, sir. *5.* Uh, yes, sir. *6.* Will that be all, sir? *7.* How'd you know? *8.* So, where are you from? *9.* You were right.

**[64]** *1.* Я прав здесь. *2.* Да, ты прав. *3.* Нет, ты прав. *4.* Я был прав. *5.* Он был прав. *6.* Хорошо, ты прав. *7.* И ты прав. *8.* Но ты прав. *9.* О, ты прав. *10.* Нет, он прав. *11.* Ну, ты прав. *12.* Ты так прав.
● *1.* I'm right here. *2.* Yeah, you're right. *3.* No, you're right. *4.* I was right. *5.* He was right. *6.* Okay, you're right. *7.* And you're right. *8.* But you're right. *9.* Oh, you're right. *10.* No, he's right. *11.* Well, you're right. *12.* You're so right.

**[65]** *1.* Возможно, ты прав. *2.* Да, он прав. *3.* Возможно, он прав. *4.* Конечно, я прав. *5.* Конечно, ты прав. *6.* Эй, ты прав. *7.* Но он прав. *8.* Ты всегда прав. *9.* И он прав.
● *1.* You might be right. *2.* Yeah, he's right. *3.* Maybe he's right. *4.* Of course I'm right. *5.* Of course, you're right. *6.* Hey, you're right. *7.* But he's right. *8.* You're always right. *9.* And he's right.

**[66]** *1.* Знаешь, он прав. *2.* Он хороший человек. *3.* Ты хороший человек. *4.* Вы хороший человек. *5.* Сколько вас человек? *6.* Я хороший человек. *7.* Ты не человек. *8.* Она хороший человек. *9.* Должно быть приятно.

● *1.* You know, he's right. *2.* He's a good man. *3.* You're a good man. *4.* You're a good person. *5.* How many are you? *6.* I'm a good person. *7.* You're not human. *8.* She's a good person. *9.* Must be nice.

**[67]** *1.* Из-за чего? *2.* Ты всегда делаешь. *3.* Как ты делаешь'? *4.* Сколько сейчас времени? *5.* Не было времени. *6.* Мы теперь вместе. *7.* Иди сюда, дорогая. *8.* Что это, дорогая? *9.* Как вы дорогая?

● *1.* Because why? *2.* You always do. *3.* How are you doin'? *4.* What time is it now? *5.* There wasn't time. *6.* We're together now. *7.* Come here, sweetheart. *8.* What is it, dear? *9.* How are you, darling?

**[68]** *1.* Дорогая, как ты? *2.* Дорогая, иди сюда. *3.* Как ты, дорогая? *4.* О, спасибо, дорогая. *5.* Как дела чувак? *6.* Иди сюда, чувак. *7.* Где ты, чувак? *8.* Вы не можете! *9.* Вы можете идти.

● *1.* How are you, sweetie? *2.* Honey, come here. *3.* How are you, dear? *4.* Oh, thank you, dear. *5.* What's up, man? *6.* Come here, man. *7.* Where are you, man? *8.* You can't! *9.* You're free to go.

**[69]** *1.* Что вы можете. *2.* Вот, возьми это. *3.* Просто возьми это. *4.* Вот, возьми мой. *5.* Я не хотел. *6.* Ты хороший друг. *7.* Где твой друг? *8.* Он просто друг. *9.* Она просто друг.

● *1.* Sure you can. *2.* Here, take this. *3.* Just take it. *4.* Here, take mine. *5.* I didn't want to. *6.* You're a good friend. *7.* Where's your friend? *8.* He's just a friend. *9.* She's just a friend.

**[70]** *1.* Давайте же теперь. *2.* Так и думал. *3.* Я не думал. *4.* Это было долго. *5.* Что так долго? *6.* Ну, как долго? *7.* Как вы сегодня? *8.* Как мы сегодня? *9.* Не видел его.

● *1.* Let's go now. *2.* Thought so. *3.* I wasn't thinking. *4.* It's been a long time. *5.* What's taking so long? *6.* Well, how long? *7.* How are you today? *8.* How are we today? *9.* Haven't seen him.

**[71]** *1.* Я видел лучше. *2.* Это было раньше. *3.* Не раньше, чем. *4.* Рад тебя видеть. *5.* Рад видеть тебя. *6.* Рад вас видеть. *7.* Приятно видеть тебя. *8.* Приятно тебя видеть. *9.* Не могу говорить.

● *1.* I've seen better. *2.* That was before. *3.* Not before. *4.* Good to see you. *5.* It's good to see you. *6.* Nice to see you. *7.* It's nice to see you. *8.* It's great to see you. *9.* Can't talk.

**[72]** *1.* Зачем ему это? *2.* Зачем ей это? *3.* Зачем говорить это? *4.* Зачем это делать? *5.* Зачем мне быть? *6.* Зачем тебе это? *7.* Что здесь происходит? *8.* Что происходит сейчас? *9.* Что там происходит?
● *1.* Why would he? *2.* Why would she? *3.* Why say that? *4.* Why do that? *5.* Why would I be? *6.* Why do you have that? *7.* What is going on here? *8.* What happens now? *9.* What's going on out there?

**[73]** *1.* Этого не происходит. *2.* Итак, что происходит? *3.* Что-то происходит. *4.* Что происходит, чувак? *5.* Это происходит снова. *6.* Ничего не происходит. *7.* Как это происходит? *8.* Что сейчас происходит? *9.* Что тогда происходит?
● *1.* This isn't happening. *2.* So what's going on? *3.* Something's going on. *4.* What's going on, man? *5.* It's happening again. *6.* Nothing's going on. *7.* How does that happen? *8.* What's happening now? *9.* Then what happens?

**[74]** *1.* Ну, что происходит? *2.* Это уже происходит. *3.* Это действительно происходит? *4.* Э, нет, спасибо. *5.* Э-э, здесь. *6.* Э-э, хорошо. *7.* Э-э, возможно. *8.* Э, что происходит? *9.* О, это здорово.
● *1.* Well, what's going on? *2.* It's already happening. *3.* Is this really happening? *4.* Uh, no, thanks. *5.* Uh, here. *6.* Uh, all right. *7.* Uh, maybe. *8.* Uh, what's going on? *9.* Oh, that's great.

**[75]** *1.* Это было здорово. *2.* Это очень здорово. *3.* Это просто здорово. *4.* Это будет здорово. *5.* Да, это здорово. *6.* Нет, это здорово. *7.* Было бы здорово. *8.* Это действительно здорово. *9.* Это так здорово.
● *1.* That was great. *2.* It's very nice. *3.* That's just great. *4.* It's gonna be great. *5.* Yeah, it's great. *6.* No, it's great. *7.* That would be lovely. *8.* That's really great. *9.* This is so great.

**[76]** *1.* Хорошо, это здорово. *2.* Эй, это здорово. *3.* Это здорово, чувак. *4.* Это здорово, дорогая. *5.* О, черт возьми. *6.* Я не знал. *7.* Я всегда знал. *8.* Я просто знал. *9.* Где вы ребята?
● *1.* Okay, that's great. *2.* Hey, that's great. *3.* That's great, man. *4.* That's great, honey. *5.* Oh, bloody hell. *6.* I didn't know. *7.* I

always knew. *8.* I just knew. *9.* Where are you guys?

[77] *1.* Как дела, ребята? *2.* А вы, ребята? *3.* Этого не достаточно. *4.* Хорошо, этого достаточно. *5.* Мне этого достаточно. *6.* Это достаточно хорошо. *7.* Теперь этого достаточно. *8.* Я видел достаточно. *9.* Нет, этого достаточно.
• *1.* How are you guys? *2.* How about you guys? *3.* That's not enough. *4.* Okay, that's enough. *5.* I've had enough of this. *6.* That's good enough. *7.* That's enough now. *8.* I've seen enough. *9.* No, that's enough.

[78] *1.* Я знаю достаточно. *2.* Я сказал достаточно! *3.* Мне здесь нравится. *4.* Мне нравится здесь. *5.* Что не нравится? *6.* Вам здесь нравится? *7.* Мне это нравится. *8.* Тебе это нравится? *9.* Ты выглядишь хорошо.
• *1.* I know enough. *2.* I said enough! *3.* I like it here. *4.* I love it here. *5.* What's not to like? *6.* Do you like it here? *7.* I kind of like it. *8.* You good with that? *9.* You look good.

[79] *1.* Ты хорошо выглядишь. *2.* Ты выглядишь лучше. *3.* Это хорошая идея. *4.* Не хорошая идея. *5.* Да, хорошая идея. *6.* О, хорошая идея. *7.* Очень хорошая идея. *8.* Хорошо, спокойной ночи. *9.* Спокойной ночи, дорогая.
• *1.* You look nice. *2.* You look better. *3.* That's a good idea. *4.* Not a good idea. *5.* Yeah, good idea. *6.* Oh, good idea. *7.* Very good idea. *8.* Well, good night. *9.* Good night, dear.

[80] *1.* Тогда спокойной ночи. *2.* Да спокойной ночи. *3.* Ладно, спокойной ночи. *4.* Я скоро буду. *5.* Откуда вам знать? *6.* Откуда мне знать? *7.* Это хорошо знать. *8.* Откуда нам знать? *9.* Это именно так.
• *1.* Good night, then. *2.* Yeah, good night. *3.* All right, good night. *4.* I'll be there soon. *5.* How would you know? *6.* How would I know? *7.* That's good to know. *8.* How do we know? *9.* That's exactly it.

[81] *1.* Кто именно вы? *2.* Где это место? *3.* Тебе место здесь. *4.* Откуда вы знаете? *5.* Вы не знаете? *6.* И знаете почему? *7.* Тогда вы знаете. *8.* Это очень плохо. *9.* Это плохо, да?
• *1.* Who exactly are you? *2.* Where is this place? *3.* You belong here. *4.* How do you know? *5.* You don't know? *6.* And do you know why? *7.* Then you know. *8.* That's too bad. *9.* That bad, huh?

**[82]** *1.* Мне будет плохо. *2.* Ты плохо выглядишь. *3.* Ну, очень плохо. *4.* Это так плохо? *5.* О, это плохо. *6.* Хорошо и плохо. *7.* Ты почти там. *8.* Мы почти там! *9.* Ты так думаешь?
● *1.* I'm gonna be sick. *2.* You don't look well. *3.* Well, too bad. *4.* Is that so bad? *5.* Oh, this is bad. *6.* Good and bad. *7.* You're almost there. *8.* We're almost there! *9.* You think so?

**[83]** *1.* Где ты думаешь? *2.* Тебе лучше пойти. *3.* Это большой день. *4.* Что сейчас произошло? *5.* Как это произошло? *6.* Когда это произошло? *7.* Что там произошло? *8.* Этого не произошло. *9.* Где это произошло?
● *1.* Where do you think? *2.* You'd better go. *3.* It's a big day. *4.* What just happened? *5.* How did this happen? *6.* When did this happen? *7.* What happened out there? *8.* It didn't happen. *9.* Where did it happen?

**[84]** *1.* Это уже произошло. *2.* Что именно произошло? *3.* Что здесь произошло? *4.* Что еще произошло? *5.* В чем дело? *6.* Как насчет этого? *7.* Как насчет сейчас? *8.* Как насчет тебя? *9.* Как насчет нее?
● *1.* It already has. *2.* What exactly happened? *3.* What has happened here? *4.* What else happened? *5.* What's wrong? *6.* How about that? *7.* How about now? *8.* How 'bout you? *9.* How about her?

**[85]** *1.* Как насчет здесь? *2.* Хорошая работа, ребята. *3.* Это хорошая работа. *4.* Хорошая работа, чувак. *5.* Это просто работа. *6.* Он хороший парень. *7.* Эй, большой парень. *8.* Ты хороший парень. *9.* Где этот парень?
● *1.* How about here? *2.* Good job, guys. *3.* That's good work. *4.* Good job, man. *5.* It's just work. *6.* He's a good guy. *7.* Hey, big guy. *8.* You're a good kid. *9.* Where is this guy?

**[86]** *1.* Где твой парень? *2.* Просто скажи мне. *3.* Скажи это снова. *4.* Скажи мне почему. *5.* Скажи еще раз. *6.* Скажи мне сейчас. *7.* Давай, скажи это. *8.* Скажи мне как. *9.* Теперь скажи мне.
● *1.* Where's your boyfriend? *2.* Just tell me. *3.* Say it again. *4.* Tell me why. *5.* Say again. *6.* Tell me now. *7.* Go ahead, say it. *8.* Tell me how. *9.* Now tell me.

**[87]** *1.* Тогда скажи это. *2.* Скажи мне, когда. *3.* Скажи мне где. *4.* Просто скажи ему. *5.* Скажи спокойной ночи. *6.* Как это звучит? *7.* Да, звучит хорошо. *8.* Это звучит здорово. *9.* Это звучит хорошо?

● *1.* Then say it. *2.* Tell me when. *3.* Tell me where. *4.* Just tell him. *5.* Say good night. *6.* How does that sound? *7.* Yeah, sounds good. *8.* It sounds great. *9.* Does that sound good?

**[88]** *1.* Это звучит плохо. *2.* Это так мило. *3.* Это очень мило. *4.* Это действительно мило. *5.* О, как мило. *6.* О, это мило. *7.* Это было мило. *8.* Да, очень мило. *9.* Ты выглядишь мило.

● *1.* That sounds bad. *2.* That's so sweet. *3.* That's very nice. *4.* That's really nice. *5.* Oh, how nice. *6.* Oh, that's sweet. *7.* It was lovely. *8.* Yes, very nice. *9.* You look cute.

**[89]** *1.* Чем могу помочь? *2.* Рад был помочь. *3.* Я рад помочь. *4.* Увидимся позже, ребята. *5.* Ладно, увидимся позже. *6.* Хорошо, увидимся позже. *7.* Мы скоро увидимся. *8.* Ну, увидимся позже. *9.* Увидимся позже, ладно?

● *1.* How can I help? *2.* Happy to help. *3.* I'm happy to help. *4.* See you guys later. *5.* Okay, see you later. *6.* All right, I'll see you later. *7.* We'll see you soon. *8.* Well, see you later. *9.* I'll see you later, okay?

**[90]** *1.* Мы увидимся снова. *2.* Это так красиво. *3.* Это было красиво. *4.* О, это красиво. *5.* Ты выглядишь красиво. *6.* Это очень красиво. *7.* Это действительно красиво. *8.* Это просто красиво. *9.* Да, это красиво.

● *1.* We'll see each other again. *2.* It's so beautiful. *3.* It was beautiful. *4.* Oh, it's beautiful. *5.* You look pretty. *6.* It's very pretty. *7.* It's really beautiful. *8.* It's just beautiful. *9.* Yes, it's beautiful.

**[91]** *1.* Нет, не будь. *2.* Просто будь там. *3.* Готов для чего? *4.* Хорошо, ты готов? *5.* Да, я готов. *6.* Я буду готов. *7.* Ты готов идти? *8.* Теперь я готов. *9.* Я готов идти.

● *1.* No, don't be. *2.* Just be there. *3.* Ready for what? *4.* Okay, you ready? *5.* Yeah, I'm ready. *6.* I'll be ready. *7.* Are you ready to go? *8.* I'm ready now. *9.* I'm ready to go.

**[92]** *1.* Я почти готов. *2.* Хорошо, я готов. *3.* Я был готов. *4.* Думаю, я готов. *5.* О, я готов. *6.* Я готов говорить. *7.* Да, довольно много. *8.* Это довольно просто. *9.* Это хороший вопрос.

● *1.* I'm almost ready. *2.* All right, I'm ready. *3.* I was ready. *4.* I think I'm ready. *5.* Oh, I'm ready. *6.* I'm ready to talk. *7.* Yeah, pretty much. *8.* It's quite simple. *9.* That's a good question.

**[93]** *1.* Это вопрос времени. *2.* Всего один вопрос. *3.* Еще один вопрос. *4.* Это большой вопрос. *5.* Это просто вопрос. *6.* Как это выглядит? *7.* Это выглядит здорово. *8.* Как оно выглядит? *9.* Все выглядит хорошо.

● *1.* It's just a matter of time. *2.* Just one question. *3.* One more question. *4.* It's a big one. *5.* It's just a question. *6.* How does it look? *7.* It looks great. *8.* How's it looking? *9.* Everything looks good.

**[94]** *1.* Это выглядит хорошо. *2.* Это выглядит мило. *3.* Он хорошо выглядит. *4.* Как она выглядит? *5.* Как он выглядит? *6.* Это выглядит красиво. *7.* Она выглядит красиво. *8.* Она хорошо выглядит. *9.* Сейчас или никогда.

● *1.* This looks good. *2.* It looks nice. *3.* He looks good. *4.* How does she look? *5.* How does he look? *6.* That looks nice. *7.* She looks nice. *8.* She looks good. *9.* It's now or never.

**[95]** *1.* Или еще что? *2.* Нет, не совсем. *3.* Ну, не совсем. *4.* Еще не совсем. *5.* Ты совсем один. *6.* Совсем не хорошо. *7.* Сколько тебе лет? *8.* Сколько ей лет? *9.* Сколько ему лет?

● *1.* Or else what? *2.* No, not really. *3.* Well, not exactly. *4.* Not quite yet. *5.* You're all alone. *6.* Not good at all. *7.* How old are you? *8.* How old is she? *9.* How old is he?

**[96]** *1.* Много лет назад. *2.* Несколько лет назад. *3.* О, да, верно. *4.* Нет, это верно. *5.* О, верно, верно. *6.* Это очень верно. *7.* Да, все верно. *8.* Это верно, да. *9.* Э-э, верно.

● *1.* Years ago. *2.* A few years ago. *3.* Oh, yeah, right. *4.* No, it's true. *5.* Oh, right, right. *6.* That's very true. *7.* Yes, alright. *8.* That's right, yeah. *9.* Uh, right.

**[97]** *1.* Да, это верно! *2.* Да, да, верно. *3.* Это так верно. *4.* Доброе утро, сэр. *5.* О, доброе утро. *6.* Доброе утро дорогая. *7.* Доброе утро тебе. *8.* Ну, доброе утро. *9.* В самом деле.

● *1.* Yeah, that's right! *2.* Yeah, yeah, right. *3.* That is so true. *4.* Good morning, sir. *5.* Oh, good morning. *6.* Good morning, darling. *7.* Good morning to you. *8.* Well, good morning. *9.* Indeed it is.

**[98]** *1.* Вы не должны. *2.* Сколько вы должны? *3.* Вы не сделали? *4*. Вы сделали достаточно. *5*. Мы не сделали. *6*. Вы, конечно, сделали. *7*. Вы хорошо сделали. *8*. Как мы сделали? *9*. Я не понимаю!

• *1*. You mustn't. *2*. How much do you owe? *3*. You didn't? *4*. You've done enough. *5*. We did not. *6*. You certainly did. *7*. You have done well. *8*. How did we do? *9*. I don't understand!

**[99]** *1*. Я вас понимаю. *2*. Теперь я понимаю. *3*. Я понимаю, почему. *4*. Ну, я понимаю. *5*. Вы готовы идти? *6*. Мы готовы идти. *7*. Ребята, вы готовы? *8*. Мы почти готовы. *9*. Готовы к этому?

• *1*. I feel the same way. *2*. Now I understand. *3*. I can see why. *4*. Well, I understand. *5*. You ready to go? *6*. We're good to go. *7*. You guys ready? *8*. We're almost ready. *9*. Ready for this?

**[100]** *1*. Не будь таким. *2*. Это так странно. *3*. Ну, это странно. *4*. Знаешь, что странно? *5*. Это действительно странно. *6*. Это очень странно. *7*. Это было странно. *8*. Это немного странно. *9*. Ты выглядишь странно.

• *1*. Don't be that way. *2*. This is so weird. *3*. Well, that's weird. *4*. You know what's weird? *5*. This is really weird. *6*. It's very strange. *7*. It was strange. *8*. It's a little weird. *9*. You look strange.

**[101]** *1*. Ладно, это странно. *2*. Мне нужно вернуться. *3*. Я должен вернуться. *4*. Я хочу вернуться. *5*. Я могу вернуться. *6*. Нам нужно вернуться. *7*. Ты хочешь вернуться? *8*. То же самое. *9*. Сейчас самое время.

• *1*. Okay, that's weird. *2*. I have to go back. *3*. I have to get back. *4*. I want to go back. *5*. I can come back. *6*. We gotta go back. *7*. You want to go back? *8*. Same here. *9*. Now is the time.

**[102]** *1*. Вы правильно сделали. *2*. Да, это правильно. *3*. Это было правильно. *4*. Правильно о чем? *5*. Это правильно, сэр. *6*. Вы сделали правильно. *7*. Это звучит правильно. *8*. Ты правильно думаешь? *9*. Это не правильно!

• *1*. You did the right thing. *2*. Yes, that's correct. *3*. It was the right thing to do. *4*. Right about what? *5*. That's correct, sir. *6*. You did right. *7*. That sounds right. *8*. You get it, right? *9*. It's wrong!

**[103]** *1*. Я так чувствую. *2*. Чувствую лучше сейчас? *3*. Что я чувствую? *4*. Ты подожди здесь. *5*. Подожди меня здесь.

*6.* Пожалуйста подожди здесь. *7.* Тоже тебя люблю. *8.* Надеюсь, ты прав. *9.* Надеюсь на это.

● *1.* That's how I feel. *2.* Feel better now? *3.* How do I feel? *4.* You wait here. *5.* Wait for me here. *6.* Please wait here. *7.* Love you, too. *8.* I hope you're right. *9.* Hope so.

**[104]** *1.* Надеюсь, что нет. *2.* Скоро, я надеюсь. *3.* Вот и надеюсь. *4.* Увидимся через несколько. *5.* Ну тогда пока. *6.* Нет, пока ничего. *7.* Пока не уверен. *8.* Легко и приятно. *9.* Это было легко.

● *1.* I should hope not. *2.* Soon, I hope. *3.* Here's hoping. *4.* See you in a few. *5.* Bye, then. *6.* No, nothing yet. *7.* Not sure yet. *8.* Nice and easy. *9.* That was easy.

**[105]** *1.* О, это легко. *2.* Легко и просто. *3.* Ну, это легко. *4.* Это очень легко. *5.* Это будет легко. *6.* Вам легко говорить. *7.* Зачем им это? *8.* Это очень смешно. *9.* Думаешь, это смешно?

● *1.* Oh, that's easy. *2.* Plain and simple. *3.* Well, that's easy. *4.* It's very easy. *5.* It'll be easy. *6.* It's easy for you to say. *7.* Why would they? *8.* That's very funny. *9.* You think that's funny?

**[106]** *1.* Это не смешно. *2.* Знаешь, что смешно? *3.* О, это смешно. *4.* Почему это смешно? *5.* Ну, это смешно. *6.* Да, очень смешно. *7.* О, очень смешно. *8.* Это действительно смешно. *9.* Да, это смешно.

● *1.* This isn't funny. *2.* You know what's funny? *3.* Oh, that's funny. *4.* Why is that funny? *5.* Well, that's ridiculous. *6.* Yeah, very funny. *7.* Oh, very funny. *8.* That's really funny. *9.* Yeah, that's funny.

**[107]** *1.* Это немного смешно. *2.* Хотите знать, почему? *3.* Хотите что-нибудь? *4.* Вы хотите больше? *5.* Хотите еще один? *6.* Это хороший мальчик. *7.* Иди сюда, мальчик. *8.* Он хороший мальчик. *9.* Ты хороший мальчик.

● *1.* It's a little funny. *2.* You wanna know why? *3.* Want anything? *4.* Do you want more? *5.* Want another one? *6.* That's a good boy. *7.* Come here, boy. *8.* He's a good boy. *9.* You're a good boy.

**[108]** *1.* Кто хороший мальчик? *2.* Есть хороший мальчик. *3.* Я большой мальчик. *4.* Где мой мальчик? *5.* Как мой мальчик? *6.* Ты большой мальчик. *7.* Он большой мальчик.

*8.* Мы будем там. *9.* Мы будем готовы.

● *1.* Who's a good boy? *2.* There's a good boy. *3.* I'm a big boy. *4.* Where's my boy? *5.* How's my boy? *6.* You're a big boy. *7.* He's a big boy. *8.* We'll be there. *9.* We'll be ready.

**[109]** *1.* Мы будем здесь. *2.* Просто иди домой. *3.* Кто ты вообще? *4.* Да, вообще-то. *5.* Ну ты вообще. *6.* Где он вообще? *7.* Сколько это стоит? *8.* Сколько стоит этот? *9.* Я всегда делаю.

● *1.* We'll be here. *2.* Just go home. *3.* Who are you anyway? *4.* Yeah, actually. *5.* Well, you do. *6.* Where is he, anyway? *7.* How much is it? *8.* How much is this one? *9.* I always do.

**[110]** *1.* Я просто делаю. *2.* Я действительно делаю. *3.* Я уже делаю. *4.* Все еще делаю. *5.* Спасибо тебе, мама. *6.* Где твоя мама? *7.* Спокойной ночи мама. *8.* Как твоя мама? *9.* Где моя мама?

● *1.* I just do. *2.* I do indeed. *3.* I already do. *4.* Still do. *5.* Thank you, ma'am. *6.* Where's your mom? *7.* Good night, Mom. *8.* How's your mom? *9.* Where's my mom?

**[111]** *1.* Никогда не поздно. *2.* Уже очень поздно. *3.* Ну, уже поздно. *4.* Он не делает? *5.* И нам ясно. *6.* Все ясно, сэр. *7.* Мы хорошие ребята. *8.* Это совершенно верно. *9.* Большое спасибо, сэр.

● *1.* It's never too late. *2.* It's very late. *3.* Well, it's getting late. *4.* He doesn't? *5.* And we're clear. *6.* All clear, sir. *7.* We're the good guys. *8.* That's exactly right. *9.* Thank you very much, sir.

**[112]** *1.* Хорошо спасибо большое. *2.* О, большое спасибо. *3.* Что-то большое. *4.* Да, большое спасибо. *5.* Спасибо, большое спасибо. *6.* Нет, спасибо большое. *7.* Большое большое спасибо. *8.* Спасибо Вам большое. *9.* Это большое дело.

● *1.* Well, thank you very much. *2.* Oh, thank you very much. *3.* Something big. *4.* Yes, thank you very much. *5.* Thank you, thank you very much. *6.* No, thank you very much. *7.* Thank you very, very much. *8.* Thank you very much indeed. *9.* It is a big deal.

**[113]** *1.* Хорошо, большое спасибо. *2.* Нет это нормально. *3.* О, это нормально. *4.* Нет, все нормально. *5.* Это было нормально. *6.* Ну, это нормально. *7.* Но это нормально. *8.*

И это нормально. *9.* Да, это нормально.

● *1.* All right, thank you very much. *2.* No, it's okay. *3.* Oh, that's okay. *4.* No, it's OK. *5.* It was okay. *6.* Well, that's fine. *7.* But that's okay. *8.* And that's okay. *9.* Yeah, that's okay.

**[114]** *1.* Это совершенно нормально. *2.* Это будет нормально? *3.* Это достаточно далеко. *4.* Не слишком далеко. *5.* Это ужасно говорить. *6.* Это было ужасно. *7.* Кто-нибудь другой? *8.* Так или другой. *9.* Один или другой.

● *1.* It's perfectly normal. *2.* Would that be okay? *3.* That's far enough. *4.* Not too far. *5.* That's a terrible thing to say. *6.* It was terrifying. *7.* Someone else? *8.* One way or the other. *9.* One or the other.

**[115]** *1.* Где другой парень? *2.* Почему ты пришел? *3.* Когда ты пришел? *4.* Я пришел один. *5.* Я пришел сюда. *6.* Насколько я знаю. *7.* Насколько это далеко? *8.* Насколько оно большое? *9.* Насколько это здорово?

● *1.* Where's the other guy? *2.* Why did you come? *3.* When did you get here? *4.* I came alone. *5.* I came here. *6.* As far as I know. *7.* How far is it? *8.* How big is it? *9.* How great is that?

**[116]** *1.* Насколько это странно? *2.* Эй, подожди секунду. *3.* Всего на секунду. *4.* Просто подожди секунду. *5.* Теперь подожди секунду. *6.* Нет, подожди секунду. *7.* Подожди, подожди секунду. *8.* Хорошо, подожди секунду. *9.* Моя жизнь здесь.

● *1.* How weird is that? *2.* Hey, wait a second. *3.* Just for a second. *4.* Just wait a second. *5.* Now, wait a second. *6.* No, wait a second. *7.* Wait, hold on a second. *8.* Okay, wait a second. *9.* My life is here.

**[117]** *1.* Какой еще парень? *2.* Ох, черт возьми. *3.* Как это работает? *4.* Это не работает. *5.* Он работает здесь. *6.* Ну, это работает. *7.* Мне просто интересно. *8.* Это так интересно. *9.* Это очень интересно.

● *1.* What other guy? *2.* Oh, goddamn it. *3.* How does it work? *4.* This isn't working. *5.* He works here. *6.* Well, it's working. *7.* I'm just curious. *8.* This is so exciting. *9.* That's very interesting.

**[118]** *1.* Мне это интересно. *2.* Это было интересно. *3.* О, это интересно. *4.* Я скоро вернусь. *5.* Я вернусь позже. *6.* Но я вернусь. *7.* Возьми это обратно. *8.* Он не делал. *9.* Никогда не делал.

● *1.* I'm interested. *2.* That was interesting. *3.* Oh, that's interesting. *4.* I'll be right back. *5.* I'll come back later. *6.* But I'll be back. *7.* Take it back. *8.* He did not. *9.* Never did.

**[119]** *1.* Ты выглядишь прекрасно. *2.* Это было прекрасно. *3.* Я прекрасно понимаю. *4.* Это звучит прекрасно. *5.* О, это прекрасно. *6.* Боюсь, что так. *7.* Боюсь, что нет. *8.* Боюсь, это так. *9.* Я так боюсь.

● *1.* You look beautiful. *2.* It was fine. *3.* I understand perfectly. *4.* That sounds lovely. *5.* Oh, that's lovely. *6.* I'm afraid so. *7.* I'm afraid not. *8.* I'm afraid it is. *9.* I'm so afraid.

**[120]** *1.* Но я боюсь. *2.* Я тоже боюсь. *3.* Я просто боюсь. *4.* Это очень важно. *5.* Это действительно важно. *6.* Вот что важно. *7.* Это так круто. *8.* Нет, это круто. *9.* Это было круто.

● *1.* But I'm scared. *2.* I'm scared, too. *3.* I'm just scared. *4.* It's very important. *5.* It's really important. *6.* That's what's important. *7.* This is so cool. *8.* No, it's cool. *9.* That was cool.

**[121]** *1.* Как это круто? *2.* Это довольно круто. *3.* Да, это круто. *4.* О, это круто. *5.* Это круто, чувак. *6.* Это не круто. *7.* Это действительно круто. *8.* Насколько это круто? *9.* Но это круто.

● *1.* How cool is that? *2.* It's pretty cool. *3.* Yeah, it's cool. *4.* Oh, that's cool. *5.* It's cool, man. *6.* It's not cool. *7.* That's really cool. *8.* How cool is this? *9.* But it's cool.

**[122]** *1.* Хорошо для них. *2.* Я не ребенок. *3.* Она хороший ребенок. *4.* Я только вернулся. *5.* Вернулся так скоро? *6.* Почему ты вернулся? *7.* Эй, ты вернулся. *8.* О, ты вернулся. *9.* Вы сейчас серьезно?

● *1.* Good for them. *2.* I'm not a child. *3.* She's a good kid. *4.* I just got back. *5.* Back so soon? *6.* Why'd you come back? *7.* Hey, you're back. *8.* Oh, you're back. *9.* Are you serious right now?

**[123]** *1.* О, ты серьезно. *2.* Да, я серьезно. *3.* Это очень серьезно. *4.* Что вы серьезно? *5.* Я серьезно, чувак. *6.* Это стоит того. *7.* Эй, не волнуйся. *8.* Да, не волнуйся. *9.* Не волнуйся, дорогая.

● *1.* Oh, you're serious. *2.* Yeah, I'm serious. *3.* This is very serious. *4.* What, are you serious? *5.* I'm serious, man. *6.* It's worth a shot. *7.* Hey, don't worry. *8.* Yeah, don't worry. *9.* Don't worry, honey.

**[124]** *1.* Не волнуйся, мама. *2.* Не волнуйся, чувак. *3.* Я точно знаю? *4.* Я точно уверен. *5.* Точно так же. *6.* Да, это точно. *7.* Это хорошая вещь. *8.* Эй, маленький человек. *9.* Мой маленький мальчик.

● *1.* Don't worry, Mom. *2.* Don't worry, man. *3.* I know, right? *4.* I'm pretty sure. *5.* Exactly the same. *6.* Yeah, it sure is. *7.* That's a good thing. *8.* Hey, little man. *9.* My little boy.

**[125]** *1.* Давай, маленький человек. *2.* Ты в безопасности. *3.* Она в безопасности. *4.* Он в безопасности. *5.* Они в безопасности. *6.* Мы в безопасности? *7.* Вы в безопасности? *8.* Они хорошие люди. *9.* Они не люди.

● *1.* Come on, little man. *2.* You're safe. *3.* She's safe. *4.* He's safe. *5.* They're safe. *6.* Are we safe? *7.* Are you safe? *8.* They're good people. *9.* They're not human.

**[126]** *1.* В последний раз. *2.* И последний вопрос. *3.* Почему вы думаете? *4.* Как вы думаете? *5.* Вы не думаете? *6.* О Боже мой. *7.* Боже мой, нет. *8.* Посмотрите, кто вернулся. *9.* Теперь посмотрите это.

● *1.* One last time. *2.* One last question. *3.* Why do you think? *4.* How do you think? *5.* You don't think? *6.* Oh, dear God. *7.* Good heavens, no. *8.* Look who's back. *9.* Now watch this.

**[127]** *1.* Теперь посмотрите сюда. *2.* Дай мне секунду. *3.* Дай мне больше. *4.* Это хорошие новости. *5.* Эй, хорошие новости. *6.* Не без вас. *7.* Я просто говорю. *8.* Я не говорю. *9.* Хорошо быть дома.

● *1.* Now, look here. *2.* Give me a second. *3.* Give me more. *4.* That's good news. *5.* Hey, good news. *6.* Not without you. *7.* I'm just saying. *8.* I'm not telling. *9.* It's good to be home.

**[128]** *1.* Ее нет дома. *2.* Ты сейчас дома. *3.* Его нет дома. *4.* Она не знает. *5.* Кто еще знает? *6.* Откуда он знает? *7.* Он уже знает. *8.* Ну, кто знает? *9.* Это было потрясающе.

● *1.* She's not home. *2.* You're home now. *3.* He's not home. *4.* She doesn't know. *5.* Who else knows? *6.* How does he know? *7.* He already knows. *8.* Well, who knows? *9.* That was awesome.

**[129]** *1.* Ты выглядишь потрясающе. *2.* Это звучит

потрясающе. *3.* Это будет потрясающе. *4.* В чем проблема? *5.* Не говори так. *6.* Ничего не говори. *7.* Не говори ему. *8.* Не говори этого! *9.* Возможно тебе следует.

● *1.* You look terrific. *2.* That sounds amazing. *3.* It's gonna be awesome. *4.* What is the big deal? *5.* Don't say that. *6.* Don't say anything. *7.* Don't tell him. *8.* Don't say it! *9.* Maybe you should.

**[130]** *1.* Возможно, нам следует. *2.* Нет, не следует. *3.* Нам следует вернуться. *4.* Удачи с этим. *5.* Нет такой удачи. *6.* Ну тогда удачи. *7.* Удачи сегодня вечером. *8.* Что здесь случилось? *9.* Итак, что случилось?

● *1.* Maybe we should. *2.* No, you shouldn't. *3.* We should get back. *4.* Good luck with that. *5.* No such luck. *6.* Good luck, then. *7.* Good luck tonight. *8.* What happened here? *9.* So, what happened?

**[131]** *1.* Ничего не случилось. *2.* Ну, что случилось? *3.* Что случилось сейчас? *4.* Это случилось снова. *5.* Мама, что случилось? *6.* Что же случилось? *7.* Что-то случилось? *8.* О, что случилось? *9.* Это хорошее место.

● *1.* Nothing's wrong. *2.* Well, what happened? *3.* What's the matter now? *4.* It happened again. *5.* Mom, what's wrong? *6.* Now, what happened? *7.* Is something up? *8.* Oh, what's wrong? *9.* It's a nice place.

**[132]** *1.* Это хорошее имя. *2.* Это хорошее время? *3.* Что-то хорошее. *4.* Спокойной ночи, папа. *5.* Папа, где ты? *6.* Как дела, папа? *7.* Добрый день, сэр. *8.* Что ж, отлично. *9.* Ты отлично выглядишь.

● *1.* That's a nice name. *2.* Is this a good time? *3.* Something good. *4.* Good night, Dad. *5.* Daddy, where are you? *6.* What's up, Dad? *7.* Good afternoon, sir. *8.* Well, great. *9.* You're looking great.

**[133]** *1.* Все было отлично. *2.* Тот же парень. *3.* Они не мои. *4.* Вот, позвольте мне. *5.* Уже почти пора. *6.* Тебе пора идти. *7.* Нам пора идти. *8.* Мне пора идти. *9.* Дом, милый дом.

● *1.* Everything was fine. *2.* Same guy. *3.* They're not mine. *4.* Here, let me. *5.* It's almost time. *6.* You have to go now. *7.* We gotta go now. *8.* I gotta go now. *9.* Home sweet home.

**[134]** *1.* Спокойной ночи милый. *2.* Он такой милый. *3.* Ты такой милый. *4.* Иди сюда, милый. *5.* Ты очень милый. *6.* Доброе утро, милый. *7.* Я лучше пойду. *8.* Я не пойду. *9.* Я пойду сейчас.

● *1.* Good night, sweetheart. *2.* He's so cute. *3.* You're so cute. *4.* Come here, honey. *5.* You're very sweet. *6.* Good morning, honey. *7.* I better go. *8.* I won't go. *9.* I'm gonna go now.

**[135]** *1.* Я пойду один. *2.* Я тоже пойду. *3.* Тогда я пойду. *4.* Куда я пойду? *5.* Я пойду туда. *6.* Я просто пойду. *7.* Что будешь делать? *8.* Когда будешь готов. *9.* Ты будешь там?

● *1.* I'll go alone. *2.* I'll go too. *3.* Then I'll go. *4.* Where am I gonna go? *5.* I'll go there. *6.* I'm just gonna go. *7.* What will you do now? *8.* When you're ready. *9.* Will you be there?

**[136]** *1.* Как дела, приятель? *2.* Иди сюда, приятель. *3.* Хорошая работа, приятель. *4.* Спокойной ночи, приятель. *5.* Где ты, приятель? *6.* Эй, маленький приятель. *7.* Я собираюсь сейчас. *8.* Я не собираюсь! *9.* Я собираюсь туда.

● *1.* How you doing, buddy? *2.* Come here, buddy. *3.* Good job, buddy. *4.* Good night, buddy. *5.* Where are you, buddy? *6.* Hey, little buddy. *7.* I'm going now. *8.* I'm not going! *9.* I'm going over there.

**[137]** *1.* Я тоже собираюсь. *2.* Собираюсь один раз. *3.* Это было давно. *4.* Вы давно здесь? *5.* Да, очень давно. *6.* Это не мое. *7.* Нет, это мое! *8.* Она очень красивая. *9.* Вы очень красивая.

● *1.* I'm going, too. *2.* Going once. *3.* That was a long time ago. *4.* Have you been here long? *5.* Yeah, a long time ago. *6.* It's not mine. *7.* No, it's mine! *8.* She's very pretty. *9.* You're very pretty.

**[138]** *1.* Ты очень красивая. *2.* Она действительно красивая. *3.* Так что вперед. *4.* Не делай этого! *5.* Где твой отец? *6.* Где мой отец? *7.* Как твой отец? *8.* Спокойной ночи, отец. *9.* Доброе утро, отец.

● *1.* You're very beautiful. *2.* She's really pretty. *3.* So go ahead. *4.* Don't do it! *5.* Where's your father? *6.* Where's my dad? *7.* How's your dad? *8.* Good night, Father. *9.* Good morning, Father.

**[139]** *1.* Куда ты идешь? *2.* Ты идешь домой. *3.* Это было сложно. *4.* Это очень сложно. *5.* Ну, это сложно. *6.*

Насколько это сложно? *7.* Это будет сложно. *8.* Ну, сложно сказать. *9.* Не слушай ее.

● *1.* Where are you going? *2.* You go home. *3.* It was hard. *4.* It's very difficult. *5.* Well, it's complicated. *6.* How hard is that? *7.* It will be difficult. *8.* Well, it's hard to say. *9.* Don't listen to her.

**[140]** *1.* Не слушай меня. *2.* Я не вижу! *3.* Теперь я вижу. *4.* Я вижу сейчас. *5.* Просто держись там. *6.* Ты держись там. *7.* Привет, как дела? *8.* Привет, как ты? *9.* Привет, доброе утро.

● *1.* Don't listen to me. *2.* I can't see! *3.* Now I see. *4.* I see now. *5.* Just hang in there. *6.* You hang in there. *7.* Hi, how are you? *8.* Hey, how are you doing? *9.* Hey, good morning.

**[141]** *1.* И тебе привет. *2.* Привет еще раз. *3.* Это более важно. *4.* Пожалуйста, не более. *5.* Более, чем достаточно. *6.* Ты такая красивая. *7.* Она такая красивая. *8.* Куда он идет? *9.* Все идет нормально.

● *1.* Hello to you, too. *2.* Hi again. *3.* This is more important. *4.* Please, no more. *5.* More than enough. *6.* You're so beautiful. *7.* She's so pretty. *8.* Where's he going? *9.* So far, so good.

**[142]** *1.* Куда она идет? *2.* Все идет отлично. *3.* Все идет хорошо. *4.* Куда это идет? *5.* Вот он идет. *6.* Давай просто пойдем. *7.* Мы пойдем вместе. *8.* Давай пойдем туда. *9.* Давай пойдем домой!

● *1.* Where's she going? *2.* It's going great. *3.* It's going well. *4.* Where does it go? *5.* Here he goes. *6.* Let's just go. *7.* We'll go together. *8.* Let's go there. *9.* Let's go home!

**[143]** *1.* Ну что, пойдем? *2.* Пойдем, моя дорогая. *3.* Мы все пойдем. *4.* Ты не сумасшедший. *5.* Я не сумасшедший! *6.* Ты сумасшедший, чувак. *7.* Ты действительно сумасшедший. *8.* Что это значит? *9.* Я так счастлив.

● *1.* Well, shall we? *2.* Come along, my dear. *3.* We'll all go. *4.* You're not crazy. *5.* I'm not crazy! *6.* You're crazy, man. *7.* You're really crazy. *8.* Well, what does that mean? *9.* I'm so happy.

**[144]** *1.* Ты сейчас счастлив? *2.* Ты счастлив сейчас? *3.* Я очень счастлив. *4.* Я был счастлив. *5.* Я счастлив здесь. *6.* Я действительно счастлив. *7.* Счастлив сделать это. *8.* Конечно, я счастлив. *9.* Он был счастлив.

● *1.* Are you happy now? *2.* You happy now? *3.* I'm very happy.

*4.* I was happy. *5.* I'm happy here. *6.* I'm really happy. *7.* Happy to do it. *8.* Of course I'm happy. *9.* He was happy.

**[145]** *1.* Больше не надо. *2.* Нет, не надо. *3.* Пожалуйста, не надо. *4.* Сколько тебе надо? *5.* Лучше не надо. *6.* Даже не надо. *7.* Ну, не надо. *8.* Не надо, ладно? *9.* В следующий раз.
● *1.* No more. *2.* No, don't. *3.* Please, don't. *4.* How much do you need? *5.* Better not. *6.* Don't even. *7.* Well, don't be. *8.* Don't, okay? *9.* Next time.

**[146]** *1.* Хорошо, кто следующий? *2.* Просто возьми деньги. *3.* Как все прошло? *4.* Все прошло хорошо. *5.* Сколько времени прошло? *6.* Прошло много времени. *7.* Как дела детка? *8.* О да, детка. *9.* Спокойной ночи, детка.
● *1.* All right, who's next? *2.* Just take the money. *3.* How'd it go? *4.* That went well. *5.* How long's it been? *6.* It's been awhile. *7.* What's up, baby? *8.* Oh, yeah, baby. *9.* Good night, baby.

**[147]** *1.* Теперь мы знаем. *2.* Это так весело. *3.* Это очень весело. *4.* Это было сильно. *5.* Это очень трудно. *6.* Тебя трудно найти. *7.* Это звучит великолепно. *8.* Ты выглядишь великолепно. *9.* Это выглядит великолепно.
● *1.* Now we know. *2.* That's so funny. *3.* It's so funny. *4.* That was intense. *5.* It's so hard. *6.* You're a hard man to find. *7.* That sounds great. *8.* You look fantastic. *9.* That looks great.

**[148]** *1.* Это было великолепно. *2.* Все прошло великолепно. *3.* Она выглядит великолепно. *4.* Это место великолепно. *5.* О, великолепно, великолепно. *6.* Это моя вина. *7.* Еще кое-что. *8.* Это было идеально. *9.* Нет, это идеально.
● *1.* That was brilliant. *2.* It went great. *3.* She looks great. *4.* This place is great. *5.* Oh, great, great. *6.* That's my bad. *7.* One more thing. *8.* It was perfect. *9.* No, it's perfect.

**[149]** *1.* Это звучит идеально. *2.* Как они могли? *3.* Я сделаю лучше. *4.* Он очень хорош. *5.* Ты был хорош. *6.* О, ты хорош. *7.* Ты очень хорош. *8.* Он действительно хорош. *9.* Ты так хорош.
● *1.* That sounds perfect. *2.* How could they? *3.* I'll do better. *4.* He's very good. *5.* You were good. *6.* Oh, you're good. *7.* You're pretty good. *8.* He's really good. *9.* You're so good.

**[150]** *1.* Я был хорош. *2.* Ты слишком хорош. *3.* Он был хорош. *4.* Этот парень хорош. *5.* Да, он хорош. *6.* Это все неправильно. *7.* Нет, это неправильно. *8.* Ты дома рано. *9.* Все еще рано.

● *1.* I was good. *2.* You're too good. *3.* He was good. *4.* This guy's good. *5.* Yeah, he's good. *6.* It's all wrong. *7.* No, that's not right. *8.* You're home early. *9.* It's still early.

**[151]** *1.* Рано или поздно. *2.* Ты пришел рано. *3.* Я слишком рано? *4.* Ты вернулся рано. *5.* Мой лучший друг. *6.* Доброе утро всем. *7.* Всем спокойной ночи. *8.* Всем доброе утро. *9.* Всем большое спасибо.

● *1.* Sooner or later. *2.* You're here early. *3.* Am I too early? *4.* You're back early. *5.* My best friend. *6.* Good morning, everyone. *7.* Good night, everybody. *8.* Good morning, everybody. *9.* Thank you all very much.

**[152]** *1.* Спокойной ночи всем. *2.* Добрый день всем. *3.* Мне очень повезло. *4.* Это отличная идея. *5.* Ни слова больше. *6.* Привет, старый друг. *7.* Он старый друг. *8.* Может быть завтра. *9.* Я вернусь завтра.

● *1.* Good night, everyone. *2.* Good afternoon, everyone. *3.* I'm very lucky. *4.* It's a great idea. *5.* Not another word. *6.* Hello, old friend. *7.* He's an old friend. *8.* Maybe tomorrow. *9.* I'll be back tomorrow.

**[153]** *1.* Как насчет завтра? *2.* Может быть, два. *3.* Нет такой вещи. *4.* Где мои вещи? *5.* Мне все равно. *6.* Но все равно. *7.* Смотри кто здесь. *8.* Смотри, куда идешь! *9.* Ну, смотри сюда.

● *1.* How about tomorrow? *2.* Maybe two. *3.* No such thing. *4.* Where's my stuff? *5.* I don't even care. *6.* But still. *7.* Look who's here. *8.* Watch where you're going! *9.* Well, looky here.

**[154]** *1.* Это хорошая история. *2.* Это отличная история. *3.* Я не скажу. *4.* Это хорошая девочка. *5.* Она хорошая девочка. *6.* Иди сюда, девочка. *7.* Как моя девочка? *8.* Есть хорошая девочка. *9.* Просто оставайся там.

● *1.* It's a good story. *2.* It's a great story. *3.* I won't tell. *4.* That's a good girl. *5.* She's a good girl. *6.* Come here, girl. *7.* How's my girl? *8.* There's a good girl. *9.* Just stay there.

**[155]** *1.* Ты оставайся здесь. *2.* Нет, оставайся здесь. *3.* Оставайся здесь, ладно? *4.* Просто оставайся здесь. *5.* Это хороший план. *6.* Хорошо, вот план. *7.* Здесь так тихо. *8.* Красиво и тихо. *9.* В другое время.

• *1.* You stay right there. *2.* No, stay here. *3.* Stay here, okay? *4.* Just stay right there. *5.* It's a good plan. *6.* Okay, here's the plan. *7.* It's so quiet. *8.* Nice and quiet. *9.* Some other time.

**[156]** *1.* Это было другое. *2.* Что-то другое. *3.* Нет, это другое. *4.* Но это другое. *5.* Ну, это другое. *6.* Нет ты первый. *7.* Где мои дети? *8.* Это было близко. *9.* Это достаточно близко.

• *1.* That was different. *2.* Something else. *3.* No, this is different. *4.* But this is different. *5.* Well, that's different. *6.* No, you first. *7.* Where are my children? *8.* That was close. *9.* That's close enough.

**[157]** *1.* Мы так близко. *2.* Ты слишком близко. *3.* Просто будь собой. *4.* Я большая девочка. *5.* Ты большая девочка. *6.* Идти спать сейчас. *7.* Не могу спать. *8.* Теперь иди спать. *9.* Просто иди спать.

• *1.* We're so close. *2.* You're too close. *3.* Just be yourself. *4.* I'm a big girl. *5.* You're a big girl. *6.* Go to sleep now. *7.* Can't sleep. *8.* Now go to bed. *9.* Just go to sleep.

**[158]** *1.* Было приятно познакомиться. *2.* Очень приятно познакомиться. *3.* Так приятно познакомиться. *4.* Приятно познакомиться, сэр. *5.* О, приятно познакомиться. *6.* Привет, приятно познакомиться.

• *1.* It was nice to meet you. *2.* It's very nice to meet you. *3.* It's so nice to meet you. *4.* Nice to meet you, sir. *5.* Oh, nice to meet you. *6.* Hey, nice to meet you.

**[159]** *1.* Не смотри вниз! *2.* Он идет вниз. *3.* Вы уверены, что? *4.* Уверены в этом? *5.* Вы совершенно уверены? *6.* Вы действительно уверены? *7.* Я был занят. *8.* Я немного занят. *9.* Нет, я занят.

• *1.* Don't look down! *2.* He's going down. *3.* Are you sure about that? *4.* Sure about that? *5.* Are you quite sure? *6.* Are you really sure? *7.* I was busy. *8.* I'm kind of busy. *9.* No, I'm busy.

**[160]** *1.* Не имеет значения. *2.* Этого не произойдет. *3.* Что произойдет тогда? *4.* Вот что произойдет. *5.* Что произошло дальше? *6.* Что будет дальше? *7.* Еще немного дальше. *8.* А что потом? *9.* Что случилось потом?

● *1.* Doesn't matter. *2.* That's not gonna happen. *3.* What happens then? *4.* Here's what's gonna happen. *5.* What happened next? *6.* What happens next? *7.* Just a little further. *8.* And then what? *9.* What happened then?

**[161]** *1.* Сейчас и потом. *2.* Это еще хуже. *3.* Я не понял. *4.* Я правильно понял. *5.* Я понял, ладно? *6.* Я почти понял. *7.* Вот, я понял. *8.* Все еще понял. *9.* Только одна вещь.
● *1.* Now and then. *2.* That's even worse. *3.* I didn't understand. *4.* Got that right. *5.* I get it, okay? *6.* I've almost got it. *7.* Here, I got it. *8.* Still got it. *9.* Just one thing.

**[162]** *1.* Еще одна вещь. *2.* Она была одна? *3.* Она не одна. *4.* Она совсем одна. *5.* Всего одна ночь. *6.* Где твоя машина? *7.* Где моя машина? *8.* Добрый вечер сэр. *9.* Добрый вечер всем.
● *1.* Just one more thing. *2.* Was she alone? *3.* She's not alone. *4.* She's all alone. *5.* Just one night. *6.* Where's your car? *7.* Where's my car? *8.* Good evening, sir. *9.* Good evening, everyone.

**[163]** *1.* О, добрый вечер. *2.* Добрый вечер, Отец. *3.* Ах, вот оно. *4.* Ах, это хорошо. *5.* Ой, подожди секунду. *6.* Куда ты ушел? *7.* Куда он ушел? *8.* Почему ты ушел? *9.* Когда он ушел?
● *1.* Oh, good evening. *2.* Good evening, Father. *3.* Ah, here it is. *4.* Ah, that's good. *5.* Oh, wait a second. *6.* Where did you go? *7.* Where's he gone? *8.* Why'd you leave? *9.* When did he leave?

## Difficulty Level: 3

**[1]** *1.* Я здесь, я здесь. *2.* Нет, это не так. *3.* Это не так просто. *4.* Нет, я не был. *5.* И где ты был? *6.* Нет у меня нет. *7.* Тебя здесь не было. *8.* У тебя все хорошо. *9.* Очень хорошо, очень хорошо.
● *1.* I'm here, I'm here. *2.* No, it's not. *3.* It's not as simple as that. *4.* No, I wasn't. *5.* And where were you? *6.* No, I have not. *7.* You weren't here. *8.* You're doing good. *9.* Very good, very good.

**[2]** *1.* Это было очень хорошо. *2.* Это хорошо, это хорошо.

451

*3.* Да, это было хорошо. *4.* Это было так хорошо. *5.* Ну и где он? *6.* Ну, это было так. *7.* Ну, это не так. *8.* Ну, я не был. *9.* Ну, это очень просто.

● *1.* That was really good. *2.* That's good, that's good. *3.* Yeah, it was good. *4.* That was so good. *5.* Well, where is he? *6.* Well, it was. *7.* Well, it wasn't. *8.* Well, I wasn't. *9.* Well, it's very simple.

**[3]** *1.* Нет, его здесь нет. *2.* Я все еще здесь. *3.* Так почему мы здесь? *4.* О, да, да, да. *5.* О, хорошо, ты здесь. *6.* Это не о тебе. *7.* Это была не она. *8.* Что сейчас не так? *9.* Ну, я сейчас здесь.

● *1.* No, he's not here. *2.* I'm still here. *3.* So why are we here? *4.* Oh, yeah, yeah, yeah. *5.* Oh, good, you're here. *6.* This isn't about you. *7.* It wasn't her. *8.* What's wrong now? *9.* Well, I'm here now.

**[4]** *1.* И где он сейчас? *2.* И где она сейчас? *3.* Ну, ты сейчас здесь. *4.* Нет я в порядке. *5.* Что-то не так. *6.* Это где-то здесь. *7.* Я не могу сейчас. *8.* Вот почему мы здесь. *9.* О, вот и все.

● *1.* And where is he now? *2.* And where is she now? *3.* Well, you're here now. *4.* No, I'm fine. *5.* Something's wrong. *6.* It's here somewhere. *7.* I can't now. *8.* That's why we're here. *9.* Oh, here we go.

**[5]** *1.* Ну, вот и все. *2.* Хорошо, вот и все. *3.* Вот и все, да? *4.* Да, вот и все. *5.* Вот он и сейчас. *6.* Вот что не так. *7.* И почему бы нет? *8.* Это было бы хорошо. *9.* Что было бы хорошо.

● *1.* Well, that's it. *2.* Okay, here goes. *3.* So that's it, huh? *4.* Right, that's it. *5.* There he is now. *6.* That's what's wrong. *7.* And why not? *8.* That'd be good. *9.* That would be good.

**[6]** *1.* Как бы это было? *2.* Теперь все в порядке. *3.* И теперь этого нет. *4.* Ну и что теперь? *5.* И теперь ты здесь. *6.* Нет, я не знаю. *7.* Все ли в порядке? *8.* Я, не так ли? *9.* Нет, ее здесь нет.

● *1.* How would that be? *2.* It's okay now. *3.* And now it's gone. *4.* Well, what now? *5.* And now you're here. *6.* No, I don't know. *7.* Is everyone all right? *8.* I am, aren't I? *9.* No, she's not here.

**[7]** *1.* Это никогда не так. *2.* Есть что-то еще. *3.* Тебя там не было. *4.* Он все еще там. *5.* Там что-то есть. *6.* Ты там в порядке? *7.* Они все еще там? *8.* Да, я был там. *9.* Но это не так.

● *1.* It never is. *2.* There's something else. *3.* You weren't there. *4.* He's still out there. *5.* There's something out there. *6.* You okay in there? *7.* Are they still there? *8.* Yes, I was there. *9.* But you're not.

**[8]** *1.* Но я в порядке. *2.* Но я сейчас здесь. *3.* Но все в порядке. *4.* Но вот ты здесь. *5.* Но вот мы здесь. *6.* Я ничего не знаю. *7.* Только ты и я. *8.* Я здесь для тебя. *9.* И когда это было?

● *1.* But I'm fine. *2.* But I'm here now. *3.* But it's all right. *4.* But here you are. *5.* But here we are. *6.* I don't know nothing. *7.* Just you and me. *8.* I'm here for you. *9.* And when was that?

**[9]** *1.* Тогда все в порядке. *2.* Тогда почему ты здесь? *3.* Тогда почему я здесь? *4.* Тогда что это было? *5.* Ну и что тогда? *6.* Тогда почему мы здесь? *7.* Все будет в порядке. *8.* Нет, он не будет. *9.* Нет, она не будет.

● *1.* All right, then. *2.* Then why are you here? *3.* Then why am I here? *4.* Then what was it? *5.* Well, what then? *6.* Then why are we here? *7.* It'll be okay. *8.* No, he won't. *9.* No, she won't.

**[10]** *1.* И когда это будет? *2.* Действительно я в порядке. *3.* Это было действительно хорошо. *4.* Это действительно было так. *5.* Это действительно очень просто. *6.* Так как вы были?

● *1.* And when will that be? *2.* Really, I'm fine. *3.* It was really good. *4.* It really was. *5.* It's really very simple. *6.* So, how have you been?

**[11]** *1.* Я не хочу этого. *2.* Тебе бы лучше быть. *3.* У меня было лучше. *4.* Я тоже это знаю. *5.* Как мне это сделать? *6.* Не могу этого сделать. *7.* Не могу сделать что? *8.* Так же, как и. *9.* Где же он тогда?

● *1.* I don't want this. *2.* You better be. *3.* I've had better. *4.* I know that too. *5.* How do I do that? *6.* Can't do that. *7.* Can't do what? *8.* Just as well. *9.* Where is he, then?

**[12]** *1.* Я так не думаю. *2.* Этого не может быть. *3.* Как нам это сделать? *4.* Я этого не сделал. *5.* Как ты это сделал? *6.* Как ты сделал это? *7.* Ты только что сделал. *8.* Был там, сделал это. *9.* Как он это сделал?

● *1.* I don't think so. *2.* It can't be. *3.* How do we do this? *4.* I didn't. *5.* How'd you do that? *6.* How did you do it? *7.* You just did. *8.* Been there, done that. *9.* How did he do it?

**[13]** *1.* Тогда что ты сделал? *2.* Что он сделал сейчас? *3.* Почему ты это сделал? *4.* Что ты сделал сейчас? *5.* Так что ты сделал? *6.* Ты это сделал, да? *7.* Когда ты это сделал? *8.* Что еще ты сделал? *9.* Мне это не нужно.
● *1.* Then what did you do? *2.* What's he done now? *3.* Why have you done this? *4.* What have you done now? *5.* So what'd you do? *6.* You did, huh? *7.* When did you do this? *8.* What else did you do? *9.* I don't have to.

**[14]** *1.* Что еще вам нужно? *2.* Что еще тебе нужно? *3.* Я их не знаю. *4.* Да, мне очень жаль. *5.* Что у нас здесь? *6.* Ты знаешь, где она? *7.* Знаешь, я не знаю. *8.* Да, ну, знаешь что? *9.* Знаешь, почему я здесь?
● *1.* What else do you want? *2.* What else do you need? *3.* I don't know them. *4.* Yeah, I'm sorry. *5.* What have we here? *6.* Do you know where she is? *7.* You know, I don't know. *8.* Yeah, well, you know what? *9.* You know why I'm here?

**[15]** *1.* Тогда кто это сделал? *2.* Здесь кто то есть. *3.* Кто у нас здесь? *4.* Кто бы не был? *5.* Есть кто-то еще. *6.* Ты и кто еще? *7.* Кто еще там был? *8.* Там кто-то есть. *9.* Я знаю об этом.
● *1.* Then who did? *2.* There's someone here. *3.* Who do we have here? *4.* Who wouldn't be? *5.* There's someone else. *6.* You and who else? *7.* Who else was there? *8.* There's someone in there. *9.* I'm aware of that.

**[16]** *1.* У меня всегда есть. *2.* Почему это всегда я? *3.* Это всегда был ты. *4.* Мне очень жаль, ладно? *5.* Есть кто-нибудь там? *6.* У меня уже есть. *7.* Я уже в порядке. *8.* Он уже это сделал. *9.* Я уже это сделал.
● *1.* I always have. *2.* Why is it always me? *3.* It's always been you. *4.* I'm sorry, all right? *5.* Is someone there? *6.* I already have. *7.* I'm fine now. *8.* He already has. *9.* I already did that.

**[17]** *1.* Я здесь с тобой. *2.* Кто ты еще раз? *3.* У вас всегда есть. *4.* Мы здесь для вас. *5.* Это хорошо для вас. *6.* Что мне теперь делать? *7.* Как много ты знаешь? *8.* Почему ты это сказал? *9.* Я тебе так сказал.
● *1.* I'm here with you. *2.* Who are you again? *3.* You always

have. *4.* We're here for you. *5.* That's good for you. *6.* What do I do now? *7.* How much do you know? *8.* Why do you say that? *9.* I told you so.

**[18]** *1.* Что еще он сказал? *2.* Я бы так сказал. *3.* Я бы не сказал. *4.* Он не сказал бы. *5.* Я бы сказал нет. *6.* Он не сказал мне. *7.* Я ничего не сказал. *8.* Я прямо за тобой. *9.* Это было прямо здесь.

● *1.* What else did he say? *2.* I'd say so. *3.* I'd rather not say. *4.* He wouldn't say. *5.* I should say not. *6.* He wouldn't tell me. *7.* I didn't say nothing. *8.* I'm right behind you. *9.* It was right here.

**[19]** *1.* Он был прямо там. *2.* Он был прямо здесь. *3.* Я в этом уверен. *4.* Почему ты так уверен? *5.* Он уверен, что да. *6.* Он уверен, что сделал. *7.* А вот и он. *8.* Ты сделал это снова. *9.* О, нет, не снова.

● *1.* He was right there. *2.* He was right here. *3.* I'm sure of it. *4.* What makes you so sure? *5.* He sure is. *6.* He sure did. *7.* Here he comes. *8.* You did it again. *9.* Oh, no, not again.

**[20]** *1.* О, вот и снова. *2.* Итак, где мы были? *3.* Итак, что ты сделал? *4.* Итак, что мне делать? *5.* Итак, почему ты здесь? *6.* Итак, что это будет? *7.* Итак, вот и все. *8.* Итак, что он сказал? *9.* Итак, о чем это?

● *1.* Oh, here we go again. *2.* Now, where were we? *3.* So what did you do? *4.* So, what do I do? *5.* So, why are you here? *6.* So, what's it gonna be? *7.* So there you go. *8.* So, what did he say? *9.* So, what's this about?

**[21]** *1.* Нет, ты не можешь! *2.* В то же время. *3.* Конечно, я это сделал. *4.* Конечно, так и есть. *5.* Как у нас дела? *6.* Разве ты не знаешь? *7.* Был ли он один? *8.* Еще один, еще один. *9.* Такой же как ты.

● *1.* No, you can't! *2.* Same time. *3.* Sure I did. *4.* Sure does. *5.* How we doing? *6.* Don't you know? *7.* Was he alone? *8.* One more, one more. *9.* Same as you.

**[22]** *1.* Нет, я не такой. *2.* Возможно, он это сделал. *3.* Нет, я не буду. *4.* Эй, ты в порядке? *5.* Эй, что не так? *6.* Эй, это снова я. *7.* Не все из нас. *8.* Я не сказал ему. *9.* Сколько у тебя есть?

● *1.* No, I ain't. *2.* Maybe he did. *3.* No, I won't. *4.* Hey, you okay? *5.* Hey, what's wrong? *6.* Hey, it's me again. *7.* Not all of us. *8.* I didn't tell him. *9.* How much you got?

**[23]** *1.* Нет это не правда. *2.* Я в порядке, правда. *3.* Все в порядке, правда. *4.* Ну, это было быстро. *5.* Сколько я вам должен? *6.* Он должен быть здесь. *7.* Я не могу сказать. *8.* Как бы это сказать? *9.* Можешь мне сказать почему?
- *1.* No, that's not true. *2.* I'm fine, really. *3.* It's okay, really. *4.* Well, that was fast. *5.* How much do I owe you? *6.* He should be here. *7.* I can't say. *8.* How do I put this? *9.* Can you tell me why?

**[24]** *1.* Разве это не приятно? *2.* Как приятно для тебя. *3.* Не давай мне этого. *4.* Ты сейчас со мной. *5.* Нет, я не мог. *6.* Как ты мог сказать? *7.* Где он мог быть? *8.* Я в порядке, спасибо. *9.* Ну и дела, спасибо.
- *1.* Isn't this nice? *2.* How nice for you. *3.* Don't give me that. *4.* You're with me now. *5.* No, I couldn't. *6.* How could you tell? *7.* Where could he be? *8.* I'm fine, thank you. *9.* Gee, thanks.

**[25]** *1.* Так что спасибо тебе. *2.* Спасибо, что вы здесь. *3.* Не для меня, спасибо. *4.* Нет, мы не можем. *5.* Я рад за тебя. *6.* Рад, что ты здесь. *7.* Хороший день для тебя. *8.* Сейчас я должен идти. *9.* Теперь мы можем идти?
- *1.* So thank you. *2.* Thank you for being here. *3.* Not for me, thanks. *4.* No, we can't. *5.* I'm happy for you. *6.* Glad you're here. *7.* Good day to you. *8.* I have to go now. *9.* Can we go now?

**[26]** *1.* Ты не можешь идти. *2.* Теперь ты можешь идти. *3.* Почему тебе нужно идти? *4.* Мне не нужно идти. *5.* Что ж, спасибо тебе. *6.* Меня даже здесь нет. *7.* Ты даже не знаешь. *8.* Ты ей не сказал? *9.* Где ты это хочешь?
- *1.* You can't go. *2.* Now you can go. *3.* Why do you have to go? *4.* I don't have to go. *5.* Well, thank you. *6.* I'm not even here. *7.* You don't even know. *8.* You didn't tell her? *9.* Where do you want this?

**[27]** *1.* Иди сюда, иди сюда. *2.* Так оно и есть. *3.* Оно все еще здесь. *4.* Как у него дела? *5.* Что, если это правда? *6.* Что ж, спасибо, сэр. *7.* Мне очень жаль, сэр. *8.* Сэр, вы в порядке? *9.* Все в порядке, сэр.
- *1.* Come here, come here. *2.* That's just the way it is. *3.* It's still there. *4.* How is he doing? *5.* What if it's true? *6.* Well, thank

you, sir. *7.* I'm very sorry, sir. *8.* Sir, are you okay? *9.* It's all right, sir.

**[28]** *1.* Вот и мы, сэр. *2.* Да, сэр, прямо сейчас. *3.* Откуда ты это знаешь? *4.* Я думаю ты прав. *5.* И он был прав. *6.* Что ж, он прав. *7.* Это должно быть хорошо. *8.* Чего ты здесь хочешь? *9.* Чего я не знаю?

● *1.* Here we are, sir. *2.* Yes, sir, right away. *3.* How do you know that? *4.* I think you're right. *5.* And he was right. *6.* Well, he's right. *7.* This ought to be good. *8.* What do you want here? *9.* What don't I know?

**[29]** *1.* Что ты здесь делаешь? *2.* У меня нет времени. *3.* Мне нужно больше времени. *4.* Сколько времени вам нужно? *5.* Мы в этом вместе. *6.* Все в порядке, дорогая. *7.* Я не знаю, дорогая. *8.* Ты в порядке, чувак? *9.* Мне очень жаль, чувак.

● *1.* What are you doing here? *2.* I don't have time. *3.* I need more time. *4.* How much time do you need? *5.* We're in this together. *6.* It's okay, honey. *7.* I don't know, sweetheart. *8.* You okay, man? *9.* I'm so sorry, man.

**[30]** *1.* Как вы можете сказать? *2.* Я не хотел этого. *3.* Как дела мой друг? *4.* У нее все хорошо. *5.* Извините за это, сэр. *6.* Я так и думал. *7.* Как долго я здесь? *8.* Это было так долго? *9.* Что ты делаешь сегодня?

● *1.* How can you tell? *2.* I didn't want this. *3.* How are you, my friend? *4.* She's doing well. *5.* Sorry about that, sir. *6.* I thought so. *7.* How long have I been here? *8.* Has it been that long? *9.* How you doing today?

**[31]** *1.* Я его не видел. *2.* Я видел это раньше. *3.* Приятно видеть вас снова. *4.* Я рад тебя видеть. *5.* Тоже рад видеть тебя. *6.* Рад тебя видеть, чувак. *7.* Эй, рад тебя видеть. *8.* Я не хочу говорить. *9.* Зачем ты это сделал?

● *1.* I haven't seen him. *2.* I've seen it before. *3.* Good to see you again. *4.* I'm glad to see you. *5.* Nice to see you, too. *6.* Good to see you, man. *7.* Hey, good to see you. *8.* I don't want to talk. *9.* Why did you do that?

**[32]** *1.* Эй, что здесь происходит? *2.* Вот как это происходит. *3.* Никогда этого не происходит. *4.* Э-э, знаешь что? *5.* Э-э, нет, нет. *6.* Это было бы здорово. *7.* Где, черт возьми, все? *8.* Не в этот раз! *9.* Я бы не знал.

● *1.* Hey, what's going on here? *2.* That's how it goes. *3.* It never does. *4.* Uh, you know what? *5.* Uh, no, no. *6.* That'd be great. *7.* Where the hell is everybody? *8.* Not this time! *9.* I wouldn't know.

**[33]** *1.* Ребята, вы в порядке? *2.* Рад вас видеть, ребята. *3.* Мне очень жаль, ребята. *4.* У меня было достаточно. *5.* Этого должно быть достаточно. *6.* Я думаю, этого достаточно.

● *1.* You guys okay? *2.* Good to see you guys. *3.* I'm sorry, you guys. *4.* I've had enough. *5.* That should be enough. *6.* I think that's enough.

**[34]** *1.* Мне это не нравится. *2.* Ты выглядишь очень хорошо. *3.* Да, это хорошая идея. *4.* Он скоро будет здесь. *5.* Как я должен знать? *6.* Ты хочешь знать почему? *7.* Ты действительно хочешь знать? *8.* Откуда мне это знать? *9.* Ты не мог знать.

● *1.* I don't like this. *2.* You look very nice. *3.* Yeah, that's a good idea. *4.* He'll be here soon. *5.* How should I know? *6.* You want to know why? *7.* Do you really want to know? *8.* How do I know that? *9.* You couldn't have known.

**[35]** *1.* Откуда ты мог знать? *2.* Откуда мне было знать? *3.* Мне нужно знать, почему. *4.* Почему ты хочешь знать? *5.* Зачем вам это знать? *6.* Я буду именно там. *7.* Что именно ты делаешь? *8.* Мне здесь не место. *9.* Вы этого не знаете.

● *1.* How could you know? *2.* How was I supposed to know? *3.* I need to know why. *4.* Why do you wanna know? *5.* Why do you need to know? *6.* I'll be right there. *7.* What exactly are you doing? *8.* I don't belong here. *9.* You don't know that.

**[36]** *1.* Очень плохо для тебя. *2.* Да, я почти уверен. *3.* Так что ты думаешь? *4.* Думаешь, это хорошая идея? *5.* Куда ты хочешь пойти? *6.* Могу я пойти сейчас? *7.* Мы можем просто пойти? *8.* Это произошло так быстро. *9.* Но этого не произошло.

● *1.* Too bad for you. *2.* Yeah, I'm pretty sure. *3.* So what do you think? *4.* You think that's a good idea? *5.* Where do you want to go? *6.* May I go now? *7.* Can we just go? *8.* It happened so fast. *9.* But it didn't.

**[37]** *1.* Что же тогда произошло? *2.* Вот в чем дело. *3.* А что насчет тебя? *4.* Как насчет прямо сейчас? *5.* Так как насчет этого? *6.* Как у тебя работа? *7.* Скажи мне, где он. *8.* Скажи, что тебе жаль. *9.* Да, это звучит хорошо.

● *1.* So then what happened? *2.* Here's the thing. *3.* So, what about you? *4.* How about right now? *5.* So how about it? *6.* How's work? *7.* Tell me where he is. *8.* Say you're sorry. *9.* Yeah, that sounds good.

**[38]** *1.* Звучит как хорошая идея. *2.* Я этого не говорил. *3.* Ты говорил это раньше. *4.* Разве это не мило? *5.* Ты выглядишь очень мило. *6.* Я здесь, чтобы помочь. *7.* Как мы можем помочь? *8.* Увидимся ли я позже? *9.* Разве это не красиво?

● *1.* Sounds like a good idea. *2.* I didn't say that. *3.* You said that before. *4.* Isn't that sweet? *5.* You look very pretty. *6.* I'm here to help. *7.* How can we help? *8.* Will I see you later? *9.* Isn't it beautiful?

**[39]** *1.* Ты выглядишь так красиво. *2.* Ты выглядишь очень красиво. *3.* Ты готов сделать это? *4.* Я еще не готов. *5.* Я просто не готов. *6.* Это было довольно хорошо. *7.* Ты готов к этому? *8.* Это только вопрос времени. *9.* Это да или нет?

● *1.* You look so beautiful. *2.* You look really pretty. *3.* You ready to do this? *4.* I'm not ready yet. *5.* I'm just not ready. *6.* That was pretty good. *7.* You ready for this? *8.* It's only a matter of time. *9.* Is that a yes or a no?

**[40]** *1.* Или я так думал. *2.* Я не совсем уверен. *3.* Сколько тебе было лет? *4.* Это верно, это верно. *5.* Ты делаешь доброе дело. *6.* Да, в самом деле. *7.* Мы должны идти сейчас. *8.* Они этого не сделали. *9.* Ну, вы это сделали.

● *1.* Or so I thought. *2.* I'm not really sure. *3.* How old were you? *4.* That's right, that's right. *5.* You make a good point. *6.* Yes, indeed. *7.* We have to go now. *8.* They didn't. *9.* Well, you did.

**[41]** *1.* Теперь вы сделали это. *2.* Мы уже это сделали. *3.* Конечно, вы это сделали. *4.* Я-я не понимаю. *5.* Вы готовы к этому? *6.* Они готовы для вас. *7.* Я думаю, мы готовы. *8.* Ты всегда был таким. *9.* Странно, не так ли?

● *1.* Now you've done it. *2.* We already did. *3.* Sure, you did. *4.* I-I don't understand. *5.* Are you ready for this? *6.* They're ready for you. *7.* I think we're ready. *8.* You always have been.

*9.* Strange, isn't it?

**[42]** *1.* Я могу вернуться позже. *2.* Что ж, самое время. *3.* Это то же самое. *4.* Мне то же самое. *5.* Не то же самое. *6.* Я хорошо себя чувствую. *7.* Подожди, мне очень жаль. *8.* Я тоже тебя люблю. *9.* Я надеюсь на это.

● *1.* I can come back later. *2.* Well, it's about time. *3.* It's the same. *4.* Same for me. *5.* Not the same. *6.* I feel fine. *7.* Wait, I'm sorry. *8.* I love you, too. *9.* I should hope so.

**[43]** *1.* Надеюсь, все в порядке. *2.* Надеюсь ты в порядке. *3.* Вам легко это говорить. *4.* Зачем им это делать? *5.* Разве это не смешно? *6.* Что вы еще хотите? *7.* Мы будем в порядке. *8.* Ну, что будем делать? *9.* Я хочу пойти домой.

● *1.* I hope that's okay. *2.* I hope you're okay. *3.* That's easy for you to say. *4.* Why would they do this? *5.* Isn't it funny? *6.* What more do you want? *7.* We'll be fine. *8.* Well, what are we gonna do? *9.* I want to go home now.

**[44]** *1.* Как это вообще возможно? *2.* Почему ты вообще здесь? *3.* Сколько тебе вообще лет? *4.* Возможно, нам стоит пойти. *5.* Я действительно так делаю. *6.* Ты можешь уйти сейчас.

● *1.* How is that even possible? *2.* Why are you even here? *3.* How old are you anyway? *4.* Maybe we should go. *5.* I really do. *6.* You can leave now.

**[45]** *1.* Мы не можем уйти. *2.* Все в порядке, мама. *3.* Мне очень жаль, мама. *4.* Лучше поздно, чем никогда. *5.* Слишком поздно для этого. *6.* Нет, уже слишком поздно. *7.* Но уже слишком поздно. *8.* Ну, уже слишком поздно. *9.* Что он здесь делает?

● *1.* We can't leave. *2.* It's okay, Mom. *3.* I'm sorry, Mother. *4.* Better late than never. *5.* Too late for that. *6.* No, it's too late. *7.* But it's too late. *8.* Well, it's too late. *9.* What's he doing here?

**[46]** *1.* Она этого не делает. *2.* Как она это делает? *3.* Она всегда так делает. *4.* Нет, не сегодня вечером. *5.* У нас все ясно. *6.* Я в порядке, ясно? *7.* Я просто хочу поговорить. *8.* Приятно с тобой поговорить. *9.* Мы можем поговорить позже?

● *1.* She doesn't. *2.* How is she doing? *3.* She always does. *4.* No, not tonight. *5.* We're clear. *6.* I'm fine, okay? *7.* I just want to talk. *8.* Nice talking to you. *9.* Can we talk later?

**[47]** *1.* Теперь мы можем поговорить. *2.* Ты куда-то собираешься? *3.* Ну, спасибо вам большое. *4.* Если ты так говоришь. *5.* Нет, это не нормально. *6.* Он не в себе. *7.* Я чувствую себя ужасно. *8.* Возможно, в другой раз. *9.* Почему ты пришел сюда?
- *1.* Now we can talk. *2.* You going somewhere? *3.* Well, thank you so much. *4.* If you say so. *5.* No, it's not okay. *6.* He's not himself. *7.* I feel horrible. *8.* Maybe another time. *9.* Why did you come here?

**[48]** *1.* Я буду на секунду. *2.* Ты знаешь, какой он. *3.* Ох, ну и дела. *4.* Вот как это работает. *5.* Это должно быть интересно. *6.* Почему вам так интересно? *7.* Я вернусь к вам. *8.* Что ты делаешь обратно? *9.* Я этого не делал!
- *1.* I'll just be a second. *2.* You know how he is. *3.* Oh, gee. *4.* That's how it works. *5.* This should be interesting. *6.* Why are you so interested? *7.* I'll get back to you. *8.* What are you doing back? *9.* I didn't do it!

**[49]** *1.* Что он там делал? *2.* Что ты там делал? *3.* Что ты здесь делал? *4.* Он всегда так делал. *5.* Ты всегда так делал. *6.* Что ты делал раньше? *7.* Он делал это раньше. *8.* Что он здесь делал? *9.* Это было бы прекрасно.
- *1.* What was he doing there? *2.* What were you doing up there? *3.* What were you doing here? *4.* He always has. *5.* You always did. *6.* What did you do before? *7.* He's done it before. *8.* What was he doing here? *9.* That would be great.

**[50]** *1.* Я чувствую себя прекрасно. *2.* Прекрасно, не так ли? *3.* Вот чего я боюсь. *4.* Это важно для меня. *5.* Разве это не круто? *6.* Не все из них. *7.* Как у них дела? *8.* Хорошо, что ты вернулся. *9.* Вот почему я вернулся.
- *1.* I feel great. *2.* Lovely, isn't it? *3.* That's what I'm afraid of. *4.* It's important to me. *5.* Isn't that cool? *6.* Not all of them. *7.* How are they doing? *8.* It's good to have you back. *9.* That's why I came back.

**[51]** *1.* Я вернулся за тобой. *2.* Нет, вам не обязательно. *3.* И тебе того же. *4.* Но что с того? *5.* Не волнуйся о ней. *6.* Я не знаю точно. *7.* Теперь ты в безопасности. *8.* Это в последний раз. *9.* Ну, что вы думаете?

● *1.* I came back for you. *2.* No, you don't have to. *3.* Same to you. *4.* But so what? *5.* Don't worry about her. *6.* I don't know exactly. *7.* You're safe now. *8.* This is the last time. *9.* Well, what do you think?

**[52]** *1.* Боже, надеюсь, что нет. *2.* Он всего лишь ребенок. *3.* Ну, посмотрите, кто здесь. *4.* Вот, посмотрите на это. *5.* Просто посмотрите на него. *6.* Теперь посмотрите на это.
● *1.* God, I hope not. *2.* He's just a kid. *3.* Well, look who's here. *4.* Here, look at this. *5.* Just look at him. *6.* Now look at this.

**[53]** *1.* Просто посмотрите на это. *2.* Просто посмотрите на нее. *3.* Просто дай мне секунду. *4.* Не дай ей уйти! *5.* У меня хорошие новости. *6.* Я не это говорю. *7.* Я скоро буду дома. *8.* Ты далеко от дома. *9.* Он этого не знает.
● *1.* Just look at this. *2.* Just look at her. *3.* Just give me a second. *4.* Don't let her get away! *5.* I've got good news. *6.* That's not what I'm saying. *7.* I'll be home soon. *8.* You're a long way from home. *9.* He doesn't know that.

**[54]** *1.* Это было бы потрясающе. *2.* Так в чем проблема? *3.* Есть ли здесь проблема? *4.* Ну, что это такое? *5.* Нет, не говори так. *6.* И вам тоже следует. *7.* Тебе следует идти сейчас. *8.* Да, удачи с этим. *9.* Что случилось с ним?
● *1.* That would be amazing. *2.* So what's the problem? *3.* Is there a problem here? *4.* Well, what is it? *5.* No, don't say that. *6.* So should you. *7.* You should go now. *8.* Yeah, good luck with that. *9.* What's wrong with him?

**[55]** *1.* Разве ты не слышал? *2.* Я слышал это раньше. *3.* Как у всех дела? *4.* Потому что это правда. *5.* Было приятно тебя увидеть. *6.* Папа, ты в порядке? *7.* Добрый день вам, сэр. *8.* У тебя все отлично. *9.* Ну вот и отлично.
● *1.* Haven't you heard? *2.* I've heard that before. *3.* How's everybody doing? *4.* Because it's true. *5.* It was good to see you. *6.* Dad, are you okay? *7.* Good day to you, sir. *8.* You're doing great. *9.* Well, that's great.

**[56]** *1.* Отлично, не так ли? *2.* Теперь это твой дом. *3.* Один и тот же. *4.* Мои дела в порядке. *5.* Вот, позвольте мне помочь. *6.* Мне правда пора идти. *7.* Разве он не милый? *8.* О, ты такой милый. *9.* Нет, я не пойду.
● *1.* Great, isn't it? *2.* This is your home now. *3.* One and the

same. *4.* I'm doing good. *5.* Here, let me help. *6.* I really have to go. *7.* Isn't he cute? *8.* Oh, you're so sweet. *9.* No, I won't go.

**[57]** *1.* Нет, ты не будешь. *2.* Ты в порядке, приятель? *3.* Я собираюсь идти сейчас. *4.* Как давно ты здесь? *5.* Это было так давно. *6.* Давно тебя не видел. *7.* Но это было давно. *8.* Вы давно его знаете? *9.* Это было очень давно.

● *1.* No, you won't. *2.* You okay, buddy? *3.* I'm going to go now. *4.* How long have you been here? *5.* It's been so long. *6.* Haven't seen you in a while. *7.* But that was a long time ago. *8.* Have you known him long? *9.* It's a long time ago.

**[58]** *1.* Я думаю ты красивая. *2.* Разве она не красивая? *3.* Нет, ты иди вперед. *4.* Пожалуйста, не делай этого. *5.* Прямо как твой отец. *6.* Ты не мой отец. *7.* Он не мой отец. *8.* Как нам его найти? *9.* Эй, куда ты идешь?

● *1.* I think you're beautiful. *2.* Isn't she pretty? *3.* No, you go ahead. *4.* Please don't do this. *5.* Just like your father. *6.* You're not my father. *7.* He's not my dad. *8.* How do we find him? *9.* Hey, where are you going?

**[59]** *1.* Никто не знает почему. *2.* Это было так сложно? *3.* Слушай, я не знаю. *4.* Слушай, мне очень жаль. *5.* Я вижу это сейчас. *6.* Вы знаете друг друга? *7.* Но не более того. *8.* Пожалуйста, более чем пожалуйста. *9.* Вот он снова идет.

● *1.* Nobody knows why. *2.* Was that so hard? *3.* Look, I don't know. *4.* Look, I'm really sorry. *5.* I see that now. *6.* You know each other? *7.* But no more. *8.* You're more than welcome. *9.* There he goes again.

**[60]** *1.* Тогда пойдем со мной. *2.* Давай просто пойдем домой. *3.* Теперь дело за вами. *4.* Ты думаешь, я сумасшедший? *5.* Что это вообще значит? *6.* Ты должен быть счастлив. *7.* Так тебе и надо. *8.* Нет, пожалуйста, не надо. *9.* Возможно, в следующий раз.

● *1.* Then come with me. *2.* Let's just go home. *3.* It's up to you now. *4.* You think I'm crazy? *5.* What does that even mean? *6.* You should be happy. *7.* Serves you right. *8.* No, please, don't. *9.* Maybe next time.

**[61]** *1.* Это всего лишь деньги. *2.* Так как все прошло? *3.* Все в порядке, детка. *4.* Мне очень жаль, детка. *5.* Что не так, детка? *6.* Откуда мы это знаем? *7.* Разве это не весело? *8.*

Ты мне нужен здесь. *9.* Зачем я тебе нужен?

● *1.* It's only money. *2.* So how'd it go? *3.* It's okay, baby. *4.* I'm sorry, babe. *5.* What's wrong, baby? *6.* How do we know that? *7.* Isn't this fun? *8.* I need you here. *9.* Why do you need me?

**[62]** *1.* В это трудно поверить. *2.* Ну, ты выглядишь великолепно. *3.* Да, это звучит великолепно. *4.* Это не твоя вина. *5.* Есть кое-что еще. *6.* Разве это не идеально? *7.* Я обязательно это сделаю. *8.* Пока нет, но сделаю. *9.* Ты хорош в этом.

● *1.* It's hard to believe. *2.* Well, you look great. *3.* Yeah, that sounds great. *4.* This isn't your fault. *5.* There is something else. *6.* Isn't it perfect? *7.* I certainly will. *8.* Not yet, but I will. *9.* You're good at that.

**[63]** *1.* Просто делаю свою работу. *2.* Вы этого не видели? *3.* Ты мой лучший друг. *4.* Что ж, вам повезло. *5.* Просто повезло, я думаю. *6.* Не говори ни слова. *7.* Возможно, я смогу помочь. *8.* Что ж, увидимся завтра. *9.* Скажи мне все равно.

● *1.* Just doing my job. *2.* You didn't see it? *3.* You're my best friend. *4.* Well, you're in luck. *5.* Just lucky, I guess. *6.* Don't say a word. *7.* Maybe I can help. *8.* Well, see you tomorrow. *9.* Tell me anyway.

**[64]** *1.* Не смотри на него. *2.* Смотри, куда ты идешь. *3.* Ну, смотри, кто вернулся. *4.* Есть только один путь. *5.* Я скажу тебе позже. *6.* Как ты получил это? *7.* Хорошая девочка, хорошая девочка. *8.* Звучит как хороший план. *9.* Я бы не стал.

● *1.* Don't look at him. *2.* Watch where you're going. *3.* Well, look who's back. *4.* There's only one way. *5.* I'll tell you later. *6.* How did you get it? *7.* Good girl, good girl. *8.* Sounds like a good plan. *9.* I wouldn't.

**[65]** *1.* Это мой первый раз. *2.* Я был так близко. *3.* Это было слишком близко. *4.* А сейчас иди спать. *5.* Мне тоже приятно познакомиться. *6.* Рад познакомиться с вами. *7.* Вы уверены в этом? *8.* Мы уверены, что сделали. *9.* Мы уверены, что да.

● *1.* It's my first time. *2.* I was so close. *3.* That was too close. *4.* Now go to sleep. *5.* Nice to meet you, too. *6.* Glad to meet you. *7.* You sure about that? *8.* We sure did. *9.* We sure do.

**[66]** *1.* Они уверены, что есть. *2.* Я немного занят сейчас. *3.* Это не имеет значения. *4.* Как ты себя чувствуешь? *5.* Я знаю, это тяжело. *6.* Этого никогда не произойдет. *7.* Ну и что дальше? *8.* Вот что случилось потом? *9.* Как ты это понял?

● *1.* They sure are. *2.* I'm kind of busy right now. *3.* It doesn't matter. *4.* How you feeling? *5.* I know it's hard. *6.* That's never gonna happen. *7.* So, what's next? *8.* Then what happened? *9.* How did you get that?

**[67]** *1.* Я только что понял. *2.* Теперь я тебя понял. *3.* Я все еще понял. *4.* Да, да, я понял. *5.* О, еще одна вещь. *6.* Есть только одна проблема. *7.* Ах, я не знаю. *8.* Ах, вот и все. *9.* Ах, все в порядке.

● *1.* I just got it. *2.* I got you now. *3.* I still got it. *4.* Yeah, yeah, I got it. *5.* Oh, one more thing. *6.* There's just one problem. *7.* Ah, I don't know. *8.* Ah, here we go. *9.* Ah, it's okay.

**[68]** *1.* Вот почему я ушел. *2.* Как ты меня нашел? *3.* Что еще можно сделать? *4.* Боюсь, это будет невозможно. *5.* Что мы здесь делаем? *6.* Это был единственный путь. *7.* Ты мой единственный друг. *8.* Нет, я не голоден. *9.* Извините о том, что?

● *1.* That's why I left. *2.* How'd you find me? *3.* What else can you do? *4.* I'm afraid that won't be possible. *5.* What are we doing here? *6.* It was the only way. *7.* You're my only friend. *8.* No, I'm not hungry. *9.* Sorry about what?

**[69]** *1.* Вопрос в том, почему? *2.* Да, извини за это. *3.* Извини, я должен идти. *4.* У меня никого нет. *5.* Она этого не сделала. *6.* Больше чем что либо. *7.* Где ты это взял? *8.* Я не твой брат. *9.* Рад тебя видеть, брат.

● *1.* The question is, why? *2.* Yeah, sorry about that. *3.* Sorry, I have to go. *4.* I'm single. *5.* She didn't. *6.* More than anything. *7.* Where did you get this? *8.* I'm not your brother. *9.* Good to see you, brother.

**[70]** *1.* Разве это не глупо? *2.* Мы должны уйти немедленно. *3.* Ты знаешь, какая она. *4.* Я тебе не верю! *5.* Держись подальше от меня. *6.* Мне жаль это слышать. *7.* Я рад слышать, что. *8.* Я никому не скажу. *9.* Я вернусь через минуту.

• *1.* Isn't that silly? *2.* We must leave immediately. *3.* You know how she is. *4.* I don't believe you! *5.* Stay away from me. *6.* I'm sorry to hear it. *7.* I'm happy to hear that. *8.* I won't tell anybody. *9.* I'll be back in a minute.

**[71]** *1.* Да, ты, наверное, прав. *2.* Наверное, мне стоит пойти. *3.* Наверное, это хорошая идея. *4.* Наверное, тебе стоит пойти. *5.* Наверное, мне пора идти. *6.* Ты не моя мать.
• *1.* Yeah, you're probably right. *2.* I should probably go. *3.* That's probably a good idea. *4.* You should probably go. *5.* I should probably get going. *6.* You're not my mother.

**[72]** *1.* Прямо как твоя мать. *2.* Вам никогда не придется. *3.* Давай сделаем это снова. *4.* Вот что мы сделаем. *5.* Ты в порядке, малыш? *6.* Как долго это займет? *7.* Ты можешь остаться здесь. *8.* Как вы это делаете? *9.* Это было бы чудесно.
• *1.* Just like your mother. *2.* You never have. *3.* Let's do it again. *4.* Here's what we'll do. *5.* You okay, kid? *6.* How long will that take? *7.* You can stay here. *8.* How did you do this? *9.* That would be nice.

**[73]** *1.* Мы все еще друзья. *2.* Ну, значит, нас двое. *3.* Где вы двое были? *4.* Не делай мне больно. *5.* С чего мне начать? *6.* Когда ты можешь начать? *7.* О, как твои дела? *8.* Я был здесь первым. *9.* Позвольте мне пойти первым.
• *1.* We're still friends. *2.* Well, that makes two of us. *3.* Where have you two been? *4.* Don't hurt me. *5.* Where do I start? *6.* When can you start? *7.* Oh, how do you do? *8.* I was here first. *9.* Let me go first.

**[74]** *1.* Нет, ты идешь первым. *2.* Почему это имеет значение? *3.* Оставайся рядом со мной. *4.* А теперь сделай это. *5.* Как вы меня нашли? *6.* Ты думаешь, я глупый? *7.* Это что-то новое? *8.* Это ваш последний шанс. *9.* Вы не можете понять.
• *1.* No, you go first. *2.* Why does it matter? *3.* Stay close to me. *4.* Now do it. *5.* How did you find me? *6.* You think I'm stupid? *7.* Is that new? *8.* This is your last chance. *9.* You can't understand.

**[75]** *1.* Как ты это узнал? *2.* Я только что узнал. *3.* Они прямо за нами. *4.* Что они здесь делают? *5.* Где она могла быть? *6.*

Ты сам по себе. *7.* Как ты здесь оказался? *8.* Вы можете быть правы. *9.* Они были не правы.

• *1.* How did you know that? *2.* I just found out. *3.* They're right behind us. *4.* What are they doing here? *5.* Where could she be? *6.* You're on your own. *7.* How did you end up here? *8.* You may be right. *9.* They were wrong.

**[76]** *1.* Мы уже на месте? *2.* Ну, посмотри на это. *3.* Ой, посмотри, кто здесь. *4.* Разве это не безумие? *5.* Может быть, ты сможешь. *6.* Я уверен, ты понимаешь. *7.* Как такое могло быть? *8.* Могло бы и так. *9.* Надеюсь, ты не против.

• *1.* Are we there yet? *2.* Well, look at that. *3.* Oh, look who's here. *4.* Isn't that crazy? *5.* Maybe you can. *6.* I'm sure you understand. *7.* How could that be? *8.* Might as well. *9.* Hope you don't mind.

**[77]** *1.* Мы будем тут же. *2.* Тут ничего не происходит. *3.* О чем тут говорить? *4.* Хорошо, я буду тут. *5.* Оставить нас в покое! *6.* Что еще она сказала? *7.* Говорит, что это важно. *8.* Оно не может ждать. *9.* Она права, ты знаешь.

• *1.* We'll be right there. *2.* Here goes nothing. *3.* What's there to talk about? *4.* Okay, I'll be right there. *5.* Leave us alone! *6.* What else did she say? *7.* Says it's important. *8.* It can't wait. *9.* She's right, you know.

**[78]** *1.* Речь идет об этом? *2.* Вот о чем речь. *3.* Что, если он вернется? *4.* И здесь мы идем. *5.* Оставь ее в покое. *6.* Не в последнее время. *7.* Сейчас не лучшее время. *8.* У нас хорошая команда. *9.* Я думаю, ты молодец.

• *1.* Is that what this is about? *2.* That's what this is about. *3.* What if he comes back? *4.* And here we go. *5.* Leave her alone. *6.* Not lately. *7.* This isn't a good time. *8.* We make a good team. *9.* I think you're great.

**[79]** *1.* Так что вы говорите? *2.* Просто дай мне минутку. *3.* Только одну минутку, пожалуйста. *4.* Это всего лишь игра. *5.* Большое спасибо, что пришли. *6.* Все в порядке, сладкий.

• *1.* So what are you saying? *2.* Just give me a minute. *3.* Just one moment, please. *4.* It's just a game. *5.* Thank you so much for coming. *6.* It's okay, sweetie.

**[80]** *1.* Мне очень жаль, сладкий. *2.* Разве он не сладкий? *3.* Пожалуйста, оставь меня одного. *4.* Все в порядке, сынок. *5.*

Я хочу это вернуть. *6.* Вот куда я иду. *7.* Это наш последний шанс. *8.* Держи это вот здесь. *9.* Как вы это получили?
● *1.* I'm sorry, sweetie. *2.* Isn't he sweet? *3.* Please leave me alone. *4.* It's all right, son. *5.* I want it back. *6.* That's where I'm going. *7.* This is our last chance. *8.* Hold it right there. *9.* How did you get this?

**[81]** *1.* Что мы здесь получили? *2.* Это никогда не сработает. *3.* Я это хорошо помню. *4.* Ты видишь меня таким? *5.* Кто хочет пойти первым? *6.* Что в этом хорошего? *7.* Вы уже это сказали. *8.* А что насчет другого? *9.* Как прошел твой день?
● *1.* What we got here? *2.* It'll never work. *3.* I remember it well. *4.* Is that how you see me? *5.* Who wants to go first? *6.* What good is that? *7.* You already said that. *8.* What about the other one? *9.* So how was your day?

**[82]** *1.* У меня нет выбора. *2.* Мило с вашей стороны. *3.* Для вашей же безопасности. *4.* Я буду прямо снаружи. *5.* Добро пожаловать, добро пожаловать. *6.* Какое тебе здесь дело?
● *1.* I don't have any choice. *2.* Nice of you. *3.* For your own safety. *4.* I'll be right outside. *5.* Welcome, welcome. *6.* What's your business here?

**[83]** *1.* Будьте осторожны с этим. *2.* Что произошло прошлой ночью? *3.* Мы еще не закончили. *4.* Не волнуйся обо мне. *5.* Как ваши дела, сэр? *6.* Ты не можешь прийти. *7.* Я еще не закончил. *8.* У вас прекрасный дом. *9.* Мне нравится так думать.
● *1.* Be careful with it. *2.* What happened last night? *3.* We're not finished. *4.* Don't worry about me. *5.* How do you do, sir? *6.* You can't come. *7.* I haven't finished. *8.* You have a lovely home. *9.* I like to think so.

**[84]** *1.* О чем тут думать? *2.* Нет, это слишком опасно. *3.* Вернитесь в свою комнату. *4.* Видите, как это работает? *5.* Вы этого не видите? *6.* Рад, что смог помочь. *7.* Ты должен быть осторожен. *8.* Так что будь осторожен. *9.* Просто будь осторожен, ладно?
● *1.* What is there to think about? *2.* No, it's too dangerous. *3.* Go back to your room. *4.* See how that works? *5.* You don't see it? *6.* Glad I could help. *7.* You have to be careful. *8.* So be careful. *9.* Just be careful, okay?

**[85]** *1.* Сделайте что-нибудь еще. *2.* Я просто пытаюсь помочь. *3.* Как долго я спал? *4.* Вы можете войти сейчас. *5.* Но это не реально. *6.* Ну, как вам угодно. *7.* Может быть где угодно. *8.* Куда бы я пошел? *9.* Разве ты не помнишь?

● *1.* Do something else. *2.* I'm just trying to help. *3.* How long have I been asleep? *4.* You can go in now. *5.* But it's not real. *6.* Well, suit yourself. *7.* Could be anywhere. *8.* Where would I go? *9.* Don't you remember?

**[86]** *1.* Я едва тебя знаю. *2.* Сейчас все по-другому. *3.* Этого не может случиться. *4.* Как это могло случиться? *5.* Просто позвольте этому случиться. *6.* Не больше, чем обычно.

● *1.* I barely know you. *2.* Things are different now. *3.* That can't happen. *4.* How could that happen? *5.* Just let it happen. *6.* No more than usual.

**[87]** *1.* У нас мало времени. *2.* Как она себя чувствовала? *3.* Действительно ли это необходимо? *4.* Вы будете в порядке. *5.* Как он себя чувствовал? *6.* У меня плохие новости.

● *1.* We haven't much time. *2.* How was she? *3.* Is this really necessary? *4.* You'll be okay. *5.* How was he? *6.* I've got some bad news.

**[88]** *1.* И тебя это устраивает? *2.* Как нам остановить это? *3.* Но теперь все кончено. *4.* Дайте мне это прямо. *5.* Просто дайте этому время. *6.* Как в старые времена. *7.* Разве он не великолепен? *8.* Я не слышу тебя! *9.* Я никуда не пойду.

● *1.* And you're okay with that? *2.* How do we stop it? *3.* But it's over now. *4.* Give it to me straight. *5.* Just give it time. *6.* Just like old times. *7.* Isn't he great? *8.* I can't hear you! *9.* I ain't going nowhere.

## Difficulty Level: 4

**[1]** *1.* Нет, нет, это не так. *2.* Нет, это не так просто. *3.* Нет, это был не я. *4.* Не так, как ты и я. *5.* Нет, все было не так. *6.* Так было и у меня. *7.* Да, все это не я. *8.* Да, у меня все хорошо. *9.* Это очень хорошо, что вы.

● *1.* No, no, it isn't. *2.* No, it's not that easy. *3.* No, it wasn't me. *4.* Not like you and me. *5.* No, it wasn't like that. *6.* So was mine. *7.* Yeah, everyone is not me. *8.* Yeah, I'm fine. *9.* It's very nice of you.

**[2]** *1.* Это было не очень хорошо. *2.* Ну, это был не я. *3.* Ну у меня его нет. *4.* Да, я все еще здесь. *5.* У меня его еще нет. *6.* Почему ты все еще здесь? *7.* Почему нет, у меня нет. *8.* О, нет, это не так. *9.* О, ты все еще здесь?

● *1.* It wasn't very good. *2.* Well, it wasn't me. *3.* Well, I don't have it. *4.* Yeah, I'm still here. *5.* I don't have one yet. *6.* Why are you still here? *7.* Why, no, I haven't. *8.* Oh, no, you're not. *9.* Oh, you're still here?

**[3]** *1.* О, хорошо, ты все еще здесь. *2.* Ну и где он сейчас? *3.* Все в порядке, все в порядке. *4.* Я в порядке, я в порядке. *5.* Да, да, я в порядке. *6.* Нет, нет, я в порядке.

● *1.* Oh, good, you're still here. *2.* Well, where is he now? *3.* It's okay, it's okay. *4.* I'm fine, I'm fine. *5.* Yeah, yeah, I'm fine. *6.* No, no, I'm good.

**[4]** *1.* О да, я в порядке. *2.* Ты в порядке, ты в порядке. *3.* Да, нет, я в порядке. *4.* О, нет, я в порядке. *5.* Нет, нет, нет, я в порядке. *6.* Нет, я не в порядке! *7.* Да, я в порядке, я в порядке. *8.* Я в порядке, как ты? *9.* О, нет, он в порядке.

● *1.* Oh, yeah, I'm fine. *2.* You're okay, you're okay. *3.* Yeah, no, I'm fine. *4.* Oh, no, I'm fine. *5.* No, no, no, I'm fine. *6.* No, I'm not okay! *7.* Yeah, I'm fine, I'm fine. *8.* I'm fine, how are you? *9.* Oh, no, he's fine.

**[5]** *1.* Нет, я в порядке, я в порядке. *2.* Я в порядке, в порядке. *3.* Нет, нет, он в порядке. *4.* Нет, мы не в порядке. *5.* Она в порядке, она в порядке. *6.* Так что ты в порядке.

● *1.* No, I'm good, I'm good. *2.* I'm fine, fine. *3.* No, no, he's fine. *4.* No, we're not okay. *5.* She's okay, she's okay. *6.* So you're good.

**[6]** *1.* Здесь что-то не так. *2.* Я все еще не могу. *3.* Ну вот мы и здесь. *4.* Вот почему я все еще здесь. *5.* Да почему бы и нет? *6.* Что еще это было бы? *7.* Было бы это так просто. *8.* Все было бы в порядке. *9.* Ну, это был бы я.

● *1.* There's something wrong. *2.* I still can't. *3.* Well, here we are. *4.* That's why I'm still here. *5.* Yeah, why not? *6.* What else would it be? *7.* Would that ih twuuuuuuh so simple. *8.* That'd be all right. *9.* Well, that would be me.

**[7]** *1.* Вот где я был бы. *2.* Я знаю, почему ты здесь. *3.* Я знаю, что это не так. *4.* Я знаю, что что-то не так. *5.* Нет, я не знаю, где она. 6. Я просто знаю, вот и все. 7. Я знаю, что это не я. 8. Я не так хорошо тебя знаю. 9. Я не очень хорошо тебя знаю.

• 1. That's where I'd be. 2. I know why you're here. 3. I know it isn't. 4. I know something's wrong. 5. No, I don't know where she is. 6. I just know, that's all. 7. I know it's not me. 8. I don't know you that well. 9. I don't know you very well.

[8] 1. Это был ты, не так ли? 2. Было ли что-то еще? 3. Все ли было в порядке? 4. Так все ли в порядке? 5. Нет, я ее не знаю. 6. У меня никогда не было. 7. Это никогда не так, не так ли? 8. Что еще у тебя есть? 9. Он есть, не так ли?

• 1. It was you, wasn't it? 2. Was there something else? 3. Was it all right? 4. So is everything okay? 5. No, I don't know her. 6. I never have. 7. It never is, is it? 8. What else you got? 9. He is, isn't he?

[9] 1. Она есть, не так ли? 2. Они есть, не так ли? 3. У меня есть, не так ли? 4. Да это так и есть. 5. Я знаю, что ты там. 6. У тебя там все в порядке? 7. Тебя никогда там не было. 8. Мне хорошо там, где я есть. 9. У тебя там что-то есть.

• 1. She is, isn't she? 2. They are, aren't they? 3. I have, haven't I? 4. Yes, that's how it is. 5. I know you're in there. 6. You all right there? 7. You were never there. 8. I'm fine where I am. 9. You've got something there.

[10] 1. Что еще у тебя там есть? 2. Нет, меня там не было. 3. Он там, не так ли? 4. Нет, я никогда не был там. 5. Нет, его там не было. 6. Но я все еще здесь. 7. Но тебя там не было. 8. Но что-то не так. 9. Но это не так, не так ли?

• 1. What else you got in there? 2. No, I wasn't there. 3. He's there, isn't he? 4. No, I've never been there. 5. No, he wasn't there. 6. But I'm still here. 7. But you weren't there. 8. But something's wrong. 9. But it's not, is it?

[11] 1. Но я не могу, не так ли? 2. Но у меня никогда не было. 3. Но меня там не было. 4. Но это было не так. 5. Я все еще в этом. 6. В этом что-то не так. 7. У меня его больше нет. 8. Я больше не могу есть. 9. Я больше ничего не знаю.

• 1. But I can't, can I? 2. But I never have. 3. But I wasn't there. 4. Except it wasn't. 5. I'm still in it. 6. There's something wrong with that. 7. I don't have it anymore. 8. I can't eat any more. 9.

I don't know anything anymore.

**[12]** *1.* У тебя на меня ничего нет. *2.* У меня сейчас ничего нет. *3.* Это только ты и я. *4.* Он только что был здесь. *5.* Она только что была здесь. *6.* У меня только что было это.

● *1.* You ain't got nothing on me. *2.* I have nothing now. *3.* It's just you and me. *4.* He was just here. *5.* She was just here. *6.* I just had it.

**[13]** *1.* Она только что была там. *2.* Здесь нет ничего для тебя. *3.* Это было не для меня. *4.* Не для меня, это не так. *5.* Ну, это все для меня. *6.* О, это не для меня. *7.* Что еще у тебя есть для меня? *8.* Я знаю, что для тебя хорошо. *9.* Я знаю, что хорошо для меня.

● *1.* She was just there. *2.* There's nothing for you here. *3.* It wasn't for me. *4.* Not to me, it doesn't. *5.* Well, that's it for me. *6.* Oh, it's not for me. *7.* What else you got for me? *8.* I know what's good for you. *9.* I know what's good for me.

**[14]** *1.* Тогда почему ты все еще здесь? *2.* Тогда где бы я был? *3.* О, тогда все в порядке. *4.* Все у тебя будет хорошо. *5.* Никогда не было и никогда не будет. *6.* Это будет не так просто.

● *1.* Then why are you still here? *2.* Then where would I be? *3.* Oh, that's all right, then. *4.* You'll be all right. *5.* Never have, never will. *6.* It's not gonna be that easy.

**[15]** *1.* Ну и что это будет? *2.* Я знаю, что он не будет. *3.* Так вот как это будет? *4.* Я его действительно не знаю. *5.* Это было действительно что-то. *6.* Да, это было действительно хорошо.

● *1.* Well, what's it gonna be? *2.* I know he won't. *3.* So that's how it's gonna be? *4.* I don't really know him. *5.* That was really something. *6.* Yeah, it was really good.

**[16]** *1.* Вы были там, не так ли? *2.* Они только что были здесь. *3.* Ну и где мы были? *4.* Мы никогда не были здесь. *5.* Нет, я не хочу этого. *6.* Я хочу быть там, где ты. *7.* Лучше бы это было хорошо. *8.* Я знаю тебя лучше этого. *9.* Так лучше, не так ли?

● *1.* You were there, weren't you? *2.* They were just here. *3.* Well, where were we? *4.* We were never here. *5.* No, I don't want it. *6.* I want to be where you are. *7.* This better be good. *8.* I know you better than that. *9.* That's better, isn't it?

**[17]** *1.* Я тоже этого не хочу. *2.* За то, что ты здесь. *3.* Что еще я могу сделать? *4.* И как мне это сделать? *5.* Я не знаю, как это сделать. *6.* Ну и как мне это сделать? *7.* Ну, я не знаю, как это сделать. *8.* Тогда почему бы тебе не сделать это? *9.* И почему я хочу это сделать?

● *1.* I don't want that either. *2.* For being here. *3.* What else can I do? *4.* And how do I do that? *5.* I don't know how to. *6.* Well, how do I do that? *7.* Well, I don't know how to do that. *8.* Then why don't you do it? *9.* And why would I wanna do that?

**[18]** *1.* Да, почему бы тебе не сделать это? *2.* Так где же мы были? *3.* И все же, вот вы здесь. *4.* Ну и что же тогда? *5.* И все же вы здесь. *6.* Что же это было тогда? *7.* И все же я здесь. *8.* И все же ты все еще здесь. *9.* И все же я есть.

● *1.* Yeah, why don't you do that? *2.* So where were we? *3.* And yet, here you are. *4.* Well, what is it, then? *5.* And yet here you are. *6.* What was it, then? *7.* Yet here I am. *8.* And yet you're still here. *9.* And yet I am.

**[19]** *1.* Вот о чем это все. *2.* Я не знаю, о чем ты. *3.* Но это было больше чем то. *4.* Я знаю его лучше, чем ты. *5.* Нет, я так не думаю. *6.* Я думаю, что я в порядке. *7.* Думаю, я знаю, почему ты здесь. *8.* Это все, о чем я думаю. *9.* Думаю, это только ты и я.

● *1.* That's what it's all about. *2.* I don't know what you're on about. *3.* But it was more than that. *4.* I know him better than you do. *5.* No, I don't think so. *6.* I think I'm good. *7.* I think I know why you're here. *8.* It's all I think about. *9.* I guess it's just you and me.

**[20]** *1.* Я думаю, это было бы хорошо. *2.* Ну, я думаю, все в порядке. *3.* Что еще это может быть? *4.* Она не может этого сделать. *5.* Ну, может быть, я так и есть. *6.* Он не может этого сделать!

● *1.* I think that would be fine. *2.* Well, I guess it's all right. *3.* What else could it be? *4.* She can't do that. *5.* Well, maybe I am. *6.* He can't do that!

**[21]** *1.* Нет, нет, этого не может быть. *2.* Ну, может быть, так и будет. *3.* Но он не может этого сделать. *4.* Сейчас он ничего не может сделать. *5.* И как нам это сделать? *6.* Нет, я этого не сделал.

• *1.* No, no, it can't be. *2.* Well, maybe this will. *3.* But he can't do that. *4.* There's nothing he can do now. *5.* And how do we do that? *6.* No, I didn't.

**[22]** *1.* Что ты только что сделал? *2.* Сделал ли он это сейчас? *3.* Тогда почему ты это сделал? *4.* Он это сделал, не так ли? *5.* Я думаю, ты только что это сделал. *6.* Думаю, я только что это сделал.

• *1.* What did you just do? *2.* Did he now? *3.* Then why did you? *4.* He did, didn't he? *5.* I think you just did. *6.* I think I just did.

**[23]** *1.* Так почему ты это сделал? *2.* Что бы ты сделал тогда? *3.* Но как ты это сделал? *4.* Ты действительно сделал бы это для меня? *5.* И что ты тогда сделал? *6.* Ну и что он сделал?

• *1.* So why did you? *2.* What would you do then? *3.* But how did you do it? *4.* You'd really do that for me? *5.* And what did you do then? *6.* Well, what did he do?

**[24]** *1.* Ты бы сделал это, да? *2.* Ты бы действительно сделал это? *3.* Ну, ты только что это сделал. *4.* Вот почему ты это сделал? *5.* Ну, что бы ты сделал? *6.* О, да, ты это сделал.

• *1.* You would, huh? *2.* You'd really do that? *3.* Well, you just did. *4.* Is that why you did it? *5.* Well, what would you do? *6.* Oh, yeah, you did.

**[25]** *1.* Вот как он это сделал. *2.* Вот почему он это сделал. *3.* И ты тоже это сделал. *4.* Как ты когда-то сделал. *5.* Ты только что это сделал? *6.* О, он это сделал, да? *7.* Так как ты это сделал? *8.* И почему ты это сделал? *9.* И тогда он это сделал.

• *1.* That's how he did it. *2.* That's why he did it. *3.* And you did, too. *4.* As you once did. *5.* Did you just do that? *6.* Oh, he did, huh? *7.* So how did you do it? *8.* And why did you do that? *9.* And then he did.

**[26]** *1.* И как ты это сделал? *2.* То, что ты только что сделал. *3.* Да, ну, ты это сделал. *4.* Да, ты действительно это сделал. *5.* Я знаю, как он это сделал. *6.* Ты только что сделал это.

• *1.* And how did you do that? *2.* What you just did. *3.* Yeah, well, you did. *4.* Yeah, you really did. *5.* I know how he did it. *6.* You just did that.

**[27]** *1.* Ты сделал это очень хорошо. *2.* Да, он это сделал, не так ли? *3.* Тебе нужно что-то еще? *4.* Мне это не нужно было. *5.* Тебе это нужно больше, чем мне. *6.* Вам это не нужно было.

● *1.* You did it very well. *2.* Yeah, he did, didn't he? *3.* Do you need anything else? *4.* I didn't need to. *5.* You need it more than I do. *6.* You didn't need to.

**[28]** *1.* Нам нужно сделать это сейчас. *2.* Нет, мне это не нужно. *3.* Мне это сейчас не нужно. *4.* Теперь вам это не нужно. *5.* Мне не нужно быть здесь. *6.* Я знаю его слишком хорошо.

● *1.* We need to do this now. *2.* No, I don't need it. *3.* I don't need this right now. *4.* Now you don't have to. *5.* I don't need to be here. *6.* I know him too well.

**[29]** *1.* Их здесь никогда не было. *2.* У меня их больше нет. *3.* Я знаю, и мне очень жаль. *4.* Мне так, так, так жаль. *5.* У нас все в порядке. *6.* У нас здесь что-то есть. *7.* Для нас здесь ничего нет. *8.* Что еще у нас здесь есть? *9.* Так что же у нас здесь?

● *1.* They were never here. *2.* I don't have them anymore. *3.* I know, and I'm sorry. *4.* I'm so, so, so sorry. *5.* We're fine. *6.* We got something here. *7.* There's nothing for us here. *8.* What else we got here? *9.* So what have we got here?

**[30]** *1.* Но это не о нас. *2.* Знаешь ли ты, где ты? *3.* Ты знаешь меня лучше, чем это. *4.* Ты знаешь, что это не так. *5.* Ты действительно что-то, ты знаешь это? *6.* Я думаю, ты знаешь, почему я здесь.

● *1.* But this isn't about us. *2.* Do you know where you are? *3.* You know me better than that. *4.* You know I'm not. *5.* You're really something, you know that? *6.* I think you know why I'm here.

**[31]** *1.* Ты знаешь, я бы этого не сделал. *2.* Знаешь, что ты только что сделал? *3.* Ты знаешь ее лучше, чем я. *4.* Знаешь, почему бы и нет? *5.* Ты знаешь, что его здесь нет. *6.* Знаешь, почему он это сделал?

● *1.* You know I wouldn't do that. *2.* You know what you just did? *3.* You know her better than I do. *4.* You know, why not? *5.* You know he's not here. *6.* Do you know why he did it?

**[32]** *1.* Знаешь, о чем я сейчас думаю? *2.* Ты не знаешь, что я могу сделать. *3.* Знаешь, я так не думаю. *4.* Есть ли кто-то еще? *5.* Я не знаю, кто они. *6.* Так кто же это сделал?

● *1.* You know what I'm thinking now? *2.* You don't know what I can do. *3.* You know, I don't think so. *4.* Is there someone else? *5.* I don't know who they are. *6.* So who did?

**[33]** *1.* Ты знаешь, кто я, да? *2.* Кто же это был тогда? *3.* Кто вы и почему вы здесь? *4.* Теперь я знаю, кто ты. *5.* Я не знаю, кто ты! *6.* Я не знаю, кто я! *7.* Я не знаю, кто это. *8.* Кто же тогда это сделал? *9.* Ну, я знаю, кто ты.

● *1.* You know who I am, right? *2.* Who was it, then? *3.* Who are you and why are you here? *4.* Now I know who you are. *5.* I don't know who you are! *6.* I don't know who I am! *7.* I don't know who this is. *8.* Who did it, then? *9.* Well, I know who you are.

**[34]** *1.* Так кто же ты тогда? *2.* Я не знаю об этом. *3.* Ну и что ты об этом знаешь? *4.* Я всегда здесь для тебя. *5.* Всегда было и всегда будет. *6.* Это всегда было о тебе. *7.* То же, что и всегда. *8.* Так же, как и всегда. *9.* У меня всегда все в порядке.

● *1.* So what are you, then? *2.* I don't know about this. *3.* Well, what do you know about that? *4.* I'm always here for you. *5.* Always have, always will. *6.* It's always been about you. *7.* The same as always. *8.* Same as it ever was. *9.* I'm always all right.

**[35]** *1.* Да ладно, все в порядке. *2.* Я не хочу, чтобы ты был здесь! *3.* Вот что мне нужно, чтобы ты сделал. *4.* Есть ли еще что-нибудь? *5.* Вы когда-нибудь были там? *6.* Ты когда-нибудь был здесь?

● *1.* Come on, it's okay. *2.* I don't want you here! *3.* Here's what I need you to do. *4.* Is there anything else? *5.* You ever been there? *6.* Have you ever been there?

**[36]** *1.* Ну, я могу что-нибудь сделать? *2.* Ты знаешь что-нибудь об этом? *3.* Но ты это уже знаешь. *4.* Я думаю, что у нас уже есть. *5.* Что с тобой не так? *6.* С тобой все будет в порядке.

● *1.* Well, is there anything I can do? *2.* You know something about this? *3.* But you already know that. *4.* I think we already have. *5.* What's wrong with you? *6.* You're gonna be okay.

**[37]** *1.* Я просто хочу быть с тобой. *2.* С тобой все было в порядке. *3.* С тобой сейчас все в порядке? *4.* Теперь с тобой все в порядке. *5.* С тобой там все в порядке? *6.* Я хочу быть с тобой всегда.

• *1.* I just want to be with you. *2.* You were fine. *3.* Are you all right now? *4.* You're all right now. *5.* Are you okay in there? *6.* I want to be with you forever.

**[38]** *1.* С тобой все будет в порядке, ладно? *2.* Я хочу быть здесь с тобой. *3.* О, с тобой все будет в порядке. *4.* Теперь с тобой все будет в порядке. *5.* Хорошо, с тобой все в порядке? *6.* Да, с тобой все будет в порядке.

• *1.* You're gonna be fine, okay? *2.* I want to be here with you. *3.* Oh, you'll be fine. *4.* You'll be all right now. *5.* Okay, you all right? *6.* Yeah, you'll be fine.

**[39]** *1.* Но с тобой все будет в порядке. *2.* И с тобой все будет в порядке. *3.* Есть ли там кто-нибудь с тобой? *4.* Ну, с тобой все в порядке? *5.* Нет, с тобой все будет в порядке. *6.* Что это было еще раз?

• *1.* But you're gonna be all right. *2.* And you'll be fine. *3.* Is there someone there with you? *4.* Well, are you all right? *5.* No, you'll be fine. *6.* What was that again?

**[40]** *1.* Что еще я могу сделать для вас? *2.* Было ли это хорошо для вас? *3.* Ну, теперь у вас есть. *4.* Может быть, у вас есть. *5.* Но у вас уже есть. *6.* У вас есть, не так ли?

• *1.* Anything else I can do for you? *2.* Was it good for you? *3.* Well, now you have. *4.* Maybe you have. *5.* But you already have. *6.* You have, haven't you?

**[41]** *1.* У вас все еще есть это. *2.* Почему они у вас есть? *3.* Это будет хорошо для вас. *4.* И теперь у вас есть. *5.* Это может быть хорошо для вас. *6.* У вас все в порядке?

• *1.* You've still got it. *2.* Why do you have them? *3.* It will be good for you. *4.* And now you have. *5.* It might be good for you. *6.* Y'all okay?

**[42]** *1.* Ну, у вас есть это. *2.* Я думаю, у вас уже есть. *3.* Они у вас еще есть? *4.* Что же нам теперь делать? *5.* Я больше не могу этого делать. *6.* Вам не нужно этого делать.

• *1.* Well, you've got it. *2.* I think you already have. *3.* Do you still have them? *4.* What do we do now? *5.* I can't do this anymore. *6.* You don't need to do this.

**[43]** *1.* Я не хочу этого делать. *2.* Я больше не хочу этого делать. *3.* Ну и что мне было делать? *4.* Нет, я не хочу этого делать. *5.* Мне не нужно ничего делать. *6.* Я не знаю, что мне делать.

● *1.* I don't mean to. *2.* I don't wanna do this anymore. *3.* Well, what was I supposed to do? *4.* No, I don't want to do that. *5.* I don't need to do anything. *6.* I don't know what I should do.

**[44]** *1.* Почему вам нужно это делать? *2.* Я не хочу ничего делать. *3.* Я знаю, что мне нужно делать сейчас. *4.* Я просто не могу больше этого делать. *5.* Но я не знаю, что еще делать. *6.* Я не могу просто ничего не делать.

● *1.* Why do you have to do that? *2.* I don't want to do anything. *3.* I know what I have to do now. *4.* I just can't do this any more. *5.* But I don't know what else to do. *6.* I can't just do nothing.

**[45]** *1.* Это лучше, чем ничего не делать. *2.* Ты знаешь, что тебе нужно делать, да? *3.* Это слишком много для меня. *4.* Нам так много нужно сделать. *5.* Ты уже так много сделал. *6.* Что я только что сказал?

● *1.* It's better than doing nothing. *2.* You know what you have to do, right? *3.* It's too much for me. *4.* We have so much to do. *5.* You've done so much already. *6.* What did I just say?

**[46]** *1.* Почему ты просто не сказал мне? *2.* Почему он мне не сказал? *3.* Почему ты мне этого не сказал? *4.* Нет, я бы так не сказал. *5.* Почему ты мне не сказал? *6.* Это не то, что он сказал.

● *1.* Why didn't you just tell me? *2.* Why didn't he tell me? *3.* Why didn't you tell me this? *4.* No, I wouldn't say that. *5.* Why did you not tell me? *6.* That's not what he said.

**[47]** *1.* Я сказал тебе, я в порядке. *2.* Я так сказал, не так ли? *3.* Все так, как ты сказал. *4.* Я бы никогда этого не сказал. *5.* И почему ты мне не сказал? *6.* Что еще ты мне не сказал?

● *1.* I told you, I'm fine. *2.* I said so, didn't I? *3.* It's just like you said. *4.* I would never say that. *5.* And why didn't you tell me? *6.* What else haven't you told me?

**[48]** *1.* Это не то, что он мне сказал. *2.* Почему ты нам этого не сказал? *3.* О, почему ты так не сказал? *4.* Почему он не сказал нам? *5.* Это не то, что ты сказал. *6.* Ну, почему ты ничего не сказал?

- *1.* That's not what he told me. *2.* Why didn't you tell us this? *3.* Oh, why didn't you say so? *4.* Why wouldn't he tell us? *5.* It's not what you said. *6.* Well, why didn't you say something?

**[49]** *1.* Тогда почему ты это сказал? *2.* Почему ты мне ничего не сказал? *3.* Почему он просто не сказал мне? *4.* Почему ты ничего не сказал? *5.* Ты мне ничего не сказал. *6.* Он мне ничего об этом не сказал.

- *1.* Then why did you say it? *2.* Why didn't you say anything to me? *3.* Why didn't he just tell me? *4.* Why haven't you said anything? *5.* You haven't told me anything. *6.* He didn't say anything to me about it.

**[50]** *1.* Тогда почему ты ничего не сказал? *2.* Кто сказал, что у меня нет? *3.* Ты сказал, что все в порядке. *4.* Он сказал, что это не так. *5.* Ты бы мне сказал, да? *6.* Так почему ты ничего не сказал?

- *1.* Then why didn't you say something? *2.* Who says I haven't? *3.* You said it was okay. *4.* He said he wasn't. *5.* You'd tell me, right? *6.* So why didn't you say anything?

**[51]** *1.* Ты не просто так мне это сказал. *2.* Как я уже сказал, я не знаю. *3.* Он ничего мне не сказал. *4.* Я не знаю, почему он это сказал. *5.* Кто сказал, что это не так? *6.* Так что тебе от меня нужно?

- *1.* You did not just say that to me. *2.* Like I said, I don't know. *3.* He wouldn't tell me anything. *4.* I don't know why he said that. *5.* Who said it wasn't? *6.* So what do you need from me?

**[52]** *1.* Я не могу сделать это прямо сейчас. *2.* У меня есть это прямо здесь. *3.* Да, я прямо за тобой. *4.* Я уверен, что это так. *5.* Я бы не был слишком уверен. *6.* Ты уверен, что все в порядке?

- *1.* I can't do this right now. *2.* I have it right here. *3.* Yeah, I'm right behind you. *4.* I'm sure it is. *5.* I wouldn't be too sure. *6.* Are you sure it's all right?

**[53]** *1.* И ты уверен в этом? *2.* Ты уверен, что не знаешь его? *3.* И ты в этом уверен? *4.* Почему ты так уверен в этом? *5.* Мне нужно, чтобы ты был уверен. *6.* А кто у нас здесь?

- *1.* And you're sure about this? *2.* You sure you don't know him? *3.* And you're sure of that? *4.* What makes you so sure of that? *5.* I need you to be sure. *6.* And who do we have here?

**[54]** *1.* Да, а почему бы и нет? *2.* Мне очень жаль, а ты? *3.* А ты этого не сделал? *4.* Ну, может быть, а может и нет. *5.* Ну а что еще это может быть? *6.* А теперь есть что-нибудь еще?
● *1.* Yeah, why wouldn't I be? *2.* I'm sorry, you are? *3.* And you didn't? *4.* Well, maybe, maybe not. *5.* Well, what else could it be? *6.* Now, is there anything else?

**[55]** *1.* Ну, а ты бы сделал это? *2.* Ну а что бы еще? *3.* А почему бы и нет? *4.* Это не я, а ты. *5.* Ну а что еще есть? *6.* Ну а почему бы и нет? *7.* Я не знаю, а ты? *8.* Ну, а почему ты это сделал? *9.* Я хочу его, а не тебя.
● *1.* Well, would you? *2.* Well, what else would it be? *3.* And why shouldn't you? *4.* It's not me, it's you. *5.* Well, what else is there? *6.* Well, why wouldn't I? *7.* I don't know, can you? *8.* Well, why did you? *9.* I want him, not you.

**[56]** *1.* Я бы сделал это снова. *2.* Ну вот мы и снова. *3.* И вот мы снова здесь. *4.* Итак, что нам теперь делать? *5.* Итак, у нас все хорошо? *6.* Итак, что же у нас здесь? *7.* Итак, вот и все, да? *8.* Итак, о чем все это? *9.* Итак, что тебе от меня нужно?
● *1.* I'd do it again. *2.* Well, here we are again. *3.* And here we are again. *4.* So, what do we do now? *5.* So, we good? *6.* So, what do we have here? *7.* So, that's it, huh? *8.* Now, what's all this about? *9.* So, what do you need from me?

**[57]** *1.* Итак, что у тебя есть для меня? *2.* Итак, что еще у тебя есть? *3.* Как ты можешь быть так уверен? *4.* Нет, ты не можешь этого сделать. *5.* Ты ничего не можешь сделать. *6.* Почему ты не можешь этого сделать?
● *1.* So, what do you have for me? *2.* So, what else you got? *3.* How can you be so sure? *4.* No, you can't do that. *5.* You can't do anything. *6.* Why can't you do it?

**[58]** *1.* Я знаю, что ты не можешь. *2.* Ну, что ты можешь сделать? *3.* Только ты можешь это сделать. *4.* Больше ты ничего не можешь сделать. *5.* Нет, нет, ты не можешь этого сделать. *6.* Но ты не можешь этого сделать.
● *1.* I know you can't. *2.* Well, what can you do? *3.* Only you can do that. *4.* There's nothing more you can do. *5.* No, no, you

can't do that. *6.* But you can't do this.

**[59]** *1.* Ты можешь это сделать, ладно? *2.* Нет, я думаю, ты не можешь. *3.* Ты не можешь это сделать? *4.* Теперь ты ничего не можешь сделать. *5.* Ну, ты не можешь этого сделать. *6.* Теперь ты можешь это сделать?

● *1.* You can do this, okay? *2.* No, I guess you can't. *3.* You can't do it? *4.* There's nothing you can do now. *5.* Well, you can't do that. *6.* Now, can you do that?

**[60]** *1.* Нет, нет, нет, ты не можешь. *2.* Ты знаешь, что не можешь этого сделать. *3.* Ты не можешь, а я могу. *4.* Пожалуйста, ты не можешь этого сделать. *5.* Ты не можешь сделать это снова. *6.* Что ты можешь сделать тогда?

● *1.* No, no, no, you can't. *2.* You know you can't do that. *3.* You can't, but I can. *4.* Please, you can't do this. *5.* You can't do that again. *6.* What can you do then?

**[61]** *1.* У нас еще есть время. *2.* Где ты был все это время? *3.* Я был здесь все время. *4.* Он был здесь все это время. *5.* Ты был здесь все это время? *6.* Сейчас не время для этого.

● *1.* We still have time. *2.* Where have you been all this time? *3.* I was here all the time. *4.* He's been here all along. *5.* Have you been here the whole time? *6.* Now is not the time for this.

**[62]** *1.* То же, что и мой. *2.* Конечно, почему бы и нет. *3.* Конечно, я могу это сделать. *4.* Нет, конечно, ты этого не сделал. *5.* Конечно, ты этого не сделал. *6.* Ну, конечно, я это сделал.

● *1.* Same as mine. *2.* Sure, why not. *3.* Sure, I can do that. *4.* No, of course you didn't. *5.* Sure you didn't. *6.* Well, of course I did.

**[63]** *1.* Ну, конечно, ты это сделал. *2.* Ну, конечно, ты бы сделал это. *3.* Конечно, я знаю, где это. *4.* Конечно, я все еще здесь. *5.* Нет, конечно, он этого не сделал. *6.* Ну, конечно, он это сделал.

● *1.* Well, of course you did. *2.* Well, of course you would. *3.* Of course I know where it is. *4.* Of course I'm still here. *5.* No, of course he didn't. *6.* Well, of course he did.

**[64]** *1.* А как у тебя дела? *2.* Ну и дела, я не знаю. *3.* Ну и дела, мне очень жаль. *4.* Разве это не что-то? *5.* Разве он не

был с тобой? *6.* Разве она не была с тобой? *7.* У меня уже есть один. *8.* Я не хочу быть один. *9.* Я сделал это один раз.
● *1.* And how are you? *2.* Gee, I don't know. *3.* Gee, I'm sorry. *4.* Isn't that something? *5.* Wasn't he with you? *6.* Wasn't she with you? *7.* I already have one. *8.* I don't wanna be alone. *9.* I did it once.

**[65]** *1.* Я могу сделать это один. *2.* Я не хочу, чтобы ты был один. *3.* Я не могу быть один. *4.* Ну, может быть, только один. *5.* Ты сделал это один раз. *6.* Но он был не один.
● *1.* I can do it alone. *2.* I don't want you to be alone. *3.* I can't be alone. *4.* Well, maybe just one. *5.* You did it once. *6.* But he wasn't alone.

**[66]** *1.* Это было только один раз. *2.* Я не могу сделать это один! *3.* Может быть, больше, чем один. *4.* Кто сказал, что я один? *5.* Я никогда не был один. *6.* Ты не такой, как они.
● *1.* It was only once. *2.* I can't do this alone! *3.* Maybe more than one. *4.* Who says I'm alone? *5.* I've never been alone. *6.* You're not like them.

**[67]** *1.* У меня есть такой же. *2.* Возможно, я так и сделал. *3.* Возможно, у меня уже есть. *4.* Возможно, это был не он. *5.* Возможно, у нас здесь что-то есть. *6.* Я буду прямо за тобой.
● *1.* I have one just like it. *2.* Maybe I did. *3.* Maybe I already have. *4.* Maybe it wasn't him. *5.* We may have something here. *6.* I'll be right behind you.

**[68]** *1.* Нет, я не буду этого делать. *2.* Я больше не буду этого делать. *3.* Я всегда буду здесь для тебя. *4.* Я не буду, я не буду. *5.* Я не буду делать это снова. *6.* Эй, что с тобой не так?
● *1.* No, I won't do it. *2.* I won't do it anymore. *3.* I will always be there for you. *4.* I won't, I won't. *5.* I'm not doing it again. *6.* Hey, what's wrong with you?

**[69]** *1.* Эй, эй, все в порядке. *2.* Эй, ты не можешь этого сделать! *3.* Эй, я тебя не знаю? *4.* Эй, эй, эй, все в порядке. *5.* Эй, ты все еще здесь. *6.* Эй, эй, ты в порядке?
● *1.* Hey, hey, it's okay. *2.* Hey, you can't do that! *3.* Hey, don't I know you? *4.* Hey, hey, hey, it's okay. *5.* Hey, you're still here. *6.* Hey, hey, you okay?

**[70]** *1.* Ты теперь один из нас. *2.* Ну и что из этого? *3.* Я здесь из-за тебя. *4*. Мне ничего из этого не нужно. *5*. Но не из-за меня. *6*. Это был не кто-то из нас. *7*. Разве у вас не будет немного? *8*. Я ему так и сказал. *9*. Ему это было не нужно.

● *1*. You're one of us now. *2*. Well, what of it? *3*. I'm here because of you. *4*. I don't need any of that. *5*. But not because of me. *6*. It wasn't any of us. *7*. Won't you have some? *8*. I told him so. *9*. He didn't need to.

**[71]** *1*. Ему больше ничего не нужно. *2*. Ему лучше там, где он есть. *3*. Сколько еще у нас есть? *4*. Ты знаешь, что это правда. *5*. Мне очень жаль, но это правда. *6*. Нет, я в порядке, правда.

● *1*. He doesn't need anything anymore. *2*. He's better off where he is. *3*. How much longer do we have? *4*. You know it's true. *5*. I'm sorry, but it's true. *6*. No, I'm fine, really.

**[72]** *1*. Но это правда, не так ли? *2*. Нет, правда, я в порядке. *3*. Ну, это правда, не так ли? *4*. Нет, правда, все в порядке. *5*. Нет, все в порядке, правда. *6*. Так быстро, как только могу.

● *1*. But it's true, isn't it? *2*. No, really, I'm fine. *3*. Well, it's true, isn't it? *4*. No, really, it's fine. *5*. No, it's fine, really. *6*. As fast as I can.

**[73]** *1*. Не так быстро, не так быстро. *2*. Ты не должен был этого делать. *3*. Я не должен быть здесь. *4*. Ты мне так много должен. *5*. Я должен был быть там. *6*. Он уже должен быть здесь.

● *1*. Not so fast, not so fast. *2*. You shouldn't have. *3*. I'm not supposed to be here. *4*. You owe me that much. *5*. I should have been there. *6*. He should be here by now.

**[74]** *1*. Почему я должен это делать? *2*. Он уже должен был быть здесь. *3*. Я должен был быть здесь. *4*. Я должен сделать это один. *5*. Я должен был быть уверен. *6*. Почему это должен быть я?

● *1*. Why do I have to? *2*. He should have been here by now. *3*. I should have been here. *4*. I have to do this alone. *5*. I had to be sure. *6*. Why does it have to be me?

**[75]** *1*. Он должен быть где-то здесь. *2*. Разве я не должен быть? *3*. Я ему ничего не должен. *4*. Я так много тебе должен. *5*. Он не должен быть здесь. *6*. Итак, что я тебе должен?

● *1*. He must be here somewhere. *2*. Shouldn't I be? *3*. I don't owe him anything. *4.* I owe you that much. *5.* He's not supposed to be here. *6.* So, what do I owe you?

**[76]** *1.* Он должен быть в порядке. *2.* Ну, кто-то должен это сделать. *3.* Нет, а почему я должен быть? *4.* Почему это должен был быть он? *5.* Я должен быть где-то. *6.* Я должен, не так ли?
• *1.* He should be fine. *2.* Well, somebody's got to do it. *3.* No, why should I be? *4.* Why did it have to be him? *5.* I gotta be somewhere. *6.* I should, shouldn't I?

**[77]** *1.* Должен ли я сделать это снова? *2.* Я ничего тебе не должен. *3.* Ты можешь сказать это снова. *4.* Ну что я могу сказать? *5.* Мне так много нужно тебе сказать. *6.* Это все, что я могу сказать.
• *1.* Should I do it again? *2.* I don't owe you a thing. *3.* You can say that again. *4.* Well, what can I say? *5.* I have so much to tell you. *6.* This is as far as I go.

**[78]** *1.* Я не могу ему сказать. *2.* Что еще я могу сказать? *3.* Не могу сказать, что у меня есть. *4.* Не могу сказать, что да. *5.* Что еще я могу вам сказать? *6.* Я не могу этого сказать.
• *1.* I can't tell him. *2.* What more can I say? *3.* Can't say that I have. *4.* Can't say that I do. *5.* What else can I tell you? *6.* I can't say that.

**[79]** *1.* Я не знаю, что сказать. *2.* Я ничего не могу сказать. *3.* Должен ли я сказать вам, почему? *4.* Я не могу сказать вам. *5.* Почему бы тебе не сказать мне? *6.* Могу я просто сказать что-нибудь?
• *1.* I wouldn't know what to say. *2.* I can't say anything. *3.* Shall I tell you why? *4.* I cannot tell you. *5.* Why wouldn't you tell me? *6.* Can I just say something?

**[80]** *1.* Почему бы тебе не сказать мне это? *2.* Этого я не могу тебе сказать. *3.* Это все, что я могу сказать сейчас. *4.* Как я могу тебе сказать? *5.* Я не могу вам этого сказать. *6.* Я не могу вам здесь сказать.
• *1.* Why wouldn't you tell me that? *2.* That I can't tell you. *3.* That's all I can say right now. *4.* How can I tell you? *5.* I cannot tell you that. *6.* I can't tell you here.

**[81]** *1.* Что еще я должен сказать? *2.* Почему бы тебе просто не сказать мне? *3.* Вам есть что еще сказать? *4.* Я никогда не знаю, что сказать. *5.* Этого я не могу сказать. *6.* Почему бы тебе не сказать так?

● *1.* What else should I say? *2.* Why don't you just tell me? *3.* Do you have anything else to say? *4.* I never know what to say. *5.* That I cannot say. *6.* Why don't you say so?

**[82]** *1.* Я не могу ему этого сказать. *2.* Я больше ничего не могу сказать. *3.* Больше чем я могу сказать. *4.* Мне тоже есть что тебе сказать. *5.* Как я могу сказать нет? *6.* Я действительно не знаю, как это сказать.

● *1.* I can't tell him that. *2.* I can say no more. *3.* More than I can say. *4.* I have something to tell you too. *5.* How can I say no? *6.* I don't really know how to say this.

**[83]** *1.* Я не знаю, что ему сказать. *2.* Я так много хочу сказать. *3.* Ты знаешь, я не могу сказать. *4.* Я могу сказать вам прямо сейчас. *5.* Почему бы тебе не сказать мне сейчас? *6.* Я не могу сказать вам, почему.

● *1.* I don't know what to say to him. *2.* There's so much I want to say. *3.* You know I can't say. *4.* I can tell you right now. *5.* Why don't you tell me now? *6.* I can't tell you why.

**[84]** *1.* Я хочу сказать, что мне очень жаль. *2.* Да, ну что я могу тебе сказать? *3.* Тебе есть что еще сказать? *4.* Я никогда не могу сказать. *5.* Я не знаю, как это сказать. *6.* Я-я не знаю, что сказать.

● *1.* I want to say I'm sorry. *2.* Yeah, well, what can I tell you? *3.* You got anything else to say? *4.* I can never tell. *5.* I don't know how to put this. *6.* I-I don't know what to say.

**[85]** *1.* Да, ну что я могу сказать? *2.* Ну, я не могу вам сказать. *3.* Я не могу сказать, что да. *4.* Я могу сказать тебе, где он. *5.* Теперь я могу вам сказать. *6.* Ну, разве это не приятно?

● *1.* Yeah, well, what can I say? *2.* Well, I can't tell you. *3.* I can't say I do. *4.* I can tell you where he is. *5.* Now I can tell you. *6.* Well, isn't that nice?

**[86]** *1.* Как приятно, что ты здесь. *2.* О, не давай мне этого. *3.* Со мной все будет в порядке. *4.* Что со мной не так? *5.* Как ты можешь сделать это со мной? *6.* За что ты так со мной?

● *1.* It's so nice to have you here. *2.* Oh, don't give me that. *3.* I'll be all right. *4.* What's wrong with me? *5.* How can you do this to me? *6.* Why do you do this to me?

**[87]** *1.* Со мной что-то не так? *2.* Почему ты сделал это со мной? *3.* Что ты только что со мной сделал? *4.* Ты не можешь сделать это со мной! *5.* Его не было со мной. *6.* Вот что со мной не так.
● *1.* Is there something wrong with me? *2.* Why would you do this to me? *3.* What did you just do to me? *4.* You can't do that to me! *5.* He wasn't with me. *6.* That's what's wrong with me.

**[88]** *1.* Не со мной, а с тобой нет. *2.* Она не может сделать это со мной. *3.* Как ты мог это сделать? *4.* Где еще я мог бы быть? *5.* Я сделал все, что мог. *6.* Я просто не мог этого сделать.
● *1.* Not with me, you're not. *2.* She can't do this to me. *3.* How could you do that? *4.* Where else would I be? *5.* I did the best I could. *6.* I just couldn't do it.

**[89]** *1.* Я уверен, что ты мог бы. *2.* Я действительно не мог сказать. *3.* Нет, я не мог этого сделать. *4.* Я не мог быть уверен. *5.* О, нет, я не мог. *6.* Что еще я мог сказать?
● *1.* I'm sure you could. *2.* I really couldn't say. *3.* No, I couldn't do that. *4.* I couldn't be sure. *5.* Oh, no, I couldn't. *6.* What else could I say?

**[90]** *1.* Может быть, я мог бы. *2.* Не то чтобы я мог сказать. *3.* Где еще он мог быть? *4.* Почему ты не мог мне сказать? *5.* Я никогда не мог этого сделать. *6.* О, я не мог этого сделать.
● *1.* Maybe I could. *2.* Not that I can tell. *3.* Where else could he be? *4.* Why couldn't you tell me? *5.* I never could do that. *6.* Oh, I couldn't do that.

**[91]** *1.* Этого я не мог тебе сказать. *2.* Я мог бы, но не сделал этого. *3.* Ну, думаю, я мог бы. *4.* Но я просто не мог. *5.* Нет, я думаю, ты не мог. *6.* Нет, я в порядке, спасибо.
● *1.* That I couldn't tell you. *2.* I could have, but I didn't. *3.* Well, I guess I could. *4.* But I just couldn't. *5.* No, I guess you couldn't. *6.* No, I'm fine, thanks.

## Difficulty Level: 5

**[1]** *1.* Нет, нет, все в порядке, все в порядке. *2.* Но это было не так, не так ли? *3.* Есть ли в этом что-то не так? *4.* Ну, я не знаю, что я могу сделать. *5.* Есть ли что-то, о чем я не знаю? *6.* Я думаю, что у меня здесь что-то есть.

● *1.* No, no, it's okay, it's okay. *2.* But it wasn't, was it? *3.* Is there anything wrong with that? *4.* Well, I don't know what I can do. *5.* Is there something I don't know about? *6.* I think I got something here.

**[2]** *1.* Ну, я думаю, здесь только ты и я. *2.* Не знаю, но это не может быть хорошо. *3.* Но ты этого не сделал, не так ли? *4.* Я не думаю, что ты бы это сделал. *5.* Нет, я не думаю, что я это сделал. *6.* Это было бы слишком просто, не так ли?

● *1.* Well, I guess it's just you and me. *2.* I don't know, but it can't be good. *3.* But you didn't, did you? *4.* I don't think you would. *5.* No, I don't think I did. *6.* That would be too easy, wouldn't it?

**[3]** *1.* Мне очень жаль за то, что я сделал. *2.* Я думаю, у нас здесь что-то есть. *3.* Я думаю, у нас сейчас все в порядке. *4.* Ты знаешь это так же хорошо, как и я. *5.* Ты знаешь, почему я здесь, не так ли? *6.* Но ты же об этом не знаешь, не так ли?

● *1.* I'm really sorry for what I did. *2.* I think we got something here. *3.* I think we're all right now. *4.* You know that as well as I do. *5.* You know why I'm here, don't you? *6.* But you wouldn't know about that, would you?

**[4]** *1.* Не то чтобы в этом было что-то не так. *2.* Что я могу сделать, чтобы сделать это лучше? *3.* Хорошо, вот что я хочу, чтобы ты сделал. *4.* Есть ли что-нибудь еще, что вам нужно? *5.* Но ты уже это знаешь, не так ли? *6.* С тобой все в порядке, с тобой все в порядке.

● *1.* Not that there's anything wrong with that. *2.* What can I do to make it better? *3.* Okay, here's what I want you to do. *4.* Is there anything else you need? *5.* But you already know that, don't you? *6.* You're all right, you're all right.

**[5]** *1.* Мне очень жаль, что я сделал это с тобой. *2.* У меня есть как раз то, что нужно. *3.* Могу ли я сделать что-нибудь еще для вас? *4.* Вот, я хочу, чтобы у вас было это. *5.* Я не знаю, почему ты мне не сказал. *6.* Да, это то, что я только что сказал.

● *1.* I'm so sorry I did this to you. *2.* I have just the thing. *3.* Can I do anything else for you? *4.* Here, I want you to have this. *5.*

I don't know why you didn't tell me. *6.* Yeah, that's what I just said.

**[6]** *1.* У меня есть все, что мне нужно, прямо здесь. *2.* Это все, что я могу сделать прямо сейчас. *3.* Ты уверен, что с тобой все в порядке? *4.* Я бы не был в этом так уверен. *5.* Я бы не был в этом слишком уверен. *6.* Да, я уверен, что он бы это сделал.
- *1.* I have everything I need right here. *2.* That's all I can do right now. *3.* You sure you're okay? *4.* I wouldn't be so sure of that. *5.* I wouldn't be too sure of that. *6.* Yeah, I'm sure he would.

**[7]** *1.* О, я уверен, что ты бы это сделал. *2.* Ты уверен, что я ничего не могу сделать? *3.* Может быть да, а может быть и нет. *4.* Ну, а что я могу для тебя сделать? *5.* Ну а почему бы и мне не быть? *6.* Как ты можешь быть в этом так уверен?
- *1.* Oh, I'm sure you would. *2.* You sure there's nothing I can do? *3.* Maybe yes, maybe no. *4.* Well, now, what can I do for you? *5.* Well, why shouldn't I be? *6.* How can you be so sure of that?

**[8]** *1.* Разве ты не можешь сделать что-то лучше? *2.* Эй, ты уверен, что с тобой все в порядке? *3.* Я просто сделал то, что должен был сделать. *4.* Разве это не то, что ты должен делать? *5.* Нет, я не могу сказать, что у меня есть. *6.* Я просто хочу сказать, что мне очень жаль.
- *1.* Can't you do better than that? *2.* Hey, are you sure you're okay? *3.* I just did what I had to do. *4.* Isn't that what you're supposed to do? *5.* No, I can't say that I have. *6.* I just want to say I'm sorry.

**[9]** *1.* Это все, что я могу вам сказать прямо сейчас. *2.* Есть ли у вас что-нибудь еще сказать? *3.* Есть ли что-нибудь еще, что ты можешь мне сказать? *4.* Почему бы тебе не сказать мне, что тебе нужно? *5.* Я сказал, что со мной все в порядке. *6.* Я думаю, что со мной что-то не так.
- *1.* That's all I can tell you right now. *2.* Have you anything further to say? *3.* Is there anything else you can tell me? *4.* Why don't you tell me what you need? *5.* I said I'm fine. *6.* I think there's something wrong with me.

**[10]** *1.* Ты бы не сделал этого со мной, не так ли? *2.* Нет, ты не можешь сделать это со мной! *3*. Я хочу, чтобы ты был там со мной. *4*. Я хочу, чтобы ты был здесь со мной. *5*. Я уверен, что ты сделал все, что мог. *6*. Ну, я думаю, ты мог бы так сказать.

• *1*. You wouldn't do that to me, would you? *2*. No, you can't do this to me! *3*. I want you to be there with me. *4*. I wish you were here with me. *5*. I'm sure you did everything you could. *6*. Well, I suppose you could say that.

**[11]** *1*. Есть ли что-нибудь еще, что мы можем сделать? *2*. Я рад, что с тобой все в порядке. *3*. Что ж, я рад, что ты это сделал. *4*. Что ж, я могу вам сказать вот что. *5*. Что ж, я рад, что с тобой все в порядке. *6*. Ну и что ты хочешь, чтобы я сделал?

• *1*. Is there anything else we can do? *2*. I'm glad you're all right. *3*. Well, I'm glad you did. *4*. Well, I can tell you this. *5*. Well, I'm glad you're okay. *6*. Well, what do you want me to do?

**[12]** *1*. Есть ли что-нибудь еще, что ты хочешь? *2*. Ты не хочешь этого делать, не так ли? *3*. Я не думаю, что ты хочешь этого сделать. *4*. О, я уверен, что так оно и есть. *5*. Я не думаю, что оно у тебя есть. *6*. Сейчас мы ничего не можем для него сделать.

• *1*. Is there anything else you want? *2*. You don't wanna do that, do you? *3*. I don't think you want to do that. *4*. Oh, I'm sure he does. *5*. I don't think you have it. *6*. There's nothing we can do for him now.

**[13]** *1*. Если бы я это сделал, я бы тебе не сказал. *2*. Если только ты не хочешь, чтобы я этого сделал. *3*. Но что, если бы он этого не сделал? *4*. А что, если бы это было не так? *5*. Я знаю тебя откуда-то, не так ли? *6*. Я знаю, что меня не должно быть здесь.

• *1*. If I did, I wouldn't tell you. *2*. Unless you don't want me to. *3*. But what if he didn't? *4*. What if I wasn't? *5*. I know you from somewhere, don't I? *6*. I know I shouldn't be here.

**[14]** *1*. Ну, должно же быть что-то, что ты можешь сделать. *2*. Есть ли что-то, чего ты не можешь сделать? *3*. Нет ничего, чего бы я не сделал для тебя. *4*. Ты уверен, что это то, чего ты хочешь? *5*. Я не знаю, чего ты от меня хочешь! *6*. Ты больше этого не делаешь, не так ли?

● *1.* Well, there must be something you can do. *2.* Is there anything you can't do? *3.* There's nothing I wouldn't do for you. *4.* You sure this is what you want? *5.* I don't know what you want from me! *6.* You don't do that anymore, do you?

**[15]** *1.* Да, я знаю, что ты этого не делаешь. *2.* Я уверен, что ты делаешь все, что можешь. *3.* Что я могу сделать для тебя, моя дорогая? *4.* Можете ли вы сказать мне, о чем это? *5.* Я просто хотел сказать, что мне очень жаль. *6.* Это то, чего ты хотел, не так ли?

● *1.* Yeah, I know you don't. *2.* I'm sure you're doing everything you can. *3.* What can I do for you, my dear? *4.* Can you tell me what this is about? *5.* I just wanted to say I'm sorry. *6.* This is what you wanted, isn't it?

**[16]** *1.* Я бы не хотел, чтобы ты это сделал. *2.* Спасибо за то, что ты такой хороший друг. *3.* Я не думал, что в тебе это есть. *4.* Я думал, ты сказал, что не знаешь его. *5.* Я даже не знаю, о чем я думал. *6.* Ну и дела, я никогда об этом не думал.

● *1.* I wouldn't want you to. *2.* Thank you for being such a good friend. *3.* I didn't think you had it in you. *4.* I thought you said you didn't know him. *5.* I don't even know what I was thinking. *6.* Gee, I never thought of that.

**[17]** *1.* Ты не думал об этом, не так ли? *2.* Нет, это не то, о чем я думал. *3.* Я думал, что у нас все в порядке. *4.* Да, я не знаю, о чем я думал. *5.* Мне жаль, что меня так долго не было. *6.* Почему ты не сказал мне об этом раньше?

● *1.* You didn't think about that, did you? *2.* No, that's not what I was thinking. *3.* I thought we were okay. *4.* Yeah, I don't know what I was thinking. *5.* I'm sorry I was gone so long. *6.* Why didn't you tell me this earlier?

**[18]** *1.* Рад видеть, что с тобой все в порядке. *2.* Что бы это ни было, теперь этого нет. *3.* Я никогда ни в чем не был так уверен. *4.* Можем ли мы не говорить об этом прямо сейчас? *5.* Я не должен был говорить то, что сказал. *6.* Я не могу говорить об этом с тобой.

● *1.* Glad to see you're all right. *2.* Whatever it was, it's gone now. *3.* I've never been more sure of anything. *4.* Can we not talk about this right now? *5.* I shouldn't have said what I said. *6.* I can't talk about this with you.

**[19]** *1.* Ты знаешь, я не могу об этом говорить. *2.* Эй, что, черт возьми, с тобой не так? *3.* Как долго тебя не будет на этот раз? *4.* Но ты уже знал это, не так ли? *5.* Я не знал, что ты все еще здесь. *6.* Даже если бы я знал, я бы тебе не сказал.
● *1.* You know I can't talk about that. *2.* Hey, what the hell is wrong with you? *3.* How long will you be gone this time? *4.* But you already knew that, didn't you? *5.* I didn't know you were still here. *6.* Even if I knew, I wouldn't tell you.

**[20]** *1.* Я не знал, что здесь кто-то есть. *2.* Я знал, что с тобой все будет в порядке. *3.* Я не знаю ничего, чего бы ты не знал. *4.* И я просто хотел, чтобы ты это знал. *5.* Я уверен, что с ней все будет в порядке. *6.* Я бы не знал, что с этим делать.
● *1.* I didn't know anyone was in here. *2.* I knew you'd be okay. *3.* I don't know anything you don't know. *4.* And I just wanted you to know that. *5.* I'm sure she'll be fine. *6.* I wouldn't know what to do with it.

**[21]** *1.* В этом и есть идея, не так ли? *2.* Но я не думаю, что это хорошая идея. *3.* Я действительно не думаю, что это хорошая идея. *4.* Я просто не думаю, что это хорошая идея. *5.* Есть ли что-нибудь еще, что мне нужно знать? *6.* Я должен был знать, что что-то не так.
● *1.* That's the idea, isn't it? *2.* But I don't think it's a good idea. *3.* I really don't think that's a good idea. *4.* I just don't think it's a good idea. *5.* Is there anything else I need to know? *6.* I should have known something was wrong.

**[22]** *1.* Мне нужно знать, что с ней все в порядке. *2.* Я просто хочу знать, что с тобой все в порядке. *3.* Мне нужно знать, что с тобой все в порядке. *4.* Думаю, у меня есть именно то, что нужно. *5.* Вы здесь именно для этого, не так ли? *6.* Это именно то, что я хочу, чтобы ты сделал.
● *1.* I need to know that she's okay. *2.* I just want to know you're okay. *3.* I need to know that you're okay. *4.* I think I have just the thing. *5.* That's what you're here for, isn't it? *6.* That's exactly what I want you to do.

**[23]** *1.* Не все было так плохо, не так ли? *2.* Что ж, мне жаль, что ты так думаешь. *3.* Ты думаешь, что знаешь меня, но это не так. *4.* Как думаешь, с ней все будет в порядке? *5.* Может быть, ты мог бы пойти со мной. *6.* Я не хотел, чтобы это

произошло вот так.
- *1.* It wasn't all bad, was it? *2.* Well, I'm sorry you feel that way. *3.* You think you know me, but you don't. *4.* Do you think she'll be all right? *5.* Maybe you could come with me. *6.* I didn't want it to happen like this.

**[24]** *1.* Вот в чем все дело, не так ли? *2.* Скажи ей, что со мной все в порядке. *3.* Скажи ему то, что ты только что сказал мне. *4.* Скажи мне что-нибудь, чего я не знаю! *5.* Просто скажи мне, что я сделал не так. *6.* Просто скажи ему то, что ты сказал мне.
- *1.* That's what this is all about, isn't it? *2.* Tell her I'm fine. *3.* Tell him what you just told me. *4.* Tell me something I don't know! *5.* Just tell me what I did wrong. *6.* Just tell him what you told me.

**[25]** *1.* Что бы это ни было, просто скажи это. *2.* Я никогда не говорил, что ты это сделал. *3.* Я говорил тебе, что все будет в порядке. *4.* Я говорил тебе, что со мной все в порядке. *5.* Почему ты никогда не говорил мне этого раньше? *6.* Говорил тебе, что со мной все в порядке.
- *1.* Whatever it is, just say it. *2.* I never said you did. *3.* I told you it would be all right. *4.* I told you I was good. *5.* How come you never told me that before? *6.* Told you I was fine.

**[26]** *1.* Могу ли я помочь вам с чем-нибудь еще? *2.* Мне жаль, что я не мог больше помочь. *3.* Что ж, мы можем помочь вам в этом. *4.* Все в порядке, я здесь, чтобы помочь тебе. *5.* Я не знаю, готов ли я к этому. *6.* Это выглядит не очень хорошо, не так ли?
- *1.* Can I help you with anything else? *2.* I'm sorry I couldn't be more help. *3.* Well, we can help you with that. *4.* It's okay, I'm here to help you. *5.* I don't know if I'm ready for this. *6.* It doesn't look good, does it?

**[27]** *1.* Я должен был сделать это много лет назад. *2.* Можете ли вы сказать мне, сколько вам лет? *3.* Я уверен, что с ним все будет в порядке. *4.* Я думаю, что с ним что-то не так. *5.* Чего ты на самом деле хочешь от меня? *6.* Ну, а может ли это быть на самом деле?
- *1.* I should have done this years ago. *2.* Can you tell me how old you are? *3.* I'm sure he'll be fine. *4.* I think there's something

wrong with him. *5.* What do you really want from me? *6.* Well, of all things Can it be really?

**[28]** *1.* Так что ты на самом деле здесь делаешь? *2.* Скажи мне, что ты на самом деле думаешь. *3.* Но теперь я знаю, кто я на самом деле. *4.* На самом деле, я думаю, что это так. *5.* Так что же ты хочешь, чтобы мы сделали? *6.* Что ж, я рад, что они это сделали.
- *1.* So what are you really doing here? *2.* Tell me what you really think. *3.* But now I know who I really am. *4.* Actually, I think it is. *5.* So what do you want us to do? *6.* Well, I'm glad they did.

**[29]** *1.* Вы сделали именно то, что должны были сделать. *2.* Ну, я не понимаю, почему бы и нет. *3.* Я понимаю, почему ты сделал то, что сделал. *4.* Я не понимаю, чего ты от меня хочешь. *5.* А вот и я, готовы вы или нет. *6.* Ты бы сделал то же самое для меня.
- *1.* You did exactly what you had to do. *2.* Well, I don't see why not. *3.* I understand why you did what you did. *4.* I don't understand what you want from me. *5.* Ready or not, here I come. *6.* You'd have done the same for me.

**[30]** *1.* Знаешь, все то же самое, то же самое. *2.* Я мог бы сказать то же самое о тебе. *3.* Я мог бы сказать вам то же самое. *4.* Хотел бы я сказать то же самое о тебе. *5.* Я могу сделать то же самое для тебя. *6.* О, вы знаете, все то же самое, то же самое.
- *1.* You know, same old, same old. *2.* I could say the same about you. *3.* I could say the same to you. *4.* Wish I could say the same for you. *5.* I can do the same for you. *6.* Oh, you know, same old, same old.

**[31]** *1.* Я хочу сделать то же самое для тебя. *2.* Это не может быть правильно, не так ли? *3.* Как, черт возьми, ты думаешь, как я себя чувствую? *4.* На самом деле, я чувствую себя довольно хорошо. *5.* Я чувствую то же самое, что и ты. *6.* Что ж, я надеюсь, ты знаешь, что делаешь.
- *1.* I want to do the same for you. *2.* That can't be right, can it? *3.* How the hell do you think I am? *4.* I feel pretty good, actually. *5.* I feel the same way you do. *6.* Well, I hope you know what you're doing.

**[32]** *1.* Для тебя это так легко, не так ли? *2.* Я никогда не говорил, что это будет легко. *3.* Я не думаю, что это будет так легко. *4.* Скажи им то, что ты только что сказал мне. *5.* Это то, чего вы хотите, не так ли? *6.* Так что же мы будем с этим делать?

● *1.* It's so easy for you, isn't it? *2.* I never said it was gonna be easy. *3.* I don't think it's gonna be that easy. *4.* Tell them what you just told me. *5.* That is what you want, isn't it? *6.* So what are we gonna do about it?

**[33]** *1.* Давай никогда больше не будем об этом говорить. *2.* Я вообще не должен был быть здесь сегодня. *3.* Я не думаю, что нам стоит больше этого делать. *4.* На самом деле, да, я так и делаю. *5.* Я не знаю, что я делаю не так. *6.* Я даже не знаю, что я делаю больше.

● *1.* Let's never speak of it again. *2.* I'm not even supposed to be here today. *3.* I don't think we should do this anymore. *4.* Actually, yeah, I do. *5.* I don't know what I'm doing wrong. *6.* I don't even know what I'm doing anymore.

**[34]** *1.* Я этого не сделал, но теперь я это делаю. *2.* Я делаю то, что хочу и когда хочу. *3.* Я уверен, что это было не так уж плохо. *4.* Не так уж плохо, не так уж плохо. *5.* Не так уж и много, не так ли? *6.* Выглядит не так уж плохо, не так ли?

● *1.* I didn't, but now I do. *2.* I do what I want, when I want. *3.* I'm sure it wasn't that bad. *4.* Not too bad, not too bad. *5.* Not much, is it? *6.* It doesn't look too bad, does it?

**[35]** *1.* Не так уж и много выглядит, не так ли? *2.* На самом деле не так уж и плохо. *3.* На самом деле, не так уж и хорошо. *4.* Уже немного поздно для этого, не так ли? *5.* Я не думаю, что кто-то так делает. *6.* Сегодня вечером мы больше ничего не можем сделать.

● *1.* Doesn't look like much, does it? *2.* Not too bad, actually. *3.* Actually, not so good. *4.* It's a little late for that, isn't it? *5.* I don't think anyone does. *6.* There's nothing more we can do tonight.

**[36]** *1.* Я не могу сейчас говорить об этом, ясно? *2.* Есть ли где-нибудь, где мы можем поговорить? *3.* Может быть, ты мог бы поговорить с ним. *4.* Я хотел бы поговорить с тобой еще раз. *5.* Вот о чем я хочу с тобой поговорить. *6.* Почему бы нам не поговорить об этом позже?

- *1.* I cannot talk about this right now, okay? *2.* Is there somewhere we can talk? *3.* Maybe you could talk to him. *4.* I'd like to talk to you again. *5.* That's what I wanna talk to you about. *6.* Why don't we talk about this later?

**[37]** *1.* Почему бы тебе не пойти поговорить с ней? *2.* Ну и что ты собираешься с этим делать? *3.* Большое вам спасибо за то, что вы здесь. *4.* Есть ли что-то, о чем ты мне не говоришь? *5.* Если только ты не чего-то нам не говоришь. *6.* Ты очень уверен в себе, не так ли?

- *1.* Why don't you go talk to her? *2.* Well, what are you gonna do about it? *3.* Thank you so much for being here. *4.* Is there something you're not telling me? *5.* Unless there's something you're not telling us. *6.* You're very sure of yourself, aren't you?

**[38]** *1.* Ну, может быть, как-нибудь в другой раз. *2.* Извините, я думал, что вы кто-то другой. *3.* Вот что я пришел сюда, чтобы сказать вам. *4.* Почему ты не пришел и не сказал мне? *5.* Можем ли мы поговорить об этом на секунду? *6.* Ох, я бы не был так уверен в этом.

- *1.* Well, maybe some other time. *2.* Sorry, I thought you were someone else. *3.* That's what I came here to tell you. *4.* Why didn't you come and tell me? *5.* Can we talk about this for a second? *6.* Oh, I wouldn't be so sure about that.

**[39]** *1.* Что бы это ни было, мне это не интересно. *2.* Я не хочу, чтобы ты что-нибудь делал. *3.* Ты никогда не делал этого раньше, не так ли? *4.* На самом деле нет, я этого не делал. *5.* На самом деле это не так уж и важно. *6.* Я не знал, что у тебя есть ребенок.

- *1.* Whatever it is, I'm not interested. *2.* I don't want you to do anything. *3.* You've never done this before, have you? *4.* Actually, no, I didn't. *5.* It's really not that big of a deal. *6.* I didn't know you had a child.

**[40]** *1.* Я здесь только для того, чтобы помочь тебе. *2.* Мне очень плохо из-за того, что произошло. *3.* Не волнуйся, со мной все будет в порядке. *4.* Я просто хочу, чтобы ты был в безопасности. *5.* Это был последний раз, когда я видел ее. *6.* Ты еще не видел меня в последний раз.

- *1.* I'm just here to help you. *2.* I feel really bad about what happened. *3*. Don't worry, I'll be fine. *4*. I just want you to be safe. *5*. That was the last time I saw her. *6*. You haven't seen the last of me.

**[41]** *1*. Когда он у вас был в последний раз? *2*. Я не имел в виду то, что сказал. *3*. Как вы думаете, сколько времени у нас есть? *4*. Я все еще надеюсь, Боже мой, я все еще надеюсь. *5*. Ну, боже мой, почему ты так не сказал? *6*. Я не могу поверить, что я это сделал.
- *1*. When was the last time you had one? *2*. I didn't mean what I said. *3*. How long do you think we have? *4*. Still I hope, my God, still I hope. *5*. Well, golly, why didn't you say so? *6*. I can't believe I did that.

**[42]** *1*. Если бы я только мог в это поверить. *2*. Вот именно то, что я имею в виду. *3*. Я имею в виду, почему бы и нет? *4*. Я имею в виду, я надеюсь на это. *5*. Я имею в виду, я этого не делал. *6*. Я имею в виду, чего еще ты хочешь?
- *1*. If only I could believe that. *2*. That's exactly what I mean. *3*. I mean, why not? *4*. I mean, I hope so. *5*. I mean, I didn't. *6*. I mean, what more do you want?

**[43]** *1*. Я имею в виду, насколько это может быть плохо? *2*. Ну, я имею в виду, я не знаю. *3*. Дай мне знать если тебе нужно что-нибудь еще. *4*. Дай мне знать, что с тобой все в порядке. *5*. Что ж, у меня есть новости для вас. *6*. Пожалуйста, скажи мне, что у тебя есть хорошие новости.
- *1*. I mean, how bad could it be? *2*. Well, I mean, I don't know. *3*. Let me know if you need anything else. *4*. Let me know you're okay. *5*. Well, I got news for you. *6*. Please tell me you have some good news.

**[44]** *1*. Я не знаю, что бы я делал без тебя. *2*. Я думаю, ты знаешь, о чем я говорю. *3*. Я никогда раньше в жизни ее не видел. *4*. Разве ты не хочешь знать, что это такое? *5*. Не говори мне, что ты не думал об этом. *6*. Есть ли что-нибудь еще, что мне следует знать?
- *1*. I don't know what I'd do without you. *2*. I think you know what I'm talking about. *3*. I never saw her before in my life. *4*. Don't you wanna know what it is? *5*. Don't tell me you haven't thought about it. *6*. Is there anything else I should know?

**[45]** *1*. Я не думаю, что тебе следует этого делать. *2*. Я не думаю, что тебе следует это делать. *3.* Я не думаю, что мне следует это делать. *4.* Я все еще думаю, что нам следует уйти. *5.* Я не хочу, чтобы это случилось с тобой. *6.* Мне очень жаль, что это случилось с тобой.

• *1.* I don't think you should do this. *2.* I don't think you should be doing that. *3.* I don't think I'm supposed to. *4.* I still think we should leave. *5.* I don't want that to happen to you. *6.* I'm so sorry this happened to you.

**[46]** *1.* Разве ты не слышал, что я только что сказал? *2.* Потому что я не хочу, чтобы ты этого делал. *3.* Я пришел сюда не для того, чтобы увидеть тебя. *4.* Папа, я не знаю, о чем ты говоришь. *5.* Я не был уверен, что ты будешь здесь. *6.* Ты никогда не был и никогда не будешь.

• *1.* Did you not hear what I just said? *2.* Because I don't want you to. *3.* I didn't come here to see you. *4.* Dad, I don't know what you're talking about. *5.* I wasn't sure you'd be here. *6.* You never were and you never will be.

**[47]** *1.* И это именно то, что я собираюсь сделать. *2.* Кажется, это было очень давно, не так ли? *3.* Точно так же, как это сделал твой отец. *4.* Никто никогда не делал этого для меня раньше. *5.* Это было не так уж сложно, не так ли? *6.* Я не могу поверить в то, что вижу.

• *1.* And that's exactly what I'm gonna do. *2.* Seems like a long time ago, doesn't it? *3.* Just like your father did. *4.* No one's ever done that for me before. *5.* That wasn't so hard, was it? *6.* I can't believe what I'm seeing.

**[48]** *1.* После этого я больше никогда ее не видел. *2.* Все, что у нас есть, это друг друга. *3.* Возможно, это была не такая уж хорошая идея. *4.* Что, черт возьми, с вами не так, люди? *5.* Я не знаю, значит ли это что-нибудь. *6.* Я знаю, как много это значит для тебя.

• *1.* I never saw her again after that. *2.* All we have is each other. *3.* Maybe this wasn't such a good idea. *4.* What the hell's wrong with you people? *5.* I don't know if it means anything. *6.* I know how much it means to you.

**[49]** *1.* Я знаю, как много он для тебя значит. *2.* Потому что я хочу, чтобы ты был счастлив. *3.* Я никогда в жизни не был так счастлив. *4.* Ну, если ты счастлив, то и я счастлив. *5.* Знаешь ли ты, как сильно я тебя люблю? 6. Где ты был, когда ты мне был нужен?

● 1. I know how much he means to you. 2. Because I want you to be happy. 3. I've never been so happy in my life. 4. Well, if you're happy, I'm happy. 5. Do you know how much I love you? 6. Where were you when I needed you?

[50] 1. Я знаю, что это должно быть трудно для тебя. 2. Есть кое-что, что я тебе не сказал. 3. И позвольте мне сказать вам кое-что еще. 4. Есть кое-что, о чем ты нам не говоришь. 5. У меня тоже есть кое-что для тебя. 6. У меня есть для тебя кое-что еще.

● 1. I know this must be difficult for you. 2. There's something I haven't told you. 3. And let me tell you something else. 4. There's something you're not telling us. 5. I got something for you, too. 6. I have something else for you.

[51] 1. Здесь есть кое-что, что вы должны увидеть. 2. Вот, у меня есть кое-что для тебя. 3. Я знаю кое-что, чего ты не знаешь. 4. Есть кое-что, о чем я хочу с тобой поговорить. 5. Ну, у меня есть кое-что для тебя. 6. Есть кое-что, о чем ты мне не говоришь.

● 1. There's something here you should see. 2. Here, I got something for you. 3. I know something you don't know. 4. There's something I wanna talk to you about. 5. Well, I have something for you. 6. There is something you're not telling me.

[52] 1. Есть еще кое-что, что тебе следует знать. 2. Не могли бы вы сделать это еще раз? 3. Да, ну, может быть, я так и сделаю. 4. Да ладно, ты же знаешь, что я хорош для этого. 5. Мне так повезло, что ты у меня есть. 6. Я не думаю, что смогу больше это делать.

● 1. There's something else you should know. 2. Could you do that again? 3. Yeah, well, maybe I will. 4. Come on, you know I'm good for it. 5. I'm so lucky to have you. 6. I don't think I can do this anymore.

[53] 1. Я не знаю, смогу ли я это сделать. 2. Тебя не должно было быть здесь до завтра. 3. Как бы то ни было, мне все равно. 4. Что, если я скажу что-то не то? 5. Я скажу тебе, что со мной не так. 6. Я счастлив, потому что получил то, что хотел.

- *1.* I don't know if I could do that. *2.* You weren't supposed to be here till tomorrow. *3.* Whatever, I don't care. *4.* What if I say the wrong thing? *5.* I'll tell you what's wrong with me. *6.* I'm happy, coz I got what I wanted.

**[54]** *1.* Я никогда раньше не видел тебя в своей жизни. *2.* Я имею в виду, кто бы не стал? *3.* Нет, ты бы не стал, не так ли? *4.* Я бы не стал, если бы я был тобой. *5.* Так близко и в то же время так далеко. *6.* Я не могу есть, я не могу спать.
- *1.* I've never seen you before in my life. *2.* I mean, who wouldn't? *3.* No, you wouldn't, would you? *4.* I wouldn't, if I were you. *5.* So near and yet so far. *6.* I can't eat, I can't sleep.

**[55]** *1.* Вы уверены, что это то, чего вы хотите? *2.* Он ничего под этим не имеет в виду. *3.* Разве ты не можешь сказать, что я занят? *4.* Сейчас это не имеет значения, не так ли? *5.* Я рад видеть, что ты чувствуешь себя лучше. *6.* Я имею в виду, как ты себя чувствуешь?
- *1.* Are you sure this is what you want? *2.* He doesn't mean anything by it. *3.* Can't you tell, I'm busy? *4.* Doesn't matter now, does it? *5.* I'm glad to see you're feeling better. *6.* I mean, how do you feel?

**[56]** *1.* Не очень хорошо себя чувствуешь, не так ли? *2.* Я знаю, что ты чувствуешь то же самое. *3.* Я знаю, что это должно быть тяжело для тебя. *4.* Я нашел тебя именно там, где я хочу. *5.* Я не могу поверить, что мы делаем это. *6.* Я имею в виду, что мы здесь делаем?
- *1.* Doesn't feel so good, does it? *2.* I know you feel the same way. *3.* I know this must be hard for you. *4.* I got you right where I want you. *5.* I can't believe we're doing this. *6.* I mean, what are we doing here?

**[57]** *1.* Дело не в том, что я тебя не люблю. *2.* Я не могу поверить, что она это сделала. *3.* Я знаю это лучше, чем кто-либо другой. *4.* Это все, о чем ты когда-либо думал? *5.* Все, что я когда-либо хотел, это ты. *6.* Это все, что я когда-либо хотел для тебя.
- *1.* It's not that I don't love you. *2.* I can't believe she did that. *3.* I know that better than anyone. *4.* Is that all you ever think about? *5.* All I ever wanted was you. *6.* That's all I've ever wanted for you.

**[58]** *1.* Это все, чем я когда-либо хотел быть. *2.* Ничего из того, что я когда-либо видел раньше. *3.* Это все, что я когда-либо хотел сделать. *4.* Я не думаю, что ты когда-либо это делал. *5.* С чего ты взял, что у меня нет? *6.* Я не знал, что у тебя есть брат.

● *1.* That's all I've ever wanted to be. *2.* Nothing I've ever seen before. *3.* That's all I ever wanted to do. *4.* I don't think you ever did. *5.* What makes you think I haven't? *6.* I didn't know you had a brother.

**[59]** *1.* Почему ты не пришел ко мне с этим? *2.* Я не верю в это ни на секунду. *3.* Ты чертовски хорошо знаешь, о чем я говорю. *4.* Что ж, это очень мило с твоей стороны. *5.* Я не думаю, что у меня есть выбор. *6.* Я не вижу, чтобы у нас был выбор.

● *1.* Why didn't you come to me with this? *2.* I don't believe that for a second. *3.* You know damn well what I'm talking about. *4.* Well, that's very nice of you. *5.* I don't think I have a choice. *6.* I don't see that we have a choice.

**[60]** *1.* Я никогда раньше не видел тебя с этой стороны. *2.* Почему бы тебе не остаться здесь со мной? *3.* Могу ли я остаться с тобой сегодня вечером? *4.* Это то, что вы делаете, не так ли? *5.* Нет, на самом деле мы просто хорошие друзья. *6.* Я верю, что вы двое знаете друг друга.

● *1.* I've never seen this side of you before. *2.* Why don't you stay here with me? *3.* Can I stay with you tonight? *4.* That's what you do, isn't it? *5.* No, actually we're just good friends. *6.* I believe you two know each other.

**[61]** *1.* Мне просто нужно, чтобы ты сделал одну вещь. *2.* Тебя никогда нет рядом, когда ты мне нужен. *3.* Я не хочу, чтобы ты был рядом с ним. *4.* Я знаю, что меня не было рядом с тобой. *5.* То, чего я никогда о нем не знал. *6.* Возможно, вы нашли того, кто вам больше нравится.

● *1.* I just need you to do one thing. *2.* You're never around when I need you. *3.* I don't want you anywhere near him. *4.* I know I haven't been there for you. *5.* Things I never knew about him. *6.* Maybe you found someone you like better.

**[62]** *1.* Ты, должно быть, думаешь, что я такой глупый. *2.* Мне бы хотелось, чтобы все было так просто. *3.* Как бы мне хотелось, чтобы ты был здесь. *4.* О, тебе бы этого хотелось, не так ли? *5.* Мне бы хотелось, чтобы ты этого не делал. *6.* Мне бы хотелось, чтобы ты этого не говорил.

● *1.* You must think I'm so stupid. *2.* I wish it was that simple. *3.* I wish you were here. *4.* Oh, you'd like that, wouldn't you? *5.* I wish you hadn't. *6.* I wish you hadn't said that.

**[63]** *1.* Мне бы хотелось, чтобы я мог сделать больше. *2.* Мне бы хотелось, но я этого не делаю. *3.* Мне бы очень хотелось, чтобы ты этого не делал. *4.* Мне бы хотелось, чтобы он этого не делал. *5.* Нам бы этого не хотелось, не так ли? *6.* Мне бы хотелось, чтобы ты мне этого не говорил.

● *1.* I wish there was more I could do. *2.* I wish I did, but I don't. *3.* I really wish you wouldn't. *4.* I wish he hadn't. *5.* We wouldn't want that, would we? *6.* I wish you hadn't told me that.

**[64]** *1.* Мне бы очень хотелось, чтобы вы это сделали. *2.* У нас есть только один шанс на это. *3.* Я просто не могу понять, как это сделать. *4.* Я не знал, что у тебя есть компания. *5.* По крайней мере, мы есть друг у друга. *6.* По крайней мере, ты можешь мне это сказать.

● *1.* I really wish you would. *2.* We only have one shot at this. *3.* I just can't figure out how. *4.* I didn't realize you had company. *5.* At least we have each other. *6.* You can tell me that at least.

**[65]** *1.* Ты уверен, что не хочешь пойти с нами? *2.* Вчера вечером он так и не пришел домой. *3.* Почему ты не сказал мне об этом вчера вечером? *4.* Я имею в виду, просто посмотри на него. *5.* Скажи мне еще раз, что это не безумие. *6.* Я не думал, что ты сможешь это сделать.

● *1.* You sure you don't want to come along? *2.* He never came home last night. *3.* Why didn't you tell me this last night? *4.* I mean, just look at him. *5.* Tell me again this isn't crazy. *6.* I didn't think you could do it.

**[66]** *1.* Ты думаешь, что ты довольно умный, не так ли? *2.* Я не думаю, что он был бы против. *3.* У кого-нибудь еще есть проблемы с этим? *4.* У меня никогда раньше не было этой проблемы. *5.* Раньше у нас никогда не было этой проблемы. *6.* Почему ты не можешь просто оставить нас в покое?

● *1.* You think you're pretty smart, don't you? *2.* I don't think he'd mind. *3.* Anybody else have a problem with that? *4.* I've never had this problem before. *5.* Heretofore, we never had this problem. *6.* Why can't you just leave us alone?

**[67]** *1.* Все в порядке, ты можешь оставить это себе. *2.* Она сказала, что с ней все в порядке. *3.* Разве это вам ни о чем не говорит? *4.* Он говорит, что с ним все в порядке. *5.* Она говорит, что с ней все в порядке. *6.* Есть кое-что, о чем он нам не говорит.

• *1.* It's okay, you can keep it. *2.* She said she's fine. *3.* Doesn't that tell you something? *4.* He says he's fine. *5.* She says she's fine. *6.* There's something he's not telling us.

**[68]** *1.* Все, что мы можем сделать сейчас, это ждать. *2.* Вот о чем речь на самом деле, не так ли? *3.* Я не думаю, что речь идет об этом. *4.* Можете ли вы сказать мне, куда мы идем? *5.* Держите руки так, чтобы я мог их видеть. *6.* Я просто подумал, что тебе интересно это знать.

• *1.* All we can do now is wait. *2.* That's what this is really about, isn't it? *3.* I don't think that's what this is about. *4.* Can you tell me where we're going? *5.* Keep your hands where I can see them. *6.* I just thought you'd like to know.

**[69]** *1.* Я подумал, может быть, ты сможешь мне помочь. *2.* Знаешь, я только что подумал кое о чем. *3.* Да, я только что подумал о том же. *4.* Эй, я только что подумал кое о чем. *5.* О, я только что подумал кое о чем. *6.* Я не знаю, почему я об этом подумал.

• *1.* I thought maybe you could help me. *2.* You know, I just thought of something. *3.* Yeah, I was just thinking the same thing. *4.* Hey, I just thought of something. *5.* Oh, I just thought of something. *6.* I don't know why I thought of that.

**[70]** *1.* Я не видел тебя здесь в последнее время. *2.* Что с тобой не так в последнее время? *3.* Что ты сделал для меня в последнее время? *4.* В последнее время он был не в себе. *5.* Я знаю, что ты имел в виду добро. *6.* Хорошо, давайте посмотрим, что у нас здесь есть.

• *1.* I haven't seen you around lately. *2.* What's wrong with you lately? *3.* What have you done for me lately? *4.* He hasn't been himself lately. *5.* I know you meant well. *6.* All right, let's see what we got here.

**[71]** *1.* Я не знаю, о чем вы говорите, сэр. *2.* И не говорите мне, что вы не знаете. *3.* Я никогда раньше не видел такого в своей жизни. *4.* Я имею в виду, что в этом такого? *5.* Что у нее есть такого, чего нет у меня? *6.* Что у него есть такого, чего нет у меня?

● *1.* I don't know what you're talking about, sir. *2.* And don't tell me you don't know. *3.* I've never seen that before in my life. *4.* I mean, what's the big deal? *5.* What does she have that I don't? *6.* What's he got that I haven't?

**[72]** *1.* Что ты знаешь такого, чего не знаю я? *2.* Я не видел ни одного уже много лет. *3.* Почему бы тебе не пойти со мной, сынок? *4.* Если бы я мог вернуть это, я бы это сделал. *5.* Я не могу оставаться здесь и ничего не делать. *6.* Ты все еще любишь его, не так ли?

● *1.* What do you know that I don't? *2.* I haven't seen one in years. *3.* Why don't you come with me, son? *4.* If I could take it back, I would. *5.* I can't stay here and do nothing. *6.* You still love him, don't you?

**[73]** *1.* Я знаю, что ты все еще любишь меня. *2.* Я рад, что ты видишь это именно так. *3.* Здесь есть кто-то, кто хочет вас увидеть. *4.* Можем ли мы поговорить о чем-то другом? *5.* У меня действительно нет выбора, не так ли? *6.* Мне очень жаль, но у меня нет выбора.

● *1.* I know you still love me. *2.* I'm glad you see it that way. *3.* There's someone here to see you. *4.* Can we talk about something else? *5.* I don't really have a choice, do I? *6.* I'm sorry, but I have no choice.

**[74]** *1.* Мне очень жаль, у меня не было выбора. *2.* Это было бы очень мило с вашей стороны. *3.* Почему бы тебе не пойти работать на меня? *4.* Что, черт возьми, случилось с тобой прошлой ночью? *5.* Что ты на самом деле думаешь обо мне? *6.* Нет, это не то, о чем я могу думать.

● *1.* I'm sorry, I had no choice. *2.* That would be very nice of you. *3.* Why don't you come work for me? *4.* What the hell happened to you last night? *5.* What do you really think of me? *6.* No, not that I can think of.

**[75]** *1.* Ты не можешь думать ни о чем другом? *2.* Вам хотелось бы так думать, не так ли? *3.* Мы поговорим об этом как-нибудь в другой раз. *4.* Я не знаю, что вы в нем видите.

*5.* Я так рад, что ты смог это сделать. *6.* Я не смог бы сделать это без тебя.

● *1.* Can't you think of anything else? *2.* You'd like to think that, wouldn't you? *3.* We'll talk about it some other time. *4.* I don't know what you see in him. *5.* So glad you could make it. *6.* I couldn't have done this without you.

**[76]** *1.* Сам я не смог бы сделать это лучше. *2.* Ты не смог бы этого сделать, не так ли? *3.* Кем бы ты сказал, что ты был еще раз? *4.* Мы не будем двигаться дальше в этом деле. *5.* Я никогда раньше не был в твоей комнате. *6.* Я не могу позволить ей увидеть меня таким.

● *1.* Couldn't have done it better myself. *2.* You couldn't do it, could you? *3.* Who'd you say you were again? *4.* We will proceed no further in this business. *5.* I've never been in your room before. *6.* I can't let her see me like this.

**[77]** *1.* Нет, я не могу позволить тебе сделать это. *2.* Боюсь, я не могу позволить тебе сделать это. *3.* Не то чтобы это имело какое-то значение. *4.* Мне нужно, чтобы ты пошел со мной сейчас. *5.* Куда бы ты ни пошел, я буду там. *6.* Я бы хотел, чтобы все было по-другому.

● *1.* No, I can't let you do that. *2.* I'm afraid I can't let you do that. *3.* Not that it makes any difference. *4.* I need you to come with me now. *5.* Wherever you go, I'll be there. *6.* I wish it were different.

**[78]** *1.* Что ж, рано или поздно это должно было случиться. *2.* Ты вполне уверен в себе, не так ли? *3.* Я бы хотел, чтобы тебе не пришлось идти. *4.* Мне очень жаль, что тебе пришлось это увидеть. *5.* Ему пришлось уйти, потому что он вернулся поздно. *6.* Я никогда в жизни не чувствовал себя лучше.

● *1.* Well, it had to happen sooner or later. *2.* You're pretty sure of yourself, aren't you? *3.* I wish you didn't have to go. *4.* I'm so sorry you had to see that. *5.* He had to leave, to be back late. *6.* I never felt better in my life.

**[79]** *1.* Я не чувствовал себя так хорошо уже много лет. *2.* Да, в последний раз я чувствовал себя так! *3.* Я хочу, чтобы ты чувствовал себя в безопасности. *4.* Я просто хочу, чтобы ты чувствовал себя в безопасности. *5.* У меня есть хорошие новости и плохие новости. *6.* Я имею в виду, если тебя это устраивает.

- *1.* I haven't felt this good in years. *2.* Yes, the last time I Felt like this! *3.* I want you to feel safe. *4.* I just want you to feel safe. *5.* I got good news and bad news. *6.* I mean, if it's okay with you.

**[80]** *1.* Все кончено, когда я говорю, что все кончено. *2.* Дайте нам знать, если вам нужно что-нибудь еще. *3.* Я не могу поверить в то, что слышу! *4.* Я не слышу ни слова из того, что ты говоришь. *5.* Я бы не позвонил, если бы это не было важно. *6.* Вы еще не слышали об этом в последний раз.

- *1.* It's over when I say it's over. *2.* Let us know if you need anything else. *3.* I can't believe what I'm hearing! *4.* I can't hear a word you're saying. *5.* I wouldn't have called if it wasn't important. *6.* You haven't heard the last of this.

**[81]** *1.* Я уверен, что у вас есть много вопросов. *2.* У меня просто есть к вам несколько вопросов. *3.* В этом нет ничего плохого, не так ли? *4.* Я просто хочу, чтобы ты оставил меня в покое. *5.* Поэтому я подумал, что у меня тоже будет такой. *6.* Я мог бы спросить тебя о том же.

- *1.* I'm sure you have a lot of questions. *2.* I just have a few questions for you. *3.* Nothing wrong with that, is there? *4.* I just want you to leave me alone. *5.* So I thought I'd have one as well. *6.* I could ask you the same thing.

**[82]** *1.* Могу ли я спросить вас кое-что еще? *2.* Я просто хочу спросить тебя кое о чем. *3.* Что ж, позвольте мне спросить вас об этом. *4.* Я просто хотел у тебя кое-что спросить. *5.* Я пришел сюда, чтобы спросить тебя кое о чем. *6.* Э-э, позвольте мне спросить вас кое-что.

- *1.* Can I ask you something else? *2.* I just want to ask you something. *3.* Well, let me ask you this. *4.* I just wanted to ask you something. *5.* I came here to ask you something. *6.* Uh, let me ask you something.

**[83]** *1.* Как ты мог вообще спросить меня об этом? *2.* Я знаю, что это не имеет никакого смысла. *3.* Он чувствовал себя глупо из-за того, что забыл. *4.* Ну, в любом случае это не имеет значения. *5.* В любом случае, я подумал, что ты должен знать. *6.* В любом случае, было приятно с вами поговорить.

● *1.* How could you even ask me that? *2.* I know it doesn't make any sense. *3.* He felt dumb for forgetting. *4.* Well, it doesn't matter anyway. *5.* Anyway, I thought you should know. *6.* Anywho, it was nice talking to you.

**[84]** *1.* Я любил ее так же сильно, как и ты. *2.* Это самое красивое, что я когда-либо видел. *3.* Я так рада, что ты смог это сделать. *4.* Я так рада, что с тобой все в порядке. *5.* Если ты этого не сделаешь, я сделаю это. *6.* Может быть, ты сделаешь это, а может быть, и нет.

● *1.* I loved her as much as you did. *2.* It's the most beautiful thing I've ever seen. *3.* I'm so glad you could make it. *4.* I'm so glad you're okay. *5.* If you don't, I will. *6.* Maybe you will, maybe you won't.

**[85]** *1.* Есть ли у вас идеи, с чего начать? *2.* Я думал, что больше никогда тебя не увижу. *3.* Может быть, я когда-нибудь увижу тебя снова. *4.* Мне никогда в жизни не было так страшно. *5.* И это именно то, что мы собираемся сделать. *6.* Мы собираемся в одно и то же место.

● *1.* Do you have any idea where to start? *2.* I thought I'd never see you again. *3.* Maybe I'll see you again sometime. *4.* I've never been so scared in my life. *5.* And that's exactly what we're gonna do. *6.* We're going to the same place.

**[86]** *1.* Я не уверен, что понимаю, что вы имеете в виду. *2.* Позвони мне, когда у тебя что-нибудь будет. *3.* Я не ожидал, что ты вернешься так скоро. *4.* Что бы ты ни собирался делать, делай это быстро. *5.* Мне никогда в жизни не было так стыдно. *6.* Мы не можем просто оставить это без внимания.

● *1.* I'm not sure I know what you mean. *2.* Call me when you have something. *3.* I didn't expect you back so soon. *4.* Whatever you're gonna do, do it fast. *5.* I've never been so embarrassed in my life. *6.* We can't just let this go.

**[87]** *1.* Никто здесь не является именно тем, кем кажется. *2.* Я просто хотел быть тем, кем ты хотел. *3.* Вы не можете иметь и то, и другое. *4.* Что ж, я буду иметь это в виду. *5.* Я не могу иметь с тобой дело прямо сейчас. *6.* А что, если что-то пойдет не так?

● 1. No one here is exactly what he appears. 2. I just wanted to be what you wanted. 3. You can't have it both ways. 4. Well, I'll keep that in mind. 5. I can't deal with you right now. 6. And what if something goes wrong?

**[88]** 1. Теперь все это имеет смысл, не так ли? 2. Плохие мальчики, плохие мальчики. Что ты собираешься делать? 3. Я уверен, что с ними все будет в порядке. 4. Я понятия не имею, о чем ты говоришь. 5. Вы понятия не имеете, что вы только что сделали. 6. Я понятия не имел, что уже так поздно.
● 1. It all makes sense now, doesn't it? 2. Bad boys, bad boys What you gonna do? 3. I'm sure they'll be fine. 4. I've no idea what you're talking about. 5. You have no idea what you've just done. 6. I had no idea it was that late.

**[89]** 1. Я понятия не имел, что ты будешь здесь. 2. Я не чувствую себя хорошо по этому поводу. 3. Могу я вернуться к вам по этому поводу? 4. Позвольте мне вернуться к вам по этому поводу. 5. Откуда мне знать, что я могу тебе доверять? 6. Я не знаю, могу ли я тебе доверять.
● 1. I had no idea you would be here. 2. I don't feel good about this. 3. Can I get back to you on that? 4. Let me get back to you on that. 5. How do I know I can trust you? 6. I don't know if I can trust you.

**[90]** 1. Я говорил тебе, что мы не можем ему доверять. 2. Вы понимаете, что я имею в виду, да? 3. Если бы ты мог, ты был бы свободен. 4. В комнате было слишком темно, чтобы что-либо увидеть. 5. Так что будьте осторожны, очень осторожны, молодой человек. 6. Как вы думаете, что вы делаете, молодой человек?
● 1. I told you we couldn't trust him. 2. You know what I mean, right? 3. If you could, you would be free. 4. The room was too dar to see anything. 5. So be careful, very careful, young man. 6. What do you think you're doing, young man?

**[91]** 1. Я знаю, что мне не следовало этого делать. 2. Я знал, что нам не следовало доверять тебе. 3. То, что мне следовало сделать много лет назад. 4. Я до сих пор не знаю, что это значит. 5. Я думаю, у нас всё будет в порядке. 6. Я понятия не имею, как я туда попал.

● *1.* I know I shouldn't have. *2.* I knew we shouldn't have trusted you. *3.* What I should have done years ago. *4.* I still don't know what that means. *5.* I think we're gonna be okay. *6.* I have no idea how I got there.

**[92]** *1.* Дела идут не очень хорошо, не так ли? *2.* Это еще не конец, пока все не закончится. *3.* Это была самая большая ошибка в моей жизни. *4.* Есть ли у тебя что-то, ради чего стоит жить? *5.* Вот ради этого я и пришел к тебе. *6.* Он никогда бы не сделал этого ради тебя.
● *1.* It's not going well, is it? *2.* It ain't over till it's over. *3.* It was the biggest mistake of my life. *4.* Do you have anything worth living for? *5.* That's what I came to see you about. *6.* He'd never do it for you.

**[93]** *1.* Чего бы я не сделал ради этого человека? *2.* Тебе не обязательно было делать это ради меня. *3.* Не могу поверить, что я это сказал, придурок. *4.* Почему мы до сих пор говорим об этом? *5.* Я не могу поверить, что мы говорим об этом. *6.* И у меня есть для вас небольшой сюрприз.
● *1.* What wouldn't I do for that man? *2.* You didn't have to do that for me. *3.* I can't believe I said that, you knucklehead. *4.* Why are we still talking about this? *5.* I can't believe we're talking about this. *6.* And I have a little surprise for you.

**[94]** *1.* Между вами что-то уже произошло, не так ли? *2.* Я на самом деле с нетерпением жду этого. *3.* И я с нетерпением жду того, что будет дальше. *4.* Почему бы тебе не посмотреть, куда ты идешь? *5.* Я просто хотел посмотреть, как у тебя дела. *6.* Я знаю, что ты всего лишь пытался помочь.
● *1.* Something already happened between you two, hasn't it? *2.* I'm actually looking forward to it. *3.* And I look forward to what comes next. *4.* Why don't you look where you're going? *5.* I just wanted to see how you're doing. *6.* I know you were only trying to help.

**[95]** *1.* С тех пор я ничего о нем не слышал. *2.* И с тех пор ты его не видел? *3.* Так что же нам делать до тех пор? *4.* Прошло много времени с тех пор, как я вернулся. *5.* Мы не такие уж разные, ты и я. *6.* Мы просто хотим, чтобы вы были в безопасности.

● *1.* I haven't heard from him since. *2.* And you haven't seen him since? *3.* So what do we do till then? *4.* Been a long time since I've been back. *5.* We're not so different, you and I. *6.* We just want you to be safe.

**[96]** *1.* Что я могу получить для тебя сегодня вечером? *2.* Ну, не всегда можно получить то, что хочешь. *3.* Вы когда-нибудь видели что-нибудь настолько красивое? *4.* Я сожалею о том, что я сделал с тобой. *5.* Я хочу, чтобы ты остался здесь со мной. *6.* Я не могу справиться с этим прямо сейчас.

● *1.* What can I get for you tonight? *2.* Well, you can't always get what you want. *3.* Have you ever seen anything so beautiful? *4.* I'm sorry for what I did to you. *5.* I want you to stay here with me. *6.* I can't deal with this right now.

**[97]** *1.* Ничего, с чем я бы не смог справиться. *2.* Нет ничего, с чем я не смог бы справиться. *3.* Ничего, с чем ты не смог бы справиться. *4.* Я не позволю, чтобы с тобой что-нибудь случилось. *5.* Что ж, я позволю тебе вернуться к работе. *6.* Я думаю, мы оба знаем, что это неправда.

● *1.* Nothing I couldn't handle. *2.* It's nothing I can't handle. *3.* Nothing you can't handle. *4.* I'm not gonna let anything happen to you. *5.* Well, I'll let you get back to work. *6.* I think we both know that's not true.

**[98]** *1.* Я знал, что ты не сможешь остаться в стороне. *2.* Мне очень жаль, что я заставил вас ждать. *3.* Я хочу сказать тебе кое-что очень важное. *4.* У меня есть к тебе вопрос кое-что важное. *5.* Я не думаю, что ты мне больше нравишься. *6.* Это был самый счастливый день в моей жизни.

● *1.* I knew you couldn't stay away. *2.* I'm so sorry to have kept you waiting. *3.* I have something very important to tell you. *4.* I've got something important to ask you. *5.* I don't think I like you anymore. *6.* That was the happiest day of my life.

**[99]** *1.* Я точно знаю, что ты имеешь в виду. *2.* Не говори этого, если ты не имеешь это в виду. *3.* Мама, папа, я не ждал тебя так рано. *4.* Он должен быть здесь с минуты на минуту. *5.* А если он этого не сделает, то это сделаю я. *6.* По крайней мере, один из нас это сделает.

● *1.* I know exactly what you mean. *2.* Don't say it if you don't mean it. *3.* Mum, dad, I wasn't expecting you so early. *4.* He should be here any minute. *5.* And if he doesn't, I will. *6.* At least one of us will.

**[100]** *1.* Что ж, вам просто придется подождать и посмотреть. *2.* Я не знаю, что бы мы делали без тебя. *3.* Сделайте что-то, чего вы никогда раньше не делали. *4.* Вы не делали этого раньше, не так ли? *5.* Вы когда-нибудь делали что-нибудь из этого раньше? *6.* Очень мило с вашей стороны, что это удалось.
● *1.* Well, you'll just have to wait and see. *2.* I don't know what we'd do without you. *3.* Do something you've never done before. *4.* You haven't done this before, have you? *5.* Have you ever done one of these before? *6.* Nice of you to make it.

**[101]** *1.* Я никогда не думал об этом таким образом. *2.* Знаешь, что мне только что пришло в голову? *3.* Я так горжусь тем, что я твоя жена. *4.* Он использовал это слово только в этот раз. *5.* Когда-нибудь ты скажешь мне спасибо за это. *6.* Ну, я не скажу, если ты не скажешь.
● *1.* I never thought of it that way. *2.* You know what just occurred to me? *3.* I'm so proud to be your wife. *4.* He used the word only for this nonce. *5.* You'll thank me for this someday. *6.* Well, I won't tell if you won't.

**[102]** *1.* Ну, я не скажу, если ты этого не скажешь. *2.* Тебе столько лет, на сколько ты себя чувствуешь. *3.* Расскажи мне, что ты на самом деле чувствуешь. *4.* Это все, что я получил на данный момент. *5.* На данный момент со мной все в порядке. *6.* Разве я не должен тебя об этом спрашивать?
● *1.* Well, I won't tell if you don't. *2.* You're only as old as you feel. *3.* Tell me how you really feel. *4.* That's all I got so far. *5.* I'm all right for the moment. *6.* Shouldn't I be asking you that?

**[103]** *1.* Как ты вообще можешь спрашивать меня об этом? *2.* Это было не очень умно, не так ли? *3.* Я знаю, ты не хочешь причинить мне боль. *4.* Я не хотел, чтобы это закончилось вот так! *5.* Когда ты разговаривал с ней в последний раз? *6.* С тех пор я с ним не разговаривал.
● *1.* How can you even ask me that? *2.* That wasn't very smart, was it? *3.* I know you don't want to hurt me. *4.* I didn't want it

to end this way! *5.* When did you talk to her last? *6.* I haven't talked to him since.

**[104]** *1.* Я не разговаривал с ним какое-то время. *2.* Да, мне бы хотелось, чтобы это было правдой. *3.* Ты правда только что спросил меня об этом? *4.* Чем меньше вы об этом знаете, тем лучше. *5.* Как ты думаешь, почему я привел тебя сюда? *6.* Просто оставь меня в покое на некоторое время.

● *1.* I haven't talked to him in a while. *2.* Yeah, I wish that were true. *3.* Did you really just ask me that? *4.* The less you know about it, the better. *5.* Why do you think I brought you here? *6.* Just leave me alone for a while.

**[105]** *1.* Просто забудь, что я что-то сказал, ладно? *2.* Для этого я должен стать кем-то другим. *3.* Почему бы вам не стать немного ближе друг к другу? *4.* Ты не можешь продолжать делать это со мной. *5.* Я не могу продолжать делать один и тот же выбор. *6.* Ты никогда не говорил мне, что ты женат.

● *1.* Just forget I said anything, okay? *2.* To do this, I must become someone else. *3.* Why don't you get a little closer together? *4.* You can't keep doing this to me. *5.* I can't keep making the same choices. *6.* You never told me you were married.

**[106]** *1.* С тех пор, как я впервые увидел тебя. *2.* Я, честно говоря, не знаю, о чем вы говорите. *3.* Вы не можете принять это на свой счет. *4.* Я хочу, чтобы это было сделано как можно скорее. *5.* Мне бы хотелось, чтобы мы никогда не встречались. *6.* Я не думаю, что мы когда-либо встречались.

● *1.* Since I first saw you. *2.* I honestly don't know what you're talking about. *3.* You can't take it personally. *4.* I want it done as soon as possible. *5.* I wish we'd never met. *6.* I don't think we've ever met.

**[107]** *1.* С ним все будет в порядке, я обещаю. *2.* Я не могу объяснить это вам прямо сейчас. *3.* Я имею в виду, ты знаешь, как это бывает. *4.* Я знаю, это звучит безумно, но это правда. *5.* Мне нужно, чтобы ты был честен со мной. *6.* Ты хочешь, чтобы я был честен с тобой?

● *1.* He'll be fine, I promise. *2.* I can't explain it to you right now. *3.* I mean, you know how it is. *4.* I know it sounds crazy, but it's true. *5.* I need you to be honest with me. *6.* You want me to be honest with you?

**[108]** *1.* Ну, дайте мне знать, если вам что-нибудь понадобится. *2.* Я здесь для тебя, когда тебе что-нибудь понадобится. *3.* Я даже не знал, что у тебя есть дочь. *4.* Когда у тебя в последний раз было свидание? *5.* Не с тех пор, как я встретил тебя. *6.* Не с тех пор, как я был ребенком.
● *1.* Well, let me know if you need anything. *2.* I'm here for you when you need anything. *3.* I didn't even know you had a daughter. *4.* When's the last time you had a date? *5.* Not since I met you. *6.* Not since I was a kid.

**[109]** *1.* У меня был один, когда я был ребенком. *2.* Говорила ли она о нем еще что-нибудь? *3.* Это всегда одна и та же старая история. *4.* Положите руки так, чтобы я мог их видеть. *5.* Я имел в виду то, что сказал ранее. *6.* Есть ли что-нибудь еще, что вы хотели бы знать?
● *1.* I had one when I was a kid. *2.* Did she say anything else about him? *3.* It's always the same old story. *4.* Put your hands where I can see them. *5.* I meant what I said earlier. *6.* Is there anything else you'd like to know?

**[110]** *1.* Я не думаю, что ты в это веришь. *2.* Ты так говоришь, как будто это что-то хорошее. *3.* Не говори обо мне так, будто меня здесь нет. *4.* У меня такое чувство, будто я тебя уже знаю. *5.* Я выгляжу так, будто со мной все в порядке? *6.* У меня такое чувство, будто я тебя откуда-то знаю.
● *1.* I don't think you believe that. *2.* You say that like it's a good thing. *3.* Don't talk about me like I'm not here. *4.* I feel like I already know you. *5.* Do I look like I'm okay? *6.* I feel like I know you from somewhere.

**[111]** *1.* Эй, ты не можешь со мной так разговаривать. *2.* Потому что я не хочу с тобой разговаривать. *3.* Я даже не могу сейчас с тобой разговаривать. *4.* Ты так говоришь, как будто это что-то плохое. *5.* Я не позволю, чтобы с тобой случилось что-то плохое. *6.* Есть ли что-нибудь еще, что ты можешь вспомнить?
● *1.* Hey, you can't talk to me like that. *2.* Because I don't want to talk to you. *3.* I can't even talk to you right now. *4.* You say that like it's a bad thing. *5.* I won't let anything bad happen to

you. *6.* Is there anything else you can remember?

**[112]** *1.* Я бы не принял это на свой счет. *2.* Никто никогда не спрашивал меня об этом раньше. *3.* Возможно, когда-нибудь мы сможем сделать это снова. *4.* Это самое хорошее время, как и любое другое. *5.* На данный момент больше никаких вопросов, Ваша Честь. *6.* Для меня большая честь наконец встретиться с вами.

● *1.* I wouldn't take it personally. *2.* No one's ever asked me that before. *3.* Maybe we can do it again sometime. *4.* It's as good a time as any. *5.* No further questions at this time, Your Honor. *6.* It's an honor to finally meet you.

**[113]** *1.* О, тебе бы это понравилось, не так ли? *2.* Это всегда возвращается к этому, не так ли? *3.* Не могу дождаться, чтобы увидеть тебя в нем. *4.* Вы действительно в это верите, не так ли? *5.* Вы действительно имели в виду то, что сказали? *6.* Это все, что я когда-либо хотел услышать.

● *1.* Oh, you'd love that, wouldn't you? *2.* It always comes back to that, doesn't it? *3.* Can't wait to see you in it. *4.* You really believe that, don't you? *5.* Did you really mean what you said? *6.* That's all I ever wanted to hear.

**[114]** *1.* Я просто хочу услышать, как ты это скажешь. *2.* Это именно то, что мне нужно было услышать. *3.* Почему бы вам не рассказать нам об этом? *4.* Почему бы тебе не рассказать мне, что происходит? *5.* Можете ли вы рассказать нам, что именно произошло? *6.* Я с нетерпением жду встречи с вами снова.

● *1.* I just wanna hear you say it. *2.* That's exactly what I needed to hear. *3.* Why don't you tell us about it? *4.* Why don't you tell me what's going on? *5.* Can you tell us exactly what happened? *6.* I look forward to seeing you again.

**[115]** *1.* Иди сюда, я хочу тебе кое-что показать. *2.* Я не думаю, что тебе следует здесь находиться. *3.* Ты даже не можешь находиться рядом со мной. *4.* Возможно, вы могли бы использовать один из них. *5.* Никогда не одно и то же место дважды. *6.* Чего бы это ни стоило, мне очень жаль.

● *1.* Come here, I want to show you something. *2.* I don't think you should be here. *3.* You can't even stand to be around me. *4.* Maybe you could use one of these. *5.* Never the same place twice. *6.* For what it's worth, I'm sorry.

**[116]** *1.* Ну, мы никогда не узнаем, не так ли? *2.* Что заставляет вас думать, что что-то не так? *3.* Разве это не заставляет вас чувствовать себя хорошо? *4.* Я никогда и ни о чем тебя не просил. *5.* Я пришел за тобой, как ты и просил. *6.* Я говорил тебе, что нам не следовало приходить сюда.
● *1.* Well, we'll never know, will we? *2.* What makes you think something's wrong? *3.* Doesn't that make you feel good? *4.* I never asked you for anything. *5.* I came for you, just like you asked. *6.* I told you we shouldn't have come here.

**[117]** *1.* Вы не знаете, когда остановиться, не так ли? *2.* Я имею в виду, в этом нет ничего страшного. *3.* Она чувствовала себя ужасно из-за этой ситуации. *4.* Я чувствую то же самое по поводу ситуации. *5.* Что ж, это очень любезно с вашей стороны. *6.* Как любезно с вашей стороны позволить мне прийти.
● *1.* You don't know when to quit, do you? *2.* I mean, it's no big deal. *3.* She felt lousy about the situation. *4.* I feel similarly about the situation. *5.* Well, that's very kind of you. *6.* How kind of you to let me come.

**[118]** *1.* Я не знал, что вы двое были так близки. *2.* Что заставляет тебя думать, что ты такой особенный? *3.* Или что-нибудь еще, если уж на то пошло. *4.* И это пошло куда бы я ни пошел. *5.* Ни за что на свете не пропустил бы этого. *6.* Она должна быть здесь с минуты на минуту.
● *1.* I didn't know you two were so close. *2.* What makes you think you're so special? *3.* Or anything else, for that matter. *4.* And it went wherever I did go. *5.* Wouldn't miss it for the world. *6.* She should be here any minute.

**[119]** *1.* Это была всего лишь одна из тех вещей. *2.* Пусть папа сделает это, папа делает это хорошо. *3.* Я даже не знаю, почему меня это беспокоит. *4.* Не могли бы вы выйти из машины, пожалуйста? *5.* Что, черт возьми, не так с этим парнем? *6.* Мы не могли держать руки подальше друг от друга.
● *1.* It was just one of those things. *2.* Let Daddy do it, Daddy does it good. *3.* I don't even know why I bother. *4.* Would you step out of the car, please? *5.* What the hell is wrong with this

guy? 6. We couldn't keep our hands off each other.

**[120]** *1.* Можете ли вы сказать мне, как туда добраться? *2.* Есть в ней что-то, чему я не доверяю. *3.* Это самая глупая вещь, которую я когда-либо слышал. *4.* Но есть одна вещь, которую ты не знаешь. *5.* Это лучшая новость, которую я слышал за весь день. *6.* Девушка, которую я никогда не думал, что увижу снова.

● *1.* Can you tell me how to get there? *2.* There's something about her I don't trust. *3.* That is the stupidest thing I've ever heard. *4.* But there's one thing you don't know. *5.* That's the best news I've heard all day. *6.* A girl I never thought I'd see again.

**[121]** *1.* Я позабочусь о том, чтобы она это получила. *2.* Я позабочусь, чтобы с ней все было в порядке. *3.* Мои мысли были где-то в другом месте. *4.* У меня все еще есть чувства к тебе. *5.* Я не могу себе представить, как это сделать. *6.* Ты самое прекрасное, что я когда-либо видел.

● *1.* I'll make sure she gets it. *2.* I'll make sure she's okay. *3.* My mind was elsewhere. *4.* I still have feelings for you. *5.* I can't imagine how. *6.* You're the most beautiful thing I've ever seen.

**[122]** *1.* Есть что-то, что не увидишь каждый день. *2.* Они жили в мире, где всем было все равно. *3.* О, слава богу, с тобой все в порядке. *4.* О, слава богу, что ты все еще здесь. *5.* Почему бы тебе не пойти и не узнать? *6.* Не то чтобы я мог об этом подумать.

● *1.* There's something you don't see every day. *2.* They lived in a world where noone cared. *3.* Oh, thank God you're okay. *4.* Oh, thank God you're still here. *5.* Why don't you go and find out? *6.* Not that I can think of.

**[123]** *1.* Я не причинил тебе вреда, не так ли? *2.* Я не думал, что он сможет это сделать. *3.* Зависит от того, как ты смотришь на это. *4.* Я мог бы задать вам тот же вопрос. *5.* Это не имеет большого значения, не так ли? *6.* Во всяком случае, то, что от него осталось.

● *1.* I didn't hurt you, did I? *2.* I didn't think he could do it. *3.* Depends on how you look at it. *4.* I could ask you the same question. *5.* It doesn't really matter, does it? *6.* What's left of it, anyway.

**[124]** *1.* Я не хочу иметь с этим ничего общего. *2.* Она не хочет иметь со мной ничего общего. *3.* Я не могу поверить, что ты мне не доверяешь. *4.* У него была другая точка зрения на этот счет. *5.* Ты не сможешь избавиться от меня так просто. *6.* Мне жаль, что тебе пришлось через это пройти.

● *1.* I don't want anything to do with this. *2.* She doesn't want anything to do with me. *3.* I can't believe you don't trust me. *4.* He had a different standpoint on the matter. *5.* You can't get rid of me that easy. *6.* I'm sorry you had to go through that.

**[125]** *1.* Я не могу пройти через это еще раз. *2.* За последнее время тебе пришлось через многое пройти. *3.* Огромное спасибо за то, что вы у нас есть. *4.* Я не хочу, чтобы ты был в моем доме. *5.* Я не виню тебя за то, что ты расстроен. *6.* Мы могли бы очень весело провести время вместе.

● *1.* I can't go through it again. *2.* You've been through a lot lately. *3.* Thank you so much for having us. *4.* I don't want you in my house. *5.* I don't blame you for being upset. *6.* We could have a lot of fun together.

**[126]** *1.* Возьмите это из этого, если это будет иначе. *2.* Вы когда-нибудь видели что-нибудь подобное раньше? *3.* Мне жаль, что я так поступил с тобой. *4.* Извините, это заняло у меня так много времени. *5.* Ну, я ничего не могу с этим поделать. *6.* Знаешь, что может заставить тебя чувствовать себя лучше?

● *1.* Take this from this if this be otherwise. *2.* Have you ever seen anything like this before? *3.* I'm sorry to do this to you. *4.* Sorry it took me so long. *5.* Well, I can't help it. *6.* You know what might make you feel better?

**[127]** *1.* Я не могу заставить тебя поверить в это. *2.* Ты не можешь заставить меня что-либо сделать. *3.* И это должно заставить меня чувствовать себя лучше? *4.* Не могли бы вы дать нам несколько минут? *5.* Я здесь, чтобы дать тебе то, что ты хочешь. *6.* Я не думаю, что это было бы разумно.

● *1.* I can't make you believe it. *2.* You can't force me to do anything. *3.* And that's supposed to make me feel better? *4.* Could you give us a few minutes? *5.* I'm here to give you what you want. *6.* I don't think that would be wise.

**[128]** *1.* Это то, что ты сказал в прошлый раз. *2.* Все будет не так, как в прошлый раз. *3.* Вы когда-нибудь думали о том, чтобы выйти замуж? *4.* Спасибо, что встретились со мной в такой короткий срок. *5.* Поднимите руки так, чтобы я мог их видеть. *6.* Я не буду играть с тобой в эту игру.

● *1.* That's what you said last time. *2.* It won't be like last time. *3.* Have you ever thought about getting married? *4.* Thanks for seeing me on such short notice. *5.* Get your hands where I can see them. *6.* I'm not gonna play this game with you.

**[129]** *1.* Откуда ты узнал, что у меня день рождения? *2.* Ты лучший друг, который у меня когда-либо был. *3.* Есть только один человек, который может мне помочь. *4.* Это был опыт, который бывает раз в жизни. *5.* Мы с тобой не похожи друг на друга. *6.* Их отношения не похожи ни на какие другие.

● *1.* How did you know it was my birthday? *2.* You're the best friend I've ever had. *3.* There's only one person who can help me. *4.* It was a once-in-a-lifetime experience. *5.* You and I are nothing alike. *6.* Their relationship is unlike any other.

**[130]** *1.* Почему бы нам просто не забыть об этом? *2.* Я не хочу, чтобы ты куда-то уходил. *3.* Делайте то, что у вас получается лучше всего. *4.* У меня это получается лучше, чем у тебя. *5.* Это самая странная вещь, которую вы когда-либо видели. *6.* Не веди себя так, как будто ты не знаешь.

● *1.* Why don't we just forget it? *2.* I don't want you to go anywhere. *3.* Do what you do best. *4.* I'm better at it than you are. *5.* It's the weirdest thing you ever saw. *6.* Don't act like you don't know.

**[131]** *1.* Возможно, у нас больше никогда не будет такой возможности. *2.* Это самая сумасшедшая вещь, которую я когда-либо слышал. *3.* Что ж, это очень щедро с вашей стороны. *4.* У меня есть для тебя кое-что особенное. *5.* Его реакция на эту новость была просто «черт возьми». *6.* На этот раз тебе это не сойдет с рук.

● *1.* We may never have this opportunity again. *2.* That's the craziest thing I've ever heard. *3.* Well, that's very generous of you. *4.* I got something special for you. *5.* His reaction to the news was simply, 'drat'. *6.* You won't get away with it this time.

**[132]** *1.* Я бы никому не позволил причинить тебе боль. *2.*

Это то, что вы сказали в прошлом году. *3.* Ты никогда не спрашиваешь меня, чего я хочу. *4.* Зависит от того, как вы на это смотрите. *5.* Мы будем там прежде, чем ты это узнаешь. *6.* И есть еще много всего, откуда это взялось.

● *1.* I wouldn't let anybody hurt you. *2.* That's what you said last year. *3.* You never ask me what I want. *4.* Depends how you look at it. *5.* We'll be there before you know it. *6.* And there's plenty more where that came from.

**[133]** *1.* Я не буду отвечать ни на какие вопросы. *2.* Если бы я сказал тебе, ты бы мне не поверил. *3.* Я просто хочу, чтобы ты снова мне поверил. *4.* Мне нужно, чтобы ты поверил мне прямо сейчас. *5.* Как насчет того, чтобы я купил тебе выпить? *6.* Я упал, но со мной все в порядке.

● *1.* I will not be taking any questions. *2.* If I told you, you wouldn't believe me. *3.* I just want you to trust me again. *4.* I need you to trust me right now. *5.* How about I buy you a drink? *6.* I took a tumble but I'm okay.

**[134]** *1.* Не могли бы вы подойти сюда на секунду? *2.* Рэй сказал, что у тебя все равно проблемы. *3.* Я бы хотел, чтобы мы остались здесь навсегда. *4.* На самом деле, я беру свои слова обратно. *5.* Я не могу поверить, что ты солгал мне. *6.* Ей нужно было больше денег, чтобы купить машину.

● *1.* Could you come here for a second? *2.* Ray said you were in trouble anyway. *3.* I wish we could stay here forever. *4.* Actually, I take that back. *5.* I can't believe you lied to me. *6.* She needed more dosh to buy the car.

**[135]** *1.* В конце концов, это было не так уж и плохо. *2.* Я уверен, что у него были свои причины. *3.* Смотри на меня, когда я с тобой разговариваю. *4.* Я хотел убедиться, что с тобой все в порядке. *5.* Я уверен, что мы сможем что-нибудь придумать. *6.* У меня нет особого выбора, не так ли?

● *1.* After all, it wasn't so bad. *2.* I'm sure he had his reasons. *3.* Look at me when I'm talking to you. *4.* I wanted to make sure you were okay. *5.* I'm sure we can work something out. *6.* I don't have much choice, do I?

**[136]** *1.* О, Боже мой, я не могу этого вынести. *2.* Что самое худшее, что ты когда-либо делал? *3.* Я имею в виду, что самое худшее может случиться? *4.* У меня есть кое-что интересное, чтобы показать вам. *5.* Всего один человек может изменить вашу жизнь навсегда. *6.* Случалось ли что-нибудь подобное когда-нибудь раньше?

● *1.* Oh, my God, I can't take it. *2.* What's the worst thing you've ever done? *3.* I mean, what's the worst that can happen? *4.* I have something interesting to show you. *5.* Just one person can change your life forever. *6.* Has anything like this ever happened before?

**[137]** *1.* Я рад, что вы, ребята, смогли это сделать. *2.* У меня очень плохое предчувствие по этому поводу. *3.* С таким же успехом это мог быть я. *4.* Я дам вам знать, когда это будет сделано. *5.* Ну и что, по-твоему, мне следует делать? *6.* У меня было предчувствие, что я найду тебя здесь.

● *1.* I'm glad you guys could make it. *2.* I have a really bad feeling about this. *3.* It might as well be me. *4.* I'll let you know when it's done. *5.* Well, what do you think I should do? *6.* I had a feeling I'd find you here.

**[138]** *1.* Вы действительно хотите, чтобы я ответил на это? *2.* Забудьте все, что вы знали, и начнем все сначала. *3.* В последнее время у меня часто болит голова. *4.* Мне жаль, что я не мог быть более полезным. *5.* Это значит, что он все еще в моих руках. *6.* Наверное, я никогда особо об этом не думал.

● *1.* You really want me to answer that? *2.* Forget what you know and let's start fresh. *3.* I have had frequent headaches lately. *4.* I'm sorry I couldn't be more helpful. *5.* That means he's still mine to find. *6.* I guess I never really thought about it.

**[139]** *1.* Я говорю вам это для вашего же блага. *2.* Ради вашего блага, я надеюсь, что вы правы. *3.* Иди сюда, позволь мне кое-что тебе показать. *4.* Я не виню тебя за то, что ты ненавидишь меня. *5.* Почему ты не можешь быть больше похож на своего брата? *6.* Ну ты и сам не так уж и плох.

● *1.* I'm telling you this for your own good. *2.* For your sake, I hope you're right. *3.* Come here, let me show you something. *4.* I don't blame you for hating me. *5.* Why can't you be more like your brother? *6.* Well, you're not so bad yourself.

**[140]** *1.* Ты знаешь это лучше, чем любой из нас. *2.* Ты самый сильный человек, которого я когда-либо встречал. *3.*

Почему я должен верить всему, что ты говоришь? *4.* Можем ли мы купить еще что-нибудь из этих вещей? *5.* Я надеюсь увидеть вас снова в ближайшее время. *6.* Я просто не хочу, чтобы кто-нибудь пострадал.

● *1.* You know that better than any of us. *2.* You're the strongest person I've ever met. *3.* Why should I believe anything you say? *4.* Can we buy some more of these things? *5.* I hope to see you again soon. *6.* I just don't want anybody to get hurt.

**[141]** *1.* Ты знаешь, я не могу на это ответить. *2.* Не могли бы вы ответить на несколько вопросов? *3.* Где-то, где ты его никогда не найдешь. *4.* У тебя есть что-то еще на уме? *5.* Вы ведь ничего об этом не знаете, не так ли? *6.* Мы ведь не встречались раньше, не так ли?

● *1.* You know I can't answer that. *2.* Would you mind answering a few questions? *3.* Somewhere you'll never find it. *4.* You have something else in mind? *5.* You wouldn't know anything about that, would you? *6.* We haven't met before, have we?

**[142]** *1.* Ты ведь за этим пришел сюда, не так ли? *2.* Вы выбрали не того человека для этой работы. *3.* Мне нужно мое одеяло, чтобы чувствовать себя уютно. *4.* Вы понятия не имеете, на что я способен. *5.* Что бы ни случилось, я всегда буду любить тебя. *6.* Я бы не хотел, если вы не возражаете.

● *1.* That's what you came here for, isn't it? *2.* You've got the wrong man for the job. *3.* I need my blankie to feel cozy. *4.* You have no idea what I'm capable of. *5.* Whatever happens, I will always love you. *6.* I'd rather not, if you don't mind.

**[143]** *1.* У меня есть для тебя очень важная работа. *2.* Не делайте это сложнее, чем оно уже есть. *3.* Но к тому времени было уже слишком поздно. *4.* Что ж, это то, что нам нужно выяснить. *5.* Что вы когда-либо делали со своей жизнью? *6.* Я только что разговаривал с ним по телефону.

● *1.* I have a very important job for you. *2.* Don't make this harder than it already is. *3.* But by then it was too late. *4.* Well, that's what we need to find out. *5.* What have you ever done with your life? *6.* I just got off the phone with him.

**[144]** *1.* Мы бы не пропустили это ни за что на свете. *2.* Ты просто пытаешься заставить меня чувствовать себя лучше. *3.* Я бы не сделал этого на твоем месте. *4.* Тебе не следовало идти на все эти неприятности. 5. Если этого не сделаете вы, это сделает кто-то другой. 6. Он был в ярости, когда узнал об этом.

• 1. We wouldn't miss it for the world. 2. You're just trying to make me feel better. 3. I wouldn't do that if I was you. 4. You shouldn't have gone to all this trouble. 5. If you don't, somebody else will. 6. He was livid when he found out.

[145] 1. Надеюсь, ты не с чем-то не справишься. 2. Я не могу поверить, что я был таким глупым. 3. Что ж, ваше предположение так же хорошо, как и мое. 4. Ты только что это придумал, не так ли? 5. Вы не услышали ни слова из того, что я сказал. 6. Ты имеешь в виду, что тебя не услышали?

• 1. I hope you're not coming down with something. 2. I can't believe I was so stupid. 3. Well, your guess is as good as mine. 4. You just made that up, didn't you? 5. You haven't heard a word I've said. 6. You mean you ain't heard?

[146] 1. Я бы никогда не попросил тебя сделать это. 2. Я не вижу причин, почему бы вам этого не сделать. 3. Вы так и не ответили на мой вопрос. 4. Вы уверены, что это был не несчастный случай? 5. Я получил те же приказы, что и ты. 6. Она оставила сообщение, но оно осталось без ответа.

• 1. I would never ask you to do that. 2. I see no reason why you shouldn't. 3. You still haven't answered my question. 4. Are you sure it wasn't an accident? 5. I got the same orders as you. 6. She left a message, but it remained unanswered.

[147] 1. Твоя догадка так же хороша как и моя. 2. Дорогая, ты уверена, что с тобой все в порядке? 3. Я расскажу тебе как-нибудь в другой раз. 4. Я никогда не мог обмануть тебя, не так ли? 5. Мы не знаем, с чем здесь имеем дело. 6. Я пришел сюда не для того, чтобы спорить.

• 1. Your guess is as good as mine. 2. Honey, are you sure you're okay? 3. I'll tell you some other time. 4. I never could fool you, could I? 5. We don't know what we're dealing with here. 6. I didn't come here to argue.

[148] 1. Двое мужчин около 20 лет, оба без сознания. 2. Вы можете уйти в любой момент, когда захотите. 3. Знаешь, что заставило бы меня чувствовать себя лучше? 4. Ситуация была слишком сложной, чтобы ее можно было решить. 5. Я

не буду стоять у тебя на пути. *6.* Ты знаешь, я никогда не причиню тебе вреда.

● *1.* Two men, mid-20s, both unconscious. *2.* You can leave anytime you want. *3.* You know what would make me feel better? *4.* The situation was too complex to solve. *5.* I won't stand in your way. *6.* You know I'd never hurt you.

**[149]** *1.* Я понятия не имею, как оно туда попало. *2.* Ты ни на что не похожа на нее. *3.* Не делайте тех же ошибок, что и я. *4.* Но на этот раз ты зашел слишком далеко. *5.* Я не могу поверить, что ты заставляешь меня это делать. *6.* Ты слышал, как он меня только что назвал?

● *1.* I have no idea how it got there. *2.* You don't look anything like her. *3.* Don't make the same mistakes I did. *4.* But this time you've gone too far. *5.* I can't believe you're making me do this. *6.* Did you hear what he just called me?

**[150]** *1.* Они не будут действовать, поэтому я решил, что буду. *2.* Я надеялся, что больше никогда тебя не увижу. *3.* Вы никогда ни к чему не относитесь серьезно. *4.* Я не могу снова пойти по этой дороге. *5.* Ты заставляешь меня чувствовать себя очень, очень некомфортно. *6.* Я не хочу, чтобы ты чувствовал себя некомфортно.

● *1.* They wouldn't act, so I decided I would. *2.* I was hoping I'd never see you again. *3.* You never take anything seriously. *4.* I can't go down that road again. *5.* You're making me feel very, very uncomfortable. *6.* I don't want you to feel uncomfortable.

**[151]** *1.* Дайте мне знать, если найдете что-нибудь еще. *2.* Извините, что вы проделали весь этот путь зря. *3.* Как можно быть таким спокойным по этому поводу? *4.* Я не хочу, чтобы ты об этом беспокоился. *5.* Что, черт возьми, не так с вами двумя? *6.* Только еще один человек знает, чем я занимаюсь.

● *1.* Let me know if you find anything else. *2.* Sorry you came all this way for nothing. *3.* How can you be so calm about this? *4.* I don't want you to worry about it. *5.* What the hell is wrong with you two? *6.* Only one other person knows what I do.

**[152]** *1.* Я думал, что посмотрю, как у тебя дела. *2.* Когда вы в последний раз разговаривали с ним? *3.* Что ж, нам нужно с чего-то начинать. *4.* Я имел в виду это в хорошем смысле. *5.* Жаль, что я не смог приехать сюда раньше. *6.* Я не плачу вам за то, чтобы вы думали.

● *1.* I thought I'd see how you were doing. *2.* When did you last speak to him? *3.* Well, we have to start somewhere. *4.* I meant it in a good way. *5.* Sorry I couldn't get here sooner. *6.* I don't pay you to think.

**[153]** *1.* Чем меньше вы знаете, тем в большей безопасности вы находитесь. *2.* Мне жаль, что я даже поднял этот вопрос. *3.* Мне нужно побыть какое-то время в одиночестве. *4.* В этом и суть дела, не так ли? *5.* Я не могу пойти домой в таком виде. *6.* Ребята, могу ли я принести вам что-нибудь еще?

● *1.* The less you know, the safer you are. *2.* I'm sorry I even brought it up. *3.* I need to be alone for a while. *4.* That's the deal, isn't it? *5.* I can't go home like this. *6.* Can I get you guys anything else?

**[154]** *1.* Я знаю, как сильно ты заботишься обо мне. *2.* Сейчас самое подходящее время, как и любое другое. *3.* Мне нужно было сделать так, чтобы это выглядело хорошо. *4.* Ты можешь бежать, но ты не можешь спрятаться. *5.* Никто и никогда не сможет занять твое место. *6.* Это может занять больше времени, чем мы думали.

● *1.* I know how much you care about me. *2.* Now is as good a time as any. *3.* I had to make it look good. *4.* You can run, but you can't hide. *5.* No one could ever take your place. *6.* That might take longer than we thought.

**[155]** *1.* То же самое касается и остальных из вас. *2.* Сэм, у тебя в голове не был Бог. *3.* У тебя никогда не было никакой надежды, брат. *4.* Нет причин, по которым вам это следует делать. *5.* Я рад, что у нас состоялся этот разговор. *6.* У меня так и не было возможности попрощаться.

● *1.* Same goes for the rest of you. *2.* It wasn't God inside your head, Sam. *3.* There was never any hope for you, brother. *4.* There's no reason why you should. *5.* I'm glad we had this talk. *6.* I never got a chance to say goodbye.

**[156]** *1.* Я говорил тебе, что он что-то задумал. *2.* Думаю, я буду скучать по тебе больше всего. *3.* Ты должен идти туда, куда он тебя приведет. *4.* С этого времени так я считаю твою любовь. *5.* Он так и не узнал, что его поразило. *6.* Я дам вам знать, когда мы его найдем.

● *1.* I told you he was up to something. *2.* I think I'll miss you most of all. *3.* You gotta go where it takes you. *4.* From this time such I account thy love. *5.* He never knew what hit him. *6.* I'll let you know when we find it.

[157] *1.* Они думают, что никогда больше нас не найдут. *2.* У меня не хватило сил сказать тебе это лично. *3.* Она получила травму и поэтому не сможет играть. *4.* Я понятия не имею, о ком ты говоришь. *5.* Я думаю, ты знаешь, о ком я говорю. *6.* Ты не заботишься ни о ком, кроме себя.

● *1.* They think that they'll never find us again. *2.* I wasn't strong enough to tell you face-to-face. *3.* She was injured, hence she cannot play. *4.* I have no idea who you're talking about. *5.* I think you know who I'm talking about. *6.* You don't care about anyone but yourself.

[158] *1.* Я сделаю ему предложение, от которого он не сможет отказаться. *2.* Мне жаль, что я звоню тебе так поздно. *3.* Я просто хочу, чтобы меня оставили в покое. *4.* Вы хотите, чтобы вас оставили в полном одиночестве? *5.* Больше всего он хотел, чтобы его оставили в покое. *6.* Я не имел в виду те вещи, которые сказал.

● *1.* I'll make him an offer he can't refuse. *2.* I'm sorry to call you so late. *3.* I just wanna be left alone. *4.* Do you long to be left all alone? *5.* He chiefly wanted to be left alone. *6.* I didn't mean those things I said.

[159] *1.* Расскажите нам что-нибудь, чего мы не знаем. *2.* Назовите мне хотя бы одну причину, почему бы и нет. *3.* Им не хватало сотрудников, и им требовалось больше сотрудников. *4.* Я же говорил тебе, что ты не поймешь. *5.* С тех пор, как я была маленькой девочкой. *6.* Ей стало плохо, и ей пришлось бросить мяч.

● *1.* Tell us something we don't know. *2.* Give me one reason why not. *3.* They were short-staffed and needed more staffers. *4.* I told you you wouldn't understand. *5.* Ever since I was a little girl. *6.* She felt sick and had to hurl.

[160] *1.* Призрак исчез так же быстро, как и появился. *2.* Я чувствую то же самое по отношению к тебе. *3.* Ну, ты не можешь винить меня за попытку. *4.* Я бы не доверял ему на

твоем месте. *5.* Я не тот человек, о котором ты думаешь. *6.* Это тот парень, о котором я тебе говорил.

• *1.* The apparition vanished as quickly as it appeared. *2.* I feel the same way about you. *3.* Well, you can't blame me for trying. *4.* I wouldn't trust him if I were you. *5.* I'm not the man you think I am. *6.* This is the guy I told you about.

**[161]** *1.* К счастью, короткая встреча оставила время для обеда. *2.* Я никогда раньше ни в кого не стрелял. *3.* Вам не обязательно быть злым по этому поводу. *4.* Я добрался сюда так быстро, как только мог. *5.* Он был в восторге от предложения о работе. *6.* Верите ли вы в любовь с первого взгляда?

• *1.* The mercifully short meeting left time for lunch. *2.* I never shot anyone before. *3.* You don't have to be mean about it. *4.* I got here as fast as I could. *5.* He was ecstatic about the job offer. *6.* Do you believe in love at first sight?

**[162]** *1.* Я не имею в виду это в плохом смысле. *2.* Позвольте мне еще раз взглянуть на эту карту. *3.* Я не веду себя неразумно, не так ли? *4.* Где ты был в ту ночь, когда она исчезла? *5.* Ты действительно беспокоишься о нем, не так ли? *6.* Он нуждается в тебе сейчас больше, чем когда-либо.

• *1.* I don't mean that in a bad way. *2.* Let me see that map again. *3.* I'm not being unreasonable, am I? *4.* Where were you the night she disappeared? *5.* You're really worried about him, aren't you? *6.* He needs you now more than ever.

**[163]** *1.* Почему бы тебе не взять на себя управление? *2.* Слушай, я не тот, кем ты меня считаешь. *3.* Я люблю острую пищу, а он предпочитает острую. *4.* Что бы вы ни делали, не трогайте это. *5.* Вы не ожидали, что это произойдет, не так ли? *6.* Что, черт возьми, не так с этими людьми?

• *1.* Why don't you take over? *2.* Look, I'm not who you think I am. *3.* I like spicy food, whereas he prefers mild. *4.* Whatever you do, don't touch it. *5.* Didn't see that one coming, did you? *6.* What the hell is wrong with these people?

**[164]** *1.* Они случайно прибыли в одно и то же время. *2.* Я не могу в таком виде выходить на публику. *3.* Они были в долгу перед ними за помощь. *4.* Я здесь не для того, чтобы сражаться с тобой. *5.* Давайте продолжим с того места, на котором мы остановились. *6.* Он не остановится, пока это не будет сделано.

● *1.* They coincidentally arrived at the same time. *2.* I can't go out in public like this. *3.* They were indebted to them for their help. *4.* I'm not here to fight you. *5.* Let's pick up where we left off. *6.* He will not cease until it's done.

**[165]** *1.* Ты не тот человек, каким я тебя считал. *2.* Они изо всех сил пытались дышать под водой. *3.* Как насчет того, чтобы я вызвал тебе такси? *4.* Мне просто показалось, что я что-то услышал. *5.* Она стала свободно говорить после жизни за границей. *6.* Кто лучший пилот, которого вы когда-либо видели?

● *1.* You're not the man I thought you were. *2.* They struggled to breathe underwater. *3.* How about I call you a cab? *4.* I just thought I heard something. *5.* She became fluent after living abroad. *6.* Who's the best pilot you ever saw?

**[166]** *1.* Она получила новости, которые привели ее в восторг. *2.* Я бы хотел, чтобы тебе не приходилось этого делать. *3.* Я не верю ничему из того, что ты говоришь. *4.* Я думаю, нам стоит встретиться с другими людьми. *5.* Я знаю, что ты никогда не сможешь меня простить. *6.* Поможет ли вам от этого почувствовать себя лучше?

● *1.* She received news that left her ecstatic. *2.* I wish you didn't have to. *3.* I don't believe anything you say. *4.* I think we should see other people. *5.* I know you can never forgive me. *6.* Would that make you feel better?

**[167]** *1.* Я знаю, что поможет тебе почувствовать себя лучше. *2.* Так рада, что вы смогли присоединиться к нам. *3.* Как мило с вашей стороны присоединиться к нам. *4.* Ключ был слишком ржавый, чтобы его можно было использовать. *5.* Баффи не похожа ни на кого другого в мире. *6.* Есть ли у меня неприятный запах изо рта?

● *1.* I know what'll make you feel better. *2.* So glad you could join us. *3.* How nice of you to join us. *4.* The wrench was too rusty to use. *5.* Buffy's like nobody else in the world. *6.* Do I have bad breath?

**[168]** *1.* Что ж, я здесь, если я тебе понадоблюсь. *2.* Я буду прямо снаружи, если я тебе понадоблюсь. *3.* Я совершил самую большую ошибку в своей жизни. *4.* Лучшая работа, которая у меня когда-либо была. *5.* Я здесь не для того, чтобы судить тебя. *6.* Мне не следовало быть с ним так строгим.

● *1.* Well, I'm here if you need me. *2.* I'll be right outside if you need me. *3.* I made the biggest mistake of my life. *4.* Best job I ever had. *5.* I'm not here to judge you. *6.* I shouldn't have been so hard on him.

**[169]** *1.* Пьяный водитель изо всех сил пытался не заснуть. *2.* Как я могу внести свой вклад в команду? *3.* Я не буду принимать это на свой счет. *4.* Он вел себя бесполезно, когда она нуждалась в нем. *5.* Я сам не смог бы выразить это лучше. *6.* Я люблю тебя больше, чем могут выразить слова.

● *1.* The groggy driver struggled to stay awake. *2.* How can I contribute to the team? *3.* I won't take it personally. *4.* He acted unhelpful when she needed him. *5.* I couldn't have put it better myself. *6.* I love thee more than words can wield.

**[170]** *1.* Он был слишком упрям, чтобы изменить свое мнение. *2.* Следите за тем, чтобы он держал рот на замке. *3.* Ты никогда не звонишь, ты никогда не пишешь. *4.* Ты боишься или что-то в этом роде? *5.* Мне жаль, что я потратил так много времени. *6.* У нас с тобой есть что-то общее.

● *1.* He was too stubborn to change his mind. *2.* Make sure he keeps his mouth shut. *3.* You never call, you never write. *4.* Are you scared or something? *5.* I'm sorry I took so long. *6.* You and I have something in common.

**[171]** *1.* От природы она была талантлива в игре на фортепиано. *2.* Когда вы в последний раз видели своего мужа? *3.* А теперь иди домой и поцелуй свою жену. *4.* Ты правда думаешь, что у папы есть план? *5.* Она регулярно занимается игрой на фортепиано каждый день. *6.* Мы думали, что больше никогда тебя не увидим.

● *1.* She was naturally talented at playing the piano. *2.* When did you last see your husband? *3.* Now go home and kiss your wife. *4.* Do you really think dad has a plan? *5.* She routinely practices her piano every day. *6.* We thought we'd never see you again.

**[172]** *1.* Ты не слушаешь ни слова, которое я говорю. *2.* Не в то время, которое у нас есть. *3.* Я не думаю, что нас должным образом представили. *4.* Ты под кайфом или что-то в этом роде? *5.* По крайней мере, это было похоже на бутылку. *6.* Что-то не так с твоей ногой, мальчик?

● *1.* You're not listening to a word I'm saying. *2.* Not in the time we have. *3.* I don't think we've been properly introduced. *4.* Are you high or something? *5.* At least, it looked like a bottle. *6.* Something wrong with your leg, boy?

**[173]** *1.* Я не думаю, что я следую за тобой. *2.* Вы даже не знаете, что означает это слово. *3.* Я просто рассказываю вам то, что я видел. *4.* Я могу отвезти тебя к нему прямо сейчас. *5.* Они жили внутри страны и редко видели океан. *6.* Волосы у нее были темные, как черное дерево.

● *1.* I don't think I follow you. *2.* You don't even know what the word means. *3.* I'm just telling you what I saw. *4.* I can take you to see him now. *5.* They lived inland and rarely saw the ocean. *6.* Her hair was as dark as ebony.

**[174]** *1.* Робот вышел из строя и вышел из строя. *2.* Хотя он так и не стал моим мужем. *3.* С тех пор он вырос в геометрической прогрессии. *4.* У них была сильная зависимость друг от друга. *5.* Читали какие-нибудь хорошие книги в последнее время? *6.* Я подумал, что ты, возможно, захочешь пойти с нами.

● *1.* The robot malfunctioned and went haywire. *2.* Although he never became my husband. *3.* It's grown exponentially since then. *4.* They had a strong dependence on each other. *5.* Read any good books lately? *6.* I thought you might like to come along.

**[175]** *1.* Вы будете говорить только тогда, когда с вами разговаривают. *2.* У него была внутренняя реакция на эту новость. *3.* Я был так же удивлён, как и ты. *4.* Она позвонила больной, потому что ей было плохо. *5.* Я рад, потому что у меня хорошие оценки. *6.* Они были так же удивлены, как и мы.

● *1.* You will speak only when spoken to. *2.* He had a visceral response to the news. *3.* I was as surprised as you were. *4.* She called in sick because she was unwell. *5.* I'm happy cus I got good grades. *6.* They were as surprised as we were.

**[176]** *1.* Он поцеловал меня, но он меня не любит. *2.* Я надеюсь, что у вас была приятная поездка. *3.* Мне жаль, что я когда-либо сомневался в тебе. *4.* Я ни на секунду не сомневался в тебе. *5.* Почему бы тебе не пригласить ее на свидание? *6.* Оставайся на низком уровне, оставайся на низком уровне.

● *1.* He kissed me, but he doesn't love me. *2.* I trust you had a pleasant trip. *3.* I'm sorry I ever doubted you. *4.* I never doubted you for a second. *5.* Why don't you ask her out? *6.* Stay low, stay low.

**[177]** *1.* Пообещай мне, что больше не будешь этого делать. *2.* Я же говорил тебе никогда не называть меня так. *3.* У тебя есть другие вещи, о которых стоит беспокоиться. *4.* Я сказал некоторые вещи, которых мне не следовало говорить. *5.* Это самая крутая вещь, которую я когда-либо видел. *6.* В любви и на войне все средства хороши.

● *1.* Promise me you won't do it again. *2.* I told you never to call me that. *3.* You've got other things to worry about. *4.* I said some things I shouldn't have. *5.* This is the coolest thing I've ever seen. *6.* All's fair in love and war.

**[178]** *1.* Это самая смешная вещь, которую я когда-либо слышал. *2.* Меньшее, что ты можешь сделать, это поблагодарить меня. *3.* Даже несмотря на то, что ты спал с моей женой. *4.* Что-нибудь конкретное я могу вам помочь найти? *5.* Успех компании до сих пор не имел себе равных. *6.* Новая политика может поставить под угрозу их шансы.

● *1.* That's the most ridiculous thing I've ever heard. *2.* The least you could do is thank me. *3.* Even though you slept with my wife. *4.* Anything in particular I can help you find? *5.* The company's success had hitherto been unmatched. *6.* The new policy could jeopardize their chances.

**[179]** *1.* Эх, у меня есть сомнения на этот счет. *2.* Вы действительно ожидаете, что я поверю в это? *3.* Даже если бы я захотел, я бы не смог. *4.* Не могли бы вы извинить нас на секунду? *5.* Один неверный шаг может стать для вас последним! *6.* Мы не виделись с тобой какое-то время.

● *1.* Ehh, I have my doubts about it. *2.* Do you really expect me to believe that? *3.* Even if I wanted to, I couldn't. *4.* Could you excuse us for a second? *5.* One false step could be your last! *6.*

We haven't seen you in a while.

**[180]** *1.* Буря прошла так же быстро, как и возникла. *2.* Вы действительно отправили бы свою жену в тюрьму? *3.* Что ж, ни одно доброе дело не остается безнаказанным. *4.* Я говорю тебе это уже в шестой раз. *5.* Я не получал столько удовольствия уже много лет. *6.* Я не хочу, чтобы ты в этом участвовал.

● *1.* The tempest passed as quickly as it came. *2.* You'd actually send your wife to prison? *3.* Well, no good deed goes unpunished. *4.* This is the sixth time I've told you. *5.* I haven't had this much fun in years. *6.* I don't want you involved.

**[181]** *1.* Мне нужно, чтобы ты был со мной откровенен. *2.* Я уверен, что у него есть веская причина. *3.* Но я не смог довести это до конца. *4.* Он почувствовал себя одиноким после того, как его друзья ушли. *5.* Я думаю, что здесь вы совершаете большую ошибку. *6.* У тебя нет ноги, на которой можно стоять.

● *1.* I need you to be straight with me. *2.* I'm sure he has a good reason. *3.* But I couldn't go through with it. *4.* He felt lonesome after his friends left. *5.* I think you're making a big mistake here. *6.* You don't have a leg to stand on.

**[182]** *1.* Это еще одна причина, по которой я здесь. *2.* Что ж, будем надеяться, что до этого не дойдет. *3.* Пожалуйста, повесьте трубку и попробуйте позвонить еще раз. *4.* Самая проклятая вещь, которую я когда-либо видел. *5.* Ну, это один из способов взглянуть на это. *6.* Это самая печальная вещь, которую я когда-либо слышал.

● *1.* That's the other reason I'm here. *2.* Well, let's hope it doesn't come to that. *3.* Please hang up and try your call again. *4.* Damnedest thing I ever saw. *5.* Well, that's one way of looking at it. *6.* That's the saddest thing I've ever heard.

**[183]** *1.* Она не могла поверить в наглость этого придурка. *2.* На медовый месяц она купила новое нижнее белье. *3.* Давай просто забудем, что это когда-либо происходило. *4.* Это вторая пуля, которую я остановил ради тебя. *5.* И именно на этом мы стоим сегодня вечером. *6.* Я был в таком стрессе в последнее время.

● *1.* She couldn't believe the audacity of the shithead. *2.* She bought new lingerie for the honeymoon. *3.* Let's just forget it ever happened. *4.* That's the second bullet I stopped for you. *5.* And that's where we stand tonight. *6.* I've been so stressed lately.

**[184]** *1.* Задняя часть здания была окрашена в синий цвет. *2.* Я не хочу, чтобы эти два убийства были связаны. *3.* Ее прямой подход к решению проблем оказался эффективным. *4.* Просто ведите себя так, как будто вы принадлежите. *5.* Молочный коктейль оказался слишком густым, чтобы его можно было пить. *6.* Назови мне хотя бы одну причину не делать этого.

● *1.* The backside of the building was painted blue. *2.* I don't want the two murders linked. *3.* Her straightforward approach to problem-solving was effective. *4.* Just act like you belong. *5.* The milkshake was too thick to drink. *6.* Give me one reason not to.

**[185]** *1.* Можете ли вы научить меня, как это сделать? *2.* Я бы не стал относиться к этому слишком серьёзно. *3.* Мы добрались сюда так быстро, как только могли. *4.* В Колорадо есть множество развлечений на свежем воздухе. *5.* Я здесь только для того, чтобы предупредить тебя. *6.* Когда его спрашивали, он всегда отвечал «да, сэр».

● *1.* Can you teach me how to do that? *2.* I wouldn't take it too seriously. *3.* We got here as fast as we could. *4.* Colorado has many outdoor activities. *5.* I'm just here to warn you. *6.* He always said yessir when asked.

**[186]** *1.* Как насчет того, чтобы я пошёл с тобой? *2.* Она не могла не упасть в обморок от него. *3.* Ее онлайн-персонаж отличался от ее реальной личности. *4.* Произошло ли что-нибудь необычное во время процедуры? *5.* Почему бы тебе просто не сделать это самому? *6.* Вы бы не поверили мне, если бы я вам рассказал.

● *1.* How about I come with you? *2.* She couldn't help but swoon over him. *3.* Her online persona differed from her real self. *4.* Did anything unusual happen during my procedure? *5.* Why don't you just do it yourself? *6.* You wouldn't believe me if I told you.

**[187]** *1.* Я знал это и все равно нанял его. *2.* Я рад, что ты пригласил меня на свидание. *3.* Назовите мне хотя бы одну вескую причину, почему. *4.* Ты совершаешь самую большую ошибку в своей жизни. *5.* Ее горячая вера в справедливость никогда не колебалась. *6.* После этого он уже никогда не был прежним.

● *1.* I knew it, and I hired him anyway. *2.* I'm glad you asked me out. *3.* Give me one good reason why. *4.* You're making the biggest mistake of your life. *5.* Her fervent belief in justice never wavered. *6.* He was never the same after that.

**[188]** *1.* Он не был прежним с тех пор, как ты ушел. *2.* Мне нужно, чтобы ты отнесся к этому серьезно. *3.* Она изо всех сил пыталась понять технический жаргон. *4.* У него была особая связь со своей собакой. *5.* Было очень важно, чтобы он присутствовал на встрече. *6.* Что ж, оставим это в том же духе.

● *1.* He hasn't been the same since you left. *2.* I need you to take this seriously. *3.* She struggled to understand the technical jargon. *4.* He had an especial bond with his dog. *5.* It was vital that he attend the meeting. *6.* Well, let's keep it that way.

**[189]** *1.* Они такие же потенциальные убийцы, как и мы. *2.* Именно тогда я понял, что мне нужно измениться. *3.* Не давайте обещаний, которые вы не сможете выполнить. *4.* Я не думаю, что тебе стоит туда заходить. *5.* Я не думаю, что я в его вкусе. *6.* Хозяин позаботился о том, чтобы им было удобно.

● *1.* They're potential slayers, just like we were. *2.* That's when I realized I had to change. *3.* Don't make promises you can't keep. *4.* I don't think you should go in there. *5.* I don't think I'm his type. *6.* The innkeeper made sure they were comfortable.

**[190]** *1.* Ты имеешь в виду, что мы застряли здесь? *2.* В любом случае, давайте перейдем к следующей теме. *3.* Независимо от того, что заставляет вас чувствовать себя лучше. *4.* Я не знаю, что ждет нас в будущем. *5.* Попробуйте это, чтобы узнать глубокую и темную тайну. *6.* Это самая романтическая вещь, которую я когда-либо слышал.

● *1.* You mean we're stuck here? *2.* Anywho, let's move on to the next topic. *3.* Whatever makes you feel better. *4.* I don't know what the future holds. *5.* Try this for a deep, dark secret. *6.* That's the most romantic thing I've ever heard.

**[191]** *1.* Мы должны пойти туда, чтобы достичь места назначения. *2.* Я никогда не думал, что этот день наступит. *3.* Не заставляй меня использовать на тебе свою магию. *4.* Это расследование начинается прямо сейчас за моим столом. *5.* Наконец-то она заставила свою собаку взломать дом. *6.* Шведский стол был всем, что вы можете съесть.

• *1.* We must go thither to reach the destination. *2.* I never thought this day would come. *3.* Don't make me use my magic on you. *4.* This investigation starts at my desk now. *5.* She finally got her dog housebroken. *6.* The buffet was all-you-can-eat.

**[192]** *1.* Я не могу поверить в такой объем работы. *2.* Я бы на твоем месте не прикасался к этому. *3.* На мероприятие он был одет в классический смокинг. *4.* К сожалению, тело жертвы так и не было найдено. *5.* Действительно, милорд, вы заставили меня поверить в это. *6.* На мероприятии он был одет в мрачные цвета.

• *1.* I can't believe the volume of work. *2.* I wouldn't touch that if I were you. *3.* He wore a classic tuxedo to the event. *4.* Tragically, the victim's body was never found. *5.* Indeed, my lord, you made me believe so. *6.* He wore somber colors to the event.

---

**[1]** *1.* Меня бы здесь не было, если бы я этого не сделал. *2.* Можем ли мы поговорить об этом как-нибудь в другой раз? *3.* Все, что я говорю, это то, что здесь что-то есть. *4.* Разве ты не слышал ни слова из того, что я сказал? *5.* Это не похоже ни на что, что мы когда-либо видели раньше. *6.* Я не могу понять ни слова из того, что ты говоришь.

• *1.* I wouldn't be here if I didn't. *2.* Can we talk about this some other time? *3.* All I'm saying is there's something here. *4.* Haven't you heard a word I've said? *5.* It's like nothing we've ever seen before. *6.* I can't understand a word you're saying.

**[2]** *1.* Видите, это было не так уж и плохо, не так ли? *2.* Я до сих пор не могу поверить, что его больше нет. *3.* Просто скажи мне, что однажды с нами все будет в порядке. *4.* Я бы никогда не сделал ничего, что могло бы причинить тебе боль. *5.* Хотя она никогда этого не говорила, ей было не все равно. *6.* Они не похожи ни на что, что мы когда-либо видели раньше.

• *1.* See, that wasn't so bad, was it? *2.* I still can't believe he's gone. *3.* Just tell me one day we'll be OK. *4.* I would never do anything to hurt you. *5.* Though she never said it, she cared. *6.* They're like nothing we'd ever seen before.

**[3]** *1.* Он не похож ни на кого, кого я когда-либо встречал. *2.* Я ценю ваше беспокойство, но со мной все будет в порядке. *3.* Ты вырос с тех пор, как я видел тебя в последний раз. *4.* Вы чувствуете, что теперь у вас есть контроль, не так ли? *5.* Назовите мне хотя бы одну вескую причину, почему я должен это сделать. *6.* Она предупредила его, чтобы он не вел себя плохо на публике.

• *1.* He is unlike anyone I've ever met. *2.* I appreciate your concern, but I'll be fine. *3.* You've grown since I last saw you. *4.* You feel you now have control, don't you? *5.* Give me one good reason why I should. *6.* She warned him not to misbehave in public.

**[4]** *1.* У него была непереносимость лактозы, и он не мог пить молоко. *2.* И дети, в которых они убеждены, на самом деле не их. *3.* Я бы никогда не сделал ничего, что могло бы ему навредить.

• *1.* He was lactose intolerant and couldn't drink milk. *2.* And kids they're convinced aren't actually theirs. *3.* I would never do anything to hurt him.

**[5]** *1.* Он был в восторге от того, что у него есть сломанный домашний питомец. *2.* Речь идет о том, чтобы доставить нас туда, куда мы идем. *3.* У него было слишком много багажа, с которым нужно было справиться.

• *1.* He was thrilled to have a housebroken pet. *2.* It's about getting us to where we're going. *3.* He had too much baggage to handle.

**[6]** *1.* Он недостаточно пользуется зубной нитью и у него есть зубной камень. *2.* Первым прибыл - первым обслужен Эквивалент в русском языке: поздний гость гложет и кость. *3.* Она была технически подкована и всегда была в курсе последних событий.

• *1.* He doesn't floss enough and has tartar. *2.* First come, first served. *3.* She was tech-savvy and always up-to-date.

**[7]** *1.* С тех пор, как я начал использовать Ambadeo, нет ничего невозможного. *2.* Она смешивала краску до тех пор, пока она не стала голубоватой. *3.* Она работала над тем, чтобы привести в тонус свои дряблые мышцы.

• *1.* Since I started using Ambadeo, nothing's impossible. *2.* She mixed the paint until it became bluish. *3.* She worked to tone her flabby muscles.

Made in the USA
Las Vegas, NV
25 September 2024

95757419R00302